THE PLAYHOUSE
OF PEPYS

By
MONTAGUE SUMMERS
Author of *The Restoration Theatre*, etc.

With 24 Collotype Plates

HUMANITIES PRESS
New York
1964

First published 1935 by
Routledge & Kegan Paul Ltd.

Reprinted 1964 by
HUMANITIES PRESS, INC.
303 Park Avenue South
New York 10, N. Y.

Library of Congress Catalog Card No. 64-14678

Printed in U.S.A. by
NOBLE OFFSET PRINTERS, INC.
NEW YORK 3, N. Y.

CONTENTS

LIST OF ILLUSTRATIONS

INTRODUCTION

The following five chapters, although in themselves entirely self-contained, separate, and complete, actually form the Second Part or Volume of an extended study of the Restoration Stage, the First Volume of which appeared last year under the title *The Restoration Theatre*.

Before the student, and in a lesser though very real degree, the ordinary reader, can at all adequately appreciate the merits and genius of the dramatists of the latter half of the seventeenth century, he must have some knowledge of the conditions under which the authors of the days of Charles II wrote their plays, and if he is to form any estimate of their craft and skill, he must be able to visualize (at least to a certain degree) the stage for which they fitted their work, since the technique of an acting play is inevitably to a large extent determined by the contemporary theatre.

Accordingly in *The Restoration Theatre* as an essential preliminary I dealt in some detail, first with the art of advertisement, systems of admission, and the audience, and then with the methods and machinery of the Restoration Producer, the use of the curtain, the apron stage, lighting, scenery, and the changes of scenes; in fact the physical conditions of the playhouse.

The present volume, *The Playhouse of Pepys,* aims at covering (with certain omissions or rather deferments) the years from 1660 to 1682, a terminus *ad quem* self-marked by the Union of the Two Companies with the changes and readjustments that resulted from this coalition. Some question may perhaps be raised by the title, *The Playhouse of Pepys,* since the last entry in Pepys' keeping of his Journal is 31st May, 1669, and my survey continues yet another dozen years. I believe, however, that the name will be approved by all save the exceptious, whose whole business it is to carp and cavil and pick holes, inasmuch as, with regard to things theatrical, there was no break of continuity in 1669, although, of course, there resulted during the next twelve years important developments, which had (be it noted) well begun, and were even established and on their way before Pepys ceased his Diary.

Moreover I do not in this volume directly consider the Rhymed Heroic Drama, which was so important a feature of the period from 1663 to 1675, when at last Dryden in *Aureng-*

Zebe took formal leave of his "long-lov'd Mistris, Rhyme"
—although I hasten to add that Crowne produced *Caligula* in
1698, and indeed a remarkable group of rhymed tragedies
appeared in the last few years of the century, whilst such typical
heroic tragedies as Settle's *The Empress of Morocco* and Lee's
Sophonisba kept the stage until well within the eighteenth century,
and Dryden's own *The Indian Emperour* was drawing crowded
houses in 1734.

Thus the opening chapters of Volume III of my study will
concentrate upon Dryden, Orrery, Nathaniel Lee, Settle, and
the Rhymed Heroic Drama.

Volume III will also deal with such writers as Otway, Shadwell,
Crowne, Ravenscroft, D'Urfey.

In a History of the Drama running to several volumes it is
impossible that there should not be some postponement and
even some slight overlapping of material, particularly when,
as in the present case, the dramatists and their output are being
considered more or less biographically, and not by any purely
artificial segregation under such clouterly headings of groups
or imaginary tendencies as "Other Types of Tragedy";
"Tragedy and Opera"; "Jonsonian Element: Shadwell";
"Farce and Sentimentalism" (a rather unhappy juxtaposition,
this); all of which seem to me a very awkwardly devised
arrangement.

In the present volume I have tried to emphasize the intimate
connexion between the Theatre that was closed down in 1642
and the Theatre that reopened in 1659–1660, for actually, in
spite of violent disruption and loss, the links were never altogether
broken; the tradition as carried on and much modified, perhaps,
by Davenant, Killigrew, and others persisted.

Of Sir Robert Howard and his brothers; Porter; Flecknoe;
and of several other early dramatists with whom I deal there
has not (so far as I am aware) been given any account beyond
the notices to be found in the *Biographia Dramatica* and the
Dictionary of National Biography, and these summaries from their
very scope are necessarily so limited as to be little more than
indicative and outlines, which can offer neither adequate criticism
nor a complete review of the authors' work. I have, moreover,
been able to present a quantity of new and not unimportant
material, the results of the research of many years.

It may be considered that in their proportion I have devoted
more space to the minor writers and men of one play such as
Thompson, St. Serfe, William Joyner, Nevil *alias* Payne, Maidwell,
Whitaker, than I have given to Sedley and Wycherley. I do not
conceive that this censure would be well founded, but none the

less I should point out that where an author's work is reasonably accessible and has been edited, I have thought it less useful, however great a name he may be, to review him in such intimate detail as it seems necessary to treat smaller men, whose plays (until a *Corpus* of Restoration Drama, something on the lines of Dodsley, is collected) are difficult to obtain, and for the most part exist only in the original quartos, and of whom there has hitherto been written no adequate account. Of Sir Robert Howard, for example, a figure of prime importance, badly in need of critical care, there is no collected edition—(one disregards, of course, in this sense the two folios and the duodecimo, 1722)—whilst *The Complete Works of William Wycherley* were edited in 1924 in four volumes, with Notes upon the Sources of the four comedies, Theatrical Histories, ample Excursuses, and a critico-bibliographical Introduction of sixty-four pages.

A quarter of a century ago it was almost universally maintained that the plays of the age of Charles II could never again in any circumstances be seen upon the English stage.

When *Love for Love* was given at the Aldwych for two performances in April, 1917, there was indeed a fluttering in the dovecotes. Mrs. Grundy made shrill protest; and a gentleman, a true son of Jeremy Collier, went up and down the town declaring that in his opinion there could be no excuse, artistic or otherwise, for the acting of so vulgar a piece. Was there not a sailor in it who was too terribly frank and outspoken? Upon the production by the Phoenix Society in November, 1919, of *The Duchess of Malfi* at the Lyric Theatre, Hammersmith, Sir Leo Chiozza Money wrote to *The Daily News* " to ask what purpose is served by these revivals of the drama of blood and filth, of which the blood is by far the least objectionable ingredient. Is Webster to be followed by the Restoration blackguards of Wycherley and Shadwell, who dealt in nothing as decent as blood? " The situation does not lack humour.

Even in the ranks of the Phoenix itself some misgiving was felt when I urged the revival of *The Country-Wife,* and it was in the face of difficulty and opposition that I insisted upon and carried my point. The Phoenix presented *The Country-Wife,* which had not been acted since 1748, in February, 1924, and the result was in the words of a contemporary critic, " a revolution in taste," since " this performance of Wycherley's masterpiece was magnificent ", and " in a performance given over to the enjoyment of wit, wit alone for once was allowed to rule supreme ".

It will be readily understood, then, how dearly pleased I was with the great and deserved success of *Love for Love,* as given by

Miss Baylis at Sadler's Wells for four weeks from Tuesday, 6th March, to Saturday, 31st March, 1934. It was especially interesting to compare the Tattle of Mr. Charles Laughton with the Tattle of Mr. Ernest Thesiger seventeen years before. The conceptions of both artists differed widely; both conceptions were superlatively good and entirely individual. At Sadler's Wells in a cast where all were admirable Mr. Roger Livesey's Ben Foresight was so brilliant that I shall ever recall it as among the few great pieces of comic acting that it has been my happy fortune to see.

The master-stroke of Mr. Sydney Carroll's production at the Ambassadors Theatre of *The Country-Wife*, which enjoyed a victorious run of five months, was in a sense even more gratifying than the triumph of Congreve, for here amid the paeans of the critics I felt (if I may so say and not be misunderstood) that the cause I had fought, against, as it seemed, overwhelming odds and universal opinion, was finally and completely vindicated and approved.

Since Sir William Davenant's *The Siege of Rhodes* marks so memorable a date in this book it may be well to observe that the music of the opera is entirely lost, yet as Professor E. J. Dent acutely points out, although it is of comparatively little importance to know what the recitatives, the " variation of *ayres* " and choruses of the piece sounded like—and indeed " we can make a sufficient guess at that by looking at other compositions of the men who contributed to it—it is of the greatest interest to know what relation the music bore to the dramatic action, and how far it intensified the emotional values of the play ". These points accordingly Professor Dent has analysed and fully discussed in his masterly survey of musical drama in England during the seventeenth century, *Foundations of English Opera*, where he passes in review not only *The Siege of Rhodes*, but Shadwell, Locke and Draghi's *Psyche*, the *Macbeth* music, *Albion and Albanius*, *Dido and Aeneas*, *Dioclesian*, *King Arthur*, *The Fairy Queen*, and many more. For me to attempt to add anything to his pages would be the veriest impertinence.

The Shakespearean adaptations of Davenant and other dramatists of the reign of Charles II have been dealt with in amplest detail by Professor Hazelton Spencer in his *Shakespeare Improved*, a most excellent study which stands out as pre-eminently the best work upon the Restoration period that American scholarship has given us. I would also draw attention to Professor Spencer's *How Shakespeare Staged His Plays*, a suggestive monograph of considerable consequence and interest.

Professor George C. D. Odell in his *Shakespeare from Betterton to Irving*, whilst tracing the history of the plays in the theatre for two hundred and forty-one years, devotes much space to The Age of Betterton, 1660–1710. His rare enthusiasm—and his work has many other sterling recommendations—is a quality which of itself alone would ensure that his two volumes should take their place as of permanent value and authority. Occasionally I confess he surprises us. His judgement (Volume II, pp. 23–5) of *Measure for Measure*, for example, is to me frankly incomprehensible. On the other hand his most welcome criticism of certain more recent and more eccentric productions of Shakespeare is notably shrewd and sane, and as such practically constructive.

It is well known that France (which itself copiously conveyed from Spanish sources) was a fount whence our English dramatists of the Restoration drew without stint and often, and in this connexion the wide research of Professor H. C. Lancaster's *A History of French Dramatic Literature in the Seventeenth Century* is established as of essential importance.

It is no small pleasure to thank His Grace the Duke of Devonshire for generously granting me permission to reproduce from the Chatsworth Collections John Webb's original design for Act II, Scene I of *The Siege of Rhodes* ; and also for their kind assistance in several particulars, Mr. C. K. Adams of the National Portrait Gallery ; Mr. Sydney Carroll, for permission to reproduce photographs of his production of *The Country-Wife* ; Professor E. J. Dent ; Mr. A. I. Ellis of the British Museum ; the Rev. G. H. Salter, Vicar of S. Sepulchre's, Holborn Viaduct, who was at the trouble to examine on my behalf the Registers of his Church for details of the burial in the South vault of John Crosby on 16th April, 1724 ; Mr. Hector Stuart-Forbes.

MONTAGUE SUMMERS.

THE PLAYHOUSE OF PEPYS

CHAPTER I

SIR WILLIAM DAVENANT: HIS EARLIER WORK AND THE OPERA

Then we shall still have *Playes!* and though we may
Not them in their full Glories yet display;
Yet we may please our selves by reading them,
Till a more Noble Act this Act condemne.
Happy will that day be, which will advance
This *Land* from durt of precise Ignorance;
Distinguish *Morall Virtue,* and *Rich Wit,*
And *gracefull Action,* from an unfit
Parenthesis of *Coughs,* and *Hums,* and *Haes,*
Threshing of Cushions, and *Tautologies.*
Then the dull *Zelots* shall give way, and flye,
Or be converted by bright Poesie.
Apollo may enlighten them, or else
In *Scottish Grots* they may conceale themselves,
Then shall Learn'd *Johnson* reassume his Seat,
Revive the *Phœnix* by a second heat.
Create the Globe anew, and people it,
By those that flock to surfet on his *Wit.*
Judicious *Beaumont,* and th' Ingenious Soule
Of *Fletcher* too may move without controule.
Shakespeare (most rich in *Humours*) entertaine
The crowded *Theaters* with his happy veine.
Davenant and *Massinger,* and *Sherley,* then
Shall be cry'd up againe for Famous men.
And the Dramatick Muse no longer prove
The peoples Malice, but the peoples Love.

ASTON COKAINE. *A Prœludium to Mr. Richard
Bromes Playes,* 1653.

Le Chevalier Dauenant que le Poëme Dramatique a rendu celebre.
LE SIEUR CHAPPUZEAU. *L'Europe Vivante,* 1667.

It is both a happy and a remarkable circumstance that the actual continuity between the theatre of 1642 and the theatre which was officially established and royally recognized immediately after the Restoration, although not infrequently strained to breaking point and seemingly upon the very event of rupture and disjunction, fortuitously was never snapped and sundered. There was a coherence; there was a succession; and in spite of the desire and intention of the sour despots, who had snatched and tightly clung to the reins of government, for ever and finally to annihilate and extinguish the English stage, when at the King's return public playhouses were again reopened, favoured, and patronized, the old traditions were found to have been by no means lost, the break with the past— a past far more remote than mere count of years could tell— was seen to be in no wise irremediable, since a very real conservation and relationship trilled, and although the stream was slender the waters were clear from their source.

A large number of persons who had been connected and intimately connected with the theatre of 1642 were not only alive but deedily active. Many, too many—and those of the best—had gone; but the Argus-eyed and Briareus-handed despot, Sir Henry Herbert, Master of the Revels, who had been appointed nearly forty years before, on 7th August, 1623,[1] was busy at the very Restoration, as early indeed as June, 1660,[2] when he authorized William Beeston to " Gett, Lett, or vse " Salisbury Court as a playhouse, " wherein Comedies, tragedies, trage Comedies, Pastoralls, and Interludes, may bee Acted."

Of the actors themselves, Michael Mohun, Charles Hart, Burt, Lacy, Wintershal, Clun, Cartwright, and not a few of lesser note but waited opportunity, nay, were even anticipating opportunity and occasion to exhibit their craft. Of the dramatists, the sick and prematurely aged James Shirley, now a schoolmaster in Whitefriars, was more concerned with pedagogics than plays,[3] and, owing perhaps to his failing health, evinced little or no interest in the stage, save that a ghost for the fee's sake he would help the younger men, revising and polishing their work.[4]

Yet there were other playwrights of Shirley's own fellowship who were full of enthusiasm and fire for the theatre resurgent. There was his great patron, William Cavendish, Marquess (soon to be Duke) of Newcastle, whose two comedies *The Country Captain* and *The Varietie*,[5] produced at the Blackfriars before 1642, were presently to be revived with good applause; there was that erratic fantast Sir Robert Stapylton; there were Abraham Cowley, Sir William Lower, Sir William Killigrew, Sir William Berkeley, Lodowick Carliell, John Tatham; there was that boldly important figure, " the *Traveller, Courtier, Soldier, Writer*, and the *Buffoon*," Thomas Killigrew; and above all there was Sir William Davenant.

The services of Sir William Davenant to the English theatre it would be difficult to overestimate. It was his enterprise at a time of blank depression and even of danger which forced

recognition for the claims of the drama, and he is infinitely to
be admired for the skill and the address as well as for the courage
and self-reliance with which he not merely projected but matured
his plans. It may be argued that Davenant was not the only
Thespis in the field, that even if he had not paved the way
a resurrection of the public theatre (as every symptom showed)
was in course of time inevitable with the return of King Charles.
No doubt this is true enough, but it in no wise lessens the value
of his activities nor does it dequantitate the measure of the
obligation the stage must ever owe him. It would confessedly
be far too much to assert that his aims were purely altruistic,
that his sole ideal was the art of the theatre. Certes he could
read with adroitest prognostication such signs of the times as
the persistence and popularity of performances, however burked
and banned. No doubt he counted all these circumstances, and
since his genius lay that way, was resolved to take fullest advantage of them to his own benefit as well as to the gratification
of his patrons and supporters. Indeed a ballad to which
Langbaine has drawn attention,[6] *How Daphne pays his Debts,*
which may be dated in the spring of 1656, already tells us as
much. The poet is pestered by duns and he relies upon the
proceeds of *Gondibert*[7] to stop their mouths :—

> But when this *book* it did come forth
>   As some have given a hinting,
> The gains of his pitifull *Poetry*
>   Scarce paid for paper & printing.

> At the months end they come again,
>   Molesting him like Devils.
> *Well now Ile pay ye all,* quoth he,
>   *I must be master o' th'* Revels.

> *The State hath promis'd this to me,*
>   *As the Clerk of the Parliament saith,*
> *And I hope that you will do as I do,*
>   *Believe the PVBLIQUE FAITH.*

Davenant, a practised dramatist, a gifted and felicitous poet,
a shrewd and capable man of business, was undoubtedly in
every way qualified and equipped to exploit the situation,
to develop and pursue every possibility. His chief trait, perhaps,
was a very real love for and knowledge of the theatre, not
merely a theoretical or literary appreciation, but a practical
and experimental acquaintance with the scene. He certainly
ran serious risks for the faith that was in him. Had he been
more of a poet he would have left us dramas which, however

great as poetry, might not have had that direct stage appeal which so informs his plays and makes them such first rate playhouse fare ; had he been less of a poet and more of a business man, a Christopher Rich, he might have failed in an age which, yet pulsing with romance in life both public and domestic, demanded romance and mettle on the boards too. Davenant was at his moment the ideal manager, the ideal director, and the ideal manager must be immediately in touch with his own day.

Yet Davenant did not stand alone, for with the Restoration there appeared a powerful and energetic rival in Thomas Killigrew, himself no mean dramatist, Groom of His Majesty's Bedchamber, and a prime favourite with King Charles. Sir William Davenant, it is true, was appointed Poet Laureate (or Court Poet) by Charles I, but there is some reason to suppose that during the Royal Exile Charles II had already named Killigrew his Master of the Revels, or at any rate this is pretty plainly suggested by the following passage in the Second Part, Act V, scene 12, of *Thomaso, or, The Wanderer,* a comedy written in 1654,[8] which is largely autobiographical, many of the characters representing actual persons, and in which Thomaso (who is Killigrew himself) thus addresses his companion Ferdinando : " I promise thee, *Ferdinando,* a Patent to shew him thy self ; a favour, but that thou art a Friend to the Master of the Revels, you should not easily obtain, the shewing of your own Monster."

Careless Tom Killigrew, however, let the reins of government almost entirely slip out of his hands, whilst Davenant trained his young actors in the best possible tradition. Indeed, it was owing to his example of shrewd perseverance, of business concentration, of fair dealing with his own, and capable manage-ment, that after his death the Duke of York's company long retained a certain code of loyalty, of equity and method amongst their fellowship which traditions for many a year, in spite of domestic tiffs not a few, of disaffection, of some bad blood and individual spleen, preserved them whole and entire, and eventually gained them the monopoly of the Town. Such men as Thomas Betterton and William Smith were the result of Davenant's schooling. In theatrical history Davenant was a far greater and more important figure than Killigrew. His precedence in time may have been something of an accident, but it is a circumstance which, however fortuitous, carries weight. All Davenant's activities were designedly leading up to the establishment of the first English picture-stage, the new Duke's Theatre in Lincoln's Inn Fields, which opened on Friday, 28th June, 1661.[9]

In order adequately to estimate Davenant's position it is necessary to take into account the work that he did and the dramas which he wrote before the prohibition of the theatres in 1642, since many of these plays were revived with applause after the Restoration, and curiously enough there seems to be in this connexion no concise survey of his earlier activities which were many and important. To commence any consideration of Davenant with *The Siege of Rhodes,* or arbitrarily from the year 1655,[10] is at once lop-sided and misleading.

William Davenant was born in Oxford towards the end of February, 1606, and on 3rd March he was baptized at S. Martin's Church. His mother, " a very beautiful woman of a good wit and conversation," [11] was the wife of John Davenant,[12] a vintner and master of the well-known Crown Inn. Speaking of William Davenant, Giles Jacob says : " His father's house being frequented by the famous Shakespeare, his poetical genius in his youth was by that means very much encouraged, and some will have it that the handsome landlady, as well as the good wine, invited the tragedian to these quarters." [13] The clever anecdote related by Oldys is familiar : " Young Will. Davenant was then a little schoolboy of the town, of about seven or eight years' old, and so fond also of Shakespeare, that, whenever he heard of his arrival, he would fly from school to see him. One day an old townsman, observing the boy running homeward almost out of breath, asked him whither he was posting in that heat and hurry. He answered to see his godfather, Shakespeare. ' There is a good boy,' said the other, ' but have a care that you don't take *God's* Name in vain.' This story Mr. Pope told me at the Earl of Oxford's table upon occasion of some discourse which arose about Shakespeare's monument in Westminster Abbey ; and he quoted Mr. Betterton, the player, as his authority." [14] The tradition that William Davenant was Shakespeare's son is, of course, impossible to establish. From the very nature of the case those most concerned—if indeed any save the father and mother knew the facts—would keep silence, although Davenant himself in merry mood was wont to make reference to his paternal ancestry,[15] and the truth cannot be certainly ascertained at this time of day, although myself I see no reason at all why the story may not be accepted.

After attending the Grammar School of All Saints, William Davenant commenced to keep his terms at Lincoln College, Oxford, under Mr. Daniel Hough in 1621. The following year, upon the death of John Davenant, he left college to enter as page the service of Frances, first Duchess of Richmond. In the will of John Davenant, which was probated 21st October,

1622, William is mentioned as " being now arrived sixteen years of age ".   Presently he passed into the household of a famous poet and patron of letters, Sir Fulke Greville, first Lord Brooke, upon whose murder by Ralph Hayward, a serving-man, in September, 1628, Davenant sought and secured the patronage of that very remarkable personage, Robert Carr, Earl of Somerset, sometime minion *en titre* to King James I.   Owing to the terrible scandals which resulted from the murder by poison of Sir Thomas Overbury in September, 1613, a crime wherein Somerset was directly and maliciously implicated, and perhaps even more owing to the fact that the favourite had married Frances Howard, the divorced wife of the Earl of Essex—for, as other homosexuals, King James did not wish his Ganymedes to wed [16]—after both Earl and Countess had been tried for their lives, found guilty and sentenced to death (25th May, 1616), Somerset was disgraced, banished from court, and granted from his forfeited estates a revenue of four thousand pounds a year.   He was now living in retirement, and it is a little extraordinary that Davenant, although but a youth of twenty-two years old, should have deemed it politic or worth while to ensue the favour of one who a bare thirteen years before had not merely fallen from his high place, but fallen in a sombre blaze of turpitude and foulest infamy.   Nevertheless *The Tragedy of Albovine, King of the Lombards,* 4to, 1629, is dedicated to Somerset in a strain of studied and elaborate commendation by his " humblest creature ", who declares " You read this Tragedie, and smil'd upon't, that it might live : and therein, your Mercy was divine, for it exceeded Justice."   Moreover Edward Hyde, subsequently Earl of Clarendon and Lord Chancellor, in his verses prefixed to the printed copy warmly congratulates the poet :—

> *Thy Wit hath purchas'd such a Patrons name*
> *To deck thy front, as must deriue to Fame*
> *These Tragick raptures, and indent with Eyes*
> *To spend hot teares t'inrich the Sacrifice.*

All this can only mean that Somerset was in no wise the ruined and broken eremite that has generally been supposed. It is clear from the other writers who obliged Davenant with congratulatory verses which were prefixed to his tragedy that he had already won some repute as a wit and a poet.   " Hast thou unmaskt thy Muse ? " rhetorically asks Henry Howard [17] in his brocaded rhymes.   William Habington, the author of *Castara* ; Thomas Ellis ; Henry Blount ; Roger Lorte ; and other lesser names were quick to hail Davenant's first venture with couplet and compliment.

It has been questioned whether *Albovine* was in the first place presented upon the stage of Charles I, a doubt which apparently arises from the fact that there is no mention of any theatre [18] on the title-page of the first quarto, 1629, since this merely reads : The Tragedy Of Albovine, King Of The Lombards : *By W^m. D'auenant.* [Printer's ornament.] London, Printed for *R. M.* and are to bee sold in Saint *Dunstanes* Church-yard. 1629. Such a detail, however, must not be pressed, for several parallel cases can be cited where any reference to production in the theatre was omitted in the printed copy.[19] One thing is very certain, that in *Albovine* Davenant already shows an exceptional mastery of stagecraft, and in his very first play proves an adept in theatrical technique. It was no lack of merit that withheld *Albovine* from the boards. It is a drama of extraordinarily fine quality ; admirable enough in a practised playwright ; yet more admirable in a tiro and a mere juvenal. From the very first, then, Davenant exhibited that keenly intuitive and argute sense of the theatre which was to make him one of the most important figures in our dramatic history. *Albovine* is the first tragedy of a young man, but of a very remarkable young man. For Davenant was a great poet, and not only his dramatic work but *Gondibert* is witness to this. It is no oblique criticism, no reflection upon his originality, to say that here and there, throughout his earlier scenes, are caught echoes from—not imitations of—the most eminent of his contemporaries, Shakespeare, Beaumont and Fletcher, Webster, Ford. He emulates no lesser name.

If not indeed for the first time upon any stage, at any rate for the first time in three hundred years, *Albovine* was produced by the present writer on 27th and 28th February, 1931. The tragedy was given in the hall of Lincoln College, Oxford, being presented by the Davenant Society of that College. The characters Albovine, Paradine, Rhodolinda, Valdaura, Thesina, and all were played by undergraduates, whose success in the rôles of the court-ladies was particularly remarked.

The plot of *The Tragedy of Albovine, King of the Lombards,* to some extent turns upon the well-known incidents in the life of Alboin, founder of the Longobard dominion in Italy.[20] " You may read the story," says Langbaine airily enough, " in several Historians," [21] referring to Paulus Diaconus Casinensis [22] ; the *Historia Francorum* of S. Gregory of Tours [23] ; and to Peter Heylyn's *Cosmography*. There can, however, be little doubt that actually Davenant directly derived his theme from the *Histoires Tragiques* of François de Belle-Forest,[24] who paraphrased a novella of Bandello,[25] Parte II, novella 18.

Although it has engaged the attention of French, Spanish,

and other foreign dramatists the history of Albovine seems only once since Davenant's day to have been brought upon the English stage. We may except *Rosmunda; or, The Daughter's Revenge,* a tragedy by William Preston, barrister-at-law, as this piece which was printed in the author's *Poetical Works,* Dublin, 8vo, 1793, is not designed for representation.

In 1698 was produced at the Theatre Royal *The Revengeful Queen,* a tragedy in five acts, by William Phillips. Among his principal characters are *Alboino,* King of the *Lombards,* very Brave, but Rash, Opinionated and Cruel; *Aistolfus,* his General; *Desiderio,* his Friend; *Rosamund,* the Queen, Haughty, Proud, Revengeful; *Angellina,* Vertuous and Discreet, privately in Love with *Desiderio.* The scene is laid in Verona, and the intrigue runs on the same lines as Davenant's *Albovine.* It has, however, no spark of the genius and little of the vigour of the older poet. Alboino is killed during Act IV, whilst Act V concludes with a welter of blood and poison. As a *bonne bouche* the janty epilogue was spoken by Miss Dennis Chock, aged eight.

However, the Characters proved "*not agreeable to the present Taste of the Town*", and in his Dedication to the Duke of Ormonde, when the play was printed, 4to, 1698, Phillips very candidly avows : "*It was folly in me to Write at all, greater to Write no better, and chiefly to Print what I have Writ,*" a sentence which might very well be pondered by many a dramatist to-day. Phillips further declares : "*A considerable Time after this was Writ, I was informed, That Sir William Davenant had made a Play on the same Story; I knew it not before, nor have I yet seen it : It was very unhappy for me to happen on the same Subject with so Ingenious a Person.*"

The Florentine poet, Giovanni Rucellai (1475–1526) wrote a *Rosmunda,* a tragedy wholly upon the Senecan model, which was not only much admired in its day but also performed with great applause in the Rucellai Gardens before the author's relative Leo X, when that pontiff honoured with a state visit his native town. Unfortunately this drama is almost wholly without action, and it merely consists of a number of incidents related by Messengers to the Chorus. Thus the banquet with the fearful climax of Albuino compelling Rosmunda to drink from the " tazza del teschio d'un'uomo morto " is told by a Serva, whilst the Coro utter appropriate sentiments of horror and dread. The verse is vivid enough, but Rucellai failed to dramatize his theme.

Davenant's *Albovine* is a fine tragedy of the school of Fletcher's latest mood. Highly romantic and even sentimental, it depends less upon the display or logical development of character than upon the swift and often surprising sequence of events. We feel indeed that there is little or no scope for nice psychology—and perhaps in these days of complex and analysis, of Freud and faddle, this is some relief—for the individuals of the drama are already keyed to the highest pitch so that their loves and passions show simple and direct. It would be false to say that situations are created without regard to the propriety and influence of character, and if it is true that events are so arranged as to hold and suspend the attention in the interest of a subtly-contrived and perhaps theatric *dénouement,* it should be borne in mind that these events are historical happenings.

The psychology of *Albovine* certainly rings false in one point, and this flaw is especially luckless since if we are not content to take the drama as it is, a well-told legend of barbaric blood, and lust that crushes love, the whole motif is marred. In Act I Paradine, the favourite of Albovine, is thus greeted by the Lombard monarch who is about to enter Verona in triumph :—

> My Boy, I bring thee home my chiefe Trophy :
> Thou dost delight me more then victory.
> Retire ; I am in loue too violent.
> My embraces crush thee, thou art but yet
> Of tender growth—

But Albovine is enamoured of Rhodolinda ; and Paradine loves Valdaura, although there is a hint this latter union will not altogether please the King.[26]   The bisexual temperament is actually not rare,[27] yet it is difficult to suppose that a person should simultaneously be so violently attracted towards both sexes as Albovine is represented.   There will be a marked pre-dominance in one direction ; and if Davenant, which one can hardly suppose to have been the case, had in view King James I, who married Anne of Denmark, but was swayed by his favourites, the poet must have known that shortly after her marriage the Queen was " deprived of the nightly company of her husband ", and consoled herself with many lovers, the Earl of Gowrie ; one Stuart of the household of the Earl of Murray ; Buly, a Dane ; and other gallants of the court.[28]

It is remarkable that Davenant's second play *The Cruell Brother* (4to, 1630), which was licensed by Sir Henry Herbert, 12th January, 1626–7, and produced by the King's Men at the Black-friars, a most wealthy and fashionable theatre,[29] has as the principal character Lucio, a Count, the favourite of the Duke of Siena—" molles Senae " Beccadelli once sang—where the scene is laid. Foreste, the Cruel Brother, whose sister Corsa is presently wedded to Lucio, thus addresses him :—

> Young Lord, . . .
> You are the Dukes Creature ! who doates by Art,
> Who in his loue, and kindnesse, Method keepes :
> He holdeth thus his Armes, in fearefull care
> Not to bruse you with his deere embracements.

Certes one can hardly wonder to find a uranian romanticism, that exotic flower of the Renaissance garden, so marked in the drama of this date. Davenant's serious plays, the tragedies and tragi-comedies, all deal with the intrigues, politic or amorous, of persons in most exalted station ; his scene is Lombard Verona,[30] Siena, Florence, Pisa, Savoy ; we walk in council-chambers, in banqueting-halls, in royal galleries, in palaces where sweet odours are burned and flung about the air, where soft and easy-fingered lutes sound behind the arras, and the couches are spread with green Persian tapestries.[31] During his most impressionable years Davenant had lived at court and in noble households, and inevitably he would draw the picture of his princely halls, far off in time and place, from Whitehall and Theobalds at home. It is true that, as Mrs. Hutchinson tells us in her *Memoirs of Colonel Hutchinson,* " The face of the court was much changed in the change of the king, for King Charles was temperate, chaste, and serious ; so that the fools and bawds, mimics and catamites, of the former court, grew out of fashion ; and the nobility and courtiers who did not quite abandon their debaucheries, yet so reverenced the king as to retire into corners to practise them," yet how often must Davenant have heard the whispered tale of the minions of King James, who, as Sir Anthony Weldon says, " was not uxorious but loved favourites whom he often changed," such magnificent Gitons as Sir George Hume, Earl of Dunbar ; Richard Preston, Earl of Desmond ; Sir Philip Herbert, Earl of Montgomery and Pembroke, " carressed by King James for his handsome face, which kept him not long company " [32] ; Sir James Hay, Earl of Carlisle ; Sir Robert Carr, Earl of Somerset ; and above all the omnipotent Buckingham. Consequently Albovine must have his Paradine ; and Siena's Duke his Lucio.

The Cruell Brother, in the conduct of which Davenant would appear to have been generally influenced by Ford, is a tragedy of great merit, and the scene of the death of Corsa, whom Foreste in his loathing for the Court—a rank disgust which seems to swell and break like some ripe imposthume—hideously murders since that she has been ravished by the Duke, rises to heights of real power. It will not escape notice that Foreste if not modelled upon, owes something to, Daniel de Bosola. In this play Castruchio, "A satirical Courtier," may be recognized as not too exaggerated a caricature of the puritan poet, George Wither, whose *Abuses Stript and Whipt* (first published in 1611) [33] is actually mentioned in Act II where Dorido smartly says :—

> You remember your Vices-strip'd, and whip'd.
> Your trimme Eclogues, the Fulsome Satyr too,
> Written to his Grace.

The "trimme Eclogues" are *The Shepherds Hunting: Being, Certaine Eglogs . . . By George Wither,* 1615 (two editions), a book composed during the author's imprisonment in the Marshalsea. The "fulsome satire" is *A Satyre: Dedicated To His Most Excellent Maiestie. By George Wither,* 1614.

I find myself obliged entirely to differ from Genest who says of *The Cruell Brother* "this is Davenant's worst play",[34] indeed, on the contrary, in my opinion it takes high rank among his theatre.

On 22nd July, 1629, Sir Henry Herbert licensed Davenant's *The Colonel,* now generally identified with *The Siege,* a tragi-comedy first published in the folio of 1673. There can be no doubt that there have been additions and alterations, probably even fairly extensive excisions, and the very text bears evidence of tampering by some unskilled hand. In this drama Pisa is invested by the Florentines, a young officer of whose number, Florello, loves passionately Bertolina, daughter of the Governor of the beleaguered city. Unable to negotiate a peace Florello deserts to the Pisans, whereupon the lady rejects him as treacherous and dishonoured. She contrives that he shall return to his own camp, and in the next assault, hoping to be slain, he fights with such valour that Pisa is captured. Although Florello would now resign Bertolina to his noble rival Soranzo, she bestows her hand upon her lover as quit and clean of his revolt. The Governor of Pisa is assured of grace and pardon by Castracagnio, the Florentine general. All this appears to me extremely artificial ; and, truth to tell, with its depressing atmosphere of militarism and fighting, the play is more than a little tedious. There are comic episodes which are no better than the rest, although it is only fair to add that these scenes seem especially disjointed and inchoate. The character of Piracco, a poor *esquisse,* is borrowed from that of the Humorous Lieutenant, an original far better left untouched.

The Just Italian, licènsed by Herbert, 2nd October, 1629, and produced at the Blackfriars, is a typical tragi-comedy of the later Caroline school in which, so far as the serious scenes at all

events are concerned, until a certain point it is doubtful whether
the intrigue will take a tragic turn or develop on lighter and
happier lines. These plays indeed evolve their action in a manner
very imitative of the scapes, quick shifts, and surprises real life
unfolds and probably afforded far more markedly and frequently
then than now, it may be in the realm of grave and notable
affairs wherein the dramatists move, or it may be in the petty
sphere of domestic businesses and a journeyman ambit.

The Just Italian, although the hint which concludes Carew's
complimentary verses prefixed to the first quarto, 1630, suggests
that at its production it did not meet with the success it most
certainly deserved,[35] is an interesting and well-written drama with
some passages of fine poetry. That there can be traced any
resemblance between Davenant's Alteza and Margarita in *Rule a
Wife and Have a Wife* [36] is surely fanciful.[37]

For about three years Davenant's pen lay idle, a silence doubtless to be attributed to an obstinate illness, since in his prologue
to *The Witts* the author speaks of himself as " our long-sick
Poet ". The script of *The Witts,* Davenant's first comedy, was
submitted by him for the purposes of licensing in December, 1633,
to Sir Henry Herbert, who promptly returned the MS. with
various passages, and in particular such expressions as " faith ",
" 'slight ", and " death ", deleted.[38] But the poet did not tamely
brook such peddling interference, and handed the play to a
great patron of literature, the accomplished Endymion Porter,
requesting his good offices with the King. Porter, nothing
loath, for the autocratic and sullen puritanism of the censor
had long become a nuisance, carried *The Witts* to Charles I
and begged him to cast an eye over the offending pages. The
sequel is best told in Herbert's own words : " This morning,
being the 9th of January, 1633[-4], the kinge was pleased to
call mee into his withdrawinge chamber to the windowe, wher
he went over all that I had croste in Davenant's play-booke,
and allowing of *faith* and *slight* to be asseverations only,
and no oathes, markt them to stande, and some other few
things, but in the greater part allowed of my reformations.
This was done upon a complaint of Mr. Endymion Porters in
December.

" The kinge is pleased to take *faith, death, slight,* for asseverations,
and no oaths, to which I doe humbly submit as my masters
judgment ; but, under favour, conceive them to be oaths, and
enter them here, to declare my opinion and submission. The
10 of January, 1633, I returned unto Mr. Davenant his playe-
booke of *The Witts,* corrected by the kinge.

" The kinge would not take the booke at Mr. Porters hands ;

but commanded him to bring it unto mee, which he did, and likewise commanded Davenant to come to me for it, as I believe :
otherwise he would not have byn so civill." [39]

The Witts accordingly was licensed on 19th January, 1633–4,
and almost immediately produced at the Blackfriars. It was
given at Court on Tuesday, 28th January, the King and Queen
being present. Herbert comments : " Well likt. It had a various
fate on the stage, and at court, though the kinge commended
the language, but dislikt the plott and characters." [40] When
printed, quarto, 1636, Davenant, not unmindful, dedicated his
piece to " The Chiefly Belov'd of All That are Ingenious and
Noble, Endymion Porter ", thanking him for having rescued
the " work from a cruel faction ".

If we except the altered *Tempest,* this was certainly long the
most popular of all Davenant's comedies, perhaps indeed the
most popular of all his original plays. Downes tells us that
when it was revived after the Restoration at Lincoln's Inn Fields :
" The Part of the Elder *Palatine,* Perform'd by Mr. *Betterton ;*
The Younger *Palatine* by Mr. *Harris,* Sir *Morgly Thwack* by
Mr. *Underhill,* Lady *Ample* by Mrs. *Davenport* : All the other
Parts being exactly Perform'd ; it continu'd 8 Days Acting
Successively." [41] The comedy was seen several times by Pepys,
who notes on Thursday, 15th August, 1661 : " To the Opera,
which begins again to-day with ' The Witts ' never acted yet with
scenes ; . . . and indeed it is a most excellent play." On Thursday,
18th August, 1667, he writes : " To the Duke of York's house,
and there saw ' The Witts ', a play I formerly loved, and is now
corrected and enlarged : but though I like the acting yet I like
not much in the play now." These additions which together
with a new Prologue and Epilogue were duly printed in the
1673 folio consist for the most part of an amplification of the
low comedy episodes wherein Constable Snore, his spouse,
and Mistress Queasy are concerned. They contain a good deal
of humour, and are certainly an improvement, for we are glad
to see more of the merry watchmen and their mates. After
some ten or fifteen years *The Witts* began to be given less frequently, although it did not entirely fall out of the repertory
until the second decade of the eighteenth century. Probably
the latest revival was that by the summer Company at Lincoln's
Inn Fields on 19th August, 1726. It was said, and perhaps truly,
not to have been acted for sixteen years. Various alterations
were made on this occasion, when the Elder Pallatine was played
by Ogden ; the Younger Pallatine, William Milward ; Sir
Morglay, Morgan ; Lady Ample, Mrs. Vincent, *née* Binks,
" a very promising young actress," says Chetwood ; and

Mrs. Queasy, Mrs. Martin, who was the original Mrs. Peachum and Diana Trapes.

When speaking of Fletcher's *Wit at Several Weapons* Langbaine [42] wrote that this diverting comedy " possibly was the Model on which the Characters of the Elder *Pallatine* and Sr. *Morglav Thwack* were built by Sr. William D'Avenant, in his Comedy call'd *The Wits* ", but there seem to be insufficient grounds for this suggestion. [43]

The Cruell Brother was dedicated to Lord Weston, Lord High Treasurer ; *The Just Italian* to the Earl of Dorset ; and there can be no doubt that these bids for high patronage were attaining their ends.   For Davenant was warmly welcomed into that circle of court poets and wits which included such literary figures as Henry Jermyn, afterward Earl of St. Albans ; Endymion Porter ; Jack Young [44] ; and Sir John Suckling, who in spite of his pungent pasquils remained on the best of terms with those he satirized.   However, Davenant's most substantial preferment was due in the first place to Inigo Jones.   The quarrel between Jones and Ben Jonson which had taken place in 1630 over the question of precedence on the title-page of *Chloridia : Rites to Chloris and her Nymphs* [45] was not merely kept warm but even exacerbated by the poet's satires on his umquhile colleague, who not unnaturally forthwith invited other writers to collaborate with him in the famous masques. He turned to Aurelian Townsend, Shirley, Heywood, Carew, and Davenant.   Nor were the younger men slow to seize their excellent opportunities ; and, as may well be supposed, so far from insisting upon their due and enforcing the rights Ben Jonson claimed, they were amply satisfied to accord entire precedence to " that admirable Artist, Mr. Inego Jones, Master surveyor of the King's worke, &c.", as Heywood saluted him with ceremonious compliment in the preface to *Love's Mistress : Or, The Queen's Masque,* when it was printed quarto, 1636.   For although Jones's name does not indeed actually occur on the title-page the poet insists that it was he " Who to every Act, nay almost to every Sceane, by his excellent Inventions, gave such an extraordinary Luster ; upon every occasion changing the stage, to the admiration of all the Spectators ; that, as I must Ingeniously confesse, It was above my apprehension to conceive, so to their sacred Majesties, and the rest of the Auditory ".

On Shrove Tuesday, 1634, *The Temple of Love,* [46] a masque, " By Inigo Jones, Surveyor of his Maties Workes, and William Davenant, her Maties Servant," was presented by Henrietta Maria and her ladies at Whitehall.   This extremely elaborate, and it must be allowed well contrived, spectacle proved an admirable introduction for the poet to the Queen, who from that time afforded him her particular grace and protection. In 1673, when dedicating the folio works to Charles II, Davenant's widow reminds her royal patron " that your Most Excellent Mother did graciously take him into her family ; that she was often diverted by him, and as often smiled upon his endeavours ".

A second masque, *The Triumphs of the Prince D'Amour*,[47] was " devis'd and written in three days " for the entertainment of Karl Ludwig, Prince Palatine of the Rhine, second son of the King and Queen of Bohemia, and nephew of King Charles I. The Prince, a lad of eighteen, had come to England in November, 1634, and on 24th February, 1635, the gentle Company of the Middle Temple rendered this masque as " an expression of their Loves " to a visitor whom they greeted as both " ornament and feast ". It should be noted that Prince d'Amour was the title officially given by members of the Middle Temple to the Principal whom they elected to superintend and direct their Christmas revels. *The Prince D'Amour* is actually of itself no great thing, but it is very well farced with stately show, poetic bijoutry, and compliment, which after all was precisely the end in view. It may be remarked that save for a short prologue the masque was entirely set to music, the composition of William and Henry Lawes,[48] of whom the latter had but a few months before played the Attendant Spirit and associated with Milton in *Comus*.[49] The two brothers were pupils of the Italianized Englishman, Coperario, and they clearly belong to the school of Giulio Caccini. Some of the music by William Lawes has survived, and is preserved in the Bodleian Library.[50]

On 20th November, 1634, Sir Henry Herbert had licensed *Love and Honour,* which was produced at the Blackfriars, and Sir Henry Mildmay enters a note, 12th December, 1634 : " To a play of Love and Honour." Actually this tragi-comedy was not printed for fifteen years ; 4to, 1649. The name itself is extremely significant, and might indeed stand as a sort of text or motto not merely for the heroic drama which was to come, but also for the Rambouillet romances of Gomberville, La Calprenède, Georges and Madeleine de Scudéry, whose heroes, be it in drama, in epic, or in novel, all resemble the gallant Gouveneur de Nostre Dame's Alaric,[51] " le vainqueur des vain- queurs de la terre," the conqueror of the world, but in his turn to be conquered by Love. Originally it was intended that *Love and Honour* should be called *The Courage of Love,* and afterwards at Davenant's suggestion Herbert proposed *The Nonpareilles, or the Matchless Maids,*[52] but there can be little doubt that the title finally adopted is the most fitting as it is the most effective.

Love indeed is the predominant interest of the play, but it is a love that is constantly crossed and checkmated by a sense of honour which seems (to me at any rate) sickly and scrupulous to excess. There is, moreover, a deal of actual or potential self-sacrifice, for the three men who are enamoured of the heiress of Milan, Evandra, are eager to offer themselves as love's martyrs, and revel in their destiny. At the close of Act III Evandra, although such a course may involve her death, compels Leonell to pursue a polity dictated by mere morbid punctiliousness. In fine the heroine stands for honour as it is fantastically understood, an extravagant and non-ethical conception ; whilst the hero more sensibly and more really subordinates everything to love. That there are persons who give rein to these ultra-quixotic vagaries and idealistic calentures experience only too surely demonstrates. We may well tolerate this psychology in the drama or in a romance, but in life it will inevitably lead to misery and wasted days. This is not to say that it does not afford a very effective subject for the stage, and the subtly-drawn conflict of emotions will command, if not our approval, our applause. The stichomythia of Love and Honour is the fundamental motive of the heroic play. But how often do we feel that the atmosphere upon these sublime heights is too rarified for us to linger long ? It was in sooth no unnatural juxtaposition of ideas which set as a relievo beside *Almanzor and Almahide ; The Destruction of Jerusalem* ; and *Ibrahim, The Illustrious Bassa ;* the comedies of Wycherley ; of Tom D'Urfey ; and Ravenscroft's *The London Cuckolds.*

After the Restoration *Love and Honour* was revived on Monday, 21st October, 1661, with much success. Downes notes : " Love and Honour, wrote by Sir *William Davenant* : This Play was Richly Cloath'd ; The King giving Mr. *Betterton* his Coronation Suit, in which, he Acted the Part of Prince *Alvaro* ; The Duke of *York* giving Mr. *Harris* his, who did Prince *Prospero* ; And my Lord of *Oxford,* gave Mr. *Joseph Price* his, who did *Lionel* the Duke of *Parma*'s Son ; The Duke was Acted by Mr. *Lilliston ; Evandra* by Mrs. *Davenport,* and all the other Parts being very well done : The Play having a great run, Produc'd to the Company great Gain and Estimation from the Town." [53] It was seen no less than three times by Pepys in the week commencing Monday, 21st October, 1661.

The lighter episodes of *Love and Honour* deal with the wooing of an old Widow by a hot-spark Colonel Vasco, whose merry comrades, Altesto, Frivolo, and Tristan entertain themselves vastly at the progress of his suit. The ancient sibyl herself is excellently drawn, and was not forgotten by Mrs. Behn when she designed Lady Youthly in *The Younger Brother; or, The Amorous Jilt*.

On 11th January, 1720, was produced at Lincoln's Inn Fields a farce in three acts, *The Half-Pay Officers,* in which a principal rôle was acted by Peg Fryer, "it being the first time of her appearance on any stage since the reign of Charles II." The farce is professedly a compilation from Shakespeare, something from *Much Ado about Nothing*; and from *Henry V*, Fuellin entire with a character, Culverin, to supply Pistol; from Shirley, Lodam, Rawbone, and Camelion, from *The Wedding*; from Davenant, the Widow with some other matter from *Love and Honour*. The piece was printed, 12mo, 1720. Although anonymous it is ascribed by Whincop in his *English Dramatic Poets* [54] to Charles Molloy, who says in the Preface, " the part of Mrs. Fryer is in an old play called Love and Honour, which she acted when she was young, and which was so imprinted in her memory, she could repeat it every word; and it was to an accidental conversation with her, this Farce owed its being; she acted with so much spirit and life, before two or three persons who had some interest with the house, that we judged it would do upon the stage; she was prevailed upon to undertake it; upon which this Farce was immediately projected and finished in 14 days." In the printed copy the name of Mrs. Vandervelt stands to the Widow Rich, so we are to take it that Mrs. Vandervelt and Peg Fryer were the same person. The prologue has :—

> To-night strange means we try your smiles to win,
> And bring a good old Matron on the scene :
> Kindly she quits a calm retreat to show
> What acting pleased you fifty years ago.
> When you behold her quivering on the stage,
> Remember, 'tis a personated age :
> Nor think, that no remains of youth she feels,
> She'll show you, e're she's done—she has it in her heels.

Whincop writes : " Peg Fryer was 85. Her character in the Farce was that of a very old woman; she went through it very well, but when, the Farce being done, she was brought upon the stage again to dance a jig, which had been promised in the bills, she came tottering in, as if ready to fall and made two or three pretended offers to go out again, but all on a sudden, the music striking up the Irish Trot, she danced and footed it away almost as nimbly as any wench of 25 could have done." Having danced this Irish Trot in one of the intervals, she also gave a character dance " The Bashful Maid " in John Leigh's farce *Hob's Wedding* which followed. *The Half-Pay Officers* and *Hob's Wedding* were played together seven times in all, the authors being jointly accorded two benefits, on the third and sixth nights.[55]

Peg Fryer acted Mrs. Amlet in *The Confederacy* at Lincoln's Inn Fields on 28th March, 1720, this being her last appearance on the stage. According to Whincop she afterwards set up a public house at Tottenham Court, whither resorted large numbers of people to see her out of curiosity.

If Whincop may be relied upon Peg Fryer would have been born about 1635, and therefore was in her early twenties when *Love and Honour* was revived at the Restoration. It is, of course, obvious that we must not stress her exact age to within two or three years. It appears from the narrative that she played the Old Widow when Betterton was Alvaro; Lilliston, the Duke; and Mrs. Davenport, Evandra, as Downes chronicles. But so far as I am aware the name Mrs. Fryer is recorded in no Restoration cast. Yet we need not be overmuch surprised to find no mention of the lady. There are several Restoration actresses, belonging to both houses, of whom we know nothing save their names, or at most that they filled some one insignificant rôle. Such are Mrs. Verjuice, Mrs. Brown, Mrs. Yates, Mrs. Dalton, Mrs. Yockney, Mrs. Child, Mrs. Merchant, all of Killigrew's company; Mrs. Slaughter, Mrs. Dixon, Mrs. Williams, Mrs. Spencer, Mrs. Crofts, Mrs. Moyle, of the Duke of York's theatre. However, in the case of Ruggle's *Ignoramus*,[56] which, translated by Ferdinando Parkhurst, was played before the King and Queen at Whitehall on Saturday evening, 1st November, 1662, the part of Nell, a waiting-maid,[57] is assigned to Pegg. It is just possible this may have been a surname,[58] but it is far more likely to have been the actress's Christian name. In the prompt-book of Shirley's *The Sisters,* which I have described in detail,[59] made for a revival at the Theatre Royal, 1668–1671, when Nell Gwyn is required the prompter, Charles Booth, always marginally noted " Mrs. Ellen ", " Ellen ", or " Mrs. Nelle " to remind him of that lady's call, whereas we have Mrs. Hughes and Mrs. Nep (Knepp) jotted down *interiore nota* anticipating the several entrances of Angellina and Paulina, the rôles sustained by these two actresses.[60]

I suggest then that Pegg who played Nell, the waiting-maid, in *Ignoramus* is Peg Fryer, and I also believe that she is the " pretty woman " referred to by Pepys, who calling at the Theatre Royal on Thursday, 7th May, 1668, notes : " Here I did kiss the pretty woman newly come called Pegg,[61] that was Sir Charles Sidly's mistress, a mighty pretty woman, and seems, but is not, modest." I understand " newly come " as meaning that she had transferred her services from the

Duke's house, for these migrations among the lesser actors were very common, and only checked with the greatest difficulty. Peg Fryer, then, an early actress of Davenant's company, seems to have left Lincoln's Inn Fields when she went into keeping by Sir Charles Sedley, and it was no doubt owing to his influence —his first play *The Mulberry-Garden* was produced at the Theatre Royal on 18th May, 1668—that she was subsequently enrolled among Killigrew's corps.

Among the many nebulous inaccuracies of Mr. Vivian de Sola Pinto's *Sir Charles Sedley* [62] we find a loose conjecture that Mrs. James, who was a member of Killigrew's company from 1668 to 1677, " *might be* identical with Pepys's ' Pegg '," " *if it could be shown that* her Christian name was Margaret." So far as I am aware there is no ground at all for any such random surmises, and these fond capricious speculations are not merely nugatory, but as being fruitful sources of error must not be indulged.

After the romance of *Love and Honour* Davenant returned to plain comedy, and on 1st August, 1635, Herbert licensed *News of Plimouth,* which was first printed in the folio, 1673. In Davenant's *Poems* the Epilogue is given as the Epilogue to a Vacation Play (unnamed) at the Globe, so there can be no doubt the piece was produced upon licensing at that theatre, the second of the name, being built in 1614 upon the site of the house which was burned down 29th June, in the previous year.[63] *News from Plimouth* is a well-written and amusing comedy although perhaps somewhat lacking in plot, for which deficiency the author indeed seems to apologize in the Prologue when he says :—

we could not raise
From a few Seamen, wind-bound in a Port
More various changes, business, or more sport.

Captain Cable, in particular, is in his mood almost Chaucerian, and his description of the town " dearer then *Jerusalem* " is admirably witty :—

If you walk but three turnes
In the High-street, they will ask you Mony
For wearing out the Pebles.

Apparently the locale was originally Portsmouth for Widow Carrack speaks of her house :—

The best in *Portsmouth,* and hath entertain'd
An Admirall, and his Mistress too ; but they
Have laine in several chambers on mine Honour.

Davenant soon turned back again to a more etherealized theme. In a letter from Westminster, 3rd June, 1634, James Howell writing to Philip—afterwards Sir Philip Warwick, at Paris, says that of Court there is " little news at present, but that there is a Love call'd Platonick Love which much sways there of late. It is a Love abstracted from all corporeal, gross impressions and sensual appetite, but consists in contemplations, and ideas of the mind, not in any carnal fruition. This Love sets the Wits of the Town on work, and they say there will be a Masque shortly on it, whereof her Majesty and her Maids of Honour will be a part ". It would appear as if this new fashion were an effort to popularize transcendental mysticism ; and, as every such attempt must, it was bound to vaporize into feckless failure. The ecstasy of the cloister and the hermitage cannot be translated into vulgar terms and common use. Hence in our own day the futility, and worse than futility, of such peptonized manuals as *Practical Mysticism for Normal People,* and other horn-books, which in truth inculcate a kind of Catharism. *Sacramentum Regis abscondere bonum est.*

The " Platonick Love " fashionable at the Court of Charles I had, needless to say, nothing of Plato in it. Its dream-world had been mapped out by such writers as Federigo Luigino of Udine, who in *Il Libro della Bella Donna* [64] delicately delivers his praises of æsthetic loveliness and feminine beauty. His images are as exquisite as they are insincere, and beneath all this green and luxuriant foliage in vain do we seek for fruit. An effete and frivolous society sought to translate lyrical emotions in the terms of real life ; and women whose nights were those of Messalina and Faustine sought to be worshipped as something " ensky'd and sainted " by troubadours who perhaps were not altogether ill content to use this amorous nonsense as a cloak for their hardly concealed preference for Giton and Earinus.

With his keen dramatic instinct Davenant was quick to see that here was excellent matter for the stage, and on 16th November, 1635, Herbert licensed his new tragi-comedy *The Platonick Lovers,* which was produced at the Blackfriars. The play was published, quarto, 1636, and one might well take as its motto the words of Buonateste in Act II :—

> I still beseech you not to wrong
> My good old friend *Plato,* with this court calumnie ;
> They father on him a Fantastick Love
> Hee never knew, poore Gentleman.

The Platonic Lovers are Theander, a Sicilian Duke, and

Eurithea, sister to Phylomont, a Duke whose territory borders Theander's domain. Confident that all they woo " is the spirit, face, and heart ", Theander and Eurithea allow themselves considerable liberties such as night visits and private rendez-vous. When Phylomont, however, seeks to wed Ariola, the sister of Theander, he finds his suit frowned upon by his friend, who preaches matrimony without consummation. Indeed, on their marriage night Theander and Eurithea forgetting that as Jason Pratensis says (*De morbo cerebri*, xix) there is no better remedy for love *quam ut amanti cedat amatum,* retire to several apartments, but by a plot whose engine is one Fredeline, himself dishonourably desiring the bride, Theander is made to suppose that his wife has played him false. After a brief spell of un-happiness the villainy is discovered, and so the play ends with sufficient content and a promise of more natural things in the future. Buonateste is a good character ; but Gridonell, although an amusing fellow, is something too improbable. Davenant's ridicule of the prevailing fashion is certainly poetical, and doubtless that was the best manner to use. Had he essayed something more in the vein of Turlupin and Jodelet no question his scenes must have been vastly funnier, yet he could scarcely have avoided farce and some honest bawdry to boot, which likely enough might have injured his prospects of advancement at Court.

On the Sunday after Twelfth Night, 1637, there was given at Whitehall a masque of altogether exceptional and even extravagant magnificence, in which the King himself took part, *Britannia Triumphans,* " By Inigo Jones, Surveyor of his Majesties Workes, and William D'Avenant, her Majesties Servant." [65] This was printed 4to, 1637, but curiously enough finds no place in the folio, 1673.

On 16th April, 1638, Herbert licensed Davenant's *The Unfortunate Lovers,* which was produced at the Blackfriars, and in 1643 with a dedication to Philip, Earl of Pembroke, printed, quarto, " as it was lately acted with great applause." This tragedy certainly takes a very high place amongst Davenant's dramas, and several passages have a power and effectiveness which elsewhere he seldom approached and assuredly never surpassed. In the first appearance of Arthiope jailored by the grim and silent monk and her recognition in the garb of shame by the heart-broken Altophil there is something truly touching, whilst the poetry is pregnant with the pathos of the situation. Amaranta again appears a figure of tender and flower-like loveliness, and even when we remember the supreme beauty of the lost Aspatia we would not withhold our tribute to her death :—

Amaranta. Go tell *Arthiope* she needs not fear
          Her Rival now, my Bridal Bed is in the Earth.
Altophil. Oh, stay ! there may be help !
Amaranta. When you come near my grave, if any Flower
          Can grow on such unlucky ground, pray water't with
          A single tear, that's all I ask : Mercy Heaven—

We are not too far from Webster here, and praise can reach no higher.

The plot of *The Unfortunate Lovers* turns upon the machinations of a villainous statesman, Galeotto, whose plots well-nigh destroy Verona. He has suborned false witnesses to accuse Arthiope, betrothed to Altophil, of incontinence, wherefore she is condemned to do public penance in a white sheet. Ascoli, the prince of Verona, banishes Galeotto for his crime, and the traitor immediately admits the Lombard enemy into the city. Heildebrand, their chieftain, ravishes Arthiope, when Altophil in despair slays both the new Tarquin and the recreant Galeotto. Arthiope expires of a broken heart, whilst her lover dies in her arms from the mortal wounds he has received in the conflict. Ascoli recovers his sovranty. Amaranta, the virtuous daughter of Galeotto, loves Altophil who cannot return her passion.

The Unfortunate Lovers was revived immediately after the Restoration for it occurs in a list of plays acted at the Red Bull, and it was given at Vere Street, Monday, 19th November, 1660. But, as was natural, Davenant soon claimed the monopoly of his popular tragedy, which remained a stock play. Downes tells us that Arthiope was played by Edward Kynaston, " he being then very Young Made a Compleat Female Stage Beauty, performing his Parts so well, especially *Arthiope* and *Aglaura,* being Parts greatly moving Compassion and Pity ; that it has since been Disputable among the Judicious, whether any Woman that succeeded him so Sensibly touch'd the Audience as he." [66] Various additions were made after the Restoration, the lighter episodes in particular which deal with Rampino, a gallant young soldier ; Fibbia, a widow to whom he is indebted ; and Friskin, a comic tailor ; being amplified with fresh dialogue. A new character whose business is to sing two songs, " Run to love's lott'ry " and " 'Tis in good truth ", Orna, the " little cousin " of Amaranta, makes her appearance, and there can be no doubt that this rôle was written in for the little girl, whose dancing and singing Pepys so much admired when he saw *The Law against Lovers* on Tuesday, 18th February, 1661–2. We do not know which actress succeeded Kynaston as Arthiope, but it is stated in the Elegy on the death of Edward Angel (1673) [67] that this actor was famous in the part of Friskin :—

Adieu, dear *Friskin*: Unfort'nate Lovers weep,
Your mirth is fled, and now i' th' Grave must sleep.

It may be noted that the new additions to this tragedy were first printed in the folio, 1673. Pepys records that he saw the play three times.

It were, of course, impertinent to remark the anachronisms which occur in Davenant's tragedies, since these have their own romantic setting, but it cannot escape notice that in Act I of *The Unfortunate Lovers* Arthiope appears attended in her open penance by a Carthusian monk. S. Bruno, the founder of this great Order, who died 6th October, 1101, was installed with six companions at Chartreuse by S. Hugh, Bishop of Grenoble, in the year 1084. Hildebrand, the Longobard king, who is a prominent character in the play, reigned in 744, and was succeeded that same year by Rachis. If this confused chronology were taken as a blemish no doubt Davenant would reply in the phrase of Georges de Scudéry, who in the Preface to *L'Illustre Bassa* writes: "*Now for fear it may be objected unto me, that I have approached some incidents nearer than the History hath shewed them to be, great* Virgil *shall be my warrant, who in his divine Æneads hath made* Dido *appear four Ages after her own.*" [68]

Although not published until the folio, 1673, *The Fair Favourite*,[69] licensed by Herbert on 17th November, 1638, was doubtless produced this month, and at the Blackfriars, as we may reasonably conjecture. In order to join Otranto to the kingdom of Naples his councillors have persuaded the King to marry the lady, a portion of whose dowry is the new province. This they could only do by persuading him that Eumena, whom he loved, was dead. At the nuptial banquet he discovered Eumena to be alive, and forthwith, renewing his suit, refused to know his wife. Oramont, Eumena's brother, supposes that his sister's interest at Court is due to her having become the King's mistress, but Amadore, his friend, champions her purity. After various accidents the King is reconciled to his Queen and consummates, whilst Eumena weds Amadore. The play is good and well-designed, yet I do not know that it calls for any especial remark or commendation.

On 16th August, 1637, Ben Jonson died, and upon 13th December, 1638, was issued a Patent from Charles I giving and granting William Davenant the annuity or yearly pension of one hundred pounds " in consideraĉon of seruice heretofore done and hereafter to be done vnto vs by Willm̄ Davenant gentl ". It has been very amply discussed whether Jonson did actually hold the post of poet laureate, and whether Davenant succeeded him in that office. Perhaps it might be more technically precise to say that both Jonson and Davenant were "Court poets", and that the first poet laureate in the full connotation of that term, as we take it, was John Dryden. It may certainly be argued that Davenant was not a poet laureate in the same sense as Colley Cibber and Alfred Austin were poets laureate; he was not "a stipendiary poet . . . bound to furnish twice a year a measure of praise and verse, such as may be sung in the chapel, and, I believe", (says Gibbon) [70] "in the presence, of the sovereign." Davenant would have refused to grind out New Year's Odes and Birthday Odes such as Cibber churned [71]; nor would he have been guilty of such sluttery as *England's Darling*. None the less we may truly say that he was recognized both at Court and generally by the public as holding the laureate's office, however inexactly that may have been defined in official documents. Six days after Davenant's death a warrant was issued "for a grant to John Dryden of the Office of Poet Laureate, void by the death of Sir William Davenant".[72] Nothing could be more explicit. Aubrey often refers to Davenant as Poet Laureate, and writes that "after Ben Jonson's death [Davenant] was made Poet Laureate".[73] Again on 19th May, 1668, he writes to Wood : "Sir William was Poet Laureate, and Mr. John Dryden hath his place." [74] The publisher of the 1673 folio, Herringman, who was Davenant's friend, expressly declares : "My Author was Poet Laureate to two Great Kings." It hardly skills then to inquire precisely in what details the office differed from that held by Tennyson or Bridges, it is enough that Davenant was both officially and popularly recognized as laureate from 1637, although perhaps the duties and obligations which later attached to that position had not so early taken definite shape.

Davenant now had sufficient influence to secure from King Charles on 26th March, 1639, a royal patent [75] under the Great Seal of England to erect a theatre "upon a parcel of ground lying near unto or behind the Three Kings Ordinary in Fleet Street, in the parishes of Saint Dunstan's in the West, London, or in Saint Bride's, London, or in either of them ; or in any other ground in or about that place, or in the whole street aforesaid, already allotted to him for that use, or in any other place that is or hereafter shall be assigned or allotted out to the said William Davenant by our right trusty and right well-beloved cousin and counsellor, Thomas, Earl of Arundel and Surrey, Earl Marshall of England, or any other of our commissioners for building for that time being in our behalf ". The new house was to have "necessary tiring and retiring rooms, and other places convenient, containing in the whole forty yards square at the most, wherein plays, musical entertainments, scenes, or

PLATE II

SIR WILLIAM DAVENANT

[face p. 24

other like presentments may be presented ". The warrant, which is extraordinarily verbose, authorizes the patentee " his heirs, executors, administrators, and assigns, from time to time to gather together, entertain, govern, privilege, and keep, such and so many players and persons, to exercise action, musical presentments, scenes, dancing, and the like " as he or they " shall think fit or appear for the said house ". Davenant and his heirs, etc., are also empowered to " exercise music, musical present-ments, scenes, dancing, or other the like, at the same, or other, hours, or times, or after the plays are ended, peaceably and quietly, without the impeachment or impediment of any person or persons whatsoever, for the honest recreation of such as shall desire to see the same ". There can be no question that Davenant purposed to introduce painted scenery in his new theatre, and the large building was necessary for the accom-modation of the Italian system of scenes and machines he had in mind. It is clear too from the term " musical presentments " that productions of opera [76] were being planned.

But Davenant's scheme never came to fruition and it cannot now definitely be ascertained why his project was defeated. Chalmers supposed that it was " on some disagreement with the Earl of Arundel, the landlord " [77] ; whilst Collier vaguely hints that the royal permission was withdrawn,[78] which we know was actually not the case. There was, it is true, some hostility on the part of established theatrical proprietors, and not unlikely there may have been a certain amount of opposition from the citizens and merchants living in the vicinity of the proposed house. I would further suggest that when Davenant came to practical details he probably found that certain of his backers were not so ready with their financial assistance as they had promised. Clouds were already gathering on the political horizon, and not only wise men were beginning to look to their hilts. Whatever the difficulties may have been, Davenant did not surrender his patent, but on 2nd October, 1639,[79] he made indenture waiving his right to erect a theatre in Fleet Street and undertaking indeed not to build any other playhouse in London or Westminster " unless the said place shall be first approved and allowed by warrant under His Majesty's sign manual, or by writing under the hand and seal of the said Right Honourable Thomas, Earl of Arundel and Surrey ". None the less, although the patent was thus suspended, Davenant never relinquished his rights, and the validity of his claim under the royal warrant of 26th March, 1639, was fully recognized and allowed at the Restoration,[80] what time he publicly perfected his plan of more than twenty years past. It was because of his ready compliance in the matter of this projected theatre that he was appointed Governor of the company acting at the Cockpit when, as will shortly be noted, William Beeston forfeited that position.

The paramount importance and full significance of Davenant's undertaking will only be realized when we recall that it was but two years before, in 1637, that the first public opera-house was opened, the Teatro San Cassiano in Venice,[81] a theatre which had been planned and built for movable scenes. Evelyn on 19th November, 1644, being at Rome speaks of Bernini, " a Florentine sculptor, architect, painter, and poet, who, a little before my coming to the citty, gave a publiq opera (for so they call shews of that kind) wherein he painted the scenes, and the statues, invented the engines, compos'd the musiq, writ the comedy, and built the theater." In France, during the earlier years of the minority of Louis XIV, Cardinal Mazarin, a great lover of music, was continually striving to establish Italian opera as a permanent institution at the French Court, and it may be said that opera—although at first given to a select and limited audience—was actually introduced in 1645, when the Queen and certain of the Court assisted at a performance, which, although it cannot certainly be identified, was probably the pastoral *Nicandro e Fileno,* set by Marco Marazzoli, whilst in December of the same year was seen *La Finta Pazza,* no doubt with the music of Francesco Sacrati, as it had been produced at Venice.[82] It is obvious that Davenant in England was well in the forefront of the new movement, and it seems clear that he would have established painted scenery in his new theatre in Fleet Street so soon as the house had been built, that is according to his hopes and plans, 1639-40.

On 30th November, 1639, Herbert licensed a play by Davenant entitled *The Spanish Lovers,* which undoubtedly is to be identified with *The Distresses,* first printed in the folio of 1673. The scene is laid in Cordova, and the complicated intrigue, the nocturnal serenatas, the wooing of Amiana by Don Androlio, the flight of Claramante in boy's disguise from her brother's house, the constant bustle of the duello—the scene opens with a surgeon binding up Don Balthazar's wound—

> Such climbing
> Into Windows, clambering over house-tiles
> And scratching for Females,

all point to a Spanish original or originals, for I think more than one *comedia* has been utilized. Longfellow's description of these pieces is, of course, playfully exaggerated but it has some truth :—

There were three duels fought in the first act,
Three gentlemen receiving deadly wounds,
Laying their hands upon their hearts, and saying,
" O, I am dead ! " a lover in a closet,
An old hidalgo, and a gay Don Juan,
A Doña Inez with a black mantilla,
Followed at twilight by an unknown lover,
Who looks intently when he knows she is not ! [83]

In reading *The Distresses* I am constantly reminded of *The Chances,* and although it is hard precisely to point out any one incident or character that may be borrowed, I cannot think that Fletcher's fine comedy was very far from Davenant's mind. I would hazard indeed that Orco, " a merry gentleman," was prompted by Antonio, and Androlio has a spice of Don John.

It has been said that the pride and beauty of the great masques were brought to an appropriate climax by the performance at Whitehall in January, 1640, of *Salmacida Spolia,* written by Davenant, a pageantry in the mounting of which Inigo Jones was assisted by John Webb, a relative and pupil of that great architect. The early co-operation of Webb and Davenant is particularly to be noted, for it was Webb who some sixteen years later designed the scenes for *The Siege of Rhodes,* and incidentally thus preserved the continuity of theatrical spectacle. The name *Salmacida Spolia* is derived from a verse of Ennius quoted by Festus : *Salmaci da spolia, sine sanguine, et sudore.* Upon which Scaliger glosses : " Ergo spolia quae in-cruenta sunt," reading " Salmacida ", one word, rather than " Salmaci da ", two words.[84] Davenant cites the " ancient adages " :

> Salmacida Spolia sine sanguine sine sudore, potius quam
> Cadmia victoria, ubi ipsos victores pernicies opprimit.

The original drawings of Jones for *Salmacida Spolia* are still preserved, Lansdowne MS. 1171, and have been several times reproduced. They may conveniently be consulted in P. Reyher's *Les Masques Anglais* (1909). It should be noticed that they comprise a complete system of flats or drawn scenes. I do not know upon what authority Chetwood in the brief prefatory note to his reprint of *Salmacida Spolia,* Dublin, 12mo, 1750, says : " The painting was designed by the inimitable Peter Paul Rubens." *Salmacida Spolia,* in addition to an antimasque of Furies which opened the piece after the flying up of the curtain, has a succession of no less than twenty " Entries of Antimasques " all entirely different from one another, and disconnected. In Antimasque the Eighteenth Geoffrey Hudson, the famous mannikin who is the subject of Davenant's poem *Jeoffreidos*,[86] played " a little Swiss ". Of the principal Masques the gentlemen were led by the King ; the ladies by the Queen. The music was composed by Louis Richard, the French Master of the Queen's Music, but as none of his work appears to be extant, " we have no means of judging," says Professor Dent, " how he differentiated the characters of his dancers." [87] It would seem as though every recourse of art, money, and talent were exhausted to pomp it on this occasion,[88] and the masque " was generally approved of, especially by all strangers that were present, to be the noblest and most ingenious that hath been done here in that kind ".

At the end of April, 1640, the King's and Queen's Boys, who were playing at the Cockpit, or Phoenix, in Drury Lane under the management of William Beeston,[89] with incredible foolishness gave great offence to Charles by performing an unlicensed piece which had some dangerous reference to the royal journey into Scotland. The Lord Chamberlain upon the 3rd May [90] issued a warrant for the arrest of Beeston, who on the following morning, Monday, 4th May,[91] was taken and lodged in the Marshalsea, whilst the house was promptly closed down for several days. The script of the play was confiscated by Sir Henry Herbert, whom also the King had reprimanded bidding him punish not too lightly those who proved at fault. Considerable trouble ensued in consequence of the temerity and insubordination of the actors, who were pretty severely brought to book. Beeston himself was promptly removed from his office as Governor of the Company, and the position was bestowed upon Davenant, 27th June, 1640.[92] He was empowered " to take into his government and care the said company of players, to govern, order, and dispose of them for action and presentments, and all their affairs in the said house, as in his discretion shall seem best to conduce to His Majesty's service in that quality ". Every person connected with the theatre was " to obey the said Mr. Davenant and follow his orders and directions, as they will answer the contrary ".[93] It is clear, then, that he had almost unlimited control of his new charge, and the very extent of his authority shows how entirely he was trusted and how highly he was regarded. If it be inquired why he did not introduce at the Phoenix his long-considered design of painted scenes the answer is not far to seek. In the first place his duty was divided, since other concerns of State importance pressed, and, as it proved, his tenure was brief ; moreover, it was not the time for novelties, especially when such fresh decorations would have been costly and were certainly neither looked for nor awaited ; again, the Phoenix was a small house and he could not have found sufficient scope to carry out in their entirety plans which any cramping or curtailment must have impaired if not vitally marred. James Wright tells us that " The *Black-friars, Cockpit,* and *Salisbury-court,* were called Private Houses, and were very small to what we see now . . . they were all three Built almost exactly alike, for Form and Bigness ".[94]   The Blackfriars was, we know, constructed in a hall forty-six feet broad by sixty-six feet long ; and Salisbury Court was erected on a plot of ground forty-two feet broad by one hundred and forty feet long ; hence we are able to form some rough estimate of the approximate size of the Phoenix.

It is certain that Davenant at this time held some post in the royal army,[95] but he remained in charge of the Phoenix until the first week of May, 1641, when he fled to avoid being taken by the Parliament owing to his being concerned in the promoting of a most excellent design to bring the army from Yorkshire to London for the safer protection of His Majesty, and thus to quell the disorders which angry faction was everywhere fomenting. The revolting party carried their insolence to such a degree that proclamation was made for the loyal hearts who had devised this project, and Davenant being apprehended at Faversham was sent up to London, when he was brought before the House and some while detained in custody.   After two months he was bailed, and eventually reached France, but not before he had again been arrested.   He sojourned on the continent until the close of the year 1642, when he returned with supplies for the King, and was made Lieutenant-General of the Ordnance.   At the siege of Gloucester in September, 1643, he was knighted. He remained with the royal forces until the sad defeat of Marston Moor, 2nd July, 1644, after which disaster in common with many others he withdrew to France

It is hardly necessary to follow Davenant's political fortunes in detail here.   Suffice to say that having been converted to the Catholic Faith by the famous Franciscan, François Faure, Bishop of Amiens,[96] he stood high in favour with Queen Henrietta Maria who in October, 1646, entrusted him with a mission to the King then at Newcastle-upon-Tyne.   In February, 1649–50, Davenant was appointed to supersede Lord Baltimore as Governor of Maryland,[97] but he had scarcely set sail for America, and was yet in the Channel, when his ship was captured by a Parliamentary frigate, and he was ordered to close confinement in Cowes Castle, Isle of Wight.   Early in 1651 he was transferred to the Tower, and for some time was in extremest jeopardy. After much difficulty his life was saved [98] and a pardon secured. In October, 1652, he was finally released from close imprisonment, and granted certain restricted privileges. But his troubles had not ceased, for although no longer a penned prisoner his goods and monies had all been escheated, and he was not only stripped, but severely harassed by his creditors. In these straits he did what many another man has done both before and after, he sought to refurnish himself and establish his fortunes through a lucky marriage, since at this time he was a widower, left with one daughter by Mary, his first wife. In the same month as his release from the Tower he wedded Dame Anne Cademan, whose second husband, Sir Thomas Cademan, a well-known physician of stout Royalist principles, had died in 1651.[99] Anne Cademan was the mother of a family of four, having three sons by Thomas Cross, her first husband, Thomas, Paul, and John ; and by Sir Thomas Cademan, one son, Philip, aged nine. Her jointure from her late husband's estate amounted to nearly eight hundred pounds, and this Sir William utilized, either wholly or in greater part, to satisfy his more pressing debts. He was therefore under a bond decently to maintain his stepsons until he should pay each one a several sum of one hundred pounds on or before 7th February, 1654-5. He failed, however, to discharge this obligation and we learn from his petition of 22nd March, 1654, praying to be freed from surveillance by the Lieutenant of the Tower that he was then greatly embarrassed by the constant molestations of those to whom he yet owed various sums that perforce remained undischarged. Naturally he was casting about him all the while to find some means of substantially and permanently replenishing his purse, and although the theatres were officially closed down and suppressed [100] the fact that clandestine performances, even if attended with no small degree of danger both to audience and actors, were so eagerly followed and supported, must have suggested to him that he should essay his old profession of manager and dramatist. He was in close touch with the majority of those who could be counted upon to assist and contribute to such a movement,[101] but the way was difficult and any plans must develop slowly, almost furtively, since the thing he designed stank in the nostrils of the rebels in power as a heathenish abomination and lewd vanity of Canaan, whilst he himself was a marked malignant. He laid his foundations well.

It is not without significance that in the " *Preface* to the Reader " which Flecknoe prefixed to his *Loves Dominion,* 12mo, 1654, the poet speaks of public Representation on the stage as

" much longed for still, by all the noble and better sort, and during the silent years various other writers did not hesitate to put forward a sober and measured defence of the drama. James Shirley in the famous preface " To The Reader ", which presents the 1647 folio of Beaumont and Fletcher, pens a most eloquent tribute to the theatre. His commencing periods are rarely writ : " Poetry *is the Child of* Nature, *which regulated and made beautifull by* Art, *presenteth the most Harmonious of all other compositions ; among which (if we rightly consider) the* Dramaticall *is the most absolute, in regard of those transcendent* Abilities, *which should waite upon the* Composer ; *who must have more than the instruction of Libraries (which of it selfe is but a cold contemplative knowledge) there being required in him a* Soule *miraculously knowing, and conversing with all mankind, inabling him to expresse not only the Phlegme and folly* of thick-skin'd men, *but the strength and maturity* of the wise, *the Aire and insinuations of the Court, the discipline and Resolution of the Soldier, the Vertues and passions of every noble condition, nay the councells and characters of the greatest Princes."*

Certain private performances were continually being essayed throughout the whole period of the King's exile, and if not generally approved ceremonial masques were upon occasion winked at and even by authority allowed. Thus masques were given at the Inner Temple in 1651, 1653, and 1654.[102] There is even a record of a play, otherwise unknown, by Davenant, *The Countryman,* "Acted at the Inner Temple Hall," 5th November, 1657. Bulstrode Whitelocke's influence may be discerned here. James Shirley's masque *Cupid and Death* was printed 1653, "As it was Presented. before his Excellencie, The Embassadour of Portugal, Upon the 26. of March, 1653," an official performance which presumably took place at Whitehall. In 1659 *Cupid and Death* was reprinted as "A Private Entertainment, represented with Scenes & Musick, Vocall & Instrumentall ". This second performance was given at the Military Ground in Leicester Fields, in a house belonging to the Military Company,[103] and it was for this occasion that " The Instrumentall and Vocall Musique in the Morall representation " [104] was specially composed by Matthew Locke and Christopher Gibbons. In 1659 was also printed : " *Honoria and Mammon.* Written by James Shirly Gent. . . . As it was represented by young Gentlemen of quality at a private entertainment of some Persons of Honour," at Shirley's school in Whitefriars.

Thomas Jordan's masque *Cupid His Coronation* was " Presented w^th: good Approbation at the Spittle diverse tymes by Masters and young Ladyes y^t were theyre scholers in the yeare 1654 ".

The young priest of Apollo whose speech commences the entertainment is careful to declare that nothing will be shown to wrong " Religion, Government or Modestie ". *Cupid His Coronation* has not been printed, but a MS. is preserved in the Bodleian.[105] Three years later, in 1657, was published, 4to, Jordan's masque *Fancy's Festivals,* "As it hath been privately presented by many civil persons of quality." The apology and plea for dramatic performances, as previously voiced by Apollo's priest, are emphatically repeated in the same terms in the Introduction.

Dr. Richard Whitlock in ZWOTOMIA (1654) has an essay " Profane Inspirations Plea or Poetry's Preheminence ", in which, although he entirely declines to enter the " Lists with any *Histriomastix* to maintain the *Stages Quarrell*", he maintains that the " Dramatick part of Poetry " is inferior to none for usefulness. He proceeds [106] : " Nor is it such a *Paradox* as it may seem to sound to some half-witted Eares ; for I dare aver what hath been writ for the *Stage (ancient,* or *modern)* is not inferior to any writings on the same *Theme* (excepting the *Advantages of Christianity,* and our better *Schoolmaster for Heaven)* of never so *severe* an *Authority.*"

In 1655 Sir Ralph Freeman reprinting in quarto his tragedy *Imperiale* (4to, 1639 ; 12mo, 1640), took occasion to quote various passages from Aristotle, Plutarch, and other classical authors commending the theatre, and these he introduced thus : "And therefore to manifest how Antiquity hath valu'd this kinde of Argument, I have prefixed some testimonies, that the rigid men of our age, who will be ready to say, I have been to idly busi'd may see what use the Graecians and Romans made of Tragaedy to prevaile upon the affections of the people." Leonard Willan, also, in 1658, ushers in his tragedy *Orgula, or the Fatal Error* with a " *Preface,* discovering the true nature of *Poesie,* with the proper Use and Intention of such publique Divertisements ". Although his diction is somewhat stilted he makes several good points, and particularly emphasizes the fact that plays afford an excellent means of instructing youth, an educational method which has, he insists, been admirably employed in colleges, seminaries, and schools on the Continent. This last argument and example, although greatly insisted upon and widely pursued to-day (often, perhaps, not altogether wisely) as the cream of education, would, I fear, bear little weight with the puritans, and indeed might rather tend to confirm them in their prejudices and rancour.

James Howell, again, in his *Londinopolis* comes forth as a warm advocate on behalf of the stage. He speaks of the time when

" there were more theatres in *London* than any where else ",
and continues : " It was a true observation, that those comical,
and tragical Histories, did much improve, and enrich the *English*
Language, they taught young men witty Complements, and how
to carry their Bodies in a handsome posture : Add hereunto
that they instructed them in the stories of divers things, which
being so lively represented to the eye, made firmer impression
in the memory. Lastly, They reclaimed many from Vice and
Vanity ; for though a Comedy be never so wanton, yet it ends
with vertue, and the punishment of vice."

A commendatory poem by F. Cole prefixed to George Gerbier
D'Ouvilly's *The False Favourite Disgrac'd, and the Reward of
Loyalty,* a tragi-comedy, unacted, but printed 12mo, 1657, com-
mences thus :—

> *Dramatick Poems,* though the *zealous Age*
> Will not permit them to *Adorn the Stage*)
> Are without doubt of greater Excellence
> Then *they* suppose, who *want* both *Wit* and *Sense.*
> They are the *Crowne of Vertue, Scourge of sin ;*
> Some *scape a Sermon,* whom a *Play might win.*
> Crimes of *pridigious bulk* and *purple dye,*
> Are here *dissected* and expos'd to th' eye ;
> To make them *hated* too, as well as *known*
> Few will a *Branded Malefactor* own.

It will be seen from these few examples that throughout the
literary world in London there was an undercurrent, and something more than an undercurrent, of protest against the silence
of the Stage, and even those who would have been the first to
check any undue licence or scurrility were in revolt and resented
the tyranny which sought wholly to eradicate and extinguish
the drama. Davenant could be sure of many sympathizers in his
schemes of resurrection. In March, 1655, Anne Davenant
died,[107] and some few months later Davenant obtained permission
to visit France. It is uncertain what business he pleaded, but a
pass was granted to him on 10th August of that year.[108] In France
he married for the third time, " Henrietta-Marie du Tremblay,
widow, of an ancient family in St. Germain Beaupré " of Anjou.[109]
This lady, the mother of Charles Davenant and many other sons,
plays no small part in the history of the theatre, and appears
as a shrewd and capable business woman, who not only had
confidence but materially interested herself in her husband's
ventures, since she was able to supply the money that matured
his earliest plans for reviving the drama in England. Upon
their return to London Sir William Davenant and his family
took up their residence in Rutland House, Charterhouse Yard.[110]

This had been the town mansion of Cicely, Countess Dowager of Rutland, a *grande dame* of the old school, and a staunch Catholic. On this account her estate was sequestered, and when she died in September, 1654, all her domestic goods were seized to be sold whilst Cromwell coolly pocketed the proceeds.[111] After this bit of plunder the house was handed over to George Thorn and John Hopkins the purchasers of the reversion.[112]

On Friday, 23rd May, 1656, was given *The First Dayes Entertainment at Rutland House,* the first of Davenant's regular performances under the Commonwealth. There seems no reason to dispute this accepted date, although it has been argued that entertainments had been provided by Davenant even before April, 1656. It is true that as early as February, 1656, Davenant formed a company " to build a structure for representations and shows ", and several wealthy merchants not merely signed an agreement to take up shares, of which there were to be sixteen at £275 per share, but had also in some cases made full or part payment, duly receiving receipts for the same. However, the house was never built, probably because suspicion was aroused and the puritans in power refused to tolerate any such enterprise, and eventually in 1661 the project became the subject of legal proceedings.[113] All the while Davenant was diplomatically endeavouring to obtain some kind of recognition from the authorities, for he was very well aware that without this his schemes might be crushed in a moment, his entertainments of whatsoever kind raided by the military, the audience dispersed, the actors clapped up in ward. Accordingly he approached the all-powerful Bulstrode Whitelocke, a keen amateur musician, who indeed little more than twenty years before had been generally responsible for the music of Shirley's *The Triumph of Peace,*[114] a superb masque organized by the Inns of Court in 1633–4 as a direct expression of protest against Prynne's *Histriomastix.* Whitelocke, who was very friendly disposed to Davenant, received him kindly, and encouraged him in his undertaking, the ultimate aim and scope of which we may be sure the poet was careful not to press too nearly or prematurely in the proceedings. Yet so long as there was no question of the opening of a regular theatre with profane stage-plays to give scandal, Entertainments and even Opera— a term which, it must be remembered, was then imperfectly defined—might be allowed ; nay, even encouraged. A little later Davenant addressed a memorandum [115] to John Thurloe, the republican Secretary of State, a man of great influence with Cromwell, and in this document various arguments emphasizing the utility of " moral representations " are most adroitly marshalled, none being more effective than a suggestion of the possibility of employing such entertainments for political purposes. Parliament was about to vote a vast sum for the war against Spain, a country Cromwell particularly hated, since the Catholic Spaniard " by reason of the enmity that is in him against whatever is of God " was the " natural enemy " of the Good Old Cause, and Davenant with more policy than probity proposed that one of his entertainments should show the grannam myth of the barbarities practised by the Spaniards when they conquered the Western Indies and " their severall cruelties there exercis'd ".

This, however, was when the poet was essaying to make his Entertainments something more elaborate, and it will be necessary to retrace our steps a few months in order to consider the very beginnings. That Davenant had approached Bulstrode White-locke upon the subject of these permissive " moral representa-tions " was not a secret, indeed there seems no reason why his first efforts should have been kept dark or in any wise con-cealed, and the cavalier lampoons of the day jeer him as assuming the office of Master of the Revels.[116] They forget that by no other means could he have attained his end. To have flouted the existing state of things by clandestine performances would have entirely defeated his purpose, and must merely have led to a series of raids upon the old playhouses, tennis courts, or other rendezvous where his entertainments might be given. That Davenant ever sought, or indeed would have accepted, such a position as Master of the Revels under Cromwell, even had the office been established which is in itself more than un-likely, I do not for a moment believe. It is true that Sir Henry Herbert in July, 1662, when he was entangled in multifold lawsuits with both Davenant and Killigrew, and was defending his precious monopoly and his outraged dignity in a very bellicose hogan-mogan manner, in a petition to the Lord High Chancellor and the Lord Chamberlain furiously abused Davenant as " a person who exercised the office of Master of the Reuells to Oliuer the Tyrant, and wrote the First and Second Parte of Peru, acted at the Cockpitt, in Oliuers tyme, and soly in his fauour ", but this is deliberate misrepresentation, and in his efforts to harm his adversary Herbert without conscience or scruple heaps together the most baseless scandals and untruths.

As we have seen, in February, 1656, Davenant was all agog to build a new theatre, and when this plan fell through, with his wonted cheery optimism he set about finding a convenient house where the projected Entertainment might most com-modiously be given. The pasquil *How Daphne pays his Debts* makes fine fun of his various negotiations, and in the course of these he seems to have treated for Apothecaries Hall, which indeed after the Restoration was actually used for rehearsals of *The Siege of Rhodes* and *The Witts*.

Finally after all his peregrinations and more than one false start Davenant decided that no place would better serve his purpose, and incidentally no doubt suit his purse, than his own residence, Rutland House. Here then in a narrow hall at the back of the mansion on Friday, 23rd May, 1656, was given the *First Dayes Entertainment*. The following contemporary account [117] is of considerable interest.

The Bills for Sr Will: Dauenants
Opera are thus Intitled./.

The Entertainment by Musick and Declarations [*sic*] after the manner of the Ancients./.

The Scene Athens

Upon friday the 23 of May 1656 These foresaid Declarations began att the Charterhouse and 5^{s.} a head for the entrance. The expectation was of 400 persons, but there appeared not aboue 150 auditors. The roome was narrow, at the end of which was a stage and on ether side two places railed in, Purpled and Guilt, The Curtayne also that drew before them was of cloth of gold and Purple./.

After the Prologue (wch told them this was but the Narrow passage to the Elizium theire Opera) Vp came Diogenes and Aristophanes, the first against the Opera, the other for it. Then came up A Citizen of Paris speaking broken English—and a Citizen of London and reproached one a nother wth the Defects of each Citty in theire Buildings, Manners, Customes, Diet, &c : And in fine the Londoner had the better of itt, who concluded that hee had seene two Crocheteurs in Paris both wth heavy burdens on theire backs stand complementing for ye way wth, ceste a vous Mons^{r:} Mons^{r:} uous uous Mocquies de Moy &c : which lasted till they both fell down under their burden./.

The Musick was aboue in a loouer hole railed about and couered wth Sarcenetts to conceale them, before each speech was consort Musick. At the end were songs relating to the Victor (the Protector). The last song ended wth deriding Paris and the french, and concluded

And though a shipp her scutchen bee
yet Paris hath noe shipp at sea./.

The first song was made by Hen: Lawes, ye other by Dr. Coleman who were the Composers. The Singers were Capt. Cooke, Ned Coleman and his wife, another wooman and other inconsiderable voyces. It lasted an howre and a haulfe and is to continue for 10 dayes by wch time other Declamations wilbee ready./.

Although the Contention of the Parisian and the Londoner is certainly amusing and vivacious, whilst their speeches have much that is interesting, it would, I fear, prove a tiresome business enough to sit through the lengthy harangues of the Cynic and the Poet. Yet perhaps they seemed brief to a company who must often have been compelled to listen to indeterminate Genevan discourses endlessly unwinding from the lofty pulpit their coils of seventhly and eighthly, and we may also remember the enormous sermons of the great divines; sermons which if preached as written must have taken two or three hours to deliver; sermons of Tillotson and South; sermons of Barrow who on one occasion preached unwearied, save as he said of standing so long, before the Lord Mayor for three and a half hours.

As we might expect, in the Entertainment Aristophanes easily wins the day, and certes the arguments of Diogenes are somewhat of the ninepin variety. I have no doubt that the music was exceedingly agreeable, and the audience were surely grateful for this dramatic antepast. The small number of those who assisted is easily to be accounted for, since many would fear some raid or molestation during the performance and prefer to wait before they ventured, nor could the news that such an Entertainment was to be given have reached more than a limited few, since even with permission obtained it would have been impolitic, perhaps hazardous, to have bruited the matter too widely, and it is not difficult to understand why only those who were the most enthusiastic or who were closely in touch with Davenant put in an appearance. That plenty of encouragement was forthcoming a little later is certain from the fact that Davenant shortly proceeded to far more ambitious efforts.

Mention is made of " songs relating to the Victor (the Protector) ", but these are not given in the printed copy of the *First Dayes Entertainment,* octavo, 1657, which there is reason to think may have been issued on 22nd November, 1656, as that date is written by a contemporary hand in a copy belonging to the British Museum, and a book issued late in 1656 might regularly have borne the imprint of the following year. There is no reason to doubt that such songs were sung, and their introduction would have enormously facilitated the granting of the required licence. No information has been obtained with regard to the " other Declamations " which were to be ready after the ten days " run "—if I may so employ this expression—of the *First Dayes Entertainment.* The *Satyrical Declamations, by Sir William Davenant, Knight,* advertised in *Mercurius Politicus,* 13th to 20th May, 1658; and *Satyricall Declamations at the Opera* advertised in *A Catalogue of New Books,* London, 1660, if any other than the *First Dayes Entertainment* itself have not been traced. My own view of the matter is that these two books are the octavo *Entertainment,* 1657. I am all the more inclined to believe this because Davenant's time and activities must now have been fully occupied with his preparations for the next production, an event of paramount importance in the history of the English theatre.

The first English Opera, *The Siege of Rhodes,* was announced as "A Representation by the art of Prospective in Scenes and the Story sung in Recitative Musick ". The exact date when it was first given at Rutland House is not known, but it was certainly one day early in September, 1656. Some weeks before, Davenant had sent the script, or libretto if you will, to the printer and his preface " To the Reader " is signed 17th August, 1656. From what he says it is obvious that his Opera was then near production, and on 3rd September he submitted a copy to Bulstrode Whitelocke to whom he also addressed the following letter :—

My Lord,

When I consider the nicety of the Times, I fear it may draw a Curtain between your Lordship and our Opera ; therefore I have presumed to send your Lordship, hot from the Press, what we mean to represent ; making your Lordship my supreme Judge, though I despair to have the Honour of inviting you to be a Spectator. I do not conceive the perusal of it worthy any part of your Lordship's leisure, unless your antient relation to the Muses [118] make you not unwilling to give a little entertainment to Poetry ; though in so mean a dress as this and coming from, my Lord,

Your Lordship's
most obedient Servant,
WILLIAM DAVENANT.

We probably shall not be far out if we place the production of *The Siege of Rhodes* some seven or eight days after this letter.

When Evelyn was at Venice in 1645, during Ascension Week he made the following entry in his *Diary* : " This night, having with my Lord Bruce [119] taken our places before, we went to the opera,[120] where comedies and other plays are represented in recitative musiq, by the most excellent musicians, vocal and instrumental, with variety of sceanes painted and contrived with no lesse art of perspective, and machines for flying in the aire, and other wonderful motions ; taken together, it is one of the most magnificent and expensive diversions the wit of man can invent. The history was, Hercules in Lydia [121] ; the sceanes changed thirteen times. The famous voices, Anna Rencia, a Roman, and reputed the best treble of women ; but there was an eunuch who, in my opinion, surpassed her ; also a Genoese that sung an incomprable bass. This held us by the eyes and ears till two in the morning." Indeed the great features of Italian Opera were scenic and spectacular extravagancies and surprises of the most costly and magnificent sort that could be devised, and accordingly the theme was inevitably some mythological story which gave a full scope for all the wonders and admiration of enchantment. Since the stage at Rutland House was narrow to a degree, and there was, moreover, no excess of funds, his very limitations compelled Davenant to plan something widely different from Opera as it was known in Italy or even in France. In the first place a story which would necessitate " machines for flying in the aire " and other designs of this sort was entirely out of the question, and consequently the poet-manager selected an historical theme, although at the same time he took good care that it was a story with which romance, love, and valour might well be mingled.

In this connexion it is interesting to note that Davenant (addressing Hobbes) in the Preface prefixed to *Gondibert* (1650) had already contemned the epic " machinery " : "And more closely than *Virgill* waits on *Homer* doth *Statius* attend *Virgill*, and follows him there also where Nature never comes, even into Heaven and Hell : and therefore he cannot escape such as approve the wisdom of the best Dramaticks, who, in the representation of examples, beleeve they prevail most on our manners, when they lay the Scene at home in their own Country ; so much they avoid those remote Regions of Heaven and Hell, as if the People, whom they make civill by an easie communication with reason (and familiar reason is that which is call'd the civility of the Stage) were become more discreet than to have their eyes perswaded by the descending of Gods in gay Clouds, and more manly than to be frighted with the rising of Ghosts in Smoke."

Tasso's errors in this kind " admit no pardon. Such are his Councell assembled in Heaven, his Witches Expeditions through the Air, and enchanted Woods inhabited with Ghosts ". Davenant continues with great severity that even if the elder Poets " fed the world with supernaturall Tales . . . Yet a Christian Poet, whose Religion little needs the aids of Invention, hath less occasion to imitate such Fables as meanly illustrate a probable Heaven by the fashion and dignity of Courts, and make a resemblance of Hell out of the Dreams of frighted Women, by which they continue and increase the melancholy mistakes of the People ". These are very chaste ideas,[122] and however straitly he may have maintained them so far as the Epic is concerned, when he found opportunity in the theatre he went to the other extreme, for it cannot be forgotten that it was Davenant who helped to dress *Macbeth* "in all it's Finery, as new Cloath's, new Scenes, Machines, as flyings for the Witches; with all the Singing and Dancing in it"[123]; and who, moreover, altered and elaborated *The Tempest.*

Yet for Rutland House he certainly showed no ordinary perspicacity in fixing upon such an event as the famous siege of Rhodes in 1522, when six hundred *Chevaliers* with 4,500 soldiers resisted for six months a force numbering nearly a quarter of a million.[124] " Nothing has been well lost save Rhodes ! " exclaimed the great Emperor Charles V, who afterwards bestowed Malta on the Order. The historical part of Davenant's play was derived from Richard Knolles' *The Generall Historie of the Turkes,* London, 1603, a narrative which in many respects he has fairly closely followed. He would also seem to be indebted to a work by Giacomo Bosio, *Dell'Istoria della Sacra Religione e Illma Militia di San Giovanni Gierosolimitano,* which was published at Rome in Two Parts, 1594. The hint, it is nothing more, for the romantic episodes, perhaps one ought more precisely to say the romantic emotions which have so much to do with the development of the plot, was taken from the famous work of Madeleine de Scudéry, *Ibrahim, ou l'Illustre Bassa,* which had been translated into English by Henry Cogan and published London, folio, 1652, but which Davenant knew well in its original.[125] I am aware that it has been argued that Davenant drew largely from the Solyman-Perseda group of stories and plays.[126] These would include Yver's *Le Printemps* and Mainfray's *La Rhodienne,* and in English Wotton's *Cupid's Cautels* with the old tragedy of *Solimon and Perseda.*[127] Since these stories concern the same cycle of events one is not surprised that resemblances, some of which are quite striking in themselves, can be traced and emphasized, but there is nothing that Davenant could not very well have found elsewhere.

From whatever source or sources the poet derived his plot, his chief measure of complaint is that he was obliged to curtail a narrative full of incidents and bring it down to the smallest compass, and Dryden aptly observes that even when Davenant " *review'd his* Siege of Rhodes, *and caus'd it to be acted as a just Drama . . . There wanted the fulness of a Plot, and the variety of Characters to form it as it ought* ".[128] Davenant was himself only too conscious of this, for in the preface " To the Reader " he pleads with the audience to excuse the defects, and he plainly says that it is for them to remedy these " by building us a larger room ", a matter of funds, and he pertinently adds what has been the cry of writers and artists in all ages, that those who are interested in and devoted to art for art's sake "have not alwayes money to expend in things necessary towards the making up of perfection". We cannot do better than allow him to relate the difficulties, neither few nor unimportant, with which he had to cope in his own frank phrase : "It has been often wisht that our scenes (we having oblig'd our selves to the variety of five changes, according to the ancient drammatick distinctions made for time) had not been confin'd to eleven foot in height, and about fifteen in depth, including the places of passage reserv'd for the musick. This is so narrow an allowance for the fleet of *Solyman* the Magnificent, his army, the Island of *Rhodes,* and the varieties attending the siege of the city, that I fear you will think we invite you to such a contracted trifle as that of the *Caesars* carved upon a nut.

"As these limits have hinder'd the splendor of our scene, so we are like to give no great satisfaction in the quantity of our argument, which is in story very copious ; but shrinks to a small narration here, because we could not convey it by more than seven persons ; being constrain'd to prevent the length of *recitative* musick, as well as to conserve, without incumbrance, the narrowness of the place. Therefore you cannot expect the chief ornaments belonging to a history dramatically digested into turns and counterturns, to double walks, and interweavings of design."

Since Inigo Jones had now been dead for some four years, Davenant naturally called in the assistance of the pupil and lifelong companion of that great master, John Webb, with whom, it will readily be remembered, he had been associated when his masque *Salmacida Spolia* was produced at Whitehall. Although confined to so narrow a room—"a cup-board scene " —it was obvious that poet and artist would endeavour, as far as possible, to work upon the familiar lines of the court masques of the preceding reign, and accordingly we find that a usual and striking feature of the decor of these entertainments, to wit an emblematic proscenium or Frontispiece with the conventional hatchment was provided. "The Ornament which encompass'd the scene, consisted of several columns, of gross rustick work, which bore up a large freese. In the middle of the freese was a compartiment, wherein was written RHODES." Fortunately in 1914 there were discovered at Chatsworth by Mr. William Grant Keith six drawings, finished in pen-and-ink, which he identified as the proscenium and five scenes for the first production of *The Siege of Rhodes*.[129] We are thus enabled almost completely to reconstruct the appearance of the stage. The opening was 18 ft. 4 in. wide, and 9 feet high; for

Davenant's "Eleven foot in height" includes 2 feet for the depth of the frieze. The background of the frieze consisted of ample crimson drapery, caught up at either side of the frontis-piece so that the ends hung half-way in rich foldings. At the sides of the stage (the total depth of which was but 18 feet) were set three pairs of wings, each successive pair being wider and advanced nearer to the middle of the stage, so that the space between the furthest pair could only have measured 7 feet. These side-wings were purely conventional, representing "craggy rocks and high cliffs with several verdures naturally growing" upon them, and they remained unchanged throughout the progress of the play. The changes of scene were effected by means of the five shutters, each of which measured 9 feet in length and 7 ft. 6 in. in height. The first of these, marked by Webb "1 : sceane. Rhodes. A shutter.", was a panorama of a maritime coast, whereon was depicted the true prospect of the City of Rhodes with its harbour, and upon the sea horizon, as it were a few miles distant, was painted the Turkish fleet with crowded sail making towards the city. It is evident that Webb based his drawing upon correct topographical authority, and he had clearly studied with some care the views of Rhodes given in Daniel Meisner's *Thesaurus Philo-Politicus* (tertia pars), 4to, 1625, and G. F. Camotti's *Rodi Città*, Venice, 1571. The second scene showed Rhodes "beleaguer'd at Sea and Land," writes Davenant, but Webb's design "2 : Sceane. The Towne beseige[d]. A Shutter" is a landward view of the town from the south-east. It is in fact a picture of an assault, showing on the left the walls of the town, and on the right the tents of the enemy and their artillery delivering a fierce cannonade whilst in the bay the Otto-man fleet manœuvres. The next scene was a "releieve" displaying the Royal Pavilion of Solyman, and in order to show this the back shutter opened in the middle, and the pair of flats ran off right and left. "These 'relieve' scenes, or scenes in relief," says Mr. Keith, "were apparently used when a greater effect of distance was required than could be rendered on a single back shutter, or flat, and they consequently were of composite form. Lacking detail drawings showing their working, the make-up of these scenes cannot precisely be determined, but an examination of the drawings now under consideration gives us a pretty strong clue to their disposition. They were in common use in Inigo Jones' masques, and in the plan of the stage for *Salmacida Spolia* they occupied the same position, *i.e.* between the back shutters and the back set." Shortly the scene returned to that of the town besieged, and then it was "varied to the prospect of Mount Philermus" with the Turkish army, whose

THE SIEGE OF RHODES: ACT II: SCENE I

Original design by John Webb

Copyright of His Grace the Duke of Devonshire

[face p. 42

disposition is rendered in minutest detail, drawn up in the plain below.

It should here be remarked that since it was not possible to bring a large number of supernumeraries upon the stage, Davenant followed French precedent [130] and the figures were painted upon the canvas. This established an English custom which at best could hardly have been illusive, and often must have been ludicrous to a degree.

It may be remarked that Sebastiano Serlio in his *Il Primo* [—*Quinto*] *Libro d'Architectura,* Venice, 1551, expressly condemns this practice of depicting persons as if they were characters in a play upon the canvas of the scene. Notwithstanding the device long persisted, and perhaps even to-day is not altogether unknown in the English theatre. [131]

The fifth design by Webb which he describes as : " 5 ; Sceane. The Town generally assaulted, especially at the English Bulwarke, a Shutter," very exactly tallies with the description given by Davenant which runs thus : " The Scene is chang'd into a representation of a general assault given to the town ; the greatest fury of the army being discern'd at the English station." It is a spirited and even imposing picture, for we must bear in mind that it is a picture, and does not, as later scenery was generally supposed to do, merely provide a place or background for the action. Indeed, the action itself is presented on the scene in a remarkably realistic fashion. The Turkish troops are depicted as advancing in solid battalia in their attempt to take the town by storm. That he may render this with the more vigour and boldness Webb has dispensed with his wonted topographical accuracy, not that this licence matters much in so crowded and indeed conventional a display.

The final scene of Davenant's Opera was the shutter of Rhodes " beleaguer'd ", and the performance concludes with the fate of the city left still undecided. It has been questioned whether the author first wrote his script in full, that is to say, the entire piece produced at the theatre in Lincoln's Inn Fields some five years later, and then cut down the play to befit the limitations of Rutland House, both as regards actual space and performers, or whether he first wrote the libretto as it was originally given and afterwards elaborated and enlarged it when he had the facilities to present it as he wished. It certainly seems more probable and the more natural course that he should have added to and amplified the book which was printed quarto, 1656 (reprinted with very slight differences 1659). Later he penned a second part completing the first, and in both parts he introduces, with others, the important character of Roxolana, and featly rounds the whole story.[132]

It must not escape notice that when Webb was called upon to mount *The Siege of Rhodes* he was confronted with a new problem which he solved most successfully, and that without any borrowing from the theatres either of Italy or of France. The Rutland House stage as he arranged it was in reality a simplified form of Inigo Jones's masque stage of the most developed type, and as his inspiration came from his master, so his style of composition is obviously modelled upon that of the great artist. Economization of space was certainly one of the chief considerations in the production, and had it not been for this Webb no doubt would have extended his stage as an apron in front of the proscenium, but such an arrangement must have taken up a certain amount of the seating accommodation of the theatre, and this could not be spared since the productions had to be made to pay their way and accordingly they depended upon their audiences. It was lack of room again which obliged Webb to content himself with only three wings on either side. The stage for *Salmacida Spolia* had four, and this was the usual number. As Davenant fully and most generously acknowledged, Webb played no small part in conveying from the masque and establishing the pictorial traditions of the theatre in their best developments, and although there is no actual evidence to show that he painted scenes for the public playhouses, we may well assume this to have been the case since when on 18th October, 1666, Davenant's company performed at Whitehall the Earl of Orrery's heroic tragedy *Mustapha, The Son of Solyman The Magnificent,* it was Webb who was asked to design the very beautiful and elaborate scenery, the drawings for which are still preserved in the collection at Chatsworth.

The characters in *The Siege of Rhodes* (1656) were personated as follows: Solyman, Captain Henry Cook; Villerius, Gregory Thorndell; Alphonso, Edward Coleman; the Admiral of Rhodes, Matthew Locke; Pirrhus, John Harding; Mustapha, Henry Purcell; and Ianthe, Mrs. Coleman. The Instrumental Music was composed by Dr. Charles Coleman, who had formerly been a member of Charles I's band, and Mr. George Hudson.

Although described as an Opera, *The Siege of Rhodes* does not in the least resemble the libretti of any Operas which were being produced in Italy at that time, nor has it anything in common with the gorgeous ballets which were seen at Paris.[133] In fact as regards the latter Davenant was obliged to eliminate dancing, which had been an essential feature of the Caroline masques. The numbers are " often diversify'd and fall into short fractions ;

... for frequent alterations of measure (which cannot be so unpleasant to him that reads as troublesome to him that writes) are necessary to *recitative* musick for variation of *ayres* ". The whole Opera then was in *Stilo Recitativo* alternating with arias and choruses. In its original form, Dryden did not consider *The Siege of Rhodes* " *a just* Drama ", although, as is well known, he argued that it was in some sort the first heroic play, or the prototype of an heroic play, since in his essay " Of Heroique Playes " prefixed to the first part of *The Conquest of Granada*, 4to, 1672, he says : " *For Heroick Plays, (in which onely I have us'd it [Rhyme] without the mixture of Prose) the first light we had of them on the* English Theatre *was from the late Sir* William D'Avenant : *It being forbidden him in the Rebellious times to act Tragedies and Comedies, because they contain'd some matter of Scandal to those good people, who could more easily dispossess their lawful Sovereign than endure a wanton jeast ; he was forc'd to turn his thoughts another way : and to introduce the examples of moral vertue, writ in verse, and perform'd in* Recitative Musique." [134] It might be queried, and the point is certainly not without interest, how far the recitative style of the first English Opera influenced or affected the delivery of actors who were sustaining characters in tragedy. The author [135] of *The Fairy-Queen*, 4to, 1692, says : " He must be a very ignorant Player, who knows not there is a Musical Cadence in speaking : and that a Man may as well speak out of Tune, as sing out of Tune " ; and Aaron Hill in the dedication to his tragedy *The Fatal Vision, or The Fall of Siam*, 4to, 1716,[136] condemns the affected, vicious, and unnatural tone of voice, so common on the stage at that time. Anthony Aston, whose *Brief Supplement to Colley Cibber, Esq., his Lives of the late Famous Actors and Actresses,* was probably written in 1747 or 1748, says of Mrs. Barry that she " had a Manner of drawing out her Words, which became her. ... Neither she, nor any of the Actors of those Times, had any Tone in their speaking, (too much, lately, in Use) ". It is somewhat difficult to understand what Aston means, since he certainly does not intend to convey that Mrs. Barry's voice was monotonous or without feeling. All critics are agreed that she was one of the greatest actresses who ever trod the boards, and Cibber says that her voice was " full, clear and strong, so that no Violence of Passion could be too much for her : And when Distress or Tenderness possess'd her, she subsided into the most affecting Melody and Softness. In the Art of exciting Pity she had a Power beyond all the Actresses I have yet seen, or what your Imagination can conceive ".[137] Davies tells us further : " Mrs. Barry was mistress of all the passions of the mind : love, joy, grief, rage, tenderness, and jealousy, were all represented by her with equal skill and equal effect. In the play of the Orphan, when, on leaving Castalio, in the last act, she burst out into that affecting exclamation ' O poor Castalio ! ' she never failed to shed tears herself, nor was it possible for the audience to refrain from correspondent lamentations." [138]

With regard to the great Betterton Cibber writes [139] : " In the just Delivery of Poetical Numbers, particularly where the Sentiments are pathetick, it is scarce credible upon how minute an Article of Sound depends their greatest Beauty or Inaffection. The Voice of a Singer is not more strictly ty'd to Time and Tune, than that of an Actor in Theatrical Elocution : The least Syllable too long or too slightly dwelt upon in a Period depreciates it to nothing ; which very Syllable if rightly touch'd shall, like the heightening Stroke of Light from a Master's Pencil, give Life and Spirit to the whole. I never heard a Line in Tragedy come from *Betterton* wherein my Judgment, my Ear, and my Imagination were not fully satisfy'd ; which, since his Time, I cannot equally say of any one Actor whatsoever." He also tells us : " *Betterton* had a Voice of that kind which gave more Spirit to Terror than to the softer Passions ; of more strength than Melody," whilst Aston writes : " His Voice was low and grumbling ; yet he could Tune it by an artful *Climax,* which enforc'd universal Attention, even from the *Fops* and *Orange-Girls.*" With regard to Kynaston whom Cibber praises very highly for his grave majesty of demeanour : " This true Majesty *Kynaston* had so entire a Command of, that when he whisper'd the following plain Line to *Hotspur,*

Send us your Prisoners, or you'll hear of it ! [140]

he convey'd a more terrible Menace in it than the loudest Intemperance of Voice could swell to. But let the bold Imitator beware, for without the Look and just Elocution that waited on it an Attempt of the same Nature may fall to nothing." Davies has an anecdote which may or may not be true. " I have been informed, by some of the old comedians, that, from his early representation of women's characters Kynaston had contracted some disagreeable tones in speaking, something like whining, or what we term canting. When George Powell was once discharging the intemperance of the preceding day from his stomach, during the time of action Kynaston asked him if he was sick. ' How is it possible to be otherwise,' said Powell, ' when I hear you speak.' " [141] William Mountford had a " Voice clear, full, and melodious ... His Addresses had a resistless

Recommendation from the very Tone of his Voice, which gave his Words such softness that, as *Dryden* says,

> *—Like Flakes of feather'd Snow,*[142]
> *They melted as they fell."*

Benjamin Victor in his *The History of the Theatres,* 1761,[143] tells of "the good old Manner of singing and quavering out their tragic Notes", and a little later he particularly mentions Colley Cibber's "quavering tragedy Tones". But Cibber was notoriously bad in tragedy both as an actor and a writer, so a mannerism which may have passed unnoticed, or perhaps even have been effective in a fine tragic actor might become ridiculous in a performer whose talent lay in comedy. Probably Susanna Maria Cibber was the last of the great actresses who retained the tragic elocution in vogue under Charles II, and of her declamation we have a highly interesting account by Richard Cumberland in his *Memoirs,*[144] when he describes a performance of Rowe's *The Fair Penitent* with Quin as Horatio; Garrick, Lothario; and Mrs. Cibber, Calista. "Quin presented himself upon the rising of the curtain in a green velvet coat embroidered down the seams, an enormous full-bottomed periwig, rolled stockings, and high-heeled square-toed shoes; with very little variation of cadence, and in a deep full tone, accompanied by a sawing kind of action, which had more of the senate than of the stage in it, he rolled out his heroics with an air of dignified indifference, that seemed to disdain the plaudits, that were bestowed upon him. Mrs. Cibber in a key, high pitched but sweet withal, sung or rather recitatived Rowe's harmonious strain, something in the manner of the Improvisatoires: it was so extremely wanting in contrast, that, though it did not wound the ear, it wearied it." This is all very well, but we must remember that of Quin Charles Churchill wrote:

> His words bore sterling weight, nervous and strong
> In manly tides of sense they roll'd along.
> Happy in art, he chiefly had pretence
> To keep up Numbers, yet not forfeit Sense.
> No actor ever greater heights could reach
> In all the labour'd artifice of speech.[145]

And of Mrs. Cibber he says:

> Form'd for the tragic scene, to grace the stage,
> With rival excellence of Love and Rage,
> Mistress of each soft art, with matchless skill
> To turn and wind the passions as she will;
> To melt the heart with sympathetic woe,
> Awake the sigh, and teach the tear to flow;

To put on Frenzy's wild distracted glare,
And freeze the soul with horror and despair;
With just desert enroll'd in endless fame,
Conscious of worth superior, *Cibber* came.[146]

It is evident that an actor and an actress who could merit such praise from no very sympathetic critic must both have been of the first rank.

Of Anna Maria Yates, the great tragedienne who died in 1787, Dibdin says [147]: " If she had a fault it was an emulation of the best French actresses, which gave a declamatory air to her delivery but in her it was less a fault than it would have been in any other actress, because her voice was so wonderfully well calculated for this part of acting, that what would have appeared monotonous in any other, was in her penetrating to admiration." Davies in his *Dramatic Miscellanies* greatly admired the " just elocution, noble manner, warm passion, and majestic deportment " of Mrs. Yates. Dibdin's allusion to " the best French actresses " is interesting, and he was perhaps thinking of the verse of Racine, for, as Arthur Symons has so admirably written,[148] " there was a time when Racine was looked upon as old-fashioned, as conventional, as frigid. It is realized nowadays that his verse has cadences like the cadences of Verlaine, that his language is as simple and direct as prose, and that he is one of the most passionate of poets." Speaking of Sarah Bernhardt in the rôle of Phèdre he adds : " She seems to abandon herself wholly, at times, to her " fureurs " ; she tears the words with her teeth, and spits them out of her mouth, like a wild beast ravening upon its prey ; but there is always dignity, restraint, a certain remoteness of soul, and there is always the verse, and her miraculous rendering of the verse, to keep Racine in the right atmosphere. . . . She has Racine's verse, along with Racine's psychology . . . everything is coloured by the poetry, everything is subordinate to beauty."

Davies in highly praising the Jaffier of William Brereton, an actor of Garrick's school, advises him to " avoid tones in speaking which approach to something like singing ". The same critic wrote of Mrs. Siddons [149]: " Her voice, though not so harmonious as Mrs. Cibber's, is strong and pleasing ; nor is a word lost for want of due articulation, which the comedian should always consider as his first duty." The tendency of the Kemble style of acting was to emphasize and stress the measure and rhythmic structure of verse. Macready, who aimed at belonging to the " natural " school of actors, broke away from tradition, and the *Daily News* at the time of his retirement in 1851 remarked : " In speaking he paid less attention to the modulation of his tones, and to the rhythmical flow of verse than any other great actor whom we remember." As early indeed as 1827 the critic of the *New Monthly* censured his " too fitful, hurried, and familiar " delivery of the verse in *Macbeth*.

Personally I am very certain that the style of declamation used by Mrs. Barry, Mrs. Cibber, Mrs. Yates, and many other great actresses was that which in our own day was employed by Sybil Thorndike when she played Evadne in *The Maid's Tragedy*, by Isabel Jeans when she played Aspatia, and by Edith Evans as Cressida, Evadne, and Cleopatra (*All for Love*). No elocution could be more beautiful or more effective, and its original, in my view at least, might be traced to the performance of *The Siege of Rhodes*.

Whether the audiences attracted to Rutland House by the Entertainment were small or large Davenant won a veritable triumph with his Opera, so great indeed was his success that he found it impossible to be hampered by the limitations of the cramped room which had served for his restricted stage, and he began to cast about to obtain a public theatre. This, it must be remembered, was an important move, and entailed more weighty consideration than may at first be apparent. The performances whether of the *Entertainment* or of *The Siege of Rhodes* might technically have been regarded as private, since they took place in a private house. That Opera should be given publicly and in a common theatre was a vastly different matter. It cannot but have been through the influence of Bulstrode Whitelocke that Davenant secured permission to open his old theatre, the Cockpit (or Phoenix) in Drury Lane. In any case, licence was granted, and I doubt not that the concession was extremely facilitated by the theme of the opera the poet proposed to represent, namely the very subject he had suggested in his memorandum to Thurloe, the cruelty of the Spaniards in Peru. At this time the Cockpit stood sadly in need of repairs and renovation for the interior had been damaged and even dismantled by a company of soldiers nearly ten years before, on Saturday, 24th March, 1649. However, it was refitted as speedily as might be, and the old playhouse once again welcomed crowding audiences. The exact day on which performances were commenced here is not, I think, to be ascertained, but we may say with certainty that it must have been before 25th July, 1658, since George Thomason has inscribed this date upon the printed copy he then purchased. The book is as follows : *The Cruelty of the Spaniards in Peru. Exprest by Instrumentall and Vocall Musick, and by the Art of Perspective in Scenes, &c.* The title-page informs us that the piece is " Represented daily at the *Cockpit* in *Drury-*

Lane, At Three after noone punctually ". The idea of a dramatic presentation dealing with the Conquest of Peru—that " magnificent epic " as Prescott has well termed this great action—seems to have been suggested to Davenant by an inflammatory work of John Phillips, *The Tears of the Indians : Being An Historical and true Account Of the Cruel Massacres and Slaughters of above Twenty Millions of innocent People ; Committed by the Spaniards.* Published in January, 1656, and dedicated to Cromwell, this transpontine apologue purports to be translated from the notorious narrative of the Dominican Bartolomé De Las Casas,[150] who, as is well known, waged a fierce and unbalanced crusade on behalf of the natives, and whose *Brevísima Relacion de la Destruycion de las Indias,* Seville, 1552, has been aptly described as a violent libel.[151]

Davenant's scenario served its purpose well enough, and attention must be drawn to his tact and skill in making the representation, since it was designed for public performance, far less dramatic than *The Siege of Rhodes.* Indeed, *The Cruelty of the Spaniards in Peru* is not dramatic at all. It merely consists of six entries with speeches and songs, mimic dances, and various acrobatic feats such as " the Sea-horse ", " the Spring ", " the Porpoise ", " the Double Somerset ", exhibited by the attendant of the Priest of the Sun.[152] There is, of course, a sufficiently lurid torment and torture episode. All this is nothing else than political propaganda, and it is just as preposterous as such sophisticate jockeydom must always be. No doubt it was well patronized by the sort of person who wanted to believe it, and " for those who like this kind of thing, this is the kind of thing they like ".

Yet this medley must have proved not a little offensive to many, since Charles II was greatly relying upon Spanish help to aid him in the recovery of his kingdom, whilst in the summer of 1658 James, Duke of York, now an Admiral of the Spanish Fleet, was actively engaged with the Spanish army under Don Juan, and the French Condé who for a time had entered Philip's service. We are anything but surprised to find that several satires were written against *The Cruelty of the Spaniards in Peru,* and one of these, *Peru, Or, a new Ballad,* was not only printed in *Choyce Poems,* London, 1661, but even found a place in the Third Part of Dryden's collection, *Miscellany Poems.*[153] The stanzas which jeer the bugaboo torture scenes are so amusing, and so clearly manifest the feeling with which sensible people regarded this exhibition that, particularly as the poem seems little known, it were not impertinent to quote them in full :—

The next thing was the Scene,
  And that as it was lain,
But no Man knows where in *Peru,*
  With a Story for the Nonce
  Of Raw Head and Bloody Bones,
But the Devil a word that was true.

  There might you have seen an Ape
  With his Fellow for to gape,
Now dancing and turning o'er and o'er.[154]
  What cannot Poets do ?
  They can find out in *Peru*
Things no Man ever saw before.

  Then presently the *Spaniard*
  Struts with his Winyard,
Now Heaven of thy Mercy how grim,
  Who'd have thought that Christian Men
  Would have eat up Children,
Had he not seen 'em do it Limb by Limb ?

  Oh greater Cruelty yet,
  Like a Pig upon a Spit,
Here lies one, there another boil'd to a Jelly [155] ;
  Just so the People stare
  At an Ox in the Fair
Roasted whole with a Pudding in's Belly.

  I durst have laid my head
  That the King there had been dead,
When I saw how they basted and carved him ;
  Had he not come up again
  Upon the Stage, there to complain
How scurvily the Rogues had served him.

  A little further in
  Hung a third by the Chin,
And a fourth cut out all in Quarters ;
  Oh that *Fox* had now been living,
  They had been sure of Heaven,
Or at the least been some of his Martyrs.

  But which was strange again
  The *Indians* that they had slain,
Came dancing all in a Troop ;
  But oh give me the last,
  For as often as he past,
He still tumbled like a Dog in a Hoop.[156]

And now my Signor Strugge
In good Faith you may go Jogge,
For *Sir Will.* will have something to brag on ;
Oh the *English* Boys are come
With their Fife and their Drum,[157]
And still the Knight must Conquer the Dragon.

And so now my Story is done,
And I'll end as I begun,
With a Word, and I care not who know it,
Heaven keep us great and small,
And bless us some and all,
From every such a pitiful Poet.

So great indeed proved the popularity of *The Cruelty of the Spaniards in Peru* that Davenant selected a similar subject for his next Opera or representation, the adventures and piracies of Drake : *The History of Sr Francis Drake,* " Exprest by Instrumentall and by Vocall Musick, and by Art of Perspective in Scenes, &c. *The First Part.* Represented daily at the *Cockpit* in *Drury-Lane* at Three Afternoon Punctually." [158] This opera, probably produced in the winter of 1658-9, was most obviously suggested by the success of the first piece.[159] *Sr Francis Drake,* be it observed, shows a certain amount of dramatic development. It boasts some unity of theme, and is altogether far more of a melodrame than *The Cruelty of the Spaniards in Peru.* Having paved his path with this latter, which truly was little beyond a panorama with songs, dancing, declamations, music, and an acrobat, Davenant cleverly proceeded to emphasize the theatrical qualities in his next story, whilst the other elements proportionately fell into the background. In fact he had made an important step towards the regular play. The scenery was still pictorial, that is to say the painted canvas represented the natives hunting boars, fishing, feasting their stranger guests, and at their various employments. Such stage directions as "*The prospect having continu'd a while* " ; " *This being discern'd a while* " ; " *This object having remain'd a while* " ; before any entry of characters or action plainly indicate that the scenery was regarded as a panorama and that a clear stage was left for the audience to enjoy the painting. The sixth entry showed a prospect of a caravan of mules bearing gold ingots and silver wedges down the mountain side, whilst just before the scene had opened and shown " a beautiful Lady ty'd to a tree ", a painting upon a flat.

In the winter of 1658 or early the following year Davenant further ventured to give public performances at the Cockpit of *The Siege of Rhodes,* and since this was an Opera which could not be justified or excused on political grounds, a numerous party who, apparently in spite of every plea and pretext, had been watching the performances with the utmost jealousy and suspicion began to raise a great outcry against a movement which they very justly considered was nothing else than the reopening of the theatres. On the 14th December, 1658, Rachel Newport wrote to her brother Sir R. Leveson : " It is thought the Opera will speedily go down ; the godly party are so much discontented with it." [160] There can be no doubt that the objectors were very influential ; on their side was Fleetwood, who it was whispered had been named under Cromwell's hand and seal as Protector-designate in a document since mysteriously vanished away, and presently a warrant was issued from White-hall to inquire closely into the exact nature of the performances which were being given at the Cockpit, and to ascertain upon what authority those concerned were relying. The order is as follows : " Whitehall, December 23. A course is ordered for taking into consideration the *Opera* shewed at the *Cockpit* in *Drury*-lane, and the persons to whom it stands referr'd are to send for the Poet and Actors, and to inform themselves of the nature of the work, and to examine by what authority the same is exposed to publick view ; and they are also to take the best information they can concerning the acting of Stage-playes, and upon the whole to make report, &c." [161] But the performances were still very popular, and in this connexion it is interesting to note that when *The Cruelty of the Spaniards in Peru* was printed, 4to, 1658, those who purchased the book were told that " Notwithstanding the great expense necessary to scenes, and other ornaments in this entertainment, there is good provision made of places for a shilling ". No doubt the general attitude towards Davenant was that expressed in Thomas Pecke's *Parnassi Puerperium* (1659) :

That *Ben*, whose Head, deserv'd the *Roscian* Bayes ;
Was the first gave the Name of Works, to Playes.
You his Corrival, in this Waspish Age ;
Are more than *Atlas*, to the fainting stage.
Your *Bonus Genius*, you this way display ;
And to delight us, is your Opera.

However, the agitation insistently continued, and zealot complaints were carried to the House of Lords, so that on 5th February, 1659, the following note was made in the Journal of the House : " The Lords being acquainted that, notwithstanding the Laws against stage-plays and interludes, yet there are stage-plays, interludes, and things of the like nature, called

Opera, acted, to the scandal of Religion and the Government,—Ordered a Committee." [162]

The antagonism was powerful enough to suspend all performances for a few weeks in March at least—we do not know the exact dates of silencing—but R. Greene, writing to Secretary Nicholas and dating his letter *March ye last*, 1659, speaks of " Sir Wm. Davenant and his Opera (which goes vp agen next weeke) ". [163] The feverish restlessness of public affairs was Davenant's security, nor does there seem to have been any further interruption at the theatre during several months, as under 5th May, 1659, Evelyn wrote in his Diary : " I went to visit my brother in London and next day to see a new opera after the Italian way in recitative music and sceanes much inferior to the Italian composure and magnificence : but it was prodigious that in a time of such public consternation such a vanity could be permitted. I being engaged could not decently resist the going to see it though my heart smote me for it." The performance at which Evelyn assisted was probably that of *The Siege of Rhodes*.

Less than three months after Davenant with many other Royalists was arrested by order of Mr. Secretary Thurloe on a charge of being concerned in the design of a general rising on behalf of the exiled king. The plans had been betrayed, and the movement, intended to take effect on 5th August, came to nothing on account of the preventive imprisonment of those chiefly concerned. The poet's detention, however, did not prove of long duration for Bulstrode Whitelocke interfered on behalf of his old friend, and we have the note : "Aug. 16, 1659. Sir *William Davenant* was released out of Prison." [164] Whitelocke also was one of the Council of State which upon the following day passed an order : " That it be referred to the Comitee of the Councell for Examinations to take security of Mr. Davenant upon the Act of Parlt agt. Delinqts, whereupon he is to have liberty to reside in England." [165] Advantage would certainly have been taken of his misfortune and incarceration to have closed down the Cockpit meanwhile, but in spite of this check surreptitious performances were given with the result that the house was raided and the audience mulcted there and then, a sum of three pounds, eight shillings and sixpence having been collected " at the Cockpitt Playhouse, of severall offenders, by order of the justices ". [166]

When the poet-manager came back to his theatre the performances appear to have been resumed without much let or molestation, and in February, 1660, upon the arrival of General Monk in London it seemed so certain that playhouses must shortly be reopened and officially recognized, however restricted the conditions under which they were allowed, that Davenant began to treat with Thomas Lisle for a lease of this gentleman's Tennis Court in Portugal Street, Lincoln's Inn Fields,[167] with the express intention of converting so convenient a building into a theatre. He had not, however, lost sight of his official standing at the Court, dormant though this position may have been for more than three lustra, and since it became evident that the return of the King was now only a question of a month or two at the most, Davenant very justly felt that, with a view to his own interest, he should rejoin the Master in whose cause he had wrought and suffered so much. Accordingly on the 17th March, 1660, he obtained a pass for France,[168] and when he returned to London in the royal train he was to return as a figure of no little importance, a favourite enjoying influence, prestige, and sufficient power to enable him to carry out with the King's warmest encouragement and liveliest approval those plans he had so long cherished and for the perfecting of which he had so cleverly and so tenaciously schemed and struggled during the dark and difficult years of opposition, poverty, and mistrust.

NOTES TO CHAPTER I

[1] On 20th July, 1623, Sir John Astley, who succeeded Sir George Buc, was induced to sell the Mastership of the Revels to young Henry Herbert for £150 a year. Astley remained technically the Master until his death in 1641, but the King and Court received Herbert as the Master *de facto*. Sir Henry notes : " Itt pleased the King, . . . to receive mee as Master of the Revells. At Wilton, this 7th August, 1623." Malone, *Variorum*, iii, 58.

[2] Malone, *Variorum*, iii, 243, who says with reference to the licence of Salisbury Court : " This paper appears to be only a copy, and not dated nor signed : ending as above. I believe, it was written in June, 1660."

[3] In 1649 he published *Via ad Latinam Linguam Complanata* . . . His second Latin textbook appeared in 1656 : *The Rudiments of Grammar. The Rules Composed in English Verse* . . . This was reissued in 1660 with a new title : *Manductio : or, A leading of Children by the Hand Through the Principles of Grammar*. " The second Edition, Enlarged."

[4] Several of Shirley's plays were revived at the Restoration. Downes records *The Grateful Servant ; The Witty Fair One ; Love Tricks ; The Traitor ; The Cardinal ; The Opportunity ; The Example ;* Pepys saw some eight or nine including *Love's Cruelty ;* and *Love in a Maze ;* Mrs. Pepys was bored by *The Court Secret ;* and from other sources performances have been traced of *The Sisters* and *The Constant Maid ;* nor do these dozen exhaust the list.

[5] In both of which Shirley is said to have lent the Duke much professional assistance. For fuller details see my edition of the *Works of Thomas Shadwell* (Fortune Press, 1927), vol. i, Introduction, pp. xxxiv–xxxvi.

6 *An Account of the English Dramatick Poets,* Oxford, 1691, p. 114, where having quoted various pasquils Langbaine continues : " Many other Railleries were broacht against him by his Enemies, as those lines in Sr. *John Sucklin's Session of the Poets* ; the Ballad entitled *How Daphne pays his Debts (Wits Merriment,* 8vo, p. 20), and others which I might insert, but I think 'tis time to leave these trifles." *Wits Merriment : or, Lusty Drollery* is the running title of *Sportive Wit : The Muses Merriment,* 1656, a collection which according to Marchamont's Nedham's official *The Publick Intelligencer,* 21–28 April of that year, attracted the unfavourable notice of the authorities as containing " Much Scandalous, Lascivious, Scurrilous, and profane Matter."

7 This poem, which is far better than those who have not read it may be disposed to think, was published octavo, London, 1653.

8 *Comedies and Tragedies,* Written by Thomas Killigrew, folio, general title-page, 1664 ; and the title-page to *Thomaso, or The Wanderer,* a play in Two Parts.

9 The date is from Pepys, who on Tuesday, 2nd July, 1661, " took coach and went to Sir William Davenant's Opera ; this being the fourth day that it hath begun."

10 Thus in spite of new detail, not perhaps very important, however, in itself, the account of Davenant by Mr. L. Hotson in his *The Commonwealth and Restoration Stage,* 1928, appears ill-arranged and inadequate.

11 Anthony à Wood, *Athenae Oxonienses,* ed. P. Bliss, London, 1813–1820, four vols, folio, vol. ii, col. 411.

12 He was probably first cousin of John Davenant, Bishop of Salisbury. See Campbell, *Modern Language Notes,* xviii, pp. 236 *sqq.*

13 *The Poetical Register, or, the Lives and Characters of the English Dramatick Poets,* London, 1719, vol. ii, p. 58.

14 Choice Notes (1862), privately printed with an Introduction by W. J. Thoms.

15 Anthony à Wood had the following from Aubrey : " Now Sᵣ Wm would sometimes, when he was pleasant over a glass of wine with his most intimate friends—*e.g.* Sam Butler, author of Hudibras &c.—say that it seemed to him that he writt with the very spirit that Shakespeare [did], and seemed contented enough to be thought his son."

16 It is said that James I was not pleased with the marriage of the Duke of Buckingham, who wedded the Lady Katherine Manners, a daughter of the Earl of Rutland. George Villiers, born 28th August, 1592, was introduced to the King at Apethorpe in August, 1614. His rise to high estate was singularly rapid. " Christ had His John, and I have my George," quoth King James. When he learned of Buckingham's intended marriage the King forbade the match on the pretext that the lady and her father were both Catholics. For some obscure and tangled reason the latitudinarian Williams, Bishop of Lincoln, Lord Keeper of the Privy Seal, and Dean of Westminster, an acute and shifty politician of few principles, persuaded Lady Katherine to conform, outwardly at least, to the Establishment, and in spite of the King's reluctance this prelate celebrated the marriage on 16th May, 1620. After which although seemingly Buckingham suffered no diminution in the royal favour it was rather because he had made himself necessary to the King than on account of a more personal affection. Villiers himself was clever enough to realize this full well. We hear of a youth whose face was washed " every day with posset curd ", and other younglings who were introduced to the King. Buckingham became jealous, not of these intimacies, but of his own supreme influence, and when James died at Theobalds, 27th March, 1625, little wonder that rumours which have yet entirely to be disproved accused Buckingham of having hastened the sick monarch's end. Indeed Dr. Eglisham, one of the physicians of the household, in his tract *The Forerunner of Revenge (Harleian Miscellany,* vol. ii) quite straightly inculpates Buckingham.

17 Henry Howard has a copy of verses prefixed to the Beaumont and Fletcher, folio, 1647. He was the third son of Thomas, Earl of Suffolk, and brother of Thomas Howard, created February, 1625–6, Earl of Berkshire, K.G.

18 Thus Maidment and Logan in their edition of Davenant's *Dramatic Works,* five volumes, 1872 ; vol. i, p. 3, write : "Although Kippis' ' Biographia Britannica ', in mentioning that in 1629 Davenant ' produced his first play to the world ', observes that it was ' very well received, and some very honourable recommenda-

tions were prefixed when it was printed ', there is no evidence to show that it was ever acted at that time, nor does it appear that the alterations subsequently made, and given to the public upwards of fifty years afterwards, were for stage purposes, as there is no record that even then *Albovine* was exhibited in the theatre." The word " alterations " is perhaps a little misleading, as the reference is merely to the very poor text of the mutilated tragedy given in the folio, 1673.

[19] Some two or three instances will serve. There is no mention of production upon the title-pages of the following editions of plays all of which are known to have been acted : Fletcher's *The Faithfull Shepheardesse*, first quarto, n.d., but 1609–1610, and second quarto, 1629. (The publisher of the second quarto, Richard Meigher, also published *Albovine*.) Sir William Berkeley's *The Lost Lady*, folio, 1638, a Cockpit play; William Habington's *The Queene of Arragon*, folio, 1640, a Blackfriars play. *The Bloody Brother*, by B. J. F., first quarto, 1639 ; but second quarto, 1640, adds "Acted by his Majesties Servants ".

[20] "Langobardi, gens etiam Germana feritate ferocior," *Velleius Paterculus*, ii, 106.

[21] *An Account of the English Dramatick Poets*, Oxford, 1691, p. 107.

[22] 720–799. The reference is *Historia gentis Langobardorum*, II, xxviii. There are many editions of this important work, the best being that of Bethmann and Waitz in *Monumenta Germ. Hist.: Script. Rerum Langobardarum*, 1878, 45–187.

[23] 539–594. The edition of Ruinart in Migne's *Patrologia Latina*, lxxi, is now replaced by that of Arndt and Krusch, *Scriptores Rerum Merovingivarum* in *Monumenta Germ. Hist.* (1884–5), i, pt. i, pp. 1–30.

[24] Pierre Boaistuau and François de Belle-Forest published at Paris, 1559, a French paraphrase of eighteen *novelle* from Bandello, which proved so successful that in 1565 Belle-Forest issued another eighteen *Histoires Tragiques*, and followed this up with subsequent volumes. The Albovine story is Nov. 19 of Tome IV.

[25] I have used the edition of Bandello in the *Novellieri Italiani*, Milano, 1813–16.

[26] Act I. Paradine to Valdaura :

> We will ere night
> Her black Curtaine drawes, make compleat this loue
> With marriage Rites.
>
> *Albovine.* How now, Boy ! Is my interest so decay'd
> In your young person, that you giue away your selfe
> Without my leaue !
>
> *Paradine.* Humbly on my knee I beg the vulgar
> Priuiledge due to all hearts. To loue, and not enjoy,
> Is a torture, I cannot suffer long,
> And still remaine possess'd with breath.
>
> *Albovine.* Thou hast shew'd me physick for my passion.
> Take him, *Valdaura*, and be proud ! 'Tis I
> That loue him : nor shall your ioyes be single.

[27] See Dr. Havelock Ellis, *Sexual Inversion* (*Studies in the Psychology of Sex*, vol. ii) Third Edition, 1927, pp. 278–9.

[28] Sir Edward Peyton's *Catastrophe of the House of Stuart*. See also *The Secret History of the Four Last Monarchs of Great Britain*, 1691.

[29] The Second Blackfriars, built in 1596, and demolished 6th August, 1655. There were continual complaints against and petitions for the removal of this theatre, which was especially obnoxious to the puritans.

[30] In two tragedies *Albovine* and *The Unfortunate Lovers*.

[31] *The Just Italian*, Act III.

[32] Osborne's *Traditionall Memoryes on the reign of James I*, 1658, p. 219.

[33] No copy bearing this date is now known, but Thomas Park in his *British Bibliographer* has a note showing that a copy was in the library of Mr. Herbert, and in the *Epithalamia* written for Princess Elizabeth, and printed 1612, Wither mentions this book. It was immediately suppressed. For fuller details see the Introduction with Bibliography to *The Poetry of George Wither*, edited by Frank Sidgwick, 2 vols, 1902.

[34] *Some Account of the English Stage*, vol. x, p. 79. This unfavourable judgement of Genest, who is a generous, if candid, critic seems curious and unexpected. Perhaps he used the mutilated folio edition of the tragedy. Maidment and Logan,

Davenant's Dramatic Works, vol. i, p. 111 (*Dramatists of the Restoration,* 1872), go so far as to say that *The Cruell Brother* " will, in point of plot and composition, bear favourable comparison with any work of Ford, or other of the contemporary dramatic poets."

[35] See also William Hopkins, *To my friend M. D'Avenant, on his legitimate Poem,* lines which usher in the quarto, 1630. In his Dedication to the Earl of Dorset, Davenant says that the play would have been a failure save for the favour shown it by his noble patron.

[36] Licensed by Herbert, 19th October, 1624 ; 4to, 1640.

[37] The suggestion is made by Maidment and Logan, *Davenant's Dramatic Works,* vol. i, p. 201.

[38] *The Witts,* 4to, 1636, Act II : *Sir Morglay Twack.* " Faith, I'le stride my Mule too morrow . . ." Also iii, 3, when Sir Morglay cries : " S'light, stay ; . . ." Also iii, 1, when the Elder Pallatine exclaims : " Death ! my hatband ! "

[39] *The Dramatic Records of Sir Henry Herbert,* ed. by J. Q. Adams, 1917, p. 22.

[40] Ibid., p. 54.

[41] *Roscius Anglicanus,* ed. by Montague Summers, 1928, p. 21.

[42] Langbaine, op. cit., p. 216.

[43] It is ignored by A. C. Sprague in his *Beaumont and Fletcher on the Restoration Stage,* 1926 ; and by J. H. Wilson in his *The Influence of Beaumont and Fletcher on Restoration Drama,* 1928.

[44] It was Jack Young who whilst Jonson's grave in Westminster Abbey was being covered, gave the fellow eighteenpence to cut the inscription " O rare Ben Jonson ".

[45] Presented at Court, by the Queen and her Ladies, at Shrovetide, 4to, 1630.

[46] 4to, 1634 ; and in the folio 1673.

[47] 4to, 1635 ; and in the folio 1673.

[48] See E. J. Dent, *Foundations of English Opera,* 1928, pp. 40–1.

[49] Presented at Ludlow Castle on Michaelmas Night, 1634.

[50] MS. Mus. Sch. B. 2.

[51] *Alaric,* épopée, Paris, 1654.

[52] *The Dramatic Records of Sir Henry Herbert,* ed. by J. Q. Adams, p. 36, n. 1.

[53] *Roscius Anglicanus,* ed. by Montague Summers, 1928, pp. 21–2. Queen Mary of Modena presented her Coronation Robes to Mrs. Barry, who wore them as Queen Elizabeth in a revival of Banks' *The Unhappy Favourite, or, The Earl of Essex.* The original Queen Elizabeth was Anne Quin. King James II and his consort Queen Mary were crowned 23rd April, 1685. The pageant with the robes worn are pictured in a work by Francis Sandford, Lancaster Herald at Arms, folio, 1685. The plate of the Inthronization of Queen Mary of Modena has been reproduced in my *Restoration Theatre,* 1934, no. xvii, p. 192. See also p. 283.

[54] p. 262.

[55] *The Half-Pay Officers* was revived at the Little Theatre, Haymarket, on Monday, 28th January, 1723 ; and again at the same theatre on Thursday, 12th March, 1730.

[56] This performance is noted and the cast given (folio, seventeenth century), *Hist. MSS. Comm., Rep. III,* App., p. 215a. Parkhurst's version is not recorded in the excellent edition of George Ruggle's *Ignoramus,* " accurante Johanne Sidneio Hawkins, Arm.," Londini, 1787.

[57] Nell, Ancilla Dorotheæ, Angla.

[58] So Cunningham thought, *Notes and Queries,* 24th November, 1849. It is impossible, however, that it should stand for Katherine Pegge, one of the mistresses of Charles II, for this lady in 1668 was in her fortieth year, and there is nothing to connect her with the stage. She was, by the King, the mother of Charles FitzCharles, Earl of Plymouth, who died in 1680 at the early age of twenty-three.

[59] *A Restoration Prompt Book* reprinted in *Essays in Petto,* 1928, pp. 103–110, from *The Times Literary Supplement.* In *The Restoration Theatre,* p. 142, is reproduced as an Illustration, plate xiii, a page from this prompt-book, 8vo, 1652.

[60] Marmaduke Watson of the Theatre Royal appears in the *Roscius Anglicanus,* edited by Montague Summers, 1928, p. 2, as " Mr. Duke ". See also note, ibid., pp. 77–8. Other parallels, the use of the Christian name of an actor or an actress ambiguously as a surname, might be cited.

[61] Mr. V. de Sola Pinto in his *Sir Charles Sedley*, 1639-1701, seems very much inclined to identify the Pegg of Pepys with Mrs. Margaret Hughes, in which he follows a mistake of Lord Braybrooke. Wheatley had already corrected this, and such an error is hardly pardonable even in the first editor of Pepys.

[62] *Sir Charles Sedley*, 1927 ; pp. 127-8.

[63] The (second) Globe was demolished by Sir Matthew Brend on Monday, 15th April, 1644, " to make tenements in the room of it." This is from a MS. note in the Philipps copy of Stow's *Annals* ; see *The Academy*, 28th October, 1882, p. 314.

[64] Venice, 1554 ; reprinted Milano, Daelli, 1863.

[65] The author of *The Stage Condemn'd*, 1698, pp. 12-31, gives a very particular account of this masque, and is extremely scandalized that it should have been presented on the Sabbath Day.

[66] *Roscius Anglicanus*, p. 19.

[67] Reprinted by Mr. G. Thorn-Drury in *A Little Ark*, 1921.

[68] I quote the English translation by Henry Cogan, folio, London, 1652.

[69] " The fair favourit " without any author's name appears in Warburton's list.

[70] *The Decline and Fall of the Roman Empire*, chapter lxx, Edition, 1823 ; vol. viii, p. 308, note *h*. In the text Gibbon speaks of " the title of poet-laureat, which custom, rather than vanity, perpetuates in the English court ".

[71] Yet it must be borne in mind that Davenant amongst other poems wrote a *New Year's Gift to the Queen*, 1643 ; and at the Restoration a *Poem upon His Sacred Majesty's Most Happy Return to His Dominions*, as well as a *Poem to the King's Most Sacred Majesty*.

[72] *Calendar State Papers, Domestic*, 1667-8, viii, 341.

[73] *Lives*, ed. Clark, i, p. 205.

[74] Ibid., i, p. 209. In the well-known *The Session of the Poets* (1665-8), an imitation of Suckling, stanza 3, Davenant is termed " the *Laureat* ", and, stanza 2, " wou'd fain have been Steward o' th' Court " (*Poems Relating to State Affairs*, 1705, pp. 152-3). Langbaine, *English Dramatick Poets*, Oxford, 1691, p. 106, states that Davenant was " Poet *Laureat* to Two Kings ".

[75] This is given in full in Rymer's *Fœdera*, xx, 377.

[76] The abbreviation *Opera* from " opera musicale " was as yet unknown in England. The virtuoso Evelyn first met with the term during his Italian tour in 1644-6, and particularly remarks upon it. For Dryden's definition of an *Opera* see the Preface to *Albion and Albanius*, 1685, *Dryden The Dramatic Works*, edited by Montague Summers, vol. v, 1932, pp. 344-351, and the corresponding notes, pp. 523-9.

[77] *A Supplemental Apology*, London, 1799, p. 187.

[78] *Annals of the Stage* (1879), vol. ii, p. 27.

[79] Ibid., vol. ii, pp. 28-9.

[80] J. O. Halliwell-Phillips, *A Collection of Ancient Documents . . . Relating to the Early Theatre*, London, 1870, p. 48. These (with others) were given by J. Q. Adams, *The Dramatic Records of Sir Henry Herbert*, 1917.

[81] Evelyn speaks of going to the Opera at Venice in Ascension Week, 1645. He writes : " It is one of the most magnificent and expensive diversions the wit of man can invent." The Teatro San Cassiano was in the immediate vicinity of San Cassiano, a church built in 1611. This interesting fane which lies to the west of the Canal Grande contains some notable paintings, including a Palma Vecchio of great beauty and one of the finest Tintorettos in Europe.

[82] For a history of ballet and opera in France see G. Bapst, *Essai sur l'histoire du Théâtre* (1893) ; also Professor Dent, *Foundations of English Opera*, pp. 43-52.

[83] *The Spanish Student*, i, 1, Lara's speech.

[84] The point gave rise to some discussion among the commentators. See Festus, *De Verborum Significatione*, Amstedolami, 1700, p. 475, *sub uerb*. " Salmacis ", with the notes of Scaliger and Dacier upon this passage.

[85] The acropolis of Thebes was called Cadmea, as said to have been founded by Cadmus. A version of one legend related that when Adrastus, the Argive king, was assaulting Thebes his army fell into entire disorder and so the besieged making a sally routed the enemy with great destruction. This victory, however, cost the Thebans right dear, for after the conflict very few returned alive to the city.

[86] Printed in *Madagascar with Other Poems*, 1635.

[87] *Foundations of English Opera*, 1928, p. 41

[88] This is Ben Jonson's expression in his *Expostulation with Inigo Jones*:
What is the cause you pomp it so, I ask?
And all men echo, you have made a masque.

[89] Christopher Beeston had been sworn as Governor, 21st February, 1636-7: see the Lord Chamberlain's Office-book under this date. The popular name of the Company was " Beeston's Boys ". Upon the death of his father in 1639 William Beeston succeeded and he is referred to as Governor 10th August of that year.

[90] See Collier, *History of English Dramatic Poetry* (1879), ii, 32.

[91] *The Dramatic Records of Sir Henry Herbert*, ed. J. Q. Adams, p. 66.

[92] This is the date given by Malone, Collier, and Chalmers. Mrs. Stopes " Shakespeare's Fellows and Followers ", *Shakespeare Jahrbuch*, xlvi, 99, has 5th June, but she is often very inaccurate on these points.

[93] Collier, *History of English Dramatic Poetry* (1879), ii, p. 32, n. 1.

[94] *Historia Histrionica*, 1699.

[95] *Calendar State Papers*: 17th July, 1640; and 13th April, 1641.

[96] Who also converted the Duke of York, afterwards King James II.

[97] Campbell, *Modern Language Notes*, xviii, 236 sqq.

[98] An old tradition says that Milton intervened on his behalf. Todd in his life of Milton, prefixed to his edition of the *Poetical Works of Milton*, 1801, vol. i, p. 102, observes " that the story [of Milton's intervention] had been related to Richardson (the painter) upon the authority of Pope, who received it from Betterton, the protégé of Davenant ". Aubrey attributed Davenant's escape from the scaffold to the kindly offices of " two Aldermen of York " whose liberty he had secured when the royal army was occupying the north of England during the Civil War.

[99] MS. Sloane 2149, British Museum.

[100] On 2nd September, 1642, both Houses concurred in a resolution and solemn ordinance that whilst the " publike Calamities . . . doe continue, publike Stage-playes shall cease, and bee forborne ". After an entry of two plays by Kirke on 8th June, 1642, Sir Henry Herbert had already noted : " Here ended my allowance of plaies, for the war began in Aug. 1642." Malone, *Variorum Shakespeare*, 1821, vol. iii, p. 242. Plays were, of course, clandestinely given at some hazard, and on 11th August, 1647, the House of Commons ordered the sheriffs of London and the magistrates to be very diligent in " suppressing and preventing any Stage Plays ". On 22nd October following the Commons, with the assent of the Lords, passed very severe measures against all " Common Players ". On 22nd January, 1648, the Parliament scandalized and affronted at the report of surreptitious performances caused to be prepared an ordinance " for the effectual Suppression of Stage Plays . . . and for the Pulling down of the Stages " and utter demolition of all theatres. The spectators were heavily fined. In 1649 many of the playhouses were dismantled and pulled down, and although here and there, in hole and corner, plays were yet presented, raids by the military were a perpetual and very real menace. In 1654, however, the actors had assembled at the Red Bull, which was raided on 30th December whilst they were giving *Wit without Money*.

[101] Among his expenses in February and March, 1655, Daniel Fleming has : " Spent with Sir W. D. and Sir G. F. at the Playhouse, 15s. Spent in going into a play, 1s. 4d." Sir W. D. is Sir William Davenant ; and Sir G. F., Sir George Fletcher. *Hist. MSS. Comm., Rep. XII*, App., pt. 7, p. 22.

[102] J. Bruce's Williamson's *History of the Temple*, 1924.

[103] A body similar to the Honourable Artillery Company. The Military Company existed from c. 1610 to 1660, and doubtless *Cupid and Death* was given in 1659 under their patronage. For the Military Ground in Leicester Fields, which lay to the north of Leicester Square, see C. L. Kingsford's *The Early History of Piccadilly, Leicester Square, Soho*, 1925. The Masque was presumably presented in the large meeting-room of the Company, which was upstairs.

[104] B.M. Add. MSS. 17799. There has been some confusion as Grove in his *Dictionary of Music and Musicians* mistakenly wrote that Locke and Gibbons composed the music for the original performance of *Cupid and Death* in 1653. The *Dictionary of National Biography* under Christopher Gibbons repeats this error.

[105] Rawl. B. 165.

[106] *Zwotomia*, 1654, pp. 472-3.

[107] *Registers of Westminster Abbey,* ed. Chester, Harleian Society, x, 168.

[108] *State Papers,* Domestic. Interregnum, i, 76, p. 230.

[109] *Registers of Westminster Abbey, ut sup.*

[110] Davenant had previously lived in Tothill Street, Westminster. Charterhouse Yard, Aldersgate Street, was a fashionable quarter.

[111] *Calendar of Proceedings of the Committee for Compounding,* 1643–1660, p. 2189.

[112] Ibid., p. 2735.

[113] L. Hotson, *The Commonwealth and Restoration Stage,* 1928, pp. 139–140.

[114] It is said to have cost over £21,000. Whitelocke's detailed account of the masque is given in Burney's *History of Music,* iii, pp. 369 *sqq.*

[115] First printed from Rawlinson, A. 46, 293 (Bodleian) by Sir Charles Firth in the *English Historical Review,* xviii (1903), 319. Although this paper is bound up with documents dated January, 1657, Sir Charles Firth considers it to be earlier, and written before the *First Day's Entertainment.*

[116] The ballad *How Daphne pays his Debts* to which Langbaine drew attention (*English Dramatick Poets,* 1691, p. 114) has the mocking line : *I must be Master o' th' Revels.* It may be remarked that Mr. L. Hotson, op. cit., places far too much reliance upon this lampoon, and a more intimate acquaintance with old English satires would show him how much in these poems must be discounted, and that their statements are by no means to be taken so literally as he conceives. None the less the enthusiasm which proclaims that this pasquil gives us " new facts of capital importance for the history of the English theatre " is very pardonable. To suppose that " at the time the ballad was written Davenant was giving performances in at least four different houses " (p. 145) is unwarranted. Mr. Hotson (Chapter III) seems to contradict his own conclusions, and there is some confusion.

[117] *State Papers,* Domestic. Interregnum (1656), cxxviii, 108. This was reprinted by Paul Reyher, *Les Masques Anglais,* 1909, among the *pièces justificatives,* xiv, p. 515. Mr. Hotson mistakes with regard to this account. He says (op. cit., p. 149) that " the anonymous writer refers to the piece as an " opera ", it is evidently not that, but *an argument for the opera ".* The writer does not refer to the piece as an opera. I presume Mr. Hotson has not understood the nice import of "After the Prologue (wᶜʰ told them this was but the Narrow passage to the Elizium theire Opera) ". In other words, the Prologue said that this entertainment was paving the way to an Opera, which is precisely what it effected, for it was followed at an interval by *The Siege of Rhodes.*

[118] In 1628 he had been Master of the Revels for the Society of the Middle Temple, at a time when Davenant was lodging there with Hyde, the future Lord Clarendon.

[119] Thomas Bruce, first Earl of Elgin, in Scotland ; created by Charles I on 13th July, 1640, Baron Bruce, of Whorlton, Yorkshire, in the English peerage. He died in 1663.

[120] The Teatro Novissimo, San Cassiano, the first public opera house, belonged to the Tron family, and was built early in the seventeenth century. It was called " Teatro nuovo " to distinguish it from a theatre erected a little earlier in the same parish. It was burned down in 1629 and promptly rebuilt, hence " Teatro Novissimo ". In 1637 was performed here the first Venetian opera *Andromeda,* words by Benedetto Ferrari, music by Francesco Manelli. The theatre was rebuilt in 1736, and destroyed about 1800. Sir John Reresby describing his travels in Italy, 1656–7, particularly mentions the Carnival in Venice, where are performed " operas, which are usually tragedies, sung in music, and much advantaged by variety of scenes and machines ". *Memoirs and Travels of Sir John Reresby, Bart.,* ed. by A. Ivatt, 1904, p. 58.

[121] *Ercole in Lidia :* Dramma del Signor conte Maiolino Bisaccioni, gentil'huomo della camera del rè Christianissimo. Rappresentato nel Teatro Novissimo nell'anno 1645. Venetia, Giovanni Vecellio e Matteo Leni, 1645. 144 pp. Three acts and a prologue. Giovanni Rovetta is mentioned as the composer. According to Eitrer *Quellen-Lexicon* Prete Giovanni Rovetta composed large quantities of church music, which still exists in various libraries. Livio Niso Galvani (pseud. G. Salvioli), *I teatri musicali di Venezia,* 1878, and *Saggio di Drammaturgia Veneziana,* 1879, mentions two operas, of which one is *Ercole in Lidia,* but no trace of the music has been found. La Signora Anna Renzi sang Damira in *Le Fortune di Rodope e Damira,*

Venice, Teatro Sant'Apollinare in 1657. The music of *Le Fortune* is by Padre Pietro Andrea Ziani. La Signora Anna Renzi is probably the lady to whom Evelyn refers. I owe this interesting note and the preceding note to my friend Professor E. J. Dent, who suggests several books which might be useful in this connexion, amongst others, Bonlini *Le Glorie della poesia e della musica contenute nell'esatta notizic de'teatri della città di Venezia*, Venezia, 1730 ; Leone Allacci, *Drammaturgia* ; and Ademollo *I teatri di Roma.*

[122] Davenant's opinions, as here expressed, are admirably criticized by Dryden in his Essay *Of Heroique Plays* prefixed to the First Part of *The Conquest of Granada*, 4to, 1672. See *Dryden The Dramatic Works*, edited by Montague Summers, vol. iii (1932), pp. 19–25, and the notes pp. 508–514.

[123] Downes, *Roscius Anglicanus*, ed. Montague Summers, p. 33. Downes actually refers to the more splendid revival of *Macbeth* at Dorset Garden, 1673-4, but even in Davenant's day, on 7th January, 1667, Pepys was admiring the " divertisement " in *Macbeth*, " though it be a deep tragedy " ; and three months later he is delighted with the " variety of dancing and musique " which made it one of the best plays for a stage that ever he saw.

[124] *Rhodes of the Knights* by Baron de Belabre, Oxford, 1908.

[125] Segrais gives 1635 as the date of the original edition, but the earliest known edition seems to be that of 1641. The romance was reprinted in 1652, 1665, and 1723.

[126] See Campbell in *Modern Language Notes*, xiii, pp. 177 sqq.

[127] *The Tragedie of Solimon and Perseda. Wherein is laide open, Loues constancie, Fortunis inconstancie, and Deaths Triumphs.* 4to, 1599. The play is anonymous, and there does not seem sufficient reason for ascribing it to Kyd. " Turkish histories " were very popular on the Elizabethan stage.

[128] *Of Heroique Plays. Dryden The Dramatic Works*, ed. by Montague Summers, vol. iii (1932), p. 20.

[129] These were described by Mr. W. G. Keith in two articles in *The Burlington Magazine*, vol. xxv ; Nos. cxxxiii and cxxxiv ; April and May, 1914.

[130] Eugène Rigal, *Le Théâtre Français avant le Période Classique*, 1901, p. 255, having reference to a tragedy *La Pucelle d'Orléans, c.* 1642.

[131] Chetwood, op. cit., p. 154, says : " I have seen Faces painted in a Scene of a Multitude, which is generally used in *Drury-lane* Theatre at the Coronation of *Anna Bullen*, that make most ridiculous Figures."

[132] Professor E. J. Dent, *Foundations of English Opera*, 1928, pp. 54 and 55 ; 65 and 66. The Two Parts were published quarto, 1663.

[133] Ibid., p. 65.

[134] *Dryden The Dramatic Works*, edited by Montague Summers, vol. iii (1932), pp. 19–20.

[135] Possibly Elkanah Settle.

[136] The Dedication is addressed to Dennis and Gildon.

[137] *An Apology for the Life of Mr. Colley Cibber*, 1740 ; Chapter v.

[138] *Dramatic Miscellanies*, 1784, vol. iii, p. 203.

[139] *Apology* ; Chapter v.

[140] *I King Henry IV*, Act I, scene 3.

[141] Op. cit., vol. iii, pp. 336-7.

[142] *The Spanish Fryar*, ii, 1.

[143] Vol ii, p. 164.

[144] 1806 ; pp. 59-60.

[145] *The Rosciad*, 1761. Ed. by R. W. Lowe, 1891 ; p. 48.

[146] Ibid., p. 40.

[147] *Complete History of the English Stage*, 1800, vol. iii, p. 251.

[148] *Plays, Acting, and Music*, 1903, pp. 30-1.

[149] *Dramatic Miscellanies*, vol. iii, pp. 251 and 249. Tinsley, who I fear is not always very reliable, has an amusing anecdote. He writes : " The Kembles seem to have created a school of actors and acting. Young and Macready were very much of that school, which was the old delivery of lines and sentences, and point making. Perhaps it was one of the Kembles who asked his manager whether he was going to put a play on in front of the drama he was playing in, and the Manager said he could easily put one on between his sentences." *Random Recollections*, 1900, vol. ii, p. 205.

[150] Born at Seville, probably in 1474 ; died at Madrid, 1566.

[151] "A most injudicious book, glaringly partial, based upon testimony often very impeachable and always highly coloured. That so passionate and one-sided a document should have been published with the permission of the authorities argues a broad tolerance on the part of the Spanish Government." A. F. Bandelier.

[152] Even under the Commonwealth acrobatic performances and rope-dancing were extraordinarily popular. The "*Funamble Turk*", as Evelyn in his *Numismata* dubs this agile mountebank, exhibited his skill at the Red Bull, and was largely followed. See Evelyn's *Diary*, 15th September, 1657. On 13th September, 1660, at Southwark Fair Evelyn saw "monkeys and apes dance, and do other feats of activity on the high rope".

[153] This satire is given in the edition of 1716, pp. 323-5. In the Fifth Edition, 1727, The Third Part, it occupies pp. 318-320 under the title "*A Ballad against the Opera*, call'd, *The Cruelty of the Spaniards in Peru, Writ by Sir W. D'Avenant*". There is a MS. of this pasquil in the Bodleian, Ashmole 36, fol. 163 and fol. 164.

[154] At the conclusion of the First Entry, after the Song, "a Rope descends out of the Clouds, and is stretched to a stiffness by an engine, whilst a Rustic Air is played, to which two Apes from opposite sides of the Wood come out, listen, return ; and coming out again, begin to dance ; then, after a while, one of them leaps up to the Rope, and then dances to the same Air, whilst the other moves to his Measures below. Then both retire into the Wood. The Rope ascends." When *The Cruelty of the Spaniards in Peru* became Act IV of *The Play-house to be Let* all this business of the apes was omitted.

[155] The Fifth Entry. Natives and English mariners are being racked. "*Two Spaniards are likewise discover'd, sitting in their cloaks, and appearing more solemn in ruffs, with rapiers and daggers by their sides ; the one turning a spit, whilst the other is basting an Indian Prince, which is roasted at an artificial fire.*"

[156] The "Double Somerset" performed by the Priest's acrobatic attendant. These gymnastic displays were afterwards omitted.

[157] The Sixth Entry. An imaginary army of English was supposed to join with the Peruvians and rout the Spaniards. "*These imaginary English forces may seem improper . . . but yet in poetical representations of this nature, it may pass as a vision discern'd by the Priest of the Sun, before the matter was extant, in order to his prophecy.*"

[158] Printed 4to, 1659. *The Cruelty of the Spaniards in Peru* had been printed 4to, 1658. *The Siege of Rhodes* ran into a second edition, 4to, 1659.

[159] The historical basis, such as it is, of *The Cruelty of the Spaniards in Peru* is (as has been noted) derived from the English translation, *The Tears of the Indians* (1656), of the *Brevisima Relacion de la Destruycion de las Indias*, published in 1552, of Bartolomé De Las Casas, O.P., who died in 1566. The incidents which are exhibited in *Sr Francis Drake* belong to the expedition of 1572-3. In 1572 Drake landed at Nombre de Dios, and in the same year Portobello was burned. In 1573 he sacked Venta Cruz, and in this year also he returned to Plymouth. *Sr Francis Drake* is then in some sense a sequel to *The Cruelty of the Spaniards in Peru*. Dr. W. J. Lawrence blunders badly when he writes : "Although *The History of Sir Francis Drake* formed the first part of the Peru story, it seems, oddly enough, to have been produced after *The Cruelty of the Spaniards in Peru* . . . Note that when the two operas came to be revived in 1663, as portions of D'Avenant's curious composite piece, *A Playhouse to be Let* [*The Play-house to be Let*], the proper sequence was followed, the *Drake* opera comprising the third act, and *The Cruelty* the fourth." *The Origin of the English Picture Stage, The Elizabethan Playhouse*, Second Series, 1913, p. 133. Dr. Lawrence seems to have been led into his multiplication of error by the fact that on the quarto, 1659, of *The History of Sr Francis Drake* occurs "*The First Part*". No *Second Part* ever appeared. Mr. Leslie Hotson has all too trustingly followed the mistakes of Dr. Lawrence, and thus erroneously says that "the latter opera [*Sr Francis Drake*] should logically have come first, since it relates an earlier part of the *Peru* story", *The Commonwealth and Restoration Stage*, 1928, p. 159. When Davenant, for practical convenience sake, arranged *Sr Francis Drake* as the third act of *The Play-house to be Let* and *The Cruelty of the Spaniards in Peru* as Act IV, he was in fact reversing the chronological order of these two operas.

Sr Francis Drake appears to be founded upon *Sir Francis Drake revived . . . in a Third Voyage made by him into the West Indies, in the years* 1572 *and* 1573. Set forth by Sir Francis Drake Baronet (his nephew) now living. London. 1626.

[160] *Hist. MSS. Comm., Rep. V,* App., p. 146a.

[161] *Publick Intelligencer,* 20th to 27th December, 1658. Quoted by Malone, *Prolegomena,* 1813, p. 97; also by R. W. Lowe, *Thomas Betterton,* 1891, pp. 10–11.

[162] Quoted by W. L. Bowles in his *Life of Ken* (1830–1), vol. i, p. 224, from "a MS. Diurnal of the Parliament, 1658, in the possession of the descendant of Clement Walker, John Walker Heneage".

[163] *Nicholas Papers,* Camden Society, iv, 83.

[164] Whitelocke, *Memorials,* 1732, p. 682.

[165] *State Papers,* Domestic. Interregnum, i, 79, p. 453.

[166] John Parton, *Some Account of the Hospital and Parish of St. Giles in the Fields,* p. 236.

[167] Hotson, *The Commonwealth and Restoration Stage,* 1928, p. 124.

[168] *State Papers,* Domestic. Interregnum, i, 116, p. 7a.

CHAPTER II

THOMAS KILLIGREW, AND THE HISTORY OF THE THEATRES UNTIL THE UNION, 1682

Thomas Killegrevv Maître du Theatre Royal & qui a pour sa conduitte des qualitez excellentes.—LE SIEUR CHAPPUZEAU : *L'Europe Vivante,* 1667.

Our Author writ nine Plays in his Travells, and two at *London*; amongst which his *Don Thomaso,* in two parts, and his *Parson's Wedding,* will always be valu'd by the best Judges and Admirers of Dramatick Poetry.—GERARD LANGBAINE : *An Account of the English Dramatick Poets,* 1691.

Quae theatra [Londini] *fuerint, et qui circi, quorumque extent vestigia, et quae penitus conciderint.*—ALEX. AB ALEXANDRO, *Lib.* IV, cap. xxv.

Il y a donc à Londres trois Troupes d'excellens Comediens ; la Troupe Royale que jouë tous les iours pour le public, & d'ordinaire tous les Ieudys apres soupé à Vvithal : la Troupe de Monsieur Frere vnique du Roy dans la place de Lincoln, qui reussit admirablement dans la machine, & qui va maintenant du pair auec les Italiens : & une troisième en Drury-lane, qui a grand abord. Il y a vne autre Troupe entretenue à Norvvich, l'vne des bonnes Villes du Royaume, & le seiour de toute la Noblesse du Pays, sans conter les Troupes de Campagne, ou se fait le Nouitiat des Comediens. Il faut ajoûter, Que ces trois Maisons de Londres sont superbes en decorations & en changemens ; Que la Musique y est excellente & les Ballets magnifiques; Qu'elles n'ont pas moins de douze violons chacune pour les Preludes & pour les Entr-actes ; Que ce seroit vn crime d'employer autre chose que de la cire pour éclairer le Theatre & de charger les Lustres d'vne matiere qui peut blesser l'odorat ; & enfin, quoy qu'on iouë tous les iours, que ces Maisons ne desemplissent iamais & que cent carrosses en barricadent les auenues. On ne trouue rien de semblable en Ecosse & en Irlande.—LE SIEUR CHAPPUZEAU : *L'Europe Vivante,* 1667.

Thomas Killigrew, who at the Restoration made no small figure as Davenant's energetic and not unsuccessful rival in the theatrical world, was able to put forward claims at least equipollent to those of the Laureate, if not indeed of more formal weight, since there is reason to suppose that during the Royal Exile King Charles had named him Master of the Revels,[1] an appointment which in view of the uncompromising attitude adopted and the immediate resumption of the Thespian dictatorship by Sir Henry Herbert, a crusted official and one " dexterous in the ways of the Court, as having gotten much by it ",[2] Killigrew was content should be quietly lixiviated into the ambiguous but privileged " title of King's Foole or Jester ", since this carried a fee out of the Wardrobe,[3] a goodly deal of licence, and no responsibility.

Thomas Killigrew came of old Cornish stock, a family of courtiers " remarkable for its loyalty, accomplishments and wit".[4] He was the fourth son of Sir Robert and Mary Killigrew, of whose twelve children, three sons and four daughters [5] lived to make some figure in the world.

The three brothers, William the eldest son, Thomas the fourth son, and Henry the youngest, were all dramatists, and as plays written by William and Thomas before the closing of the theatres were acted after the Restoration they may both be claimed as links between the period of Shirley and the age of Dryden, in the same way as Davenant is a link, although actually in this respect they are far less important and far less a vital force than the laureate.

The work of Sir William Killigrew demands separate and fuller consideration. Henry Killigrew (1613–1700)[6] is the author of only one play, *Pallantus and Eudora,* a romantic tragedy designed for an Entertainment of the King and Queen at York House, at the nuptials of the first Duke of Buckingham's daughter, Lady Mary Villiers, and the Lord Charles Herbert, third son and heir of Philip, fourth Earl of Pembroke, on the 8th January, 1634–5. Two and a half years later the piece was publicly acted at the Blackfriars,[7] and in 1638 a draft, derived from " a false and imperfect Transcript ", slipped into the world, a contraband quarto, as *The Conspiracy.* The correct version was printed under the poet's care, folio, 1653, as *Pallantus and Eudora.* It is curious to find that in the Second Volume of *The Works of the Honourable Charles Sedley, Bart.,* 12mo, 1722,[8] is included with separate title-page, " The Tyrant King of *Crete,* A Tragedy Never before Printed," which is nothing else save a curtailed version of *Pallantus and Eudora.* It is poor stuff presented in a clouterly sort of blank verse such as can hardly be distinguished from very bad prose. Both *The Conspiracy* and *Pallantus and Eudora* are printed in that blank verse which has crumbled to disintegration, but *The Tyrant King of Crete* is the worst of the three. Yet it is by no means unlikely that this thing may not be an exercise from Sedley's pen. That *The Works* of 1722 contain spurious pieces may be allowed, but Sedley was a disappointing dramatist, and when we remember his *Antony and Cleopatra* there

PLATE IV

THOMAS KILLIGREW

Aetat. 26

is certainly no argument to be derived from internal criticism which can definitely clear him of *The Tyrant King*.[9]

Thomas Killigrew was born on Friday, 7th February, 1612, at his father's house in the parish of S. Margaret Lothbury, London.[10] Of his boyhood some part was passed at his father's Manor of Hanworth, Middlesex, and part in London. Familiar as the passage is which gives us so vivid a glimpse of the lad Killigrew, it must be quoted once again since it shows how early his love for the theatre manifested itself. Dining with Sir John Minnes on Lord Mayor's Day, 29th October, 1662, Pepys heard " Thos. Killigrew's way of getting to see plays when he was a boy. He would go to the Red Bull, and when the man cried to the boys, ' Who will go and be a devil, and he shall see the play for nothing ? ' then would he go in and be a devil upon the stage, and so get to see plays ". The Red Bull, built about 1600 and enlarged in 1632, stood at the upper end of S. John's, Clerkenwell, and accordingly it was within easy walking distance of the Killigrews' house. This popular theatre specialized in Trojan derring-do and pyrotechnic effects, such as were employed for example in Heywood's quinary of *Ages,* where are fireworks and devils galore, and it was " mostly frequented by Citizens, and the meaner sort of People ".[11]

Thomas Killigrew, says Anthony à Wood, was " not directed at any University (and therefore wanted some learning to poise his excellent natural parts) but in the Royal Court, where he was page of honour to King Charles I ".[12] There is indeed not wanting indirect but pretty conclusive evidence that Killigrew was " without Bookes, or Artes ",[13] and he even goes so far as to break a jest upon himself as an " illiterate Courtier ",[14] which, of course, must not be pressed too nearly, for his native talent and wit supplied many deficiencies, and he was not without a considerable amount of reading in Spenser and Sidney, in romances new and old, and romantic history, as his plays bear ample witness. The exact date of his introduction at Court and his appointment as a Page of Honour cannot be precisely determined, but if we name 1625–6 [15] we shall not be far out in our reckoning. At any rate by 1632 he had an established position and was in considerable favour with the King. Thereafter references to his activities are numerous. His salary from his post was £100 a year,[16] and this he strove to supplement— with no small measure of success—by all the ways and means Caroline courtiers were wont to use, and very shabby and corrupt most of these methods were.

The literary circles of the Whitehall of Charles I were important, and since it was known that Queen Henrietta Maria in particular delighted in poets and playwrights, an obvious way to her favour was by the court stage. Not a few plays which were eventually applauded in the public theatres first saw the light as royal entertainments.[17] Thomas Killigrew, then, served both as an actor [18] and author. His activities in the former rôle were negligible, but in the second character he certainly attracted a good deal of notice.

Before the closing of the theatres in 1642 Killigrew had written three dramas in the most approved style of the day, and owing to his exceedingly useful habit of informing us where he penned his several pieces it is possible to date the composition with something like certainty. On 2nd April, 1640, the Stationers' Register enters " a tragedy called The Prisoner by Master Killigrey ", and on the following 4th August it enters " a play called Claracilla by Master Killegray ". These " Two Tragae-Comedies " were printed 12mo, 1641,[19] "As they were presented at the Phoenix in Drury Lane, by her Mties Servants." In the folio Comedies, and Tragedies, 1664, the first play is The Princesse : Or, Love at first Sight, which, Pepys tells us, was acted " before the troubles ".[20] Moreover Claracilla (which in the folio becomes Claricilla) was written in Rome ; The Princesse in Naples ; The Prisoners in London.

Killigrew accompanied Walter Montagu to Italy in 1635. They left London in the late autumn, and spending some two months in France [21] arrived at Vercelli during the second week of January, 1636. The following four months were passed in the south, Rome and Naples, and Killigrew had returned to England by the beginning of June at the latest, since he married his first wife, Cecilia Crofts, at Oatlands on 29th June, 1636. This gives a close limit for the composition of Claracilla and The Princesse, which two plays must have been written in the spring of 1636. The Prisoners, is certainly earlier and belongs to the period just before Killigrew's continental travels. It is therefore to be assigned to 1634–5, and so similar are these three dramas in style and treatment that it is easy to see they can have followed one another at no very long intervals, whilst the author was in the vein. They form one definite group and are all derived from one source, namely Ariane by Jean Desmaretz, sieur de Saint-Sorlin,[22] a romance " très bien inventé " which, originally published without the author's name in two volumes, Paris, 1632, at once became exceedingly popular at both the French and English Courts, and was read with avidity by the platonic précieuses of both countries. Such a refined circle Queen Henrietta Maria had gathered about her, and nothing would have been more grateful to his royal mistress, as Killigrew very well knew, than the romantic dramas she loved, inspired by the fashionable *Ariane*.[23]

Desmaretz de Saint-Sorlin takes his place, and that is by no means unimportant in the history of the novel, with De Gomberville, Vaumorière, La Calprenède, Georges and Madeleine de Scudéry. For *Ariane*, although considerably shorter than the *romans de longue haleine*, is of the same school; nay, more it is among the earliest and is completely typical of its kind. The work consists of sixteen books, and in the noble quarto of 1643, which I have used, comprises 775 pages. As is the wont of writers of heroic romance we are at once plunged *in medias res.* " Rome commençoit à sentir avec douleur les violences & les fureurs de Néron," who during one of his midnight sallies through the streets of the city attacks and severely wounds two young Sicilians, Mélinte and Palamède, newly arrived in Rome. The main Narrative is soon interlaced with subsidiary tales such as the " Histoire d'Antonin, d'Emilie, de Decie, & de Camille ", commencing on page 29, and on page 50 combining with the " Histoire de Palamède, de Mélinte, d'Emilie, & de Camille ". Thus the crowding incidents are set in an atmosphere of pseudo-historical events ; there are mistaken identities and masqued identities ; parents or uncles obstruct the course of true love; the heroes are torn betwixt burning love and chivalrous friendship ; the heroines are distracted by the conflict of love and honour ; pirate bands, whose leader is some person of quality, play a large part in the action ; and eventually at a time of general rejoicing when peace is declared, the rough is made smooth and the several pairs of lovers are joined in the soft roseate light of Hymen's torch.

Killigrew, it is evident, was well acquainted with and drew upon other sources, upon the work of Achilles Tatius and Heliodorus, Montemayor's *Diana,* and the *Astrée,* all so closely reflected in the heroic romances, as Georges de Scudéry boasts : "Je vous diray donc seulement que i'ay pris et que ie prendray touiours pour mes vniques Modelles, l'immortel HELIODORE, et le Grand VRFE." [24] None the less *Ariane* was his most direct inspiration.

The Phoenix, or Cockpit, in Drury Lane at which were publicly performed [25] Killigrew's *The Prisoners, Claracilla,* and *The Princesse,* was a small roofed theatre, which had been built by Christopher Beeston in 1616, and opened in the following year. The three plays were produced in quick succession in 1637–8, for, as has been noted, Killigrew returned from Italy in May, 1636, and we know that the London theatres were closed owing to the plague for a period of no less than eighteen months in 1636–7. In the prologue [26] spoken in the Dublin theatre, which was built in Werburgh Street by John Ogilby in 1634,[27] to Shirley's *The Doubtful Heir,* then being originally acted under the name *Rosania,* the following lines occur :—

> Rosania ? *methinks I hear one say,*
> *What's that ?* '*Tis a strange title to a play* . . .
> *Such titles unto plays are now the mood,*
> Aglaura, Claracilla—

Suckling's *Aglaura* was first produced at the Blackfriars during Christmastide, 1637, and shortly after was given at Court. *Rosania* was licensed by Herbert on 1st June, 1640,[28] and as *The Doubtful Heir* produced at the Blackfriars.

The Prisoners are two youths, Pausanes and Hipparchas, who belong to the band of the pirate Gallippus. They rescue the King of Sicily's sister, the Princess Cecilia,[29] but are captured by her brother's troops, and at her request become the lady's " Prisoners ". There is a vast amount of heroic love, there are continual conflicts of love and honour, extreme emotions, and the dramatist employs every ornament phantasy can devise, for needless to say in the end Pausanes and Hipparchus prove to be of royal stock, sons of the co-rulers of Sardinia, an island which once at war with Sicily is united to this country in perfect amity by the nuptials of the several ruling houses. The play was well received at its original production, but there is no record of any post-Restoration revival.

The plot of *The Princesse, or Love at first Sight* is not only extremely complicated, but is further farsed by comic scenes. We have an emperor of Rome, Julius Cæsar (to be altogether distinguished from Julius the conqueror who was slain with boydkins by false Brutus and his crew) ; a Prince of Rome, Virgilius ; a Princess, Sophia ; Facertes, a Prince of Sicily, which country is conquered by Rome ; the Princess of Sicily, Cicilia, who is captured by corsairs and sold in the slave-mart at Naples, where Virgilius sees and falls in love with her. There is a good deal of fighting with bandits, and eventually recognitions all round and discoveries. When Virgilius weds Cicilia ; and Facertes, Sophia ; Rome and Sicily are bound in closest alliance.

The most popular of these three plays was undoubtedly *Claracilla,* and it is easy to see why, for the situations are more dramatic, the movement swifter, the surprises more theatrically effective.[30] The Princess Claracilla, daughter to the King of Sicily, is sought in marriage by the false Seleucus, albeit she loves Melintus, a common soldier, who is none other than the King's nephew in disguise. There is an extraordinary amount of plotting and counterplotting, masquerading and unvizarding, but in the end the villainies of Seleucus are exposed, and the King giving his consent to the nuptials of Melintus and Claracilla, all go off the stage singing " Myrtle and triumphant Bays ". A striking character is the youth Philemon, who also loves Claracilla, but who " out of a high point of honour ", as Mr. Bayes says, resigns all his pretensions in favour of his brother Melintus.

Claracilla was received with great favour, and allowing for a certain extravagance, absurdity if you will, which would have recommended it all the more to contemporary audiences, the play has the merit of vigour ; it never falters, and it is not dull. That it was an attraction is shown by the fact that the players performed it privately during the Troubles. " The poor *Comoedians* . . . adventuring not long since to Act a Play called *Claracilla* at one *Mr. Gibbions* his *Tennis Court* " were betrayed to the authorities by the treachery of one of their fellows, " an ill *Beest* [31] . . . causing the poor *Actors* to be routed by the *Souldiery*," *Mercurius Democritus*, 2nd to 9th March, 1653. At the Restoration we find *Claracilla* in the repertory of the Red Bull actors,[32] a company headed by Michael Mohun, who very soon afterwards became His Majesty's Servants under Killigrew. Moreover this play kept the boards, as we learn from Pepys, for at least a decade. On Thursday, 4th July, 1661, Pepys " went to the Theatre [Vere Street], and there I saw ' Claracilla ' (the first time I ever saw it), well acted ". On Monday, 5th January, 1663, Pepys and his wife went " to the Cockpitt, where we saw ' Claracilla ', a poor play, done by the King's house ". On Tuesday, 9th March, 1669, he took his wife and other ladies to the Theatre Royal, Bridges Street, " to see ' Claracilla ', which do not please me almost at all, though there are some good things in it."

Here then we have in all three plays precisely the same ingredients, dream countries, dream history, a riposte of love and honour, the duello betwixt perfect love and perfect friendship, most gallant heroes, peerless heroines, blackest villains, pirates, storms at sea, a stramash of fighting, an oglio of cross purposes, disguises, the most exalted sentiments, the most artificial emotions, and a general anagnorosis to top the whole.

Yet with all their faults of construction, of diction, with all their endless phantasies and disentanglements and repetitions of incident and character these dramas have something strangely attractive, even although their vogue is gone for nearly three centuries now. I do not mean to suggest that they would bear revival, in the public theatre at least, such is far from the case, though we have seen many worse things there, but they may be read with pleasure and they bring in their pages a fragrance, faint perhaps and fading fast, of the courtesies and gallantries of a better day.

The language is often rhetorical and ornate, but often vigorous and clear. Metrically it represents the final depravation of blank verse, and indeed in the folio *The Prisoners* and *Claracilla* (now *Claricilla*) are printed in prose.

After the Restoration *The Princesse* was revived at Vere Street on Friday, 29th November, 1661, under which date Pepys has the following entry : " Sir W. Pen and to the theatre, but it was so full that we could hardly get any room, so he went up to one of the boxes, and I unto the 18*d.* places, and there saw ' Love at first Sight ', a play of Mr. Killigrew's and the first time that it hath been acted since before the troubles, and great expectation there was, but I found the play to be a poor thing, and so I perceive everybody else do." Indeed if we may believe a contemporary news letter in much halting rhyme *The Princesse* was only acted twice :

> First then to speak of his Ma[jes]t[y]s Theatre
> Where one would imagine Playes should be better
> Love att the first sight did lead the dance [33]
> But att second sight it had [th]e mischance
> To be so dash't out of Countenance as
> It never after durst shew itts face
> All though its bashfullnesse as tis thought
> Be far from being the Authors ffault.[34]

The fact is that the old style of the days of Charles I was not elegant enough for the English Monsieurs who in their exile had frequented the Parisian theatres, and had returned to demand French modes on their native boards. Mr. Frenchlove's plaint was theirs : " Twould vex me plaguly were I not a Frenchman in my second nature (that is) in my fashion, discourse and cloathes. I cannot devise in this whole City of *London,* how to find out any one Divertisement." [35]

Although his three plays had brought him applause in the circle, and to a lesser degree in the theatre, from the modish and refined, Killigrew had not achieved the golden reward of popular success, and accordingly he began to sketch out a play on very different lines, a comedy which by its mordant pictures of contemporary manners, not to mention its coarseness and rough fun, should appeal to uncultured but more profitable audiences. Accident, catastrophe, indeed, delayed the production of *The Parsons Wedding* for well nigh a quarter of a century.

At the outbreak of the Civil War Killigrew showed himself active and loyal on behalf of his Master, the King, so much so indeed that he invited the very unpleasant attention of the Rebels, and was in September, 1642, committed to the custody of Sir John Lenthall, " on suspicion for raising arms against Parliament." [36]

In the brief epistle, " To the Reader," prefixed to the folio, 1664, Killigrew speaks of his " Twenty Years Banishment ", but these are of course round figures, and must not be precisely pressed. At the same time they are not so far out, for although the exact date of his leaving England cannot be determined, we know that he was exchanged by order of the House of Lords on 27th July, 1643, " for another Prisoner at Oxon." [37] Queen Henrietta Maria sailed from Falmouth, bound for France on 14th July, 1644, and Killigrew was almost certainly in her train.

Of the next few years we learn little beyond the fact he was at Paris with the court of the English Queen and in a document dated 20th April, 1647,[38] he is termed *Dilectus & fidelis serviens noster* by the Prince of Wales, who employs him on certain important businesses in Italy. In 1648 he returned from his very successful mission, and temporarily acted as Groom of the Bedchamber to the Duke of York, then in residence at The Hague. When the Prince of Wales became King on the murder of his father, Killigrew was recalled to the royal household at Paris, and was dispatched by Charles II as envoy to Savoy and Florence and Resident at Venice. It has generally and very erroneously been believed that Killigrew was dismissed from Venice in June, 1652, owing to complaints of his loose living and debauchery, a disgrace which served to smutch his name with a very black mark. Nothing could be further from the truth. The Venetian Senate, double-dealing and slippery, discarded the King of England's Resident in consequence of the secret and underhand craft of Cromwell's agents, with whom after Worcester the Republic was eager to curry favour. It is well that this point should be insisted upon and emphasized, for the old story has been repeated and widely accepted sadly to the detriment of Killigrew's character with later writers.[39]

From Venice Killigrew proceeded first to The Hague, and in 1653 to Paris where any misunderstanding with the King was soon cleared up, and he stood in highest favour. The following year the Court left Paris, and on 28th January, 1655, Killigrew was married at The Hague to a Dutch lady, Charlotte de Hesse, a fortune of ten thousand pounds. During the remaining years of the Exile he lived at Maestricht, and he was occasionally employed in the service of the States-General, as well as ever showing himself busily active—as far as might be—on behalf of his King.

On Wednesday, 23rd May, 1660, King Charles II sailed for England on the *Royal Charles,* and the following afternoon Mr. Pepys, walking upon the decks, met not a few persons of honour, " amongst others, Thomas Killigrew (a merry droll, but a gentleman of great esteem with the King)."

During the Exile Killigrew had completed one play, already sketched in part at least, *The Parsons Wedding,* and had composed no less than seven more : *The Pilgrim ; Cicilia & Clorinda, or, Love in Arms,* in two parts ; *Thomaso, or the Wanderer,* in two parts ; and *Bellamira her Dream, or, The Love of Shadows,* in two parts. In this order they stand in the folio, but it will actually be more convenient to consider *The Parsons Wedding* last, as this was the only one of these pieces to be produced in the English theatre. Incidentally it may here be mentioned that among the books representing Killigrew's plays in the portrait frontispiece to the folio is seen a piece named *The Revenge.* This may have been an alternative title for *Cicilia* or for *Bellamira,* or else it may be some play he contemplated but did not write.

The title-page of *The Pilgrim* tells us that the piece was penned at Paris in 1651. There must be a mistake here, either in date or place, for in 1651 Killigrew was in Venice. Accordingly either *The Pilgrim* was composed at Venice ; or else, which is the more likely, it was composed at Paris in 1645 or 1646.[40] *The Pilgrim,* not perhaps exactly as it now stands in print, was certainly at one time intended for the stage, and Genest is right when he says that it " is a good Tragedy—with judicious alterations it might have been made fit for representation ".[41]

The tragedy exhibits the intrigues of Julia, Duchess of Pavia, who is wedded to Alphonso, Duke of Milan. Pavia and Milan have been at war, and Julia's first husband, the Duke of Pavia, was apparently killed on the field. Sforza, Alphonso's son, now governor of Pavia, loves Fidelia, Julia's daughter by her first marriage ; whilst Julia's son, Cosmo, now general of the Milanese forces, loves Victoria, the daughter of Alphonso by a former wife. The stage seems set fair, but Cosmo is not (as all suppose) the son of the Duke of Pavia, but of Julia's gallant, Count Martino, who, erstwhile the favourite counsellor of the slain Duke, now holds Milan's ear. Julia, who is the more forceful of the adulterous pair, and her paramour resolve that Cosmo shall rule both Pavia and Milan. They essay many devices to estrange Cosmo and Sforza, but from Fidelia the former learns something of the truth. Donning a palmer's weeds he hastens towards Pavia, and on his way saves Sforza from his mother's hired assassinate. Owing to his pilgrim's disguise he gains Julia's confidence, and further plans are laid, including the accusation of Martino upon the charge of Cosmo's murder, since the youth can nowhere be found. It is thought this subtle fetch will allay suspicion. In various ways the Pilgrim endeavours all in vain to win his mother to repentance. Even when the body of Martino, whom he has slain, is exhibited she answers by thrusting a poniard swift and deep to his heart. Too late she realizes that she has slain the son by whose unwitting hand his own father fell. The dagger yet red with her son's gore seeks a sheath in her own bosom. "None but a Son to spill a Father's blood, and a Mother to revenge it!" is her last cry. The tragedy ends with the union of Sforza and Fidelia upon whom the Duke pronounces a paternal blessing, whilst Victoria abandons the world for the cloister. There is at one point a comic underplot which has something of the breadth of an old fabliau, the tale of Trevallin, the ferryman of the River Po, who debauches the serving-wench Moretta ; whilst Argentin, the ferryman's wife, intrigues with knave Bertolin their man ; a merry mournival of cuckoldoms and japeries, but impertinent.

The Pilgrim calls for considerable revision to be fit for the boards. The trial scene, when in the course of their plots Martino is cunningly set at the bar is far too long for the theatre, too prolix and sustained. The speeches need to be curtailed, so not as to hinder and impede the action which must hurry breathless to the end. It remains an excellent piece of work.

It is interesting to note echoes of Shakespeare (especially from *Hamlet*) and other dramatists. The main theme of the tragedy was clearly suggested by the situation in Shirley's *The Politician,* a drama produced at Salisbury Court about 1639–1640,[42] and there are something more than hints from Davenant's *Albovine.*

Inasmuch as *Cicilia & Clorinda, Bellamira her Dream,* and *Thomaso* were not designed for the stage, but are rather romances in dialogue than plays for the theatre, a brief notice will suffice. Each of these closet dramas is in Two Parts of five acts apiece, but since not one of the tierce has any *dénouement* to round off Part I, we may fairly say that here we have a leash of huge ten-act plays. We are the less surprised when we find that *Cicilia & Clorinda* is directly based upon *L'Histoire d'Aglatidas et d'Amestrias* in *Artamène ; ou, Le Grand Cyrus,* Part I, Book 3. The First Part of *Cicilia & Clorinda* was written in Turin ; the Second Part at Florence. This then dates the composition, and gives us November to January, 1649–1650, when Killigrew had newly arrived in the north of Italy as the ambassador of Charles II. The first volume of *Le Grand Cyrus* had been issued at Paris " chez Augustin Courbé " in 1649, and was at once the rage among the fashionable of high and low degree.[43]

Killigrew's holograph MS. of *Cicilia & Clorinda*, both parts, formerly in the Thorn-Drury library was sold at the dispersion of this well-known collection. (Sotheby, ninth day of sale, Monday, 22nd February, 1932 ; no. 2407.)

Perhaps the most striking incident in this extraordinary play is a triple duel [44] between the Roman General Lucius who loves Cicilia ; his rival Amadeo, prince of Savoy ; and Manlius, the brother of Lucius. The villain of the piece is the hunchbacked Otrante, " le plus meprise & le plus hai " as Mlle de Scudéry calls him. He wears an appropriate black hat with huge black feathers, but " *His habit must be good* ".[45] This gentleman causes a mort of mischief, but all ends happily with weddings three.

The emotions and passions and incidents which lead to this event are (it must be confessed) rather artificially elaborate and verbose and intertwined, but if *Cicilia & Clorinda* is complex *Bellamira her Dream* is a jumble—to adopt old Genest's apter phrase.[46] Both parts of the piece were written at Venice, that is to say at some time, probably with many intervals and interruptions, between the end of February, 1650, and June, 1652.

Arcadian romances, the heroic romance, and memories of old plays have all gone to make up this fantast pasticcio. We have two dream countries, Sicily and Naples, whose Kings, brothers, have fiercely waged war, in which the latter monarch was slain. The fair Bellamira and the chivalrous Leopoldo are the children of Sicily. The people rise against the King, demanding as their sovran Genorio, son of the fallen King of Naples. Where Genorio and his sister are concealed nobody knows, but actually now named Pollidor and Phillora, they have been reared as simple rustics and dwell in a cave attended by a tame satyr. Their guardian is Ravack, a lord banished by the King of Sicily for opposing that monarch's claim to Naples. Here we have some very obvious borrowing from *Cymbeline*. Bellamira loves the figure of a shepherd who has appeared to her in a dream, " by night he makes his visits still ; like the *Egyptian Apis* in a dream he comes ; the soft-foot'd God of Sleep is onely Witness to our Love," she sighs ; she dotes upon a shadow, and needless to add that shadow is Pollidor. After various incidents Leopoldo and Phillora meet in a bosky glade and promptly burn with mutual flames. Later, Pollidor finds a miniature of Bellamira which has been dropped, and is at once enamoured of the lovely face, so he too loves a Shadow. War breaks out, and in the turmoil Almanzor, a Spanish prince who has intervened, captures Bellamira ; Palantus, general of the royal army, who loves her but in vain ; Pollidor and Phillora ; and very unpleasantly prisons them in a cave chained among " other

Prisoners and dead Carcases " where Leopoldo, disguised as a Spanish soldier, is set as sentry. He, of course, aids them to escape, which they achieve by a curious device. Some Moors, also captives, have been annoyed by a warren of fierce foxes entering their cave, but where foxes get in, prisoners can get out, and this they promptly do, an incident very reminiscent of Sinbad's fourth voyage,[47] which was certainly unknown to Killigrew. The company threading the subterranean exit find themselves on the seashore. In a final conflict Almanzor is slain. The identity of Pollidor and Phillora is revealed ; the lovers are all united, Palantus consoling himself with Fidelia, a lady who has throughout been constant to her gallant unkind.

Entirely different from the heroical plays is *Thomaso, or The Wanderer*, a huge rollicking comedy of cavaliers in exile. The date of composition can be precisely fixed as the spring of 1654, hence in spite of the assertion on the title-pages that both parts were written at Madrid this is doubtful. Killigrew was in Paris, and although he may have paid a short visit to Spain it seems more likely that he took his " local colour ", such as it is, from the conversation of his fellow royalists who had been stationed at the Spanish capital. The scene of *Thomaso,* a regular pell-mell of amorous encounters, mistakes, jealousies, intrigues, and whore-hired ambuscadoes, lies very agreeably in Madrid, whither Thomaso has come on a visit to his friend Harrigo, as also to woo Serulina the sister of the Grandee, Don Pedro. Two other cavalier exiles, Edwardo and Ferdinando, accompany Thomaso on his travels. Thomaso, who is a general undertaker, is enraptured with the beauty of a lovely Venetian courtesan Angelica Bianca, whose portrait is suspended on the lintel of her house with a notice to say that the original may be purchased at a thousand crowns a night. Thomaso loudly declares his admiration of the picture, and thus comes in conflict with Don Pedro who desires the lady. The English rout the Spaniards, and Angelica at the sight of such gallantry gives herself gratis to Thomaso for whom she conceives an ardent passion. A vast deal of intrigue and masquerading follows. Various punks whom Thomaso has jilted plot to assassinate him, but the bravoes attack another stranger in mistake, and considerable bustle and excitement ensue, during which turmoil Thomaso carries off Serulina to become his bride. Interwoven with all this are the adventures of Edwardo, who falls into the meshes of a cunning bona-roba named Lucetta. This nymph finely chouses and strips him when he visits her at night, even by a trick turning him out into the dark streets without money or clothes in the nastiest pickle. Later Edwardo and Ferdinando in order to aspire to the hands and coffers of two rich Jewish monsters, the one a giantess, a very daughter of the Anakim, and the other a pigmy, employ the love philtres of a quacksalver, Lopus, who also undertakes to fit the couple of freaks with more normal bodies, " to make a Dwarf a Gyant, or Gyantize a Dwarf." Owing to a mistake in the ceremonies of the Æsonian baths the two monstrosities become even more hideously deformed, whilst other members of the mountebank's family essaying the same experiment are metamorphosed into the strangest shapes. A veritable pandemonium is the result, and it is buzzed abroad that the Holy Office is taking cognizance of the matter. The blame, however, is laid at the door of the old Hebrew guardian of the two monsters, who has indeed already been secured. The English rejoice to have scaped so narrowly and their jollification fits very admirably with the celebration of Thomaso's wedding. Angelica Bianca, Don Pedro, and other of the company hie away to Venice.

Thomaso is an immense canvas. There are more than forty characters, who fill out seventy-three crowded scenes. " The Author has borrow'd several Ornaments," [48] thus Angelica's song in Part I, Act II, scene 3, " Come hither, you that Love," is from Fletcher's *The Captain*, Act IV, The tremendous harangue of the mountebank Lopus, Part I, Act IV, scene 2, is a patchwork " from *Johnson's Fox*, where *Vulpone* personates *Scoto* of *Mantua* ". The play is even more indebted to Middleton's *Blurt Master Constable ; or, The Spaniard's Night-Walke*, 4to, 1602, and Brome's *The Novella*, produced at Blackfriars in 1632 ; 8vo, 1653. *Thomaso,* however, is largely autobiographical, and it may very well be questioned whether some of the accidents incidental to adventuring in a foreign city among the fireships and crafty Delilahs, which occur in the old comedies of Middleton and Brome, may not actually have happened to the exiled cavaliers, and have been personal passages taken from life rather than dramatic fictions derived from the stage. Such experiences were then not uncommon to travellers. Thomaso himself is of course Killigrew, and he was generally referred to under this name, as for example by Flecknoe in his very abusive lampoon *The Life of Thomaso the Wanderer*, 1667.[49] Harrigo Pogio is Henry Proger, most loyal and active of cavaliers, who in 1654 was at Madrid and of the English ambassador's household. No doubt Edwardo too, " a lost English Boy of thirty," " an *Essex* Calf with two legs, posses'd with a Colliar of *Croyden,*" portrays an actual person. There are indeed throughout *Thomaso* innumerable vivid touches, all easily recognizable, and which to a contemporary must have proved irresistibly piquant and telling.[50]

It is curious that Killigrew never pruned and abbreviated

Thomaso for the boards, the more so since when Aphra Behn with her exceptional instinct utilized such promising material in *The Rover; or, The Banish't Cavaliers*, produced at Dorset Garden 24th March, 1677, she gave the theatre one of her liveliest and longest-lived comedies.[51] Beyond question she vastly improved what she took, but her conveyances are extremely ample, and it is hardly too much to say that *The Rover* is an admirable adaptation from Killigrew. When *The Rover* appeared in print, 4to, 1677, the town very soon found " *that 'twas Thomaso alter'd* ", a report which caused Astrea to indite a Post-Script of defence, vigorous and witty enough, but not entirely consonant with the facts.

Yet *The Rover* justly belongs to Mrs. Behn, who has done a great deal more than merely fit *Thomaso* for the stage. So successful indeed was her play that rather less than three years later she returned to the material in *Thomaso* she had at first rejected, and produced *The Second Part of The Rover,* acted at Dorset Garden in February, 1680. The scene of *The Rover* is Naples ; the *Second Part* has its incidents at Madrid. In this sequel we meet not only the two monsters, but Harlequin and Scaramouch to boot.

In *The Parsons Wedding* we have a broadly humorous, occasionally coarse, and consummately clever comedy. Some of the speeches are certainly rough, but the piece has been denounced in so resonant and exceptious a strain of obloquy it seems difficult to escape the conclusion that many who have railed loudest in their abuse truthfully could claim a very slight or rather no acquaintance at all with Killigrew's play. The scene has grossnesses, it is true, but to write that *The Parsons Wedding* " is a comedy of almost unexampled coarseness ",[52] " chiefly distinguished for ribaldry and obscenity of dialogue," [53] " one of the most flagrantly indecent of Restoration productions," [54] or that the dialogue, in part at least, " is such that it might have curdled the ink with which it was written," is just to blatter that kind of polly-parrot nonsense which seems so strangely contagious.

If the situations be arraigned as immoral, this attack is answered by the fact that the initial blame cannot be charged to Killigrew since the adventures are for the most part stock old comedy fare. Thus the chousing of the Parson, who discovers himself all unwittingly bedded with an ancient bawd, and being surprised falls a victim to the designs of the Captain, Mr. Jolly, Mr. Wild, and the rest, is found among the Italian novelists, and forms the eighth story of *Les Comptes du Monde adventureux*, Paris, 1555. In English drama with some variations it had been utilized by Brome in *The Novella,* produced at the Blackfriars in 1632 ; and it was also employed by Edward Howard in *The Six Days*

Adventure, given at Lincoln's Inn Fields, March, 1671; and by D'Urfey in *Squire Oldsapp*, Dorset Garden, May, 1678. Many parallels might be cited.[55]

The "old stale trick" by which Careless and Wild circumvent Lady Wild and Mistress Pleasant into marriage, "is an Incident in several Plays, as *Ram-Alley, Antiquary*, &c. but in none so well manag'd as in this Play."[56] The two jaunty gallants who have gained secret access to the room so compromise the ladies by appearing early in the morning all unready at the window of the bedchamber and thence hailing their friends in the street below, that there is nothing for it but downright matrimony to salve the reputations of the virtuous fair.

It might also be remarked that the figure of the "old Stallion Hunting Widow", Lady Love-all, whom Killigrew has drawn with rare strokes of humour and vivacity is as common to the stage as it is to life.

When *The Parsons Wedding* was published in the folio, 1664, it is said on the title-page to have been written at Basle. Killigrew may have sketched a draft of his comedy at this town, but nothing more. It is certain from internal evidence[57] that the play was composed, at least in greater part, by 1641, and it is equally certain that it was not produced until three and twenty years later on the 5th or 6th October at the Theatre Royal, Bridges Street, when it was "acted all by women".[58] It has been mistakenly suggested that possibly *The Parsons Wedding* was seen on the stage before the closing of the theatres, but the Revels memorandum showing that a sum of £2 was paid for the licence is conclusive, this being the fee for a new play, whilst £1 was paid for a revival.[59] Pepys, also, on the 4th October, 1664, speaks of *The Parsons Wedding*[60] as "a new play".

When acted, the script of *The Parsons Wedding* was considerably cut by the hand of Killigrew himself,[61] and indeed the speeches and scenes are so long that it is impossible that it should be given entire as printed.

In 1672, at some date between March and October,[62] *The Parsons Wedding* was revived at Lincoln's Inn Theatre, recently vacated by the Duke's company and temporarily occupied by Killigrew's actors. The witty Prologue and Epilogue, especially written for this occasion, were printed in *Covent Garden Drollery*, 1672, the former address being spoken by the leading lady, Mrs. Marshall, dressed "in man's Cloathes".

From the time of his return to England in May, 1660, until the government of the playhouse passed out of his hands in February, 1677, into the charge of his second son—the elder of three brothers by his wife Charlotte—Charles, Thomas

Killigrew's activities are so intimately concerned with the stage that in great part an account of the Theatre Royal tells his story also, although, of course, as a high favourite with the King he was a prominent figure at Whitehall and much information has come down to us concerning the courtier and the man of affairs. We are, however, only concerned with the theatrical manager.

In the year 1659, John Rhodes " a Bookseller being Wardrobe-Keeper formerly (as I am inform'd) to King *Charles* the First's Company of Comedians in *Black-Friars* . . . fitted up a House then for Acting call'd the *Cock-Pit* in *Drury Lane* ",[63] where he gathered together a number of actors and recruits who gave performances under very hazardous conditions. His own company included Thomas Betterton, Thomas Sheppey, Thomas Lovel, Thomas Lilliston, Cave Underhill, Robert Turner, James Dixon, Robert Nokes, and for female rôles Edward Kynaston, James Nokes, Edward Angel, William Betterton, John Moseley and young Floid. On 4th February, Thomas Lilliston, one of Rhodes' leading men, was charged before the Middlesex Sessions with acting " a publique stage-play this present 4th February in the Cock-Pitt in Drury Lane . . . contrary to the law ".[64] On Easter Monday, 23rd April following, General Monk and his Council issued an order forbidding theatrical representations.[65] On Saturday, 12th May, Anthony Turner and Edward Shatterell of the incorrigible Red Bull were ordered to make their appearance, and answer " for the unlawfull main-taineing of Stage-Playes and enterludes att the Redd Bull in S. John's Street ".[66] As late as Saturday, 28th July, 1660, Rhodes himself was fined for illegal acting at the Cockpit.[67]

Nevertheless when Killigrew and Davenant returned to England in May, 1660, or at any rate not many weeks later, there were three companies acting in London. Rhodes was at the Cockpit with a troupe whose strength lay in the new young recruits, many destined to become famous names ; Major Michael Mohun, of the pre-Restoration Cockpit [68] and a great favourite with King Charles II—he had returned in the King's train—presided over a company of older actors at the Red Bull [69] ; and yet another muster was to be found at William Beeston's house, Salisbury Court.[70]

Immediately the energetic and unwearied Sir Henry Herbert asserted the old powers and absolutism of the Master of the Revels to the full, and the three companies of actors found themselves compelled forthwith to submit to the authority which " time out of minde whereof the memory of man is not to the Contrary, belonged to the Master of his Majesties Office of the Revels ". Beeston was licensed and allowed to continue and constitute Salisbury Court a playhouse.[71] The leash of managers, Beeston, Rhodes, and Mohun, severally each agreed to pay Herbert £4 a week whilst their three companies were performing tragedies, comedies, and the like.[72] Killigrew and Davenant, however, were almost equally swift in their countercheck. Diplomatically they combined forces and presented a united front to Herbert's claims. They decided between themselves to acquire by Royal grant a monopoly of the London theatres, to select two companies under their own names, to establish these in two playhouses, and effectually to quash all rivals, great or small. Sir William Davenant had by him his old patent of 1639,[73] granted by Charles I, but shrewdly he did not entirely rely upon this. The King had given Killigrew on 9th July, 1660, an order for a warrant " to erect one Company of players which shall be our owne Company " and directing that all other companies save the two now to be erected should be silenced and suppressed.[74] Owing to the great influence of Killigrew and Davenant with the King, on 21st August, 1660, there passed the Privy Signet the order [75] which assigned to the two managers a complete monopoly of the London theatres, authorizing them to build a couple of playhouses, placing the companies under their jurisdiction, government, and authority, and granting them the censorship of all plays ; in short, an absolute control.

What was pending, however, could not be hidden from Sir Henry Herbert who raised a shriek of protest, and was prepared to fight tooth and nail for his authority. He alleged that Killigrew and Davenant had represented to the King that the Master of the Revels was consenting to the grant, which he hotly denied. He protested vehemently against any usurpation or curtailment of his " ancient powers ", and petitioned the throne in very unequivocal terms.[76] The King referred the whole matter to the Attorney-General, Sir Jeffery Palmer, and a very great deal of debate and angry contention resulted.

In the meantime, called upon to serve many masters, the poor actors were in a pretty predicament. They could obtain no decisive answer when they asked what authority they were to obey, and Herbert actually obtained damages—although far less than he tyrannically claimed—from Mohun's company for alleged failure to pay his fees.[77] Simultaneously Killigrew and Davenant were enforcing their power over the actors, and both lodged complaints with the King that scandalous plays were being given and the prices exorbitantly raised. Herbert riposted with an official letter " To Mr. Michael Mohun and the rest of the actors of the Cockpitt playhouse in Drury Lane. The

13th of October, 1660 ", deriding the " pretended power " of Killigrew and Davenant, and severally reprimanding the troupe for " innovations and exactions not allowed by mee ". Furthermore he laid down regulations in reference to the censorship of even the older plays about to be revived.[78] Little wonder that on the same day the actors approached the King and presented " The humble Petition of Michael Mohun, Robert Shatterell, Charles Hart, Nich. Burt, Wm. Cartwright, Walter Clun, and William Wintersell ". They complain that Sir Henry harried them until it " ended in soe much per weeke to him " and a promise of his protection, which was nugatory, since under the Royal warrant Killigrew suppressed the company until they had entered into a covenant with the two patentees, Killigrew and Davenant, and bound themselves to act in a new theatre with women, " and habitts according to our sceanes." None the less Herbert persisted and had become " a continual disturbance ".[79]

The first move by the patentees, then, was an amalgamated company,[80] and this began acting at the Cockpit, a playhouse of which Rhodes was lessee, on Monday, 8th October, and continued until towards the end of the month. The company included actors from the several theatres, Mohun, Hart, Burt, Robert and Edward Shatterell, Lacy, Clun, Wintershal, Cartwright, Baxter, Loveday, as well as two new-comers to the stage, Betterton and Kynaston.[81] The arrangement soon achieved the result which had been intended by the patentees, the division of the actors into two separate companies under the several management of Killigrew and Davenant.

Killigrew selected for his troupe the older actors, the King's Company, and on Monday, 5th November, they played *Wit without Money* at the old Red Bull; on the next day they gave *The Traitor*; and on Wednesday *Beggars Bush*. On Thursday, 8th November, they opened with *I Henry IV* at Gibbons' Tennis Court, Vere Street, Clare Market, the first Theatre Royal.[82]

It must be borne in mind that Vere Street, as the house may be conveniently known, was a platform stage, hung with tapestries, and not set with scenery.[83] An oblong roofed theatre, it was the last constructed house of the Elizabethan order.

Although the history of the two companies inevitably cross and come in contact it will be simpler directly to follow the fortunes of Killigrew's actors, and then to pick up the threads of the Duke of York's servants under Davenant. A few words may not inaptly, perhaps, be given here to a brief consideration of that interesting question, Who was the first English professional actress ? It may at once be said that it is impossible to

speak with certainty upon this point, and indeed the very words
" the first professional actress " must be ambiguous, since it is
hardly to be supposed that one lady appeared at any distinct
interval before others.[84] As I have already dealt with the evidence
at some length,[85] and propose to treat it in a later chapter in
even fuller detail, it will suffice to summarize the inquiry here.
The precise phrase " professional actress " is used, speaking
by the card, to exclude that " pleasant jolly woman " Mrs. Coleman,[86] who sang Ianthe in *The Siege of Rhodes* at Rutland House
in 1656. Curll's assertion in his notoriously inexact *History of
the Stage* that Mrs. Norris was our first professional actress,
which is echoed by Davies,[87] is a mere guess and a blunder
to boot. The " received tradition " [88] that Mrs. Mary Saunderson
who married Betterton, " made her first essay " at the Red Bull
at Vere Street, and " was the first English actress " is entirely
erroneous. Bellchambers, also, says that Mrs. Saunderson was
" the first woman, before her marriage, that appeared upon the
English stage ", but he is confused and flatly contradicts himself
as he further adds that Ann Marshall " the principal unmarried
actress in the royal company is perhaps entitled to this dubious
distinction ".[89]

In a petition, printed by Mr. Albert S. Borgman in *The Times
Literary Supplement,* 27th December, 1934, which was addressed
by Mrs. Katherine Corey to the Lord Chamberlain, the Earl of
Dorset, on 11th March, 1689, praying that she should be re-
admitted into the playhouse whence she had been most unfairly
excluded, this lady represents that " she was the first and is
the last of all the Actresses that were constituted by King Charles
the Second at His restauration ", adding moreover that she had
been on the stage " for 27 yeares ". Here then we have a very
definite statement, and it is significant that Downes when giving
in the *Roscius Anglicanus* a list of the seven Women who upon
the Creation of the King's Servants belonged to " his Majesty's
Company of Comedians in *Drury-Lane* " places Mrs. Corey first.
The others follow in this order : Mrs. Ann Marshall ;
Mrs. Eastland ; Mrs. Weaver ; Mrs. Uphill ; Mrs. Knepp ;
Mrs. Hughes. Mrs. Corey's own phrase may, of course, imply
nothing further than that at the time the actors and actresses
of Thomas Killigrew's original troupe were sworn His Majesty's
Servants she was the first woman to take the oath.

Katherine Corey was certainly the last of these seven ladies
to remain upon the stage, for in 1689 more than a decade had
elapsed since the appearance of any one of the six actresses
whom Downes here names with her. As I have shown in my
essay *Pepys' " Doll Common ",* included in *Essays in Petto,*

Mrs. Corey did not retire until 1692, her last rôle probably being that of the Abbess of Cheston in a revival of *The Merry Devil of Edmonton.*

The traditional claim of Mrs. Margaret Hughes to be the first English actress in that very restricted sense in which alone so equivocal a term can reasonably be used rests upon evidence of some weight and no little interest.

On Saturday, 8th December, 1660, *The More of Venice* was acted at Vere Street, and this, we presume, was the occasion on which Mrs. Hughes appeared as Desdemona. The rôle we know from Thomas Jordan's "*A Prologue to introduce the first Woman that came to Act on the Stage in the Tragedy, called* The Moor of Venice ". It has been superfluously pointed out that there is a slight ambiguity in the rubric to Jordan's prologue, as it appears in *A Royal Arbor of Loyal Poesie,*[90] but it is quite clear on reading this address that the reference is not to the first woman who acted in *Othello,* but to the first woman who professionally appeared upon the stage, on which occasion the part she played was Desdemona. Downes [91] informs us that Desdemona was taken by Mrs. Hughes.

Incidentally John Payne Collier in his MS. *History of the Restoration Stage* (Harvard University Library), when discussing the question of the first actress, decides that it must have been Ann Marshall, and he supports himself by quoting the following doggerel, preserved, he says, in the Bridgewater House MSS., but which is doubtless a forgery.

> Who must not be partial
> To pretty Nan Marshall ?
> Though I think be it known
> She too much *does de-moan.*   (Desdemona)
> But that in the Moor
> May be right, to be sure,
> Since her part and her name
> Do tell her the same
> But none can refuse
> To say Mistress Huges
> Her rival out-does.

A little later he adds the following :—

> Yet—I swear—honest Coz.,
> With a critical oath
> That Ned beats them both.

The allusion here must, of course, be to Kynaston. But the lines are more than suspect, and the very fact of an addition being tagged on after seems in itself evidence of bad faith.

Even if these verses were genuine they do not, be it noted, decide the point. Moreover it is in the highest degree improbable that the rôle of Desdemona would have been assigned to two several actresses, Margaret Hughes and Ann Marshall, nor were these ladies rivals in any sense of the word.

We do not know which actresses originally sustained the parts of Emilia and Bianca to the Desdemona of Mrs. Hughes. Downes gives Mrs. Rutter as Emilia, but he also tells us that she did not join Killigrew's company until some time later. Indeed his cast must be subsequent to August, 1664, the date of Walter Clun's murder, for Clun was a famous Iago, in which rôle he was succeeded by Michael Mohun, and Downes has: "Jago, Major *Mohun.*"

The quarto of *Othello,* 1687, gives Mrs. Cox as Desdemona ; Mrs. Rutter, Emilia ; and Mrs. James, Bianca. Hart who used to play Cassio (now assigned to Kynaston) has followed Burt as the Moor, and the cast is certainly that of the Second Theatre Royal, which opened on 26th March, 1674.

It is not impossible, although it appears very unlikely, that young actors were at first the Emilia and Bianca to the Desdemona of Mrs. Hughes. It might be argued also that in the other case the two actresses who filled these parts at that performance have almost equal claims to priority with herself. So we arrive at over-subtle distinctions, and rather than split hairs let us say that, if we will, we can very justifiably regard Margaret Hughes as in a certain sense the first professional actress in the English theatre.

Having opened at Vere Street, His Majesty's Theatre, on Thursday, 8th October, as we have seen, Thomas Killigrew found himself by no means immune from the persecution— for it was nothing else—of the rancorous and truculent Master of the Revels. In Trinity term, 1661, Herbert filed a suit against Killigrew and Davenant for the infringement of his rights owing to the acting from the 8th to the 16th October, 1660, of their united company, and in the following Michaelmas term he brought a similar suit at Westminster. Eventually the two patentees were not only acquitted, but awarded £25 damages and costs.[92] Undeterred, nay, further exasperated, Herbert now divided his attack. Killigrew he pursued with such relentless molestations and annoy that on the 4th June, 1662, the vexed and fretted manager was compelled to come to terms with his tormentor. The first clause of the Articles of Agreement,[93] "That a firme Amity be concluded for life betweene the said Sir Henry Herbert and the said Thomas Killigrew," sounds with a bitter tang. The Articles give Herbert a sweeping victory.

Killigrew agreed to pay him all licensing fees for plays acted since the 11th August, 1660, at the rate of £2 for new plays and £1 for revivals. He also liquidated the expenses of all Herbert's litigation, and added " a noble present " of £50 for the great damages the Master of the Revels had sustained—on his own showing. Further yet, Killigrew bound himself to aid and assist Herbert in his office " and neither directly nor Indirectly to Ayde or Assiste sir William Davenante, Knight ". In return Herbert superficially extended his patronage to Killigrew, and promised not to harry him for the future. Possibly a more one-sided agreement was never signed, and Herbert appears without disguise as little other than a pitiless bloodsucker and oppressor.

Killigrew, meanwhile, was busy with the building of his new permanent theatre, the site of which was a " piece or parcell of ground scituate in Pach. Sct. Martin's in the Ffeilds and St. Paule Covent Garden, knowne by the name of the Rideing Yard ", in length from east to west 112 feet ; in breadth from north to south at the east end 59 feet, and at the west end 58 feet. This was leased on 20th December, 1661, from William, Earl of Bedford, to Killigrew ; to Sir Robert Howard, who thus early began to play an important part in the history of the theatre ; to eight actors, Hart, Mohun, Burt, Lacy, Robert Shatterell, Clun, Cartwright, and Wintershal ; and to William Hewett and Robert Clayton. An annual ground rent of £50 was to be paid, and there was a condition that before Christmas, 1662, £1,500 should have expended in building a playhouse on the aforesaid " piece or parcell of ground ".[94]

On 28th January, 1662, Hewett and Clayton sold their interest in the site, and the property was divided into thirty-six parts, nine to Sir Robert Howard, nine to Killigrew, four to Lacy, and two apiece to Mohun, Hart, Burt, Robert Shatterell, Clun, Cartwright, and Wintershal. On the same day Howard and Killigrew entered into an agreement with these eight actors, to whom were joined Theophilus Bird, Richard Baxter, Edward Kynaston, Nicholas Blagden, and Thomas Loveday, by which contract the actors bound themselves only to play at this theatre, and covenanted that the whole company should pay the building sharees a fee of £3 10s. every acting day. As Fitzgerald comments, a very business-like joint-stock speculation.[95]

When Theophilus Bird, one of the sharing actors, died early (before 28th April) in 1663, Killigrew despotically endeavoured to appropriate his share, and the company appealed to the King.[96] In the course of this dispute it becomes clear that the manager had already delegated his powers, in practice at any rate, to Mohun, Hart, and Lacy,[97] which boded ill for the true welfare of the theatre, and indeed on one occasion, at least, when there was a quarrel between Mohun and Hart the house closed down and was silenced.[98]

Scenery was used for the first time by Killigrew at his new house, the Theatre Royal, Bridges Street, which opened on Thursday, 7th May, 1663, with *The Humorous Lieutenant.* " *Note,* this Comedy was Acted Twelve Days Successively." [99] The principal actors in Killigrew's company from 1663 to 1682 were : Charles Hart ; Michael Mohun ; John Lacy ; Nicholas Burt [100] ; William Cartwright ; Walter Clun ; Richard Baxter ; Robert and William [Edward] [101] Shatterell ; Marmaduke Watson ; Thomas Hancock ; Edward Kynaston ; William Wintershal ; Thomas Bateman ; Nicholas Blagden ; Thomas Loveday ; Thomas Gradwell ; Joseph Haines ; Philip Griffin ; Cardell (Cardonell) Goodman ; Walter Lydal ; Richard Hart ; Graydon ; William Wilbraham, who was at the Cockpit in 1630, when he played Bashaw Alcade in Heywood's *The Fair Maid of the West,* Part I, and where he also played Isaac in Shirley's *The Wedding* ; William Charleton, the original Jerry Blackacre, and who is possibly to be identified with Will Cherrington the boy who played Feminia in Jordan's *Money is an Asse,* acted in the country *c.* 1637–8 ; William Shirley (upon the pre-Restoration stage better known as Sherlock) who was at the Cockpit as early as 1622 ; Henry Hailes ; Thomas Kent, who was possibly the father of Tommy Kent, a boy who commenced acting at the Theatre Royal in 1689 ; George Beeston ; Richard Bell ; Thomas Clarke ; Martin Powell ; Carey Perin ; John Wiltshire ; Nathaniel Cue ; Disney ; John Coysh ; Chapman ; Styles ; Gray ; Saunders ; Alexander (not to be confused with the actor of this name 1685–1694) ; Littlewood ; Reeves ; Hughes ; Thomas Tanner ; Jermaine ; John Power ; Henry Boutell ; and William Harris. The principal actresses were Katherine Corey ; Ann and Rebecca Marshall ; Mrs. Eastland ; Elizabeth Weaver ; Susanna Uphill ; Mary Knepp ; Margaret Hughes ; Mrs. Pratt ; Mrs. Boutell ; Nell Gwyn ; Mrs. James ; Margaret Rutter ; Anne Reeves ; Mrs. Corbet ; Anne Quin ; Elizabeth Cox ; Frances and Elizabeth Davenport ; Jane Davenport ; Mrs. Yockney ; Mrs. Elizabeth Roche ; Sarah Cook ; Mrs. Farlee (who may be the same as Mrs. Weaver) ; Mrs. Merchant ; Mrs. Vincent ; Sue Percival, who afterwards married Mountford ; Mrs. Bates ; Katherine and Frances Baker ; Elizabeth Slade ; Anna Maria Knight ; Mrs. Dalton ; Mrs. Beattie ; Mrs. Yates ; Mrs. Hall ; Mrs. Moyle ; and Mrs. Anne Child. The Book-keeper, that is to say the librarian of the theatre to whose custody were entrusted the manuscripts, was Mr. Charles Booth.

PLATE V

SIR PATIENT FANCY: THE EPILOGUE

These actors and actresses were not, of course, all in the company at the same time. Downes tells us, for example, that Bell, Reeves, Hughes, and William Harris " were Bred up from Boys, under the Master ACTORS ".[102] Clarke, again, Wiltshire, and others were later comers, as also were Katherine and Frances Baker, and the more famous Anna Maria Knight. Mrs. Cox joined the theatre about 1670, and only remained on the stage some seven or eight years. Mrs. Reeves retired to a foreign cloister in the Spring of 1675. Anne Quin left the Theatre Royal in 1668–9. Clun was murdered by highway robbers in August, 1664; Richard Bell perished during the fatal fire of January, 1672.[103]

A crushing blow was dealt to both theatres when their doors were closed for eighteen months on account of the visitation of the Plague. On 5th June, 1665, the Lord Chamberlain ordered that no performance of any kind should be attempted anywhere until he gave official sanction, and this actually was not accorded until 29th November, 1666, which day both houses began to act on condition that a large share of the takings should be assigned to charitable uses.[104] Although plays had been given at Whitehall,[105] an attempt to open the two theatres in October was quashed by the Archbishop of Canterbury, who complained to the King,[106] and even on Thanksgiving Day, 20th November, the town openly murmured that the Thanksgiving was hastened " to get ground for plays to be publicly acted, which the Bishops would not suffer till the plague was over ", the notice being suddenly given and no ceremony.[107]

During the interval Killigrew had taken advantage of the closing of the theatres to make considerable alterations in his house, particularly widening the stage in order to give room for ampler scenery, a larger number of actors, and a grander spectacle. On the 19th March, 1666, Pepys found the workmen busy, and the playhouse " all in dirt ".

The improvements effected at so doleful and difficult a time must have been extremely costly, and therefore the disaster which befell the Theatre Royal on Thursday evening, 25th January, 1672, came with overwhelming force. A fire, breaking out between seven and eight o'clock under the stairs at the back of the building, spread with incredible rapidity and consumed half the theatre, including the scenes and wardrobe. All the houses from the Rose Tavern in Russell Street on that side of the way in Drury Lane and many in Vinegar Yard were destroyed, whilst inevitable destruction was also done by the gunpowder used to blow up the houses in the way of the flames to check the conflagration. It was in one of these explosions that the young actor, Richard Bell, was killed. The damage to property was estimated at £20,000.[108]

No more terrible misfortune than the destruction of their home could have fallen upon the company, and for a time they were completely paralysed. Indeed from this date we may clearly reckon the rapid decline and disintegration of the Theatre Royal, until its final collapse some eight or nine months before the Union of the Two Companies in 1682.

Before 1672 Killigrew's actors had not only excelled in their magnificent repertory, but it was their house which presented by far the greater number of successful new plays, and in spite of the extraordinary strength of their rivals, the Duke of York's Servants, they were for a decade at any rate the established favourites of the town. Among their stock pieces were *Othello, King Henry IV, Julius Cæsar, Volpone, The Alchemist, The Silent Woman, Bartholomew Fair, The Maid's Tragedy, A King and no King, The Scornful Lady, The Chances, Rule a Wife and Have a Wife, Philaster, The Jovial Crew, The White Devil,* and many more which never failed to draw crowded houses. Dryden was their principal modern author, and *The Indian-Queen, The Indian Emperour, Secret Love, Tyrannick Love, The Conquest of Granada,* were all immensely applauded and admired. Yet even as early as February, 1667, Killigrew was complaining " how the audience at his house is not above half so much as it used to be before the late fire ".[109]

To add to the misfortunes of Killigrew's actors the rival company had only two months before moved into a new house, the magnificent Dorset Garden, where they had opened on Thursday, 9th November, 1671, with the popular Sr *Martin Mar-all,* which never failed of its attraction.[110] Hart and his fellows were obliged to occupy Lisle's Tennis Court, Lincoln's Inn Fields, the playhouse whence Betterton had so recently migrated. On Monday, 26th February, 1672, the " shipwreck'd Passengers " publicly commenced with *Wit without Money,* " that compleat Actor Major Mohun " playing Valentine and speaking a Prologue especially written by Dryden for the occasion.[111] With such costumes as they could muster they were compelled to depend upon the stock fare for many weeks ere they could hazard the mounting of a new piece. Probably the first new play given by Killigrew's company at Lincoln's Inn Fields was Dryden's *Marriage A-la-Mode,* which achieved a triumph.

The date when Killigrew's company vacated their temporary home cannot be precisely determined. There is, it is true, a warrant of the Lord Chamberlain to Killigrew, 7th June, 1673, signifying the King's pleasure " that there shall not bee acted any playes at the Theatre in Lincolnes Inne fieilds after Mid-summer day next ensueing vntill further order ", and it has been assumed that 24th June, 1673, was the date of the final performance by the Theatre Royal troupe at Lincoln's Inn Fields. None the less their new house was not ready for another nine months to come, and the warrant so far from forbidding any acting at Lincoln's Inn Fields for the future, merely suspends performances " vntill further order ". There is no reason to think that permission to resume was not granted in due course, or that Hart and his fellows were not giving plays at Lincoln's Inn Fields during the autumn and winter of 1673, indeed until towards the opening of their new house in March, 1674.

At once Killigrew set about building a new theatre, which should be more commodious than his first house in Bridges Street, and in order to provide accommodation for the scenes stretched on their frames he added a cellared scene-house in Vinegar Yard, a rear annex to the main structure. The price of this theatre, the second Theatre Royal in Bridges Street (more loosely the second Drury Lane) was " near £4,000 ",[112] a sum of money which was not raised without considerable difficulty. The building investors owned the theatre, but the cost of the scene-house, new scenery, machines, and dresses was raised by contributors in proportion to their shares, from the actor-sharers of the company.

Matters were further complicated by Killigrew's financial operations, which could not fail badly to affect the prosperity of the Theatre Royal. As early as 1st May, 1663, he had made over his own shares in the theatre to Sir John Sayer under certain conditions of assignment. On 21st June, 1673, he made over these same shares to Sir Laurence Debusty as security for a loan of £950, and a month later he borrowed £1,600 of a Richard Kent, by means of his agent James Magnes, the security being his theatrical patent and authority.[113] Thus hypothecation and re-hypothecation were forced upon him, and the second Theatre Royal, Bridges Street, which opened on 26th March, 1674, with the popular comedy *Beggars Bush* commenced its career in somewhat disadvantageous circumstances, the effects of which were very shortly to make themselves felt.

Dryden's Prologue, addressed to the King and Queen, who were present at the first performance, adroitly contrasts—giving the preference to the former—the new " Plain built House " with the rococo magnificence of Dorset Garden " shining all with Gold ", where " Scenes, Machines, and empty *Opera's* reign ".

The " homely House " would have been well enough, but

all was far from peace within. As early as 16th May, 1674, the Lord Chamberlain had been obliged to issue an order prohibiting members of either company from suddenly migrating to the rival house. The takings were dwindling, whilst during 1675 Hart, Kynaston, Cartwright, and Wintershal more than once gave in their notices, and with difficulty were persuaded to continue. Killigrew by now had long left the government in the hands of Hart and Mohun, with the result that early in 1676 the company " left off acting upon private differences and disagreements betweene themselves ", until a royal mandate on the 14th February peremptorily bade them at once resume. In the autumn of the same year owing to the quarrel between Thomas Killigrew and his son Charles, who claimed his father's promise of the Managership of the theatre and the office of Master of the Revels—held by Thomas since Sir Henry Herbert's death in 1673—the Lord Chamberlain appointed Mohun, Hart, Kynaston, and Cartwright to control the Theatre Royal. A little later Hart was commissioned to act in the capacity of manager alone. In the autumn of 1676 two leading actresses, Mrs. Marshall and Mrs. Hughes, migrated to the Duke's Company. At Dorset Garden Mrs. Hughes created Octavia in *The Wrangling Lovers* and Mrs. Moneylove in *Tom Essence,* whilst early the next year, 1677, she acted Cordelia in *A Fond Husband* with Mrs. Marshall as Maria, and Mrs. Barry, Emilia. On 22nd February, 1677, Thomas Killigrew having come to terms with his son resigned to him all power and authority over His Majesty's Comedians, and two days later he further delivered up to him the office of Master of the Revels. Thomas Killigrew died on 19th March, 1683, and is buried in Westminster Abbey.

As may be supposed, all these domestic dissensions, these variances and divisions, not unmixed with a good deal of sharp practice, to use no harsher term, utterly disorganized, and in fine practically ruined, the company. Yet during those years, 1674 to 1677, they produced many first-rate plays.

This want of harmony, however, and something worse, very plainly made themselves felt by a distinct falling-off in the audiences, and consequently a lowering of the house receipts, which were already burdened with claims that could only have been properly satisfied had the takings kept up briskly to a high-water mark of popularity. It is true that during the lean year of 1667 Pepys several times refers to the thinned audience, but this was a certain revulsion after the Plague and the Fire, largely due to extraneous circumstances and depression abroad. On Wednesday, 17th April, 1667, the Theatre Royal at *Rollo* was " very empty "; on Thursday, 1st August following, he notes at *The Custom of the Country* " the house mighty empty —more than I ever saw it " ; on Monday, 26th August, there was " very little company in the house " at *The Surprisal* ; on Monday, 16th September, at three o'clock, " there was not one soul in the pit " for *The Scornful Lady* ; whilst on Saturday, 5th October, Pepys being in the scene-room heard Nell Gwyn curse " for having so few people in the pit " at *Flora's Vagaries*. Naturally enough there were also occasions when the house was " mighty full ". But in 1675–6 there are allusions and plaints which make it fairly obvious that a good audience was an exceptional thing at the Theatre Royal. Thus Duffett's Prologue (spoken by Haines) written for a revival of *Every Man out of his Humour*, July, 1675, commences [114] :—

> So fast from Plays approv'd and Actors known,
> To drolling, stroling, Royal Troops you run,
> That *Hayns* despairing is Religious grown.
> So Crack enjoy'd, the queazy Gallants slight,
> And she, though still her beauty's in its height,
> In rage turns Nun, and goes to Heav'n in spight,
> O Novelty, who can thy pow'r oppose !
> *Polony* Bear or strange Grimace out-goes
> Our finest language and our greatest shows.

Dryden in the Prologue to *Aureng-Zebe*, November, 1675, diplomatically suggests that the rivalry between the two houses largely accounted for bad business at the Theatre Royal, a plea in which there was possibly some half-truth, but which is by no means adequate to explain the situation :—

> There needs no care to put a Play House down,
> 'Tis the most desart place of all the Town.
> We and our Neighbours, to speak proudly, are
> Like Monarchs, ruin'd with expensive War.
> While, like wise *English*, unconcern'd, you sit,
> And see us play the Tragedy of Wit.

Unfortunately the rule of Charles Killigrew proved even more unsatisfactory than the management of his father, and by the summer of 1678 the actors were clamouring to be allowed to govern themselves. In this year we find associated with Charles Killigrew as a Master Partner or Sharer his half-brother, Henry,[115] one of the most rakehelly libertines of the court of Charles II, a notorious blackguard and yet a great Wit, whose scandalous depravities have incidentally done much to slur the name of his father with whom he is constantly confused. The interest of Henry Killigrew in the Theatre Royal could be productive of little good to any concerned. Two of the younger actors, also, Cardell Goodman and Thomas Clarke, jealous of Hart and Mohun, and anxious to try their stride in the rôles these great men had made peculiarly their own, were Master Partners or Sharers, and their coalition excited much uneasiness and unrest.[116]

It is true that many of the older actors were falling out of the ranks. William Wintershal died in 1679, Burt retired in the same season.[117] Lacy who died on 17th September, 1681, had long been ill and unable to play for some years. Cartwright was an invalid, confined to his house in Lincoln's Inn Fields, so that after 1679 he was hardly in the theatre half a dozen times. Charles Hart was tortured with stone and other disorders, Mohun was a martyr to the gout. In the prologue to The *Ambitious Statesman,* produced at the Theatre Royal in the spring of 1679, Crowne laments :

> *In our poor Play-house fallen to the ground,*
> *The Times Neglect and Maladies have thrown*
> *The two great Pillars of our Play-house down.*

Elkanah Settle, also, in the Dedication, addressed to Sir Robert Owen, to *Fatal Love ; or, The Forc'd Inconstancy,* 4to, 1680 (Theatre Royal, September, 1680), writes of Charles Hart : " *the* Theatre Royal *was once all Harmony. . . . But, oh, that their Oracle should be quite silent ! . . . And when he leaves the Stage, the Reign of* Tragedy *expires.*" Again *the Calamity of the Time,* the frenzy and fury of Oates's bedlam plot which raged from 1678 to 1681 *made People not care for Diversions.*[118]

Little wonder then that whilst such misgovernment was wrecking the Theatre Royal the dramatists carried their plays to the Duke of York's company, and as early as 1678 Charles Killigrew, Hart, Burt, Goodman, and Mohun addressed a woe-begone petition [119] to the Lord Chamberlain, seeing that Dryden and Lee, the one a sharer and the other a pensioner of the house, " they being the only Poets remaining to us," took their new tragedy *Oedipus* to Dorset Garden, where indeed it was actually produced in the December of that year with Betterton in the title-rôle.

In 1678 also, whilst the Theatre Royal was closed owing to the quarrels of Charles and Henry Killigrew and the other partners, several of the younger actors amongst whom were Goodman and Clarke, apparently giving up all hope of a reasonable settlement which would afford them opportunity to continue their careers, left England for Edinburgh with Thomas Gray, the treasurer of the company,[120] who had resigned his position.

With "His Majesty's Comedians", as they called themselves, went the popular Mrs. Corey, a host in herself. It seems that the migratory Joe Haines accompanied the troupe to the north, a journey one would indeed expect of this picaresque rogue. Thomas Gray was appointed Manager of His Majesty's Servants in Scotland, and at Edinburgh they acted at the Canongate house Thomas St. Serfe the dramatist had been utilizing as a theatre. The Duke of York in his office of High Commissioner for Scotland, reached Holyrood on 27th October, 1679, and his train of courtiers immediately gave every encouragement to the actors, who at last seemed to have fallen upon easy places.

Meanwhile things at the Theatre Royal, Bridges Street, were going from bad to worse, and the Killigrews began vigorously to importune Gray, Goodman, and Clarke to return. This the actors, entirely misled by the representation that all disputes at home had been amicably and finally settled, were at length persuaded to do, on the promise that their travelling expenses should be defrayed. It so happened that in February, 1680, the Duke of York was recalled to England, and on the 24th of the month he reached London. Possibly the whole of the Scotch company of actors, at any rate Gray, Goodman, Clarke, and Haines returned in his entourage.

Edward Ravenscroft's *Titus Andronicus, or the Rape of Lavinia,* "Alter'd from *Mr. Shakespears* Works," was not printed until 1687, when it was found that the Prologue and Epilogue had been lost, for the tragedy was originally given at the Theatre Royal in the winter of 1679. Not to disappoint the buyer of his pennyworths Ravenscroft generously furnished three Prologues and an Epilogue he had by him, all of which had been written about the time of the original production of the tragedy. These addresses were not indeed intended for the piece. The first prologue and the epilogue are those spoken at the performance of William Whitaker's *The Conspiracy,*[121] given at Dorset Garden in March, 1680. The second prologue is described as " before the Vacation ", and the third prologue as " after the Vacation ", spoken by Haines. The second prologue has the following reference :—

> *Come all and pay your Foyes before you go,*
> *Else we must troop to Scotland after Jo*
> *We by the last advice for Certain hear*
> *That Haynes does head the Rebell-Players there.*

There is an allusion in the third Prologue " after the Vacation " to plays being acted at Windsor, and also to a pilgrimage made by some of the actresses to S. Winefride's Shrine :—

> *But Travelling of Late was much in Fashion,*   *Some*
> *Some Pilgrim Saints there were of our Vocation,*   *of the Actresses*
> *Only they did it a far different way,*   *Went that year*
> *Your Ladies went to sin, but ours, to pray.*   *to Holywell.*

It is interesting to note that *A Discourse Concerning the Devotions of the Church of Rome,* 4to, 1685, p. 6, speaks of " Pilgrimages . . . to *Jerusalem, Rome, Loretto, Mount-serrat,* to St. *Thomas* at *Canterbury,* St. *Winefrid's* Well ".

The prologue to Crowne's *Thyestes* produced at the Theatre Royal in March, 1680, just after the return of the actors from Scotland, pertinently says :—

> *What cursed Planet o're this Play-house reigns ?*
> *Palsies, and Gouts are all the Old mens gains ;*
> *And we young men e're we have learnt to speak,*
> *Have learnt the Old mens cursed trick to Break.*
> *Some went to* Scotland ; *they had cunning Plots*
> *Who went to sell the* English *wit to Scots.*

The Old Men are, of course, Hart and Mohun, to whose sicknesses, " Palsies and Gouts," such candid reference is made.

When upon their return Gray, Goodman, and Clarke found that they had been choused by Charles Killigrew, who undoubtedly played a pretty shameful part throughout these negotiations, and that so far from any settlement having been arrived at matters seemed even in worse case, they expressed their resentment hotly enough,[122] and strife was heaped upon strife.

The next couple of years dragged amid continual discord at the Theatre Royal. In addition to bad management, domestic quarrels, and ill-natured rivalry, there were thefts of property, books, and clothes, a wholesale pilfering (in which Henry Killigrew took no small share), losses which as Kynaston justly complained " very much contributed to and forwarded the dissolution of the said company ".[123] At rarer intervals Hart and Mohun, when their illnesses allowed, performed in some favourite revival, and " the House was fill'd as at a New Play ",[124] but the burden of the whole fell upon the younger members of a company at loggerheads with its manager. New plays were few enough. Settle's *Fatal Love, or The Forc'd Inconstancy,* produced in September, 1680, was tepidly received.

It was now clear that no amount of temporary botching and patching could save the situation. At the beginning of February, 1681, the money taken would not cover the outlay and the company ceased acting. In these circumstances the owners of the building shares were persuaded by Sheppey to accept a proportion only of their just fees on such days as the profits proved very small. The house was reopened, to close again on account of the meagre takings. On some days the audiences were so few that they were dismissed, and the money returned. In May and June, miser· ⸱le sums, less than £4, were not infrequently the only receipts.

Some months of ruinous silence elapsed, after which the first production at the Theatre Royal in 1681 was a revival of Lee's *Mithridates*, for which Dryden wrote a special prologue. Well might the poet at once launch out with—

> *After a four Months Fast we hope at length*
> *Your queasie Stomachs have recover'd strength.* . . .

Banks, it is true, scored a success with *The Unhappy Favourite, or The Earl of Essex,* given in the autumn of 1681, with Clarke as Essex; Mohun, Lord Burleigh; and Anne Quin, Queen Elizabeth. Dryden's Epilogue, however, only too plainly exhibits the disastrous conditions of the house. The couplets sound a knell of shipwreck and ruin :—

> *We Act by Fits and Starts, like drowning Men,*
> *But just peep up, and then Dop down again,*
> *Let those who call me Wicked change their Sence,*
> *For never men liv'd more on Providence,*
> *Not Lott'ry Cavaliers are half so poor,*
> *Nor broken Cits, nor a Vacation Whore,*
> *Nor Courts nor Courtiers living on the Rents,*
> *Of the three last ungiving Parliaments.*
> *So wretched, that if Pharaoh could Divine,*
> *He might have spar'd his Dream of Seven lean Kine,*
> *And chang'd the Vision for the Muses Nine.*
> *The Comet which they say portends a Dearth,*
> *Was but a Vapour drawn from Play-house Earth,*
> *Pent here since our last Fire, and* Lilly *sayes,*
> *Foreshows our change of State and thin third dayes.*

Settle's *The Heir of Morocco,* produced on the 11th March, 1682, with Goodman as Altomar; Clarke, Gayland; and Elizabeth Cox, Artemira, gave the poet cause to complain of living " *in an Age so Critical and so severe* ", when the drama was " *maliciously persecuted* ". Probably the last new play to be presented at the Theatre Royal was Southerne's first tragedy, *The Loyal Brother; or, The Persian Prince,* a very fine piece of work which, one is able to be glad to record, achieved a great success. Dryden wrote both Prologue and Epilogue in his happiest style, and the play was admirably cast. Goodman acted the Sophy Seliman; Clarke, Tachmas, the Loyal Brother; Mohun, the treacherous Ismael; Mrs. Corey, Begona, the

Queen-Mother ; Sarah Cook, Semanthe, whom Tachmas loves ; and Anne Quin, the jealous Sunamire. Yet it is not one swallow that bringeth in summer. *The Loyal Brother* was given in March, and in April, 1682, the Theatre Royal closed its doors.

Since for a long while past it must have been clear that the only end of His Majesty's Servants would be a conjunction with, or rather absorption into the company of Dorset Garden, we can hardly blame Charles Hart and Edward Kynaston, the two shrewdest members of Killigrew's company, because they privately came to terms with Charles Davenant, Betterton, and Smith, on 14th October, 1681. Kynaston had retired in 1677, after giving a formal notice of his intention to leave the house. Hart had played very seldom of later years. The terms of the agreement were that the two actors should be paid each 5*s.* for every regular acting day at the Duke's Theatre, provided they do not appear at the Theatre Royal or effectually assist Killigrew's Company. If Kynaston hereafter shall be free to act at the Duke's Theatre his pension ceases. Hart and Kynaston promise to make over to Davenant, Betterton, and Smith, all right, title, and claim they have to any plays, books, clothes, and scenes in the Theatre Royal, as also their claim to 6*s.* 3*d.* for every regular acting day at the Theatre Royal. Hart and Kynaston pledge themselves to all in their power to promote an agreement between the two houses, and Kynaston promises to do his endeavour to get free to act at the Duke's Playhouse, but he is not obliged to play unless he has 10*s.* a day allowed for his acting, whereupon his 5*s.* a day ceases. Hart and Kynaston promise to go to law at their own charges with Killigrew, if necessary, to have these articles performed.[125]

" I am sensible," comments Gildon, " that this private Agreement has been reflected on as Tricking and unfair, but then it is by those, who have not sufficiently consider'd the Matter ; for *an dolus, an Virtus quis in hoste requirit* ? All Stratagems are allow'd betwixt Enemies ; the two Houses were at War, and Conduct and Action were to decide the Victory ; and whatever the Duke's Company might fall short of in Action, it is plain they won the Field by their Conduct."

The preliminary negotiations for a projected Union of the two Companies began almost immediately after the closing of the Theatre Royal, and it is uncertain who made the first move. Killigrew liked to think that the managers of Dorset Garden came to him with their proposals. Charles Davenant, Betterton, and Smith, were decidedly of opinion that they were approached by Killigrew. On 4th May, 1682, the Articles of Union were signed by Charles Killigrew on the one part, and by Charles

Davenant, Betterton, and Smith on the other part.[126] The provisions are :—

The two Letters Patent are to be joined and united as one.

Charles Killigrew and Charles Davenant are joint managers, under whom all plays acted by the Dorset Garden company are to be given.

Charles Killigrew undertakes to disperse and dissolve the present company at the Theatre Royal within six days, and to hand over the Theatre Royal, except the scenes and scene-room, with all the plays of which the house had a monopoly and other properties to Davenant for the joint use and benefit of the two managers.

Charles Davenant is to pay Killigrew £3 a day for each acting at either house. In case the Theatre Royal cannot immediately be handed over after the company is disbanded Killigrew is entitled to 20s. 6d. a day for one whole year, this sum to be changed to £3 a day for each acting day when possession is given.

All acting profits to be divided into 20 equal shares, of which Killigrew shall have three. One share and a half upon dissolving the company, and discharging the company's debts amounting to £500, and one share and a half in recompense of his right to the Patent.

The Joint companies opened on 16th November, 1682, at the Theatre Royal, as being a more convenient and accessible house than Dorset Garden, which in future was mainly used for spectacular pieces and opera.

At the Union there disappear from the London stage both older and younger actors. Hart never acted more, he had in fact not been seen for some little time. Cartwright played Cacafogo in a revival of *Rule a Wife and Have a Wife,* and Baldwin in *The Bloody Brother,* but he very seldom returned to the boards. Even more rare were the appearances of the crippled Michael Mohun, who appeared in a few of his favourite rôles before illness entirely incapacitated him. Thus in *A King and No King,* Mardonius, which he had once played to the Arbaces of Hart, the Bessus of Lacy, and the Panthea of Nell Gwyn, he now sustained opposite Betterton as Arbaces, Anthony Leigh as Bessus, and Mrs. Barry as Panthea.[127]

It should be remarked that Michael Mohun was most shamefully used by the Articles of Union. Already he had been deliberately excluded by Hart and Kynaston from their negotiations. He had long been Hart's peer in the Theatre Royal, on behalf of which he spared himself no labour and no anxiety, more than once personally approaching Charles II and obtaining pardon and grace when some indiscretion provoked the sovran's displeasure. He was a married man, the father of five children, and wholly dependent upon his acting. In these days he was sick and ill, sadly broken in health, yet obliged to continue his profession. In fine he was now constrained to petition the King. He represented that he had served Charles I and Charles II " 48 yeares in ye quality of an Actor, and in all ye Warrs in England & Ireland & at ye Seege of Dublin was desperately wounded & 13 monethes a Prisoner, and after that yor petr served yor mate in ye Regmt of Dixmead in Flaunders & came over with yor Mate into England where yor Sacred Pleasure was that he should Act againe, as he hath ever since vpon all Occasions continued ". The petition goes on to say that, owing to the Union, instead of the share and a quarter in the scenes, clothes, and plays of the Theatre Royal, he is merely offered 20s. a day upon such days as they have any use for his services, and as it is plain that the Duke's Company could not have studied the plays belonging to the Theatre Royal he will not very often be called upon to act, therefore he humbly prays that the King " will be graciously pleased to Order the present Company to allow him the same Conditions as Mr. Hart and Mr. Kinaston have, (whos Shares were all equall before) whereby he may be enabled to support himselfe & 5 children And yor petr shall as in duty bound pray &c." The King, with whom Mohun was a prime favourite—for Charles was wont to call him " my Actor " and to say that Mohun (pronounced Moon) shone like the Sun—at once gave strictest orders through Lord Arlington that Mohun was to be granted absolutely the same conditions as Hart and Kynaston. The first order, 23rd November, 1682, urgent enough, was even reinforced by a second on 5th December following, which commanded that Mohun should have the same weekly pension, commencing from 23rd November last, as Charles Hart enjoyed, and, moreover, he was " to be imployed presently, & to have his owne parts to Act ".[128]

Mohun, whose house was in Brownlow Street (now Betterton Street), Drury Lane, died there early in October, 1684, and was buried at S. Giles in the Fields.

Of the younger men Thomas Clarke [129] is only once found upon the London stage after the Union. How then are we to account for the omission of his name ? We are on somewhat hazardous ground, it is true, and in the dark, since in many cases death or retirement from the stage are simple and possible answers to our query. On the other hand, another solution suggests itself, and although I put this forward quite tentatively it seems to me the probable explanation of the case.

The Union could not have been very grateful to Clarke, who when he was expecting to secure the rôles in Hart's repertory, Michael Perez, Arbaces, Wildblood, Brutus, Othello, and the rest, found himself entirely superseded by Betterton, Smith, and William Mountford, " now grown to the maturity of a good actor." In the year 1682, Joseph Ashbury, sometime Deputy-Master of the Revels in Ireland under John Ogilby, had upon the death of the Master through his interest with the Duke of Ormonde, the then Lord Lieutenant of Ireland, been appointed Master of the Revels in Ireland and Patentee of the Dublin Theatre, Smock-Alley.[130] Ashbury's first wife was the sister of John Richards,[131] an actor of the Duke of York's Servants. The Smock-Alley Company not infrequently visited England; they played at Oxford and Edinburgh with applause, and during these visits the astute manager was eager for recruits. On 19th August, 1682, the Earl of Arran writes to the Duke of Ormonde from Dublin : " The bearer Mr. Ashbury to whom I have given licence to go into England, I must recommend to your Grace's care and desire you would, notwithstanding your great affairs there, allow him to speak with you on a matter of great importance here ; the business is Mr. Smith of our playhouse is lately died, who you know was a great pillar of our stage, therefore your encouragement and assistance will be necessary or else the playhouse will fall." Rather more than six weeks later, on 3rd October, 1682, the Earl again writes to the Duke from Dublin. " I received yesterday your Grace's letter of the 23rd and 24th of the last, the latter by Ashbury, who has brought us a recruit of players which I hope will afford us some divertisment this winter." These letters are illuminating, and it is highly probable, then, that at the Union Thomas Clarke joined the Smock-Alley troupe, where he would shine as *jeune premier,* and so left London for Dublin.

Yet another difficulty arises. In a revival of *Richard III,* 1689–1690, Clarke played the minor character of Brackenbury. Now Chetwood, *A General History of the Stage* (p. 53), tells us that in Dublin the Smock-Alley Theatre closed down, and " Playing was discontinued during the Troubles between King *William* and *James* the Second ". The theatre did not professionally reopen—there had been an amateur performance—until 23rd March, 1692, " the Day of proclaiming the End of the *Irish* War," when *Othello* was given. Clarke then returned to London from Ireland as soon as Smock-Alley closed its doors, but that he was coldly enough received after his migration sufficiently appears by the rôle for which Betterton cast him in Shakespeare's tragedy. Whether he went back to Dublin in 1692 we do not know. Such was probably the case, since his name cannot be traced in any London list of actors. The fact that he does not occur in the casts of Etherege's three comedies as supplied to Chetwood by Griffith, who was born in 1680 and died 1744, does not carry weight, for we cannot exactly tell the dates of these productions, and it may be remarked that Joseph Ashbury, the Patentee and Manager, who was playing young Careless in *The Committee* and Don Quixote in 1715 is also absent from *Love in a Tub, She wou'd if she cou'd,* and *The Man of Mode.*

It will now be necessary to retrace our steps and take up the tale of Sir William Davenant's activities from October, 1660, when the London actors were divided into two separate companies under Thomas Killigrew and Davenant respectively. On Monday, 5th November, 1660, Sir William, who took over with some few exceptions [133] Rhodes's former Cockpit players, came to an agreement with the leading members of his troupe. The Articles are tripartite ; Sir William Davenant of the first part ; Thomas Betterton, Thomas Sheppey, Robert Nokes, James Nokes, Thomas Lovel, John Moseley, Cave Underhill, Robert Turner, and Thomas Lilliston, of the second part ; Henry Harris, painter, of the third part. Davenant constitutes, ordains, and erects the actors and their associates into a company to give performances until he has provided a new theatre with scenes ; and before they open the new theatre the general receipts are to be divided into fourteen shares, of which Davenant is to have four ; other directions as to the conduct of business until the new playhouse is ready are agreed ; and after this their profits are to be divided into fifteen shares, three of which go to Davenant for house-rent, repairs, frames for scenes, habits, properties, and scene-painting ; from the remaining dozen, which are to be divided into seven and five, seven are to go to Davenant as manager for his " paines and expences " and the maintenance of the actresses, five to the actors in several proportions, whilst the share of Harris is to be as great as that of any other player. Other clauses relate to tickets, doorkeepers, the wardrobe-keeper, hirelings whom we call " supers ", and various details of management. Thomas Killigrew is assigned a free box to seat six. Sharing actors are bound in £5,000, that is £500 apiece, to abide by their covenants. Davenant is the " Master and Superior ", and has the sole government of the company.[134]

As in his dealings with Thomas Killigrew, the outraged and outrageous Sir Henry Herbert showed himself as implacably disposed towards Davenant. Nay, the wrathful Master of the Revels was even more bitter and more inimical. He molested Davenant with succeeding persecutions at law, until the laureate was fain appeal to the King, who referred the matter to the

Chancellor and the Chamberlain. Meanwhile not only did Herbert obtain a writ against Betterton for acting " 10 new plays and 100 revived Playes " between the 5th November, 1660, and 6th May, 1662, without " the licence and allowance " of the Revels office, but in his reply on 11th July, 1662, to Davenant's petition he twits and taunts him as " Master of the Revells to Oliver the Tyrant ", sparing no pains to create a false and harmful impression with his abuse.[135] It were wearisome and profitless to thread the track of these litigations. Herbert found Davenant was harder to deal with than Killigrew, and the overbearing Master was by no means able to carry things with a high hand. Precise details are lacking, but it is certain that a compromise was eventually arrived at, since Davenant paid fees for licensing plays, but Herbert's other claims were disallowed and fell to the ground.

On 5th November, 1660, Davenant's company began to play at the Theatre in Salisbury Court, a house built on the site of the granary of Dorset House, near Fleet Street, and here they remained until the following June.

In the meantime Davenant was pressing on the alterations of Lisle's Tennis Court, Portugal Street, Lincoln's Inn Fields,[136] which was to be the first English public theatre regularly to utilize scenery, the first picture stage. A commodious scene-room was built, and Davenant's own lodgings, where he boarded his four principal actresses, Mrs. Davenport, Mrs. Saunderson, Mrs. Davies, and Mrs. Long, adjoined the theatre. Cibber speaks of Lisle's Tennis Court as " a Tennis *Quaree* Court, which is of the lesser sort ",[137] and since Julian Marshall in his *Annals of Tennis* [138] gives 100 English feet as the usual length of a *quaree* court, we may conclude that the theatre was some 75 feet in length and about 30 feet or rather more in width.

When the time drew near for the opening of the new theatre Davenant's company rehearsed [139] at Apothecaries' Hall (Cobham House) [140] the pieces with which it was intended to commence, namely *The Siege of Rhodes,* both parts, and *The Witts.*

It should be noted that although Davenant, as early as 16th May, 1661, had received an exemplification of the patent granted him by Charles I his full patent was not finally issued until 15th January, 1663.[141]

The Lincoln's Inn Fields Playhouse, as it is conveniently known, opened on Friday, 28th June, 1661, with the First Part of *The Siege of Rhodes.* On Saturday the Second Part was given. Thus *The Siege of Rhodes,* both parts, was acted on alternate afternoons for a fortnight. Various revivals followed, and on Thursday, 15th August, *The Wits* was produced and ran for eight days. On Saturday, 24th August, *Hamlet* was performed " done with scenes very well, but above all, Betterton did the Prince's part beyond imagination ".[142] *Twelfth Night* was revived on Wednesday, 11th September. After this the theatre closed for three or four weeks to allow of the stage being altered, as it was obvious the space was cramped with " contracted Scenes " in so narrow room.[143] The October attraction was *Love and Honour*, produced on the 21st of that month. Later in the year revivals of *The Bondman* and *The Mad Lover* proved very popular, whilst the new year saw the almost unprecedented success of Tuke's *The Adventures of Five Hours* and a revival of *Romeo and Juliet* " Play'd Alternately, Tragical one day, and Tragicomical another, for several days together ", since the Hon. James Howard had made a new version of Shakespeare, preserving the lovers alive.[144]

The cast [145] of *The Siege of Rhodes* was as follows : Solyman the Magnificent, Betterton ; Alphonso, Harris ; Villerius, Lilliston ; the Admiral, Blagden ; Ianthe, Mrs. Sanderson [146] ; and Roxolana, Mrs. Davenport.[147] In *The Wits* Betterton acted the Elder Palatine ; Harris, the Younger Palatine ; Cave Underhill, Sir Morgly Thwack ; and Mrs. Davenport, Lady Ample. When Betterton was studying Hamlet, Sir William Davenant, having seen Joseph Taylor of the Blackfriars, who was instructed by the author Mr. Shakespeare, play the prince of Denmark, taught him in every particle of it which gained him esteem superlative to all other plays.[148] Harris was Horatio ; Lilliston, the King ; Richards, the Ghost ; Lovel, Polonius ; and Cave Underhill, the First Grave-maker, his most famous rôle ; the Queen, Mrs. Davenport ; and Ophelia, Mrs. Saunderson. " No succeeding Tragedy for several Years got more Reputation, or Money to the Company than this."

Harris was Romeo to the Juliet of Mrs. Saunderson ; Betterton, Mercutio. In *Twelfth Night* Betterton played Sir Toby ; Harris, Sir Andrew ; Underhill, the Fool ; Lovel, Malvolio ; and Mrs. Anne Gibbs,[149] Olivia.

The Duke of York's Servants were well supplied by the new dramatists,[150] and although Dryden, it is true, was the poet of the Theatre Royal, none the less it so happened that two of his most popular plays, through accidents as it were, appeared at Lincoln's Inn Fields. When the Duke of Newcastle gave his jejune translation of *L'Etourdi* to Dryden, who transformed it into *Sʳ Martin Mar-all*, this was produced at Lincoln's Inn Fields on 15th August, 1667, and proved, as it well deserved, one of the most popular of Restoration comedies. In the Shakespearean adaptation, *The Tempest ; or, The Enchanted Island,* given at Lincoln's Inn Fields on Thursday, 7th November, 1667, with Harris as Ferdinand; Angel, Stephano; and Underhill, Trincalo; Dryden joined with Davenant, and accordingly the comedy was produced at the Duke of York's Theatre.

Sir William Davenant, in many respects the very antipodes of Thomas Killigrew, proved a careful and provident manager, who guided the fortunes of his company with both artistic and financial success. His authority he never delegated, but was always himself the active Master and Superior. The shares in his theatre accordingly increased in value. Two of his stepsons were employed in the house: Thomas Cross, the eldest, born in 1630, as treasurer; Philip Cademan the youngest, born in 1643, as an actor, although it is true his line was small comprising such rôles as Haly in the Earl of Orrery's *Mustapha;* Donalbain in *Macbeth*; Guilderstern in *Hamlet.* Unhappily whilst playing Don Lewis in *The Man's the Master,* revived at Dorset Garden in 1673, he was accidentally hit with a foil under the right eye, which touched his brain and half paralysed his right side. Owing to his loss of memory and a subsequent impediment in his speech he was paid 30*s.* a week from the theatre, thus cancelling a bond of £100 he held under Sir William Davenant's hand. Cademan was alive and still drawing his pension in 1708, when Downes wrote.[151]

Lincoln's Inn Fields was closed, of course, during the Great Plague, for the same term as the Theatre Royal. There was rivalry and there were quarrels among the actors. Henry Harris in July, 1663, demanded an extra fee for himself of £20 for every new play in which he appeared, and £10 for every revival. Upon being refused he walked out of the theatre, and it needed all Davenant's influence to persuade the King to prevent him from appearing at the Theatre Royal. For indeed, as Davenant pleaded, if Harris joined Hart and Mohun, Lincoln's Inn Fields might as well shut up house. It was not, however, for several months that Harris could be wrought upon to return to Davenant's company, and even then it was on his own terms and owing to the particular intervention of the Duke of York.[152] For some reason which is not known it seems that both theatres were closed by authority throughout the greater part of June and July, 1667. When Lincoln's Inn Fields reopened on Saturday, 20th July, the occasion was distinguished by a fray in the pit between the Duke of Buckingham and Henry Killigrew, who was soundly drubbed by His Grace.[153] In October, 1667, Betterton fell ill, and could not reappear until July, 1668, a long sickness, during which his place was poorly supplied by Young.[154]

Whilst Betterton was still absent from the stage the even tenour of the fortunes of Lincoln's Inn Fields was sadly interrupted by the death of the manager. Sir William Davenant died at his house adjoining the theatre on Thursday, 7th April, 1668, and on the following Thursday he " was Bury'd in *Westminster-Abbey,* near Mr. *Chaucer's* Monument ".[155] The whole company attended the funeral, and there were many coaches with six horses and many hacknies.[156] The decease of the laureate was signalized by the usual copies of elegiac verse.[157]

In 1668 Charles, Davenant's eldest surviving son by his widow, Dame Mary de Tremblay Davenant,[158] was a lad of twelve years old, and therefore until June, 1673, when she handed over the reins of government of the Duke's Theatre to her son, as his guardian she controlled the business activities of the company. The artistic side was in the hands of Betterton and Harris, and when the latter retired in 1681, of Betterton and Smith.

It had long been felt that the Lincoln's Inn Fields stage was too narrow and too straight, wherefore early in 1670 the company, much desirous of erecting a new theatre, viewed " the Garden Plot behind Salisbury House in the Strand to build a new Theatre ".[159] A little later, however, they preferred a more southerly part of Dorset Garden, having a frontage upon the waterway Thames, and a wharf next Dorset Stairs. Here the Dorset Garden Theatre was built at a cost of £9,000.[160]

The Theatre was designed by Sir Christopher Wren, and erected on a scale of the utmost magnificence. The first quarto, 1673, of Settle's *The Empress of Morocco* supplies elaborate sculptures or illustrations of the back stage with its rococo proscenium, as also of the façade of the house.[161] There is too, of some later date, a prospect of the Duke's Theatre, Dorset Garden, from the river.[162] The arms of the Royal Patron of the troupe, James, Duke of York, were emblazoned on the exterior entablature, whilst statues of Melpomene and Thalia crowned the lateral columns. These two Muses, as also the Ducal heraldry, reappeared in the interior over the proscenium. The upper stories of the theatre consisted of apartments, and here Betterton as " Keeper " of the playhouse had his lodgings. In similar fashion Charles Hart, before his retirement, had resided at the Theatre Royal.[163]

At this splendid house then the Duke's company opened on 9th November, 1671, with the popular comedy *Sr Martin Mar-all,* Nokes playing the title-rôle. There could have been no better choice to put the audience in a thoroughly good humour, and this revival was a happy stroke which crowded the house.

Three performances were given, followed by two performances of Etherege's *The Comical Revenge ; or, Love in a Tub*. The first novelty was Crowne's heroic drama in rhyme *The History of Charles the Eighth of France ; or, The Invasion of Naples by the French,* " all new Cloath'd," [164] with Betterton as Charles. This " Martial Play " ran its six days, which although not the success that was expected, can by no means be accounted a failure.

As has been remarked, the fortunes of the Theatre Royal rapidly waned after the disastrous fire of January, 1672, and the star of the Duke's Servants rose swiftly and bright in the ascendant. Such prolonged and public disorders as the panic of Oates' plot, *the downfal of the Stage,* [165] Dryden termed it, inevitably affected their prosperity, and occasionally there was some little trouble over a suppressed play as when Dryden's *The Kind Keeper, or, Mr. Limberham,* produced at Dorset Garden on 11th March, 1678, " was permitted to be acted only thrice. The Crime for which it suffered, was that which is objected against the *Satyres* of *Juvenal,* and the *Epigrams* of *Catullus,* that it express'd too much of the Vice which it decry'd." [166] Save for such accidents and chances, under the management of Betterton and Smith, those were halcyon days for Dorset Garden. The actors were well supported both by their poets—they gained Dryden to their house—and the town, their profits answered all expectations, they thrived apace, so that when the moment came for a Union with the remnant of the Theatre Royal, Charles Davenant, who attained his majority in 1677, Betterton, and Smith, were able to make terms most favourable for themselves with Charles Killigrew, Hart, and Kynaston.

At the Union the one combined company moved from Dorset Garden to the Theatre Royal, Bridges Street, where they opened on 16th November, 1682, the King and Queen attending in state. A Prologue and Epilogue, among the wittiest effusions of his muse, were written for the occasion by Dryden who promised—

Old men shall have good old Plays to delight 'em :
And you, fair Ladies and Galants, that slight 'em,
We'll treat with good new Plays, if our new Wits can write 'em.

The principal actors [167] in Rhodes' company as taken over by Davenant were : Thomas Betterton ; Thomas Sheppey ; Thomas Lovel ; Thomas Lilliston ; Cave Underhill ; Robert Turner ; James Dixon ; and Robert Nokes. Edward Kynaston, who a little later joined Killigrew ; James Nokes ; Edward Angel ; William Betterton ; John Moseley, and Floid, generally played female parts before actresses came. Henry Harris, Joseph Price, John Richards, joined the company in November, 1660, and a minor actor, Nicholas Blagden,[168] was also with Davenant for a short time. Something less than a year later, William Smith, Samuel Sandford,[169] Matthew Medbourne, Young, and Norris were recruited.

When Davenant opened at Lincoln's Inn Fields in June, 1661, his actresses were : Mrs. Davenport [170] ; Mary Saunderson (afterwards Mrs. Betterton) ; Mary Davies ; Mrs. Long ; Mrs. Ann Gibbs (afterwards Mrs. Shadwell) ; Mrs. Norris ; Mrs. Holden ; and Mrs. Jennings. The first four of these ladies were boarded at the manager's house.

Other early members of the company were Davenant's stepson, Philip Cademan ; Dacres ; Coggan ; Gibbons ; Revet [171] ; Francis Pavy ; Joseph Williams,[172] and John Crosby, the two last both mere lads.

Philip Cademan has already been mentioned. Dacres, whose line was the Second Grave-digger in *Hamlet* ; Coggan ; Gibbons ; and Revet ; were all very minor performers. Joseph Williams (who must be carefully distinguished from the unimportant David Williams), the original Polydore in *The Orphan*, Mellefont in *The Double-Dealer*, became a famous actor. His last appearance to be traced is as Hannibal in Cibber's tragedy *Perolla and Izadora*, produced at Drury Lane on 3rd December, 1705. John Crosby, who is said to have been remarkably good-looking and graceful, played the young lovers, Leander in Mrs. Behn's *Sir Patient Fancy*, produced at Dorset Garden in January, 1678 ; Paris in John Banks' *The Destruction of Troy* at the same theatre in the following December. He had retired from the stage in 1680-1, before the Union of the Two Companies, since he is spoken of as " a late Player " in *The True Protestant Mercury*, 29th July–2nd August, 1682, and in *The Loyal Protestant*, 3rd August, 1682. He died on Wednesday, 8th April, 1724, as appears from the following notice in *St. James's Evening Post*, 9th–11th April of that year : " On Wednesday Night last died at his House in Charter House Yard, John Crosby, Esq., in a very advanced Age. He was formerly an Actor of the Playhouse in the Reign of Charles II, and has been for a long time one of the Justices of the Peace, and of Oyer and Terminer for the County of Middlesex, and one of the Governors of the several Hospitals of Christ Church, Bethlehem and Bridewell." *Applebee's Original Weekly Journal*, 25th April, 1724, has : " On Thursday was 7–Night last, the Corpse of the late John Crosby, Esq ; lay in State at his House in Charter house Yard ; and late at Night was carry'd from thence in a Hearse, attended by several Mourning

Coaches and six Horses, to the Parish Church of S. Sepulchre in great Funeral State and Pomp, and interr'd in the great Vault of that Church. The Pall was supported by two Justices of the Peace and other Gentlemen that were Governors of the Hospital; to which 'tis said the Gentleman deceased has been a good Benefactor." The burial is registered, 16th April, 1724.

The following actors belonged to the Duke's company in the period preceding the Union : Rathband ; Burford ; Bamfield ; Sherwood ; Whaley ; Westwood ; Thomas Percival ; Anthony Leigh ; Thomas Jevon ; Gillow ; David Williams ; John Lee ; George Bright ; Thomas Creek ; Adams ; Allinson ; Jeremiah Lisle ; William Mountford ; John Freeman ; John Bowman ; John Weaver, the principal male dancer, who wrote *An Essay Towards an History of Dancing,* 1712 ; Leitherfull (a singer) ; Richard Leigh ; William Peer.

Among the Duke's actresses were : Mrs. Brown ; Mrs. Gosnell [173] ; Mrs. Norton, " the second Roxolana " ; Mrs. Wiseman ; Mrs. Margaret [174] ; Peg Fryer ; Mrs. Johnson ; Mrs. Mary Lee, *née* Aldridge, and afterwards Lady Slingsby ; Mrs. Gibbs, the sister of Mrs. Shadwell ; Mrs. Elinor Leigh, the wife of Anthony Leigh ; Mrs. Slaughter, who is probably Mrs. Margaret Osborne ; Mrs. Twyford ; Mrs. Crofts ; Mrs. Caff ; Mrs. Gillow ; Mrs. Barry ; Emily Price ; Elizabeth Currer ; Mrs. Napper ; Mrs. Le Grand ; Charlotte Butler ; Mrs. Petty ; Mrs. Seymour ; Mrs. Lilbourne ; Mrs. Dixon ; Mrs. Williams ; Mrs. Spencer ; Mrs. Burroughs ; Mrs. Wright ; Mrs. Ford ; Mrs. Clough ; Mrs. Evans, a singer.

It must be remembered that in spite of orders and enactments to the contrary the minor actors, and sometimes the principals as well, migrated from house to house. Joe Haines, in particular, was a notorious bird of passage. In 1669 he was acting at the Theatre Royal, whence he was discharged for a gross insult to Hart. In 1670 he was at Paris. He took part (as a dancer) in the first performance of *Le Bourgeois Gentilhomme* at Chambord, 14th October, 1670, and " diverted the King by severall English dances ".[175] He soon returned to England, however, and joined Lincoln's Inn Fields, where in July, 1672, he doubled the French Tutor and the Singing Master in Ravenscroft's *The Citizen Turn'd Gentleman.* In the winter of 1672 he was back again with Killigrew's company, and created Benito in *The Assignation.* Adams played Draxanes in Edward Howard's tragi-comedy *The Womens Conquest* at Lincoln's Inn Fields in November, 1670, and at the Theatre Royal in November, 1673, he acted the Second Witch in the extraordinary travesty burlesquing *Macbeth,* which serves as Epilogue to Duffett's farce *The Empress of Morocco.* Curiously enough although Thomas Percival was at Dorset Garden, his more famous daughter began her career at the Theatre Royal. She acted Winifrid in *Sir Barnaby Whigg*; November, 1681, and spoke the Epilogue. It should not be forgotten that two poets, Thomas Otway and Nat Lee, made their brief and unsuccessful appearances with the Duke of York's company. The story of Otway's failure is well known. Mrs. Behn gave him the rôle of the King in *The Forc'd Marriage,* produced at Lincoln's Inn Fields in December, 1670, "*for a Probation Part.*" " It was quite a crucial test, and Otway proved his entire inability to face the public. He trembled, was inaudible, melted in agony, and had to leave the stage. The part was given to Westwood, a professional actor, and Otway never essayed to tread the boards again." [176] "*Mr.* Nat. Lee, *had the same Fate in Acting* Duncan *in* Macbeth." [177] Lee, however, seems to have struggled a little longer than Otway as he played the tiny rôle of the Captain of the Watch in Nevil Payne's *The Fatal Jealousie,* produced at Dorset Garden early in August, 1672. [178]

Stout old John Downes, Betterton's veteran prompter, does not gloze over his own mishap. Being listed for an actor, on the opening of Lincoln's Inn Fields, 28th June, 1661, he essayed Haly, a Eunuch Bassa, in *The Siege of Rhodes,* and " was so much out that he was hissed off the stage ". [179]

Exceedingly agreeable to the King but intensely obnoxious to our English actors were the frequent visits of foreign comedians to London. As early as 30th August, 1661, Pepys took his wife " to the French comedy " at the Cockpit in Drury Lane, a performance which he sums up as " nasty and out of order and poor ". The company was that of Jean Chamnouveau, who on the 2nd December, 1661, was presented with £300 by Charles II for his good services, and who on the 16th of the same month was acting at Court, as mentioned by Evelyn. A great feature in the repertory of these French actors proved to be Chapoton's *La Descente d'Orphée aux Enfers,* produced in Paris, 1640, and revived at the Théâtre du Marais with new scenery and additional music. " The Description of the Great Machines Of the Descent of Orpheus Into Hell. Presented by the French Commedians at the Cockpit in Drury Lane," was even printed, French and English, a brochure of eighteen pages, in 1661.

In September, 1663, the French comedians again appeared in London, and Davenant found these incessant invasions an apt theme for satire in *The Play-house to be Let.*

It is hardly necessary to notice more than the most prominent and successful of the visits by French actors, such for example

PLATE VI

THE PROLOGUE TO ARIADNE

[face p. 110

as that in April, 1672, when owing to the destruction of the Theatre Royal by fire the King's players were temporarily housed at Lincoln's Inn Fields. To the popularity of the foreigners and to their custom of using coloured bills—red was the monopoly of the Hôtel de Bourgogne—Dryden has a bitter allusion in his new Prologue to a revival of Carliell's *Arviragus and Philicia*. The mordant lines tell how when the native actors in sore distress were using every endeavour to please their old patrons all their woes were topped by the fact that—

> A brisk *French* Troop is grown your dear delight ;
> Who with broad bloody Bills call you each day
> To laugh and break your Buttons at their Play . . .

This visit which lasted until May, 1673, is girded at by Dryden in his Epilogue, spoken by Hart to *The Silent Woman,* when the Theatre Royal company resorted to Oxford for the Act in July of that year. He complains that they have been visited during the summer with all the Plagues of Wit :

> A *French* troop first swept all things in its way,
> But these hot *Monsieurs* were too quick to stay . . .
> The *Italian Merry-Andrews* took their place,
> And quite debauched the stage with lewd grimace.

On 30th March, 1674, Pierre Perrin's opera *Ariane et Bacchus* was publicly performed in London " at the Theatre in Bridges-street ", and there were printed French and English versions, the latter being *Ariadne or the Marriage of Bacchus.* An Opera, Or, A Vocal Representation . . . Acted by the Royall Academy of Musick, At the *Theatre-Royal* in *Covent Garden,* 4to, 1673/4. The frontispiece, which depicts the Prologue with its setting of London Bridge and the Thames, is drawn from the Court performance in the previous January, for *Ariane,* reset by Louis Grabut, Master of the King's Music, was selected to celebrate the nuptials of the Duke of York with the Princess Mary of Modena, and it is to the Court performance of this opera Evelyn alludes in his Diary, 5th January, 1673–4, " I saw an *Italian Opera* in musiq," since, as Professor Dent explains, by an "*Italian Opera* " is not intended an Opera in the Italian language, or by an Italian composer, but simply a dramatic performance set to music, "A Vocal Representation."

The opera season at the Theatre Royal under the auspices of Grabut and the Royal Academy of Music lasted some three weeks, concluding on or near the 23rd April, 1674. It is probable that the *Pomone* of Robert Cambert, who was then resident in England, was given during the same season.

On 29th May, 1677, the King's birthnight " devant sa Majesté sur le Theatre Royal de Whitehall" was presented Madame La Roche-Guilhen's *Rare en tout*, "Comedie meslée de musique et de Balets," but Charles soon showed himself "aweary on't". Actually there were two French troupes in London during 1677, the one (which doubtless was responsible for *Rare en tout*) in the spring, and another at Whitehall in the winter of the year. The latter did not leave London until April, 1678, and thus we can understand why Porter in the Epilogue (spoken by a Monsieur) to *The French Conjurer,* a Dorset Garden comedy (June, 1677), should so violently attack "the French troop at toder end o' Town", that is to say performing at Whitehall. The troupe which arrived in the winter is by some supposed to have stayed here fifteen or even eighteen months, but actually their visit can hardly have lasted so long. Yet there were a number of not undistinguished artists in the company, which throve under the management of Henri Pitel, whose daughter Françoise (later to achieve fame as Mlle Raisin) was so sweet and beautiful that she set aflame all the rakes in Town, whilst the greatest gentleman in England bootless sighed for her favours.

A visit to London in 1684 of the Prince of Orange's French players under François Duperier belongs to later history. Whilst French comedians were crowding to England we should not omit to say that Betterton visited Paris more than once, and that the facetious Joe Haines delighted Louis XIV by his admirable dancing at Chambord, in the ballets at the *première* of *Le Bourgeois Gentilhomme,* 14th October, 1670. It was at the direct suggestion of Betterton, who had seen the *comédie-ballet* of *Psyché* in 1671, that Shadwell wrote his elaborate opera-tragedy *Psyche,* produced at Dorset Garden on 27th February, 1674-5. Betterton was also in Paris in August, 1683, under instructions from the King, "to endeavour to carry over the Opera", which was, however, found to be impracticable.

The Italian Comedians were even better known in London than the French. On 22nd October, 1660, Charles granted a patent to Giulio Gentileschi to build a theatre for Italian musicians, and hardly a year—save in the intervals of the Plague and Great Fire—seems to have passed without "A *Trivilino,* or a *Skaramuchio*" attracting crowds by their performances of the *commedia dell'arte.* In 1672 the King issued an order allowing Antonio Di Voto, a famous "punchenello" to perform all sorts of Drolls and Inter-ludes, provided that no London actor was admitted into his company, and that he did not take any pieces or scenes from plays belonging to the Theatre Royal or the Duke's house.

In April, 1673, another Italian troupe arrived in England under the conduct of the famous Scaramuccio, Tiberio Fiorelli, and here they remained until September, returning in 1675 when they acted in Whitehall, which gave considerable offence since money was taken at the doors, as Marvell complains in a letter of 24th July, 1675, when he comments on " Scaramuccio acting daily in the hall on Whitehall, and all sorts of people flocking thither, and paying their money as at a common play-house ". Even a twelvepenny gallery was erected so that the grave Evelyn who saw " the Italian Scaramuccio " at Whitehall on 29th September of the same year, thought it very scandalous that such payment for admission was allowed. So well did Fiorelli line his pockets that he led his troupe to London again in November, 1678, and enjoyed a four months' season of prosperity. In the summer of 1683 they were playing at Windsor for the King's especial entertainment.

There are numberless references to the *commedia dell'arte* in play, prologue, and epilogue. To name but a few : in the prologue to St. Serfe's *Tarugo's Wiles,* Lincoln's Inn Fields, October, 1667, there is a grumble at the popularity of *Trivolino* and *Skaramuchio* ; at the conclusion of Shadwell's *The Sullen Lovers,* Lincoln's Inn Fields, 2nd May, 1668, " *a Boy in the habit of* Pugenello " danced a jigg ; " the surprizing ways of Harlequin " and the antics of " Scaramouchys " are alluded to in the Prologue, " spoken by Mr. *Hayns* " to the revival of *Every Man out of his Humour,* Theatre Royal, July, 1675 ; in Otway's *Friendship in Fashion,* Dorset Garden, April, 1678, Lady Squeamish is loud in her admiration of Harlequin, as he acted " at the *Louvre* or *Whitehall* ", and to amuse her Malagene " *speaks in* Punchinello's Voice " (Act III) ; whilst Harlequin and Scaramouch are characters in Mrs. Behn's *The Second Part of the Rover,* Dorset Garden, February, 1680. Ravenscroft's *Scaramouch A Philosopher, Harlequin A School-Boy, Bravo, Merchant, and Magician,* " A Comedy After the Italian Manner," produced at the Theatre Royal on 5th May, 1677, is a complete *commedia dell'arte.* Italian is spoken in the course of the play, and pantomime tricks are played on the stage. Griffin was Scaramouch, and Joe Haines, Harlequin.

As rivals to the regular theatre puppet-plays stoutly persisted. Thus Pepys on the 8th April, 1667, frankly acknowledges that he had three times more sport at Polichinello than was afforded him by Sir Robert Howard's *The Surprisal* at the Theatre Royal. Even before the days of the Commonwealth *The Actors Remonstrance or Complaint* (24th January, 1643), written by the actors of the " private houses ", that is to say the leading companies, grumbles that " Stage-playes, only of all publike recreations are prohibited ; the exercise at the Beares Colledge, and the motions of Puppets being still in force and vigour ".

When the King joyfully came to his own again, not only English but foreign puppet-plays, and the Italian in particular drew crowding audiences. Antonio Di Voto was licensed by Herbert as master of a puppet-show almost immediately after the Restoration, and it was probably his show which Pepys saw on Friday, 9th May, 1662, when he went to Covent Garden " to see an Italian puppet play, that is within the rayles there, which is very pretty, the best that ever I saw, and great resort of gallants ". The King himself was immensely diverted by the puppets, and all good subjects shared his tastes. Pepys records very frequent visits to the puppets. On 6th August, 1663, although it was as late as nine o'clock at night he could not resist turning into " a puppet play in Lincolnes Inn Fields, when there was the story of Holofernes, and other clockwork, well done ". On 22nd August, 1666, at Moorfields Pepys saw the popular *Polichinello* which pleased him mightily, and which he saw again and again, " prettier and prettier "—and " which I like the more I see it ", he enthusiastically records. At Bartholomew Fair, on 29th August, 1668, he saw " a ridiculous, obscene little stage-play, called ' Marry Andrey ' ; a foolish thing, but seen by everybody ". At Bartholomew Fair and Southwark Fair puppet plays were one of the chiefest attractions, and patronized by the highest quality as well as the mobile. Thus on 30th August, 1667, Lady Castlemaine was at a puppet-play *Patient Grizill* at Bartholomew Fair, and on 21st September, 1668, at Southwark Fair Pepys " saw the puppet-show of Whittington, which was pretty to see ; and how that idle thing do work upon people that see it, and even myself too ! "

When introduced into the regular theatre the puppet-plays transported out of their own *milieu* did not prove so successful. Pepys very much preferred *Bartholomew Fair* without puppets, which he considered " to be a lessening " to this admirable comedy. The First (Dorset Garden, May, 1694) and Second (Dorset Garden, June, 1694) Parts of D'Urfey's *The Comical History of Don Quixote* were received with unbounded favour by the Town, but the Third Part (Drury Lane, November, 1695) was very nearly, if not quite a failure, and it was remarked that the Puppet-Play of Gines de Passamonte in no small degree contributed to the miscarriage of the piece, the audience complaining that Don Gayferos and the rest were placed so that they could neither be seen nor heard by the greater part of the house.

The history of the later puppet-plays and of that little crooked fellow Powell who exhibited with such extraordinary skill and reputation, the tale of the puppet-theatre in the Piazza, all belong to a subsequent chapter.

It may not be impertinent here to mention an entertainment which was eagerly thronged in the London of Charles II, " Paradice, shown at Hatton-house in Holborn from 3 of the clock to 8 every afternoon," as announced in *The City Mercury,* 17th–24th February, 1675.

Having followed the fortunes of the two theatres to this point, it is necessary now to retrace our steps a little. Immediately after the Restoration performances were being given in London by three companies, Mohun's players ; the troupe of John Rhodes ; and Beeston's actors. As we have seen, the two patentees, Killigrew and Davenant, obtained a monopoly of the London theatres, and when for a very brief space an amalgamated company had played at the Cockpit in October, 1660, two separate companies were selected by the patentees for their several houses.

Beeston in 1664 joined His Majesty's Servants at the first Theatre Royal, Bridges Street. It is possible that he attempted some clandestine and sporadic performances, but he must soon have given up an independent struggle, doomed to failure from the very first.

An individual far more disquieting to Killigrew and Davenant appeared in the figure of George Jolly, an experienced, courageous, and obstinate actor-manager. The date when and the circumstances in which Jolly left England are altogether uncertain, but at the end of April, 1648, he arrived in Cologne with a troupe of fourteen actors. It is useless to speculate whether Jolly was driven abroad by the Parliamentarian ordinances against the theatre of 1642 and subsequent years, or whether he had been trying his Thespian luck in foreign climes at an even earlier date. Nor need the history of the English players across the seas detain us here, full of interest and important as it is.[180] It should be remarked, however, that Jolly not only used scenery " in the Italian manner ", but also employed " skilful women " in his troupe. It is, moreover, particularly to be noted that at Frankfort, in September, 1655, King Charles II, the Duke of Gloucester, the Princess Royal, and a small party came incogniti to enjoy the fun of Frankfort Fair. The identity of the royal visitors could not long be maintained, and their patronage was soon secured by Jolly, who at once styled his company " The King's Servants ".

Owing largely to his despotism and ungovernable temper, in spite of his acknowledged eminence in his profession, the career of George Jolly in Germany was tempestuous enough, and finally on 31st January, 1660, he was expelled from Nuremberg on account of his violence and stomachful behaviour.

At the Restoration he was naturally all agog to seek his native country once more, and late in 1660 he made his appearance in London with a petition to the King for a licence to act. Not unmindful of the plays he had witnessed at Frankfort five years before, Charles II on 24th December, 1660, granted the request and formally permitted George Jolly to give " publique Presentations of Tragedies and Comedies "—this licence to be effectual notwithstanding any former grant to Thomas Killigrew, Esq., Sir William Davenant, Kt., " or any other person or persons whatsoever to the contrary." [181]

Jolly at once hired the Cockpit in Drury Lane, and although after Davenant's company had removed from Salisbury Court, he was for a while at this latter house, he was certainly playing at the Cockpit during the greater part of the year 1662. Among the jotted memoranda of Dr. Edward Browne [182] occur the names of a large number of plays which he saw, some at Norwich, "At the King's Armes," some at Cambridge, "At the Cardinalls Cap " ; some at the London theatres at the end of 1662. At the Cockpit in Drury Lane he saw *The Silent Woman* opposite which he notes " K. P.", that is the King's Players, Killigrew's company. At the same theatre later in the list he writes : " Dr. Fostus [183] 1.0 Licens: Players." These Licensed Players must have been Jolly's company, thus distinguished by Browne from the King's Players under Killigrew and from Davenant's actors, for besides these two regular troupes there were no other Licensed Players in London.

Sir Henry Herbert in January, 1663, granted Jolly a licence to raise a company of touring actors, who might give public performances in any town or place save only the Cities of London and Westminster and the suburbs of the two said Cities.

Killigrew and Davenant who had been biding their time now took advantage of this opportunity to oust their rival from the field in what, I am afraid, can only be deemed a very dishonest and underhand manner. In December, 1662, they had obtained Jolly's grant from the King in return for a pension of four pounds a week for life. This grant they alleged they were about to use to set up a company of actors, and it was agreed that (plague times only being excepted when the theatres were necessarily closed) if the stipulated pension was in arrears more than ten days the royal warrant must be returned. Jolly departed with his company on tour, and as we shall see more particularly later, made Norwich his centre. Meanwhile in July, 1663, the two patentees representing to the King that they had purchased the warrant outright, petitioned for a new licence to be made out in their own names giving them permission to erect a new playhouse which was to serve as a Nursery for the training of young recruits for the two established theatres. Their representations, entirely false, were believed, and a warrant for the new licence was prepared, and Jolly's grant declared to be revoked. In order the more securely to cover their tracks and complicate the business the more completely the two patentees requested that Colonel William Legge of the King's Bedchamber, with whom they had a private understanding, should be licensee of the Nursery, although actually the direction was in their own hands.[184]

Owing to this concerted fraud a very great deal of trouble ensued,[185] and Killigrew showed himself particularly brutal and malicious. In fact his character as a double-dealer and swindler is exhibited in the worst possible light.[186]

It is not known when Jolly came back to London, but it is improbable that his return (for any stay at all events) was before the autumn of 1664. In pursuance of their blackguardly scheme the two managers then defaulted, and returned him his warrant. Jolly at once gathered a company and began to act, whereupon Killigrew descended and the mine was sprung. However, Jolly was made of hard stuff, and in spite of a warrant from the Lord Chamberlain he kept the Cockpit open and gave very successful performances there until the Plague closed all the theatres early in June, 1665.[187] Samuel Chappuzeau, who visited London during 1664-5, in his *L'Europe Vivante*, 1667, precisely mentions three theatres, Killigrew's, Davenant's, " & une troisième en Drury lane, qui a un grand abord."

Upon the reopening of the playhouses Killigrew, amongst whose activities during the interval of enforced silence had been the preparation of a Nursery in Hatton Garden, under the direction of Captain Edward Bedford, was now more than ever determined entirely to crush George Jolly, whose story it may be well briefly to conclude as far as may be before the Nursery itself is discussed, although the two are hardly to be separated, After much dispute and ill-will, when Jolly threatened to carry his plaint to the King and Privy Council the patentees, well aware their conduct would not stand investigation, came to terms and it was compromised that Jolly should raise a company for the Nursery, and for his lifetime have control of the recruiting house. Even thus he would in effect only be a sub-manager under Killigrew and Davenant. The Nursery was to draw two-thirds of the takings of the house, the patentees claiming one-third. Should another manager for any reason be appointed in his place he was to receive six and eightpence for every acting day at the Nursery.[189]   It is plain that these terms were not very advantageous for George Jolly, and at some date between the spring of 1673 and early in 1677 he made a formal complaint of his hard usage due to the chicanery of the patentees. Lady Davenant, appreciating the justice of his case, supported his petition, but as yet nothing has come to light concerning the result of his efforts to obtain redress. Speculation is not merely hazardous but useless, and we must perforce take leave of Jolly with the hope that he obtained what was undoubtedly his due, and his disappearance from the scene denotes (we should like to think) a pensioned security.

Early in 1667 Killigrew opened his Nursery under the direction of Captain Edward Bedford in Hatton Garden.[190]   It was, of course, Davenant's training-house as well, but Killigrew seems to have been the leading spirit and in this business the more active of the two patentees. In *The Life of the Famous Comedian Jo Haines* (1701) by Tobyas Thomas we are told that Joe commenced his stage career in Town at the Nursery. " He [*Haines*] comes to *London*; a timely arrival to Cap. *Bedford,* who at present was looking for such sparks, as raising a Company of Actors. *Cosh* and *Hains* list themselves under the Captain, become his Principal Men, whilst the Play House in Hatton Garden lasted, which this Captain *Bedford* Built." [191] Pepys on 7th March, 1668, speaks of the excellent dancing at the Theatre Royal of " one Haines, only lately come thither from the Nursery ". There was published, 4to, 1667, Shirley's *The Constant Maid: or, Love will finde out the Way,* "As it is now Acted at the new Play-house called the Nursery in Hatton-Garden." [192]   The Prologue to John Dover's tragedy *The Roman Generalls: or, the Distressed Ladies,* not acted, 4to, 1667, licensed for printing 7th November, 1667, commences :

> *The Poet had design'd His Play should be*
> *Bestow'd on Both the Houses* Nursery.[193]
> *His modest Judgement, deemed it most fit,*
> *In Nurseries to plant Young Twiggs of Wit.*
> *Thinking to shun A Publick Censure, since*
> *They count Ten People There, an Audience.*

There seems to be a good deal of truth in Dover's lines for Pepys tells us that when on 24th February, 1668, he saw Kyd's *The Spanish Tragedy* at the Nursery " the house is better and the musique better than we lookd for, and the acting not much worse, because I expected as bad as could be : and I was not much mistaken, for it was so ". On the following day he went again to the Nursery and " saw them act a comedy, a pastorall, ' The Faythfull Shepherd,' [194] having the curiosity to see whether they did a comedy better than a tragedy ; but they do both alike, in the meanest manner ".

At some date—probably not very long—before 22nd April, 1669, the Nursery had removed to the Vere Street Theatre (Gibbon's Tennis Court), Killigrew's old house, for on 23rd April, 1669, Mrs. Pepys saw " a play at the New Nursery, which is set up at the house in Lincoln's Inn Fields, which was formerly the King's house ".

In November, 1669, Bedford left the Nursery, and his place, under Jolly's direction, was taken by John Perin, who was doubtless a brother or some near relation of Carey Perin,[195] a small part actor of the Theatre Royal. John Perin erected a " booth or playhouse " on a plot of ground he owned in Finsbury Fields, Bunhill. Here in the late spring and early summer of 1671 his little company acted for nine weeks, but upon some difference between himself and Lady Davenant the undertaking came to grief, and just before Christmas the builder carried off most of the structure.[196]

Lady Davenant none the less was of the opinion that a Nursery was essential for recruiting the Duke's company, and in 1671 she proceeded to build in Barbican a new house which is the best-known and longest-lived of the Nurseries. There was the inevitable and fruitless opposition on the side of the City Authorities, traditionally opposed to any theatre within their jurisdiction. The house, none the less, was erected in Playhouse Yard, a court whose entrance is a narrow alley leading out of Barbican, and almost half-way down the main thoroughfare, which extends from Redcross Street to Aldersgate Street.[197] Percy Fitzgerald in his *New History of the English Stage*, 1882, has the following reference to the Barbican Nursery : " Only a couple of years ago there was to be also seen the remains of another old theatre in Playhouse Yard . . . let out in common lodgings. A visitor clearly distinguished the gallery in the strangely sloping floor, which had been altered and " converted ". But the district has been in part cleared, streets widened, and the old theatre has shared in the general demolition." [198]

The Barbican Nursery held its own with success for a period of eleven years from 1671 to 1682. Hither Hillaria in *The Careless Lovers* (Act IV) invited her cousin with " Come, Cozen, we'l spend this Afternoon in a Frolique, we'l go see a Play at the Nursery ". Mr. Bayes too, when esteeming himself sadly disobliged by the Actors, announced his resolve to bend his thoughts " wholly for the service of the *Nursery,* and mump your proud

Players I gad ".[199] The Nursery repertory was inevitably drawn from the Elizabethan and Jacobean dramatists for the most part, and Langbaine, who mentions *Revenge for Honour* under George Chapman, notes : " This play I have seen acted many years ago at the *Nursery* in *Barbican*." Of *The Imperial Tragedy*, published anonymously but almost certainly by Sir William Killigrew, he remarks : " This Play was printed Fol. *Lond*. 1669, and has been acted (if I mistake not) at the Nursery in *Barbican*." [200]

Famous as the passage is, Dryden's lines which have immortalized the house in *Mac Flecknoe* must be quoted :—

Close to the Walls which fair *Augusta* bind,
(The fair *Augusta* much to fears inclin'd)
An ancient fabrick raised t'inform the sight,
There stood of yore, and *Barbican* it hight :
A watch Tower once, but now, so Fate ordains,
Of all the Pile an empty name remains.
From its old Ruins Brothel-houses rise,
Scenes of lewd loves, and of polluted joys,
Where their vast Courts the Mother-Strumpets keep,
And, undisturb'd by Watch, in silence sleep.
Near these a Nursery erects its head,
Where Queens are formed, and future Hero's bred ;
Where unfledged Actors learn to laugh and cry,⎫
Where infant Punks their tender voices try, ⎬
And little *Maximins* the Gods defy.[201]   ⎭
Great *Fletcher* never treads in Buskins here,
Nor greater Johnson dares in Socks appear.
But gentle *Simkin* just reception finds
Amid this Monument of vanisht minds ;
Pure Clinches, the suburbian Muse affords ;
And *Panton* waging harmless war with words.

There is some dispute as to the exact date when Dryden wrote *Mac Flecknoe*,[202] but this admirable satire was at any rate published, 4to, 1682.[203] Accordingly the Barbican Nursery must then still have been acting or can only just have ceased, for otherwise a considerable point in the poem were slurred, and Dryden was not the man to miss his hits. There is no precise evidence regarding the particular period when the Nursery was abandoned and recruits [204] joined themselves to the regular theatre, but it seems likely that this took place after the closing down of the Theatre Royal and a little before the Union of the two Companies. At least we are able to say that the Nursery had come to an end, no doubt to the great relief of the City Authorities by the autumn of 1682.

In the winter of 1671 whilst the Barbican Nursery was building the puritanical element in the City became mightily alarmed and the Lord Mayor even had the insolence to approach the King praying him that the new theatre should be demolished. Charles dismissed the petition with a characteristic stroke of humour, "That Playhouses should be pulled down when the Meeting houses were."

Bearing in mind this happy retort, it seems indeed a strange irony that the Barbican Nursery immediately after its abandonment by the actors should have been used as a surreptitious conventicle. There had been very active proceedings against clandestine meeting-houses in the autumn of 1682, and on 15th January, 1683, the Lord Mayor issued a Proclamation [205] giving public notice that in obedience to a letter from His Majesty, "All *Conventicles* and *Unlawful* Meetings" within the City and the Liberties would be prevented and suppressed. Shortly after was issued "A List of the Conventicles or Unlawful Meetings Within the City of London", and among these occur "Pauls Ally *in* Red-cross-street, *at the* Old Play-house, Anabaptist", and "Clare-market *at the* Old Play-house, *Presbyterian*", where one Farringdon was minister.[206] The best accounts of the suppression of these conventicles are to be found in the various numbers of "The Conventicle Courant : Setting Forth the Proceedings against Unlawful Meetings, By the King's Command".[207] The First Number was issued on 14th July, 1682.

The conventicle in Red-cross-street was raided, and according to *The Conventicle Courant*, 6th–15th November, 1682, "On Saturday the Goods of Mr. Plant, Preacher in the *Old-Play-House* in *Red-Cross-street*, were seized at his Wives Shop in *Fore-street*, near *Cripplegate*." Mr. Plant himself had levanted, as also did a Mr. Cockin, a preacher living in Red-Cross-Street, who "escaped through a Neighbour's House, that opened into *White-Cross-Street*".

The interesting point is that the Barbican Nursery had at once become a secret Anabaptist conventicle, and is described as being in Pauls Alley in Red-Cross-Street since it was more privately entered from the east than from the north.[208] The first care of the conventiclers on acquiring a building adaptable for their meetings was to devise with no little ingenuity extra doors, close passages, and other avenues whereby the preacher might escape when the Officers of Justice descended. As we learn from the records in contemporary journals the ministers more frequently than not were able to rub off in this way, and show the magistrates a clean pair of heels.

Thus from 1675 to 1682 the old Theatre Royal in Vere Street was most obstinately used by the sectaries as a presbyterian place of worship, and in *The Conventicle Courant*,[209] No. 28,

Wednesday, 24th January, to Wednesday, 31st January, 1682/3, we have : On Sunday, the 21st instant, the Magistrates " went to the *Old Play-house* near *Clare Market*, but Sir *John* has so fortified himself there, that makes it in a manner impossible to take him, by which means he escaped, notwithstanding all imaginable industry was used to prevent him, the Conventiclers several names were taken in order to their being proceeded against as the Law directs. On *Sunday* the 28*th* Several of the Justices of the said *Western* Division, attended by Constables and other Officers of the Peace, repaired to said *Old Play-house,* where the Preacher again escaped ; after which the names of the several persons Assembled were taken ; as also the places of their respective abode, to the end they may be punished as the Law directs ; and such was the obstinacy of these people that they immediately upon the Justices, *&c.* being gon, Re-assembled, and continued their unlawful Seditious, and Riotous Convention, as if no Law was of force enough to punish them for their Wickedness ".

Subsequently the Vere Street Old Playhouse became a carpenter's shop, and later a slaughter-house. It was destroyed by fire on 17th September, 1809,[210] and in recent years upon (or very near) the site it once occupied arose the London Opera House, now Stoll's Picture Theatre, Kingsway.

The interior of the Fortune Theatre, situate in Golden Lane, afterwards Red Cross Street, was completely dismantled in 1649,[211] yet in 1658 Davenant was planning (rumour said) to reopen this house as appears from a letter of 15th October of that year, addressed by Dr. Thomas Smith to Sir Daniel Fleming of Rydal Hall, Westmorland. It is thus summarized in the *Historical MSS. Commission* (12th Report, App. VII, 1890) : News from H[umphrey] R[obinson]. Sir William Davenant has obtained permission for stage plays, and the Fortune Playhouse is being trimmed up. The scheme, however, even if seriously entertained was not pursued in respect to this house, and the whole building was demolished shortly after the Restoration.[212] In 1819 Robert Wilkinson published in his *Londina Illustrata* [213] a picture of the façade of a brewery in Golden Lane, which he described as the exterior of the Fortune Theatre. Although this attribution is, as research has shown, altogether impossible, it was long accepted and repeated.[214] The façade in question is decorated with the Royal Arms, whose emblazoning, since the Irish Harp is quartered,[215] certainly cannot be earlier than the reign of James I. There are also symbolical figures, one of which represents a woman with children clinging to her skirts. The Arms indicate that the building was either royally endowed or erected under a patent. To sum up it may be said that this building was certainly neither the Fortune Theatre, nor (as was once hazarded) the Nursery situate in Barbican, but beyond these negations all is problematical.

It has already been mentioned that George Jolly, who had very short-sightedly farmed his London patent to his two rivals in the field, Killigrew and Davenant, in January, 1663, under the double protection of a letter from the King (29th January, 1663), and a warrant from the Master of the Revels (1st January), led a touring company in the provinces. In April of this year he was giving performances at the King's Arms, Norwich, having duly submitted his credentials to the Mayor and civic authorities. There is evidence that his season—perhaps with some intervals—lasted until September, which seems an unusually long sojourn for a touring company in one place in Restoration days, unless indeed the manager made Norwich his centre, so to speak, and rendezvous. This was, I doubt not, the case, for at the end of the seventeenth century after London, Bristol and Norwich, each with some 29,000 inhabitants, were the chief towns in the Kingdom. Dr. Edward Browne, whose memoranda have been quoted above,[216] records the names of nine old plays which he saw acted by Jolly's troupe at the King's Arms, Norwich : *Tu quoque ; Ignoramus ; The Pinner of Wakefield ; Muliasses ; A Girle worth gold ; Tis pity Shee is a whore ; The little Thief ; A new way to pay old debts* ; and *The faire quarrell.*[217]

Flushed with success, Jolly returned to Norwich in the following year, and opened his repertory season towards the end of June. It is to Jolly's company that Chappuzeau refers when, having mentioned the London theatres, he adds : " Il y a vne autre Troupe entretenue à Norwich, l'vne des bonnes Villes du Royaume, & le seiour de toute la Noblesse du Pays." [218]

Before Jolly visited Norwich there had been earlier exhibitions by strolling players, since on 29th December, 1660, the civic authorities ordered that " Thomas Knowles & other p̄sons that came to this city to sett vp a playe in the same & did beate their drummers wth out allowance & have played twice or thrice shall not from henceforth act any playe any more in this city vpon payne of incurringe the vtmost penalty the lawe will inflict ". These unfortunate strollers were to be expelled the town. But on 7th January, 1661, Robert Williams, Samberlain Harvey, and Nicholas Calvert, the leading members of this troupe, although licensed by Sir Henry Herbert, most humbly submitted to the Mayor and Court, praying for pardon and acknowledging their offence. Upon this they were allowed to continue their performances for a while, and they even acquired a new Thespian, a boy, John Taylor. In February, 1661, Gabriel Shad and his company upon showing Herbert's licence were permitted to give certain plays in Norwich.

On 25th May, 1672, Cornelius Saffery was accorded " liberty with his associate to act comedies and tragedies, pastorals and interludes, until this day sen-night in this city " Norwich.

On 6th August, 1672, a better known name, John Coysh, Esq.,[219] and his company were licensed to act plays in Norwich. On 21st April, 1683, Plays at the Red Lion were licensed to Coysh ; and again on 25th February, 1685, at which time all London theatres were closed on account of the King's death, John Coysh, gent., and his company were granted liberty to act plays for one week. In the following year, on the 16th October, he had leave to act plays in the City during the stay of His Grace the Duke of Norfolk in the City.

On 21st October, 1676, Mr. Robert Parker was licensed to act pieces of plays and drolls at the Red Lion, S. Stephen's. Two years later, on 26th October, 1678, Mr. Robert Parker " Master of the Players, [was] licensed to act plays, comedies, and tragedies ; he observing good orders and house, and not acting or keeping company together after 9 at night ".

Mr. Mountford Ballydon [had] leave to play plays, drolls, farces, and interludes at the Red Lion on 9th March, 1687, and on 14th November, 1688, Mr. John Power was given " leave to show of a play called the Newmarket Company ", that is *The Muse of New-Market,* three farces originally acted before the King and Court at Newmarket, and printed 4to, 1680.

On 24th December, 1687, for their Christmas jollity, an order was made by the Mayor for " The soldiers belonging to Col. Hefford's to have liberty to make show of a play called the Critics ", of which nothing is known, unless perhaps it is to be identified with the famous *Rehearsal.*

It is interesting to remark that in addition to more regular performances puppet shows and motions were very popular in Norwich. In Davenant's *The Play-house to be Let,* Lincoln's Inn Fields, summer of 1663, Act I, the House-Keeper alludes to " the new motion men of Norwich, Op'ra-puppets ". *The Merchant's Daughter of Bristol, Whittington and his Cat, The Wisdom of Solomon, Fair Rosamond, Edward IV and Jane Shore, The Creation of the World,* and other old favourites never failed to attract thronging audiences, but perhaps Mr. Peter Dallman's *Pollichanella* which with his three dancing monkeys and curious piece of waterwork often visited the town pleased best of all.[220]

Among companies of strolling players we number the Duke of Monmouth's Servants and the Duchess of Portsmouth's Servants.[221]

The former, licensed in the winter of 1669, were under the management of Captain Edward Bedford, who was, as we have already remarked, the first director of the Hatton Garden Nursery. Chappuzeau in *L'Europe Vivante* (p. 215) speaks of " les Troupes de Campagne, ou se fait le Nouitiat des Comediens ".

The troupe called the Duchess of Portsmouth's Servants can scarcely have been formed before the latter part of 1673. Coysh was the manager, and one of their leading men was Martin Powell. In Duffett's *New Poems*,[222] 1676, is printed " *Prologue* to The Indian Emperor, *Acted by the Duchess of* Portsmouth's *Servants, spoken by Mr.* Poel ", which is followed by " *Epilogue to the same, spoken by a Girl* ". Martin Powell and Coysh, both of whom joined the Theatre Royal, London, sustained Montezuma and Cortez respectively.

There is a record of a visit to Oxford in 1677 of the Dublin company, led by Joseph Ashbury,[223] from the Theatre Royal, Smock Alley. This troupe perhaps played at some other towns. Their appearance at the University was fated to cause considerable trouble to the Vice-Chancellor and Authorities, who found themselves involved in a sad dilemma.

Year by year at Oxford there was allowed one period of relaxation during the cloistral round, the Act, *Comitia,* that chartered period of Academic ceremonies and public exercises in the Schools, which was calendared to commence on the Monday following the 7th July, when Gown and Town made joyous revelry. The ancient Act, now faintly echoed in our modern Commemoration, was an hour of boisterous fun, retaining a spice of the reckless spirit of mediaeval licence, and exhibiting all the time-honoured buffooneries of the *Terrae Filius* when he mounted the rostrum " with a merry oration . . . interspers'd with secret history, raillery, and sarcasm ". Naturally at such a waking-time the whole countryside trooped into Oxford, and there forgathered from all quarters the tumblers and clowns and jugglers and rope-dancers, the puppet-shows and motions to set the rustic folk agape and empty their pockets to boot. There was, in fine, all the fun of Bartholomew or Southwark Fair.

In Thomas Baker's comedy, *An Act at Oxford,* 4to, 1704, Act I, scene I, Bloom, the gentleman-commoner, says : " Why, faith, this publick Act hath drawn hither half the Nation." Moreover, " The younger commoners have sold their Books to run to Plays."

The Act, as one might suppose, during the Puritan ascendancy was sternly denuded of its mirth and joyousness, the festive spirit being quenched by sermonizing orations " perstringeing

Episcopacy ", grave disputations and the like,[224] so it is hardly surprising that when the King came to his own again loyal Oxford was eager to celebrate the Act with more than wonted frolic and carnival. At the Restoration the heroics exhibited, nay even flaunted, diversions and amusements which might vex the precisians of the sour old régime, and as Wood tells us, on 19th July, 1660, " or thereabouts, the young loyall scholars of Oxford acted a play [Cowley's *Guardian*] at the new dancing school against S. Michael's church on purpose to spite the Presbyterians who had been bitter enemies to these things." [225]

It was natural that the London actors, following old custom and Elizabethan tradition, should turn their thoughts to Oxford at this especial period. In July, 1661, professional players and in their company actresses, the most recent innovation, accordingly journeyed to Oxford and set up their stage in the spacious yard of the King's Arms, Holywell, where they performed twice daily, in the morning and afternoon. Wood notes : " July 3rd. Wednesday, a play acted at the Kings Armes in Halywell, called Tu quoque." On Thursday he saw in the morning Rowley's *All's Lost by Lust,* in the afternoon Shirley's *The Young Admiral ;* Friday, *A mad world, my Masters,* and *The Merry Milkmaids of Islington ;* Saturday, *The City Wit* and *Tu quoque ;* Monday, *The Young Admiral ;* and *The Rape of Lucrece ;* Tuesday, *All's lost by lust* and *The Milkmaids ;* Wednesday, *The City Wit* and Daborne's *The poor man's Comfort ;* Thursday, *Tu quoque ;* and Massinger's *A very woman ;* Saturday, *The Rump* and *The Young Admiral.* But " these playes wherein women acted (amongst which was Roxolana,[226] married to the Earl of Oxon) made the scholars mad, run after them, take ill c[o]urses—among which Hyde of Allsouls, A.B. afterwards hanged ". It does not appear why the unfortunate baccalaureus Hyde should have come to such a sad and abrupt end owing to this visit of the actors, but it is clear that the beauty of the new actresses so amorously inflamed the notoriously susceptible hearts of the young Oxonians, that the Vice-Chancellor for a considerable time after would suffer no further dramatic entertainments from abroad.

Of all the undergraduates there was no more fond and love-sick swain than Richard Walden of Queen's College, who attended the first eight performances "At the (*Quondam-Antelope,* now) King's Arms in Holywell ", and straightway lost his heart " To The Transcendently Formose, and (as far as can be concluded from the *Topicks* of Ommatology) Most Heroically Virtuous Mrs. Anne Gibbs ". The " indelible characters imprinted on his heart by the emissive Organ of her fulgerant Eye " he felt inspired to celebrate in an " Encomiostick Decameron ", in other words a leash of poems privately printed in the year 1662, a little volume of which the only known copy is preserved in the British Museum. The first of these, *Io Ruminans,* is chiefly interesting as recording certain of the rôles Anne Gibbs acted. She played Gertrude in *Tu Quoque* ; Harebrain's wife in *A Mad World, my Masters* ; Rosinda in *The Young Admiral* ; Dionysia in *All's lost by Lust* ; A lady in *The Merry Milkmaids* ; and Lucretia in *The Rape of Lucrece.* Walden, however, found that Mrs. Gibbs was not judged to be a Lucrece in private life, in fact her reputation had been considerably blown upon, and his muse impelled him to a " Deplumation of Mrs. *Anne Gibbs* ". Her fascinations, however, proved too powerful, and immediately there followed *Fama Vapulans,* a Retractation addressed to Mrs. Anne Gibbs " By her real Convert and Re-admirer, R.W."

It may be deduced that a watchful tutor or guardian speedily conveyed Richard Walden beyond the sphere of the siren's witchery, and after a sojourn in Warwickshire the youth retired to Carmarthen. The spell was so far broken that in 1663 inconstant Richard married another lady, but in his *Parnassus Aboriens, or Some Sparkes of Poesie,* 1664, he has a poem (p. 15) " To Erycina, *Upon her retirement to* Norwich ", and for Erycina we may read Anne, whose father was Thomas Gibbs, " proctor and publick Notary " of Norwich.[227]

Some years later, in 1669, when there was " a very great and splendid Act " for the Dedication of the Sheldonian, on Friday, 9th July, the Lincoln's Inn Fields company was permitted to play in Oxford during the celebrations. They performed in the Guildhall yard, where on 8th July Wood paid half a crown to see *Love in a Tub.* He noted : " The players (d of Y) came and acted at the Guildhall yard—carried away *de claro* 1500 *li.* . . . Scholars pawn'd books, bedding, blankets—laughed at in London —but afterwards they grew wiser."

In 1670 there was no Act, but Betterton and his company returned to Oxford in 1671. They played at the New Tennis Court, and Wood notes on Wednesday, 12th July : " Cambises, King of Persia,[228] a tragedie acted at the New Tennis Court ; made by Elkanah Settle, lately a commoner of Trinity Coll." There is extant " The Prologue to the Oxford Schollers at the Act there, 1671 ". This highly complimentary address [229] commences—

Gentlemen
    Your civil kindness last year shown,   }
A second time hath brought your Creatures down,
From the unlearned and Tumultuous Town.

The Lincoln's Inn Fields company were again at Oxford in July, 1672, and the popular *Cambyses* did not cease to attract. Settle wrote a topical and rather clever Prologue for his tragedy which was " spoken by Betterton in a riding habit ".[230] He is profuse in gratitude for the applause given the company at former " solemn Acts " in spite of disadvantages and drawbacks :

> But then our House wants ornament and Scene,
> Which the chief grandeur of a Play maintain.
> But to excuse this want, we must confess,
> We are but Travellers in a riding dress.

Since the King was the idol of Oxford, " a city which always rewarded Charles's confidence with the most abject devotion," says Green,[231] it may seem surprising that His Majesty's own players—for after all the King was the official patron of the Theatre Royal—did not visit Oxford rather than the Duke's men. And indeed Killigrew's actors, who had heard with some natural envy of the enthusiastic receptions the rival London company had met with at the University, were resolved that Betterton should not enjoy this monopoly as his own prerogative. Accordingly in July, 1673, it was the King's men who were performing at Oxford. They opened with *The Silent Woman,* the Prologue and Epilogue being written for the occasion by Dryden, and spoken by Hart. In 1674 they paid a return visit, but unhappily the younger members of the company so intolerably misconducted themselves as to bring a considerable amount of odium on the whole troupe, and in 1675 they were prevented by authority from coming to Oxford, the ostensible reason being that small-pox was " frequent " there. Of their outrageous conduct during the sojourn of the previous year we learn something from a letter, 28th July, 1674, written by Humphrey Prideaux to John Ellis : " The players parted from us with small gains, not having gained so much, after all things payed, to make a dividend of 10*l.* to the chiefe sharers ; which I hope will give them noe encouragement to come again. Neither, I suppose will the University for the future permit them here, if they can be kept out, since they were guilty of such great rudenesses before they left us, going about the town in the night breakeing of windows and committeing many other unpardonable rude-nesses." [232]

In 1676 there was, says Wood,[233] " a very great Act, as many if not more company than in the great Act, 1669," and in spite of their rowdyism of two years before, the King's Players found their way again to Oxford, where they spoke Dryden's famous prologue in which he repudiates his " Mother University " for the banks of Isis. This address, which has not hitherto been correctly dated, is preserved in a MS.[234] as "A Prologue to the University of Oxford, at the Act 1676, by His Majesties Servants ". However, the Chancellor, James, Duke of Ormonde, proved by no means inclined to overlook such offences as those of which they had been so impudently guilty, and he soon found a way to punish their misbehaviours. Being also Lord Lieutenant of Ireland he brought across to Oxford for the Act in July, 1677, the first Irish troupe of players who had ever appeared in England, the company from the Theatre Royal, Smock-Alley, Dublin. Bitter indeed was the mortification of the Theatre Royal, London, and as we know from many a flick and many a sneer in Dryden's prologues and epilogues long did the slight rankle in their minds. That " such barbarous *Macs* " should be preferred to a London company seemed incredible. With regard to the Dublin company's visit, which appears to have been very satisfactory, we have a letter from the Rev. Thomas Dixon, Oxford, 1st August, 1677, to Sir Daniel Fleming, in which the writer says : " His [the Duke of Ormonde's] players, who were with us at the Act, and twenty days after, carried, it is said, 600*l*. or 700*l*. clear gains out of Oxford. They acted much at the same rate the King's and Duke's used to do." [235]

In July, 1678, no Act was celebrated, " the town and Universitie being at variance." It does not appear that any company visited Oxford in the following year, although the Act was duly held. Meanwhile the King's players, furious at having been put under the ban by the University, appealed—doubtless through Mohun—to Charles himself, who lent a ready ear to his favourite actor, and directed Arlington, the Lord Chamberlain, to convey the royal desire (or indeed command) to Dr. Timothy Halton, the Vice-Chancellor, that the actors of the King's house should be allowed to revisit Oxford at the accustomed season. Dr. Halton now found himself in a perilous quandary, since the Chancellor had already suggested that his own Irish troupe should pay a return visit. When the Duke discovered that the Irish actors were likely to be superseded by the London company, he charged his son the Earl of Ossory to interview Lord Arlington, and inform him how the land really lay. The Lord Chamberlain, wholly sympathetic and understanding, at once advised the King's men that it was impossible to go against the direct wishes of the Chancellor of the University, and that accordingly they must abandon all idea of a journey to Oxford, since he for his part declined to proceed any further in the matter. This, it might have been thought, clinched the business. No such matter. Once again the King's players contrived to get direct access to His Majesty, to whom they presented their case. Charles, careless of Ormonde's prerogative, directed Arlington to write to the Vice-Chancellor and insist that the players of the Theatre Royal, London, be received in Oxford to give performances during the Act. Ormonde's position and privileges were ignored. There remained nothing for the Chancellor, Vice-Chancellor, and University to do but submit as gracefully as they might, whilst the actors had the satisfaction—as they doubtless deemed it—of getting the better of the Lord Chamberlain, who was compelled to eat humble pie enough.

The troupe entered Oxford with flying colours, but at the same time as may be supposed they must have been only too well aware that they were but being allowed to return by *force majeure*. Accordingly they would not spare to lash the Dublin rivals who had well nigh ousted them from their position. Wood notes : 1680, " July 8. Th. king's players began to act in my brother Robert's tennis-court," and on this occasion Dryden wrote for them a Prologue first printed in the *Examen Poeticum* (*The Third Part of Miscellany Poems*), 1693. This scarifies the " Lewder tribe " in biting rhyme :

> *Teag* has been here, and to this learned Pit
> With *Irish* Action slandered *English* Wit ;
> You have beheld such barbarous *Macs* appear
> As merited a second Massacre. . . .
> When Strollers durst presume to pick your purse,
> We humbly thought our broken Troop not worse.
> How ill soe'r our Action may deserve,
> Oxford's a place where Wit can never Sterve.

It was indeed a " broken Troop " that visited Oxford in 1680, and in the following year things must have been even worse. The King who, owing to political strife, summoned his Parliament to meet at this City in March, 1681, required his actors to attend him during his sojourn. This they accordingly did, and Dryden wrote an Epilogue which was printed, broadside, Oxford and London. There are some slight differences between the London (for *Rich. Royston*) and Oxford (*L. Lichfield*) editions. The London broadside has : " Writ by Mr. *Dreyden,* Spoke before His MAJESTY at *Oxford, March* 19. 1680." The Oxford broadside has : " The Epilogue spoken to the King at the opening the Play-House at *Oxford* on Saturday last, being *March* the nineteenth, 1681." Dryden's name does not appear.[236] The play on this occasion was Charles Saunders' tragedy *Tamerlane the Great*.[237] On Monday, 28th March, the King, having dissolved parliament, left Oxford, and retired to Windsor.

PLATE VII

UNDERHILL AS OBADIAH IN THE COMMITTEE

Collection of the Author

[face p. 130

This same year, 1681, the King's players returned for the Act. But it was only a remnant, and in the following year their numbers were even more depleted, nor are we surprised to find that instead of Hart, Martin Powell spoke the prologue on 10th July, and instead of Mrs. Marshall, Mrs. Moyle delivered the Epilogue on 18th July. Both Prologue and Epilogue were printed on one leaf, 1682.[238] The Prologue deplores the pitiful estate of the players wrecked—

> By a dissenting Play-house frantick rage,
> We the poor remnant of a ruin'd Stage. . . .

In July, 1682, the Theatre Royal had been closed down at least for a couple of months, and in 1683 owing to the unsettlement in the London theatrical world consequent upon the recent Union of the two Houses no actors visited Oxford, whilst under Friday, 11th July, 1684, Wood notes : " the Act began— few company because no playes."

There is no record of a visit to Oxford by any troupe in 1685, the year of King Charles' death, but in July, 1686, the United Company was welcomed for the Act, when, however, at a performance of *The Committee*, " acted about 16th July once or twice," Anthony Leigh by some extremely offensive gag introduced into his rôle of Teague not only grossly reflected upon Dr. Obadiah Walker, the honoured Master of University College, but excessively displeased the King himself.

In 1687, 1688, 1689, 1690, 1691, 1692, there was no Act.

In 1693 the Act duly took place, and the visits of the players were resumed.

Colley Cibber, who in his *Apology*[239] gives a concise account of these theatrical peregrinations to the University, writes : " It had been a custom for the Comedians while at *Oxford* to act twice a day ; the first Play ending every morning, before the college hours of dining, and the other never to break into the time of shutting their Gates in the Evening. This extraordinary labour gave all the hired actors a title to double pay, which, at the Act in King *William*'s time, I had myself accordingly received there." Cibber remarks upon the differences of taste prevailing between London and Oxford. He notes that modern comedies, however witty and brilliant, met with little applause from a learned audience. " *Shakespeare* and *Jonson* had there a sort of classical authority, for whose masterly scenes they seemed to have as implicit a reverence, as formerly for the Ethics of *Aristotle* ; and were as incapable of allowing moderns to be their competitors, as of changing their Academical Habits for gaudy colours or embroidery." Speaking particularly of the year 1712, our historian tells us that Addison's *Cato* met with extraordinary success. " To conclude, our reception at *Oxford,* whatever our merit might be, exceeded our expectations. At our taking leave, we had the thanks of the Vice-Chancellor, for the decency and order observed by our whole Society ; an Honour which had not always been paid on the same Occasions ; for at the Act in King *William's* time, I remember some pranks of a different nature had been complained of."

In *The Times Literary Supplement,* Thursday, 31st May, 1934, Mr. Leech has drawn attention to a licence,[240] dated 14th April, 1662, issued to George Bayley of London, who with eight members of his company was allowed to present a play " called Noahs flood [241] with other Scenes ". The provincial authorities were charged to suffer him to use the Town Hall, Guildhall, or School house for his performances, which were, however, not to be given on Sundays, during Divine Service, or on any Holy Day proclaimed by Authority. The production was obviously of a very rough and ready kind, but it is curious to see how a play, a far descendant of one of the most popular of the old miracle plays, should have lingered so late, and thus have been presented, by a touring company, or strollers, in the smaller towns and English villages.

In a book of accounts kept by Sir Daniel Fleming of Rydal Hall, Westmorland, are two interesting entries having reference to Christmas entertainments given at the Hall by local players. " Dec. 27th. 1661. Given to Troutbeck players for acting here *The Fair Maid of the West.* 10.0." " Dec. 30th, 1662. Given to Longsleddell players for acting here the *Tragedy of Ferrex and Porrex.* 10.0." [242] Heywood's *The Fair Maid Of the West, Or, A Girle worth gold* was long immensely popular. The play is in two parts, and probably Part I was given at Rydal Hall. Printed 4to, 1631, it had originally been produced at the Phoenix (Cockpit), and was presented at Court " with approved liking ". As noted above, it was in the repertory of Jolly's troupe when they were acting at the King's Arms, Norwich. The latest London revival was by The Phoenix in April, 1920, and this " Tudor Odyssey ", a busy bustling picture of traditional Elizabethan adventure on land and sea, at Plymouth, on Spanish galleons and English ships, in the Azores, in black Barbary, yet proved the liveliest of entertainments.

Ferrex and Porrex, the first regular tragedy in English, was performed under the title *Gorboduc* on 18th January, 1562, as part of a " grand Christmasse " in the Inner Temple, London, and " after shewed before her Majestie ". An unauthorized text, *Gorboduc,* appeared in 1565 ; and a genuine impression as *Ferrex and Porrex* in 1570. The unauthorized issue *Gorboduc,* was reprinted in 1569, 1571, and 1590. The editions of 1565 and 1590 state that the first three acts of the play were written by Thomas Norton. The rest of the drama is from the pen of Thomas Sackville, Lord Buckhurst and Earl of Dorset, with whose name the main authorship of the work is traditionally associated. Gorboduc, King of Britain, divides his realm in his lifetime between his two sons, Ferrex and Porrex. A fatal fraticidal rivalry ensues, and the whole land is thrown into anarchical confusion. To Dryden, Oldham, and the Restoration wits *Gorboduc* was the typical old play, mouldy and stale, beloved of villagers and remoter rustics.[243]

At Cambridge annual performances were given during the fortnight of Stourbridge Fair,[244] which commenced on 19th September, but it was the Norwich Company who visited the University on these occasions, and it is related in the *Life of Jo. Hayns,* by Tobyas Thomas 1701, that this graceless droll ran away from Cambridge just after having taken his degree to join the children of Thespis. "Down comes certain strowling Players [245]; *Cosh* the chief of them, and our new Master of Arts, grows infinitely great, both Sharp, and Witty, at last *Cosh* guessing which way his Genius might tend, and that naturally he believed him of a rambling Constitution, thought it would be no hard province to induce him to become his fellow Companion, if not his Disciple, he resolves upon it, and no sooner proposes, but *Haynes* embraces : *Metamorphoses* his Cap and Gown to a Plum of Feathers, and a *Persian* Robe."

At the Cardinal's Cap, Cambridge, Edward Browne [246] saw *Philaster ; The Changeling ; The Rump* ; and *Wit without Money.*[247] Such plays indicate an excellent repertory,[248] and although London lampoons with Cockney jest never spare to speak of the strolling-players in terms of utmost contempt their performances were perhaps better than the wits allowed.[249] Yet the poorer troupes were for the most part in sorry state, even as Hogarth painted them sixty years or so later in his *Strolling Actresses Dressing in a Barn,*[250] a piece which Walpole proclaimed as being for "wit and imagination without any other end the best of all his works", and as Joe Haines, who had experience of the life, described them in his lampoon on the Greenwich Strowlers,[251] their playhouse a stable, their tiring-room a hayloft, whilst for scenery—

> I confess they have never a Scene at all,
> They wanted no copy, they had th' original,
> For the windowes being down, and most part of the roof,
> How could they want Scenes, when they had prospect enough.

NOTES TO CHAPTER II

[1] See Chapter I, p. 4.

[2] *The Autobiography of Edward Lord Herbert of Cherbury*, ed. 1896, p. 22.

[3] Pepys, 13th February, 1667-8. The Lord Chamberlain's Records contain a copy of a warrant, " Livery for y[e] jester," 12th July, 1661, " to deliver to Mr. Killigrew thirty yards of velvett, three dozen of fringe, and sixteene yards of Damaske for the year 1661." R. W. Lowe, *Thomas Betterton*, p. 70. Mr. Harbage in his recent study *Thomas Killigrew, Cavalier Dramatist*, 1930, pp. 133-4, has misunderstood " the title of King's Foole or Jester ".

[4] *Anecdotes of Painting*, Horace Walpole, ed. 1849, ii, p. 456.

[5] Charles Killigrew died soon after attaining his majority. Of Robert Killigrew (not to be confused with his cousins of the same name) who proceeded B.A. at Christ Church, Oxon, 10th June, 1630, practically nothing is known. Two sisters, Anne and Elizabeth, were maids of honour to Queen Henrietta Maria. Katherine was maid of honour to the Princess Royal of Orange. Mary, the youngest, married Sir John James.

[6] Henry Killigrew had a distinguished career. He proceeded M.A., Christ Church, Oxon, 1638, and having taken Orders was Chaplain to the King's army, 1642 ; D.D., 1642 ; Chaplain and almoner to the Duke of York, 1660 ; Master of the Savoy, 1663. In addition to his one play he published sermons and Latin verses. Thomas Killigrew in *Thomaso, or The Wanderer*, Part I, Act V, scene 1, has the following allusion to his brother : " he's a serious black fellow, he smells like Serge and old Books."

[7] Langbaine, *English Dramatick Poets*, 1691, p. 310, says that it " found the approbation of the most Excellent Persons of this kind of Writing which were in that time, if there were even better in any time ".

[8] Printed for S. Briscoe, at the *Belle-Savage* on *Ludgate-hill*.

[9] Mr. Vivian de Sola Pinto in his *Sir Charles Sedley*, 1927, p. 281, pleads that it is time Sedley " was freed from all responsibility for this shapeless mass, which has been falsely attributed to him for two centuries ", but he gives no reason at all why Sedley should be thus freed. In his *Poetical and Dramatic Works of Sir Charles Sedley*, 1928, vol. i, p. xxiv, he remarks again in reference to the same piece, " there is no good reason to suppose that Sedley had anything to do with it," an expression of opinion which lacks support.

[10] Killigrew himself made an entry of his birth in a Bible, *La Sacra Biblia, tradotta in lingua Italiana da Giovanni Diodati*, folio, 1640. The book was sold by Ellis and White in 1872, when the notes made by Killigrew were copied out by R. N. Worth, and printed in *Miscellanea Genealogica et Heraldica*, ed. J. J. Howard, New Series, i, p. 370.

[11] Wright, *Historia Histrionica*, 8vo, 1699.

[12] *Athenae Oxonienses*, iv, 692.

[13] The phrase is from the complimentary verses prefixed by Henry Bennet (afterwards Earl of Arlington) to *The Prisoners and Claracilla*, 12mo, 1641.

[14] *The Parsons Wedding*, Act V, scene 4. See *Restoration Comedies*, ed. by Montague Summers, 1921, p. 139.

[15] Mr. Harbage, *Thomas Killigrew*, pp. 49-51, argues very convincingly for 1625.

[16] *Calendar of State Papers*. Domestic, 1635, pp. 80, 444 ; ibid., 1635-6, p. 226.

[17] Lodowick Carliell in his Dedication before *The Deserving Favourite*, 4to, 1629, specifically says that his tragi-comedy " was not designed to travell so farre as the common stage ".

[18] Joseph Knight refers to an engraving in which Lord Coleraine and Thomas Killigrew are depicted as " The Princely Shepherds " in a masque.

[19] There are separate title-pages for the two plays, and that of *The Prisoners* carries the date 1640.

[20] *Diary*, 29th November, 1661.

[21] It is interesting to note that he visited Loudun and there saw the possessed Ursuline nuns, who had been ensorcelled by Urbain Grandier. The letter he wrote detailing his experiences was widely distributed in MS., and copies are not uncommon. It was printed in the *European Magazine*, 1803, pp. 102-106.

[22] Born at Paris in 1595. Under the influence of Cardinal Richelieu, Desmaretz turned his attention to the drama. Among his plays are the satirical comedy *Les Visionnaires* and the famous *Mirame*. He died 28th October, 1676.

[23] There is an English translation : *Ariana*. In Two Parts. As it was translated out of French, and presented to my Lord Chamberlaine, folio, 1636 ; 2nd ed., 4to, 1641. The original French edition was followed by reprints, 1639, 1643, and 1644. There are Dutch and German translations.

[24] "Au lecteur" prefixed to *Artamène ; ou, le Grand Cyrus*. Second ed., 10 vols., Paris, 1650-4. Vol. i (1650), "Au lecteur," unnumbered pages.

[25] They had doubtless been privately given at Court. During the long interval of the closing of the theatres a company had been organized by Christopher and William Beeston to act before the King and Queen.

[26] Printed in Shirley's *Poems*, 1646, p. 148. I quote from the Gifford and Dyce, *James Shirley*, 1833, vol. iv, p. 278. The play was acted at Dublin as *Rosania ; or, Love's Victory*, but before 7th August, 1641, the name had been changed to *The Doubtful Heir,* and under this title it was printed, 8vo, 16{2. Shirley, of course, draws attention to the new fashion of naming a drama simply from the heroine.

[27] Closed in October, 1641, by order of the Lords Justices.

[28] Malone, *Varorium Shakespeare*, iii, p. 232.

[29] In the folio edition of the play she has become the Princess Lysimella. Perhaps the name Cecilia was originally chosen in compliment to Cecilia Crofts, Killigrew's first wife. This would have been entirely in the taste of the day. The lady died on 1st January, 1638.

[30] In *Claracilla* the comic relief is supplied by a bluff old soldier, Timillus, who is at least suggested by Leontius (*The Humorous Lieutenant*), Chilax (*The Mad Lover*), the Ensign to Archas (*The Loyal Subject*), and other popular characters.

[31] Whom Mr. L. Hotson rightly identifies with William Beeston, *The Commonwealth and Restoration Stage*, pp. 49-51.

[32] *Dramatic Records of Sir Henry Herbert,* ed. J. Q. Adams, 1917, p. 82. From Malone, *Varorium*, iii, p. 272.

[33] Mr. Hotson, *Commonwealth and Restoration Stage*, p. 247, comments on this : "At Gibbons's Tennis Court—' His Majesty's Theatre '—the first new play was Tom Killigrew's *Princess : or, Love at first Sight.*" According to Pepys, however, this is inexact, for it was not a new play but a revival, and Pepys is certainly correct.

[34] British Museum, Add. MS. 34,217, fol. 31b. See also *Hist. MSS. Comm.*, Rep. X., App., pt. 4, p. 21.

[35] The Hon. James Howard, *The English Mounsieur*, 4to, 1674, p. 4.

[36] *Hist. MSS. Comm.*, Fifth Report, Appendix, Part I (1876), 63, 86 ; *Lords Journals*, v, 511 ; vi, 47.

[37] *Lords Journals*, vi, 151.

[38] British Museum, Add. MSS., 20032, f. 2.

[39] Mr. Harbage in his *Thomas Killigrew*, pp. 86-100, deals with the matter in considerable detail, and shows the utter unscrupulousness of Cromwell and his gang.

[40] Mr. Harbage, op. cit., pp. 192-3, suggests and not without likelihood that *The Pilgrim* may have been acted in Paris by the company which Charles, then Prince of Wales, struggled to maintain for a few months, July to November, 1646.

[41] *Some Account of the English Stage*, Bath, 1832, vol. i, p. 391.

[42] A. H. Nason, *James Shirley, Dramatist*, 1915, p. 307. *The Politician* was first printed 4to, 1655. Nason remarks, p. 311, "In theme and tone, *The Politician* is vaguely reminiscent both of *Hamlet* and of *Macbeth*." Both Nason, pp. 107-8 and pp. 336-343, and J. Q. Adams, *Dramatic Records of Sir Henry Herbert*, 1917, agree with F. G. Fleay, *Biographical Chronicle of the English Drama*, 1891, vol. ii, p. 246, that *The Politique Father*, licensed 26th May, 1641, is the play published as *The Brothers*, 8vo, 1652. R. S. Forsythe in his unsatisfactory and ill-digested monograph, *The Relations of Shirley's Plays to the Elizabethan Drama*, 1914, p. 45, and pp. 173-185, endeavours to dispute this, but in any case his opinion may be accounted negligible.

[43] It was inevitable that Langbaine, p. 312, should draw attention to Killigrew's source. The first edition of *Le Grand Cyrus* was Paris, chez Courbé, 10 vols., 1649-1653. The English translation appeared London, folio, 1653-4. In the 12mo edition, *Englished* by F. G., Esq., London, 1691, " *The History of* Aglatidas *and* Amestris " occupies pages 257 and 383 of volume i.

[44] In the 12mo *Artamenes,* London, 1691, this duel is illustrated with a copper-plate. The account of the duel occupies pp. 299–306, and the catastrophe in the play differs from that in the romance. Killigrew also has altered the names. His Amadeo is the Aglatidas of De Scudéry; Lucius, Megabise; and Manlius, Arbate. Cicilia stands for Amestris.

[45] *Comedies and Tragedies,* folio, with general title-page, 1664. *The First Part of Cicilia and Clorinda,* 1663, p. 217.

[46] *English Stage,* vol. i, p. 391.

[47] Actually derived from the story of Aristomenes the Messenian who was delivered from the Spartan cave by a fox. For Aristomenes see Pausanius, iv, 14–24, 34. Mrs. Centlivre's farce *A Bickerstaff's Burying, or, Work for the Upholders,* Drury Lane, 27th March, 1710, 4to [1710], which was sometimes played as *The Custom of the Country,* is suggested by the Oriental tale.

[48] Langbaine, op. cit., pp. 313–14.

[49] Reprinted from what is probably a unique copy by Mr. G. Thorn-Drury in 1925. The cause of Flecknoe's wrath, which is very scurvil in its expression, obviously lies in the fact that Killigrew was not eager to produce his plays. The wounds of vanity are the worst sores and take longest to heal. Flecknoe's tirades must be considerably discounted.

[50] In the margin of the folios, p. 456, *Thomaso,* Part II, Act V, scene 7, we even find printed precise identification of persons to whom allusion is made. Thus Will Crofts, Killigrew himself, Sir John Denham, and Davenant are named.

Embassadour Will, Resident Tom,
John the Poet with the Nose ;
All *Gondiberts* dire Foes.

Gondiberts indeed has no gloss here, but the reference is not to be mistaken.

[51] See *The Works of Aphra Behn,* edited by Montague Summers, 1915, vol. i, pp. 1–213. The two plays are here reprinted and furnished with Theatrical Histories, Notes on the Source, and other excursuses. The first part of *The Rover* was popular throughout the first half of the eighteenth century. In March, 1790, a poor version by J. P. Kemble, *Love in Many Masks,* was presented at Drury Lane. This was acted eight times that season.

[52] Mr. F. E. Schelling, *The Cambridge History of English Literature,* vol. viii, 1912, chap. v, p. 120.

[53] Miss Helen McAfee, *Pepys on the Restoration Stage,* 1916, p. 169, n. 2. One of Miss McAfee's great discoveries is a Restoration theatre, hitherto unknown as a playhouse and unrecognized. This is " Chyrurgeon's Hall ". The evidence is Pepys, 29th August, 1668, " To Chyrurgeon's hall . . . and there to see their theatre, which stood all the fire."

[54] Mr. J. R. A. Nicoll, *A History of Restoration Drama,* 2nd ed., 1928, p. 23. On p. 171, n. 2, Mr. Nicoll speaks of "A study of Killigrew's *Comedies and Tragedies*", which, however, I can find no evidence at all that he has made.

[55] See my edition of *The Parsons Wedding* in *Restoration Comedies,* 1921, Introduction, pp. xxv–xxvi.

[56] Langbaine, p. 313. See my *Restoration Comedies,* p. xxv. *Ram Alley,* 4to, 1611, is a capital comedy by David Oge Barry (Lording Barry). *The Antiquary,* 4to, 1641, is by Shackerley Marmion. Christopher Bullock in *Woman is a Riddle,* 4to, 1717, produced at Lincoln's Inn Fields, 4th December, 1716, has cleverly introduced the same situation in his Fifth Act.

Owing to an ambiguous expression in Charles Dibdin's *Complete History of the Stage,* ed. 1800, iv, p. 64, it was supposed that *The Parsons Wedding* is largely based upon Calderon's famous *La Dama Duende.* Actually the two plays do not bear the slightest resemblance in any particular. The whole point is treated at length in my *Restoration Comedies,* xxi–xxv. It is much to be regretted that not only do we remark Mr. F. Schelling in his chapter on the Restoration drama (see n. 52 *supra,*) and so superficial a writer as Mr. Nettleton, *English Drama of the Restoration,* 1914, p. 45, emphasizing this absurdity, but even scholars have been misled. In spite of the fact that this crusted mistake has been so carefully corrected we are not, of course, at all surprised to find Mr. J. R. A. Nicoll, *Restoration Drama,* 2nd ed., 1928, p. 180, blithely follows the bell-wether of error in most docile fashion.

[57] The whole atmosphere of the scene is pre-Restoration. There are also such references as *Banks's* ordinary, " The spiritual Non-sence the age calls Platonick Love " (*Restoration Comedies*, p. 29) ; Patent-snow (p. 70) ; Joseph Taylor (p. 113), and Stephen Hamerton (p. 140), the actors ; and many more.

[58] Pepys, 4th October, 1664.

[59] *The Dramatic Records of Sir Henry Herbert*, ed. J. Q. Adams, p. 138. It should be carefully noted that the date of the first item, 3rd November, 1663, applies to *Flora's Vagaries* alone, and is the date of licensing this play. The following items all belong to 1664. Mr. Harbage, *Thomas Killigrew*, p. 190, n. 16, argues that the fee of £2 paid for *The Parsons Wedding* is not conclusive, since £2 was also paid for " the licensing of " Henry 5th " which was scarcely an unacted play ". Mr. Harbage is confusing Shakespeare's *Henry V* with the Earl of Orrery's *Henry the Fifth*, produced at Lincoln's Inn Fields, on 11th August, 1664, and licensed for a fee of £2. Strictly speaking the memorandum is not that of Herbert but that of his deputy, Edward Hayward, to whom he had farmed out his office in July, 1663.

[60] 4th October, 1664. *The Parson's Dreame* is of course *The Parsons Wedding*. On 11th October, 1664, Luellin told Pepys " what a bawdy loose play this ' Parson's Wedding ' is, that is acted by nothing but women at the King's house, and ", adds the diarist, " I am glad of it."

[61] Killigrew's own copy of the folio *Comedies and Tragedies*, 1664, is preserved in the Library of Worcester College, Oxford. A note by him directs that certain passages in three of the plays should be cut out as marked, and he has made further corrections throughout the volume. In a private letter to myself, 22nd December, 1921, Mr. G. Thorn-Drury wrote : " I have to-day seen a large paper copy of Killigrew's plays which was apparently his own property : several of the plays have very extensive cuts made by him, I suppose, for representation. It is disappointing that there is comparatively speaking nothing in the way of correction of the text—in most cases he has simply cut out whole chunks."

[62] Killigrew's company opened at Lincoln's Inn Fields on 26th February, 1672. *Covent Garden Drollery* is in *The Term Catalogues*, ed. Arber, vol. i, p. 117, for Michaelmas (21st November), 1672.

[63] Downes, *Roscius Anglicanus*, edited by Montague Summers, 1928, p. 17. For Rhodes' repertory, ibid.

[64] *Middlesex County Records*, A. J. C. Jeaffreson, vol. iii, p. 282.

[65] Whitelocke, *Memorials*, 1732, p. 699. Downes' statement (p. 17) that Rhodes obtained " a Licence from the Governing State " is incorrect.

[66] *Middlesex County Records, ut sup.*, pp. 279, 280.

[67] Parton, *Some Account of the Hospital and Parish of St. Giles in the Fields*, p. 236.

[68] James Wright, *Historia Histrionica*, 1699. See also my edition of Downes, pp. 71–2.

[69] For their repertory see *Dramatic Records of Sir Henry Herbert*, ed. J. Q. Adams, p. 82.

[70] This theatre, built in 1629, stood on the site of the old granary of Dorset House, near Fleet Street. It was completely destroyed in the Great Fire, 1666.

[71] *Dramatic Records of Sir Henry Herbert*, ed. J. Q. Adams, p. 81.

[72] Ibid., p. 121.

[73] See Chapter I, p. 24.

[74] *State Papers*. Domestic, Entry Book V, 158.

[75] Malone, *Variorum*, iii, p. 249.

[76] *Dramatic Records of Sir Henry Herbert*, ed. J. Q. Adams, pp. 85–7.

[77] *The Commonwealth and Restoration Stage*, L. Hotson, pp. 203–4.

[78] *Dramatic Records of Sir Henry Herbert*, ed. J. Q. Adams, pp. 93–4.

[79] Ibid., pp. 94–6.

[80] R. W. Lowe, *Thomas Betterton*, 1891, pp. 68–9.

[81] Gildon says that both Betterton and Kynaston were apprentices to Rhodes the bookseller.

[82] The Theatre Royal, Bridges Street, the house burned down in January, 1672. For the repertory and order of plays at the Red Bull and Vere Street, see Malone, *Variorum*, iii, p. 273.

[83] There are allusions to the tapestries in Sir Robert Howard's *The Surprisal*, produced at Vere Street, 23rd April, 1662, Act II, scene 1, where Brancadoro says : " Wou'd I were hid under a Bed, or Behind the Hangings." Also in Dryden's

The Wild Gallant, produced at Vere Street on 5th February, 1662–3. See *Dryden The Dramatic Works,* 1931, edited by Montague Summers, vol. i, p. 110, where Nonsuch refers to " these Hangings " and note p. 433 ; also stage-direction at commencement of Act IV, " Table set," and note p. 429, and p. 62, Theatrical History of the play.

⁸⁴ Coryat, *Crudities,* 1611, p. 247, observes that in a Venetian theatre he witnessed " things that I never saw before, for I saw women act, a thing that I never saw before, though I have heard that it hath been some times used in London ". There is no record of actresses in an English theatre at this date, not even experimentally, and Coryat may have been mistaken or misinformed. Perhaps the allusion is to the dancing of ladies in Masques at Whitehall. Prynne, *Histriomastix,* 1633, p. 215, refers to " Frenchwomen actors in a play " at Blackfriars, in Michaelmas term, 1629, and girds angrily at " some Frenchwomen, or monsters rather " who attempted to act in a French comedy at Blackfriars, " an impudent, shameful, unwomanish, graceless, if not more than whorishe attempt," p. 414. The foreign innovation did not please, and the Frenchwomen were " hissed, hooted, and pippin-pelted from the stage ", see the contemporary letter in J. P. Collier's *Annals of the Stage,* 1831, vol. ii, p. 23. In Brome's *The Court Beggar,* produced at the Cockpit, 1632, 8vo, 1653, Lady Strangelon has the following scomm : " To your business Gentlemen ; if you have a short speech or two, the boy's a pretty Actor ; and his mother can play her part," women-Actors now grow in request."

⁸⁵ In my edition of the *Roscius Anglicanus,* pp. 93–5. In her work *Enter the Actress,* 1931, Rosamond Gilder has a chapter, vii, " Enter Ianthe, Veil'd—The First Actress in England," pp. 132–143. Wisely enough, Miss Gilder does not venture to decide the point. Unfortunately this chapter as well as the following chapters, xiii, " Mary Betterton," and ix, "Aphra Behn," all three betray the most superficial acquaintance with the Restoration stage. Miss Gilder has paid me the compliment of quoting from and generally paraphrasing my work at great length (although it is true without acknowledgement), but I would beg that in future she will at least report me correctly.

⁸⁶ Pepys met the lady more than once. See the Diary, 31st October, 6th December, 8th December, 31st December, 1665 ; and 3rd January, 1666.

⁸⁷ *Dramatic Miscellanies,* 1784, vol. ii, p. 364.

⁸⁸ *The Life and Times of that Excellent and Renowned Actor Thomas Betterton,* 1888, pp. 69–71.

⁸⁹ *An Apology for the Life of Mr. Colley Cibber,* ed. Edmund Bellchambers, 1822, pp. 69–70, *n.*

⁹⁰ We also have in this same book a Prologue to Fletcher's *The Tamer Tam'd* given on 24th June, 1660, and a corresponding " Epilogue *Spoken by the Tamer, a Woman* ", but this merely refers to the fact that in the comedy the Tamer was a female character, Maria ; it does not indicate that Maria was played by a woman.

⁹¹ The cast Downes gives, pp. 6 and 7, of *The Moor of Venice* is demonstrably not in every particular that of the earliest revival after the Restoration, but the discrepancies are of no importance as regards the present point.

⁹² *The Commonwealth and Restoration Stage,* L. Hotson, 1928, p. 211.

⁹³ Malone, *Variorum,* iii, 269.

⁹⁴ Percy Fitzgerald, *A New History of the English Stage,* 1882, vol. i, pp. 81–3, and notes.

⁹⁵ Ibid., p. 83.

⁹⁶ *State Papers.* Domestic, Charles II, lxxii, 45.

⁹⁷ Chalmers, *Apology,* 1797, p. 529.

⁹⁸ Pepys, 7th December, 1667.

⁹⁹ *The Restoration Theatre,* Montague Summers, 1934, pp. 14–16 ; and *Roscius Anglicanus,* p. 3.

¹⁰⁰ The last trace of Burt is in 1690. He is often confused with Theophilus Bird, who, as I have noted, died before 28th April, 1663. See *State Papers.* Domestic, Charles II, lxxii, 45.

¹⁰¹ Robert was the famous brother. Unless there were three brothers William is to be identified with Edward Shatterel. See *Roscius Anglicanus,* notes pp. 76–7. An Edward Schottuel was acting at The Hague in 1644–5 ; and Edward Shatterel at the Red Bull in May, 1659. Edward apparently died before 1667.

¹⁰² *Roscius Anglicanus,* p. 2.

[103] For accounts of the several actors see my notes *passim* under the respective names in my edition of Downes.

If one is to accept the authority of Collier's MS. *History of the Restoration Stage,* now in the Harvard Library, Timothy Twyford should be added to the list of Theatre Royal actors. There was certainly a Timothy Twyford, a bookseller. See Stapylton's *The Step-Mother,* 4to, 1664. There was an actress of the Duke's House, Mrs. Twyford.

[104] *State Papers.* Domestic, Charles II, clxxvii, 6.

[105] Pepys, 29th October and 5th November, 1666. Evelyn, 18th October, 1666.

[106] *State Papers.* Domestic, Charles II, clxxix, 136.

[107] Pepys, 20th November, 1666.

[108] Fitzgerald, *New History of the English Stage,* 1882, vol. i, pp. 136–7. Fitzgerald, however, says " The loss was not very serious ", an amazing statement. *The Works of William Wycherley,* 1924, ed. Montague Summers, vol. i. Introduction, pp. 39–40. *Roscius Anglicanus,* ed. Montague Summers, Explanatory Notes, pp. 86–7. We note also the allusion to the bad fire at the King's House only checked after much destruction by blowing up the adjacent houses in a letter 25th January, 1671–2, to Sir Daniel Fleming of Rydal Hall, Westmorland. *Hist. MSS. Comm.,* 12th Report, App. VII, 1890.

[109] Pepys, 12th February, 1667.

[110] Downes, p. 31.

[111] *Covent Garden Drollery,* 1672. Langbaine, *Dramatick Poets,* p. 216.

[112] Genest, *Some Account of the English Stage,* vol. i, p. 160. Mr. L. Hotson has worked out the exact cost as £3,908 11*s.* 5*d.*: *The Commonwealth and Restoration Stage,* p. 255.

[113] Hotson, op. cit., pp. 256–7.

[114] *New Poems, Songs, Prologues and Epilogues,* 8vo, 1676, p. 72. The reference to the crack who " turns Nun " is an allusion to Mrs. Ann Reeve, Dryden's mistress, who left the stage to take the veil in a foreign cloister. See *Dryden The Dramatic Works,* edited by Montague Summers, vol. i, 1931, Introduction, pp. liv–lvi.

[115] See also Malone, *Prose Works of John Dryden,* 1800. " The Life of Dryden," vol. i, pt. 1, pp. 73–4; asterisked note.

[116] Cibber, *Apology.* Chapter iv speaks of the audiences of both houses falling off, and Mohun and Hart now growing old, the younger actors, Goodman, Clarke, and others were impatient to get into their parts.

[117] The date of his death is not certainly known, but it was later than 1690.

[118] Shadwell, Preface addressed to Sir Charles Sedley and signed 16th February, 1678/9, to *A True Widow,* 4to, 1679. Cf. the Prologue to Crowne's *The Misery of Civil-War,* Dorset Garden, spring of 1680 :

> *Religious Broyles to such a height are grown,*
> *All the sweet sound of Poetry they drown.*

There are continual references of this kind.

[119] Edmond Malone, *Prose Works of John Dryden,* 1800. " The Life of Dryden," vol. i, pt. 1, pp. 73–5.

[120] Hotson, op. cit., p. 262.

[121] Printed with *The Conspiracy ; or, The Change of Government,* 4to, 1680.

[122] Ibid., p. 263. Gray brought an action against Charles Killigrew, which was heard by the Lord Chamberlain on 8th February, 1684, and settled in the treasurer's favour.

[123] Hotson, op. cit., p. 268. Also p. 273.

[124] *Roscius Anglicanus,* ed. Montague Summers, p. 16. See also the anonymous *A Comparison between the Two Stages,* 1702.

It is perhaps worth while reminding ourselves that even in the palmy days of the theatre audiences were often very thin. This was not unseldom remarked by Pepys. Thus on Thursday, 1st August, 1667, at the Theatre Royal when *The Custom of the Country* was given he found " the house mighty empty—more than ever I saw it ". On Saturday, 29th August, 1668, he went to Lincoln's Inn Fields where *The Sullen Lovers* was to be performed, but, he says, " so few people there . . . as I went out ; and do believe they did not act."

[125] Given by Charles Gildon in his *Life of Betterton,* 1710, pp. 8–9. Reprinted by Fitzgerald, *New History of the English Stage,* 1882, vol. i, p. 149.

[126] Fitzgerald, op. cit., pp. 154-8. The date 14th May should, however, be 4th May.

[127] *Rule a Wife and Have a Wife*, Downes, p. 39. *The Bloody Brother*, 4to, 1685, Licensed 27th November, 1685. *A King and No King*, Genest, op. cit., vol. i, p. 403.

[128] *Roscius Anglicanus*, ed. cit., pp. 232-3. I will take this opportunity of correcting my former statement (p. 232) : " It does not appear, however, that Mohun played after the union." We know that he appeared once or twice, but very seldom, in his old rôles.

[129] Hotson, op. cit., p. 281, inaccurately says : " From the younger group, Clarke, Perin, Disney, and Watson disappeared from view." For Perin see below, n. 132. Downes, *Roscius Anglicanus*, ed. cit., p. 39, includes Mr. Duke Watson among " the Remnant " of the Theatre Royal who joined the United Companies. Disney continued with the United Company. He was a small part actor, and played Garrucca in the operatic version of *The Indian-Queen* (music by Henry Purcell), at Drury Lane in 1695. See British Museum, A.D.M.S., 31449.

[130] W. R. Chetwood, *General History of the Stage*, 1749, pp. 51-3, 79-87.

[131] Downes, *Roscius Anglicanus*, ed cit., p. 166.

[132] *Calendar of the MSS. of the Marquess of Ormonde at Kilkenny Castle*, vol. vi (1911), p. 425. L. Hotson, op. cit., p. 281, incorrectly supposes that Perin " disappeared from view " at the Union. Perin acted the Archbishop of Lyons in *The Duke of Guise*, United Companies, Theatre Royal, November, 1682. He also played Octavius in a revival of *Julius Caesar*, 1683, and Hamond in the important 1685 revival of *The Bloody Brother*. Cibber, *Apology*, chapter v, tells us that the patentees having very unwisely refused Charlotte Butler an addition of 10s. a week to her salary, Ashbury who was raising a company to open at Smock-Alley on 23rd March, 1693, offered the lady her own conditions and accordingly she crossed to Dublin to grace the Irish Stage.

[133] Kynaston, for example, was with Killigrew.

[134] Malone, *Variorum*, iii, 257. *Dramatic Records of Sir Henry Herbert*, ed. J. Q. Adams, pp. 96-100.

[135] *Dramatic Records*, ed. Adams, pp. 102-106, 108-113, 119-123.

[136] L. Hotson, *Commonwealth and Restoration Stage*, pp. 120-7 has a very elaborate and detailed history of this theatre with sketches and plans. This permits a briefer purview here.

[137] *Apology*, ed. Lowe, vol. i, pp. 314-15.

[138] *Annals of Tennis*, p. 35.

[139] *Roscius Anglicanus*, p. 20. Downes' error, which I have corrected, " Spring, 1662," should be remarked.

[140] Purchased by the Society of Apothecaries from Lady Ann Howard of Effingham in 1682 for a hall. It was destroyed in the Great Fire of 1666, and Apothecaries Hall was rebuilt in 1670.

[141] Fitzgerald, op. cit., i, pp. 73-7, prints the Patent at length. The date, however, then given " 1662. 15 Jan. 14 Car. II ", must be amended to 1662-3.

[142] Pepys, 24th August, 1661.

[143] See the Prologue to the Second Part of *The Siege of Rhodes*, and Pepys, 21st October, 1661.

[144] *Roscius Anglicanus*, p. 22.

[145] The casts are from Downes, *Roscius Anglicanus*, pp. 20-1.

[146] She married Betterton in December, 1662. The wedding licence is dated 24th December.

[147] By a bad blunder Mr. Hotson, *The Commonwealth and Restoration Stage*, identifies this actress with Elizabeth Davenport of the Theatre Royal. See my edition of Downes, pp. 139-140, 171-2.

[148] There is a famous description of Betterton as Hamlet in Cibber's *Apology*, chapter iv. See also *The Laureat*, 1740.

[149] Afterwards Mrs. Shadwell. See my edition of *Shadwell's Works*, 1927, Introduction, pp. xxviii-xxxi. Also concerning her visit to Oxford in 1661, later in this chapter.

[150] It should, perhaps, be remarked that Malone is inexact in his account of the dramatists who were (he says) attached to the rival houses, *Prose Works of John Dryden*, vol. i, pt. i, 1800, " The Life of Dryden," pp. 72-3, n. 3.

[151] *Roscius Anglicanus*, p. 31, and note pp. 200-1.

[152] Pepys, 22nd July, 24th October, 10th December, 1663.

[153] Pepys, 22nd July, 1667.

[154] Pepys, 16th October, 1667, and 6th July, 1668.

[155] *Roscius Anglicanus*, p. 30.

[156] Pepys, 9th April, 1668.

[157] *An Elegy Upon the Death of Sr William Davenant*, Bodleian, Wood 429, f. 27. Printed in *A Little Ark*, 1921 (p. 35), ed. G. Thorn-Drury.

[158] The third wife. The first wife was Mary Davenant. The second wife Dame Anne (Cademan) Davenant. Dame Anne's first husband was Thomas Cross; her second husband Sir Thomas Cademan.

[159] L. Hotson, *The Commonwealth and Restoration Theatre*, p. 229.

[160] Ibid., p. 232.

[161] *The Restoration Theatre*, by Montague Summers, 1934, facing pp. 32, 104, and 206, has reproductions from *The Empress of Morocco*, 4to, 1673.

[162] Ibid., facing p. 66. The river view is from an engraving by R. Page, 1825.

[163] This fact incidentally comes out in *The Life of the late Famous Comedian Jo Hayns*, 1701.

[164] *Roscius Anglicanus*, p. 32.

[165] Prologue to Shadwell's *A True Widow*, produced at Dorset Garden in December, 1678.

[166] See *Dryden The Dramatic Works*, edited by Montague Summers, vol. iv, 1932, pp. 263–342, and pp. 531–568.

[167] For accounts of these actors see my edition of the *Roscius Anglicanus* under the separate names.

[168] Blagden played the Admiral in *The Siege of Rhodes* at the opening of Lincoln's Inn Fields in June, 1661, and the next year was at the Theatre Royal.

[169] It has been stated with persistent error that although William Smith acted Banquo in *Macbeth* Sandford played the *Ghost of Banquo*! William Archer delivered himself of some characteristic nonsense to the effect that "We should be shown the horrid vision of his victim as it appears to the murderer's heated imagination. The elegant Smith probably declined to ' bedabble his face with gore ' ". " *Macbeth* on the Stage," *English Illustrated Magazine*, December, 1888 (vi, p. 234). He should have known that at the conclusion of *Venice Preserv'd*, " The Ghosts of Jaffier and Pierre *rise together both bloody*." Smith acted Pierre. There are, of course, other examples. I corrected the old blunder in an article, *Notes and Queries*, vol. 159, No. 19, 8th November, 1930, where I showed that this attribution of the Ghost arose owing to a misprint in the *Macbeth*, 4to, 1674.

[170] Concerning this "fair and famous comedian", as Evelyn calls her, 9th January, 1662, there has been a good deal of confusion. The history of the blackguardly deception practised on her by Aubrey de Vere, twentieth Earl of Oxford, who seduced the lady by a mock marriage, is well known. She must be carefully distinguished from the two sisters Elizabeth and Frances Davenport of the Theatre Royal. Mrs. Davenport was celebrated in the rôle of Roxolana, *The Siege of Rhodes*, and is often called by this name. She also created Roxolana in Orrery's *Mustapha*, produced at Lincoln's Inn Fields, 3rd April, 1665. For full details see my edition of the *Roscius Anglicanus*, pp. 171–2. A subsequent article by Dr. W. J. Lawrence, " Who was Roxolana ? ", printed in *The Stage*, 14th February, 1929, added nothing to my notes beyond the totally erroneous conclusion that Mrs. Davenport is to be identified with a very minor actress of Killigrew's company, Jane Davenport. (Incidentally it is ridiculous to describe Mrs. Davenport as " singing herself into fame ".) Unfortunately his errors have been repeated by Henry Wysham Lanier in *The First English Actresses*, New York, The Players, 1930, p. 56, who writes *inter alia* that " W. J. Lawrence has secondly shown that it was almost certainly Jane (Davenport) who was the deceived Roxolana ", which, I fear, is very far from being the case. A Mrs. Davenport created Rosalinda in Lee's *Sophonisba* at the Theatre Royal in April, 1675. The rôle was very shortly taken over by Mrs. Boutell.

[171] L. Hotson, *The Commonwealth and Restoration Stage*, p. 215, on no grounds whatsoever identifies this Revet with Edward Revet, the dramatist. This " M. in Monmouth, M. in Macedon " guess-work grows tedious. There was an Eldred Revett, whose *Poems*, 12mo, were " *printed by E.T. for the Authour. Anno Dom.*1657 ".

[172] I do not know what authority L. Hotson, op. cit., has for giving 1663 as the date of Joseph Williams' birth.

[173] Sometime a maid-companion to Mrs. Pepys. See Pepys, 6th, 7th, 8th, 9th December, 1662. Also 28th May, 1663, when Pepys saw her " walk on " in *Hamlet*. Also 29th May, 1663 ; and 10th September, 1664. There are frequent other references to Mrs. Gosnell in the *Diary*.

Mrs. Norton, " a fine woman, indifferent handsome," is mentioned by Pepys, on 1st and 27th December, 1662, and again on 2nd July, 1666. She passed from Davenant's company to the Theatre Royal, and left the stage in 1669–1670.

According to Downes, *Roscius Anglicanus*, p. 26, Mrs. Betterton succeeded Mrs. Davenport in the rôle of Roxolana in Orrery's *Mustapha,* and Mrs. Wiseman followed Mrs. Betterton.

[174] This actress is not to be identified with Mrs. Hughes. But Mrs. Margaret who created Mrs. Mopus in Wilson's *The Cheats* at the Theatre Royal, Vere Street, March, 1663, is Mrs. Hughes.

[175] A letter from Paris, 25th October, 1670, addressed by William Perwick to Sir Joseph Williamson.

[176] Sir Edmund Gosse, *Thomas Otway.* See Downes, *Roscius Anglicanus,* p. 34 ; *The Works of Aphra Behn,* ed. Montague Summers, 1915, vol. iii, p. 284 ; *The Works of Thomas Otway,* ed. Montague Summers, 1926, vol. i, Introduction, pp. xix–xx. A Mr. Jyotish Chandra Ghosh, *The Works of Thomas Otway,* 2 vols, 1932, being unable to fit the facts to his theories, in speaking of Otway's failure is " led to suppose that it happened on the occasion of a revival of the play, and that Downes either forgot or did not think it worth while to record that. It would be quite like him to do either ", vol. i, p. 12, n. 1. Mr. Ghosh writes queer English, and his meaning is often as unintelligible as his phrases are ungrammatical. Otway's first appearance was his last. Mr. Ghosh, however, tells us that " the evidence of the earliest and contemporary authorities is to the contrary ". This is groundless. Mr. Ghosh on nearly every page exhibits completest and most blank ignorance of Restoration Stage history and conditions, which one cannot but feel is a drawback in a would-be editor of Otway.

[177] Downes, p. 34.

[178] *Roscius Anglicanus,* notes, pp. 211–12.

[179] Downes, p. 34. Pepys, 2nd July, 1661.

[180] Jolly's activities have been dealt with in some detail by Dr. E. Herz in his *Englische Schauspieler und englisches Schauspiel zur Zeit Shakespeares in Deutschland,* 1903, whence Mr. L. Hotson has derived very considerable material for chapter iv of his *Commonwealth and Restoration Stage.* See also Theodor Hampe, *Die Entwicklung des Theater wesens in Nurnberg,* 1900 ; and E. Mentzel, *Geschichte der Schauspielkunst in Frankfurt,* 1882.

[181] *State Papers.* Domestic, Charles II, xxiv, 37.

[182] British Museum, MS. Sloane, 1900.

[183] There is an edition of *Dr. Faustus,* " Printed with Additions as it is now acted " ; 4to, 1663.

[184] The licence, March, 1664, to Legge empowered him " to erect a nursery for breeding players in London or Westminster under the oversight and approbation of Sir Wm. Davenant and Thos. Killigrew to be disposed of for the supply of the theatres ". *State Papers.* Domestic, 1663–4, p. 539. Killigrew at first contemplated Moorfields as a possible site for the Nursery ; Pepys, 2nd August, 1664.

[185] Mr. L. Hotson, *Commonwealth and Restoration Stage,* pp. 176–194, has treated the whole passage in detail.

[186] Mr. A. Harbage in his *Thomas Killigrew,* 1930, p. 119, has done his best to say something in Killigrew's favour, but even if Jolly had shown himself venal and unpleasant this does not excuse Killigrew and Davenant from their concerted fraud. Lady Davenant, at any rate, after Sir William's death bestirred herself o Jolly's behalf and was far from approving of Killigrew's proceedings.

[187] The Lord Chamberlain's order for the closing down of the theatres is dated 5th June, 1665.

[188] *L'Europe Vivante,* . . . à Genève, 1667, p. 213.

[189] British Museum, Add. MS. 34729, ff. 124–5.

[190] There has been a good deal of confusion concerning the Nursery, and many of the details are still obscure and difficult owing to our lack of data. Mr. Hotson,

The Commonwealth and Restoration Stage, pp. 187-194, has cleared up several particulars and enabled us to recognize various errors, but even thus much remains problematical. After a good deal of independent cogitation and research I have tried to tell the story as concisely as possible, and I am glad to have this opportunity of correcting a note which I made more than a quarter of a century ago and which is printed in my edition of *The Rehearsal,* 1914, pp. 96-7.

[191] *The Life of the Late Famous Comedian Jo. Hayns,* 1701, p. 5. (The British Museum copy is dated by a contemporary hand, 23rd June. Published anonymously, the book was written by Tobyas Thomas.)

[192] British Museum : 644, c. 70.

[193] It is perfectly plain from these lines that there was one Nursery which supplied both the regular theatres. It has been suggested, however, absurdly enough, that in the second line " Nursery " is an adjective, and therefore the reference is to " *Both the* Nursery *Houses* ", that is the two Nurseries. Not only would such an interpretation be awkward to a degree, but one might inquire how a poet should bestow one play on two Houses ?

[194] A translation from Guarini's *Il Pastor Fido,* " by D. D. Gent.," 12mo, 1633.

[195] Carey Perin played such rôles as Cicco in *The Amorous Old-woman* by Duffett (Langbaine, p. 526) whilst Killigrew's company was at Lincoln's Inn Fields in 1674 ; Meleager in *The Rival Queens,* 1677 ; Sir Geoffrey Jolt in *The Rambling Justice,* 1677 ; The Third Physician in *Trick for Trick,* 1678 ; Benedick in *Sir Barnaby Whigg,* 1681 ; Meroin in *The Heir of Morocco* ; and after the Union, The Archbishop of Lyons in *The Duke of Guise,* 1682 ; Octavius in a revival of *Julius Caesar,* 1683 ; and Hamond in *The Bloody Brother,* 1685. See note 132, *supra.*

[196] Mr. L. Hotson, op. cit., pp. 189-190.

[197] Mr. L. Hotson, op. cit., p. 192, reproduces a portion of Ogilby's *Large and Accurate Map of the City of London,* 1677, showing the exact site of the Barbican Nursery.

[198] Vol. i, p. 66. Fitzgerald's account is very confused, but his reference is almost certainly to the Nursery, which he does not recognize.

[199] *The Rehearsal,* ed. by Montague Summers, The Shakespeare Head Press, 1914, p. 21.

[200] *English Dramatick Poets,* Oxford, 1691, p. 64 ; and p. 535.

[201] Maximin, the Tyrant of Rome, in Dryden's own tragedy *Tyrannick Love* ; Simkin, in the popular droll *The Humours of Simpkin.*

[202] See G. Thorn-Drury, *Some Notes on Dryden,* n.d. (1925), pp. 6-9, " The Date of Mac-Flecknoe." Mr. G. Thorn-Drury argues that *Mac Flecknoe* was probably written in 1678 and had widely circulated in MS. copies. In 1678 the Barbican Nursery was flourishing.

[203] Malone, *Prose Works of John Dryden* (1800), " The Life of Dryden," vol. i, pt. 1, p. 169. Narcissus Luttrell inscribed upon his copy of *Mac Flecknoe,* 4th October, 1682, which was the date of acquisition and not necessarily the date of publication.

[204] See, for example, Cibber's account of his entrance on the stage, *Apology,* chapter vi. Also Chetwood, *A General History of the Stage,* pp. 88, 91, 117, 164, and *passim.*

[205] Bodleian Library ; Ashmole, 1674, cxxiv.

[206] Bodleian, ibid., cxxiii.

[207] Bodleian, *Nichol's Newspapers,* vols. 4 and 5, 1681-4.

[208] See Ogilby and Morgan's *Map of London,* 1677, a square of which has been reproduced by J. Q. Adams, *Shakespearean Playhouses,* p. 270.

[209] Bodleian, *Nichol's Newspapers,* vol. 5.

[210] There is a view of the Remains of Gibbons' Tennis Court in Robert Wilkinson's *Londina Illustrata,* 1819, vol. ii.

[211] *The Academy,* xxii, p. 315.

[212] *Middlesex Sessions Books,* Cal. January, 1656-*July,* 1664, p. 156. Mention is made of houses " erected upon the piece of ground where the Fortune Playhouse formerly stood ".

[213] Vol. ii, p. 141.

[214] A fine etching of the plate from Wilkinson's *Londina* was given as the frontispiece to the selection of Dekker's plays in the Mermaid Series, 1888, and a note added (p. xlvi) on " The Old Fortune Theatre ".

215 The Harp, as a device for Ireland, first appears on the Great Seal in that of Queen Elizabeth. " In the next reign it became definitely the Arms of Ireland as it is so quartered on the Royal Shield of James I, where it has occupied the third quarter unmoved throughout the changes of its fellow quarterings." G. W. Eve, *Heraldry as Art,* 1907, pp. 108–9.

216 See note 182.

217 *Tu Quoque ; or, The City Gallant,* often known as *Greene's Tu Quoque* from the excellent acting of Thomas Greene as Bubble, was printed 4to, 1614. With some alteration by Davenant it was revived at Lincoln's Inn Fields on 12th September, 1667. *Ignoramus,* Codrington's translation, 4to, 1662, from the Latin of George Ruggle. *George a Greene, the Pindar of Wakefield,* 4to, 1599, but acted in 1593. *Muleasses the Turke* by John Mason, 4to, 1610. *The Fair Maid of the West, or A Girle worth gold,* 4to, 1631, by Thomas Heywood. No doubt Part I is intended. See later in chapter for a performance at Rydal Hall. *Tis Pitty Shees a Whore,* 4to, 1633, seen by Pepys, 9th September, 1661. A revival, by the Phoenix Society, January, 1923 ; Arts Theatre, 30th December, 1934. *The Night-Walker ; or, the Little Theife,* licensed by Herbert 11th May, 1633, as " a play of Fletchers corrected by Sherley " ; printed 4to, 1640, as by Fletcher. Seen by Pepys, 2nd April, 1661 ; 31st March, and 19th May, 1662. Massinger's *A new Way to pay old Debts,* 4to, 1633. *The faire quarrell,* by Middleton and Rowley, 4to, 1622.

218 *L'Europe Vivante,* à Genève, 1667. Licensed, 10th September, 1666, p. 215. (Bodley shelfmark : 4° J. 27, art.)

219 " *Strowling Coish* " he is called in *A Satyr on the Players,* printed for the first time in my edition of the *Roscius Anglicanus,* p. 55 and p. 285.

220 *Extracts from the Court Books of the City of Norwich,* 1666–1688, ed. by Walter Rye, Norwich, 1905.

221 Louise Renée de Keroualle was created Duchess of Portsmouth in 1673.

222 *New Poems,* 8vo, 1676, pp. 89–93.

223 For whom see Chetwood, *A General History of the Stage,* 1749, pp. 79–87.

224 See Evelyn's account of the Act of 1654 ; Evelyn's *Diary,* 6th–10th July, 1654.

225 Anthony à Wood, *Life and Times,* ed. Clark, 1891, vol. i, p. 322.

226 See above, n. 169.

227 The British Museum Press Mark of Walden's *Poems* is Huth. 163. The details can be gleaned from these effusions. It is only fair to say that Walden's marriage in 1663 took place after his inamorata married Thomas Gawdy of Claxton, Norfolk, at S. Clement Danes, 12th July, 1662. For Anne Gibbs, who *en secondes noces* married Shadwell, see *The Works of Thomas Shadwell,* ed. by Montague Summers, 1927, vol. i, Introduction, pp. xxviii–xxxi.

228 *Cambyses* was produced at Lincoln's Inn Fields early in 1671. It proved extremely popular. Downes has blundered badly in dating the play : *Roscius Anglicanus,* p. 27, and my notes, pp. 190–1.

229 Not printed, Bodley, MS. Eng. Poet, E. 4.

230 Not printed, Bodley, MS. Eng. Poet, E. 4.

231 *Studies in Oxford History,* 1901, p. 124.

232 Letters of Humphrey Prideaux to John Ellis, *Camden Society,* 1875, p. 5.

233 Op. cit., ii, 351.

234 Bodley, MS. Eng. Poet, E. 4.

235 *Hist. MSS. Comm.,* Report 12, App., Part VII, p. 139, 1890. (MSS. of S. H. Le Fleming, Esq., of Rydal Hall.)

236 For the London printing see *A Dryden Library . . . collected by Thomas James Wise,* London, Printed for Private Circulation only, 1930, p. 31, and facsimile facing p. 32. For the Oxford printing see *The Times Literary Supplement,* 5th March, 1931, letter from Mr. W. G. Hiscock, Assistant Librarian of Christ Church Library, Oxford, where the Oxford printing of the Epilogue is preserved.

237 *Tamerlane the Great* is discussed in detail in Chapter V, *infra.*

238 Bodley, G.A., Oxon, b. 111.

239 1740 ; chapter xiv.

240 Guildhall Library, MS. 2833.

241 The Chester play of " Noah and his shipp " ; the Wakefield play " Processus noe cum filiis " ; the Coventry play, being the Shipwrights' Play " Noah's Ark " ; the Cornish play " Noah and the Flood " ; and (as preserved in a list *c.* 1527) the Norwich " Noyse Shipp " ; are famous among miracle-plays. The history

of Noah and the Flood was extremely popular in dramatic form, whether acted, or by puppets in a motion. For Edward Ecclestone's rhyming Opera, *Noah's Flood; or, The Destruction of the World*, 4to, 1677 (as *The Cataclysm*, 1685; as *The Deluge*, 1690; and 12mo, 1714, as *Noah's Flood*) see Dryden *The Dramatic Works*, edited by Montague Summers, vol. i, 1931, Introduction, pp. xcv–vi. *Noah's Flood* is even parodied in Fielding's *Tom Thumb*, Haymarket, April, 1730; 8vo, 1730.

[242] *Historical MSS. Comm.*, Report 12, App., Part VII, 1890.

[243] See the note *Queen Gorboduc*, p. 440, Dryden *The Dramatic Works*, ed. by Montague Summers, vol. i, 1931.

[244] In *The Observer*, 8th April, 1934, it is said that Stourbridge Fair, granted by King John in 1211 to the Lepers' Hospital, commuted in 1539 by Henry VIII to the Corporation of Cambridge, " famous over all Europe in the Middle Ages," is likely to be held no more, as there is a strong movement for its abolition. In recent years the Fair has degenerated to a few stalls and a coco-nut shie, whilst the Mayor of Cambridge going down in his state carriage to open it proclaims the Fair to a deserted field.

[245] *The Life of the Late Famous Comedian Jo. Hayns*, 1701, pp. 4–5. " The Strowlers Prologue at Cambridge, By Sr H. Shires " is preserved in the British Museum, MS. Eg. 2623. Sir Henry Sheeres, to whom Pepys frequently refers, was knighted about 1684. " The Strowlers Prologue " may be dated *c.* 1690. Sheeres furnished Dryden with a Prologue, which was not allowed to be spoken, for *Don Sebastian*.

[216] See *supra*, n. 182.

[247] *Philaster* and *Wit without Money*, plays belonging to the Theatre Royal, were very popular upon the Restoration Stage. *The Rump; or The Mirrour of the Late Times* was produced in June, 1660, "At the Private House in Dorset Court "; 4to, 1660. *The Changeling* was licensed by Herbert, 7th May, 1622; 4to, 1653. It was seen by Pepys, 23rd February, 1661.

[218] In Gildon's *New Miscellany*, 8vo, 1701, p. 248, is a " Strowlers Prologue at Cambridge ", p. 248. Sedley's Prologue to the Strowlers, *Poems on Affairs of State*, 1698, p. 161, and British Museum, Eg. MS. 2623, f. 63, is almost certainly a Prologue to a play of this name, *The Stroulers*, and not written for any itinerant company.

[249] *Scarron's Comical Romance, or, A facetious History, of a company of Stage players*, folio, 1676, the first English translation of *Le Roman Comique*, with its anglicized incidents is of interest.

[250] The engraving was published by Hogarth in 1738 in consequence of the "Act against Strolling Players ". The original picture belonged to Mr. Thomas Wood, of Littleton Park, near Laleham, Middlesex, where it was unhappily burned in 1874.

It may be noted that by 10 Geo. II, cap. 19, " any persons whatsoever who shall for gain in any playhouse, or booth or otherwise exhibit any Stage Play, Interlude, Shew, Opera, or other Theatrical or Dramatical Performance, or act any part or assist therein within the precincts of the said University or within Five Miles of the City of Oxford or the Town of Cambridge shall be deemed rogues and vagabonds." The penalty is hard labour for one month in the House of Correction. The Chancellors of the Universities, and all University officers are deprived of all power to grant licences for such performances " notwithstanding anything in any other Statute, Law, Custom, Charter or Privilege ". So far as Cambridge was concerned this was repealed in 1894. In reference to Oxford this Act seems never to have been repealed.

[251] *Covent Garden Drollery*, 1672.

CHAPTER III

THE EARLIER RESTORATION DRAMATISTS : THE HOWARDS, STAPYLTON, FLECKNOE, WILSON, COWLEY, PORTER, SIR WILLIAM KILLIGREW, AND OTHERS.

Lisideius . . . conceiv'd a Play ought to be, *A just and lively Image of Humane Nature, representing its Passions and Humours, and the Changes of Fortune to which it is subject ; for the Delight and Instruction of Mankind.*
—JOHN DRYDEN, *Of Dramatick Poesie, An Essay,* 4to, 1668.

You Criticks (said Selinda) *make a mighty sputter about exactness of Plot, unity of Time, place and I know not what, which I can never find do any Play the least good.* (Peregrine *smild at her Female ignorance.*) *But she continued, I have one thing to offer in this dispute, which I think sufficient to convince you : I suppose the chief design of Plays is to please the People, and get the Play-House and the Poet a Livelyhood. You must pardon me Madam,* (*replyed* Peregrine) *Instruction is the business of Plays. Sir (said the Lady) make it the business of the Audience First to be pleas'd with Instruction, and then I shall allow you it to be the chief end of Plays.—The Adventures of Covent-Garden,* 12mo, 1698.

When upon the eve of the Restoration the London theatres began to open their doors, at first very tentatively and very discreetly, and then in spite of opposition with a greater boldness, the actors, especially those under Rhodes at the Cockpit and Michael Mohun's troupe at the Red Bull, were perforce bound to revive the favourite plays from their old repertories, and accordingly in these first months, Shakespeare, Beaumont and Fletcher, Jonson, Shirley, Massinger, Middleton, Chapman, Ford, Rowley, Brome, Daborne, and other of their contemporaries figure largely in the lists of the theatres.

During the Commonwealth many plays had fortunately been issued from the press,[1] but since actual stage performances were so hazardous and clandestine it was impossible that the daring spirits who ventured on the sock and buskin should do aught but present stock fare [2] and it would have been useless for a dramatist to write save for the closet and the shelves.

Thus when T.R. published his translation of Thomas Corneille's *Le Berger Extravagant* [3] as *The Extravagant Shepherd,*[4] 4to, 1654, in his Dedication " to the most virtuous lady, Mrs. Joanna

Thornhill ", he makes sad plaint that his pastoral comedy " might have enter'd the Theater, had not the Guilty Ones of this Age broken that Mirrour lest they should behold their own horrible Shapes represented ".

The printed plays of Major Cosmo Manuche, who had fought for King Charles I during the Civil Wars and suffered both imprisonment and bitter penury, belong to the decade before the Restoration. *The Just General* was published 4to, 1650; *The Loyal Lovers,* 4to, 1652; and *The Bastard,* which is almost certainly his, 4to, 1652. There are, however, a number of plays by Manuche which yet remain in MS. in the Castle Ashby Library. Among these are *The Banished Shepherdesse,* of which another MS. is in the Huntington Library, California; *The Feast,* a comedy, of which another MS. is preserved in the Library of Worcester College, Oxford; *The Mandrake,* a comedy; *Agamemnon,* a tragedy; *Lenotius, King of Ciprus,* a tragedy; *The Captives,* a comedy (unfinished); *Mariamne,* a tragedy; together with another tragedy and a comedy, both of which lack titles. Since *The Feast* has references to Tuke's *The Adventures of Five Hours,* produced at Lincoln's Inn Fields on 8th January, 1662–3, and also to Dryden and Howard's *The Indian-Queen,* produced at the Theatre Royal in January, 1663–4, it is plain that Manuche must have written this play not earlier than 1664.

Major Samuel Holland's masque *Venus and Adonis,* 4to, 1656 and 1660, is negligible. Holland in 1660–1 addressed " gratulatory " verses to King Charles. There is also preserved in the Castle Ashby Library a quarto MS., *The Enchanted Grove,* a Masque in two parts, dedicated by Holland to the Earl of Northampton. Bishop Percy was doubtless correct in his suggestion that " Major Holland (as well as Cosmo Manuche) was an Officer in the Regiment raised by the 5th Earl of Northampton in the Cause of Kg. Charles I ".

One of the first new plays—if not indeed the very first new play—to be acted after the Restoration was John Tatham's satirical *The Rump; or, The Mirrour of The Late Times* given " with Great Applause " at the Private House in Dorset-Court, June, 1660; 4to, 1660; and the Second Impression, " Newly Corrected, with Additions," 4to, 1661. As this comedy is to be more particularly considered under the political drama it will suffice to say here that Tatham presents us with the liveliest picture of the fag-end of the Rump Parliament, " the late pageantry Changeling Times." The puppet politicians, Lady Bertlam [5] (Lambert) and Prissilla her woman, are drawn with a good deal of humour, whilst the last scene, a veritable crescendo, where

Trotter (Secretary Thurloe) cries pens or ink, Prissilla peddles Seville oranges and lemons, Desborough vends turnips, cobbler Hewson bawls " old boots or shoes to mend ! ", Wareston trolls old ballads, and Gammer Cromwell with her tub of kitchen stuff exchanges Billingsgate with a rascal noise of tormenting urchins, is almost Aristophanic so many and so happy are the strokes of its mordant wit.

It is probable that a very early production after the Restoration was John Lacy's *The Old Troop ; or, Monsieur Raggou,* an amusing farce the scene of which is laid during the Civil Wars. The incidents are clearly drawn from the life, and the author spares neither Cavalier nor Roundhead, whose conduct at this time he had every opportunity of observing since he was in " 1642 vel 3, lievtenant and quartermaster to the lord Gerard ".[6] Although not printed until 1672, the script [7] shows every indication of having been written for and performed upon a platform stage. Lacy himself played Raggou. *The Old Troop* was given at the Theatre Royal, Bridges Street, in 1663,[8] and revived on 31st July, 1668.[9] It was " acted with universal Applause ".[10]

In the winter of 1660 at the Red Bull [11] the King's company gave *Wit without Money, The Traitor,* and *Beggars Bush,* on Monday, Tuesday, and Wednesday afternoons, 5th, 6th, and 7th November. On Thursday, 8th, they opened at Gibbons' Tennis Court, Clare Market, Vere Street, with *I King Henry IV.* On Friday, 9th, they acted *The Merry Wives of Windsor,* and on Saturday, 10th, *The Silent Woman.* In the following week were performed *Philaster, Love's Cruelty, The Widow,* and *The Maid's Tragedy.* On Monday afternoon, 19th November, was acted *The Unfortunate Lovers,* and that night at Court, being the first play given there after the Restoration, an entertainment offered by the Duke of Albermale to the King,[12] was performed *The Silent Woman,*[13] an occasional prologue having been written by Davenant.[14] On Tuesday afternoon, 20th November, *Beggars Bush ;* Wednesday, 21st, *The Scornful Lady ;* Thursday, 22nd, *The Traitor ;* Friday, 23rd, *The Elder Brother ;* and Saturday, 24th, *The Chances.*[15]

The importance of these older revivals, of which it is, of course, possible here to mention as illustration only a very few within some three weeks' space, and their influence upon the new dramatists who were now beginning deedily to take pen in hand must be accounted marked and long enduring. There were still alive and active some poets—Davenant and Killigrew themselves, Lodowick Carliell, Cowley, The Duke of Newcastle, Tatham—the authors of plays acted before 1642, but the greater number of writers came to the theatre as utterly inexperienced in this kind of composition, and whilst some, unable to find their feet, safely confined their efforts to adaptations from the French or Spanish as the case might be, others looked to the race before the flood for guidance in a novel technique. There was much to learn both by studying their predecessors' printed work and from actual observation at the Cockpit or the Red Bull.

The influence, then, on the Restoration theatre of our own native Elizabethan playwrights, who painted with minutest observation and the most vivid realism everyday London life as it dinged and cluttered all about them, can hardly be over-estimated. It was, of course, as time went on, permuted, re-directed, and almost infinitely varied by original thought and new design, but even a quarter of a century later, after the comedy of Etherege and Wycherley, we find such authors as Middleton and Richard Brome but a little reshaped for the boards of the fashionable Dorset Garden. Both these writers were pretty generously purloined, for example by so popular a dramatist as Mrs. Behn who borrowed and improved several excellent scenes from *A Mad World, my Masters* in her ultra-topical comedy *The City-Heiress* produced at Dorset Garden in May, 1682 ; who conveyed *No Wit No Help like a Woman's* wholesale in *The Counterfeit Bridegroom* acted at the same house in 1677 ; and who laid Brome's *A Mad Couple Well Matcht* under such copious contribution as *The Debauchee* for Dorset Garden in January, 1677. (Mrs. Behn's adaptation *Like Father, Like Son* from Randolph's *Jealous Lovers,* Dorset Garden, April, 1682, has not been printed.) Since the alterations in *The Counterfeit Bridegroom* and *The Debauchee* are really very trifling it is clear that the good old English tradition, which Dryden himself so emphatically followed in his first play, *The Wild Gallant,* Vere Street, February, 1663, was long very acceptable to a Restoration audience.

New tendencies were further introduced into the theatre from France. The chief French element was certainly most marked in the heroic drama, but Dryden himself in his Dedication to the Earl of Orrery of *The Rival Ladies,* 4to, 1664, boldly asserts that the use of rhyme in tragedy was " *not so much a New way amongst us, as an Old way new reviv'd* ". The French models, personally recommended by the King, no doubt induced Orrery to write his dramas in rhyme, but it may well be borne in mind that the heroic play does not essentially depend upon couplets as its medium. Such a tragedy as Southerne's *The Loyal Brother,* produced at the Theatre Royal in March, 1682, is in sentiment and character a typical heroic drama, although it is written in blank verse. The heroic plays of the Earl of Orrery himself are manifestly influenced by Corneille. They have a similar "Oeconomy and Contrivance", and the psychology of the Irish peer's heroes and heroines seems fashioned upon the characters of the great French poet. There is, be it noted, a vast difference between Orrery's Owen Tudor and Dryden's Almanzor, and there can be little or rather no question which of the two is nearer akin to the *héros raisonneurs* of Pierre Corneille. The form of the rhyming play, then, came from France, and in such dramas as Orrery's *Henry V* and *The Black Prince*, the matter and characterization also ; whilst in Dryden and Howard's *The Indian-Queen*, Dryden's *The Conquest of Granada*, Lee's *Sophonisba* and *Gloriana*, Settle's *Ibrahim*, Banks' *Rival Kings*, the matter was derived from the ermined romances of La Calprenède, Mlle de Scudéry, and their school.[16]

The comedies of Molière, Pierre Corneille, Thomas Corneille, Scarron, Quinault, and other French playwrights also proved immensely useful to English dramatists, and were continually being ransacked for plots and intrigue. Sometimes the foreign comedies suggest whole scenes, sometimes mere incidents and accidents of imbroglio, sometimes they are translated *en bloc*. There is, for example, hardly a play of Molière which was not rifled again and again in the forty years which succeeded the Restoration.[17] Ravenscroft even went so far as to introduce the same episodes twice over in his pieces, so that Nérine and Lucette from *Monsieur de Porceaugnac* appear as Mrs. Clappam and Mrs. Breedwell in *The Careless Lovers*, acted in March, 1673, and twenty-one years later as Mrs. Dazie and Mrs. Breeder in *The Canterbury Guests*, September, 1694. It would seem that before 1700 only *Don Garcie de Navarre*, *L'Impromptu de Versailles*, *La Princesse d'Élide*, *Don Juan*,[18] *Mélicerte*, *Les Amants Magnifiques*, and *La Comtesse d'Escarbagnas* had not been widely utilized by our English dramatists.[19]

But once Molière is transferred to the London stage how entirely native does he not become! There can hardly be any talk of French influence here ; he is metamorphosed into a regular John Bull as he is crossing the Channel. One only has to compare Lacy's *The Dumb Lady* with *Le Médecin Malgré Lui* or Shadwell's *The Miser* with *L'Avare* to realize that the Frenchman has not merely changed his language but he is as thoroughly and substantially English as if he had never lived out of the hearing of the bells of Bow. Our dramatists owe him a great debt indeed in respect of plot, although even this has been vastly over-estimated, and the most far-fetched parallels are ridiculously adduced,[20] but I should very much hesitate to say that except in rare instances we have borrowed complete characters from the

French poet. Shadwell's Goldingham and Harpagon, Mrs. Behn's Sir Patient Fancy and Argan, Caryl's Sir Salomon and Arnolphe are all entirely distinct individuals.

It may be remembered, too, that as material was taken from the French dramatists, they in their turn were debtors to Spanish sources. Sometimes thus mediately, and even more often quite directly, our English playwrights also delved in the inexhaustible mines of the Spanish theatre.[21] A very large number of Elizabethan dramas, although not now traceable perhaps to any definite Spanish originals, may without exaggeration be said to be saturated with Spanish atmosphere.

A little later the Jacobean dramatists for their part went overtly to Spanish romances for their plots, and in the Preface to *An Evening's Love,* 4to, 1671, Dryden said without exaggeration : " Beaumont *and* Fletcher *had most of theirs from* Spanish Novels : *witness the* Chances, *the* Spanish Curate, Rule a Wife and have a Wife, *the* Little French Lawyer, *and as many others of them, as compose the greatest part of their Volume in folio.*" [22] Certainly some seventeen or more of the six and twenty plays which were first published together in folio, 1647, are demonstrably derived in detail, that is to say so far as the plots are concerned, from Spanish literature. Twenty other plays, which conveniently go under the same authors' names and which appear in the folio, 1679, where are collected fifty-two pieces, are so Spanish in sentiment, in quality, and in action that although the sources may not yet have been indisputably identified we cannot be going far wrong if we attribute their origin to the Peninsula. At the Restoration the boundless treasures of the Spanish theatre were almost universally taken advantage of by our English dramatists, since there came an instant demand for new and entertaining comedies of love and honour, mistakes, accidents, disguises, intrigues, and every conceivable complication, all of which bustle and business so admirably and amply supplied by Calderón, Lope de Vega, Guillen de Castro, Alarcón, Zorilla, Moreto, and their fellows, whether reset in the London of Pepys, or whether still situate in the Madrid, Salamanca, Alicant, and Seville of carnivals and serenades, proved such an irresistible fascination and constant delight to Restoration audiences.

Thus the Earl of Bristol translated Calderón's *Mejor Está que Estaba* under the title of *'Tis Better than it Was,* and *Peor Está que Estaba* as *Worse and Worse,* and although unfortunately neither of these versions was printed, they were both produced by Davenant's company between 1662 and 1665.[23] *Elvira ; or, The Worst not always true,* produced at Lincoln's Inn Fields probably in 1663, and printed 4to, 1667, as " Written by a

Person of Quality ", almost certainly the Earl of Bristol, is Calderón's *No Siempre lo Peor es Cierto.* It is disputed whether Dryden's *The Wild Gallant,* February, 1663, may not be founded on Lope's *El Galán escarmentado,* but *The Rival Ladies,* May, 1664, was certainly suggested by a novella *Las Dos Doncellas* in the *Novelas Ejemplares* of Cervantes.[24] To confine oneself only to the five years immediately subsequent to the King's coming-in, Thomas Porter's *The Carnival,* 1664, a Theatre Royal play the scene of which is laid at Seville, stands out as a thoroughly Spanish play in every detail; whilst one of the greatest successes of Lincoln's Inn Fields in 1663 was Tuke's *The Adventures of Five Hours,* adapted from Don Antonio Coello y Ochoa's *Los Empeños de Seis Horas.* It is almost impossible to overestimate the Spanish influence in the Restoration theatre.[25]

There is extant a doggerel letter [26] to be dated about mid-June, 1662, which written to a country friend gives " The newes of all the Playes in Towne ", that is to say new productions. First, at the Theatre Royal, Vere Street, Thomas Killigrew's *The Princesse, or, Love at first Sight,* performed 29th November, 1661 (a revival), only lasted two days being " dash't out of Countenance " " att second sight " ; Sir Robert Howard's *The Surprisal,*[27] 23rd April, 1662, proved very successful chiefly owing to the acting of Lacy as Brancadoro ; Sir William Berkeley's *Cornelia,*[28] 1st June, 1662, was very witty, in fact " too witty for the vulgar sort " ; and Sir William Killigrew's *Selindra,* 3rd March, 1662, had the advantage of a good plot, but was hardly attractive.

Davenant's company were being much applauded in that " everlasting Play " *The Siege of Rhodes* with scenes ; Cowley's *Cutter of Coleman-Street,* 16th December, 1661, many preferred in its first form *The Guardian* ; whilst in his *The Law against Lovers,* 10th February, 1662, Sir William had spoiled two good plays [29] to make one bad.

Among the more important of the new dramatists to take pen in hand when the reopened theatres began to look for fresh fare were John Dryden ; Sir Robert Howard and his three brothers, Edward, James, and Colonel Henry Howard ; Lord Orrery ; Sir Robert Stapylton ; John Wilson ; John Holden ; and Fr. Richard Flecknoe.

Dryden must, of course, be considered separately ; and of the others, little is known concerning Colonel Henry Howard and John Holden. Colonel Henry Howard " made a play, called *The United Kingdoms,* which began with a funeral, and had also two kings in it ". This circumstance, it was generally believed, gave the Duke of Buckingham a just occasion to set up his two kings in Brentford, in *The Rehearsal*. *The United Kingdoms* " miscarrying on the stage the author had the modesty not to print it ".[30] John Holden, the bookseller, was a close friend of Davenant and the publisher of *Gondibert* in 1651. His daughter was one of Davenant's first actresses, although she never rose above very minor rôles.[31] Only two of his plays are known and neither of these was printed. It is of course quite possible that he wrote other dramas, which have entirely disappeared without even record of their names. *The German Princess* [32] by Holden (or as rumour had it by Davenant) [33] was produced at Lincoln's Inn Fields in April, 1664, and seen by Pepys on Friday, the 15th of that month. This piece which dealt with the notorious adventuress Mary Carleton, who in 1663 caused a great sensation throughout Town by her masquerade as an Earl's daughter of Cologne, Pepys found " very simple " although the woman herself appeared in the title-rôle. Downes [34] mentions another play by Holden, *The Ghosts,* which was given at Lincoln's Inn Fields between July, 1662, and May, 1665. It was seen on 17th April, 1665, by Pepys, who judged it " a very simple play ".

An exceedingly busy manager can spare little time to devote to dramatic composition, and it is hardly surprising that Davenant's post-Restoration plays are adaptations or translations. Of *The Secrets,* which Apollo declared " Fitting for none but a Mountebank Stage ",[35] and in which apparently the poetaster Ellis may have had some hand, we know nothing. Davenant, however, had by him two one-act plays or entertainments which have already been described, *The Cruelty of the Spaniards In Peru* and *The History of S͏ͬ Francis Drake,* both of which were fully equipped with scenes and costumes. At least the greater part of his audience could never have seen either of these, presented as they were under no easy conditions in 1658, and the idea struck him to use his stock material, fitting the two in an appropriate framework which should present four acts, each act a separate play. Now Davenant had just such a pattern as he needed in *Foure Playes (or Morall Representations) in one,* which is the last piece in the Beaumont and Fletcher folio of 1647, and it was, I believe, this model he chose for *The Play-house to be Let.*

It is the Long Vacation ; Lincoln's Inn Fields is closed down ; but the actors have put up a bill on the doors announcing that they are willing to consider a temporary occupation of the house. There are numerous applicants, and the first act which fairly dings and thuds with knockings shows us a procession of would-be tenants, each eager to show his especial craft or motion. The play commences thus : " The *SCENE* opens, and upon

two Stools are discovr'd the *Tire-woman* and *Chair-woman,* one
shelling of Beans, and the other Sowing [Sewing]."

> What, shelling of Beans ? 'tis a proper work
> For the Long Vacation.

observes a Player, who joins them in company with the House-
Keeper. A Monsieur arrives anxious to hire the house for his
Troop. " Bless us ! a Troop ? " exclaims the Tire-Woman,
who has to be informed

> they in *France*
> Call a Company of Players, a Troop.
> *Tire-Woman.* I thought he had ta'ne our long Tennis-Court [36]
> For a Stable.

Two hot Fencers next endeavour to secure a lease of the house,
but the Player sends them out a message :

> Tell 'em the *Red Bull* stands empty for Fencers.
> There are no Tenents in it but old Spiders.

A musician then appears wishing to rent the theatre, and retires
to " the Womens Tiring-room for privacy ".

> There's such a crowd at door, as if we had
> A new Play of *Gundamar,*[37]

protests the Tire-Woman. A Dancing-Master now comes to
inquire terms, and meanwhile there clamours at the door a
fanatic who—

> would hire The Turband, Scepter and
> Throne of our *Solyman* the Magnificent.[38]

" Dismiss your Doling " [39] (i.e. knipperdolling) curtly orders the
Player. They then admit "A man of Meeter, a Poet ", who brings
" Romances travesti . . . In Verse Burlesque ". He is to take
his turn last, for *Finis coronat opus.* Accordingly Monsieur with
his Farce, the spiritual Musician

> With his Seraphick Colloquies exprest
> In stilo recitativo,

and the Poet give in order a sample of their wares.

The second Act consists of a very amusing and much abridged
version in broken French of Molière's *Sganarelle, ou le Cocu
Imaginaire.*[40] The Farce, supposed to be represented by Monsieur's
troop, ends with a Dance *à la Ronde* and a song *Ah, Love is a
delicate ting* sung by Mrs. Sarah Gosnell.[41]

The Third Act is "The History of Sr Francis Drake, Exprest by Instrumental and Vocal Musick, and by Art of Perspective in Scenes, &c." (It may be remarked that the Curtain had fallen after Act II.) The Fourth Act presents "The Cruelty of the *Spaniards* in *Peru*". That is to say Davenant rather cleverly introduced here the two Entertainments he had so tentatively given at the Cockpit in the summer and winter of 1658.

The Fifth Act comprises the "Romance travesti" of Julius Caesar and Cleopatra at Alexandria. The characters, Caesar, Mark Antony, Cleopatra, Cornelia, and the rest, converse in jargoned couplets which are not without a good deal of humour, but which were to be far better managed by Cotton in his *Virgil Travestie,* when he gave the metre a new verve and swing by reducing the lines to octosyllables. Cotton was inspired—if one may use the word in this connexion—by Scarron's *Virgile travesty.*[42]

On the whole *The Play-house to be Let* is an adroitly contrived and highly comical entertainment.[43] The alternation of broad humour in Acts II and V with the miniature operas of Acts III and IV is well managed. It is a species which has gigged successors in the modern revue. Accordingly the credit—such as it is—of a most popular contemporary *entretiamento* must be given to Davenant.

In the spring of 1664 there was produced at Lincoln's Inn Fields *The Rivals,* a version of Shakespeare and Fletcher's *The Two Noble Kinsmen. The Rivals,* which is, I am bound to confess, in my opinion an extremely insipid alteration of a very fine drama receives the following enthusiastic notice from old Downes: "The Rivals, A Play, Wrote by Sir *William Davenant*; having a very Fine Interlude in it, of Vocal and Instrumental Musick, mixt with very Diverting Dances; Mr. *Price* introducing the Dancing, by a short Comical Prologue, gain'd him an Universal Applause of the Town. The Part of *Theocles,* was done by Mr. *Harris; Philander,* by Mr. *Betterton; Cunopes* the Jailor, by Mr. *Underhill*: And all the Womens Parts admirably Acted; chiefly *Celia,* a Sheperdess being Mad for Love; especially in Singing several Wild and Mad Songs. *My Lodging it is on the Cold Ground,* &c. She perform'd that so Charmingly, that not long after, it Rais'd her from her Bed on the Cold Ground, to a Bed Royal. The Play by the Excellent performance; lasted uninterruptly Nine Days, with a full Audience." [44]

The 4to, 1668, gives Heraclia, the Prince of Arcadia's niece, to Mrs. Shadwell; Celania, the Provost's daughter to Mrs. Davies; and Celania's maid, Leucippe to Mrs. Long. This cannot, however, represent the original cast entire for on the 2nd December, 1664, Pepys saw *The Rivals* a second time and notes : " The play not good, nor any thing but the good actings of Betterton and his wife and Harris." On 11th January, 1668, Mrs. Knepp gossiping with Pepys about Moll Davies told him that this lady was " for certain going away from the Duke's house, the King being in love with her ". Moreover the song *My Lodging it is on the Cold Ground* was burlesqued in James Howard's *All Mistaken*, Drury Lane, September, 1667, as *My lodging upon the cold floor is,* sung by Nell Gwyn who played Mirida. It seems more than probable that Mrs. Betterton was the original Heraclia. Pepys speaks of Mrs. Gosnell singing with Harris, but no such song for two appears in the script as we now have it, and I am inclined to suppose there were drastic alterations at the revival, the text that has been preserved. It is possible that Mrs. Gosnell was the original Celania. When *The Rivals* was revived in 1667, Mrs. Shadwell succeeded Mrs. Betterton, and Moll Davies played Celania.

" The play not good " ; there is really very little to add to Pepys' considered verdict. One fails to understand why in the first place *The Two Noble Kinsmen* should seem to have needed any alteration at all. The last London revival of this stirring drama was in March, 1928, at the Old Vic., and in spite of the unpardonable buffoonery and ill manners of the actor who played Palamon, the fine qualities of Shakespeare and Fletcher's play were more moving than one might have thought. Davenant's version certainly makes some advance in the direction of unity of action, if that is to be considered any gain, and the poet has not only smoothed and planed the verse, which in some places becomes even antithetical, but he has also knit together loosely connected incidents and episodic scenes. Thus the three mourning Queens in black disappear—a lamentable omission. Indeed the first Act of the older play is to all intents and purposes discarded.

If Davenant's alteration of *The Two Noble Kinsmen* is flaccid and poor his amalgamation of *Measure and Measure* and *Much Ado about Nothing* which, as *The Law against Lovers,* preceded *The Rivals* by some two years, being produced at Lincoln's Inn Fields on 10th February, 1662, can only be termed deplorable. He here sinks to his lowest, a nadir he never again so much as approaches, and I cannot bring myself to review this gallimaufry at any length. Suffice to say that somehow Benedick and Beatrice are foisted into *Measure for Measure* whence we lose the inimitable Pompey (for the Fool who remains is but a shadow), Mrs. Overdone, Froth, and Elbow, whilst the Mariana story is excised in its entirety. In fact the whole play falls to pieces.

The verbal alterations, the gratuitous interpolations and discordant changes are simply atrocious. It must ever prove a sad puzzle how Davenant, a dramatist and a poet capable of great things, could have taken one of Shakespeare's supremest masterpieces and thus have mammocked and degraded it. Yet Pepys thought *The Law against Lovers* " a good play and well performed ".[45] One is just owl-blasted and mazed in a damp.

On Thursday, 10th December, 1663, Pepys calling at Wotton the shoemaker's, hears news " of a rare play to be acted this week of Sir William Davenant's : the story of Henry the Eighth with all his wives ". It does not appear that Davenant made an alteration of Shakespeare and Fletcher's scenes, and by " of Sir William Davenant's " we can gather no more than that the play was performed by Davenant's company. The smart touch about " all his wives " is doubtless a mere bit of irresponsible and imaginative gossip. *Henry VIII* was very splendidly produced at Lincoln's Inn Fields with Betterton as the King ; Harris, Cardinal Wolsey ; and Mrs. Betterton, Queen Catherine.

On Thursday, 12th September, 1667, Pepys visited the Duke's house " where ' Tu Quoque ' [46] was the first time acted, with some alterations of Sir W. Davenant's ". These were probably slight enough, and in any case they were not printed.

The alterations in the Restoration acting version of *Hamlet*, 4to, 1676,[47] are verbal and were perhaps made by Davenant. Inevitably the change is for the worse, always weak, and often definitely bad. The play has not been structurally tampered with save that it was drastically cut, " such Places as might be least prejudicial to the Plot or Sense " being omitted on the stage. In 1719 there appeared an edition of *Julius Caesar*, 12mo, " Written Originally by Shakespeare, And since alter'd by Sir William Davenant and John Dryden late Poets Laureat." [48] It may at once be said that there is not the slightest authority for such an attribution. *Julius Caesar*, a Theatre Royal play, was first separately printed 4to, 1684, as given after the Union of the two Companies. Thus Betterton is Brutus ; Smith, Cassius ; Goodman, Caesar ; Lady Slingsby, Calphurnia ; Mrs. Sarah Cook, Portia ; rôles formerly (before 1672) played by Hart, Mohun, Bell, Mrs. Marshall, and Mrs. Corbet. Kynaston retained Mark Antony. This quarto, moreover, is not an acting version but presents (with one or two trifling variants and some errors) the Folio text. It was clearly in order to gain advertisement that the anonymous author who so injuriously tinkered at *Julius Caesar* foolishly sought in 1719 to father his maltreatment on Davenant and Dryden.

Davenant's additions to and changes in *Macbeth* are of course a very different and a far more important matter.

Macbeth as altered by Davenant was originally given at Lincoln's Inn Fields in 1663–4 and revived with much advertisement and splendour in 1673. Downes thus chronicles this gorgeous production : " The Tragedy of *Macbeth,* alter'd by Sir *William Davenant* ; being drest in all it's Finery, as new Cloath's, new Scenes, Machines, as flyings for the Witches ; with all the Singing and Dancing in it ; THE first Compos'd by Mr. *Lock,* the other by Mr. *Channell* and Mr. *Joseph Preist* ; it being all Excellently perform'd, being in the nature of an Opera, it Recompenc'd double the Expense ; it proves still a lasting Play." [49]

In the Introduction to my collection *Shakespeare Adaptations,* 1922, I said in a footnote, p. xxxv, " The Davenant *Macbeth* was printed in 1673." This error was very properly corrected by Professor Hazelton Spencer in his *Shakespeare Improved,* 1927, p. 152. The fact is I had unfortunately relied upon the authority of Dr. W. J. Lawrence who assured me that the *Macbeth* 4to, 1674, " does not differ very materially from its immediate predecessor," 4to, 1673 ; and that the discrepancies between the two quartos merely represent (1673) Davenant's first version of *Macbeth,* and (1674) a maturer revisal. Since I was only dealing with *Macbeth* in passing and not reprinting the play, I accepted Dr. Lawrence's statement—which I was very soon aware I ought not to have done—without further investigation. Dr. Lawrence, indeed, not only went to Furness (*Variorum Shakespeare*) for his second-hand information, but actually misunderstood what Furness wrote, for as Professor Spencer emphasizes, Furness " so far from asserting the *similarity* of the two Quartos, lays stress on their *difference* ".

It was, of course, extremely remiss in me not to have looked into the point myself, but fifteen years ago I was under the impression that one was safe in accepting an assurance from Dr. Lawrence upon a literary detail of this kind. I have not infrequently during the past twenty years and more paid ample tribute to the scope and extent of Dr. Lawrence's work, but I have so often found myself in serious peril of being misled by his conclusions that it is necessary to enter a caveat. The *ipse dixit* of which he is far too free, with me, at least, now carries no weight. Indeed Dr. Lawrence has so continually shifted his ground, contradicted his former blunders—the word is his own—restated his findings, recanted, and yet again confuted his previous rebuttals, that now it is difficult to discover what exactly may be his latest pronunciamento upon any particular question.

Professor Hazelton Spencer was, I believe, the first to insist upon the differences between the *Macbeth* quartos of 1673 and 1674. The first title-page carries : Macbeth :/A/TRAGEDY./ACTED/At the/DUKES-THEATRE./rule/[Printer's ornament]/rule./LONDON,/ Printed for *William Cademan* at the *Popes*—/*Head* in the *New Exchange,* in the/*Strand.* 1673/.⁵⁰ The second title-page carries : MACBETH,/A/TRAGEDY./With all the/ALTERATIONS,/AMEND-MENTS,/ADDITIONS,/AND/NEW SONGS./rule./ *As it's now Acted at the Dukes* Theatre./double rule./LONDON,/Printed for *P. Chetwin,* and are to be Sold/by most Booksellers, 1674/.⁵¹ The cast in 1673 is : King of Scotland, Mr. Nath. Lee ; Malcolm, Mr. Norris ; Donalbain, Mr. Cademan ; Lenox, Mr. Medburn ; Macbeth, Mr. Betterton ; Banquo, Mr. Smith ; Macduff, Mr. Harris ; Macbeth's Wife, Mrs. Betterton ; Macduff's Wife, Mrs. Long ; Heccat, Mr. Sandford. The actors' names to the other characters are not given.   1674 supplies the same list only we have " *Mr.* Lee " instead of " Mr. *Nath. Lee* ", and Sandford's name has by a printer's error been raised one line to stand opposite to Ghost of Banquo.   Hence arose the crux which has sadly puzzled all stage historians for a century and a half, to wit why the " diminutive and mean " Samuel Sandford should have played Banquo's Ghost, when Banquo himself was sustained by the athletic and handsome young William Smith.⁵² I believe I was the first to unravel the difficulty, and definitely to show that Sandford played Hecate, a rôle for which he was eminently suited.⁵³

The 4to of 1673 is a reprint of the First Folio *Macbeth* with the addition of three songs. There are, moreover, a few un-important and probably quite accidental variants. The 4to of 1674 is Davenant's alteration of the tragedy with the elaboration of the witch-scenes, and many other drastic changes of which the majority are as startling in their nature as they are obscure in their motive.

Not a few passages were varied to get rid of obsolete words and phrases, and (as it was conceived) to elucidate the meaning. Some roughness and irregularities were smoothed and pumiced with disastrous effect. For other changes I can guess no reason save the mere itch to alter. One thing, I am sure, it was all done with the best possible intentions. Act I structurally remains much the same. Seyton economically takes the place of the Bleeding Sergeant, and Macduff stands for Ross, scenes 1 and 3. Before Lady Macbeth reads her husband's letter she has a dialogue with Lady Macduff. With a good deal of garbling of text the action continues as in the original until after Duncan's murder. As we might expect, the Porter is discarded, whilst Seyton represents the Old Man with his memories of terror and affright. A new scene closes Act II, a heath, where Lady Macduff, Maid, and Servant, await Macduff, who, says the Servant "order'd me to attend him with the Chariot". He joins them, but the party is delayed by a song of witches : 1 Witch. *Speak, Sister, speak, is the Deed done?* 2 Witch. *Long ago, long ago.* This was especially admired by Restoration audiences.[54] Witches again sing and dance a round, presently prophesying to Macduff in riddling lines. Act III with verbal differences pretty nearly follows Shakespeare, save two interpolated scenes betwixt Lady Macduff and her husband who is now certain of Macbeth's guilt. The Act closes with Hecate rating the witches. After this she mounts a machine whilst *Come away Heccat, Heccat, Oh come away* is sung, and a general flighting of witches follows, which upon the stage must have been extremely effective.[55] The text is largely from Middleton's *The Witch*. Middleton is also drawn upon for the opening of Act IV, the brewing of the cauldron. Hecate answers Macbeth's demands, but curiously enough the Three Apparitions are not seen although the "*shaddow of eight Kings, and* Banquo's *Ghost after them pass by*". Seyton warns Lady Macduff of her peril, but the murderers do not actually dispatch her son on the stage. In fact the child has no part. The dialogue between Malcolm and Macduff—now transferred from England to Birnam wood—follows. A new episode, which anywhere else would have merited high praise and which is, it must be fairly acknowledged, extremely powerful, a scene between Macbeth and his wife, closes the act. Haunted by the spectre of the murdered King, she urges her husband to resign the crown. When he reminds her that she incited him to the crime, her reply is magnificent in its simplicity :

> You were a Man.
> And by the Charter of your Sex you shou'd
> Have govern'd me.

Duncan's ghost, only visible to the unhappy woman, appears and she is led out raving by her women. The great sleep-walking scene is lamentably abbreviated, and here Seyton takes the place of the Doctor. Towards the end of the play important points are continually missed or slurred, at least so it seems to me. Macbeth is slain on the stage,[56] and expires crying :

> Farewell vain World, and what's most vain in it, Ambition.

Macduff ends the whole with a conventional couplet which may be spared quotation.

With all its faults and I have not hesitated to lay them bare, Davenant's *Macbeth* theatrically proved very effective. It was not indeed for seventy years, until 7th January, 1744, that Garrick ventured to discard much of Davenant—but by no means all—and present the tragedy " as written by Shakespeare "— in his opinion. Actors and audiences were amazed. None the less the divertisements of the Witches were retained, and the Porter had not recovered his position. Neither Kemble nor Macready could dispense with the chorus of Witches. Thus in the production of the former, amid a squalid rabble of sorcerers, " the lovely Crouch " as a singing Witch " wore a fancy hat, powdered hair, rouge, point lace, and fine linen enough to enchant the spectator ".[57]

On 27th September, 1847, Phelps in his fourth Season at Sadler's Wells gave *Macbeth* " from the text of Shakespeare ", and as *The Times* remarked on the following day " There is no half-measure in this ". The music, with the interpolated words, was dropped. Only one character seems to have been omitted, the English doctor.[58] At the Princess Theatre, however, on 14th February, 1853, Charles Kean presented a magnificent spectacular production of *Macbeth,* in which he restored to the stage the Davenant witch-scenes, making place and giving time for these by banishing Lady Macduff and her son together with the drunken porter. In other respects, also, Kean was retrograde. Seyton has to do the work of a number of servants. The scene between the Old Man and Ross is omitted. Macbeth is slain on the stage.[59] Even Sir Henry Irving in his *Macbeth* of 29th December, 1888, retained some of Davenant's witch-verses,[60] the four lines of the song " Black Spirits and White ", and the ten lines of the song " Come away, come away ". Lady Macduff and her son did not return, but the porter was restored, a rôle played by Johnson.[61]

The phenomenal success of the Dorset Garden *Macbeth* aroused considerable jealousy at the Theatre Royal, whose audiences naturally thinned apace when the Town flocked to the rival house. Accordingly Thomas Duffett undertook to burlesque the tragedy, and to his farce *The Empress of Morocco,* which parodies Settle's homonymous drama, another Dorset Garden attraction (July, 1673), he affixed an extraordinary " Epilogue spoken by Witches, after the mode of *Macbeth* ". Duffett's skit on Settle was produced at the Theatre Royal in November, 1673. The title-page, 4to, 1674, of the *mock-Macbeth* epilogue runs : EPILOGUE./Being a new Fancy after the old,/and most surprising way/OF/MACBETH,/Perform'd with new and costly/MACHINES,/ [rule]/which were invented and managed/by the most ingenious Operator/Mr. *Henry VVright,* P.G.Q./[rule]/*LONDON,*/Printed in the Year 1674.[62]

The Actors' Names in the Epilogue are : Heccate, Martin Powell ; 1 Witch, William Harris ; 2 Witch, Adams ; 3 Witch, Lydal ; Thunder, Cardell Goodman ; Lightning,[63] Nathaniel Kew ; Spirits, Cats, and Musicians.

"AN EPILOGUE Spoken by *Heccate* and three WITCHES, According To the Famous Mode of MACBETH. The most renowned and melodious Song of *John Dory*,[64] being heard as it were in the Air sung in parts by Spirits, to raise the expectation, and charm the audience with thoughts sublime, and worthy of that Heroick Scene which follows.

" The Scene opens. Thunder and lightning is discover'd, not behind Painted Tiffany to blind and amuse the Senses, but openly, by the most excellent way of Mustard-bowl,[65] and Salt-Peter. Three Witches fly over the Pit Riding upon Beesomes. *Heccate* descends over the Stage in a Glorious Charriot, adorn'd with Pictures of Hell and Devils, and made of a large Wicker Basket."

The hit at the transparencies used at Dorset Garden in the storm effects of *Macbeth* will not escape notice.

Heccate addresses the three Witches, demanding—

> Where's Mack'rel back and Jilting Sue.

All the three Witches.   We want but you : we want but you.

Mack'rel back is Betty Mackarel ; and Jilting Sue, Sue Flavel, two well-known bonarobas of the day and frequenters of the theatre.[66]

In parody of *Macbeth, i, 3,* the Witches relate their exploits which are of no very decent kind, and then *Enter two Spirits with Brandy burning, which drink while it flames,* Heccate *and the three Witches Sing.*

> *To the Tune of, A Boat, a Boat,* &c.[67]
>
> Hec.   *A health, a health to Mother C——*
> *From* Moor-fields *fled to* Mill-bank *Castle,*
> *She puts off rotten new rig'd Vessel.*
>
> 1. Witch.   *A health, a health to G—— that Witch,*
> *She needs must be in spight of fate Rich,*
> *Who sells tough Hen for Quail and Partridg.*
>
> 2. Witch.   *A health, a health to Sister T——*
> *Her Trade's chief beauty and example,*
> *She'll serve the Gallant, or the Pimp, well.*
>
> 3. Witch.   *A health, a health, to Betty B——*
> *Though she began the Trade but newly,*
> *Of Country Squires there's not a few lye.*
>
> *Chorus.*
> But of all the brisk Bawdes 'tis *M——* for me,
> 'Tis *M*—the best in her degree ;
> She can serve from the Lord, to the Squire and Clown,
> From a Guinny she'll fit ye to half a Crown.[68]

Next " Heccate *speaks to the audience* ".

Hec. Hail ! hail ! hail ! you less than wits and greater !
Hail Fop [69] in Corner ! and the rest now met here,
Though you'l ne're be wits—from your loins shall spread,
Diseases that shall Reign when you are dead.
Deed is done !
War's begun !
Great Morocco's [70] *lost and won.*
Bank-side Maulkin thrice hath mew'd, no matter :
If puss of t'other house [71] will scratch, have at her.
T'appease your Spirits and keep our Farce from harm,
Of strong Ingredients we have powerful charm.

The spells are enumerated at some length.

Heccate and ⎫   ⎧ *a Hellish noise*
all the three ⎬ Huff no more ! ⎨ *is heard with-*
Witches. ⎭   ⎩ *in.*

Hec. He that wou'd damn this Farce does strive in vain,
This charm can never be o'recome by man,
'Till Whetstones Park remove to Distaff Lane.
Within Singing.
Heccate! Heccate! Come away.

Hec. Heark I am call'd——

She then mounts her Basket Chariot. Thunder and Lightning :
while they are flying up *Heccate* Sings.

The Goose and the Gander went over the Green,
They flew in the Corn that they could not be seen.
Chorus,
They flew, &c.

The three witches Sing.

Rose-mary's green, Rose-mary's green,
derry, derry, down.
When I am King, thou shalt be Queen,
derry, derry, down.
If I have Gold, thou shalt have part,
derry, derry, down.
If I have none thou hast my heart.
derry, derry, down.

And thus amid the skirling of the besom-mounted witches
through the air the farce ends. A somewhat shambling Epilogue
of more ordinary kind appealed to the audience " To get good
Plays be kind to bad Travesty ".[72]

The last play written by Sir William Davenant was *The Man's
the Master* which is thus noticed by Downes. " The Man's
the Master, Wrote by Sir *William Davenant,* being the last Play

he ever Wrote, he Dying presently after ; . . . This Comedy in general was very well Perform'd, especially, the *Master,* by Mr. *Harris ;* the *Man,* by Mr. Underhill : Mr. *Harris* and Mr. *Sandford,* Singing the Epilogue like two Street Ballad-Singers." Philip Cademan played Don Lewis ; and, as Downes relates, received a terrible injury whilst acting this rôle. " Note, Mr. Cademan *in this Play, not long after our Company began in* Dorset-Garden ; *his Part being to Fight with* Mr. Harris, *was Unfortunately, with a sharp Foil pierc'd near the Eye, which so Maim'd both his Hand and his Speech, that he can make little use of either : for which Mischance, he has receiv'd a Pension ever since* 1673, *being* 35 *Years a goe."*

Pepys, who was at the first performance of *The Man's the Master* on 26th March, 1668, Thursday in Easter week, found " not anything extraordinary in it at all . . . though there was here and there something pretty : but the most of the mirth was sorry, poor stuffe, of eating of such posset and slabbering themselves,[73] and mirth fit for clownes ; the prologue but poor ". The originality of the epilogue struck him, however, although he notes that the King who was present " did think meanly " of the play. The house was crowded to excess. On a subsequent visit, Thursday, 7th May, 1668, he acknowledged that *The Man's the Master* " proves, upon my seeing it again, a very good play ".

The Persons represented in *The Man's the Master* are : Don Ferdinand, Father to Isabella ; Don John, Suitor to Isabella ; Don Lewis, his Rival ; Sancho, Steward to Don Ferdinand ; Jodelet, Servant to Don John ; Stephano, Servant to Don Lewis ; Isabella, Daughter to Don Ferdinand ; Lucilla, Sister to Don John ; Bettris, Isabella's Maid ; and Laura, Lucilla's Maid. The Scene Madrid. And in one House.

It is midnight and after, but Don John d'Alverad who has just arrived in Madrid from Burgos attended by Jodelet, his man, resolves to visit the house of Donna Isabella de Rochas, whose father has proposed her hand to him with a dower of 20,000 crowns. Don John receiving the lady's picture in little has fallen in love with his intended bride, and has in return sent her his portrait. Jodelet, however, roguishly dispatched his own likeness instead of his Master's. They see Don Lewis descending from the balcony of the house. Actually this gallant had been admitted by Bettris to visit Lucilla, of whom he is enamoured and who is lodging privately in the house. In order to spy out the land Don John determines to assume the character of a valet, and makes Jodelet pass as the Master. Don Ferdinand and Isabella are disgusted with this clownish and clouterly Don John who betrays a thousand rusticities. Affairs are complicated by the fact that Don Lewis, who is Don Ferdinand's nephew, has owing to an error in the darkness of the night killed at Burgos Don Diego, brother to Don John. Although Isabella deems Don John a serving-man she falls in love with him, and in the last scene when he resumes his proper character they are united and all is happiness. It appears, moreover, that Don Diego has recovered from his wound, although the fact was not bruited abroad, and when Don Lewis openly sues for the hand of Lucilla d'Alverad "a knot of Friendship" is tied, and "all offences past shall vanish like the dreams of Infancy", cries Don John as he embraces his new brother-in-law. There is some amusing comedy with Sancho, Stephano, Bettris, and Laura.

The Man's the Master was revived at Lincoln's Inn Fields on 15th July, 1726, as "not acted 12 years". Milward played Don John; Bullock, Sancho; and, her first appearance, Miss Fenton [74] (the original Polly), Lucilla.. The play was given twice.

Fifty years later on 3rd November, 1776, it was revived at Covent Garden with some slight alterations attributed to Woodward, and played four times that season with the following cast : Don Ferdinand, Dunstall; Don John, Lewis; Don Lewis, Wroughton; Jodelet, Woodward; Stephano, Lee Lewes; Sancho, Quick; Donna Isabella, Miss Leeson; Donna Lucilla, Mrs. Bulkley; and Bettris, Mrs. Mattocks.

The Man's the Master is to a large extent an adaptation of Scarron's famous comedy *Jodelet, ou le Maître-Valet,* which was produced in the spring of 1645, achieving a veritable triumph. It was published "chez Quinet" at the end of April of that year, and copies were soon in every hand. It was reprinted twice during Scarron's life, in 1653 and 1659. *Jodelet* long remained in the repertory, being given with applause as late as 16th January, 1780.

Written in three weeks, *Jodelet* is itself taken from a comedy of Francisco de Rojas Zorilla (1607–1648), *Donde hay agravios no hay zelos, y Amo criado,* produced in 1635 or 1636. This excellent dramatist in 1643 took the habit of Santiago. In 1642 the *parte primera* of his comedies issued from the press at Madrid.[75]

Davenant has perhaps taken a few hints for Jodelet's awkward rusticities which so disgust Don Ferdinand and Isabella from Filipin's extravagant behaviour in the salon of Hélène de Torrez in Scarron's *L'Héritier ridicule, ou la Dame intéressée,* a capital comedy produced in 1649. The disguised valet is, of course, a common character in comedy, and Molière's Mascarille in *Les Précieuses Ridicules* clearly looks back to Jodelet and Filipin. It were unnecessary to pursue the type throughout the English and French theatres, but perhaps a passing reference should be made to Pedrillo in John O'Keefe's *The Castle of Andalusia*,[76] which was produced at Covent Garden 2nd November, 1782, and achieved an immense popularity. The servant Pedrillo (Edwin) is taken for Don Ferdinando (Mattocks) who humours the mistake, and dresses himself in livery instructing his man to act the master. O'Keefe has borrowed more than a suggestion from Davenant here. The dialogue also reveals that he had pretty carefully read the older play.

There was, perhaps, no person of greater importance and influence in the earlier days of the Restoration theatre than the sixth son of the first Earl of Berkshire, Sir Robert Howard, poet, playwright, historian, critic, theologian, statesman, an " Ingenious Person " " equally conspicuous for the lustre of his Birth, and the Excellency of his parts ",[77] and almost equally conspicuous as a butt for irresistible satire, a fantastic figure " pretending to all manner of arts and sciences, . . . not ill-natured but insufferably boasting ".[78]

Since of his very many talents only his dramatic genius and his connexion with the theatre must be considered to concern us here a very slight sketch of his life will suffice in this place. I regret not to be able to give a longer account [79] of one who in spite of his eccentricities and whimsicality, his gasconading and encyclopædic pretensions to a universality of art,[80] learning, and literature, was a strangely arresting and in some sense a noble gentleman.

Born in 1626, Robert Howard proceeded whilst quite young to Magdalen College, Oxford.[81] At the outbreak of the Great Rebellion he enlisted in the Royalist forces, and was knighted upon the field for his gallant rescue of Lord Wilmot at Copredy Bridge, on 29th June, 1644. On 1st February, 1646, he married Ann, daughter of Sir Richard Kingsmill, of Malshanger, Church Oakley, Hants. During the King's exile Sir Robert was for a time imprisoned in Windsor Castle, and stood in danger of death. At the Restoration he was created a Knight of the Bath, returned member for Stockbridge in Hampshire, and appointed Secretary to the Commissioners of the Treasury.[82] He immediately displayed a keen interest in literature and things theatrical. Mixing freely among and patronizing the new dramatists, becoming closely intimate meanwhile with his future brother-in-law John Dryden,[83] publishing his *Poems*,[84] written in captivity, with Henry Herringman, the well-known bookseller of the New Exchange, Sir Robert Howard, a stout Whig—if we may by a few years anticipate the term—yet high in favour at Whitehall, established himself as a power in the Thespian world, the

PLATE VIII

SIR ROBERT HOWARD

Collection of the Author

more so since he furnished a full quarter of the money for the building of the Theatre Royal in Bridges Street, of which he held nine shares of the total six and thirty. Yet another and more domestic tie between Sir Robert and the theatre was his liaison with the beautiful Susanna Uphill,[85] whom Downes mentions as one of Killigrew's earliest actresses.[86] This amour did not escape the shafts of satire, for when Shadwell in his *The Sullen Lovers*, Lincoln's Inn Fields, 2nd May, 1668, so cruelly caricatured Sir Robert as Sir Positive At-all,[87] he exhibited Mrs. Uphill as Lady Vaine "A Whore, that takes upon her the name of a Lady ". A scurrilous political pamphlet[88] of 1677 under Hampshire notes Stockbridge, and says : " *Sir Robert Howard,* Auditor of the Receipts of the Exchequer, with 3,000*l.* per annum : many great Places and Boons he has had, but his *W—— Uphill* spends all and now refuses to Marry him." The canard seems a baseless jeer, for on the death of his second wife, Lady Honora,[89] daughter of the Earl of Thomond, in 1678, Susanna Uphill was wedded to her constant admirer. She died about 1691-2, for on 26th February, 1693, Sir Robert " (aged near 70), . . . married young Mrs. (Annabella) Dives, maid of honour to the princesse, aged about 18 ".[90]

To go back a little, on 4th February, 1679, Howard was returned member for Castle Rising, Norfolk, from which year, with the exception of 1683, he sat in all Parliaments until June, 1698. In February, 1689, he was admitted to the Privy Council, and early in June, 1690, appointed to command all the regiments and troops of Militia horse throughout England drawn together under the generalship of John, Earl of Marlborough. It is unfortunate that in his later years he was so strong an advocate for the Revolution that by his obstinacy and pride he made many enemies,[91] and was a great favourite with Mary II.[92]

Sir Robert Howard died on the 3rd September, 1698, " aged near 80," says Luttrell,[93] and he was buried with great pomp in Westminster Abbey.

It may well be supposed that Sir Robert proved no mere sleeping partner when, as a capitalist, he advanced so considerable a sum in December, 1661, towards the building of a new playhouse. He showed himself, indeed, a very important and active factor in the development of the Restoration stage, whilst his opponents did not scruple to say that he was as interfering as he was influential. Even as late as 1694 he was an arbiter in theatrical disputes, for when Betterton and the actors petitioned against Sir Thomas Skipwith and the patentees, the Lord Chamberlain invoked the aid of Sir Robert, and all parties concerned were bidden to present themselves on Monday morning, 17th December, before Lord Dorset and Howard at the latter's house in Westminster, " betweene 10 & 11 a Clock."

So remarkable, so extravagant, so forceful and conspicuous a figure was bound to be made " the subject of comedy " as Evelyn has it,[94] and when Buckingham in 1663–4 was penning the first draught of *The Rehearsal* he pricked down Howard as Robert Bilboa,[95] the swashbuckling [96] pretentious poet. However, as all the world knows, when the play came to be shaped finally nearly a decade had passed, and the protagonist of the burlesque took on the traits of Dryden, being immortally dubbed Mr. Bayes.

In *The Sullen Lovers,* as mentioned a little before, Shadwell drew Sir Robert Howard full length, a portrait which set the whole town a-talking and crowded the theatre.[97]

Howard's works were also travestied and burlesqued ; *The Duell of the Stags,* 4to, 1668,[98] was coarsely parodied by Lord Buckhurst in *The Duel of the Crabs* [99] ; there are constant scomms and fleers at his poem *Against the Fear of Death* [100] ; his *Reflections upon the Reigns of* Edward *and* Richard II, 8vo, 1690, and *The History of Religion,*[101] 8vo, 1694, were criticized with great severity and great justice, for they are certainly very dangerous and hurtful pieces.

Fortunately, however, we are only concerned with Sir Robert Howard's plays, and to these he devoted his earlier and better years. His first essay in the dramatic kind, *The Blind Lady,* described by the author as "A Comedy ", but to our idea perhaps more nearly answering to the term tragi-comedy, was never acted.

Mironault, Vaiwode of Lithuania ; and Phylanter, son of the Vaiwode of Ruthenia, Albertus ; both love the Princess Mirramente of Poland, who is secretly enamoured of the former although she conceals her passion. Mironault, whilst visiting the Princess, is attacked by his jealous rival, and barely escapes with his two friends, Hyppasus and Pysander, taking refuge (under the pretext that they have been set upon and spoiled by brigands) in the house of Cæca, an old Blind Lady, very anxious for another husband. Taking a great fancy to Pysander, a nimble soldier, she whispers in his ear :—

> When my last husband Sir *Percivall* died
> I little thought to have had another suiter ;
> But you men have the power to winn us,
> And I can tell you, such a Tempting Gentleman.

Acting on the adage

> old Lutes
> Still sound the sweetest,

Pysander makes fierce love to the venerable dowager, and also slyly courts her ancient waiting-woman, Quinever.[103] Presently he is given such complete control that he is able to assemble the tenants of his mistress and fortify her manor-house against Phylanter and his troops who are pursuing Mironault. Meanwhile Mirramente accompanies the royal forces dispatched by her father King Sigismond to rescue Mironault and punish Phylanter. Another contingent is accompanied by Amione, Mironault's sister, who hastens to her brother's aid. Phylanter rescuing Amione from the rude assault of certain plundering soldiers falls a victim to her charms, and craves forgiveness for his revolt, declaring his heartfelt repentance. The influence of Amione and the generosity of the Princess secure his pardon. Mironault is made happy with the hand of Mirramente, who confesses she has long loved him.

Pysander consents to make the wealthy Cæca a joyous bride, upon the persuasion of Mirramente :—

> Come *Pysander*,
> The god of Love himself is blind,
> She, or her estate (I hear) is very fair.

The actual plot of *The Blind Lady* seems to be original with Howard, but the play throughout in dialogue, incident, and atmosphere most plainly copies Fletcher. We recognize suggestions from *Philaster* in the first act ; " sweet Mistress *Quinever* " is closely modelled upon the famous Abigail ; and Pysander has much of Rutilio, Monsieur Thomas, and Don John. Phylanter's change of affection from the Princess to Amione is psychologically wholly in the vein of Fletcher's school.

Howard's piece is certainly far too irregular in the action, and it cannot be denied that the interest tends to shift from Mironault to Pysander and Cæca, with Quinever, her man Peter, and the rest of her household. The Princess Mirramente is nearly a lay figure ; or at any rate her character is not sufficiently sustained in the latter part of the play.

None the less the comic episodes are very good, and, if in some measure derivative, well-written and decidedly amusing. It was no doubt the disparity of the serious plot which hindered *The Blind Lady* from being brought upon the stage.

The first of Howard's plays to be acted was *The Surprisal* produced at the Theatre Royal, Vere Street, on Wednesday, 23rd April, 1662. The rhyming letter to which reference has already been made [104] says that this piece took well and got the actors money, for which they have to be thankful " That Lacy plaid Brankadoros part ".[105] The scene is Siena, and the principal characters are Castruccio; his nephew, Miranzo; Cialto, friend to Miranzo; Brancadoro, a rich Senator's son; Villerotto, a bold fellow in Brancadoro's service; Moreno, father to Emilia; Samira, Miranzo's sister; Emilia; and Taccola, her Governess. The plot, to use Howard's own expression, is "a pretty mingle". Miranzo, newly returned from travel, finds his old uncle on the eve of marriage with a young maid, Emilia. His sister, Samira, is sadly distressed since her lover Cialto, being ruined through the vileness of the wealthy father (now deceased) of the foolish fop Brancadoro, shrinks from pressing his suit, and her uncle actually designs her for Brancadoro. This latter in order to rid himself of a rival employs one Villerotto to waylay and kill Cialto. Now Villerotto is none other than the base Borazzo, who owing to rape and plunder was cashiered from his military command by Cialto, whom he pursues with mortal hate. Miranzo falls in love with Emilia, and in order to delay their marriages the two ladies escape to take a refuge in a nunnery, on the road to which, however, they are surprised (hence the title of the play) and carried off by Villerotto and his assassinates who are stalking Cialto. Samira and Emilia, whom the ruffian is on the point of ravishing, are rescued by Miranzo, who has disguised himself as a friar. Villerotto, sore wounded, is handed over to justice; Brancadoro owing to the bad part he has played is frightened into restoring the estate of which Cialto has been choused; and the lovers are severally united in happiness. Genest considered *The Surprisal* as "on the whole a moderate piece",[106] and one hardly cares to go beyond this verdict. There are good moments, and some well-written dialogue, which, however, is not sufficiently sustained.

That Howard's next play *The Committee,* produced at Vere Street in October, 1662, although as regards literary merit not perhaps the best of his pieces—from this point of view that place must be claimed for *The Great Favourite*—yet proved the most long-lived and by far the most popular is not at all surprising, since so cheery and amusing a comedy may well in blithe triumph keep the boards for a century and plus, when other more serious and solid work is consigned to a respectful oblivion. If the province of Thalia be to hold the mirror up to life, to entertain and whilst entertaining to instruct, *The Committee* as amply fulfilling all these conditions must be given a very high place in the English theatre.[107] The characters are drawn with the most admirable strokes, "galloping Abel" the loutish son and heir of the "Chairman of the honourable Committee of Sequestrations"; starched Obadiah with his fustian coat; the shrewd slippery Nehemiah Catch and snuffling Master Headstrong; even the impertinent twattling neighbour Chat and the Days' precisian servant with his "forsooth" and "a pretty while"; whilst Mr. and Mrs. Day themselves are worthy to be named in the same breath as some of the minor characters of Dickens.

The time of the play is the later years of the King's exile, the darkest hours before the dawn, whilst the Roundhead Covenanters and Committees of Sequestration were crushing all good men with their iron-handed tyranny and most audacious pillage. So photographic are the details, so unexaggerated the picture, that Howard's stark realism can hardly be termed a castigation, unless the truth itself be plain satire. It may briefly be said that "Covenanting work" was the Parliamentary despotism which compelled all men to subscribe to the Solemn League and Covenant (not to be confused with the Scotch National Covenant of 1638). This Covenant bound all subscribers under oath to join in the extirpation of "Popery and Prelacy, superstition, heresy, schism and profaneness" and to follow the example of "the purest churches", in other words to root out Christianity for the cant of the vilest conventicles. It was, of course, a political move to extirpate the Royalists.[108] Some cavaliers, being Catholics, were altogether exempted from pardon or grace; others were forced to compound for their refusal to subscribe by sequestration, a process which meant that the rebels seized their estates, which could only be recovered by the lawful owners yielding from a sixth to a half of the value. In 1657 unless a man took an oath which was tantamount to a denial of Christianity, he forfeited two-thirds of his estate to Cromwell.

The Committee, which gives its title to Howard's play, is the Committee of Sequestrations, whose Chairman is Mr. Day. This worthy, instigated and helped by his wife, a domineering termagant, who is an adept at such little practices as forgery and fraud, accomplishes the sequestration of the estates of two cavaliers, Careless and Blunt. Mrs. Day, moreover, has brought up as her own daughter, Ruth, actually Annice the child of the wealthy Sir Basil Throughgood, who died in the King's service. She is also scheming to marry her son Abel to Arbella, "a rich Heir of one of the Cavalier Party", whose estate is under sequestration, and whom the Days have inveigled to their house. The Committee when appealed to make no bones about putting the lady and her estate into Day's hands. Now Careless loves Ruth, and Blunt is enamoured of Arbella, and it requires all their wit to thwart the ambitions of Gillian Day. However, by the happy accident of securing old Day's keys and rifling his papers they completely turn the tables. Not only do they obtain the writings of their own estates, but they are able to shut Mrs. Day's mouth by evidence of state letters she has counterfeited. As for Mr. Day, Ruth discovers some very incriminating correspondence betwixt him and his wenches, when he sent them certain emmenagogic prescriptions, which one damsel however refused to take, so a young one came into this wicked world for want of the preventing dose. Perforce then all agree to be friends and dance at the double wedding.

The most famous character in *The Committee* was that of Teg,[109] the loyal blundering Irish servant,[110] who is so devoted to his new master, Careless, and so agreeably saucy to the Days, the Headstrongs, and Scrapes. This Handy Andy rôle was created by Lacy, a performance contemporary critics judged as " perfection " and " beyond imagination ".[111] Of the superlative merits of Lacy as an actor there was never any question, he " perform'd all Parts that he undertook to a miracle ", says Langbaine,[112] " inasmuch that I am apt to believe, that as *this* Age never had, so the *next,* never will have his *Equal,* at least not his *Superiour.*" One might think that the genius of Lacy created Teg, and no doubt this was to a large extent true, but we find the popularity of *The Committee* generally ascribed to Teg alone, as for example when in *The Lives of the Poets,* 1753, which went under the name of Theophilus Cibber, it is remarked, " This comedy is often acted, and the success of it chiefly depends upon the part of *Teague* being well performed," [113] and Scott in 1808 could write : " *The Committee,* alone, of Howard's plays kept possession of the stage till our time ; and that solely supported by the humours of Teague, an honest, blundering Irish footman, such as we usually see in a modern farce." [114]

After Lacy's death the rôle of Teg was taken by Anthony Leigh, who in July, 1686, when playing at Oxford at the Act much displeased King James II by some grossly offensive gag he had the effrontery to introduce into his lines.[115] Amongst other famous actors who supported Teg in the eighteenth century were Bowen ; Miller ; little Tom Griffith [116] ; Quin ; Macklin ; Jack Johnstone, who portrayed the part " in the most exquisite colours " [117] ; Barrington ; John Moody, " probably inferiour to Barrington, but was greatly superiour to any actor who has succeeded him ", and Rock, who, Boaden says, was considered too vulgar in his humour.

It is not known who originally acted Obadiah, but after the Union of 1682 Cave Underhill appeared in this rôle with great applause. In the eighteenth century Ben Johnson, Hippisley,

PLATE IX

THE COMMITTEE: ACT IV

Collection of the Author

Arthur, Suett, William Parsons, and Munden were [118] famous
Obadiahs. Many actresses of the first rank have not disdained
to support Mrs. Day, and even " the most beautiful woman
that ever adorned a theatre ",[119] Peg Woffington, in Mrs. Day
in The *Committee,* " made no scruple to disguise the beautiful
countenance by drawing on it the lines of deformity and the
wrinkles of old age ; and to put on the tawdry habiliments and
vulgar manners of an old hypocritical city vixen."

Chetwood [120] gives an interesting cast of The *Committee* as
performed at the Dublin Theatre Royal, Smock Alley, in 1715 :
Careless, Joseph Ashbury, then aged over seventy [121] ; Blunt,
Thomas Elrington ; Abel, Quin ; Obadiah, Joe Trefusis,
" a Person of infinite Humour and Shrewd Conceits," who was
(scandal said) a natural son of Oliver Cromwell [122] ; Teg,
Griffith ; Arbella, Mrs. Ashbury ; Ruth, Mrs. Thurmond ;
Mrs. Chat, Miss Schoolding, who after married the celebrated
Dancer, Moreau ; and Mrs. Day, Mrs. Martin, the original
Mrs. Peachum and Diana Trapes in *The Beggar's Opera.*

At Drury Lane *The Committee* was revived (for Moody's benefit)
as late as 21st April, 1778, and as " not acted 3 years " on
7th February, 1788, when *Selima and Azor,* a musical entertainment, first given at Drury Lane on 5th December, 1776, was
an added attraction. Previously on 29th December, 1760,
The Committee had been performed at Drury Lane as " Not acted
10 years ". Turned into a farce of two acts by Thomas Knight
and produced as *The Honest Thieves* at Covent Garden on 9th May,
1797, Howard's maltreated play achieved considerable popularity.

The Indian-Queen, produced at the Theatre Royal, Bridges Street,
in January, 1663-4, is the joint production of Howard and
Dryden,[123] and since it is very certain that the latter had by
far the greater hand in writing the drama it may more fittingly
be dealt with at length in the chapter of my work which surveys
Dryden and the vogue of heroic tragedies.[124] It will suffice to
remark here that the performance was arranged on a scale of
especial magnificence, with new scenery, and new costumes.
Original and elaborate effects were devised, for Killigrew and
Howard spared no expense to display the golden splendours of a
legendary Peru and a fabled Mexico. Ann Marshall, the leading
tragedienne of the day, created the title rôle, Zempoalla.

Enthusiastic Pepys who found the play " a most pleasant
show ", and that " the eldest Marshall did do her part most
excellently well ", tells us how even at revivals the whole world
doted upon Nan Marshall's acting, and talked of her excellence.[125]
Evelyn, a severe judge and censor, declared *The Indian-Queen*
to be " a tragedy well written, so beautiful with rich scenes

as the like has never been seen here, or haply (except rarely)
elsewhere on a mercenary theatre ".[126] The result was, as indeed
the play deserved, an artistic triumph in the theatre. Whether
it equally proved a financial success for the management is
doubtful, since in a masque introduced into Major Cosmo
Manuche's unprinted play *The Feast,* Northampton MS., Castle
Ashby, a character appears (p. 68) " drest in Antick feathers :
personating an Indian Queene ", whilst Shelter comments :—

> This is an Indian : Queene : whose speckle'd plumes,
> Brought such an Audience : fil'd the players roomes.
> And (without doub) had fil'd their pocketts to,
> Had not the ffeather makers claimed their due.

The Indian-Queen opens with the refusal of the Ynca of Peru
to bestow his daughter Orazia upon Montezuma, his conquering
general.   In consequence of this rebuff Montezuma transfers
his allegiance to the enemy, the Mexicans, and accordingly
restores to liberty the captive Prince Acacis, whom he has taken
in battle. Zempoalla, the Usurping Indian Queen, who maintains her empire by the aid of her paramour and general, Traxalla,
falls passionately in love with her new ally.   Fortune turns ;
the Ynca and Orazia are captured by the Mexicans. Now Acacis
also loves Orazia, whose beauty farther excites the lust of Traxalla.
Zempoalla is madly jealous of the Peruvian princess, and when
Montezuma rejects her love she determines to sacrifice in the
Temple of the Sun, the Ynca, his daughter, and the man who
scorns her desires.   At the crucial moment Acacis stabs himself,
and whilst his mother wails over his death, news is brought
that Amexia, the lawful queen of Mexico, has entered the city
at the head of vast forces.   Traxalla is slain by Montezuma who
is recognized as Amexia's son, and therefore a royal consort
for Orazia, whose father joins their hands.   Zempoalla drives
a dagger to her heart, exclaiming :

> The greatest proof of courage we can give,
> Is then to dye when we have power to live.

The story of *The Indian-Queen* is derived from the " Histoire
de Zelmatide heritière de l'Empire des Incas, et de la Princesse
Izatide " in volume I of De Gomberville's *Polexandre,* 8vo,
1641.[127]

The Indian-Queen kept the stage at intervals until the commencement of the eighteenth century.   One of the latest revivals was
in July, 1715, at Drury Lane.   An operatic version with music
by Henry Purcell, produced between May and October, 1695,
was represented at the Theatre Royal with overwhelming
success. Mrs. Knight acted Zempoalla ; and Powell, Montezuma.

The Vestal-Virgin, or The Roman Ladies, produced at the Theatre Royal in 1664, owes some slight suggestion to two romances, La Calprenède's *Cléopâtre,* 12 volumes, 1646–1658 ; and Mlle de Scudéry's *Clélie,* 10 volumes, Paris, 1656–1660. It has, moreover, all the panached and exotic equipage of these famous romances, and is (it must be confessed) singularly lacking in classical atmosphere. This, moreover, in spite of allusions to " the *Flavian Bridge* ", " *Janus's Gates* ", " the *Tiber* ", " *Numa's Grove* ", " the great *Flaminian* way ", " the *Tarpeian Rock* " (in the tragic version), and so forth, although it is rather hard to say with Genest that Howard " was superlatively ignorant of Roman manners ".[128]

There is much heroic passion in *The Vestal-Virgin* : Tiridates, the younger brother of the Armenian Prince Artabaces, " now a Prisn'er at large in *Rome,* and kept as Hostage," loves Hersilia, daughter of Emilius, "A Roman Senator of great Quality ". Sertorius, " One that had been a General," also loves Hersilia, but afterwards he is enamoured of Marcellina, her cousin, whom when " *it was Acted the Comical way* " he weds, whilst Artabaces upon rescuing from her father's burning house the Vestal Verginia, Hersilia's sister, at once falls a victim to the charms of this fair innocence. The brother of Sertorius, Sulpitius, who is " of a treacherous Nature ", lusts after Hersilia, whom he is resolved to possess at all costs. Accordingly he proceeds to sow quarrels leading to duello between Sertorius and Tiridates, and with the aid of Mutius, a villain, engenders other dark schemes including the setting on fire of the house of Emilius in order to carry off Hersilia in the confusion. Verginia falls into the hands of Mutius and he incontinently declares himself a slave to her beauty. Plot and counterplot involve the situation in so complex and horrid businesses that at the end of the piece all the lovers, gallants and ladies, are killed or fall by their own hands, leaving the monster Sulpitius with his crimes unripped to be dragged to justice and doom whilst Emilius pronounces :—

> The World shall weep for me when ever Fame
> Does but relate the *Vestal-Virgin's* Name.

This was felt to be too bloodthirsty, and so Howard by some changes in the Fourth Act and rewriting the greater part of Act V provided an alternative finale, in which only Mutius falls,[129] whilst Sulpitius as a punishment is sore wounded, but Hymen happily unites the leash of lovers.

Blood-boltered as the tragedy may be, it is preferable to this conclusion, which strikes one as inadequate and an anti-climax. Howard, no doubt, took the idea—a poor one—from Suckling's

Aglaura, originally acted at the Blackfriars, Christmas, 1637, and printed folio, 1638, of which Langbaine (1691) says : " This Play is much priz'd at this Day, and has this Remarkable, That the last Act is so altered, that 'tis at the pleasure of the Actors, to make it a Tragedy, or Tragi-comedy : which was so well approv'd of by that Excellent Poet Sir *Robert Howard,* that he has followed this president, in his *Vestal Virgin.*"

It may be remembered that the Hon. James Howard altered *Romeo and Juliet* " preserving Romeo and Juliet alive ", and that there are printed two alterations (both said to be by Waller) of the last act of *The Maid's Tragedy* in each of which the King, Evadne, Amintor, and Aspatia are left alive. In 1889 Sir Arthur Pinero was obliged upon production to alter the ending of his play *The Profligate* (written 1887), as the death of the principal character was deemed too tragical.

The Great Favourite ; *or, The Duke of Lerma,* was produced at the Theatre Royal on Thursday, 20th February, 1668, before a most brilliant audience, including the King and Court. Howard tells us in the Preface to the printed play, 4to, 1668, how he came to write this tragedy. A play called *The Duke of Lerma,* had been left with the King's Company to dispose of as they pleased. This was submitted to Howard for his opinion, who when he read it found the script frankly impossible although the historical events certainly gave opportunity for a good drama. Thereupon Charles Hart, knowing that Sir Robert was going into the country, persuaded him to employ his leisure on a piece on the same subject.[131]

The pious but feeble Philip III of Spain (born 1578 ; reigned 1598–1621) gave up the whole government of the kingdom to his favourite Don Francisco de Sandoval y Rojas, Marquis of Denia, and (1599) Duke of Lerma, who became all powerful. The splendid extravagance of Lerma who lived and ruled " in a whirlwind of squandering waste, surrounded by pompous pride and unscrupulous dishonesty " drained to exhaustion the wealth of the very Indies and dragged the Spanish Empire to ruin.[132] Don Rodrigo Calderon, the favourite of the favourite, and Franquesa, the clerk of the council of finance, for years hoarded huge masses of gold and silver, and waxed more insolent and more lavish with the wealth of others. The Queen, Margaret of Austria, raised her voice against the wanton riot, and in 1611 Calderon, now Marquis de Siete Iglesias, was dismissed. When the Queen shortly after died in childbirth, rumour at once declared that she had been poisoned. Encouraged by Aliaga, the King's confessor, Lerma's false son the Duke of Uceda began to engineer his father's fall, a scheme in which he was powerfully aided by Gaspar de Guzman, Count of Olivares. On the 4th October, 1618, Lerma obtained the red hat from Pope Paul V, but was presently banished from Court, and retired to Valladolid, whither, when he hurried to Court to the dying King in March, 1621, he was curtly bidden to return. Philip III expired on 31st March, and within a few days Calderon's head fell on the scaffold in the Plaza Mayor at Madrid; the Duke of Uceda was disgraced and breathed his last a prisoner; even Aliaga was exiled; and Lerma himself was not spared, although he fought stoutly for his plunder. He died in 1625.

Philip IV, with whom the theatre was a passion, in 1627 saw upon the Madrid stage, Maria Calderon, the *Calderona,* who became his best-loved mistress and the mother of Don Juan José of Austria, who was legitimatized in 1642.

Sir Robert Howard's drama commences when Philip III lies at the point of death, and it has been remarked that his " version of this history is a model of adaptation ".[133] The Duke of Lerma, who in spite of Philip's command forbidding his presence at Court is stealthily prowling to and fro in the corridors of the palace at Madrid, has resolved with the help of Caldroon (Rodrigo Calderon) and the Confessor (Aliaga) to recover his estate and power, for which end he seeks to employ the beauty of his daughter Maria, a character in some sense drawn from the Duke of Uceda and the actress Maria Calderon. The Queen-Mother, who is inimical to Lerma, is disposed of by a subtle poison. The young King, as her father devised, falls passionately in love with Maria, who is torn between her country's shaken honour and her own. After a struggle she causes Lerma's plans to fail and lends her aid to his opponent the Duke of Medina. The confessor, learning of this at Naples, makes an end by a venomed draught; Caldroon is led to instant execution; and Lerma is summoned before the Council. There are few more effective scenes than when he appears not as a suppliant or guilty, but in all the pomp of pontifical state, clad in his sweeping scarlet robes, My Lord Cardinal, a sovran prince, whose sacred person the Grandees dare not touch nor molest. Baffled they can but snarl and gnash their teeth as with serene front and matchless dignity he passes from their presence to a safe retreat and secure retirement. The King, who is not married, and his whole Court fall at the feet of Maria, whom they salute as the saviour of her country, whilst her royal lover pleads with her not in vain to share his bed and throne.

There is a grandeur, an unexpected force in this climax which rises to very great heights of power and concentration, and

here at any rate Howard shows a genius, which to my mind
informs the whole play, but which save for *The Duke of Lerma*
might have been denied him. It has been well said that Howard's
" treatment of the original story is not only brilliant in the
matter of selection, omission, and addition, but is daringly
successful in its novel untragic seriousness. . . . His language
is always good . . . and at times is full of such bold fancy that
it is almost great. His characterization is admirable, Lerma,
Caldroon, the weak but charming King, the finely gracious
Queen, Maria—all are more than types, they are real human
beings in whose fate the audience must be interested ".[134]

Pepys who judged *The Duke of Lerma* " a very good and
most serious play " thought that it was designed to reproach
Charles II with his mistresses, which seems a little far-fetched,
indeed he expected the first performance " should be interrupted ; but it ended all well, which salved all ". The rôle
of Maria was acted by Nell Gwyn, who with Mrs. Knepp spoke
the prologue " most excellently ".

The Duke of Lerma is written in blank verse of a fine quality,
with some scenes and speeches in rhyme. The famous dispute
between Dryden and Sir Robert Howard belongs to the History
of Criticism and need hardly be glanced at here, but in the
Preface to *The Duke of Lerma* Howard very effectually disposes
of the restrictions of the Unities, and wisely remarks " *I shall
not discommend any Poet that dresses his Play in such a fashion as his
fancy best approves* ".[136]

Howard's comedy *The Country Gentleman,* designed to be
produced at the Theatre Royal on Saturday, 27th February, 1669,
caused a great stir in the world. Sir Robert had in this new
play collaborated with the Duke of Buckingham (to whom is
dedicated *the Duel of the Stags*), and this satiric nobleman introduced into these scenes a gross caricature of Sir William Coventry.
This was noised abroad and the result proved that Sir William
enraged at the insult promptly invited his Grace to measure
swords. In a news-letter [137] dated 2nd March, 1669, and sent
by John Starkey in London to Sir Willoughby Aston at Madeley,
near Stone, Staffs, the writer relates in reference to the affair :
" The occasion this, there was a new play to be acted on Saturday
last called the Country gentleman said to be made by the Duke
& Sʳ Robt. Howard, wherein tis said that the Earle of Clarendon,
Sʳ W: Coventry and some other Courtiers are plainly personated,
but especially Sʳ William in the midst of his table of writinge,
this he (or some of his relations) would not brooke, but whether
he or the Lᵈ Hallifax was to fight the Duke is not knowne, but
the King hath prevented all ; and the play is not acted." On

4th March, Coventry was committed by the King to the Tower on account of his challenge to Buckingham, a Privy Councillor. He was not released until 20th March, but during his confinement to the great chagrin of the Duke's party he was visited by a very notable number of important men, desirous of openly showing their sympathy and respect.[138]

On 3rd September, 1697, Dryden writing from Denham Court, Bucks, to his two sons, Charles and Henry, at Rome, says: "After my return to town, I intend to alter a play of Sir Robert Howard's, written long since, and lately put by him into my hands : 'tis called *The Conquest of China by the Tartars*. It will cost me six weeks' study, with the probable benefit of an hundred pounds." In December of the same year he tells Tonson : "I have broken off my studies from *The Conquest of China*, to review Virgil."[139] In the British Museum is a small folio volume, Add. MSS. 28692, which contains, folio 3*a*–69*a*, a version of Rochester's alteration of Valentinian under the title *Lucina's Rape ; Or, The Tragedy of Vallentinian*. In the same hand, folio 70*a*–75*b*, is "A Scaen of Sr Robert Howard's Play, written by the Earl of Rochester " : a vigorous piece of rhyming verse.[140] The scene opens with the Chinese army awaiting the Tartar attack. There are three battalions. The Empress Amacoa leads the main body ; on the right hand is Hyachian ; on the left Lycungus.[141] Even on the field itself there is a good deal of love and jealousy, and Lycungus deeming that the Empress prefers Hyachian withdraws his advancing troops and bids them stand still, quiet, nor fight a stroke. It is evident from a letter of Sir Robert Howard to Rochester written on 7th July, 1672, that he was then busy with his play. Howard speaks to Rochester, who is at Adderbury, of the scene which the Earl is writing for his play, and adds " nor shall I repine to see how far you can exceed me ".

At Dorset Garden on 28th May, 1675, was produced Elkanah Settle's tragedy *The Conquest of China, By the Tartars*,[142] in which it may be remarked there is a character, played by Sandford, Lycungus, Prince of China, who is a traitor and a villain. Sir Robert Howard was interested in the Theatre Royal and to this house he would have given his tragedy. It is not impossible that the production of *The Conquest of China* by the rival theatre caused him indefinitely to lay aside his script.

Sir Robert's elder brother Edward and his younger brother James were also dramatists, although neither proved in any sense his equal. Edward, indeed, was the chiefest butt of the wits of the day. Lacy, the actor, once roundly told him that he was " more a fool than a poet ", whilst Rochester, Buckingham,

Buckhurst, kept emphasizing the same unwelcome news in pasquil and lampoon. He is described as being insufferably conceited, and he was the one person in the world (they said) who took himself seriously. In order to show his light-hearted jocund wit he was wont to introduce into his gait and gestures a silly thousand affectations which ill accorded with the blankness of his long foolishly-solemn face and codfish eyes. " There goes the Melancholy Knight ! " the maids and courtiers used to cry as Ned Howard stalked down the corridor at Whitehall.[143]

Shadwell drew him in *The Sullen Lovers* as "A conceited Poet, always troubling men with impertinent Discourses of Poetry, and the repetition of his own Verses "; Poet Ninny, and the name stuck. Buckingham immortalized Edward Howard at a rehearsal of one of his own sterile plays. Ever restless, ever interrupting the actors, ever bragging, ever praising his own scenes, his mouth full of whimsical phrase and petty boast, he used to cry out to his friends in an excess of admiration : " Gad, it will pit, box, and gallery with any play in Europe." If one of the assistants happened to commend an actor, and remark, " Sir, he does it admirably," "Ay, pretty well," the author grudgingly replied, " but he does not hit me in't ; he does not Top his part "—a great word with Mr. Edward Howard.[144]

The Honourable Edward Howard, the fifth son of the Earl of Berkshire, was baptized at S. Martin-in-the-Fields on 2nd November, 1624. Of his life little beyond his literary activities is certainly known. His first play *The Usurper,* a tragedy, was produced at the Theatre Royal, Bridges Street, on Saturday, 2nd January, 1664, although it was not given to " *the Stages Tyring-House* " the press until 1668.[145]

The scene is laid in Sicily, and the characters are Damocles, the Usurper ; his son, Dionysius ; Cleander, " *The true King disguis'd like a Moor, under the name of* Hiarbas " ; Cleomenes, *a faithful noble Person* ; Demaratus, a worthy senator ; his son, Parmenis ; Hugo, *A Parasite and Creature of the Usurpers* ; Arisba, *A Moor, and Servant to King* Cleander ; various Commanders under the Usurper and his son ; Senators ; Soldiers ; Timandra, "*An* Affrican *Queen that preserv'd and lov'd the King* Cleander " ; Calanthe, the King's Sister ; and Ladies.

The first act which is interesting and well-written shows Sicily groaning under the tyranny of Damocles and his military, headed by Hugo de Petra, Colonel Strato, and other ruffians. The usurper convenes the Senate at Timoleon's Tomb, in order, as he persuades the nobles, to resign his power and place. Actually he coerces the assembly with considerable violence, his soldiers knocking down and wounding all who resist him, and when their weary General (as he dubs himself) proffers to give up his sword and place, the well-schooled cravens invite him to the crown with cries of " long live *Damocles* King of *Sicily* ". At this juncture Dionysius returns from the African wars, bringing with him as captive Queen Timandra of Numidia, in whose train is the Moor Hiarbas, being none other than the true King of Sicily, Cleander, supposed drowned. His sister, Calanthe, disguised as a page and called Polydore, is taken into the service of Damocles, who falls in love with Timandra only to find a rival in his son Dionysius. A good deal of intrigue results, during which the Usurper when his son prevents him from raping Timandra does not stickle to cut the youth down with " Villain, Bastard ! " Timandra is ordered to captivity, and Hiarbas who falls under suspicion is to lose his head. However, Lord Cleomenes, who has been working loyally in the dark, turns the tables and introduces Cleander to the Senate as their lawful sovran. He is rewarded with the hand of Calanthe, and the King takes Timandra to his throne. Damocles on being haled before the royal justice stabs himself to the heart, whilst the abominable Hugo de Petra is led away to prison and the gallows tree.

It is very easy to recognize that Damocles represents Oliver Cromwell ; Hugo de Petra, Hugh Peter ; Cleomenes, Monk, Duke of Albermarle ; and in some sort Cleander is Charles II. The play is political,[146] but the resemblances must not be pressed too far and it would be foolish, for example, to see Minette— the Princess Henrietta of England and Madame of France— in Calanthe.

Even without the topical reference the play may be read with no little pleasure, and when produced it met, as it well deserved, " *grateful Acceptation from the Judicious,*" as Edward Howard informs us.[147]

A persistent rumour asserted that old James Shirley helped Edward Howard in the composition of his pieces,[148] and if so it must have been *The Usurper* which thus benefited, although it is hardly possible to trace the hand of the greater dramatist.

On Monday, 15th April, 1667, Pepys going to the Theatre Royal found it was the first day of a new piece, and consequently the house was crowded, the King and Queen, the Duke and Duchess, and all the Court there. " The play called ' The Change of Crownes ' ; a play of Ned Howard's, the best that ever I saw at that house, being a great play and serious ;   only Lacy did act the country-gentleman come up to Court, who do abuse the Court with all the imaginable wit and plainness about selling of places, and doing every thing for money. The play took very much." The King was mighty angry, " and it was bitter indeed, but very true and witty." According to a news letter of 23rd April, 1667, Lacy was promptly imprisoned because he had introduced offensive gags into his part, a point which should be emphasized as sometimes it is missed. " 22nd. Lacy, the famous Comedian, is at length by great intercession, released from his durance under the groom porter, where he stood committed by his Majesty's order for having on his own head, added several indiscreet impressions [expressions] in the part he acted in a late play called *The Change of Crownes* written by Mr. Edward Howard." The house was forbidden to act again until Mohun, Charles' favourite, obtained leave to act but not this play. In his anonymous attack on Steele, *The Characters and Conduct of Sir John Edgar, call'd by Himself Sole Monarch of the Stage in Drury-Lane; and his Three Deputy-Governors,* 8vo, 1720, John Dennis says that in Restoration days those of the King's players who gave offence were sent to Whitehall and whipped at the Porter's Lodge, " and I have heard *Jo Haines* more than once ingenuously own, that he had been whipt twice there." [149] It seems as though Lacy had been thus flagellated over *The Change of Crownes* affair, and further trouble ensued when the actor, upon his release from the Porter's Lodge, smarting no doubt in a very real sense, met Edward Howard " who congratulated his release ; upon which Lacy cursed him as that " it was the fault of his nonsensical play that was the cause of his ill usage ". The poet promptly struck him in the face with his glove, whereat Lacy retaliated with a blow from his cane. The world wondered that Howard did not run him through on the spot, but, no, a complaint to the King did the business ; and " Whereas John Lacy hath both in abusive words and actions abused the honourable Edward Howard Esquire " he was re-arrested, and the house once more closed down in anger. The order for Lacy's second arrest for his abuse of Edward Howard, dated 20th April, 1667, requires him to be delivered " into the Custody of the Knight Marshall or the Deputy " and there is an order dated 25th April that the actor should be brought before the Lord Chamberlain. As there has been some confusion over the whole episode it is well that it should be clearly understood that there were two arrests upon two several and separate accounts, the assault upon Howard being subsequent to Lacy's first imprisonment and tawing.

The Change of Crownes was never printed, but in reviewing Howard's work we ought at least to remember that in this drama we have lost what one cannot doubt was a very remarkable play.

Of *The London Gentleman* entered in the Stationers' Register on 7th August, 1667, but seemingly not printed, nothing is known.

Edward Howard's fourth play *The Womens Conquest*, a tragicomedy, was produced at Lincoln's Inn Fields early in November, 1670, and printed 4to, the following year. In the long and interesting Preface the author has given us a valuable piece of criticism, which seems to be universally neglected and unknown. His remarks upon heroic plays,[150] the historical drama, and indeed upon tragedy and comedy in general, are both keen and just, and worthy of serious consideration. The fable of *The Womens Conquest,* he tells us, is entirely new, but " The misfortune it had in having some of the Parts ill and imperfectly performed, as also the laying down of it, the sixth day of its being presented, when the Audience was very near as considerable, as the first day it was Acted, as also an intermission hitherto occasioned by the long absence of some principal Actresses, could not but prejudice the esteem it gain'd, and might have been improved in a further time ".

The scene is Scythia, and the long cast included : Henry Harris, Tysamnes, a Persian Prince, Marry'd to the Queen of Scythia, Parisatis, Mrs. Betterton ; Bassanes, A General and Prince of the Blood of Scythia, Young ; William Smith, Foscaris, a Gentleman of Quality, who longs for his Wife Clarina (Mrs. Shadwell) after he had parted from her ; John Crosby, Andrages, Another Husband, who loves his Wife Melvissa (Mrs. Dixon) so well that he cannot part from her, though she seems to provoke him to it ; Toxaris, Alvanes, and Araxis, Scythian courtiers, Sandford, Cademan, and Norris ; Draxanes and Eumenes, friends to Bassanes, Adams and Westwood ; Mrs. Long, Madana, Queen of the Amazons ; Mrs. Lilbourne and Mrs. Wright, Cydane and Renone, her Embassadresses ; Mrs. Johnson, Statyra, a great Persian Lady, formerly belov'd by Tysamnes ; and Mrs. Mary Lee, Daranthe, Chief Commandress of the Amazons.

A law exists in Scythia that any husband may at his own mere caprice without cause or reason divorce and separate from his wife. Bassanes, returning from a glorious conquest over the " grim-look'd Tartars " is ill at ease when he finds that Queen Parisatis has married Tysamnes, since this Persian Prince was aforetime contracted to Statyra, who indeed presents herself at Court to seek revenge. Tysamnes, however, has her straitly confined to her own lodgings.

Mandana, Queen of the Amazons, refusing to suffer in the neighbouring realms a law so derogatory to the honour of the female sex, demands that it shall be repealed, and when her request is refused the virago host invade Scythia and carry all

before them so that the land is " inclos'd By female powers "
and Mandana is greeted with

> Glad tidings, mighty Queen, the King and all
> His power is now surrender'd to your General.

It is decreed that Tysamnes shall be sacrificed at the temple
altar, and meanwhile a Moorish damsel Zeriffa is appointed
his guard. Bassanes, however, with Zeriffa's aid contrives the
escape of the royal prisoner, and then whilst all the female
warriors are assembled to celebrate the Women's Conquest he
enters with a vast following of soldiers and points the way to
a nobler victory. Parisatis enters in state and reveals that she
was the dusky Zeriffa. Mandana accepts the love of the noble
Bassanes, and it is resolved that all the Amazon ladies shall
be united to Scythian nobles, the old law of divorcement being
incontinently repealed for more hallowed and surer matrimony,
the pattern being

> what's most
> Laudable, the form of happy *England*.

Statyra generously declares that she has found the fullest accomplishment of her wishes in the universal happiness.

Some lighter episodes agreeably diversify the more romantic
scenes. Foscaris, who for an idle whim has divorced his wife,
falls passionately in love with her and they come together again.
Melvissa so cleverly manages her husband that although he
seems to have every inducement to avail himself of the law
he never seeks to profit by its provisions. In her popular comedy
Every One has his Fault,[151] produced at Covent Garden, on
29th January, 1793, Mrs. Inchbald has adopted these characters
from Howard, for quite plainly Sir Robert Ramble (Lewis) is
Foscaris ; Miss Wooburn (Mrs. Esten), Clarina ; Placid (Fawcett)
Andrages ; and Mrs. Placid (Mrs. Mattocks), Melvissa.

The Womens Conquest boasts no less than three Prologues.
The first is a dialogue between Angel and Underhill, who are
presently joined by Nokes. A Changeling enters to give the
Prologue, " *the Farce way exactly*." First he dances ; " *then is
heard a noise with Thunder and Lightning, at which time* Ben. Johnson
personated rises from below." The actors retire, "After which
Ben. Johnson personated, goes up to the Audience and speaks
a Prologue." Yet a Third Prologue is delivered by another
actor. The Epilogue, written in triple rhymes, is " Spoken by
the Queen of *Amazons* ", Mrs. Long.

The most tolerable scenes of *The Womens Conquest* are those
of Foscaris and Clarina, Melvissa and Andrages. It is a disappointing play, altogether too artificial when it sets out to be

romantic and poetical. So with difficulty it ran its six nights, and was laid to rest.

Howard's next essay *The Six Days Adventure, or The New Utopia* was produced at Lincoln's Inn Fields in March, 1671, with the following cast : Sir Adam Meridith, Underhill ; Sir Grave Solymour, Medbourne ; Featlin, his son, Crosby ; Mr. Franckman, Harris ; Polidor, Young ; Tom Foppering, Nokes ; Mr. Peacock, Angel ; Euphorbus, Sherwood ; Orlando Curioso, Sandford ; Serina, Mrs. Betterton ; Celinda, Mrs. Shadwell ; Crispina, Mrs. Long ; Eugenia, Mrs. Mary Lee ; Petilla, Foppering's wife, Mrs. Dixon ; Two Ladies, Mrs. Ford and Mrs. Clough. There also appear a Blackamoor Boy, " disguiz'd like a Woman," Magistrates and Citizens of Utopia. The Scene, Utopia.

The constitution of Utopia has a statute directing that the government of the country may alternately be in the hands of either sex, and the ladies announce their intention of handling the reins. Amid a noise of drums and trumpets the female parliament is set, and the citizens deliver up mace, sword, and charter to Madam Serina, the President. Tom Foppering boasts that he cares not, as he has so lustily swinged his wife that she is brought into most absolute obedience to her lord and master, a vaunt his fellows take leave to doubt when upon the entrance of Petilla he hastily runs off to conceal himself in very henpecked fashion. Some are perturbed ; some look upon the situation as a fine jest ; whilst Jack Peacock, an adonized dandiprat who piques himself upon his new habit of gaudy feathers, is supremely indifferent who may rule the roost. Eventually all these political tangles are set straight by the dissolution of the republic, when Polidor, a prince of the old Utopian blood, ascends the throne, taking Serina as his Queen, and monarchy succeeds anarchy.

Sir Grave Solymour, who affects the most precisian severity although secretly given to chambering and private fornication, has cruelly used and discarded his son Featlin, but pursues Celinda, whom the lad loves, and delivers himself of such edifying precepts as " Love, and be secret ", and " 'Tis scandal that makes sin, not Sin the scandal " together with a gift of jewels that she promises to receive him in her chamber, when he will find her a-bed and expectant of his embraces. The old lecher hurriedly throws off his gown, chuckling to himself, "And with thee I put off my gravity," and is just about to pop between the sheets, when as he draws back the curtains there thrusts out her head a black-a-moor wench darker than Hades, and he deems that some cacodemon or sooty bogle is come to punish his hypocrisy, whilst Featlin his own son and other company rush in and catch him fast. It is pronounced he must marry the lady of whatever complexion she may be. He has indeed infringed a new statute of the female senate :—

> Our most sacred law of love by making your
> Lascivious attempt on this Lady . . .
> For which you are censur'd by our body politick
> To espouse this beautiful Black.

The Ethiop is greeted with all ceremony as my Lady Solymour, and Featlin encouragingly remarks :—

> I have heard those sun-burnt females are most
> Delicious in embrace,

whilst Franckman jeers :—

> If you get a Mag-py Child (as there may be some
> Danger) I'll invite my self Gossip.

At the end when Featlin receives the hand of Celinda, she releases her poor father-in-law from his sad predicament by discovering that the Moorish trull is but her black page in petticoats.

Intercalated with the main design of the play are the episodes of Jack Peacock, the new Narcissus, a " Bird of Manhood ", who owing to the strange arts and Paracelsian Recipes of the quack Orlando Curioso is persuaded that he has begotten another self, as he expounds—

> the same man as I am—out of me . . .
> By which means I am now in love with my self twice
> Over, (that is to say) I am doubly the same.

Shortly after " *Enter* Peacock *and* Euphorbus *drest like him, hugging one another* ". " He is call'd *Euphorbus,* in honour of *Pythagonas's* own Transmigration," [152] the sage Orlando comments. Finally Peacock is seen " *half naked and weeping* ", as he wails " Euphorbus, my other lovely being in my self " has vanished. Whilst he was asleep, his fine Vest of Feathers, and a pocketful of money were filched. "A good moral of self love," Franckman warns him, and he is told " that self of thine was but a Link-Boy Design'd to abuse thy Credulity . . . 'twas a just punishment of thy humour Of self affection, and may all that doat too much Upon themselves deceive themselves accordingly ". But they cannot cure Jack Peacock. He forgives the theft of the money, and sets off to try all the feather shops in Town, either to recover his old suit or fashion him a new one.

The Six Days Adventure, if a fantastic, is a highly amusing comedy. The characters of Sir Adam, the " first Man of mirth ", and Sir Grave, of opposing humours, seem suggested by old Mr. Merry-thought and the wealthy Merchant, Luce's father, in *The Knight of the Burning Pestle.*[153] Some few hints for the plot may have been afforded by *The Sea-Voyage,*[154] of which there was an important revival at the Theatre Royal on 25th September, 1667, and which held the stage with applause for some years. The trick played upon Sir Grave is a variant of Jonson's *Epicœne ; or, The Silent Woman,* as Howard's contemporaries did not fail to observe.[155] None the less Howard's episode of the black-a-moor is nearer to the Italian comedies, Machiavelli's *La Clizia,* v, 23, Nicomaco's account of his adventure with Siro ; Lodovico Dolce's *Il Ragazzo* (1541), iii, 2, and iv, 1 and 7, particularly when Giacchetto tells Ciaco of the event of his assignation with Messer Cesare ; and also the whole intrigue and climax of Aretino's admirable comedy *Il Marescalco* (1533). Eighteenth-century gossip said that a similar Ethiop trick—perhaps even suggested by the *Six Days Adventure*—had once been played upon Fleetwood, the Drury Lane manager of Garrick's earlier years.

Upon the stage *The Six Days Adventure* was a complete failure, and although Howard had himself paid out no less than three hundred pounds to produce his play, it could not win through for more than a couple of performances :—

> And it kept up the Second Night :
> And suddenly Utopia fell,
> Damn'd to the lowest pit of Hell.[156]

The author, no doubt justly, attributed his disaster to a furious clique of his enemies, who seem to have caused something like a riot in the theatre, which practically prevented the actors from continuing the comedy.

The last (and worst) play by Edward Howard, *The Man of Newmarket,* was produced at the Theatre Royal in March, 1678, with the following cast: Wiltshire, Passal ; Burt, his friend Maldrin ; Martin Powell, Sir Ralph Nonsuch, a publick ridiculous pretender, and a Luxuriast ; William Harris, Whiffler, a finical fop ; Swiftspur, Trainsted, and Bowser, three gentlemen-racers of Newmarket, Clarke, Goodman and Griffin ; Carey Perin, Plodwell, a lawyer ; Mohun, Breakbond, a wild gentleman, obliging the Sex of Women ; Coysh, Pricknote, an hypocritical sectary and knave ; Mrs. Corbet, Clevly ; Mrs. Baker, Jocalin ; Mrs. Corey, Quickthrift, a lady of wit, but proud and covetous, courted by Plodwell ; Mrs. Farlowe, Luce, a pretended Miss to

Sir Ralph. To Flora, Jocalin's "Twin and onely" sister, there is no actress's name. Scene, London.

I fear we cannot dissent from Genest's verdict on *The Man of Newmarket*: "This is a very poor comedy by the Hon. E. Howard—it has neither plot nor incident—nor has the dialogue anything in it to make up for the deficiency in other respects." [157] Swiftspur and Trainsted are in London, lodging for a night or two at the Red Lion in Holborn, as we gather from the gossip of five jockies whose talk opens the First Act. Swiftspur and Bowser indeed prate of nothing but horse-races, matches at Newmarket, the royal hawks and hounds. We catch a glimpse of Plodwell courting Mrs. Quickthrift, and later (in the Second Act) we have the puritanical Sir Ralph Nonsuch, comparing notes with other precisians, and pluming himself on having "no small intrigue in burning the Pope's Image on last *November*." [158] Luce, Plodwell, Mrs. Quickthrift, Clevly, Jocalin, Passal, wander in and out, seemingly almost at random, and the jockies discuss the stables with Trainsted. A dance by the characters [159] concludes Act II. Whiffler and Isaac Pricknote make love to Luce, and Plodwell presses his suit on Mrs. Quickthrift. Act IV: "*The Scene opens with the 3d and 4th* Jockey *mounted on the shape of two Horses.*" Presently we are regaled with "*A dance of* Jockeys, *with their whips in their Hands.*" Plodwell tries the effect of new modish clothes, a feather and sword, upon Mrs. Quickthrift, and when the lady finds that if she marries any other save this persevering suitor she must pay £5,000 out of her estate she easily consents to reward his constancy. Maldrin is united to Mrs. Clevly, and there are other weddings, the play concluding with a general resolution to take the road to Newmarket for the next race-meeting.

A prose Induction spoken by Robert Shatterel and Joe Haines, was followed by a Prologue in verse delivered by Clarke. Mrs. Baker spoke the Epilogue.

It was especially this piece which caused Dr. Doran [160] to write of Edward Howard: "His characters 'talk', but they are engaged in no plot; and they exhibit a dull lack of incident." It seems almost superfluous to add that *The Man of Newmarket* was a failure, absolute and complete.

As we have said, the wits made Edward Howard their particular prey,[161] and it cannot be denied that *The Man of Newmarket* is poor stuff. We must, however, remember the high opinion that Pepys formed of *The Change of Crownes*, whilst of Howard's extant plays *The Usurper* and *The Six Days Adventure* are not without considerable merit. They lack, for example, that touch of amateurishness which so often mars the work of his younger

brother James, a defect that might conceivably be covered up
to a great extent in the theatre by brilliant acting, but which
is hardly to be so disguised in the cold perusal of the closet.
Yet could James have but written with a surer touch, if he had
but in some sort revised and more firmly gripped his work,
he would incontestably have proved far the better dramatist
of the two.

James Howard was the youngest son of the Earl of Berkshire.
Of his life practically no details are known, but it would seem
from an allusion in *The Session of the Poets* [162] that he was a mere
lad when he turned dramatist :—

> *James Howard* being call'd for out of the Throng,
>   Booted and spur'd to the Bar did advance,
> Where singing a damn'd nonsensical Song,
>   The Youth and his Muse were sent into *France.*

The English Monsieur is to be dated as early as the summer
of 1663, but we will first notice Howard's Shakespearean adaptation, for the sole mention of which we refer to Downes, who
having chronicled a revival by Davenant of *Romeo and Juliet*
adds : " This Tragedy of *Romeo* and *Juliet,* was made some time
after into a Tragi-comedy, by Mr. *James Howard,* he preserving
Romeo and *Juliet* alive ; so that when the Tragedy was Reviv'd
again, 'twas Play'd Alternately, Tragical one Day, and Tragicomical another ; for several Days together." Nor would this
have appeared to a Restoration audience at all extraordinary.

Henry Harris played Romeo ; Betterton, Mercutio ; and
Mrs. Betterton, Juliet. It was in Howard's version that
Count Paris's Wife, acted by Mrs. Holden, appeared. Downes
speaks of " a Fight and Scuffle " between " the House of *Capulet,*
and House of *Paris* ", and records that famous slip of the lady's
tongue which convulsed the house with laughter.[163]

The English Monsieur, although not printed until 1674, was
produced at the Theatre Royal not later than July, 1663. This
date is fixed by an entry (quoted by Miss Ethel Seaton in a letter
to *The Times Literary Supplement,* 18th October, 1934) which
occurs in the Diary (*Itinerarium*) of the celebrated Danish scientist
Oluf Borck, who visited England in the summer of 1663, and
who saw this comedy on the 30th July of that year.

" The Names of the Persons " are : Mr. Welbred, a wild
Gentleman, Servant to the Lady Wealthy ; Mr. Comely, his
Companion ; Mr. Frenchlove, the English Mounsieur ; Mr. Vaine,
one who to gain the reputation of a Debauch belyes himself,
and all women he knows ; Jack Arch, his foot-boy ; Two
Parsons ; Gripe, a scrivener ; A Hector ; an English Taylor ;

an English Milliner; a French Taylor; a French Merchant; William, a Wiltshire Clown; Lady Wealthy, a rich widow, in love with Welbred; Two Ladies of her acquaintance; the First Mrs. Crafty, a courtezan, Mistress to Frenchlove; the Second Mrs. Crafty, a courtezan, her sister, mistress to Vaine; Elsbeth (or Elsba) Pritty, a Country Lass, sweet-heart to William. Scene, London.

Welbred has long courted the Lady Wealthy, a rich widow, but she only rallies him when he presses his suit with, " I'le lay a wager thou hast lost all thy money at Play, for then you'r alwaies in a marrying humor." He brings a little levite to her house and urges her to take him then and there. She consents, but declares he must satisfy a vow she once made, namely that the parson who tacked them together must have a fee of ten Pieces in Gold ere he commence. "A very Pious Lady," the minister ejaculates. Welbred's pockets are empty, and she laughs at him heartily for having left his money at the Groom-Porter's. Moreover she refuses him any future admittance unless he can show an hundred pound in Gold before he is received into her presence. To no purpose does he try to effect an entrance, the door is shut fast in his face, and Lady Wealthy from her window derides his plight. Welbred now bargains with an old scrivener, Gripe, who goes with him to the door and knocks. Gripe lends Welbred an hundred Pound in Gold to display to the maid who answers, and instantly retrieves his cash. The same trick is played a second time, but the maid spies how the gold is slipped back into Gripe's hands, and informs her mistress, who challenges Welbred to a game of ombre, which he manages to decline, whereupon she summons a parson, and promises to become his bride directly the fee of ten pieces is produced. As he stands confounded and abashed she banters him on the ill event of his stratagem, but later she passes her word to marry him, and although when he sends a billet-doux on the happy morning to delay the ceremony as hour or so as he is at play and winning largely she pardons him after a little fret and they are duly united.

Mr. Comely is a young gentleman who, in spite of his having indulged in a liaison with (the second) Mrs. Crafty, has never known what love may be, and is weary of a town-life, its amours and its pleasures. He states his resolve " that for my future health i'le retire into the Countrey for Air, and there Hunt and Hawk, Eat and Sleep so sound, that I will never dream of a woman, or any part about her ". He bids farewell to Welbred and the ladies, but just as booted and spurred he is about to mount and ride off, he meets a country-lass, Elsbeth Pritty, escorted by William, a yokel, whom she is about to marry. Instantly he falls in love with her sweet face, and no longer proceeds on his journey. The ladies may laugh and quiz, but in spite of the Maid's rustic garb " a straw Hat, a Quaif, a red Wastcoat, and a green Petticoat not long enough by two handfuls ", he dotes upon her fresh innocence and beauty. He offers to marry her, and seeks to tempt her with " holland smocks lin'd with Lace of 40s. a yard, Gold Petticoats and Wastcoats, Diamonds in your Ears, Pearls about your neck, Bracelets of Rubies about your hands, Silk Stockings on your legs, and Gold and Silver Shooes on your feet ". Nothing, however, will wean her affections from William, her Wiltshire swain. (It may be remembered that the Earl of Berkshire, James Howard's father, had a seat at Charlton, Wilts.) Comely so approves of her fidelity that although his heart is well-nigh breaking he settles a portion upon her of £100 a year, and can but hope to seek forgetfulness and consolation in foreign travel, distance and long absence from home.

Frenchlove, the English Mounsieur, is a capital character. " That I should have an English father and mother, and they a French son," he laments. " I confess though an English Nurse taught me to go, a French Dancing-master taught me to walk," he boasts. The first Mrs. Crafty, most cunning of the harlot kind, draws him into her net (with the help of her old lover, Welbred), by a supreme affectation of everything of " the pretty French fancie " and the trout is rarely tickled. When, seeing that he is well within ear-shot, she directs her discourse to the disparagement of " the dull English fancy " and the English ladies, the fop on the hook murmurs to himself " This must be some person of Quality that has been in *France,* I know by her despising the English women ", and in a few moments he is praising her " Celestial beauty " as well as letting her know " I adore the truths I heard spoke by your fair tongue ". Then with a congée to the ground : " O—Madam your opinion is beautiful as well as your face." There is an amusing episode when two English tradesmen, who have formerly served French-love, enraged at losing his custom, wait for two French tradesmen whom he now patronizes, bully and fairly challenge the unfortunate Monsieurs until they perforce consent to sell Frenchlove English fashions supplied by the native workmen as French, and hand over the money. Our exquisite coxcomb who is very complete in his capricio infinitely prefers a " French noise " to a noise made in England. From his mistress he takes " a denyal with a French tone of a voyce, so that it was agreeable ", and as the lady leaves him he observes " she walks away with a

French step ", which when Vaine cannot see he raps out " Not see't *mort dieu*—then draw your Sword ".

It will be readily remembered that Wycherley in *The Gentleman Dancing-Master* has drawn an exceedingly diverting picture of the English Gallomaniac, who was so common a type at that time, whilst Dryden's Melantha in *Marriage A-la-Mode* with her affectations and her famous lists of French words which begin at *Sottises* and end *en Ridicule* is an exquisite piece of purest comic wit.

Charles Lamb, however, found something even more particularly pleasant in the fopperies of James Howard's Frenchlove, and such admiration is no mean praise.[164]

Vaine and Jack Arch, his foot-boy, are an amusing couple. The master pretends to be a great conqueror of the fair sex, a very Alexander in love and intrigue, so that when he is in company young Mercury must needs bring him sweet sugared messages from the ladies, or deliver obvious billets-doux. For this service Jack demands freightage, and extorts many a vail and fee under such threats as " I am resolv'd to go serve Mr. *Welbred,* if you will not now raise my wages—and tell the whole course of your life ", whilst his master can but grumble, " Well sirrah i'le give you twenty shillings a year more ; this humour of mine keeps me in awe of my own foot boy, and yet I cannot leave it," since in reality Vaine is diffident and a bungler, but nevertheless he is trepanned at last into matrimony by the second Mrs. Crafty, Comely's blowing.

It is possible that for the two sisters Crafty Howard took a hint from the *sorores meretrices,* Bacchis of Athens and Bacchis of Samos, in the *Bacchides* of Plautus.

Pepys regarded *The English Mounsieur* which he saw on Saturday, 8th December, 1666, as " a mighty pretty play, very witty and pleasant ". He further remarks : "And the women do very well ; but, above all, little Nelly, that I am mightily pleased with the play." On the occasion of another visit, Tuesday, 7th April, 1667, he judged that " the play hath much mirth in it as to that particular humour ". Nell Gwyn acted Lady Wealthy, but she could not, of course, have originally created this rôle, as in 1663 she was not upon the stage. Hart was Welbred ; Kynaston, Comely ; and Lacy, Frenchlove. Mrs. Knepp also appeared in this comedy, but it is uncertain whether she sustained the first Mrs. Crafty or Elsbeth Pritty.

The scene where Comely, about to leave London, changes his resolve on seeing Elsbeth is parodied in *The Rehearsal,* iii, 5, when Bayes introduces " *Prince* Volscius, *going out of Town* ". Volscius meets Parthenope, and falls in love. Uncertain whether to go or stay, he sits down to pull off his boots debating all the while, and finally " *Goes out hopping with one Boot on, and the other off* ".[165] This speech of Volscius occurs in a MS. with the heading : " On the humour in Mr. Howards Play, where Mr. Kinaston disputes his staying in, or going out of Town, as he is pulling on his Boots. In Imitation of the Earle of Orrery." [166]

The third play by James Howard, *All Mistaken, or The Mad Couple* was probably produced at the Theatre Royal in September, 1667, during which month it was seen by Pepys, but there is no record of the first performance. In the quartos the cast is not given, but the Actors' Names are listed as follows : The Duke (Archemedos) ; Ortellus, next of Kin to the Duke, of an Ambitious and Trecharous Nature ; Arbatus, suppos'd Brother to Artabella ; Philidor, a Mad Kinsman of the Duke, in Love with Mirida ; Zoranzo, The Dukes Prisoner of War, in love with Amarissa ; Pinguister and Lean-man, Two Rediculous Lovers of Mirida ; Doctor to Pinguister ; Taylor to Lean-man ; Taylor ; Amphelia, in love with the Duke ; Artabella, the Dukes Sister, but taken for the Sister of Arbatus ; Mirida, Philidor's mad Mistress ; Amarissa, in love with Zoranzo ; 6 Ladies ; 3 Nurses with Children. Scene, Italy.

The play opens with the state entry of the " Duke *from War, in Tryumph, leading in his hand* Artabella, *a Woman of that Countrey from whence he came with* Arbatus *her Brother, and* Zoranzo *Prisoner, and on the other side* Amphelia *and* Ortellus *and Guard* ". In spite of the fact that he is passionately enamoured of Amphelia, who also dearly loves him, the Duke announces his forthcoming marriage with Artabella. It appears that he has been led to suppose he is scorned by Amphelia, whom his pride forbids him to supplicate under such conditions. The lady for her part has been persuaded that he holds her beauty cheap, and in the full flush of her resentment she feigns she is about to bestow her hand on Ortellus, who, however, is soon rebuffed when he ventures to urge a suitor's right. Zoranzo is condemned to die, but before the execution Amphelia, admiring his brave spirit, visits him in his dungeon and promises to contrive his escape. Ortellus, learning where she has been and conceiving that she is enamoured of the captive, not only informs the Duke, but plans that the next interview between Zoranzo and Amphelia shall both be seen and overheard by his royal master, who mad with jealousy commands " lay 'um in Shackles both ", and proceeds to order that they shall both be beheaded. Ortellus being next heir to the dukedom should the Duke leave no issue, reveals to Arbatus who is something surprised his sister's nuptials should be so strangely procrastinated, that the Duke does not intend to marry Artabella, and prompts the wrathful young soldier to revenge the injury. That night escorted by Ortellus, Arbatus appears at the Duke's bed-side and threatens the " drowsy Devil *Duke* ", but Artabella enters in the nick, and confesses that it is she who has done the wrong since she refused the Duke's hand in spite of his pleadings. Stunned and confounded, his sword falling from his grasp, Arbatus staggers from the room, whilst Artabella bursts into a flood of tears as the Duke all wildered asks :

> Oh *Artabella,* why didst take my
> Sin upon thy selfe, hiding Thy Innocence
> With a face of Guilt . . .

Artabella. Because I love you, Sir.

There now arrives Amarissa, who is betrothed to Zoranzo, since finding Amphelia chained beside her lover she believes him false, and begs the Duke to hasten their doom. Upon the very scaffold the headsman has sharpened his axe when the Duke cries aloud that he will die himself the first ; his pride is vanquished and he falls at Amphelia's feet. She reveals how she came to mistrust his love, and the treacheries of Ortellus are exposed. This base lord is only granted his life because he holds a secret, which he confesses to be that Artabella is the Duke's very sister. Zoranzo and Amarissa are united ; happiness reigns supreme.

As Genest says,[167] the comic scenes of this play are very good, Philidor and Mirida, the Mad Couple, being excellent characters. They fall in love with each other, but protest against marriage. Philidor is persecuted by three nurses, " Plaguy hunting Bitches," who have the charge of a leash of children, his by-blows. Nor is this all, for six ladies, with whom he has been a little too intimate upon promises of marriage, chase hard at his heels, and wherever he goes Mrs. Mary, Mrs. Margaret, Mrs. Sarah, Mrs. Martha, Mrs. Alice, and Mrs. Elinor come following after. In vain he essays every turn and trick to evade their attentions. Mirida has two suitors, Pinguister, an exceeding fat man, and Lean-man, who is thin as a rake. She pledges herself to marry the former when he is slim and elegant, and she vows to give her hand to the latter so soon as he has put on ample flesh, and is comely plump. Lean-man employs a tailor to bombast out his clothes, but Pinguister has recourse to more drastic methods. A doctor administers a swingeing purge, and the sudden effects are " ludicrous, but the humour is of the lowest species ". Philidor eventually has to pretend to be suddenly deceased, and Mirida summons her two lovers, the six ladies, and the three nurses, to hear the will, which has such bountiful bequests

> Of Moneys and Legacies, I leave to be
> Rais'd and Paid out of my Mannor
> Of *Constantinople,* in which the
> Great Turke is now Tennant for Life . . .

that all follow the bier in a long mourning train to the family vault. Philidor and Mirida slip out, and clap to the door. A little later Philidor as a town-crier with huge clanging bell cries the lost folk through the streets. When he is near the vault the captives flock to the grate, and hail him lustily, but he feigns neither to see nor hear. Mirida then presents herself at the grate, and pretending to console them jeers the poor wretches, whose intolerable position is now made unsavoury to a degree on account of the diarrhœal evacuations of the luckless Pinguister. When the party have set their several hands to a paper discharging and quitting Philidor from all promises and all arrears of nursing, the key is thrown to them through the bars, but Philidor and Mirida have vanished ere the dishevelled and discomfited company emerge from their weary confinement.

Although, of course, by no means the prototypes, we recognize in Philidor and Mirida that couple of madcap lovers whom Dryden was so fond of portraying, and who attain a perfection of wit and humour with Celadon and Florimel [168] in *Secret-Love ; or, The Maiden-Queen.* Pinguister and Lean-man are suggested by the fat gentleman and the thin citizen in Shirley's *The Wedding,*[169] Lodam, and Rawbone, who court Mrs. Jane, but Howard has greatly improved the hint.

The serious plot of *All Mistaken* in outline owes something to *A King and No King,* and a hint for one of the episodes is from *The Maid's Tragedy,* which were two of the most applauded Beaumont and Fletcher plays in the Restoration theatre.

There is a reference in a letter written by Henry Savile from London, 4th May, 1665, to his brother Sir George Savile (first Marquess of Halifax), which mentions a comedy wherein the humour seems to have been much the same as that of Pinguister's remedies, and it is curious two pieces should have exhibited so similar incidents : " I am newly come from my Lord of Orrery's new play called The Widow, whose character you will receive from better hands. I will only say that one part of it is the humour of a man that has great need to go to the close stool where there are such indecent postures as would never be suffered upon any stage but ours, which has quite turn'd the stomach of so squeamish a man as I am, that am used to see nothing upon a theatre that might not appear in the ruelle of a fine lady." [170] It only remains to add that no play *The Widow* of Orrery's writing is known, and certainly the incident Savile describes seems very foreign to that noble author's vein.

Full as romantic and even more rococo than the plays of the Howards are the dramas of Robert Stapylton (Stapleton), who died in 1669, aged about seventy years. The third son of Richard Stapylton of Carlton by Snaith, Yorkshire, and his wife Elizabeth, daughter of Sir Henry Pierrepoint of Holm Pierrepoint,[171] Robert Stapylton was educated at S. Gregory's, Douai, the Benedictine Monastery of the English Congregation,[172] and here on 30th March, 1625, he was solemnly professed.[173] His ill-balanced and wayward temperament unfortunately soon exhibited itself, and he proved so capricious and infatuate as even to break his vows, a tergiversation amply justifying the opinion of Sir Edmund Gosse that Stapylton was "an apparently lunatic person".[174] Having returned to his native home the ex-monk, whose Benedictine training had made him a scholar of no mean pretensions so that he was "not only Known, but Admired throughout all *England*",[175] found himself welcomed at Whitehall, and as his loyalty (whatever his faults and follies) was conspicuous, he was appointed one of the gentlemen of the Privy Chamber to Prince Charles. Warmly attached to the King's service, he was knighted at Nottingham,[176] 13th September, 1642 ; and after Edgehill, 23rd October, he accompanied Charles I to Oxford, where he was created D.C.L. in the following month. Here he remained devoting his whole time to study until the city surrendered to Fairfax in May, 1645. Stapylton then withdrew to a country house where he lived in close retirement, surrounded by books, and left comparatively unmolested owing to his extreme seclusion. He now wrote his first play, *The Royal Choice,* entered on the Stationers' Register, 29th November, 1653, but not printed. At the Restoration his appointment as one of the Gentlemen Ushers of the Royal Privy Chamber was confirmed by Charles II, and he became a familiar figure at Whitehall. He died on the 10th or 11th July, 1669, and on the 15th July was buried near the vestry door of Westminster Abbey.[177] By a will dated 11th June, 1669, and proved on 29th July by Elizabeth Simpson, widow, he left her practically his whole estate on account, it was stated, of her great care during his long illness. His wife, for one regrets to say he had married, is barely mentioned. She was a Mrs. Hammond, *née* Mainwaring. His talent lay much towards translation, and beside his plays he is the author of many works, amongst which are the following : *Pliny's Panegyricke,* Oxford, 4to, 1644 ; *The First Six Satyrs of Juvenal,* Oxford, 8vo, 1644 : *The Loves of Hero and Leander,* Oxford, 4to, 1645, and London,

PLATE X

SIR ROBERT STAPYLTON

8vo, 1647 : *Juvenal's Sixteen Satyrs*,[178] London, 8vo, 1647 ; folio, 1660 ; 8vo, 1673 : *De Bello Belgico* [179] of Famianus Strada, S.J., London, folio, 1650 and 1667. He also on occasion obliged his friends with copies of complimentary verses.[180] Of Stapylton's *Juvenal* it may candidly be allowed that although overesteemed by Langbaine and obscured by Dryden this version has merits not a few.

After the Restoration *The Slighted Maid* was "Acted with Great Applause " [181] at Lincoln's Inn Fields, being first given during February, 1663. Henry Harris played Salerno, "*An aery young Prince, who (being refused by his Love) is a pretender unto Mistresses* "; Betterton, Iberio, " *The Prince's Friend, a jealous Lover* "; Medbourne, Filomarini, " *The Prince's Uncle, a prudent and pleasant old Lord* "; Smith, Lugo, " *Filomarini's son, who will not be governed by his father* "; Philip Cademan, Arviedo, "*A name which conceals the poverty of* Giulio, *the young Heir to the Family, Honour, and Valour of the Great Captain* Gonsalvo " ; Young, Corbulo, "*A valiant Lieutenant, constrained by his wants to be* Decio's *Porter* "; Underhill, Peralta, "*A desperate Sea-captain, who (being pardon'd for Pyracy) falls to cheating* "; Robert Nokes (the elder), Gioseppe, " *Master of a Ship, a Vigilant Spie upon* Menanthe "; Sandford, Vindex, "*Decio's Slave, who by his faithful Ingenuite merits his Freedom* "; Mrs. Gibbs (afterwards Mrs. Shadwell) Decio, " *The Slighted Maid, Ericina, who (to revenge her refusal by* Iberio) *assumes the person of her dead Brother,* Decio " ; Mrs. Betterton, Pyramena,[182] "*A passionate Lady, who (having the Jealousie of him she loves) marries one She knows not* "; Mrs. Long, Diacelia, " *Elder Daughter to the Prince of* Bulgaria " ; Mrs. Williams, Leandra, " *Younger daughter to the Prince of* Bulgaria " ; James Nokes (the younger), Menanthe, "*An Impudent Cheat, a* Greek *Impostress, who takes upon her to be mother to* Leandra " ; and Robert Turner, Joan, "*A fat merry Hostess.*" "*The Instrumental, Vocal, and Recitative Musick, was composed by* Mr. Banister." The Scene, Naples. The time contemporary. The Turkish war in Candy is spoken of, and the Infidel landed there in 1645, not finally reducing the capital city until 1667.

Young Lugo Filomarini was designed by his father, the guardian of Diacelia, to wed that princess, but on the eve of his nuptials he falls in love with Leandra, whose supposed mother, the Greek Menanthe, passes in Naples " for an Illustrious Lady ". To the surprise of all, old Lord Filomarini will not stay even for the marriage-banquet, but early on the morning of the very day declares that he must set forth at once on a sea-voyage, to which the most urgent business presses him. Now the Prince of Salerno had been a suitor for Diacelia's hand, but she preferred his cousin Lugo, and upon the rejection of his suit he vows he will henceforth be a fickle libertine in love. Iberio, his friend, once wooed Pyramena, but upon some quarrel owing to his jealous humours she gave herself in a pique to Decio, a Venetian gentleman, the brother of the lady Ericina, the Maid whom Iberio slighted, and who died heart-broken at his cold indifference and scorn. Iberio realizes that Decio, a mortal enemy, is studying revenge. As Diacelia, squired by the Prince, her quondam suitor, is about to proceed to the church, Gioseppe disguised hands her a letter from Lord Filomarini bidding her beware as Lugo intends to " fly off " the match. Iberio visits Pyramena at her home, only to learn from the Prince of Salerno that Decio, having (it seems) already failed to dispatch his hated rival by poison, is plotting to assassinate him. Iberio manages, however, to evade the trap. Upon the adjournment of her marriage Diacelia, under the directions of Filomarini, who has secretly returned to Naples, disguising herself as a Spaniard and calling herself Fritilla, takes service with Menanthe. Filomarini himself as Draco, and Gioseppe as Hosepe, are also employed as domestics in the same house in order to rescue Leandra, whom the beldame, supposed her mother, carried off from Candy, and whose beauty is to be set up for market. Arviedo becomes very friendly with Decio, and they are busy arranging a masque for

St. *Gennaro's* day,
Patron of *Naples,*

that is to say 19th September. Menanthe marries Peralta, the Spanish pirate who has courted her for her wealth. He then begins to lay siege to Fritilla, and proposes they shall escape to Rome with his old wife's store of gold and jewels. Arviedo's masque is presented exhibiting the Evening " *in a Crown of Shadow'd Stars, and a Clowdy Vest with some small Stars upon it, brought in with Winds* ", and Jack-with-the-Lantern " in a black Suit border'd with *Glow-worms,* a Coronet of shaded Beams on his head, over it a Paper Lantern with a Candle in't ". It is very charming but brief, and curiously enough it is presented to Decio and Pyramena rather casually, and almost intrudes on the business of the play. Even the poetry hardly excuses this interruption, and this is probably why it was burlesqued in *The Rehearsal,* Act I, where the Prologue to Mr. Bayes' play is spoken by Thunder and Lightning.

Peralta confides in Filomarini, whom he deems Draco the serving-man, that he designs to elope with Fritilla carrying off the hag Menanthe's diamonds. Leandra rejects with disdain Lugo's hand reproaching him with his desertion of Diacelia, whilst

Menanthe urges her to become the Prince of Salerno's mistress. Peralta conveys Fritilla to fat Joan's osteria near the harbour, where, however, he encounters Menanthe, who has been fore-warned by Draco (Filomarini). Much confusion ensues, and Menanthe being brought to the bar of justice with her accomplices confesses that Leandra is the younger daughter of the Prince of Bulgaria, and that with the jewels committed to her charge she stole away this lovely child when the Turks invaded Candy. Peralta and Menanthe are banished; Filomarini discovers him-self; Lugo is accepted and forgiven by Diacelia, and the Prince of Salerno weds Leandra. Decio who has at length secretly contrived to poison Iberio and Pyramena invites the whole company to a masque. " *The Scene* Vulcan's *Court, over it is writ,* Foro del Volcane. *Soft Musique.*" Aurora and Phoebus sing a very sweet dialogue, which is interrupted by the noise of the Cyclops at their forges. Vulcan enters with four half-drunken Cyclops, who fall into a dance. Mars and Venus are to be awakened from their amorous slumbers : " Iberio *and* Pyramena *discover'd lying on a Bed, at the Bed's feet sits* Cupid *weeping.*" Decio appears with a flashing rapier in his hand. In place of poison he has administered an opiate, and then thus exposed their embraces to the whole assembly. He declares he will revenge himself upon Iberio for his treachery to the Slighted Maid, Ericina, and upon Pyramena for cuckolding him. Pyramena declares her innocence, and Decio proclaims :—

<blockquote>You shall live Man and Wife, . . .
Behold the *Slighted Maid.*</blockquote>

" Decio *puts off his Night-gown, & discovers himself to be a Woman,*" Ericina herself. All ends happily with the nuptials of the Slighted Maid and Arviedo, who is really Giulio, heir to the Great Captain Gonsalvo.

The worst fault of *The Slighted Maid* is that the incidents are extremely intricate yet disconnected. It is not difficult to see that the plan was quite clear in the poet's mind, but he has not been at the trouble to give his episodes any logical sequence or natural coherence, and Dryden in the Preface to *Troilus and Cressida ; or, Truth found too Late,* 4to, 1679, when discussing Dramatic Action which must have integral Order, criticizes the Spanish Plots where accident is heaped pell-mell upon accident, instead of one accident inevitably producing another, adding : " *Of this nature, is the* Slighted Maid ; *where there is no Scene in the first Act, which might not by as good reason be in the fifth.*" [183] This, of course, is altogether going too far, but it is true none the less that Stapylton's baroque comedy lacks the entirely just decorum of regularity.

Genest [184] on the other hand gives it as his opinion that the plot is complicated but orderly conducted, a lenient judgement, to which few (I fear) will be found to subscribe. Perhaps it is better to regard *The Slighted Maid* with its masques and music as a kind of embryo opera and to allow it the contemporary fantastries of that species. With all faults—to use a phrase beloved of the booksellers—Stapylton's comedy remains a very delightful piece.

The plot would seem to be original. Decio's epitaph pronounced upon Iberio and Pyramena is from Martial, Liber I, Ep. xiv, *De Arria et Paeto*.[185] Arviedo's masque of the Evening and Jack-with-the-Lantern is parodied in *The Rehearsal*,[186] Act V, when Bayes makes " the Earth, Sun, and Moon come out upon the Stage, and dance the Hey " [187] to represent an eclipse, and confesses " I took the first hint of this out of a Dialogue, between *Phoebus* and *Aurora* in the *Slighted Maid* ".[188]

The cast of Stapylton's second acted play produced at Lincoln's Inn Fields in November, 1663, *The Step-Mother,* was as follows : Sandford, Sylvanus, Prince of Verulam ; Betterton, Filamor, his Son ; Young, Adolph, Son to Pontia, by the Prince of Malden ; Underhill, Tetrick, favourite to Sylvanus ; Price, Fromund, Filamor's Tutor ; Smith, Crispus, Pontia's general ; Medbourne, Capito, his lieutenant-general ; Lovell and Robert Nokes, Gracchus and Sergius " *Two Gladiators, which the* Romans *call'd the* Retiarius *and Sequutor* " [189] ; Mrs. Williams, Pontia, Princess of Malden, second Wife to Sylvanus ; Mrs. Betterton, Cæsarina, her daughter by the Prince of Malden ; Mrs. Davies, Violinda, daughter to Sylvanus ; and Mrs. Long, Brianella, Pontia's Favouritess, The Scene, Verulam. " *The Instrumental, Vocal, and Recitative Musick, was compos'd by Mr.* Lock."

Prince Filamor, who has just returned from Italy, still wooes in spite of her coldness the Princess Cæsarina, daughter by a former husband to his step-mother Pontia, of whom the scholar Tetrick observes :—

> Pluto could not have rak'd him out of hell
> Such a *Step-Mother,* she reigns o're his Father.

It may at once be remarked that the essential weakness of *The Step-Mother* lies in the psychology of Pontia. I will not say that her character is impossible, because in these days of Freud and post-Freudianism perhaps anything is possible, but she is at least presented as acting from such sudden and seemingly capricious motives that her moods are as many and as diverse as the changes of Proteus. Filamor wooes the Princess Cæsarina with a short masque, such as Stapylton greatly favoured, of Cupid and a Flamen. This entertainment, pretty enough in itself, but intrusive, is observed from a balcony by Pontia, her son Adolph, and her confidante Brianella. The Queen entirely approves Cæsarina's unkindness, and discloses to her two children a scheme she has pondered for sending Filamor

> To Hell :
> Nor shall he go so far alone ; his Father,
> *Sylvanus,* And his Sister *Violinda*
> Shall bear him Company.

Accordingly she has summoned her forces from Malden, intending to seize Verulam for her own, and in order to find out the event of her plans

> she leaves
> The Temples of the Gods, to consult Witches.

However, Tetrick masquerades as a conjurer and Fromund as a witch to divert her with their artifices and false predictions. Sylvanus, Filamor, and Violinda meet in Barnet Woods, where apparently the old King hopes to escape for a while from the tyranny of his young wife. Pontia now visits the haunted beech to consult the powers of evil. " *In the Bard's Cave is discovered a Man with a grey beard, in a Russet Gown, sleeping with a Harp in his hand.*" Pontia writes her wish :—

> DIS MANIBUS. Pontia *devotes to hell*
> Filamor, Violinda, *and* Sylvanus.

Familiars appear, " *an he and a she,*" and the Bard awaking sings to his harp an ambiguous enough prophecy, such as seers use. Then " *The Scene of the Bard is shut up* ", and Pontia gives her general Crispus the commission to capture Verulam, which he refuses. The paper is conveyed to Sylvanus, who is unwilling, in spite of his danger, to strike :

> Shall I destroy my wife for her first fault ?

he asks. A masque of Apollo, Phaeton, and Daphne is now introduced wherein Filamor plays Cephalus and Adolph Actaeon. Filamor after the interlude dances a corant with Cæsarina, but Pontia has hired two gladiators to assassinate him meanwhile. The swordsmen seize Cæsarina and Violinda, who are rescued by Filamor, whilst Pontia thinking to kill the Prince stabs her own son Adolph, upon which Filamor swoons at his friend's feet. In spite of all this confusion we learn that the " Mask goes on ", and Sylvanus is to appear as the woodland god, his namesake. Adolph has not been seriously hurt since his mother's poniard glanced off a " Gold Tablet next his heart ", a locket containing " Princess *Violinda's* Picture ". Pontia enters dressed as Diana, Cæsarina as Flora, Brianella as Procne, and a Second Masque is given, in which Violinda is Philomel. In a long rhyming speech Pontia (apparently for no reason) confesses various dark stratagems and murderous intents, declaring her "Publick Penitence" and joining the hands of Filamor and Cæsarina, Adolph and Violinda. None the less Sylvanus rejects his wife's prayer and orders her to instant execution. The tables are completely turned by the arrival of the Malden troops at the critical moment, and Pontia ascending the throne of judgement sentences Sylvanus, Filamor, and Violinda. To her husband she observes :—

> Your wither'd narrow heart could afford me
> But half an hour ; I'l give you a whole hour.

To which he returns with some spirit :—

> Bountiful wife, you are extream obliging.

Adolph resolves to save Filamor and Violinda, and at last Cæsarina weds the Prince, and Violinda her rescuer. All, however, are surrounded and brought before Pontia together with Sylvanus led by an executioner. Pontia declaring

> So, now I'm all that I can wish to be ;
> O 'tis the Queen of all Felicities
> To have full pow'r to *reward* and *revenge,*

suddenly gives her full consent to the marriage of Filamor and her daughter, bestows the Principality of Malden upon her son and Violinda,

> For I'l depend only upon my husband :
> For whose pardon and love thus low I beg.
> *Sylvanus.* Rely on me, and you'l be a good Wife,
> Then I shall study to forget your Evill,
> And love you for your Goodness.

As Crispus remarks :—

> Now *Pontia,* like the Planet of the Night,
> Breaks from her Clowd, and shews us her pure light.

So we take our leave of this curiously fantastic and improbable play.

The legend of the lovers of Abydos had long fascinated Stapylton's imagination. In 1645 he published, quarto, "Ἐρωτοπαίγνιον. *The Loves of* Hero and Leander, A Greek Poem, Written by Musæus,[190] Translated by *Sir* Robert Stapylton *Knight, Gent. in Ordinary of the Privy Chamber to the* Prince." (This was reprinted with some revision, 12mo, 1647.) Stapylton has added Leander's Epistle to Hero and her answer "Taken out of *Ovid*", with elaborate annotations and excursuses.

Late in 1668 (*Term Catalogues,* November) Stapylton issued quarto *The Tragedie of Hero and Leander,* " Licensed [for printing] August 25. 1668.   Dedicated to the Duchess of Monmouth this piece is duly equipped with a Prologue and a brief Epilogue. The Scene is : *The Towers and Towns of* Sestos *and* Abydos, *the* Hellespont *flowing between them.*" [191]   Leander, a Prince of Troy, and his brother Orosis, land at Sestos during the Great Feast of Venus and Adonis.   The goddess is represented in a triumphal procession by Hero's sister Theamne, with whom Orosis falls in love.   Tiresias, Supreme Magistrate of Sestos, the father of Hero and Theamne, has dedicated the former for one year as cloistered Priestess of Venus and promised the latter to Mentor, Admiral of Athens.   Hero and Leander love passionately at first sight.   Leander swims from Abydos to the tower of Hero at Sestos.   He enters "*in his Vest and Night-Cap*", but the old Nurse [192] to Hero and Theamne, a busy beldame who is very active in promoting the happiness of fond couples, has provided a perfumed bath, and when he has washed the brine from his limbs and hair he enters Hero's bed.   Meanwhile Mentor has arrived from Athens, and confesses to his Vice-Admiral, " divine Musæus," that he is enamoured of Celena, sister to Leander. Hero is entertained in her garden by a curious diversion : the Master's Mate of Leander's ship, " Stredon *and his Ship-Boyes like Blacks enter, and dance ; first one, then another washing at the Fountain, at last all appears White.*"   In spite of a raging storm Leander determines to swim across to Sestos.   Hero awaits him, but her torch is extinguished in the wind, and as the dawn breaks she spies her lover's body floating in the waves, whereupon she flings herself into the sea.   A curious scene is "*A Bar hung with Black*", to which are brought Orosis and Celena, only to be released when Theamne declares that such is the will of the gods. Surprisingly enough when it is discovered that Sestos has been captured by Mentor, and the Nurse enters with the news of Hero's death nobody seems in the least concerned.   Theamne reveals that she is wedded to Orosis, and Celena bestows her hand on Mentor, murmuring to herself :—

> Wisdom and Valour adorn *Mentor*'s Mind ;
> Why, to his Form, was Nature so unkind ?

"*All kiss the Brides, and Bride-Groome's hands,*" whilst the delighted Admiral proclaims :—

> Time cannot ruine what *Musæus* builds ;
> He to the World a Poem will present
> For *Hero* and *Leander*'s MONUMENT.

Genest [193] has been as kind as is compatible with any semblance of truth when he writes of *Hero and Leander* : " This is an indifferent tragedy chiefly in rhyme, it is founded on the poem of Musæus which consists of 338 lines, the original story being very simple Stapylton was obliged to make large additions to it, in order to form 5 acts, he has not been happy in these additions, he makes Musæus one of his Dramatis Personae."

The fact is that the story of Hero and Leander is not adapted for the stage as it does not present sufficient material for drama in itself, and it does not admit of any extension. This proved to be the case when on 2nd June, 1892, after having been tried out (9th May) at the Prince's Theatre, Manchester, there was produced at the Shaftesbury Theatre, London, *Hero and Leander,* a " Play, in Three Acts, by Kyrle Bellew, suggested by Grillparzer's Version of the Mythological Legend ", that is to say a free adaptation of *Hero und Leander,* by Franz Grillparzer (1791–1872). The scenery was especially beautiful ; the chorus, dances, and music were much admired. The play, however, lacked incident. "As a ballet," wrote one critic, " *Hero and Leander* is agreeable enough, as a play it is empty and undramatic." Kyrle Bellew acted the lover, and Mrs. Brown-Potter Hero. " The leading characters were thankless," and hence the piece disappeared from the stage after a very brief run. Indeed the classical legend of the lovers of Sestos and Abydos will only just suffice for an opera with all the help that music gives, as is shown by Luigi Mancinelli's *Ero e Leandro,* the libretto of which was from the pen of Tobia Gorrio.

There is a burletta by Isaac Jackman, *Hero and Leander,* 8vo, 1787, acted at Goodman's Fields, which is very poor stuff. Even worse is Thomas Horde's [194] tragedy in fustian prose *Leander and Hero,* printed 8vo, 1789, " For the Author."

Wycherley has a mock poem *Hero and Leander in Burlesque,*[195] 4to, 1669, which had probably been shown about the Town in MS. and which seems especially to have annoyed Stapylton, a sworn votary of Musæus, since in his Prologue he complains that the song the old Greek poet sang was now a theme for low burlesque, and the sweet love story had become a farce for fantoccini.

It will be readily remembered that the very coarse but very amusing motion exhibited to the company in the Fifth Act of *Bartholomew Fair* vaunted a resonant mock-title : " The Ancient Modern History of Hero and Leander, otherwise called the Touchstone of true Love, with as true a trial of Friendship between Damon and Pythias, two faithful friends o' the Bankside." Stapylton must indeed have read the popular mock-poem

The Loves of Hero and Leander,[196] 8vo, 1651, 8vo, 1653, 12mo, 1662 (12mo, 1677, and 12mo, 1705), but he can scarcely have known the parodies of the two Ovidian epistles [197] (*Leander Heroni* and *Hero Leandro*) which occur in Alexander Radcliffe's *Ovid Travestie*,[198] 8vo, 1673.

Stapylton abandoned the Catholic Church and shamefully broke his religious vows, but there appears a contemporary dramatist who has accidentally attained a greater, if indeed a lean and wizened fame, a priest who was faithful to his sacred obligations, and thus in spite of his own unhappy temper and maugre poverty, neglect, literary contumely, and no common misprise, preserved not without dignity his sacerdotal character and a certain constant honour.

Not since that long summer afternoon what time Camillo Querno, as he recited his epic *Alexias,* consisting of twenty thousand verses, and quaffed deep draughts to aid, was interrupted by the Roman scholars who clamorously greeted him as *Archipoeta* and placed upon his head a coronal interwoven with the leaves of vine, of cabbage, and of laurel,[199] has there been such another coronation as that when Dryden's hand set the wreath not of bays—but of dock and darnel upon Flecknoe's brow. And yet so fortuitous, if so secure, is this immortality of Richard Flecknoe that we know practically nothing certain of " the good old Syre ".

He is hardly to be identified with the William Flexney who was born in Oxfordshire about 1575 and in 1611 entered the Society of Jesus, who may or may not be the Fleckney (Flaxenus) recorded in the *Douay Diaries* as having been ordained priest on 1st April, 1600. Richard Flecknoe is spoken of as a " mendicant Irish priest ", but another account says that he was born at Oxford, and was in fact the nephew of William Flexney, S.J. Flecknoe was educated at foreign Jesuit Colleges, but there is hardly sufficient evidence to bear out the assertion that he joined the Society. According to his own account in the form of letters in *A Relation of Ten Years Travells In Europe, Asia, Affrique and America,* 1656, he went abroad in 1640, first spending three or four years in the Low Countries. In 1644-5 he travelled to Rome, where during the reign of Pope Innocent X he was recognized as something of a virtuoso, and appears chiefly to have been occupied with pictures and statues. The " Pilgrim's Book " of the English College contains four entries which mention his name. Of these the first is : " 1645. Circa fine Januarii venit D. Richardus Fleckno, Sacerdos Anglus Londiniensis mansit in Collo : ritus hospitis ad 4 dies." On the Feast of S. Thomas of Canterbury, the College festa, 29th December,

1645, Flecknoe and a large company were entertained to dinner at the College. On 7th February, 1646, Flecknoe and others "coenati sunt" at the College, and on 21st July, 1646, "D. fflecknow hic pransus in Refectorio." Marvell's satire, "Fleckno, *an English Priest at* Rome," describing his visit to "this *Basso Relievo* of a Man", so thin and tall, shrunken and starved, who lodged in a tiny chamber "three Stair-Cases high", is famous. The allusion to Flecknoe's connexion with Lord Brooke has not been explained,[200] although in 1640 Flecknoe had dedicated *The Affections of a Pious Soule* to Lady Nevill Brooke. In any case it seems clear that he must have been residing in or near Rome from the commencement of 1645 to the autumn of the following year. Leaving Rome Flecknoe visited Constantinople, and afterwards he travelled in Portugal, and in 1648 made a voyage to Brazil. From South America he returned to Flanders, and thence to England, where in 1652 he made London his home. His first book, *Hierothalamium,* had been published as early as 1626, and now he began to pour out a number of miscellaneous works, many of which being printed for private circulation have become excessively rare. Thus of his last production *A Treatise of the Sports of Wit,* 1675, only two copies have been traced. Flecknoe died in 1676–7, aged about seventy-seven years.

The very reason of Dryden's contempt for Flecknoe is obscure. It may have been, as is not now for the first time suggested, the disdain of a great poet for a mongrel rhymster. Southey surmised that : "Perhaps Dryden was offended at his invectives against the obscenity of the stage, feeling himself more notorious, if not more culpable than any of his rivals, for this scandalous and unpardonable offence." This is a little ridiculous, and it is far more likely, I think, that Flecknoe, who was essentially of a meddlesome quality, had thrust himself in upon some literary dispute, and that Dryden very justly resented this intrusion. I believe, moreover, it is possible to identify the actual occasion.[201] In 1668 was printed, 4to, "A Letter from a Gentleman to the *Honourable* Ed. Howard, Esq. ; Occasioned By a *Civiliz'd Epistle* of Mr. Dryden's Before his Second Edition of his *Indian Emperour.*"[202] The writer signs himself "R. F.", and the pamphlet of eight leaves is nothing else than a scurrilous and railing attack upon the laureate. It is entirely uncalled for, and such a gratuitous assault may well have angered Dryden and rankled. These backbiting tracts were, one regrets to say, Flecknoe's speciality. In 1925 the late Mr. G. Thorn-Drury discovered and reprinted (from what is believed to be a unique original) an eight-leaved lampoon, *The Life of Tomaso the Wanderer,*

8vo, 1667,[203] an ill-natured and angry indictment of Thomas Killigrew, the reason for which is far from plain.[204] It seems within the bounds of possibility that there are similar prose pasquils from Flecknoe's pen which have not yet come to light, for in his repeated efforts to compel the theatres at the Restoration to produce his plays Flecknoe not only quarrelled violently with the two managers, Davenant and Thomas Killigrew, but crossed the actors as well, and when hurt he is by no means sparing of his invective.

The first play which Flecknoe wrote is of very considerable interest, since during the Commonwealth in 1654 he published *Loves Dominion,* a "Dramatique Piece . . . Written as A Pattern for the Reformed Stage", which he dedicated to the Lady Elizabeth Claypole [205] with a plea for the restoration of the stage, and the directing it to its "first institution; of teaching Virtue, reproving Vice, and amendment of Manners". Thus he takes occasion to be very severe upon "some who have written obscenely and scourrilously", and he sharply reprehends the general "disreglement" of the theatre.

After the Restoration, having made some alterations in this play, he reissued it, 12mo, 1664, as *Love's Kingdom,* "A Pastoral Tragi-Comedy." With certain variations upon which the actors insisted, *Love's Kingdom* had been produced at Lincoln's Inn Fields in March of that year, but Flecknoe was resolved to print the piece as he wrote it "which was onely in an innocent and harmless way". The Prologue is spoken by Venus from the clouds, and the chief Persons represented are: Theotimus, Loves Arch-Flamin, and Governour of Cyprus; Palaemon, a noble Cypriot in Love with Bellinda, and lov'd by Filena; Pamphilus, a vicious young fellow, stranger to Love's Kingdom, and imagining all as vicious as himself; Philander, a noble Cretian, Bellinda's betroth'd; Bellinda, a noble Cretian Nymph stranger in Love's Kingdom; Filena, a noble Cyprian Nymph; The Popa,[206] or sacred Executioner; together with a rout of Lovers and Nymphs. The Scene, Cyprus,[207] which is Love's Kingdom; "*It never goes out of the view or prospect* of Love's Temple," and all the unities are strictly preserved.[208]

Palaemon loves Bellinda, who has been shipwrecked on the coast of Cyprus, and now after three months residence, upon the Feast of Venus [209] must swear she loves some one in the Island. This she is fortunately able to do as in the company she catches sight of her betrothed Philander, who has just arrived on shore in search of her.

The best character in the play is Pamphilus, a stranger, who seeks "a Love that has some substance in it". Upon arriving in Love's Kingdom he supposes that the nymphs will offer him ample opportunity and scarcely " apprehend the loss of a maidenhead ". When he is rebuffed, he murmurs to himself, " This is a strange Countrey, where a man can't get a wench neither for love nor money," and blames himself for " handling 'um with so much ceremony " for " women shou'd be handled like nettles, but press them hard and you may do any thing with them ". However, he is very pointedly reminded that he is in " Love's Kingdom " " But not in Lust's ", and that " for all leud and lascivious speeches we have a gentle punishment here, called whipping . . . And for fowl libidinousness an other excellent remedy call'd castrating that takes it clean away ", whilst unruly gallants are disciplined " by marrying 'um unto old women of fourscore, there's a cooler for you ". In the end Pamphilus decides " it is no place for me ". Genest is doubtless correct in his surmise [210] : " Harris probably acted Pamphilus."

The fault of *Love's Kingdom* lies in the fact that the atmosphere is so highly artificial and etherialized that it is impossible to be interested either in the characters or the events. Flecknoe should have been content to have written it as a masque. A great poet might have achieved his aim by the beauty and music of his verse, but although *Love's Kingdom* is not without a quota of pretty passages it almost entirely lacks that melody of numbers which alone can commend such rarified conceits.

Downes [211] tells us that " *Love's Kingdom,* Wrote by Mr. *Fleckno* . . . Expir'd the Third Day ", and it is hardly surprising that this piece seems never to have been revived.

We have noted how the actors quite justly required that they should be allowed to make some practical alterations in the conduct of the play as a condition of producing *Love's Kingdom,* and Flecknoe, although obliged to agree, took their necessary and well-meant corrections very hardly since he not only advertised his vexation when he published the piece,[212] but further in his *Epigrams of All Sorts,* 1670 (pp. 73–4), he included some lines *On the spoyling, and mangling of one of his Plays,* which plainly show that he was nursing his grievance :—

> Alas poor Play! for never *Orpheus*
> By frantick hands was torn and mangled thus ! . . .
> 'Tis th' common fate of *Poets* now-a-days,
> T'have such as these mangle & Spoil their Plays ;
> And there is scarcely any one that scapes,
> Th' unskilful tampering of these *Poet-Apes ;*
> For which, all th' harm that I could wish to them,
> May never *Poet* write for them agen :

But they be forc'd to Act *old Plays* like those
For want of new, are forc'd to wear *old Cloathes;*
And come o' th' *Stage* all tattered and poor,
In old cast sutes, which *Field* and *Burbadge* woar.

Actually Flecknoe's first play to be seen in the theatre was *Erminia, Or The Chaste Lady*, "A Trage-Comædy" but this was not printed until 1665, 8vo. It was originally produced at the Theatre Royal, Vere Street, in 1662, and seems to have remained in the repertory for about a couple of years. The cast was: The Duke of Missena (Mycenae), Theophilus Bird, and after his death in April, 1663, William Cartwright; The Prince, his Son, Hart; Cleander, his General, Mohun; Amynter, the General's friend, Burt; Anthenor, a courtier of Missena, Robert Shatterel; Leontius, a courtier of Argos, William Wintershal; Clinias and Cleobulo, two of Cleander's slaves, Clun and Lacy; Aurindo, alias Cyrena, Princess of Argos, Mrs. Ann Marshall; The Duchess, Mrs. Margaret Rutter; Erminia, wife to Cleander, Mrs. Weaver; Althea, her woman, Mrs. Michel (which is, I suspect, a misprint for Mrs. Rebecca Marshall). The Scene, Missena in Greece. The habits, romantic.

Cleander, the brave general of Missena, has been sent to the wars not so much from necessity of state "as more to facilitate the Dukes access unto his lady the admir'd *Erminia*". This lady, however, who is chaste as Lucrece and as fond of her absent husband as Penelope, keeps the strictest retirement. Whilst one day she is addressing her vows to Mars, before his image, on her lord's account the statue stirs and answers, descending from the pedestal and proving to be the Prince, the Duke's son, who has fallen in love with her, and now declares his passion which she coldly rejects. The Duke is announced, and the Prince hastily leaps back upon the base, whence he perforce hears his father wooing Erminia. Cleander returns from the field secretly, resolving to watch his wife since he suspects the Duke's design, and disguised as a deaf and dumb Ethiop he is presented to her as a servant by his friend Amynter who is in the plot. Thus her husband is able to witness the Duke's courtship. Matters are complicated by the fact that the Duchess dotes upon Aurindo, a beautiful page of the Prince's suite, who is none other than Cyrena, Princess of Argos, in male attire. Cyrena has secretly fled to the court of Mycenae, following the Prince whom she loves, and who was intended to marry her, which he seemed willing to do until he became enamoured of Erminia. The Duchess is angered at finding the Duke visits Erminia, and reproaches him for his treachery. The Prince now employs his page to plead his suit with Erminia, whereupon

Aurindo makes known to the lady the secret, and as she embraces the " sweet *Cyrena* " they are espied both by the Duchess and Cleander, whom the sight enrages and torments. Dimagoras, a soldier, is hired by the Duke to beguile Erminia with a false report of Cleander's death ; but at the sight of her sorrow he acknowledges the fiction. Erminia persuades Aurindo to assume a woman's attire and present herself as Cyrena. Whilst the ladies are together Cleander rushes in thinking he will catch his wife in dalliance with the page and is abashed to discover a woman. He stares so wildly that Erminia begins to fear her Moorish servant is frantic. Erminia now gives the Prince an assignation where her place is supplied by Cyrena. He solemnly promises marriage, deeming Cleander dead, and upon their being discovered she reveals that she is the Princess of Argos, to whom he is now twice pledged. He falls at her feet begging forgiveness, and when Cleander reveals himself all are made happy, the Duke declaring " Noble Cleander, I must demand your pardon for trying *Erminia's* constancy in your absence, assure your self 'twas done with good intent ", to which the General, a true courtier replies, bowing low, " I shall believe it."

Erminia is undoubtedly Flecknoe's best play. It seems to have met with some success in the theatre,[213] and was also presented at Court before the King, to whom a special Prologue is addressed with a neatly turned compliment.

The disguise of Cleander as a Moor has given the author of *Emilia,* 8vo, 1672, a suggestion for the precisely similar device of Calimachus in this play, although possibly both Flecknoe and the later dramatist drew from Aureli's *La Costanza di Rosmonda,* 12mo, 1659.

Killigrew certainly from time to time rejected plays which the importunate poet pressed upon his notice. Of these *The Physician against His Will,* an adaptation of *Le Médecin malgré Lui,*[214] for which Flecknoe has a Prologue in his *Epigrams,* was one, and *The Damoiselles A La Mode* another. This latter refusal seems particularly to have angered the poet, who had a very high opinion of his work, since in his Preface to *The Damoiselles A La Mode,* when printed octavo, 1667, he boldly announces : " This *Comedy* is taken out of several Excellent Pieces of *Moliere.* The main plot of the *Damoiselles* out of his *Pretieusee's Ridiculee's ;* the Counterplot of *Sganarelle,* out of his *Escole des Femmes,* and out of the *Escole des Marys,* the two *Naturals* ; all which like so many *Pretieuse* stones, I have brought out of *France* ; and as a Lapidary set in one Jewel to adorn our *English Stage.*" Nay more the poet boasts : " I have not only done like one who makes a posie out of divers flowers in which he has nothing of his own (besides the collection, and ordering them) but like the *Bee,* have extracted the spirit of them into a certain Quintessence of mine own." The result of this Bee's labour is the sorriest amalgam that ever called itself a comedy. Even Molière is lost when strained through Flecknoe's colander. In some slip-slop fashion he has, as he so naïvely plumes himself, lumped together I know not how a paltry version of *Les Précieuses Ridicules* and excerpts from *L'École des Maris,* adding a crude travesty of Alain and Georgette from *L'École des Femmes,* his " two *Naturals* ", to make the thing slab. " For the Acting it, those who have the Governing of the Stage, have their Humours, and wou'd be intreated ; and I have mine, and w'ont intreat them," wrote Flecknoe in the true vein of Mr. Bayes, so it seemed as if this " Jewel " would never sparkle in the eyes of the public. But Flecknoe was not to be outdone, and when his play was printed " Together with the Persons Represented " he was obliging enough to set down the Comedians whom he intended " shou'd Represent them, that the Reader might have half the pleasure of seeing it Acted, and a lively imagination might have the pleasure of it all intire ". The Persons Represented are : Bonhomme, Father to the Damsels (designed for Cartwright) ; Valerio, in love with Isabella (C. Hart) ; Ergasto, his Friend (W. Winterson, i.e. Wintershal) ; Du Buisson and La Fleur, suitors to the Damsels (Burt and Kynaston) ; Sganarelle, Guardian to Isabella (Lacy) ; Marquis Mascarillio and Count Jodelet, Two Laquys disguis'd (Mohun and Robert Shatterel) ; Two Natural Fools, Sganarelle's Houskeepers (Alexander and Wilbraham) [215] ; Mademoiselle Mary and Mademoiselle Anne, the Damoiselles (The Two Marshalls) ; Isabella, a witty damoiselle (Mrs. Rutter) ; and Lysette, the Damoiselles waiting woman (Nel Guin). The Scene, Paris. " The Unity of Persons, Time, and Place, exactly observed."

One of the few alterations Flecknoe makes is to introduce the Damoiselles after their " conversion ". " *Enter Madamoiselle Mary with a Book, Anne with a Gally pot in her hand, &c.*" The book is supposed to be a godly manual the *Spur of Devotion,* but it proves to be the first part of the *Grand Cyrus,* and the gallipot contains no unguent or salve but a lady's face-pomatum. However, they throw away the book and pot, a sham which they only paraded to show that compulsion cannot do what gentle persuasion may effect.

It is hard to believe that *The Damoiselles A La Mode* pleased the King, as the author insinuates, *Epigrams,* 1670 (p. 74). Yet for some reason although at first rejected—and we cannot help feeling very properly rejected—by the actors, Flecknoe contrived to force his *Damoiselles* into the theatre with the inevitable result, a horrid failure, for which he most unfairly held Killigrew to blame. *The Damoiselles A La Mode* was produced at the Theatre Royal on Monday, 14th September, 1668. The cast was probably that which appears in the printed book. Pepys, who was present on the second day, found it " so mean a thing as, when they come to say it would be acted again to-morrow, both he that said it, Beeson, and the pit fell a-laughing, there being this day not a quarter of the pit full ".[216] It was, perhaps, the influence of Flecknoe's patrons, the Duke and Duchess of Newcastle, to whom this comedy is dedicated, that shoved the mangled Molière on to the stage.

Be that as it may, even if so signal a defeat did not damp the dramatist's poetic fire it at least gave the Theatre Royal sufficient grounds absolutely to decline any other play of his making. However, since it is ill parting from him in a pet we may say that some of his poems have distinct merit and are to be read with pleasure, whilst his " Discourse of the English Stage " which all will agree with Langbaine in taking " to be the best thing he has extant " is ably written, acute and often just in its criticisms, and thus may deservedly be commended. "A vain busy coxcomb," a critic in *The Retrospective Review* [217] calls him, yet adds : " But although he has not the slightest claim to be considered a man of genius, we cannot deny him the praise of fancy and ingenuity." A writer in *Chambers' Encyclopædia of English Literature* [218] has higher, but yet not undeserved, praise for Flecknoe when he says : " Flecknoe was not a great poet, but some of his verses are pretty, his thoughts felicitous, and his conceits not so strained as those of many contemporaries." As a miscellaneous writer he is entitled to far higher consideration than as a dramatist.

If Richard Flecknoe was no playwright, another Catholic poet in his one very successful play " was awakening delusive hopes of a great new dramatist ".[219]

Samuel Tuke was the youngest son of George Tuke of Frating,[220] Essex. An ardent royalist, he at once attached himself to the King, and served with great distinction throughout the rebellion. In March, 1644, he was in command at Lincoln ; he fought bravely at Marston Moor in the following July ; and in 1645 he was serving in the west of England under the heroic Lord Goring. In 1648 Tuke took part in the gallant defence of Colchester against Fairfax, and when that city was forced to capitulate, he acted as one of the commissioners for the beseiged. During Cromwell's usurpation he very wisely remained on the Continent. Evelyn met him at Paris in October,

1649,[221] and we find that he was greatly trusted by that excellent lady, Queen Henrietta Maria, who recommended him as Secretary to the Duke of York, but owing to the underhand dealing of Hyde he failed of this appointment. In March, 1653, he was in attendance upon the Duke of Gloucester. At a period of not more than six years after he had openly declared himself a Catholic, and about the time of the Restoration Charles II, with whom he was a prime favourite, employed his services in several missions of great importance and most delicate secrecy to the French court. He was knighted 3rd March, 1663-4,[222] and created a baronet on the 31st March following. On the 9th June, 1664, Sir Samuel married in S. James' Chapel Mary Guldeford, kinswoman to Lord Arundel of Wardour. She died in childbirth at Paris on the 30th August, 1666, and he married a second time on Thursday, 2nd July, 1668, Mary, the daughter of Edward Sheldon, of Stratton. This lady, who was one of the Queen's dressers, survived her husband. They had one son,[223] Charles, baptized at Somerset House, 19th August, 1671, when the King honoured him by standing godfather. Sir Samuel Tuke died at Somerset House in the Strand on the 26th January, 1673-4, and was buried in the chapel there.

Sir Samuel Tuke throughout his life was very active on behalf of his fellow Catholics and urged some remission of the penal laws. He was one of the first members of the Royal Society, and as there is ample contemporary evidence to prove regarded by all men, high and low, with unfeigned respect and admiration as " a person of complete honour and ingenuity ".[224]

In the preface to the third edition of *The Adventures of Five Hours*, " Revis'd and Corrected by the Author," 4to, 1671, Tuke says : " The *Plot* needs no *Apology* ; it was taken out of *Dom Pedro Calderón*, a celebrated *Spanish* Author, the Nation of the World who are the happiest in the force and delicacy of their *Inventions*, and recommended to me by *His Sacred Majesty*, as an *Excellent Design* ; whose Judgment is no more to be doubted, than his Commands are to be Disobey'd." Tuke, in fact, took the Spanish play with him into the country, and worked upon it whilst he was a guest at Aldbury, the seat of his good friend the Right Honourable Henry Howard of Norfolk.

It will not escape notice that Tuke has gained one hour, and turned the *Seis Horas* of the original into *Five*.

Los Empeños de Seis Horas (*The Complications of Six Hours*) although certainly long ascribed to Calderón actually is not the work of that great dramatist. The play seems to have been written about 1641, or a few years later, and in that vast library of Spanish drama, which from 1652 to 1714 was published under the general title *Comedias Nuevas de los Mejores Injenios de España,* it appears under the name of Calderón, but it is not admitted into the various collections of that author's works, and it seems almost certain that it was written by Don Antonio Coello y Ochoa (1611–1652). About the middle of the seventeenth century was issued *Lo que Pasa en una Noche* (*What happens in One Night*), Comedia famosa de Don Antonio Coello, and this is practically the same play as *Los Empeños de Seis Horas,* which was printed at Madrid in 1657, and attributed to Calderón in the eighth volume of the *Comedias Nuevas,* mentioned above. Calderón, however, definitely declared that this comedy was not his work, and Don Emilio Cotalero, the distinguished Spanish scholar, in his *Life of Coello,* says that possibly neither is it to be attributed to this dramatist. " Calderón declaró que no era suya esta comedia. Quizá tampoco lo sea de Coello." [225] In fact the play so much resembles Calderón that it has been suggested it may be by some close and not unskilful imitator of the master.

On Tuesday, 23rd December, 1662, Evelyn notes : " I went with Sr. George [Samuel] Tuke to hear the comedians con and repeate his new comedy, ' The Adventures of 5 Hours,' a play whose plot was taken out of the famous Spanish poet Calderón." At the first performance, at the Duke's house, which took place on Thursday, 8th January, 1663, both Evelyn and Pepys were present as they have recorded in their several Diaries. Evelyn remarks that it took " universally ", whilst Pepys judged it one of the best plays for the variety and most excellent continuance of the plot to the very end that ever he saw or could hope to see, " and the House, by its frequent plaudits, did show their sufficient approbation." [226] Downes in the *Roscius Anglicanus* [227] thus records the enthusiastic reception of *The Adventures of Five Hours :* " This Play being Cloath'd so Excellently Fine in proper Habits, and Acted so justly well. Mr. *Betterton,* Acting *Don Henriq* ; Mr. *Harris, Antonio* ; Mr. *Young, Octavio* ; Mr. *Underhill, Diego ;* Mr. *Sandford, Ernesto* ; Mr. *Smith,* the *Corrigidor* ; Mr. *Price, Silvio* ; Mrs. *Davenport, Camilla* ; Mrs. *Betterton, Portia* ; Mrs. *Long, Flora.* It took Successively 13 Days together, no other Play Intervening." An uninterrupted run of thirteen days was justly considered a complete triumph, for we must bear in mind from how restricted a public the audiences were drawn. When in January, 1693, *The Old Batchelour* achieved a continuous run of fourteen days, this indeed was something so extraordinary as actually to become a piece of theatrical tradition.[228]

The somewhat complicated plot of *The Adventures of Five Hours* may be briefly summarized as follows : The Scene is Seville : Don Henrique, who is described as " Cholerick, Jealous,

Revengeful ", has by proxy contracted his sister Porcia, " Ingenious, constant, and severely vertuous," to Don Antonio
de Mendoza, who is a soldier, haughty and of exact honour,
without the lady even having seen her betrothed. Furthermore
she is in love with and beloved by Don Octavio, a valiant and
accomplish'd cavalier. Don Antonio duly arrives in town and
meets his friend Octavio, who, as he declares embracing him,
" was my *Camerade* when I first bore Arms." Ernesto, Antonio's
servant, brings his master the key of the apartment which
has been assigned him in Henrique's house, " that opens on
Saint *Vincent*'s Street." Porcia has granted Octavio an interview. He arrives accompanied by Antonio who is anxious to
serve his friend in the love affair confided to him and, entirely
ignorant of the identity of the lady, would rescue her for Octavio
from her tyrant brother. Henrique encounters them in the
garden, swords are drawn, and much scuffling ensues. During
the confusion Porcia escapes with Octavio in the moonlight.
Don Henrique is beside himself with fury at the elopement—
" the Funeral of my own Honour," he cries. Antonio congratulates himself that he has seen " My Friend and his fair Mistress
safely Lodg'd ", and now resorts to Don Henrique's to find all
at sixes and sevens. Here he sees Camilla, the sister of Don
Carlos, a near kinsman of Henrique. Antonio had fallen in
love with Camilla whom he had met at Brussels, and whom he
had gallantly rescued during the Flanders campaign. Meeting her
in Henrique's house he takes her to be Porcia, more especially
as Henrique had told Ernesto, the servant, that Porcia will be
without a veil. In her flight Porcia had taken her cousin Camilla's
veil, and Ernesto now confirms his master's mistake with

Sir, 'tis *Porcia,*
A Lovely Living Woman, and your Bride.

Camilla realizes Antonio's error but as she is enamoured of her
brave soldier, she does not undeceive him. Presently she retires,
and when Don Henrique enters to greet Antonio with shame
and sorrow he learns from his guest that Porcia has entertained
him and delighted him with her beauty and sweet conversation.
Henrique is planet-struck and puzzled beyond measure. Porcia,
fearing she may be exposed to scandal through the negligence
of Diego, a great coward, Octavio's man, and even compelled
to separate from her lover, puts herself under the protection
of Antonio, since Henrique must assuredly trace her to Octavio's
house but will not be able to find her if she is guarded by an
honourable gentleman, a stranger, Octavio's friend. Don Antonio
conveys her in a chair to his lodging, which is an apartment

in her own house. Antonio tells her " Madam, My Wife will suddenly attend you ", and introduces Camilla. Henrique is more bewildered than before at finding his sister and her cousin together in the house.

What can this be ?
These sure are Riddles to pose an *Oedipus,*

he exclaims. Other little cross accidents occur to entangle the situation, which is finally cleared up by a long explanation that takes place, and then Octavio is united to Porcia, and Camilla to Antonio, the latter remarking :—

Thus end the strange *Adventures of Five Hours ;*
As sometimes Blustring Storms, in Gentle Showres.

The Adventures of Five Hours is a very important, a very interesting, and, I think we may truly claim, a very excellent drama. It is remarkable for its lofty ideals, and the purity, one might say the nobility, of its language. Surely it is not insignificant that a Restoration audience who are often crassly condemned as if their one itch and joy was ever to listen to bawdy jests and lickerish repartee should have received Tuke's scenes with enthusiasm and delight ; surely it is not unimportant to remember that so clear and continent a play achieved a run of unprecedented length, a veritable triumph which passed into a tradition of the stage.

Tuke's complete mastery of his technique is for the author of one single piece amazing in its sureness and dexterity, nor is his skill altogether due to the Spanish original, although of course *Los Empeños* stood him in unfailing service throughout. Very agreeably does the light gossip of the servants over their chocolate — and each, the butler, the usher, the groom, is cleverly individualized—relieve the grave scenes of Castilian dignity and pride, nor are the humours of honest Diego unamusing. In fact, the laughter is admirably managed, nor is the jest preserved too long. The serious intrigue at times appears to be so entangled that we are wellnigh afraid it cannot be unravelled without some violent snap or jar, and yet the author patiently and perseveringly weaves the perfect pattern of his play with the utmost simplicity and the utmost naturalness to its very end.

The Adventures of Five Hours remained popular until the end of the seventeenth century, and was revived with some not very important changes at the Haymarket, 3rd February, 1707, and again at Drury Lane, 9th October, 1727. On 31st January, 1767, an adaptation was produced at Covent Garden, *The Perplexities,* a comedy by Thomas Hull, who in the Advertisement to the printed play, 8vo, 1767, acknowledges himself " entirely indebted to an old play ", *The Adventures of Five Hours.* The *Perplexities* was given about a dozen times during the season, " having been treated," says Hull, " with very distinguished marks of candour and encouragement, in the representation."

On 19th June, 1893, at the Lyceum Theatre, Edinburgh, was produced *The Adventures of a Night,* a comedy in three acts founded by Meyrick Milton upon *The Adventures of Five Hours.* At the Strand Theatre, London, on the afternoon of 21st July, 1893, Milton's play was presented with the author himself in the cast supported by W. H. Vernon, Luigi Lablache, Miss May Whitty, and Miss Ada Ferrar.

A loyal heart, and not unlike Sir Samuel Tuke also in having given extraordinary promise, unhappily left unfulfilled, in one early play, was John Wilson, the son of Dr. Aaron Wilson of Caermarthen, archdeacon of Exeter, vicar of Plymouth, and chaplain to Charles I. The Rev. Aaron Wilson who died in 1643 was a stout royalist, and much regarded by the King. John, who was born in London, 1626,[229] matriculated being aged seventeen at Exeter College, Oxford, on 5th April, 1644. He did not proceed to a degree, but was admitted at Lincoln's Inn 31st October, 1646, and called to the Bar 10th November, 1652.[230] After the Restoration Wilson enjoyed the favour of James, Duke of York, by whom he was recommended to a position in the household of James Butler, first Duke of Ormonde. Wilson was appointed recorder of Londonderry by Charles II on 20th December, 1666, and he occupied this position until 1679–1680. His term of office was certainly a stormy one, and at last " a troublesome brangle " which he had with the city forced him to leave Ireland for London, " a better place for lawyers and poets." Here he continued to reside until his death at his lodging " near Leicester Fields ", 1695.[231] Wilson's first play, *The Cheats,* written as the first quarto expressly tells us in 1662, at once brought him very prominently into notice.

The Cheats is an excellent comedy, something—but by no means slavishly, for it has great originality—in the Jonsonian manner. Afterwitt, a gentleman of an encumbered estate is aided by his friend Jolly in his suit for the hand of Beatrice, daughter of old Alderman Whitebroth, a covetous and hypochondriacal hunks who secretly intrigues with the wife of Double-Diligence, a Puritan Constable, and who prefers for his daughter's hand Tyro, a foolish young Squire. Mrs. Whitebroth, Mrs. Double-Diligence, and Mrs. Mopus, the wife of one Mopus, a charlatanry Astrological Physician who pills and potions the Alderman, are prominent members of the flock of Mr. Scruple, an oily canting nonconformist Minister. Mrs. Mopus entertains as her lover Titere-Tu,[232] a hector who usurps the name of Captain, whilst his boon-companion Major Bilboe both lodges with Mrs. Double-Diligence and cuckolds her husband. When Beatrice consults Mopus, who her maid Cis assures her " can shew one, ones Sweethearts face in a glass ", Master Rosicrucian has just been surprised by Afterwitt and Jolly as he is ruffling Mrs. Double-Diligence, and his palm further greased with a round bribe in compliance with their orders he shows the lass her future husband in the mirror she holds, the face of course being that of Afterwitt who steals up behind her chair and after softly peeping over her shoulder for a few minutes retires. Beatrice is delighted, and presently a little levite is pressed into service to tie the nuptial knot. Moreover Afterwitt and Jolly, having learned from Mopus of the Alderman's gallantries with the Constable's easy spouse, set Bilboe and Titere-Tu to catch him as he is about to board the lady, and thus extort a thousand pounds from the poor old lecher, who also discovers that when he deemed he was signing his will, by a device in which lawyer Runter and Mr. Scruple had their share, he has made a settlement upon his daughter and her husband, which leaves him no alternative save to receive the couple into favour.

It is interesting to note that according to the MS. Squire Tyro finds himself wedded to Cis, whom he takes for Beatrice's sister, but who is in reality her maid. This has disappeared from the printed play.

The actors whose names are first given in the fourth quarto, 1693, were as follows : Whitebroth, Cartwright ; Runter, Wintershal ; Afterwitt, Burt ; Jolly, Hart ; Scruple, Lacy ; Mopus, Mohun ; Bilboe, Clun ; Titere-Tu, Shatterel ; Double-Diligence, Loveday ; Mrs. Whitebroth, Mrs. Corey ; Mrs. Mopus, Mrs. Margaret ; Mrs. Double-Diligence, Mrs. Marshall.[233] It is hardly possible to imagine a finer cast, and the ensemble must have been indeed superb. John Lacy, in particular, excelled as the vehement upholder of the Good Old Cause and Holy Covenant. He was much admired by Charles II, and exactly how he looked we know from Wright's painting.[234] The dress, gesture, expression are all inimitable. It was obviously this photographic figure—for there is hardly any exaggeration— which excited the spleen of his brethren of the kirk, and set the whole theatre out of kelter. The part of this Restoration Stiggins and Chadband is indeed written with an exquisite zesto which rivals even if it does not surpass Dickens' humours of the " shepherd " and the " vessel ". The scene where whilst the old Alderman is shaking with an obstinate cough the " good sisterly women " gather round Scruple and administer the caudle which he pretty dextrously sups down as " though the Bowle be scandalous, 'tis pity the good creature should be spoil'd " ; the scene where he debates whether " If a young woman, of a godly Parentage, do fall into a holy Fornication (not out of Lust, but Love) and thereupon prove with Child ", may procure abortion—a very modern touch—and decides that it is lawful " provided alwayes, it be not done, with an intention of Murder, but only to save Life, or Reputation " ; the scene of the " new-spiritual-mouth-waterings " ; the scene where he resolves " Three hundred pounds a year, and conform ", but by the arguments of the " good comfortable women " is persuaded to " 400*l*. a year, and not Conform " ; the final pronunciamento on music, dancing, the wedding sack-posset, which may be " Raggs of the Whore " ; are all in the rarest and richest vein of comedy.

There is preserved in the library of Worcester College, Oxford, a manuscript copy of *The Cheats,* as submitted to Sir Henry Herbert, wherein important passages have been censorially marked for deletion, not to be spoken on the stage, and presumably (he would have desired) not to be printed, although of course this fell outside his province and the printing licence belonged to another authority.[235] The Worcester College script bears the autograph licence of the Master at the end : " This Comedy, of the Cheates, may be Acted, As Allowed for the stage, the Reformations strictly obserued, to the Kings Company of Actors by Henry Herbert. Master of the Reuells. Marche. 6. 1662[-3]."

The Cheats, originally given at the Theatre Royal, Vere Street, in the third week of March, 1663,[236] was received with the great applause so thoroughly merited by such lively and telling scenes, but a disgruntled adverse faction set hard against the piece, and on 28th March, Abraham Hill writing to John Brooke says in a postscript : " The new play, called the Cheats, has been attempted on the stage ; but it is so scandalous, that it is forbidden." [237] The circumstances of the first production of Wilson's play are certainly curious and not altogether easy to understand. It is surprising that puritan opposition should have proved sufficiently powerful to drive from the boards a comedy duly licensed by the Master of the Revels, yet such undoubtedly was the case, since there is a minute dated 22nd March, 1663, by Sir Henry Bennet, Secretary of State (Baron Arlington, 1665 ; Viscount Thetford and Earl of Arlington, 1672), of a letter sent to the manager, Thomas Killigrew, signifying the Royal pleasure that *The Cheats* " be no more represented " until the script had been examined and reviewed by Sir John Denham and Edmund Waller, the latter of whom was advised in the following

missive : " Sr His Ma^{ty} beeing informed, that there ware in
a New Comedy lately acted at ye Theater many things of a Scandalous offensive nature hath Commanded mee to Signifie his
Pleasure to you y^t you and Sr John Denham immediately
send for ye saide new play and reading it ouer together giue jointly
to his Ma^{ty} yor Opinion of it, that if there bee cause for it it
may be suppreesed. Y^e pretended approbation it is said to haue
had from his Ma^{ty} hauing I can assure you noe further ground
then That a matter of twenty or thirty lines of it being shown
him wch had been excepted against his Ma^{ty} was pleased to
say if there bee nothing worse it may bee acted, adding
further to the player, that their Company should take heed in
this as in all their other Playes, to expose upon ye Stage any thing
y^t was either prophane Scandalous or Scurrilous observing which
they should be protected & no longer." Denham received a
similar dispatch.[238]

The player who had audience of the King and who ventured
to read the incriminated passages was, no doubt, Mohun ;
a great favourite with Charles II, and one who upon several
occasions interceded at court with success when the actors
had by some misbehaviour or mishap incurred official displeasure
and rebuke.[239]

There is something sublimely ironical in the whole situation,
and particularly in the sober admonishment supposed to have
fallen from the lips of the King when we remember Old Rowley's
censure of Crowne's comedy as the dramatist read it to the
monarch in the Royal Cabinet at Whitehall. " This Play is
the famous *Sir Courtly Nice* which the King highly approv'd
of, only he said it wanted a little more of what *Collier* calls
Smut in his View of the Stage." [240]

That the report of Waller and Denham was favourable is
clear from the Second Prologue to *The Cheats,* " intended upon
the revival of the Play, but not spoken " ; an address put in
the mouth of Scruple which commences :—

> *Sad News my Masters ; And too true, I fear,*
> *For us—Scruple's a silenc'd Minister* [241] *;*
> *Would ye the Cause ?—The Brethren snivle, and say,*
> *'Tis scandalous that any Cheat, but they :*
> *Well—To be short ; H'as been before the Tryers,*
> *And (by good Fortune) is got out o' th' Bryers ;*
> *Where, if he lost a Limb to save the rest,*
> *No hurt—Here's yet enough to know the Beast :*
> *Nor let the sisters pule—(I'll tell y' a thing)*
> *He may be libb'd, and yet have left, a string.* [242]

The Cheats remained a stock play for wellnigh half a century, and Benjamin Griffin, who, as Davies tells us, was much admired for his just representation of the canting puritanical preacher, Tribulation Wholesome in *The Alchemist*,[243] proved equally great in the rôle of Wilson's nonconformist. At Lincoln's Inn, Fields *The Cheats* was revived as late as 11th December, 1727, when Hippisley [244] appeared as Scruple. It was printed 4to, 1664; 1671, 1684, and 1693.

The manuscript preserved in Worcester College Library affords very interesting and very ample evidence of Herbert's deletions. A superficial account of the MS. has been given by Mr. F. S. Boas in a collection of papers entitled *Shakespeare and the Universities* (1923), but he can claim no particular knowledge of the Restoration stage and, as might be supposed, this essay from so pretentious yet otiose a pen can only be regarded as a piece of jerry-journalism and as such unsatisfactory. Mr. Boas artlessly enough insinuates his "discovery" of the MS., the existence of which was very well known long before. In 1931 I gave some time to an inspection of the Worcester College Library MSS., but a full and detailed description of this particular script, *The Cheats,* is the particular province of an editor, and I conceive that a few general remarks alone are here required.[245]

It would appear that Herbert had as keen an eye in 1663 as in 1634 for any word or phrase that might be thought remotely to smack of the expletive, and accordingly " Faith; troth; by the good Morglay [246]; fore George ", are all cancelled and not to be spoken. It is even more astonishing to note that such puny asseverations as " by this good light; by all that's good; by the light of pharoh; by this hand "; and " as I am an Alderman ", were sternly disallowed. Out goes the fanatic Constable's mealy " Odds Niggs ", a typical roundhead expression [247]; and consequently Bilboe's comment is excised : " I hate those Puritan Oaths. If thou must swear, swear like a man of Office." Odds Nigs is a ridiculous old oath at which the dramatists were never tired of poking fun, and there could be no clearer evidence of Herbert's petty piddling ways than the excision of so harmless if entirely foolish and unmeaning a juramento.

We are the less surprised then to find that several mildly innocuous and not very amusing carwichets and quarterquibbles that flick the Welsh offended Herbert's tender susceptibilities, for he was a man of one skin for his country, and hence these are marked for omission. The Master's closest attention, however, was demanded by Scruple, many of whose best speeches were ruthlessly castrated or expunged. I confess myself unable to grasp the reason for these mutilations, more especially as one might have supposed that Herbert as a loyal servant of the

King would have been far from displeased that the fanatics should appear in their own true ridiculous but hateful colours upon the boards, and there is nothing extravagant, although there is much that is most nicely exact, in the drawing of the pliant Levite, Mr. Scruple.

Following the practice of his father Ben, Wilson has garnered his material for *The Cheats* from many sources, and he has indeed donned the " learned sock " to good purpose. Thus we recognize in his scenes not a few well-contrived hints, and perhaps something more than hints, from Latin authors, as also echoes from the great Elizabethans. There is some direct conveyance from Erasmus, whose *Moriae Encomium* he was later to english in its entirety. The Rosicrucian Iatros Iatrophilus Mopus closely reflects such contemporary astrologers as John Heydon and William Lilly, even drawing upon their published works. The Incantation, Act V, scene 1, which commences with the Hebrew " Mazal Tob " (*Greetings*), discourses extracts from the *Miles Gloriosus,* Rabelais, Manilius, a word or two of Aristotle and Tacitus, and a few letters from the Greek and Hebrew alphabets. It seems almost superfluous to say that Mr. F. S. Boas proved quite unable to recognize any of these. He found himself *au bout de son Latin,* was fairly flummoxed, and accordingly wrote [248] : " The manuscript, strangely enough, leaves a blank where the quartos insert the dog-Latin jargon headed *Mazal Tob.*" Imprimis, the Incantation is not " dog-Latin jargon " but a very clever and interesting mosaic of words, whilst one might have supposed that it required no extraordinary acumen to appreciate the reason for this lacuna in the manuscript. Witty and apposite as the piece is in the reading, on the boards it would be even more effective for Mohun as Mopus to insert some bombast abracadabra of his own, and simpler far than for the actor to commit to memory and declaim a long and difficult passage in three tongues.

In the days of Wilson, the two men o' Memphis, Titere-Tu and Bilboe, might have been met at wellnigh every London tavern or ruffling up and down the streets, and our author assuredly drew these game-cocks from the life,[249] but he has also cast an eye upon *The Hectors, or, The False Challenge,* a comedy written in 1655, and printed, quarto, the following year. It has been assigned by Phillips and Winstanley to Edmund Prestwich.

The casuistry of Scruple which gave so grave offence to Herbert is to be traced in large part to Pascal's bitter caricature of the moral teaching of the great Jesuit doctors, Antonio Escobar y Mendoza, Étienne Bauny, Gabriel Vasquez, Vincenzo Filliucci,

Thomas Sanchez, and the rest. The *Lettres Provinciales* were published from 1656 to 1657, and appeared in English during this latter year as *Les Provinciales, Or, The Mystery of Jesuitisme* (Second Edition corrected ; 1658).

Wilson's next play to be given to the world was of an entirely different kind, and from the Dedication, which is dated 15th January, 1663, it would seem that actually it had been written " long since ". *Andronicus Commenius,* a Tragedy, was printed 4to, 1664,[250] without prologue or epilogue, and never appeared upon the stage.[251] It is not easy to conjecture why such should have been the case, for Wilson's scenes are interesting and powerful, and if some of the poetical speeches are perhaps too protracted for the theatre, there could have been no difficulty in judiciously cutting the script. The dramatist has used his material with skill and effect. The history of Andronicus I. Comnenus " the Liberator " who waded through blood and treachery to the Byzantine throne, which he held from 1183–5, may most conveniently be read in Gibbon, chapter xlviii, who graphically portrays the extraordinary character and adventures of this emperor. In his departures from fact, his selection and compressions, Wilson seems almost justified having regard to the dramatic end in view. The characters are well drawn, in particular that of Philo, Andronicus's zany, who is of course the creation of the author. It seems evident that in the second scene of Act III where Basilius presses the crown upon Andronicus, and also in the third scene of Act IV, the wooing of Anna [252] by Andronicus, Wilson has closely copied *Richard III* since some of Shakespeare's lines are nearly reproduced.

John Wilson was a scholar and a man of wide reading, and his obligations to Shakespeare's tragedy are, no doubt, due to his study of the printed text, but at the same time since neither Odell nor Hazelton Spencer have anything to tell us of *Richard III* before the famous alteration by Cibber, it may not be impertinent, inasmuch as new and unprinted evidence has come to light, to devote a brief word to the history of this play as it appeared on the Restoration stage.

Richard the Third was one of the plays allotted to Killigrew's company, and hence it was the monopoly of the Theatre Royal. The " *Prologue to* Richard *the third* " printed in *Covent Garden Drollery,* 1672, affords proof of a revival at some time before (and probably near to) this date. We are, I think, safe in assigning this revival to the first Theatre Royal, Bridges Street.

In his *Apology,* speaking of Samuel Sandford, Cibber tells us that had Sandford lived in Shakespeare's time the poet would assuredly have selected him above all other actors to fill the rôle of Richard. Accordingly when Cibber's alteration of *Richard III* was produced at Drury Lane, since Sandford was then engaged at Lincoln's Inn Fields and not available, Cibber, who himself appeared as the King, modelled his performance in every detail exactly upon that which Sandford would have given. "I imagin'd I knew how *Sandford* would have spoken every Line of it," he writes ; and Sir John Vanbrugh assured him he was a second Sandford, having not only borrowed that actor's gait, but every look, gesture, speech, and motion.

Cibber's phrase is unintentionally a little ambiguous, and taken by itself the wording leaves us in doubt whether he meant that he played Richard III as Sandford had acted the part, or as Sandford *would* have acted the part had the piece ever been revived. Since no definite record of a revival had hitherto been traced, the latter meaning was accepted. However, there are generally overlooked two references (quoted in my notes, 1927, to *Covent Garden Drollery*), one of which at any rate points to contemporary performances. In Henry Higden's *A Modern Essay On the Thirteenth Satyr of Juvenal*, 4to, 1686, we have :—

Bath'd in cold Sweats he frighted Shreiks
At visions bloodier than King *Dicks*.

Upon this the author has a note : "*Vision Dicks*. In the Tragedy of *Richard* the 3rd." Again in D'Urfey's *A Fool's Preferment,* Dorset Garden, April, 1688, iii, 2, the distracted Lyonel cries out : "A Horse ; a Horse ; my Kingdom for a Horse," an allusion which the author must have expected to be taken up by the audience. (The significance of this point, as indeed of many others, has been entirely missed by Mr. R. S. Forsythe in his blundering and slipshod reprint of the play, 1917.)

In addition, more important and conclusive evidence has come to light, since a copy of the 1634 quarto of Shakespeare's *Richard III* has been found to contain, written in a contemporary hand, a post-Restoration cast of the play. This runs as follows : Edward IV, Betterton ; Clarence, Kynaston ; Richard, Duke of Gloucester, Sandford ; Buckingham, Joseph Williams ; Hastings, Haines ; Richmond, Mountford ; Norfolk, Smith ; Derby, Bowman ; Rivers, Hodgson ; Grey, Alexander ; Stanley, Powell ; Brakenbury, Clarke ; Sir Thomas Vaughan, Michael Leigh ; Catesby, Bowen ; Tyrrell, Bright ; Prince Edward, Tommy Kent ; Richard, Duke of York, a Little Boy ; The Duchess of York, Mrs. Betterton ; Queen Margaret, Mrs. Knight ; Queen Elizabeth, Mrs. Barry ; and Lady Anne, Mrs. Bracegirdle.

Several points of interest and great importance arise in con-nexion with this cast, but only a pertinent few can be touched on here. In the first place, it is established that Sandford actually did appear as Richard III. The date of the revival must have been after the Union of the two Companies, November, 1682, and before the death of Mountford, December, 1692. It can indeed by various indications be considerably narrowed down, and as I have shown in Chapter II we shall not (I think) be far out if we put it at 1689–1690. If we argue from Higden's allusion we may incline to 1686, but I rather believe that this is a literary reference. The difficulty with regard to the presence of Clarke in the cast and his appearance in so small a part has been dealt with in the second chapter.

It should perhaps be added that in Baron Caryl's *The English Princess ; or, The Death of Richard III,* a heroic tragedy produced at Lincoln's Inn Fields, 3rd March, 1667, Betterton acted the King.

Andronicus, a Tragedy, " Impieties Long Successe, or Heavens Late Revenge," unacted, 12mo, 1661, a drama upon the same subject as Wilson's play, is anonymous. Tumid and tame, it is of no value.

The Projectors, a comedy so far in the Jonsonian tradition as to be plainly modelled upon *The Devil is an Ass,* was published by Wilson, 4to, 1665 (Imprimatur, 13th January, 1664),[253] and presumably produced at the Theatre Royal either late in 1664 or in the first week of January, 1665. Genest questioned whether this comedy had ever been given in the theatre, but the *Biographia Dramatica* [254] is probably correct when it says that *The Projectors* " met with good success on the stage ". At the same time although this piece contains at least one excellent character and some few brisk scenes it sadly lacks incident, whilst a great deal of the business with the projectors is unwieldy and overweighted.[255] In spite of the fact that Wilson took the suggestion from the *Aulularia* [256]—and indeed some of the language even is from Plautus—Suckdry the usurer is drawn with wholly admirable strokes, and is a true original, but when he leaves the stage the scene immediately drops. Had there gone towards the other characters a tithe of the vigour which created Suckdry *The Projectors* would take no mean place in the English theatre. As it is, we cannot but judge it the least successful of Wilson's work, and we are all the more sorry to see so brilliant a portraiture overcast in so arid an environment. The rather dull scene of the She Senate in the third Act is from Aristophanes, but the humour is lost. The device of Ferdinand, who when he courts Nancy, the usurer's daughter, appears in mean habiliments and suits his conversation to his clothes, has been employed by William Harrison Ainsworth in that first-rate romance *The*

Miser's Daughter,[257] when Philip Frewin dressed in a shabby worn suit presents himself to woo Hilda Scarve.

A quarter of a century elapsed before Wilson's last play followed. *Belphegor ; or, The Marriage of the Devil* was produced at Dorset Garden late in June, 1690, and proved a complete failure. Yet the old story is handled with considerable skill, the dialogue is lively and well-written, the characters individual and animated. It is strongly to be suspected that Wilson's acknowledged Jacobitism, his noble fidelity to the King, must be held accountable for this want of success, and indeed himself he hints as much. The scene of *Belphegor* is laid at Genoa. Here Belphegor, passing as Roderigo, a Spanish merchant from the Indies, is married to the fair Imperia. The play follows the lines of the old story. The wanton extravagant Imperia brings her husband to ruin, intrigues with gallants, and henpecks him to the depths of misery. Being by his very bargain subjected to the conditions of humanity the demon flies, and is sheltered from his enemies by Mattheo, a vineyard-keeper, whom he repays by possessing a great lady. Thus when Mattheo, feigning himself an exorcist, is called in to deliver her, he can make his own terms since Belphegor has promised to remove only at his bidding. This the demon pledges he will do twice, but no more. The two tricks are played, and Belphegor next possesses Julia, the Duke of Genoa's daughter. Mattheo is summoned, but the demon will not dislodge. Whereupon the crafty winedresser tries a subtle fetch. With a horrid hubbub and hullaballoo, whilst Mattheo is delivering Julia a regular jobation, there enters a lady veiled. " Your Wife's in chase of ye," bawls Mattheo, and whoop! off and away scampers the choused cacodemon.

With this fable, to divert the tediousness of a single walk, Wilson has introduced Montalto a noble Genoese who has sunk his fortune in serving the Republic, but whose needs are generously helped, unknown to him, by his friend Grimaldi, and whose occasions of discontent are sweetened by his loving wife, Portia. So solaced and serene does Montalto become that when the Senate elect him Duke, he refuses and turns his back on giddy ambition.

The bravo, Don Hercio ; the two pugs attending Roderigo as his valet and page ; Quartilla, matrona to Imperia ; and the abigail, Scintilla, are good comic characters. *Belphegor* was printed, 4to, 1691 ; Licensed 13th October, 1690 ; Term Catalogues, February, 1691. The author's original MS. of *Belphegor,* 86 folio sheets, was described in a catalogue of Messrs. Pickering and Chatto about 1910, and is now, I understand, preserved in an American private library. A note said : " This MS. bears all the evidence of having been used as the prompter's copy for more than one production."

An early play upon the subject of Belphegor [258] is *Grim, the Collier of Croydon,* not printed until 1662, but almost certainly to be identified with Haughton's *The Devil and his Dame,* mentioned in Henslowe's *Diary* under March, 1600.

Wilson informs us that he took his theme from Machiavelli's novella, although he confesses he cannot say which is the earlier, Machiavelli or Straparola.   Actually Machiavelli's *Nove la di Belfagor arcidiavolo* (leaving on one side possible variants in Serbian folklore) is the earliest Western form of the story. The author's original MS. is preserved in the Florentine National Library.   The legend of an old Latin MS. containing *Belphegor* which was in the Library of St. Martin de Tours cannot be substantiated. Professor Fausto Lasinio considers that Machiavelli derived the theme, orally no doubt, from the Oriental fiction of the *Forty Viziers,* which in the first place comes from India. From Machiavelli it was adopted by Giovanni Brevio, and is the fourth Novella in his *Novelle* and *Rime* published at Rome in one volume, 8vo, 1545.   It is the fourth Novella of the Second Night of Straparola's *Tredeci piacevoli notte,* Venice, 8vo, 1550.   So great was its popularity that it is also to be found in Sansovino's *Novelle,* in Part II of Doni's *Libreria,* and in Canto III of that extraordinary poem *Tristarello.* For further details one may conveniently consult Gargani's reprint of *Belfagor arcidiavolo,* Florence, Dotti, 1869.   Perhaps the most famous modern version is the story as told with lively wit by La Fontaine.

The Cheats, which must certainly be esteemed Wilson's best play, draws a very realistic picture of Commonwealth days in London, so true to life indeed that many being galled much misliked the humour and were little sparing of their censure, to whom the poet has amply made reply.   Yet another comedy by another poet as stoutly loyal as Wilson's self was fated to encounter considerable opposition on the very same score, for in *Cutter of Coleman-Street* Cowley was held not only to have satirized the puritans, but also some of the rag-tag of the King's party, and the consequence was that, as will presently be noted, at its first performance this piece met with no very favourable reception.

Cutter of Coleman-Street is an alteration, to a large extent a re-writing, of *The Guardian,* which was acted before Prince Charles at Trinity College, Cambridge, on 12th March, 1641.   *The Guardian* was printed, 4to, 1650, and Cowley tells us several times performed "*privately during the troubles* ", as also at Dublin in

1662 or 1663 "*with good approbation*". Curiously enough it was revived in 1668 at Lincoln's Inn Fields at which theatre on 5th August of that year Pepys "saw 'The Guardian'; formerly the same, I find, that was called 'Cutter of Coleman Street'".259

Cutter of Coleman-Street was produced at Lincon's Inn Fields on Monday, 16th December, 1661.

It should be noted that a cutter was a bully or a bravo, one who all too quickly resorted to the argument of weapons. Coleman Street runs from Lothbury to Fore Street, Cripplegate. During the seventeenth century it was infested by puritans and a good deal of treason was hatched here. (See for example the evidence in the trial of Hugh Peter.)

The scene of the play is London in the year 1658. Colonel Jolly, a Gentleman whose Estate was confiscated in the late troubles, is father to Aurelia and guardian to Lucia. Owing to this impoverishment he wishes to dispose of his ward to advantage himself, and cooly offers her hand both to Cutter, a sharking fellow who pretends to have been a Colonel in the King's army, and also to Worm, a feigned Royalist captain, on condition that he is presented with a thousand pounds for his goodwill and her estate is so settled that he can manage it as he pleases. Lucia, however, rejects both these sharks with scorn, the more especially as she is in love with Truman, whose testy old father has exacted an oath from his son that he will neither see nor speak with her. She contrives to visit him muffled in a long veil, and writes what she wishes to say. Eventually they are married. Their courtship is materially aided by Aurelia, who subtly contrives to wed Puny, a rich fop, suitor to Lucia. Colonel Jolly himself takes as his wife Mistress Barebottle, the widow of a soapboiler, who had bought his estate. She is a pretended Saint of the Fifth Monarchy sect, and no less a fanatic is her daughter Tabitha. Cutter pretends to have been converted by inspiration; "I had a Vision which whisper'd to me through a Key-hole, Go call thy self *Abednego*!" he proclaims. "The wonderful Vocation of some Vessels," sighs Tabitha. He dresses himself in a sad-coloured suit, draws a long face, whines, snivels and cants how "Major General *Harrison*260 is to come in Green sleeves from the North upon a Sky-colour'd Mule, which signifies heavenly Instruction". When he informs Sister Tabitha that "we two, who are both holy Vessels" must be joined in matrimony as is shown by a vision he experienced what time she rode behind him on a Purple Dromedary, the good Sister cannot withstand the supernal prompting, and they are made man and wife. But

PLATE XI

CUTTER OF COLEMAN-STREET: ACT V: SCENE 6

no sooner is the knot tied than Cutter bursts into song, throws off his steeple hat and linen bands, dons a brave periwig, a hat and feather, sports a belt and sword, and in fine equips himself in a " roaring habit of Perdition ".   Next he summons the fiddlers, in spite of Tabitha's shrill protests, but anon after the sack has been merrily tippled the wench foots it with the best. These scenes are exquisitely humorous, and one might have thought would have ensured an overwhelming success for any play, even were it vastly inferior to the well-written and lively *Cutter.*

John Dennis, however, tells us in the Epistle Dedicatory to *The Comical Gallant : or, The Amours of Sir John Falstaffe,* 4to, 1702 : " *The only Play that ever Mr.* Cowley *writ, was barbarously treated the first night, as the late Mr.* Dryden *has more than once informed me, who has told me that he went to see it with the famous Mr.* Sprat, *now Bishop of* Rochester, *and that after the Play was done, they both made a visit to Mr.* Cowley, *whom the Death of his Brother had obliged to keep the House, and that Mr.* Cowley *received the news of his ill success, not with so much firmness, as might have been expected from so great a man.*"

Pepys, indeed, who was present at the first performance and judged it " a very good play ", does not mention any disapproval, although he remarks the comedy was " made in the year 1658, with reflections much upon the late times ", but Langbaine [261] notes that it " met with some Opposition ", and in his Preface Cowley himself complains that *Cutter* " *met at the first with no favourable reception, and I think there was something of Faction in it. . . . Afterwards it got some ground, and found Friends as well as Adversarys* ".   The first clamour raised was " *That it was a piece intended for abuse and Satyre against the King's party* ".   This accusation seems to have cut the poet to the heart and he stoutly defended himself, pointing out that some knaves must be found in any Party, for the Royalists will hardly " *assume the Name of the Congregation of the Spotless* ", and knaves are a fit subject for comedy.   He pleads well, but none the less Cutter and Worm can hardly be supposed figures a stout cavalier would be anxious to see paraded in the public theatre, and there is little doubt that the suspicion which had been engendered stuck in many minds.   Moreover Colonel Jolly himself was not an over-scrupulous nor yet a very honourable and honest heroic. Cowley pleads that he did not intend the Character one of exemplary Virtue but " *an ordinary jovial Gentleman* ", although it is to be feared that Jolly falls very far below even that standard.   His bargains with Cutter and Worm for Lucia are ugly work.   The next objection, says the poet, " *is enough to knock a man down, and accuses me of no less than Prophaneness.*" Here Cowley is on sure ground, and can defend himself right well. "*Is it Prophane to speak of* Harrison's *return to Life again, when some of his friends really profest their belief of it and he himself had been said to promise it?*" Such an accusation is truly "*very false and malitious*", and although we might allow that his portraiture of Cutter and Worm was perhaps a trifle indiscreet at the moment, and that Colonel Jolly once or twice almost makes us guess at darker shades in his character, this last charge of profanity is utterly baseless and absurd. Even if there be small blemishes—and this is open to question—*Cutter of Coleman-Street* is an admirable play, and once established in popular favour it seems to have taken a fairly permanent place in the repertory, for Langbaine speaks of having "seen it acted with universal Applause". It was revived at Drury Lane on 1st August, 1712, with a new Prologue spoken by Pack who played Puny. On 3rd January, 1723, there was a revival at Lincoln's Inn Fields, as "Not acted 30 years" (at this theatre) with Quin as Jolly; Ryan, Cutter; Hippisley, Worm; and Mrs. Egleton, Tabitha. It enjoyed a run of seven nights during the season, but it does not appear to have been given at any later date.

Downes has the following record :—

"*Cutter* of *Coleman-street*; Written by Mr. *Abraham Cowley*; Colonel *Jolly*, perform'd by Mr. *Betterton*; Old *True-man*, by Mr. *Lovel*; Young *True-man*, Mr. *Harris*; *Cutter*, Mr. *Underhill*; Captain *Worme*, Mr. *Sandford*, Parson *Soaker*, Mr. *Dacres*; *Puny*, Mr. *Nokes*; *Will.*, Mr. *Price*; *Aurelia*, by Mrs. *Betterton*; *Lucia*, Mrs. *Ann Gibbs*; Laughing *Jane*, by Mrs. *Long*: This Comedy being Acted so perfectly Well and Exact, it was perform'd a whole Week with a full Audience." [262]

Note, This Play was not a little injurious to the Cavalier Indigent Officers; especially the Character of *Cutter* and *Worm.*

It is a pity that the names of the original representatives of the Widow Barebottle and Tabitha are not preserved.

There could scarcely be a figure more dissimilar to that of the gentle Abraham Cowley than our next dramatist, the ruffling Major Thomas Porter. The fourth son of Endymion Porter, Thomas, who was born in 1636, began to show his spirit at a sufficiently early age since on 24th February, 1655, he carried off Anne Blount, daughter of Mountjoy Blount, Earl of Newport. For this abduction he was imprisoned, the contract being declared null and void.[263] None the less a valid marriage took place immediately after since Porter had a son, George, by the lady.[264] In the same year, 1655, on 26th March, Porter killed a soldier Thomas Salkeld in Covent Garden, and was put upon his trial for murder. He pleaded manslaughter, was found guilty, and being allowed the benefit of clergy was burned in the hand.[265] After the Restoration Porter achieved a marked success as a dramatist, and it may not untruly be said that his very scenes seem to echo the clash and click of toledo blades which were so resonant in his own life. On Sunday evening, 28th July, 1667, Porter quarrelled upon a slight silly word with his dear friend Sir Henry Bellassys, both being something in their cups. They fought, those two gallant hot-headed gentlemen, in Covent Garden, and Bellassys received a mortal wound, from which after lingering a few days he died, whilst the world talked " of them as a couple of fools, that killed one another out of love ".[266] Porter, although badly hurt, fled the kingdom, and wisely sojourned in France until his pardon—not without difficulty—had been sealed. When he returned he was a thought steadier, and had the good sense to keep more in the background. Left a widower he married Roberta Anne, the daughter of Sir Thomas Colepepper.[267] He died in 1680.

Porter's first play *The Villain* was produced at Lincoln's Inn Fields on Saturday, 18th October, 1662. The characters are : Clairmont, the General ; La Bar, Gentleman of his Horse ; D'orvile, Governor of the Town ; Brisac, a young Colonel ; Beaupres, his friend ; Malignii, his Major and a Villain ; Boutefeu, D'elpeche, Lamarch, Officers in Brisac's regiment ; Colignii, an impertinent young scrivener ; Cortaux, his father ; Bellmont, sister to Brisac ; Charlotte, daughter to the Governour ; Mariane and Francibell, Colignii's two sisters ; Luyson, a waiting-woman to Bellmont ; a Surgeon ; a Friar ; mine Host and his Wife.

The scene is Tours, and the play opens well with all the bustle and stir consequent upon the arrival in the town of a new regiment whose officers are being quartered for the winter upon various citizens. No doubt these incidents were drawn from Porter's own experience, and are realistically enough portrayed. Colonel Brisac requests his friend Beaupres to escort his sister Bellmont from their county seat to Tours. Now Beaupres and Bellmont have long loved, and by pre-arrangement they are married secretly by a good friar. Both Brisac and the General, Clairmont, are passionately enamoured of Charlotte, the daughter of D'orvile, Governor of Tours. With some difficulty Bellmont induces Charlotte to confide that she loves Brisac. This scene is admirably written. The ladies are conversing as they pace the paths of an old-world garden, and the dialogue as they walk to and fro is conceived with a true knowledge of the human heart. Charlotte is cold to Clairmont, and eventually the General and

Brisac meet in a duel. The former is killed on the field, the latter mortally wounded. He is carried home and laid on a bed, but the surgeon sadly declares to his friends : " He cannot last an hour." Brisac who more than suspects that Malignii is a villain with his last breath gasps out to Beaupres " Have a care of *Malignii* ". This is misunderstood, and those standing around the bed suppose him to be commending Malignii to their regard. As Charlotte is carried out swooning, to die broken-hearted, crazed with sorrow, Malignii snivels :—

> Alas, my Colonel took care, you see, at last,
> For me, unworthy me ; I shall grow blind with grief.

Malignii, although he realizes his suit were hopeless, has long lusted after Bellmont's beauty, and discerning that Beaupres loves Bellmont he makes it his business to sow discord and jealousies. He is the more eager to do this because meeting the lady at night in the garden he attempts to ravish her, but the house is roused by her cries. She escapes his grasp, yet through fear of her brother's hot temper she does not disclose the real reason for her alarm. Malignii has already stirred up strife between Beaupres and Boutefeu, and he forthwith convinces the latter that Bellmont secretly dotes upon him, alleging this as the real reason why Beaupres has quarrelled with him. Boutefeu is further persuaded to disguise himself in a friar's habit and meet her when she is walking in the garden by the riverside. The villain next slyly informs Beaupres that his wife has consented " to meet A man disguis'd and privately ". He then tells Bellmont that her confessor wishes to speak with her about making up the difference between her husband and Boutefeu, and to that end is awaiting her " Below the Garden, by the Riverside ". The lady forthwith proceeds to the spot only to recognize Boutefeu when the religious hood is thrown back. Malignii at this moment introduces Beaupres who, mad with jealous rage, mortally wounds his wife, and kills the supposed friar. At that moment Malignii runs at Beaupres with his sword, but is disarmed and seized by the servants as they rush to the place. Bellmont expires in her husband's arms, and the whole of Malignii's black treacheries are revealed. He is ordered to instant punishment, and when the Governor and a company arrive on the scene his screams are heard, a door is opened and " Malignii *discover'd pierct with a stake* ". Beaupres, who has been wounded in the struggle, falls and expires with one sigh :—

> Forgive me dear *Bellmont;* forgive a Crime
> Caus'd by my too much Love—

There are some good lighter episodes in which Cortaux, his son

Colignii, two officers Lamarch and D'elpeche, with Mariane and Francibell take part. The famous scene in Act III where the Host regales his guests by producing veal and salad from various parts of his garments, sausages from his belt, a capon from his helmet, a tansy from the lining of his cap, finally pouring cream out of the scabbard of his sword, is parodied in *The Rehearsal* at the appearance of Pallas who fills two bowls with wine from her lance, furnishes a pie from her casque, and lays on the table a buckler made of cheese.

The Villain, which was one of the great theatrical successes of the decade 1660 to 1670, is thus noticed by Downes : " The Villain, Written by Major *Thomas Porter* ; this Play by its being well perform'd, had Success extremly beyond the Company's Expectation. Mr. *Betterton*, Acting *Monsieur Brisac* ; Mr. *Harris, Monsieur Beaupré* ; Governour, *Mr. Lilliston ; Boutefeu*, Mr. *Young. Maligni*, the Villain, Mr. *Saunford ; Coligni*, the Scriveners Son, by that Inimitable Sprightly Actor, Mr. *Price* ; (especially in this part) ; *Bellmont*, by Mrs. *Betterton* : It Succeeded 10 Days with a full House to the last."

Downes, Cibber, Anthony Aston, all testify to the excellence of Samuel Sandford in the rôle of Malignii. Thus Sir Quibble Queere, who is " perpetually asking Questions about the Playhouse ", whilst strolling on Richmond Hill with Mr. Quickwit, a London visitor, inquires : " Does Mr. *Sandford* act the Villain still, prithee ? " This was in March, 1693, as D'Urfey tells us in his comedy *The Richmond Heiress, Or, A Woman Once in the Right,* Act I, scene 1. In fact Porter's tragedy may be said to have expired with this famous actor. There is an allusion in *The Tatler,* 16th February, 1709, to his celebrated performance : " When poor *Sandford* was upon the stage, I have seen him groaning upon a wheel, stuck with daggers, impaled alive, calling his executioners, with a dying voice, cruel dogs and villains, and all this to please his judicious Spectators, who were wonderfully delighted with seeing a man in torment so well acted." Colley Cibber tells us that Joseph Price who died 1670–1 was succeeded some three or four years later in " the Scrivener's great booby Son, in the *Villain* " by Anthony Leigh, who awoke the loudest laughter as Colignii.

Pepys saw *The Villain* several times. Young Killigrew praised it " as if there had never been any such play come upon the stage ", and although the diarist confesses that after such eulogium he was at first a little disappointed " in over-expecting ", he acknowledged on a subsequent visit that he had much undervalued this true and allowable tragedy.

The Villain is a powerful drama, very ably written and

interesting throughout. Had Porter given us two or three more pieces of the same excellence his name would indeed stand high among English dramatists. Upon the stage one can well imagine that these scenes would be more than ordinarily effective, and they afford great scope for the actor. It would have been easy for a less skilful hand to have cast all the officers in the same mould, but Porter finely differentiates and individualizes even his minor personages. We feel that they actually live. Bellmont and Charlotte again are admirably drawn, and the episode in the garden where the latter faltering and with blush-mantled cheeks confesses her love for Brisac is not the only scene which has insight and beauty. The death of Brisac and the figure of the poor distracted girl crooning snatches of an old ballad as she complains that she is cozened, cozened of her happiness, have real pathos.

Of the date of production at the Theatre Royal of Porter's second play *The Carnival* there is no record, and so far I have been unable to trace any material contemporary allusions. This comedy was printed 4to, 1664, and accordingly it is safest to surmise that it first trod the boards during the preceding year, 1663.

The principal characters in *The Carnival* are : Don Ferdinando, betrothed to Beatrice ; Don Felices, a wild fellow, his brother ; Don Alvaredo, brother to Beatrice ; Don Lorenzo, his half-uncle ; Don Antonio, half-brother to Elvira ; Sancho, a fantastick Clown ; Donna Beatrice and Donna Miranda, Alvaredo's sisters ; Quinta-gona, their Governante ; Donna Elvira, Alvaredo's mistress ; and Bianca, her woman. The scene, Seville. No cast is given.

Don Ferdinando is betrothed to Beatrice, the sister of his friend Alvaredo, who loves Elvira. Don Alvaredo takes Ferdinando to visit Elvira. After they have left the house Ferdinando returns, and tells the lady he is passionately enamoured of her. She is not slow to let him understand that his affection is reciprocated, since she could never more than esteem Don Alvaredo. Torn between love and honour, Ferdinando resolves to leave Seville for a while and retire to Salamanca. Beatrice suspecting some disloyalty follows him, disguising her-self as a man. They both fall into the hands of thieves, who set them free when they have filched their purses, and themselves ridden off on the horses. The thieves, however, as they disappear throw back their two swords, a true Porter touch. Beatrice informs Ferdinando that she is

Alonzo, Brother to *Alvaredo,*
A Student late at *Salamanca,*

and demands satisfaction. Ferdinando laments his fickleness and shame, refusing to fight but crying

> I am willing to expiate my crime,
> Forgive, fair *Beatrice,* thy dying Martyr.
>
> [*Offers to kill himself.*

The supposed youth thereupon reveals he is Beatrice. They return together to Seville and are married. Elvira, although doting upon Ferdinando, is so moved by the generosity of Alvaredo, that his nobleness wins her steady affection and she makes him happy with her hand.

Don Lorenzo, Don Antonio, Sancho, and the duenna Quintagona, are capital comic characters and take part in some amusing scenes which, however, have little or no connexion with the plot. Felices, Ferdinando's brother, and Miranda prove a lively enough pair who considerably help the course of the comedy.

" This is a good Comedy by Porter," says Genest,[268] and I really do not know that there is anything to add more. I am inclined to think that the author has borrowed from some Spanish original, but I have not yet come across this in my reading.

That Thomas Porter was the " T.P. Gent." who wrote *A Witty Combat: Or, The Female Victor* there seems no reason to doubt. This short piece dramatizes a sensational contemporary scandal, and was published quarto, 1663, "As it was *Acted* by Persons of Quality in *Whitson*-Week with great applause." In that year Whit Sunday fell on 7th June, and it is plain that the "*Acted* by Persons of Quality " does not refer to any performance of this piece, but ironically to the real individuals concerned in the affair.

The "Female Victor " is the notorious adventuress Mary Carleton. This woman, whose father's name was Moders, was born at Canterbury in 1634 or 1635. She ran away from her first husband, Thomas Stedman, a shoemaker, in 1658, and then married a second time at Dover a chirurgeon, Thomas Day, only escaping punishment for bigamy owing to the non-appearance of her first husband Stedman as a witness. She then disappears until 1663 when her exploits became the talk of London.

A Witty Combat lists as "Actors Names " : Old Mr. Carleton ; Mr. G. Carleton, his Eldest Son ; Mr. J. Carleton, " his youngest Son in love with the *Germaine Princess* " ; Mr. King, his Son-in-Law ; A Parson ; Two or three Gentlemen ; Two or three Young Clarkes ; Two Watermen ; Drawers ; a Cellarman ; Fiddlers ; Mrs. King ; Madam Moders ; Old Mrs. Carleton ; and Cook Maid.

The play follows very nearly the actual adventures of Mary Moders, and therefore it is hardly necessary to give her career in detail. Act I commences with two Watermen gossiping over their ale at Billingsgate in a tavern. A gentleman comes in to inquire which way a lady took whom they carried on the boat, but who was whipped off by " a dry bon'd Parson " before he could talk with her, yet he gets little satisfaction for his pains. In the second scene the said Parson appears escorting Madam Moders and unctuously declaring : " In verity it is a cold bleak morning, a little of the Creature would do well : a Glass of Malligo is very comfortable, yea, even unto the Spirits, with a Toast ; it does regenerate, and quicken much, and in a way does elevate, and stir the blood to action ; it does assuredly." Madam Moders would shake him off : " Sir, I fear you give yourself too great a trouble, thus to follow me, I cannot reach your meaning." " Verily 'tis sincerity of love I bear to strangers," snivels her companion, ". . . assuredly we should love one another, yea, so the Word is . . ." They enter the King's tavern and drink, and the minister softly says : " the Weather may allow us to come neerer one another, verily, without offence, or misconstruction ; for it is raw and cold, yea very cold." He presently grows a little wanton, and Madam Moders checks him with a " Hands off " whilst the landlord King also has his rebuke "A man of your Coat d'ye see to do these things d'ye see, it is a shame d'ye see, d'ye marke me that ". The minister pays the shilling for their drinks and rubs off muttering " he that takes a Woman for his friend takes a wrong Sow by the Ear, yea, verily ".

The piece proceeds with a good deal of ingenuity. King tells his wife of the Gentlewoman of Quality staying in the house, and presently Mrs. King, making many an apology, fetches her down to dinner. King, his wife, and young Carleton discuss the stranger, and mine host shows himself a trifle suspicious. As for the rest all goes on swimmingly. Mary Moders contrives that the maid shall catch sight of jewels and money in her bed-chamber, and ingenuously confesses that she is Maria van Wolway, the daughter of an Earl dwelling near Cologne, all of which is promptly reported to Mrs. King who proceeds to " lordifie " John, and sing my Lord's praises to her guest. Next Old Mr. Carleton and his wife with son George appear, but Madam Moders is very bashful and retiring, which naturally but lures them the more, until at the beginning of Act V his Lordship is all agog to hurry her " into the Armes of Hymen ". The wedding is kept with music, and the company are as merry as the maids. Next day we see the young clerks laughing among themselves at the marriage of Lord John Carleton to a German

Princess. The happy pair are keeping "their Court and State at *Durham* House i' th' *Strand*". The play now huddles to a conclusion. Up to this point there has been some witty and indeed realistic writing, but with the entrance of Old Carleton bawling out to John that the virtuous Princess is "A very Puss-cat, a subtle Carrion, and a cursed Cheat", we have but mere snatches of scenes. Madam Moders laughs the Carletons to scorn with a "Is that all? Ha, ha, ha", when her father-in-law thunders: I'll "hang you Whore for having of two Husbands". Next follow a couple of speeches between the two Kings, and then "*Enter two Gentlemen as from the Sessions-house*". They express some sympathy with young Carleton but a noise within proclaims that Mary Moders is acquitted. She passes over the stage, and when all have gone off, to end the play "*Enter Moders alone, applying herself to the Auditory*" in a brief but pointed Epilogue of ten lines.[269]

A Witty Combat was clearly not intended for the public stage, but John Holden the bookseller and friend of Davenant utilized the notorious scandal for a play *The German Princess*[270] which was produced at Lincoln's Inn Fields in April, 1664, with Mary Moders herself in the title-rôle. Pepys who saw the piece on 15th April judged that "never was any thing so well done in earnest, worse performed in jest upon the stage". Holden's topical comedy was never printed, and it has sometimes been identified with *A Witty Combat,* a blunder that should not have been made.[271]

More than a decade was to pass before the appearance of Porter's last play—that is if *The French Conjurer,* as there is some reason to suppose, be actually from his pen. This comedy, printed quarto, 1678,[272] was produced at Dorset Garden in the late spring of 1677 with the following cast: Jevon, Avaritio, a rich old covetous Spaniard; Crosby, Claudio, a noble young Spaniard; Gillo, Dorido, in love with Clorinia; Norris, Horatio, his friend; Percival, Truro, Claudio's servant; Anthony Leigh, Monsieur; Richards, Audacio, Horatio's bravo; John Lee, Pedro, a gold-wire-drawer; Mrs. Barry, Clorinia, Avaritio's daughter; Mrs. Hughes, Leonora, Pedro's wife; Mrs. Norris, Sabina, a servant to Claudio; and Mrs. Leigh, Scintillia, Clorinia's maid. Scene: Seville.

Senior Claudio, doting upon the fair Leonora, wife to Pedro, a gold-wire-drawer, is so enamoured that he declares: "I'll spend the value of half a *Spanish* Plate-Fleet, but I'll have her." His chief agents are Monsieur, a sharking French astrologer, and the adroit Sabina. This latter pretends to be a confidential servant of the Lady Abbess of the Convent of S. Sylvester, and

in this character is constantly visiting Pedro's house with orders
for gold wire. Delighted at obtaining the custom of the convent,
as he thinks, Pedro is most anxious to ingratiate himself with the
messenger, never failing to accord her a most favourable reception.   Sabina takes Leonora to visit the Abbess, but on the
way declares she must call for a moment upon Donna Beatrix,
a lady of her acquaintance.   They knock at the door of a fine
mansion and are ushered into a dining-room, when Leonora is
desired to wait.   A moment later Claudio enters and explains
the trick to Leonora, who after a little decent remonstrance
very readily yields to his embrace.   Clorinia and Dorido love
one another, but it is certain that Avaritio, her miserly father,
will never listen to a poor man's suit for his daughter.   Horatio
lays siege to Clorinia, although he soon realizes he has no chance
to succeed save by treachery.   He comes to her window at night
when he knew she was expecting Dorido and gives the signal
by whistling.   Supposing him to be her lover she hands him
a letter through the casement, and whilst taking the paper he
stabs her in the arm.   Next by means of Audacio he immediately
conveys the letter and the bloody dagger into the pocket of
Dorido, upon whom they are thus found, since by Horatio's
contrivance the watch seize him as he hastens to the spot upon
hearing Clorinia's shrieks.   The lady discovers Horatio's schemes,
and when her father loses a valuable necklace of pearl entrusted
to his care with the help of Claudio she persuades him to consult
the famous Astrologer.   Accordingly they repair to Monsieur's
house, and whilst the adept in long stellated robes is conjuring
and exorcizing amain and Avaritio is trembling and quaking,
Dorido and Clorinia are joined in matrimony, a match which
the old man begins to regard with singular complacency when
he hears that the bridegroom is heir to his uncle, the wealthy
Fabricio, of whose death at Madrid the news most opportunely
arrives at Seville.   A rather clever Epilogue is delivered by
Monsieur, who speaks in stagey broken English throughout the
play.   This is a capital comedy, the dialogue being well written,
always easy and often witty, the episodes happily designed in
a manner which does much credit to the talent and technical
skill of the author.

The plot of *The French Conjurer* is taken and varied from two
novels in the famous romance of *Guzman d'Alfarache,* namely,
" The Story of Dorido and Clorinia " and "A true and strange
story of a Merchant in Sevill ".   In the play Dorido and Clorinia
are made happy, but Aleman gives their adventures, the scene
of which is laid at Rome, a tragic turn.   " The Merchant in
Sevill " relates the intrigues of Claudio and Dorotea (Leonora).

" Dorido and Clorinia " may be read in Mabbe's translation of *Guzman de Alfarache,* third edition, folio, 1634, Part I, pp. 255–267 ; and the " Merchant in Sevill ", Part II, pp. 194–208.

Not dissimilar in certain respects to *The French Conjurer* and derived from the same source was a slightly earlier play, *Guzman,* the first comedy of Roger Boyle, Earl of Orrery. The more important dramatic work and influence of Orrery, one of the most prominent figures in the theatre of the decade immediately succeeding the Restoration, will be fittingly considered in a later chapter when treating of heroic tragedy, but it will be well to devote a little place here to his lighter fare, a brace of comedies which notably stand apart from the rest of his productions. Although not printed (folio) until 1693, *Guzman* was produced at Lincoln's Inn Fields on 16th April, 1669. To Pepys, who was present, the play seemed " very ordinary ", and he was astonished when Shadwell, whom he met in the pit told him " that my Lord of Orrery did write this play, trying what he could do in comedy, since his heroique plays could do no more wonders ". Shadwell's opinion may be pretty heavily discounted, and there was a very personal note in his criticisms. Henry Harris, the actor, who had no part in the new play was sure on the first day that it would not take, but Downes [273] informs us that it " took very well ".

The scene of *Guzman* is at Salamanca. Guzman himself is "*An Old Covetous Rich Amorous Cowardly Buffoon*". We also have Francisco, Guivarro, and Alvares, three Brothers, Gentlemen of decay'd Fortunes, left to shift by their Wits, with a complement of sisters, confederates in their designs, Maria, Lucia, and Julia. The last is serving as woman to Leonora, a rich widow, with two daughters, great fortunes, Antonia and Pastrana. The mother and her daughters are " all three practised upon by the forementioned Alvares and his Brothers ". Oviedo and Piracco are " Two Young Foppish Dons, of plentiful Fortunes, Pretenders to Antonia and Pastrana ". Salazar and Ferdinando, " Uncles and Guardians to Oviedo and Piracco ", encourage the courtship of their wards, but " instead of discharging their Trust " the two spectacled wiseacres are themselves practised upon, and at the end find themselves severally married to Tirelesa and Tireletta, whom they suppose to be Maria and Lucia, whereas they are but these ladies' abigails. Upon conditions and payment, however, at their plaints the old gentlemen are released from the matrimonial yoke by Francisco who uses the simple expedient of pulling off the priest's periwig, when her woman's hair tumbles about her ears, and a laundress in cassock stands revealed. Francisco indeed holds most of the threads

of the extremely complicated intrigue in his own hands, and
he large manipulates events in the guise of the Great Alcanzar,
an astrological fortune-teller to whom nearly all the characters
resort for direction and advice. In Act II we find : " *The new
Black Scene.* [*Flashes of Fire ready.* The Scene opens, and *Francisco*
appears in a Magical Habit (with his Closet painted about with
Mathematical Instruments and Grotesque Figures) with a Laurel
on his Head, and a White-Wand in his Hand, Knocks with his
Foot, and four Boys appear within the Scene." [274] These are
his confederate hobgoblins, who presently when Guzman is
consulting the wizard appear " *at several Doors* [275] *in hideous
Dresses, making great Noises and Hums* ".

The plot of *Guzman,* which does not seem to have kept the
stage, is taken from incidents in *Guzman d'Alfarache,* and these
certainly have not gained in clarity by adaptation to fit five acts.

Orrery's second comedy also did not issue from the press
during the lifetime of the author. Although not printed until 1690
(Licensed by J. Fraser, 27th August, 1689), *Mr. Anthony* was
produced at Dorset Garden in 1671 with the following cast :
Sir Timothy [Mr. Sandford] ; Mr. Anthony, Nokes ; Mr. Plot,
Joe Haines ; Mr. Art, Betterton ; Mr. Pedagog, Underhill ;
Mr. Cudden, Angel ; Trick, Mr. Samford ; Mrs. Philadelphia,
Mrs. Jennings ; Mrs. Isabella, Mrs. Betterton ; Mrs. Nell,
Mrs. Long ; Goody Winifred, [Mrs.] Norris. The names of the
actresses who played Sir Timothy's Lady and Mrs. Nan are
not given. There are errors in the cast owing to the late publication. Thus it was almost certainly Sanford who played
Sir Timothy, and not the small rôle of Trick ; Mrs. Norris
not Mr. Norris was Goody Winifred. The text also is carelessly
printed after nearly twenty years, and in the script Mrs. Nell
is often called Mrs. Betty. The Prologue prefixed to *Mr. Anthony*
was first printed in *Covent Garden Drollery,* 1672. Described as
"A second Prologue intended but not spoken " it is to be found
before Duffett's *The Amorous Old-woman,* 4to, 1674, and it again
appeared as the Prologue to D'Urfey's *The Fool Turn'd Critick,*
4to, 1678.

Sir Timothy is desirous that his wards Mrs. Philadelphia
and Mrs. Isabella should marry his son Mr. Anthony and his
nephew Mr. Cudden, who are two coxcombly fools. Mr. Pedagog,
Anthony's bear-leader and dominie, greatly mislikes Jack Plot's
influence over his pupil. " Go Mr. *Tony,*" he threatens, " . . . learn
from your Tutor *Plot,* to Drink, Swear, Whore, Lye and Quarrel :
. . . while I Dedicate my Oil and Labour to Cultivate the Intel-
lectuals of Mr. *Nicholas,* your Junior by Birth, but your Fathers
Heir by Merit." None the less they discover that Mr. Pedagog

PLATE XII

THE INDIAN-QUEEN: ACT IV: SCENE 1

Collection of the Author

had forced old Mrs. Winifred the housekeeper to accept a certain courtesy, much as Square was found with Molly Seagrim, and they hold his wenching *in terrorem* over him, vowing they will peach to Sir Timothy unless he wink at their pranks. Anthony whose twenty-first birthday is being celebrated huffs and picks a quarrel with his cousin Cudden over the two ladies, and the brace of noodles resolve on a duel. Cudden furnishes himself with two crab-tree cudgels with basket hilts, whilst Anthony dresses in complete armour and appears at the rendezvous armed with a bow and arrows. There is an amusing but farcical scene which fairly brought down the house.[276] Anthony and Cudden are reconciled and engage three fiddlers to serenade their mistresses, who appear on the balcony. The fiddlers suddenly present pistols in the faces of the silly swains whom they strip to their very shirts whilst the ladies laugh at the proceedings. After the thieves have rubbed off, the puppies fall to fisticuffs. Sir Timothy who has an itch for Mrs. Nell invades her bed-chamber whilst she is a-bed and proceeds to slip between the sheets, " 'tis time to Storm you " the new Tarquin cries in a paroxysm of amorous impatience. " Help, help," she shrieks and at her vociferations, Sir Timothy's wife, Philadelphia, Isabella, Nan, and the old housekeeper come rushing into the room.[277] Sir Timothy is dragged from behind the curtains and Goody Winifred runs out to return immediately exclaiming : " Oh, Madam, by the happiest chance in the World, I met in the Street, just at the door, the three Chastizers of the Parish, newly risen from sitting in Judgment on a young Fornicator, who they have handled without Mittings, and therefore will feague an old Adulterer." On 10th May, 1650, the rebels had passed "An Act for suppressing the detestable sins of Incest, Adultery and Fornication " all such offences to be adjudged felony, death being the penalty of the two first, with imprisonment for the latter. The Chastizers were Parish Officers who inquired in the first place regarding such accusations. Three Elders enter with a snuffle and a hum, of whom one proclaims on hearing the charges against Sir Timothy : " My Brothers, here's a Covy of Vices complicated ; Fornication, as she is a single Woman ; Adultery, as he is a Marry'd Man, and Incest as he is an Unkle," Mrs. Nell being his wife's niece. The wretched delinquent when harangued by the leash of Elders is ready to agree to any terms. He assigns portions to Mrs. Nell and Mrs. Nan giving them in marriage to Anthony and Cudden ; he leaves Mrs. Philadelphia and Mrs. Isabella to be at their own disposal when they forthwith accept Tom Art and Jack Plot as their husbands ; he settles money on Anthony and Cudden, and for ever resigns the Sovereignty of the House to his injured wife. When the trembling Miscreant-Penitent has signed and sealed, confirmed and ratified before the whole company as witnesses, the three Elders pluck off their disguises and prove to be Anthony, Cudden, and Pedagog. "Well, I am Noos'd I confess," sadly mutters the luckless and choused old wretch.

Mr. Anthony is farcical no doubt, but it is an extremely amusing piece, funnier I venture to think than *Guzman,* which is a play by no means lacking in wit and humorous incident, although (as I have remarked) a little too involved in the intrigue. It is a pity that when Orrery's dramatic works were collected in two volumes by Dodsley, 1739, *Mr. Anthony* (without a word of explanation) was replaced by the rather tame and colourless *As You Find It* [278] by Charles Boyle (afterwards Earl of Orrery), grandson of the First Earl.

The Widow, a comedy attributed to Roger Boyle, but not printed and of which actually little is known, has been mentioned above.

Since of his three—or if we count the masque—his four dramatic pieces one only was written (but unacted) after the Restoration it might be argued that Sir Aston Cokayne is scarcely entitled to a place here, and indeed it has chiefly been his lot to fall between two stools. Cokayne was born from an ancient family of Ashbourne, Derbyshire, at Elvaston the residence of his maternal grandfather Sir John Stanhope. His mother, Anne, was the half-sister of Philip, first Earl of Chesterfield. He was baptized at Ashbourne, 20th December, 1608, and educated at Chenies, Bucks. Thence he proceeded to Trinity College, Cambridge, and afterwards " for fashion's sake " entered one of the Inns of Court, London. In 1632 he set out upon an extensive tour in France and Italy, and upon his return married Mary, daughter of Sir Gilbert Knyveton, Bart., of Mercaston, Derbyshire. At his father's death, on 26th January, 1639, he succeeded to Pooley Hall, Warwickshire, his favourite place of residence. Ashbourne went to his mother, and did not become his estate until her death, 29th August, 1664. On 10th January, 1642, he was created a baronet by Charles I, but actually the patent, although always recognized, was never enrolled. In the same year Oxford conferred upon him the degree of M.A., but this was not registered. "A perfect boon fellow " he was no niggard in his living, but his impoverishment was due to the heavy losses he suffered and the crushing fines as a " popish delinquent ". During the frenzy of Oates' plot the persecutions in Lancashire and Derbyshire were especially bitter, and Cokayne was obliged to sell all his estates, eventually in 1683 even parting with Pooley

Hall. He died broken-hearted in lodgings at Derby in February, 1684. Having survived his wife, and only son, he left what little remained to him to his two daughters, both of whom were married. With him the baronetcy became extinct.

The Masque, which was presented on Twelfth Night, 1639, at Brethie in Derbyshire before the poet's relation Philip, the first Earl of Chesterfield and his Countess, " Two of their Sons acting in it," is an extremely pleasing and poetical little piece, not perhaps without at one point some trifling suggestion from *Comus*.[279] It was first printed in *A Chain of Golden Poems,* 8vo, 1658.

The manuscript of *The Obstinate Lady* had been lent by the author on leaving London for the country to a friend, who unhappily died rather suddenly, whereupon his papers were accidentally dispersed, and the play chanced to come into the hands of a bookseller, William Godbid. The last leaf had been torn off, but Godbid supplying a brief conclusion printed the " new Comedy ", 4to, 1657. On hearing of this, Cokayne collected together a number of his poems together with a second play *Trappolin,* and these were published by Godbid in one volume, 8vo, 1658, wherein was also included the revised and correct text of *The Obstinate Lady* with the original ending and epilogue.

With regard to the writing *The Obstinate Lady* may be judged not without merit in parts, but it is obviously the work of a lover of poetical drama rather than of a practised dramatist. It is at best an intensely imitative specimen of the lesser school of playwrights about 1635 to 1642. The scene is London, but the persons are romantically introduced under such names as Philander, Carionil, Falorus, Lucora, Vandona, Nentis. The characters of Carionil, and Lucora " the Obstinate Lady ", must be at once recognized as closely modelled upon Don John Antonio and Almira in *A Very Woman*,[280] unfortunately without a tithe of Massinger's genius to make them live. Not only do we meet the inevitable love-lorn lass, disguised as a page in the service of the object of her passion, but we also have the incomprehensible masquerade of Rosinda, the mother of three marriageable children, as Tandorix, a servant in her husband's household. In fine the sentiments, the situations, and the characters are all too artificial and strained to arouse, much less to enchain, any interest in these scenes.[281]

It is all the more surprising how adroitly Cokayne has manged the twists and turns of *Trappolin creduto Principe ; or, Trappolin Suppos'd a Prince,* and what brisk facile dialogue, eminently adapted for stage effect, he has composed. This " Italian Trage-Comedy " is farcical to the last degree, nay more, it might not untruly be dubbed a pantomime, but for all that it remains an extremely spirited and amusing piece of work. Although doubtless better suited for actual performance than for reading, even in the closet it cannot fail to please, and this in itself may be advanced as a proof of very high merit. Cokayne tells us that his scenes are far from being a mere translation. He saw the original piece twice during a visit to Venice, and the design so liked him by its ingenuity and real fun that he employed it with most admirable result for an English play. Criticism naturally approaches an *entretiamento* of this sort from one only standpoint. We ask to be amused, and assuredly Trappolin is the most laughable fellow. What matter if it is, as the *Biographica Dramatica* complains, " a most absurd piece of work, every rule of character, probability, and even possibility, being absolutely broken through," a little nonsense now and then is relished by the wisest men.

Lavinio, the Great Duke of Tuscany, departing for Milan to wed the matchless Isabella, leaves as governors Lord Barbarino and Lord Machavil. Now the former has an itch towards Trappolin's sweetheart, the pretty Flametta, and consequently whip-snitch Master Trappolin is banished, exiled, and all that. However Mago, a conjurer (who in the end proves to be his own natural father), meets him and presents him with a magic hat, mirror, and cloak with various subtle powders, all of which possess strange virtues. Suffice to say that by these ensorcelled properties Trappolin is enabled to appear exactly as the Great Duke. He comes back to Florence, punishes Barbarino and Machavil, playing a thousand pranks in a thousand corners. When Lavinio himself returns the confusion is, of course, doubly confounded. At the end Mago having secured a general pardon acknowledges the sleight, whilst Trappolin is not only forgiven but rewarded by the Turin prince to whom during his mock dukedom he has done a good turn, and he is able to wed his faithful Flametta.

To look for the source of the magic gifts, familiar to us all from the nursery, would be to trace far and wide the boundless stores of oriental fiction, and in fine the folklore of the world. The conduct of Trappolin in the scene with the petitioners may be paralleled with an old story in the Sieur D'Ouville's *Contes aux heures perdues*,[282] where are collected a vast number of tales and anecdotes from *Cento Novelle Antiche*, *Le Tombeau de la Mélancholie*, *Le Moyen de Parvenir*, from Poggio, Domenichi, and a score of other writers. Trappolin, who is no better than a practised pimp, in his examination before the Lords, Act I, 2, very nearly resembles Pompey before Escalus in

Measure for Measure. There are, indeed, even exact verbal conveyances.

Trappolin Suppos'd a Prince was first produced nearly twenty years after it had been written at the Theatre Royal in 1675 with Joe Haines as Trappolin. A new Prologue composed for the occasion by Duffett and printed in his *Poems,* 8vo, 1676, was spoken.

On 3rd November, 1684, at the Theatre Royal was given *A Duke and no Duke,*[283] a farce by Nahum Tate, being an alteration of Cokayne's play. This proved extremely to the taste of the town, and Anthony Leigh as Trappolin "A Parasite, Pimp, Fidler, and Buffoon" immensely amused the King. The vitality of Trappolin indeed under various forms was so extraordinary that he remained a favourite even in the nineteenth century. Among the many alterations perhaps the most notable were John Thurmond's pantomime in grotesques, *A Duke and No Duke,* produced at Drury Lane in 1720; Robert Drury's farcical ballad opera *The Devil of a Duke; or, Trapolin's Vagaries,* Drury Lane, August, 1732, of which a version attributed to Allan Ramsay was given in Edinburgh the following year; and an anonymous *A Duke and No Duke,* a London success of 1757–8, printed 8vo, 1758. In July, 1818, a comic melodramatic burletta, *The Duke and the Devil,* in which Fitzwilliam[284] as Trappolin "kept the house in a continual roar of laughter", was very favourably received at Covent Garden. At minor theatres and in the provinces Trappolin was welcomed until well nigh the middle of the last century.

It is impossible to conjecture owing to what circumstance Cokayne's last play *The Tragedy of Ovid,* published 8vo, 1669, as "Intended to be Acted shortly", never saw the boards. It seems at any rate not less interesting than many contemporary pieces which were given with approval and applause. It is a highly sensational drama, the main plot of which concerns Bassanes, a young lord of Tomos, who wrongfully suspecting his bride Clorina, murders Pyrontus whom she has repelled more icily than Lucrece, and binds her in a chair fastening the heart of the supposed adulterer in her hands. There she expires, sighing out her innocence. Punishment follows, however, for Bassanes falls in love with and dotes upon the beauteous Caralinda, who is none other than the brother of Pyrontus, Phœbianus, in disguise. The youth having sorely taunted the brutal Bassanes kills him in a duel. The not unimportant episodes of the lewd Italian captain, Hannibal, who in bravado bids a corpse from a gibbet to supper, and when the carrion, having accepted the welcome and presented himself at the appointed hour, returns the invitation, thereon duly repairs to a fearful feast at the gallows-tree, whence he is borne off to bale by a hideous train of furies and ghosts, is a variant of the Don Juan legend.[285] Langbaine, probably correctly, suggests that this passage is borrowed from the Italian play, *Il Ateista Fulminato*.[286] The author and date of *Il Ateista Fulminato* are quite unknown, but M. Simone Brouwer found in a Roman library eight and forty *lazzi* or outlines of plays, and among them was the draft of this tragedy. Ovid, from whom Cokayne's drama rather maladroitly has its name, is hardly concerned in the action. " I know not why the Author gave this Play the Title of *Ovid's Tragedy,* except that he lays the Scene in *Tomos,* and brings him to fall down dead with grief at the News he received from *Rome,* in sight of the Audience : otherwise he has not much business on the Stage." [287] The part of the comely youth Phœbianus, who masquerades as Caralinda, was designed for Edward Kynaston.

The name, character, and cruelty of Bassanes are derived from *The Broken Heart,* produced at the Blackfriars, and printed 4to, 1633. In Ford's tragedy the young lovers, Orgilus and Penthea, have been separated by the lady's ambitious brother Ithocles, who compels her to wed the insanely jealous Bassanes. Penthea dies broken-hearted, refusing food and starved to death. She has refused to give herself to Orgilus, although loathing the bond which unites her to Bassanes. Her lover determines to revenge her, which he does by entrapping Ithocles in a chair contrived to hold and fetter the occupant powerless to move.[288] Orgilus then stabs his victim to death. Many of Penthea's speeches are echoed by Clorina, and the device of the chair in which she is manacled was plainly suggested by Ford's engine.

Throughout Cokayne's work his dependence upon and borrowings from earlier dramatists are most marked and frequent.

The dramas of Sir William Lower (1600–1662), both in character and treatment, strictly belong to the period before the Restoration, and therefore though full of interest must from our point of view be rather summarily dismissed.

The first of Lower's plays *The Phaenix in her flames,* 4to, 1639, is an exceedingly exotic and highly romantic tragedy where we meet the King of Arabia ; and his daughter, Phoenicia ; the Princes of Damascus and Persia ; with other persons of quality and a whole complement of banditti and assassinates. When Amandus, Prince of Damascus, is slain, Phoenicia who loves him resolves to imitate the Phoenix, and her Doctor instructs her :

'Tis true I can compose variety
Of gummes, of drugges and spices mixt together,
And make a perfume not unlike unto
The *Phoenix* Funerall fire, whereby you may,
Be sweetly smother'd lying in your bed.

Accordingly she swoons to death amid the fume of frankincense
and thick breath of Sabean odours.

The Phaenix in her flames was, I think, suggested by Heliodorus.
Although perhaps there are no incidents which can be exactly
paralleled, the adventures with the Arabian robbers are not dissimilar to episodes in *Theagenes and Chariclea,* and one is conscious
of a relationship of genre.

Polyeu tes ; or, The Martyr, 4to, 1655, is a translation by
Lower from Pierre Corneille's *Polyeucte, Martyr, tragédie
Chrétienne,* produced at Paris in 1640,[289] and published 4to, 1643.
The *Roman Martyrology* under 13th February celebrates the
birthday (the heavenly birthday and entrance into bliss) of
S. Polyeuctus,[290] who suffered in the persecution of Decius at
Melitina in Armenia. There is little to be said of Lower's version
save that it is extremely mediocre and commonplace and entirely
misses the genius of the original. Genest [291] quaintly enough
remarked that there was matter in this piece to which a good
Protestant might object. For aught I can tell such may be the
case, and at any rate I suppose Genest knew.

A second translation from Corneille, Lower's *Horatius :
A Roman Tragedie,* 4to, 1656, is so pedestrian as to be easily
the worst of the English versions of *Horace.* The blank verse
is merely prose chopped up into lengths, such as defy the reader
and would be impossible to speak.

The Three Dorothies ; or, Jodele' Box'd was translated by Lower
in 1657 from Scarron's *Les Trois Dorothées, ou, le Jodelet Souffleté,*
produced in 1646, and printed 1651 as *Jodelet duelliste. The Three
Dorothies,* of which the original MS. was formerly in the Skeffing-
ton collection, has not been printed.

Unprinted also is Lower's *Don Japhet of Armenia,* a version made
in 1657 of Scarron's famous comedy *Dom Japhet d'Arménie,* 1652.
Lower's autograph MS. is preserved in the British Museum.[292]

In June, 1658, Lower published at The Hague (Adrian Vlack)
The Enchanted Lovers, a pastoral, the scene of which is " in the
Island of Erithrea in Portugal ", of which domain the Princess
is " an Inchantress " of Zoroaster's line, Melissa. This lady
by her spells complicates the romantic adventures and wooings
of a leash of lovers, amours which truth to tell already seem
sufficiently intricate and involved. However, in Scena Ultima
the Goddess Diana descends to set all straight and unite the

several fond pairs. *The Enchanted Lovers* is suggested in part, at any rate, by D'Urfé's incomparable *Astrée*, and rococo, even bizarre, as Lower's scenes must be acknowledged to be this piece should by no means have been so carelessly omitted from W. W. Greg's *Pastoral Poetry and Pastoral Drama*, 1906, where it receives no mention.

Almost equally baroque is *The Noble Ingratitude*, "A Pastoral-Tragi-Comedy," The Hague, 12mo, 1659, a translation by Lower from Quinault's *La Généreuse Ingratitude* (1654), and by him dedicated to the Queen of Bohemia. "*The Scene is in the Forrest of Argier*," and the conflicting passions of love are panached and plumed beyond all measure. Zelinda, of the Abencerage house, who is promised to Zegry follows him in disguise as a youth, Osmin, to Argier. Zegry loves Fatima who dotes on Abidar, but he is cold to her charms having given his heart to Zegry's sister, Zaida, who shuns his addresses since she loves and is beloved by Almansor, the brother of Zelinda. So the tangle works itself out, the "Noble Ingratitude" being the transfer of Zegry's affection from Fatima to Zelinda. The French original is a charming piece ; the English a very poor translation.[293]

The Amorous Fantasme, a tragi-comedy, "Acted at Court," The Hague (John Ramzey), 12mo, 1660, is Lower's fairly close but woefully tepid version of Quinault's *Le Fantôme Amoureux*, Hôtel de Bourgogne, 1659. Lower has shifted the scene from Milan to Ferrara,[294] whose Duke enamoured of Climene orders her betrothed Fabritio to be assassinated. A stranger is killed in the dark streets by mistake for Fabritio, and thus supposed dead he lies hid in his father's house whence " a secret mine " enables him to appear to his mistress, who soon realizes that this " deceitfull Fantasme " is her lover in the flesh. The Duke meeting the ghost is horror struck, and a happy conclusion is reached owing to his repentance and remorse.

The original, Calderón's *El Galan Fantasma,* is wholly delightful, and Quinault certainly has a quality the English lacks. *The Amorous Fantasme* is furnished with a Prologue and Epilogue, spoken at Court, and therefore it was probably acted before Charles II at Whitehall in 1661. There is no record that it was ever produced in the public theatre.

The other works of Lower, mostly translations from the French,[295] do not fall within our scope. Dr. Richard Lower told Wood in a letter that Sir William Lower " was an ill poet, and a worse man ". The former is, I fear, incontestable. Let us hope that the latter was merely a kinsman's spleen, for Sir William was not on good terms with his relations.

It may not be amiss here to consider another dramatist whose work solely consists of translations from the French and Italian, John Dancer, whom there seems no adequate reason to identify with John Dauncy, a contemporary miscellaneous writer. Of Dancer practically nothing is known save what he himself tells us in his Dedications, whence we gather that he was in the service of and a favourite with the Duke of Ormonde. At the Restoration, on 4th November, 1661, this most honoured nobleman was again appointed Lord-Lieutenant of Ireland, although actually it was not until 27th July, 1662, that he landed and entered Dublin in state. It was under his semi-royal patronage and with his personal encouragement that Dancer's two plays were produced at Smock Alley.

Dancer's earliest work was a version (not intended for the stage) of Tasso *Aminta,* published 8vo, 1660, as *The Famous Pastoral. Written in Italian By Signor Torquato Tasso.* And Translated into English Verse By *John Dancer.* Together with divers Ingenious *Poems.*

Nicomede, his translation from Corneille, was published London, 4to, 1671, by Francis Kirkman. (Licensed for printing *Dec.* 16, 1670. *Roger L'Estrange.*) Perhaps the most interesting feature of this quarto is that it furnishes " an Exact Catalogue of all the English *Stage-Plays* printed, till this present Year 1671 ". " I have done it as perfectly as I can," says Kirkman of this list, which if not indeed complete is of considerable value. There are 806 titles of plays, and Kirkman tells us he also has " some quantity in Manuscript ".

Nicomede is dedicated to Ormonde's son, the Earl of Ossory, at whose particular desire Dancer undertook the English version, which " passed the Suffrage of the Stage " in 1662–3.

Corneille's *Nicomède* was produced in 1651. The poet derived his subject from Justin's *Historiae,*[296] Lib. xxxiv, c. 4, a brief account which he has considerably modified to suit the special design of his drama.

The characters of Dancer's *Nicomede* (alternately called Nicho-mede) are : Prusias, King of Bithinia ; Flaminius, the Roman Ambassador ; Arsinoe, second wife to King Prusias ; Nicomede, eldest son of Prusias by a former venture ; Attalas, son of Prusias and Arsinoe ; Laodice, Queen of Armenia ; Araspes, Captain of the Guards ; and Cleone, confidante to Arsinoe. The Scene is Nicomedia (modern Ismid), situated in a north-eastern angle of an island in the Propontis. Prusias is Prusias II, the Hunter, who reigned 192–148 B.C. ; Titus Quinctius Flaminius was consul in 198 B.C., and ambassador in 183. Nicomedes II (Philopater) reigned over Bithynia 148 B.C–91 B.C., succeeding Prusias.

Nicomede and Attalus are both enamoured of Laodice, who loves the former. Through the influence of Arsinoe, Prusias, wishing Laodice to marry Attalus, puts Nicomede under a guard intending to dispatch him as a hostage to Rome. The populace rise and rescue the prince, who appeases their fury. Prusias is reconciled to Nicomede, whose friendship and forgiveness are also sought by Arsinoe and Attalus. Even Flaminius declares that the Senate of Rome must admire so great and generous a spirit :—

> And if the name of friend they can't allow,
> They'l think to have found in you a worthy foe.

In actual history Prusias for the sake of his sons by his second Queen intended to have killed Nicomedes, but the prince discovering his father's subtle designs made open war upon him with the help of the King of Pergamus. " Nicomedes having beaten the army of his father, killed him in the temple whither the unfortunate king had fled, and it was only by an impious murder that Nicomedes possessed himself of the government and ascended the throne of Bithynia." Thus Diodorus Siculus.[297] Hence Nicomedes was in derision termed Philopater. Genest speaks of the " coldness and declamation " of *Nicomede,* and Dancer's version is in truth a dull, disappointing piece.

Agrippa, King of Alba : Or, The False Tiberinus was received with great applause upon its production at Dublin. It was published, 4to, 1675, with a Dedication to the Lady Mary Cavendish, daughter of Ormonde, who favoured this play with very marked approval. It is a translation in heroic couplets from Quinault's *Agrippa, Roy d'Albe, ou le Faux Tiberinus,* a tragi-comedy produced in 1661 at the Hôtel de Bourgogne. " Cette Tragedie," says Parfaict,[298] " eut un succès marqué ; lorsqu'elle parut au Théâtre, et elle s'y est conservée depuis." "*The Scene is the Palace of the Kings of* Alba, *in the Princess* Lavinia'*s Abartment.*" The intrigue is sufficiently intricate, but never confused. Tiberinus, King of Alba, having been drowned in the river Albula, Tyrhenus " a Prince of Æneas's blood " persuaded his son Agrippa, who exactly resembles Tiberinus, to assume the character of the dead monarch. The scheme perfectly succeeds. The real Tiberinus was enamoured of Agrippa's sister, Albina, and was beloved by her. The false Tiberinus (Agrippa) loves Lavinia, a Princess of the Blood Royal. Mezentius, nephew to the drowned King, is also a suitor for the hand of Lavinia, who rejects him although she detests the false Tiberinus, since she believes him to have murdered Agrippa, whom she fondly loved. Accordingly she lays her commands on Mezentius to kill the false Tiberinus (Agrippa), and this he vows to do, since as he tells the lady,

> To be gainsaid, Love's power is too divine . . .
> You in my heart do bear the highest sway,
> And Loves laws are the first I should obey.

Shortly after the false Tiberinus privately acknowledges to Lavinia that he is in reality Agrippa :—

> 'Twas Tiberinus who alone was drown'd,
> And you in me that happy love have found.

He requests his father to witness the truth of this, but far from doing so Tyrhenus insists that his son Agrippa has been murdered at the royal command.   Lavinia questions him further, but even as they are talking an officer named Faustus brings the news that the false Tiberinus has been slain by Mezentius and his soldiers, whereupon Tyrhenus overcome with grief confesses that it is indeed his son Agrippa who has fallen.   Almost immediately after it appears that Albina, deeming him to be the real Tiberinus who once loved her, has saved Agrippa's life by hurrying him through a garden gate, whence he made his way to the fort and put himself at the head of his cohorts.   Seeing all lost Mezentius kills himself, by whose death, now that the real Tiberinus is no more, Lavinia becomes rightful Queen of Alba.   Tyrhenus presents her with the crown, which she bestows with herself upon Agrippa :—

> Thus then let all the world my faith approve,
> And see your Son crown'd here by Me and Love.

In spite of the easy criticisms of the Abbé du Bos in his *Réfléxions sur la Peinture et la Poësie*,[299] *Agrippa, Roy d'Albe* is a delightful baroque play.   Dancer's translation, moreover, is not without merit, and often he is very happy in his turns.   The plot is romantic fiction.   Dionysius Halicarnassensis (Lib. I, cap. 71) mentions the story, and Ovid [300] also in the *Fasti,* ii, 389–390, refers to the old legend of Tiberinus, King of Alba Longa, the most ancient town in Latium, who was drowned in the river Albula, thereafter known as the Tiber :—

> Albula, quem Tibrin mersus Tiberinus in unda
> Reddidit, . . .

To conclude this chapter we may devote some attention to the work of an author who has been long and most unjustly neglected.   It was the ill hap of William Killigrew to furnish the playhouse after the Restoration with tragi-comedies that belonged to an earlier period, pieces whose vogue had passed away and was clean forgot of the newer school.   The eldest brother of Thomas Killigrew, William, was born at Hanworth in 1605.   He entered S. John's College, Oxford, 1623, and three years later was knighted by James I.   He sat in Parliament for

Penryn, Cornwall, 1628–9, and was appointed Governor of Pendennis Castle by Charles I, who held him in high esteem. In 1642 Oxford created him a Doctor of Civil Laws. William Killigrew had unhappily sunk his whole patrimony in a useless scheme of draining the fen lands, and during the interregnum he fell upon days of great difficulty. At the Restoration he was conspicuously favoured by the Queen-Mother, in whose household he had been appointed Vice-Chamberlain, and for whom he wrote plays of the kind in which she especially delighted. Henrietta Maria, however, left England in 1665. From 1664 to 1678 Killigrew sat as member for Richmond, Yorkshire, and he occupied the post of Vice-Chamberlain to the Queen-Consort, Catherine of Braganza. The Revolution destroyed the world for this fine old courtier, who died in 1693 broken-hearted and undone.[301]

Langbaine made no specific mention of the production in the theatre of Sir William Killigrew's four plays, and it was apparently in consequence of this omission that a quite erroneous idea became generally established among the more superficial and bell-wethered to the effect that, as a recent pundit is pleased to inform us : " Probably only one of his four plays was ever acted on the stage : both from their manner of printing and from their style they seem to have been intended for closet dramas." [302] Nothing could be further from the actual truth, and this inept pronunciamento only serves to betray a slender knowledge of the Restoration drama and Restoration stage conditions. The blunder must speedily have been corrected had the writer been at the trouble to acquaint himself with a few examples of the many romantic dramas of the tradition in which Sir William Killigrew so narrowly trod. Moreover Downes (to mention no other authority) records the acting of *Selindra* and *Pandora* ; the script of *The Seege of Urbin* prepared and cut for performance is preserved ; and if the Complimentary Verses prefixed to the *Four New Playes,* folio, Oxford, 1665, mean anything at all they certainly indicate that *Ormasdes* was given in the theatre.

Selindra was produced at the Theatre Royal, Vere Street, on Monday, 3rd March, 1662 ; *Pandora* at Lincoln's Inn Fields in 1663 ; *Ormasdes* in 1664, but it is uncertain at which theatre ; and *The Seege of Urbin* at the Theatre Royal, Bridges Street, early in 1665. *Selindra* is mentioned by Henry Herbert as a new play, and also in a contemporary doggerel letter,[303] where it is said :—

> A good Plott though ill writt lookes more like a Play
> Then all your fine lines when the Plott is away.

Edmund Waller addressed some verses to William Killigrew "Upon his altering his Play *Pandora* from a Tragedy, into a Comedy, because not approved on the Stage ".[304]   It would appear that from blank verse Killigrew had turned his dialogue into prose. Both versions seem to have been acted.

The Scene of the first of Sir William Killigrew's plays, the highly romantic "Tragy-Comedy" *Selindra,* "Is the *Emperors Palace* at *Bizantium,*" and in addition to a fairly long cast "a great attendance of Lords, Ladies, Officers, Guards, Pages, and Servants" is required.

Prince Phillocles, son of the Emperor Lascaris of Greece, has defeated the German invaders of Hungary in a decisive battle, but jealous of his victory the treacherous allies King Trebello of Hungary and his elder son Bazanes plan to seize their champion. The younger son of King Trebello, Prince Pollinesso, discovers the plot to Phillocles, whereupon the King and Barzanes in terror take to flight, compelling Pollinesso to accompany them. News is brought that they have been drowned in crossing a river, and since Astella, the Princess of Hungary, has disappeared and been mysteriously concealed before the war, the grateful nation of Hungary lay the crown at the feet of Phillocles. To his father's wrath, he refuses the throne, and being of heroic temper resolves to seek out the fair Astella. "Is this a time to act Romances in?" angrily chides the Emperor. Phillocles is in love with Selindra, the daughter of a Cypriot lord, Periander, dwelling in Byzantium, but the Emperor, designing that his son shall marry Astella if ever the lady be found and so secure the crown of Hungary, insists that Selindra shall wed Cleonel, the son of Cecropius, a base favourite. There is much rivalry between Phillocles and Cleonel, which so enrages the Emperor that he determines Selindra must be dispatched by poison, and gives her to the custody of Cecropius, who plots strange villainies, and even attempts to ravish her. Cleonel informs Selindra of her impending fate, which she can only escape by his means. He swears honourably to escort her to Belgrade, but no sooner are they on their way than she realizes he is devising treachery, and she is only rescued by a party of travellers amongst whom is Pollinesso, who cuts down Cleonel. The Prince at once recognizes Selindra as his sister Astella; but Phillocles, mad with jealousy, has pursued Selindra and Cleonel, and there are a good many cross accidents before the riddle is read. Swayed by Cecropius, burning to avenge his son, the Emperor yet designs to compass Selindra's death, but when Pollinesso at the head of the Hungarian forces arrives before the gates of Byzantium and in solemn state leads in his sister Astella (heretofore Selindra), the dark plots of Cecropius crumble. He is banished, and Lascaris bestows imperial benisons on the marriage of Phillocles and Astella, whilst to Pollinesso is given the Princess Ordella of Byzantium, alliances binding the two empires in perpetual kinship and amity.

Selindra, which (as we have it) is written in prose, seems more to resemble a romance in dialogue than a play. There are some good scenes, but dramatically much appears thin-spun and weak. The events are many, and at times a little confusing, so frequent are the disguises, changes, and conspiracies. The Emperor Lascaris is a particularly unprincipled and unpleasant character throughout.

The cast of *Selindra* is not printed. Downes [305] mentions it without comment in a list of eleven pieces, all of which were successful, so we may presume that it was tolerably well approved.

It is curious, in view of Sir William's relationship to Tom Killigrew, that his next play *Pandora, or, The Converts* should have been given at Lincoln's Inn Fields. Waller's lines are too vague in their allusion to enable us to surmise with any exactness how Killigrew was able to change the tragedy which failed into the comedy as we now have it.

The scene is Syracusa, the heir of which Principality, Lonzartes, is being led into wild courses and debauch by his rake-helly companion, Clearcus, a great hunter of the game, whom for a merry jest Pandora, urged thereto by other ladies, resolves to turn into a very Platonic lover. " I do fancy his conversion might be wrought by her, and his Eclips'd virtues made to shine brighter then his vices do," says Lonzartes of his friend. Actually the Princess Theodocia and her cousin Pandora are loud in their praises of a single life. Silvander and Lindamira are passionate but philosophical lovers. Lonzartes is sighing perpetually for a certain Cloris, under which name he designs Theodocia, who eventually rewards his devotion, a match extremely pleasing to the Three Estates of Syracusa. Clearcus and Pandora, in spite of their supposed aversion to matrimony, find themselves " fool'd into the *Platonick* pound ", and become mere man and wife, since

> This happy issue of so strange contest,
> Wrought by the gods, must by the gods be blest.

Pandora, commencing with a couple of good brisk scenes, soon trails off into lengthy and undramatic dialogues and discussions upon themes which however well written in themselves seem more suited to the fine-drawn casuistries of a Provençal Parliament of Love than adapted to the quick traffic of the candle-lit stage. Neither as a tragedy, nor when metamorphosed to comedy,

did the play prove a success.   In some vague far-off manner
Clearcus and Pandora remind one of Dryden's Celadon and
Florimel, although Killigrew's lay figures have not a spark of
the vivacity of that delightful pair.

> *I judge, that by* Ormasdes, *you designe,*
> *To teach how Friendship's, more then Love, divine!*

says Sir Samuel Tuke in a Poem addressed to Killigrew upon
his next play, *Ormasdes,* which was in effect afterwards named
Love and Friendship.   The scene lies in the Island of Citherea,
of which the Queen Cleandra, being enamoured of a Grecian
Prince, her General, Ormasdes, very coldly receives the
Embassador from Valerianus, King of Treconia, who sues for
her hand.   The Embassador, only too truly suspecting the cause
of the rejection, is in high dudgeon and quarrels with Ormasdes,
when as swords are actually drawn, Mariana, the Embassador's
sister, cries out that he is King Valerianus himself, thus revealing
herself to be the Princess Valeriana.   The King departs in fury,
but Valeriana returns to the court of Citherea, and presently
falls sick of love.   Queen Cleandra, out of her heroic ideals of
friendship, stifling her own affection for Ormasdes would have
him marry the Princess.   This lady, however, fears that the
love of Ormasdes may be rather compassion than the heart's
affection she demands.   She is finally convinced, as he watches
all night by her couch, that her burning love is fully returned,
and accordingly they are united at Hymen's altar.   It is easy
to see that *Ormasdes* is pitched upon the very highest and most
artificial note of love and heroic friendship.   With all the salient
and somewhat exaggerated characteristics of Killigrew pushed
to an extreme, it is such a play as Madelon and Cathos would
have immensely admired.   The writing lacks neither elegance
nor fire, and the conception is in the first place noble and pure.
Perhaps we feel that Cleandra's love for Ormasdes is singularly
wanting in depth to be so easily overcome.   When Dryden was
to treat a not dissimilar theme in *Secret-Love, or, The Maiden-Queen*
his genius gave nature instead of artifice, and the figure of the
Queen of Sicily loses no jot of its sovranty, although the woman's
heart bleeds and breaks beneath her ermined robe.

Killigrew's fourth play *The Seege of Urbin,* "A Tragy-Comedy,"
which was produced at the Theatre Royal early in 1665, is far
more dramatic and far better suited to the theatre than his former
work.   The folio, 1666, gives no cast but the author's MS.[306]
has the names of seven performers who filled the most important
of the many rôles. The Duke of Urbin, Hart; Fernando (Lorenzo,
Duke of Florence), Florio (Celestina), and Pedro (Melina), three

strangers, Mohun, Mrs. Anne Martiall [Marshall], and Mrs. Nell [Gwyn]; Silviana, the Duke of Urbin's sister, Mrs. Weaver; Clara, maid to Mariana the daughter of old lord Corbino, Mrs. Bettie [Elizabeth Davenport]; and Lodovico, Duke of Ferrara, Burt.[307]

Lodovico of Ferrara has laid siege to Urbin, hoping " by force to get the Princess *Silvania* for his Wife; against her Brothers and her own Consent ". In order to escape a marriage she abhors Celestina, the cousin of the Duke of Florence, disguised as Florio and attended by her woman Melina disguised as Pedro, have chanced to take refuge in Urbin on the very eve of the investment of the city. As they come up to the gate through the darkness their approach puts to flight some five banditti who are attacking a traveller, Fernando. In gratitude he takes them to his lodging, and the next day the three strangers proffer their services to the Duke. He at once takes a great fancy to the handsome young Florio. So distinguished a favour together with the bravery shown in the field by Fernando (who is none other than Lorenzo, Duke of Florence) arouses great jealousy amongst the lords of Urbin, and they by various plots including the use of forged letters, endeavour to ruin Fernando. Their treachery fails and thus betrays their own black guilt. The Princess Silvania, who is enamoured of Florio, summons the supposed youth to her presence, yet when she sends for him he but pleads the suit of Fernando who has fallen a victim to her charms. (There seems to be more than a suggestion here of Viola urging Orsino's love to Olivia in *Twelfth Night*.) When Fernando is led to believe Florio wooes Silvania, the lad avows that he is "*A wandering Woman, in so strange disguise*". In a furious assault upon the town Florio, being wounded, is discovered to be Celestina. The Duke instantly crowns her as she swoons with a diadem and dresses her in robes of state as Duchess of Urbin; the Princess Silvania rewards Duke Lorenzo's love with her hand; and Duke Lodovico who has been captured whilst his troops are utterly routed is at last compelled to realize that his hopes are vain.

The Seege of Urbin, which is written in prose, is for all that a highly poetic and romantically interesting play. In the printed copy it may appear somewhat lengthy, but the script prepared for the stage shows extensive cutting. Thus the whole of scene 1 at the very commencement is omitted, and in many other places entire pages of dialogue have been scored through, whilst other passages are condensed and in part rewritten. In fact it almost seems as though clarity had been sacrificed to brevity, and in a drama of so complicated intrigue this might prove a fault.

PLATE XIII

MISS HOPKINS AS ARETHUSA IN PHILASTER

Collection of the Author

If one may trust the allusions in complimentary verses by Sir Samuel Tuke and Sir Robert Stapylton *The Seege of Urbin* was by no means unsuccessful in the theatre.[308]

It seems curious that the Latin play *Zeno* which was " very much Altered ", almost certainly by Sir William Killigrew, as *The Imperial Tragedy*, folio, 1669, has not hitherto been identified, especially as the original is pretty plainly indicated in the Prologue which tells us that it was acted with applause at Rome. *Zeno* tragœdia, Rome, 8vo, 1648 (and Antwerp, 12mo), is the work of Joseph Simeon or Simons, the name adopted by Emmanuel Lobb (1594–1671) upon his conversion and vocation to religion. Born at Portsmouth, he became a Catholic in Portugal, which country he visited early in life to follow mercantile pursuits. Subsequently he entered the English College at Rome, and on account of his remarkable talents attained considerable eminence in the Society of Jesus, being provincial of the English Jesuits from 1667 until his death. By many authorities it is thought that he reconciled the Duke of York to the Church in 1669, although others believe that the Duke had been previously received by the Bishop of Amiens, François Faure. Father Simons was highly esteemed as a Latin scholar of profound learning and a most elegant dramatist. He has left us five tragedies, which were frequently given with general approbation in Italy and Spain. Of these *Zeno* is the best known and extremely admired.

The Scene of *The Imperial Tragedy* is Constantinople. Zeno,[309] Emperor of Greece, reigned from 474–491. The drama opens with a Senecan ghost, the Emperor Basiliscus, lately slain, who denounces Zeno, " favourite of Hell," and presages doom. (Basilseus, who reigned for twenty months had compelled Zeno to flee. In August, 476, however, he returned and triumphed. Basiliscus was sent to Cucusus in Cappadocia, and there beheaded.) In disguise Zeno consults the wizard Euphemian, and learns that the Emperor, a monster of evil,

> *Buried before his death, within a Tombe,*
> *He shall vomit out his damn'd soul.*

It is also prophesied that he is to be thus thrown alive into the grave by a creature of the court. The Emperor's dagger is the astrologer's reward. Actually Zeno trusted greatly in the predictions of a sorcerer, Marianus, who informed him that a silentarius should succeed to the throne and wed the Augusta Ariadne.[310]

An orgy of murders and crime follows. Zeno raises his brother Longinus, *Princeps* of the Senate, to the rank of his colleague and heir. Historically this Longinus was as dissolute and cruel as he appears in the tragedy.[311] Anastasius, a lord of the court, gently entering the room whilst Longinus sleeps discovers a list of those to be quickly dispatched. The last name is, "Anastasius a plain man." A number of patricians are hurried to execution, including young Basiliscus the son of Zeno's general, Harmatius. A man of great quality, Pelagius, is by a trick accused of worshipping Jupiter, and false witnesses are suborned to swear he is a pagan. Whilst Zeno and Longinus mock and jeer, " there *appears on poles, upon the Town wall, the Heads of* Harmatius, Basiliscus, Pelagius, Gazeus, *and the Eight Captains.*" A banquet follows, but the guilty are haunted by the pale spectres of those whom they have slain. When the revels are at their height and Longinus has donned a crown and purple robes of empery, Anastasius rushes in followed by cohorts of soldiers. Longinus is cut down, and Zeno seized. " *The Scene is chang'd into a dismal Vault, set round with Coffins, in each a dead corps ; in the remote part, a small Lamp burning ; in the front, next the Stage is* Zeno *sleeping his leggs chain'd to the ground : at one corner in the outside a Guard stands.* Zeno *wakes* " and calls for water only to be utterly disregarded.

> *Anastasius* Reigns, you are in your grave,

replies a soldier. In mad terror " Zeno *thrusts his Mantle into his mouth, and choaks himself* ".

Actually the Emperor Zeno was carried off by a fit of epilepsy, 9th April, 491. His funeral took place on the following day, and on 11th April the silentiary Anastasius was crowned. He married the Augusta Ariadne on 20th May, whilst Longinus, having been compelled to take Holy Orders, was banished to a monastery in the distant Thebaid.

Langbaine tells us that *The Imperial Tragedy* was acted " at the Nursery in *Barbican* ".[312]

In spite of obvious faults which are neither negligible nor few, a lack of concentration, general diffuseness of dialogue, the crowding together of incidents as in *Selindra,* or too etiolated and artificial a theme as in *Pandora,* there is something very pleasing and very agreeable in the work of Sir William Killigrew. He had little practical sense of the theatre, and yet one regards these pieces with a tolerant affection that one denies—nor is it mere caprice—to bestow upon the far wittier and far more ingenious scenes of some other writers. This is, I apprehend, largely due to the ideals Sir William Killigrew has set forth, a little clumsily perhaps, in his beloved and thrice-pondered performances.

Upon a general consideration of the dramatists in the years immediately following the Restoration we are bound to recognize that we have here a period of extraordinary interest ; a transition period, it is true, and one which was more fertile in promise than in actual performance. This is not to say that the writers whom we have reviewed did not give us some very remarkable dramas, if indeed the word " great " may not without very little exaggeration be justly applied to so important a tragedy as Howard's *The Duke of Lerma*. *The Villain,* again, is in its kind of a quality hard to be bettered. In the lighter realm of comedy, also, the charming *The Adventures of Five Hours* hailed by contemporary critics as " One of the best Plays now extant " would reflect conscious honour on any theatre, whilst for broader fun and realistic portraiture the vivid scenes of *The Committee, The Cheats,* and *Cutter of Coleman Street* must be accounted wholly admirable.

If unequal, the general achievement was very full and varied, and even in the pages of the least names we not unseldom find a breath of poetry that fairly astonishes us by its glimpse of beauty.

We notice that whilst a few dramatists harked back, a little too keenly maybe, to the days of Fletcher, Shirley, Massinger, and Ford—some indeed with very considerable ability, and others not quite so successfully—the more talented men either felt their own way or discreetly drew upon the vast treasury of France and Spain, often transmuting, like subtle alchemists of poetry, the foreign gold to true English ore.

Although any notice, however brief, of even the earlier accomplishment of Dryden is reserved for another chapter, we cannot omit to remind ourselves that among the dramatists whom we have just considered the greatest of all Restoration writers was essaying his first footsteps on the stage, since that capital comedy *The Wild Gallant* was given at Vere Street on 5th February, 1663. It is probable (although the point is obscure) [313] that *The Wild Gallant* takes something from Spain and it certainly has a suggestion from Ben Jonson. None the less it is an entirely original work in the completest sense of the word. That " very innocent and most pretty witty play " *The Rival-Ladies,* Theatre Royal, Bridges Street, May, 1664, is vastly improved from a novella of Cervantes with a hint *en passant* from Rotrou and Quinault,[314] Spain and France and England. *The Indian-Queen* with all the young vigour of genius is the radiant Aztec dawn which heralds the glowing glory of *Almanzor and Almahide*.

NOTES TO CHAPTER III

[1] A very long list might be given to include Brome's *Five New Playes*, 8vo, 1653; Cartwright's *Comedies Trago-Comedies, With other Poems*, 8vo, 1651; Daborne's *Poor Man's Comfort*, 4to, 1655; Heywood's *Fortune by Land and Sea*, 4to, 1655; several important plays by Massinger, Shirley, and Middleton; and very many more of several authors.

[2] There are recorded performances of *A King and No King; Wit without Money; Rollo*; Cowley's *The Guardian*; Killigrew's *Claracilla*; Arthur Wilson's *The Inconstant Lady* given at the author's own college, Trinity, Oxford, in 1653; and others. Davenant's Entertainments are, of course, in a class by themselves.

[3] Corneille's play is founded upon Charles Sorel's *Le Berger extravagant*, 1628, which was translated into English as *The extravagant Shepheard, the anti-romance, or the history of the shepherd Lysis*, London, folio, 1653; second edition, 1660.

[4] *The Extravagant Shepherd*. A Pastorall Comedie. Written in French by T. Corneille. Englished by T. R., 4to, 1654.

[5] In the first edition of *The Rump* Bertlam stands for Lambert, Woodfleet for Fleetwood, Stoneware for Wareston, and so on, but it is not very easy to understand so thin an attempt at mystification.

[6] Aubrey, *Brief Lives*, ed. Andrew Clark, 1898, vol. ii, pp. 28–9. Charles Gerard, in 1645 baron Gerard of Brandon, in 1679 Earl of Macclesfield, at the outbreak of the rebellion joined the King at Shrewsbury. This fine soldier died in 1694.

[7] There may, of course, have been changes at the various revivals. The Prologue and Epilogue as printed, 4to, 1672, are certainly not those of the original production.

[8] There is an allusion in the Epilogue (spoken by Lacy) to Sir Robert Howard's *The Vestal-Virgin* when that tragedy was altered and "*Acted the Comical Way*".

> *If nothing pleases but Variety,*
> *I'll turn* Rageu *into a Tragedy.*
> *When* Lacy, *like a whining Lover dies,*
> *Though you hate Tragedies, 'twill wet your Eyes.*

[9] Pepys, 31st July, 1668: "to the King's house, to see the first day of Lacy's "Monsieur Ragou", now new acted. The King and Court all there, and mighty merry—a farce."

[10] Langbaine, *English Dramatick Poets*, Oxford, 1691, p. 318.

[11] Malone, *Variorum*, iii, 273. *Dramatic Records of Sir Henry Herbert*, ed. J. Q. Adams, 1917, p. 116.

[12] Pepys, on 20th November, 1660, found the Earl of Sandwich "in bed late, he having been with the King, Queen, and Princess, at the Cockpit all night, where General Monk treated them; and after supper a play".

[13] *Hist. MSS. Comm.*, Rep. V, App., p. 200.

[14] The prologue was printed. "The Prologue to His Majesty. At the first Play presented at the Cockpit in Whitehall; Being part of that Noble Entertainment which their Majesties received *Novemb.* 19. from his Grace the Duke of Albemarle. London, *Printed for* G. Bedell *and* T. Collins *at the* Middle-Temple Gate *in* Fleet Street 1660"; British Museum; Press Mark, 669, f. 26/30.

[15] This was Fletcher's original play before it was altered by the Duke of Buckingham.

[16] *The Indian-Queen* is to some extent founded upon the episode of Zelmatide in De Gomberville's *Polexandre*, see Dryden *The Dramatic Works*, ed. Montague Summers, vol. i (1931), Introduction, pp. xlv–xlvii, and p. 203; *The Conquest of Granada* is something indebted to Mlle de Scudéry's *Almahide, on l'Esclave Reine*, but see Dryden *The Dramatic Works*, ed. cit., vol. iii (1932), pp. 3–13; *Sophonisba* is from the Earl of Orrery's *Parthenissa; Gloriana* from La Calprenède's *Cléopâtre;* Settle's *Ibrahim* from Mlle de Scudéry's *Ibrahim, ou l'Illustre Bassa*; Banks' *The Rival Kings* from La Calprenède's *Cassandre*; Pordage's *The Siege of Babylon* from the same romance.

[17] In the Prologue to Mrs. Centlivre's *A Bold Stroke for a Wife* produced at Lincoln's Inn Fields on 3rd February, 1718, the true boast is made :—

> *Our Plot is new, and regularly clear,*
> *And not one single Tittle from* Molière.

[18] Shadwell derives the main theme of *The Libertine*, Dorset Garden, June, 1675, from Rosimond's *Le nouveau Festin de Pierre*. For full details see *The Complete Works of Thomas Shadwell*, edited by Montague Summers, 1927, vol. i, Introduction, pp. cxxii–cxl, also vol. iii, pp. 9–10.

[19] *Don Garcie de Navarre* was used by Charles Johnson in *The Masquerade*, Drury Lane, 16th January, 1719 ; *La Princesse d'Élide* was drawn upon by James Miller in *The Universal Passion*, Drury Lane, 28th February, 1737.

[20] As for example by Mr. J. R. A. Nicoll who, in his *A History of Restoration Drama*, 1923, pp. 173–6, heedlessly retails the errors and blunders of the worst German monographs. Thus he finds, or affects to find, *Le misanthrope* in *Bury Fair ; Tartuffe* in *The Assignation, The Kind Keeper,* and *The Double-Dealer ; Le médecin malgré lui* in *The Spanish Fryar ; Monsieur de Pourceaugnac* in *Love Triumphant ; Les femmes savantes* in *The Double-Dealer* again. We are also informed (p. 177) that " For his *Tyrannick Love*, Dryden could go to a comparatively insignificant and unimportant *Sainte Catherine*, for his *Dame Dobson* Ravenscroft could pass to an almost unknown comedy *La Devineresse*". In the first place Dryden borrowed nothing for *Tyrannick Love* from the *Sainte Catherine* of Desfontaines ; and secondly *La Devineresse* is not " an almost unknown comedy ". But that all these plays are unknown to Mr. Nicoll I am very ready to believe. In his *History of Early Eighteenth Century Drama*, 1925, pp. 142 and 157, Mr. Nicoll ascribes *Dame Dobson* to Shadwell.

[21] The influence of Spain upon England has been dealt with in my Introductions to *Restoration Comedies*, 1921, and to *The Adventures of Five Hours*, 1927. Martin Hume's *Spanish influence upon English Literature*, 1905, and Fitzmaurice Kelly's *The Relations between Spanish and English Literature* may be usefully consulted.

[22] *Dryden the Dramatic Works*, ed. Montague Summers, vol. ii (1931), p. 247, and note pp. 501–2.

[23] Downes, *Roscius Anglicanus*, ed. Montague Summers, p. 26 ; and notes, pp. 188–9. Pepys saw *Worse and Worse* at the Duke's house on 20th July, 1664.

[24] *Dryden The Dramatic Works*, ed. Montague Summers, vol. i (1931), p. 61 and pp. 131–2.

[25] Striking examples are Thomas St. Serfe's *Tarugo's Wiles ; or, The Coffee-House*, Lincoln's Inn Fields, 1667, founded upon Moreto y Cabaña's *No puede ser*, which itself owes something to Lope de Vega's *El Mayor impossible*, and which later was used by Crowne in *Sir Courtly Nice*, see *Restoration Comedies*, 1921, ed. by Montague Summers, Introduction, pp. xxxviii–xliii. Also Wycherley's *The Gentleman Dancing-Master*, Dorset Garden, 1672, which derives something (although not so much as has been supposed) from Calderón's *El Maestro de Danzar*, see *The Works of William Wycherley*, 1924, ed. Montague Summers, vol. i, Introduction, pp. 40–5. Mrs. Behn's *The Young King ; or The Mistake*, Dorset Garden, 1679, has important episodes from Calderón's *La Vida es Sueño*, itself at least suggested by Rojas' *Viaje Entretenido*. See *The Works of Aphra Behn*, 1915, ed. Montague Summers, vol. ii, pp. 102–3. From a stanza (41) in *The Session of the Poets, Poems on State-Affairs*, 1705, pp. 152–8, it would appear that Rhodes has written a play with a " Spanish Plot ".

[26] British Museum, Add. MS. 34217, fol. 31*b*. See also *Hist. MSS. Comm.*, Rep. X, App., pt. 4, p. 21.

[27] For the date of *The Surprisal, Cornelia* and *Selinda*, see Malone *Variorum*, iii, 273. Malone gives 25th instead of 23rd April for the first.

[28] Not printed.

[29] *Measure for Measure* and *Much Ado about Nothing*.

[30] *The Rehearsal*, ed. by Montague Summers, 1914, p. 120.

[31] Downes, *Roscius Anglicanus*, ed. by Montague Summers, pp. 20, 22, and note pp. 175–6.

[32] To be distinguished from Thomas Porter's *A Witty Combat ; or, The Female Victor*, for which see pp. 235–37.

[33] *The Session of the Poets*: Stanza 40. *Poems on State-Affairs*, 1705, p. 157.

[34] *Roscius Anglicanus*, p. 26.

[35] *The Session of the Poets*: Stanza 36. *Poems on State-Affairs*, 1705, p. 157.

[36] Lisle's Tennis Court, the first Duke's House.

[37] Middleton's famous political play *A Game at Chess*, brought out in August, 1624, at the Globe. Gondomar, the Spanish ambassador, is drawn with very

unequivocal strokes as the Black Knight. After a run of nine days to thronging houses authority prohibited the piece and trouble ensued.

³⁸ In *The Siege of Rhodes.*

³⁹ A doling is an adherent of Bernhard Knipperdolling (or Knipperdollinck) the Münster Anabaptist, who being elected burgomaster of the town in February, 1534, proceeded to set up a " New Sion " amid scenes of fearful licence and outrage. These lewd and blasphemous wretches were captured and executed in 1536.

⁴⁰ Produced at Paris, 28th May, 1660, and derived from *Il Ritratto, ove Arlecchino cornuto per opinione.* *Sganerelle* has been drawn up several times by English dramatists, notably by Rawlins in *Tom Essence,* Dorset Garden, September, 1676 ; and by Arthur Murphy in *All in the Wrong,* Drury Lane, 15th June, 1761.

⁴¹ Sometime maid to Mrs. Pepys ; see the Diary, 17th November, 1662. There are many references to her by Pepys, who particularly notes her acting and singing at the Duke's house.

⁴² 1648–1652 ; itself suggested by Giovanni Battista Lalli's *Eneide travestita,* Venice, 1633, a burlesque frequently reprinted.

⁴³ In *The Session of the Poets,* ut sup. stanza 3, it is termed a " damnable Farce ", but this carries little or no weight.

⁴⁴ *Roscius Anglicanus,* ed. cit., pp. 23–4. " Celia " should be " Celania ".

⁴⁵ 18th February, 1662.

⁴⁶ *Tu Quoque ; or, The City Gallant* by Cooke ; 4to, 1614. See Chapter II, n. 218.

⁴⁷ There are two issues of this year. *Hamlet* was reprinted 4to, 1683 ; 1695 ; and 1703, two issues.

⁴⁸ "As it is now Acted ; Mills, Caesar ; Wilks, Antony ; Booth, Brutus ; Elrington, Cassius ; Mrs. Horton, Calphurnia ; Mrs. Porter, Portia."

⁴⁹ *Roscius Anglicanus,* ed. cit., p. 33. See also notes, pp. 209–211. *Joseph Preist* should be Josias Priest.

⁵⁰ Bodley, Malone 1010.

⁵¹ Bodley, Art. 4° C. 103.

⁵² See Chapter II, n. 178. Also *Notes and Queries,* 8th November, 1930, vol. 159. Even so careful a writer as Professor Hazelton Spencer, *Shakespeare Improved,* 1927, p. 64, falls into the old error : "A curious rôle of Sandford's was Banquo's Ghost, Banquo in the flesh being played by Smith."

⁵³ Even to-day one or two of the weird sisters are occasionally played by men. During their career in the earlier part of the eighteenth century Bullock and Johnson often acted as Witches, and Davies, *Dramatic Miscellanies,* 1783, vol. ii, pp. 118–19, has a curious passage : " It has been an old complaint of stage critics, that the parts of the witches are always distributed amongst the low comedians, who, by mistaking the sense of the author, render those sentiments ridiculous which were designed by him to be spoken with gravity and solemnity. Should we suppose this charge to be well founded, it would not be a very easy task to remove it ; for the tragedians are all employed in various parts of the drama, suited to their several abilities, so that none but the comic actors are left to wear gowns, beards and coifs. But, I confess, I do not see the propriety of the accusation. There is, in the witches, something odd and peculiar, and approaching to what we call humour. The manners bestowed on these beings are more suitable to our notions of comic than tragic action, and better fitted to Yates and Edwin than Henderson and Smith . . . From the dramatis personæ of Davenant's Macbeth, we see the parts of the witches given to the low comedians of those times." Davies may have seen some cast in MS., but in the quartos the names of these actors are not given, although doubtless he is correct in his assertion. At Drury Lane in the season 1746–7 Macklin played one of the Witches. On 21st March, 1794, at Drury Lane Kemble was Macbeth ; Mrs. Siddons, Lady Macbeth ; Parsons, Moody, and Baddeley, the three Witches. When Kean acted Macbeth at Drury Lane, 10th November, 1814, Mr. Bellamy was Hecate ; Mr. Dowton, Mr. Knight, and Mr. Lovegrove, the three Witches. At Covent Garden 6th November, 1837, Macready appeared as Macbeth. The Witches were Mr. G. Bennet, Mr. Meadows, and Mr. Payne ; Mr. H. Phillips, Hecate. At Sadler's Wells, 27th May, 1844, Phelps opened in Macbeth, with Mr. Clement White, Hecate ; the three Witches, Mr. Forman, Mr. Wilson, and Mr. Morelli. In Irving's *Macbeth,* 29th December, 1888, women, Miss Marriott, Miss Desborough, and Miss Seaman, played the Witches, and Miss Ivor, Hecate.

[54] There is an amusing reference in Dryden's *The Kind Keeper,* Dorset Garden, March, 1676, Act V, 1, where Judith says to Woodall: "When I come back again, I shall knock at your door, with speak, Brother, speak; is the deed done?" (*Singing.*) Woodall takes up the jest and burden: "Long ago, long ago." See *Dryden The Dramatic Works,* edited by Montague Summers, vol. iv, 1932, p. 327, and note, p. 564.

[55] See Professor Dent's *Foundations of English Opera,* 1928, pp. 128–136.

[56] See *The Restoration Theatre,* by Montague Summers, pp. 207–8, for Garrick's version of the killing of Macbeth.

[57] Boaden, *Memoirs of the Life of John Philip Kemble, Esq.,* 1825, vol. i, p. 418.

[58] The Witches, "squalid, and unearthly, and picturesque," played by Messrs. A. Younge, Scharf, and Wilkins were highly praised. Scharf was a great Touchstone, the Fool in King Lear, and the Clown in *Twelfth Night*; Younge was famous for Dogberry, Autolycus, and Sir Andrew Aguecheek. See *The Life and life-work of Samuel Phelps,* by W. M. Phelps and John Forbes-Robertson, 1886, pp. 96–102.

[59] The programme for this occasion resembles an archæological monograph.

[60] See *The Times,* 29th December, 1888. Also for Irving's revival *The Story of My Life,* by Ellen Terry, 1908, chapter xiii, "The Macbeth Period." See *Henry Irving* by Bram Stoker, 2 vols., 1906, vol. i, pp. 107–113, and Austin Brereton, *The Life of Henry Irving,* 2 vols., 1908, vol. ii, chapter ix, pp. 134–150.

[61] In a recent (April, 1934) production of *Macbeth* at the Old Vic., scene 1 was entirely omitted, since it is "not by Shakespeare"! Maeterlinck rejected scene 2, and as the Hon. Maurice Baring pertinently remarked, *The Observer,* 15th April, 1934, before long theatrical producers "will end by being without any text of *Macbeth* at all".

[62] Duffett's *The Empress of Morocco,* 4to, 1674, is excessively rare. Only two perfect copies (with the frontispiece, reproduced in my *The Restoration Theatre,* p. 282) apparently are known.

[63] Mr. Bayes had the conceit of introducing his tragedy with a Prologue spoken by Thunder and Lightning. See *The Rehearsal,* edited by Montague Summers, 1914, pp. 12–14.

[64] Weber, who in his edition of Beaumont and Fletcher printed this popular song from Thomas Ravenscroft's *Deuteromelia* (1609), states that it is referred to as "an old three-man's song" by R. Carew, *The Survey of Cornwall* (1602).

[65] See *The Restoration Theatre* by Montague Summers, pp. 191–4, and p. 250, nn. 5 and 6.

[66] To Betty Mackarel there are in particular very many references. With Joe Haines she spoke the Introduction to the Prologue before Duffett's burlesque *The Mock-Tempest,* Theatre Royal, November, 1674. See my *Shakespeare Adaptations,* 1922, pp. 107–8, and note pp. 261-2. There is an allusion to "Betty, dear, dear, dear, Betty Mackarel" in Philips' *Don Quixote,* 1687, p. 184. In a satire addressed to Julian, and since it is often attributed to Rochester included (pp. 144–5) in the *Collected Works of John Wilmot Earl of Rochester,* Nonesuch Press, 1926, the penultimate line runs: "May *Betty Mackrell* cease to be a W——." The note, p. 384, upon this is a flagrant example of the errors which disfigure this most unfortunate reprint. "*Betty Mackrell.* Mackrell seems to be a nickname; the word is better known in French, 'maquereau maquerelle'; the meaning in this case seems to be 'Betty the procuress, or the bawd'—possibly the well-known Betty Morris." It is obvious that Mr. Hayward could never have heard of Betty Mackarel. It were to be wished that anyone who sets up as an editor—save the mark!—of Rochester should have some acquaintance with the Restoration period, and recognize the more common names continually to be met with in contemporary pasquil and lampoon.

[67] "A boat, a boat to cross the ferry" is a round by John Jenkins (1592–1678), first printed in John Hilton's collection of catches, "Catch that catch can," 1652. It was extremely popular, and has been frequently reprinted.

[68] Mother C—— is the famous, or rather infamous, Mrs. Cresswell, to whom there are innumerable references. I have collected twenty or more of these in a note, see *The Works of Thomas Otway,* edited by Montague Summers, 1926, vol. iii, pp. 274–6. Mrs. Cresswell resided in Moorfields. She was keeping house here before the Restoration, and here she died in 1683.

G——— is Mother Gifford to whom there is a reference in Dryden's *Sr Martin Mar-all*, acted in 1667, 4to, 1668, see *Dryden The Dramatic Works*, edited by Montague Summers, vol. ii, 1931, p. 116, and notes pp. 476–7. Lord Dartmouth alludes to " Mother *Temple, Bennet*, or *Gifford.*" Mother Temple is *Sister T———* of whom the Second Witch sings. In Etherege's *She wou'd if She cou'd*, v, i, produced in February, 1667–8, 4to, 1668, Freeman cries, " wou'd I were safe at *Giffords.*" In the latest reprint of Etherege, two volumes, 1927, Mr. Brett-Smith the editor, vol. ii, p. 314, guesses that the allusion is " to a fashionable eating-house " !

Betty B———, Mother Buly, alluded to in John Phillips' *Don Quixote*, folio, 1687, p. 195 ; *The Female Fire-Ships*, 4to, 1691 ; and elsewhere.

M———, Mother Moseley, who was particularly patronized by Shaftesbury, is referred to in the Epilogue to John Dover's *The Mall ; or, The Modish Lovers*, acted early in 1674, 4to, 1674 ; in Payne's *The Siege of Constantinople*, acted in November, 1674, 4to, 1675 ; and elsewhere. She resided in Durham Yard. For fuller details see my edition of Settle's *The Empress of Morocco* with the reprint of Duffett's farce.

[69] For fop-corner see my *The Restoration Theatre*, pp. 77–8.

[70] Settle's tragedy *The Empress of Morocco* produced at Dorset Garden, 3rd July, 1673.

[71] The Dorset Garden Theatre.

[72] Later burlesques of *Macbeth* are the anonymous *Macbeth Travestie*, 1818 ; Francis Talfourd's *Macbeth Travestie*, given at Henley-on-Thames, 17th June, 1847, and at the Olympic, London, in April, 1853 ; *Macbeth Mystified*, a burletta, W. H. Mason and J. E. Roe, Theatre Royal, Brighton, 3rd May, 1863 ; and *Macbeth Travestie*, Royal Naval School, New Cross, 3rd June, 1889.

[73] The business of Jodelet eating the scalding posset and sputtering when he burns his mouth, whilst Sancho slabbers it all over his beard, and scraping it off with a clasp knife, gobbles it down, occurs at the end of Act III.

[74] Lavinia Fenton, 1708–1760. *The Beggar's Opera* was produced at Lincoln's Inn Fields, 29th January, 1728. Miss Fenton retired from the stage that year and married the Duke of Bolton in 1751. Hogarth has left us portraits of this lovely actress, and her future husband in his canvas depicting " the Polly and Lucy scene ". This picture, which belongs to the Duke of Leeds, is at Hornby Castle, Yorkshire. It may be remarked that with startling inaccuracy Mr. J. R. A. Nicoll in his *History of Early Eighteenth Century Drama*, 1925, p. 239, giving a curiously inadequate account of *The Beggar's Opera*, refers to Mr. and Mrs. Peachum as " Watchem and his wife ".

[75] I have used the edition of *Donde hay agravios* in the *Tersoro del Teatro español*, tom. iv, by Eugenio de Ochoa, Paris, 1838.

[76] An alteration by O'Keefe of his *The Banditti ; or Love's Labyrinth*, a comic opera with music by Dr. Arnold, which in its original production at Covent Garden, 27th October, 1781, failed to please.

[77] Langbaine, *English Dramatick Poets*, Oxford, 1691, p. 276.

[78] Evelyn, *Diary*, 16th February, 1685.

[79] There is no separate and adequate study of Sir Robert Howard, nor is there any modern reprint of his plays, the last edition being 12mo, 1722. I have devoted several pages to him (and his brothers) in the Introduction, pp. xl–lviii, of my edition of Shadwell's *Works*, vol. i, 1927. See also my recension of *The Rehearsal*, 1914, Introduction, pp. viii–xi. Mr. C. N. Thurber's " *Sir Robert Howard's Comedy ' The Committee '*," University of Illinois Studies, vol. vii, No. 1, 1921, is unfortunately of little value. He even reprints the text of *The Committee* from a late prompt copy of 1776, which is of course worthless.

[80] Evelyn, *Diary*, 16th June, 1683, speaks of " Sir Robert Howard (that universal pretender) ".

[81] Cole, in his *Athenae Cantabrigienses*, says that Sir Robert Howard was a member of Magdalene, Cambridge, but the dramatist is here confused with his namesake and uncle, the Cantab. Sir Robert Howard.

[82] A very lucrative post. Howard, " hath got, they say, £20,000 since the King come in," Pepys, 8th December, 1666.

[83] For some time Howard and Dryden were living together in the former's house in Lincoln's Inn Fields. Thus Shadwell in his *The Medal of John Bayes,* upon the lines

Then by th' assistance of a Noble *Knight*
Th' hadst plenty, ease and liberty to write,

glosses : " *Sir R.H. who kept him generously, at his own* House." See *Dryden The Dramatic Works,* edited by Montague Summers, vol. i, 1931, Introduction, pp. xxvii–xxx, xxxiii, xxxvi–xxxviii.

[84] 8vo, 1660. A second edition, 1696. See *Dryden,* ed. cit., vol. i, 1931, Introduction, p. xxx.

[85] On 18th October, 1666, Evelyn noted his reluctance to attend public theatres, " foul and undecent women now (and never till now) permitted to appear and act, who inflaming several young noblemen and gallants, became their misses, and to some, their wives. Witness the Earl of Oxford, Sir R. Howard, Prince Rupert, the Earl of Dorset, and another greater person than any of them."

[86] Mrs. Uphill played very minor rôles such as waiting women and confidantes. See my edition of the *Roscius Anglicanus,* pp. 91–2 ; also my edition of Shadwell's *Works,* 1927, vol. i, Introduction, pp. xliii–xliv.

[87] "A foolish Knight, that pretends to understand everything in the world."

[88] "A Seasonable Argument to Persuade All the *Grand Juries* in *England,* to petition for a New Parliament, Amsterdam, Printed in the Year, 1677," ascribed to Andrew Marvell.

[89] Sir Robert married the Lady Honora O'Brien at Wotton Basset, on 10th August, 1665.

[90] Luttrell, *Brief Relation* (Oxford, 1857), vol. iii, p. 45.

[91] J. Nichols, *A Select Collection of Poems,* London, 1772, vol. i, p. 147, n.

[92] On 24th September, 1692, she dined at Sir Robert's house, Ashstead in Surrey, Luttrell, vol. ii, p. 577.

[93] Luttrell, vol. iv, p. 423.

[94] *Diary,* 16th February, 1685.

[95] The Christian name, Robert, remains (perhaps accidentally) in one passage, Act II, scene I, where Bayes says : *Experto crede Roberto.* See my edition of *The Rehearsal,* 1914, p. 19.

[96] Howard's personal bravery was never questioned. This trait is emphasized by Shadwell in several places in *The Sullen Lovers,* especially Act III, the scene where Sir Positive meets the two Clerks whom he has challenged for railing at his play.

[97] See Pepys, 2nd, 4th, 5th, 6th, 8th May, 1668. Also Shadwell's *Works,* ed. cit., vol. i, pp. xl–lx and 5–6.

[98] *Printed for Henry Herringman,* nine leaves. This poem was several times reprinted, and was included by H. Hills in his poetical tracts issued in 1709, 1710, 1711, at one penny, twopence, or threepence each.

[99] *The Duel of the Crabs* : By the Lord B——st. *Occasion'd by* Sir R. Howard's *Duel of the Stags. Poems on State-Affairs,* 1705, pp. 150–2.

[100] As for example when in *The Sullen Lovers,* Act I, Sir Positive very sententiously proclaims to Stanford " betwixt you and I, let me tell you, we are all Mortal ". See also Dryden's *A Defence of an Essay of Dramatique Poesie, The Indian Emperour,* Second Quarto, 1668 : " the Stage being one place cannot be two. This, indeed, is a great a Secret, as that we are all mortal." *Dryden The Dramatic Works,* ed. Montague Summers, vol. i, 1931, pp. 265–6, and note pp. 455–6.

[101] Printed as " Written by A Person of Quality ". Of this tract Dr. Atterbury in a sermon pointedly observed : " Some Persons who write pretended Historys of Relligion are beholden to the Real Relligion of others that their own Historys are not written."

[102] It occupies pp. 27–140 of the *Poems,* 8vo, 1660.

[103] Guinever was the traditional appellation of a withered crone. In Dekker's *Satiromastix,* 4to, 1602 (ed. Penniman, Act III, scene I, p. 823) Tucca accosts Mistris Miniver as " mother Bunch . . . Queene Gwyniver ". In Mrs. Behn's posthumous *The Younger Brother,* 4to, 1696, iv, 3, Sir Merlin salutes Lady Blunder as " Old Queen *Gwiniver* ". *The Works of Aphra Behn,* ed. by Montague Summers, 1915, vol. iv, p. 380, and note p. 422.

[104] Chapter II, note 34.

[105] The rest of the cast is not known. At a revival in 1667 Nell Gwyn acted Samira ; Pepys, 26th December, 1667. It has been said that Mrs. Knepp played Emelia, but this seems an error. If such were the case she could hardly have come " after her song in the clouds " to Pepys in the pit, and have been treated by him with " oranges, 2s." (17th April, 1668). From this it rather appears that she sang Hymen in the masque, Act III, scene 1.

[106] *English Stage*, vol. i, p. 56.

[107] Langbaine, p. 276, writes of *The Committee*, " This is an admirable Comedy, and highly commended." In Bell's *British Theatre*, vol. ix, London, 1792, a note before the play says that it is " unadorned with any brilliancy of either thought or language ", which is scarcely correct, as the characters are excellently portrayed and the language, which has a great deal of humour, suits the speakers.

[108] As Hume clearly points out, *History of England*, 1789, vol. vi, pp. 540-1. Even this writer allows that the Covenant was devoted " to the maintenance of systems still more abroad and more dangerous " than any which it opposed. Sir Harry Vane, who was a prime mover in the Covenant, met a just reward when he was executed on Tower Hill, 14th June, 1662, the King having graciously commuted the sentence of hanging at Tyburn to decapitation.

[109] Teg (Teague) had become a generic name for Irishmen very many years before the Restoration, and is given to an Irish character in *The Welsh Ambassador, c.* 1622. Teague in Farquhar's *The Twin-Rivals*, Drury Lane, 14th December, 1702, owes everything to Howard's Teg. Alfred Tellenbach in a thesis on *The Committee*, Zürich, 1913, mistakenly attempts to link up Teg with Shadwell's Tegue o' Divelly, the Irish priest, an entirely different character.

[110] Charles Howard in his *Historical Anecdotes of some of the Howard Family*, 1817, p. 111, says that " Sir Robert took the first hint of that odd composition of fidelity and blunders which he has so humorously worked up in the character of Teague " from an Irishman, who was one of his own domestics, and he tells a story relative to this suggestion. See also the *Biographia Dramatica*, 1812, vol. ii, pp. 114-15, where it is further remarked that *The Committee* " has had the second title of *The Faithful Irishman* added to it ".

[111] Evelyn, *Diary*, 27th November, 1662 ; Pepys, *Diary*, 12th June, 1663. See also Downes, *Roscius Anglicanus*, p. 16, in reference to Lacy :—

> For his *Just Acting, all gave him due Praise,*
> His *Part in the Cheats,* Jony Thump, Teg *and* Bayes.
> *In these Four Excelling ; The Court gave him the* Bays.

In one of the impressions the last two lines of this triplet run :—

> Bayes, Teg, Jony Thump *in* Love in Amaze,
> *In these three excelling the Court gave him the* Bayes.

Thumpe is Sir Gervase Simple's man in Shirley's *The Changes ; or Love in a Maze*. See my edition of the *Roscius*, notes pp. 146-7.

[112] *Dramatick Poets*, p. 317.

[113] Vol. iii, p. 59.

[114] *Dryden's Works*, vol. ii, p. 225.

[115] Colley Cibber, *Apology*, chapter xiv.

[116] He was distinguished as " little Griffith " in the bills, see Chetwood, *History of the Stage*, 1749, p. 164.

[117] *New Monthly Magazine*, 1829. Johnstone, 1749–1828, was known as " Irish Johnstone ", and, says Walter Donaldson, in his day he was one of the most popular men in London, " in consequence of his unapproachable talent in either the Irish gentleman or the peasant." For Moody, see Genest, *English Stage*, vol. iv, p. 606.

[118] In *Theatrical Anecdotes* there is a funny story of Munden and Jack Johnstone in the scene when Teg plies Obadiah with liquor. As Munden swallowed his grimace was fearful, and it was found that the property-man had mistaken a bottle containing lamp-oil for one prepared with sherry and water.

[119] T. Davies, *Dramatic Miscellanies*, 1784, vol. i, p. 57. At the Haymarket, 2nd December, 1706, Mrs. Leigh played Mrs. Day ; with Mrs. Barry, Ruth ; and Mrs. Bracegirdle, Arbella. Mrs. Baker, Mrs. Macklin, and Mrs. Hopkins were all much applauded as Mrs. Day.

[120] *History of the Stage,* 1749, p. 58.

[121] " I have seen him (Ashbury) acquit himself in the Part of *Careless* in the *Committee* so well, that his years never struck upon Remembrance." Ibid., p. 85.

[122] Ibid., p. 169, note *e.*

[123] They were then living together at the former's house in Lincoln's Inn Field. See *Dryden The Dramatic Works,* ed. Montague Summers, vol. i, 1931, Introduction, pp. xxxvi–xxxvii.

[124] Ibid., Introduction, pp. xlv–xlviii, and pp. 203–6.

[125] *Diary,* 1st February, 1664; 27th June, 1668.

[126] *Diary,* 5th February, 1664.

[127] The " Historie " occupies Tome i, pp. 238–397. It is interrupted and resumed on p. 429 to break off on p. 564. It is taken up once more on p. 589 and concludes on p. 772. For full details, as also regarding the names derived from *Polexandre,* see *Dryden,* ut sup., pp. xlv–xlvii, and p. 203.

[128] *English Stage,* vol. i, p. 58.   Mutius has one fine phrase deserving quotation :—

> O the brave days of *Julius,* when he flew
> The *Roman* Eagles at the stooping World
> And dar'd it like a Lark !

[129] In his Illinois thesis, *Sir Robert Howard's Comedy " The Committee ",* C. N. Thurber incorrectly says of *The Vestal-Virgin* : " In the comedy *no* one dies " (p. 25).

[130] *English Dramatick Poets,* p. 497–8.   *Roscius Anglicanus,* Notes, pp. 160–1.

[131] Hence probably arose the charges of plagiarism which were unfairly brought against Howard, and which are more than hinted at in *The Sullen Lovers.* There was a play by Henry Shirley, *The Spanish Duke of Lerma,* Stationers' Register, 9th September, 1652, non-extant.

[132] For details see Martin Hume's *The Court of Philip IV,* 1907.

[133] *Dryden & Howard, 1664–1668. The Text of . . . The Duke of Lerma,* edited by D. D. Arundell, Cambridge, 1929. The note on *The Duke of Lerma,* pp. 208–211, is good, but the general Introduction and the account of Howard are altogether too sketchy. The text of the two reprinted plays is marred by the intrusion of diacritical dots. For an editor to avow " I have repunctuated, respelt and reparagraphed " is surely a sad confession.

[134] Ibid., pp. 208–9, which I have slightly abridged in quotation. I am not certain about the phrase " untragic seriousness ". There are moments of tragedy and even terror in the play. Greatly as I admire *The Duke of Lerma* I feel that to say that it ranks " higher than any other serious play of the period " and that it is " the first attempt at drama of character since Shakespeare " are judgements which might be questioned. The phrase " the period " is of course vague, and may imply merely 1660–8.

[135] *Diary,* 20th February, 1668. See *The Restoration Theatre* by Montague Summers, p. 122.

[136] In the address *To the Reader* before *Four New Plays,* folio, 1665, Howard maintains that rather than classical plays or French, Italian, and Spanish pieces, " *our* English *Plays justly challenge the Preheminence,*" although he hardly approves of Tragi-comedy, considering the alternation of sadness and mirth not " *so Proper to be Presented* " as one unvaried design. He argues against the use of rhyme in plays, although he admires Lord Orrery's tragedies and was himself part-author at least of *The Indian-Queen,* whilst many scenes of *The Vestal-Virgin* are rhyme.

[137] British Museum, MS. Add. 36916.

[138] Pepys, *Diary,* 3rd March to 22nd March, 1668–9, furnishes many other details. Sir William told Pepys the matter intended for his abuse, " wherein they foolishly and sillily bring in two tables like that which he hath made, with a round hole in the middle, in his closet, to turn himself in ; and he is to be in one of them as master, and Sir J. Duncombe in the other as his man, or imitator ; and then discourse in those tables, about the disposing of their books and papers, very foolish." Coventry effectively threatened Killigrew and any actor who dared offer at such a burlesque. Pepys mentions Coventry's table, *Diary,* 4th July, 1668.

[139] *Prose Works of John Dryden,* 1800, ed. Edmond Malone, vol. i, part ii, pp. 55–6 and p. 61.

[140] Mr. J. R. A. Nicoll in an article, "Dryden, Howard and Rochester," *The Times Literary Supplement,* 13th January, 1921, p. 27, put forward the "opinion" that this scene was the first-fruits of Dryden's study of Howard's play. But Mr. Nicoll was, of course, unaware of Howard's letter to Rochester.

[141] In the reprint *Collected Works of John Wilmot Earl of Rochester,* 1926, this name, pp. 241–7, when it occurs is falsely spelled Lycurgus.

[142] 4to, 1676. *Term Catalogues,* Hilary, 10th February, 1676.

[143] See Rochester's satire *On Poet Ninny.* Needless to say the "editor of the *Collected Works of Rochester,* 1926", was unable to identify Poet Ninny, pp. 63–4.

[144] *The Rehearsal,* edited by Montague Summers, 1914, pp. 3, 31, 76–9, 109.

[145] 4to, 1668. Licensed for printing by Roger L'Estrange, 2nd August, 1667.

[146] Curiously enough Pepys did not relish this, and when he saw *The Usurper* on 2nd December, 1668, remarked that it was "a pretty good play, in all but what is designed to resemble Cromwell and Hugh Peter, which is mighty silly".

[147] The Epistle : A2 verso, 4to, 1668.

[148] *Poems on State Affairs,* 1705 ; *The Session of the Poets* ; stanzas 20 and 21, p. 155.

[149] It might be hazarded that the two occasions of castigation were, (1) when Haines was arrested on 4th November, 1675, at the complaint of Sir Edmund Wyndham whom he had abused "with ill and scandalous language, and insolent carriage", and (2) when on 18th June, 1677, he was laid by the heels "for receitinge . . . a Scurrilous and obscoene Epilogue".

[150] He had already, in The Epistle before *The Usurper,* 4to, 1668, spoken of dramatists whose works "*have their measures ador[n]ed with Trappings of Rhime, which how'ere they have succeeded in wit or design, is still thought musick, as the Heroick Tone now goes*". It is interesting to note his objection to the conventional dance concluding a comedy, "*the wresting in of Dances, when unnatural and improper to the business of the Scene and Plot, as if by an unintelligable Charm of their Muses, the Actors were like Fair[i]es Conjur'd up, that the Play might vanish in a Dance.*" See *The Restoration Theatre,* by Montague Summers, pp. 165–172.

[151] Revived by Phelps in his second season at Sadler's Wells, 15th May, 1845, with Marston and Mrs. Warner in the principal parts. *The Life-Work of Samuel Phelps* by W. M. Phelps and John Forbes-Robertson, 1886, p. 77.

[152] Euphorbus, son of Panthous, one of the bravest of the Trojans was slain by Menelaus (*Iliad,* xvi, 806 ; xvii, 1), who afterwards dedicated the shield of Euphorbus in the Temple of Hera, near Mycenae, Pausanias II, 17, 3. Pythagoras asserted that he had once been the Trojan Euphorbus, and in proof of his assertion took down at first sight the shield of Euphorbus from the many trophies in Hera's shrine. Hence the famous allusion of Horace, *Odes,* I, xxviii, 9–13 (quamvis clipeo Troiana refixo tempora testatus) ; see also Ovid, *Metamorphoseon,* xv, 160–4. Aulus Gellius, IV, xii, 14, has : Pythagoram vero ipsum, sicut celebre est, Euphorbum primo se fuisse dictitasse. See also Diogenes Laertius, viii, 4 ; the scholiast upon Apollonius, i, 30 ; and Lactantius, vii (*De Vita Beata*), xii.

[153] This point has been missed by Mr. J. H. Wilson in his *The Influence of Beaumont and Fletcher on Restoration Drama,* Columbus, Ohio, 1928.

[154] Whence also may have been drawn the Amazons of *The Womens Conquest.*

[155] Thus Aphra Behn in her Pindarics addressed to Howard does not hesitate to compare him with Jonson to the disparagement of the latter :—

> You have outdone what e'er he writ,
> In this last great Example of your Wit.
> Your *Solymour* does his *Morose* destroy
> And your *Black Page* undoes his *Barbers Boy.*

Howard is further told that he created a new Utopia, "Of which *Moor* only did the Model draw." See *The Works of Aphra Behn,* ed. by Montague Summers, 1915, vol. vi, pp. 204–7, and notes, pp. 426–7. This poem by Mrs. Behn, poems by Ravenscroft, Sam Clyat, and a certain J. T. (Tatham ?), were printed with *The Six Days Adventure,* 4to, 1671.

[156] *On Three Late Marriages,* a satire, unprinted MS., dated 1688, but probably some years earlier.

[157] *English Stage,* vol. i, p. 229. It will not escape notice that we find Carey Perin, Coysh, Mrs. Baker (Frances or Katherine ?), and Mrs. Farlowe in the cast.

[158] November, 1677. The antic Pope-burning was a commemoration of the anniversary of the accession of Queen Elizabeth, 17th November, 1558. For a full account of these impious and riotous turmoils see *Dryden The Dramatic Works,* edited by Montague Summers, vol. iv, 1932, pp. 601–3.

[159] This in spite of his spirited protest against intruded dances, even to conclude a play. See above, n. 150.

[160] *Annals of the English Stage,* ed. R. W. Lowe, 1888, vol. i, p. 197.

[161] Perhaps his " incomparable " heroic poem, *The Brittish Princes,* 8vo, 1669, was the chief object of satire. See *The Works of Thomas Shadwell,* edited by Montague Summers, 1927, vol. i, Introduction, p. lii.

[162] *Poems on State-Affairs,* 1705, p. 155, stanza 22.

[163] *Roscius Anglicanus,* 1928, p. 22, with the corresponding note, pp. 179–180. The old prompter's account offers difficulties which I have discussed *in loco.*

Mr. J. R. A. Nicoll, *A History of Restoration Drama,* 1928 (*revised* edition), p. 127, is mistaken when he writes : " Edward Howard, Downes tells us, turned *Romeo and Juliet* into a tragi-comedy."

[164] In his *Specimens of English Dramatic Poets* Lamb has an extract from *The English Mounsieur.*

[165] *The Rehearsal,* ed. by Montague Summers, 1914, pp. 39–42.

[166] Bodleian, MS. Eng. poet., *e4.*

[167] *English Stage,* vol. iv, p. 116.

[168] Created by Hart and Nell Gwyn, who were the original Philidor and Mirida.

[169] Originally produced at the Phoenix in Drury Lane ; 4to, 1629, also 1633, 1660. It was given on Monday, 9th January, 1661, at Vere Street, and had probably been revived even earlier than this.

[170] *Savile Correspondence,* Camden Society, 1858, p. 4.

[171] Dugdale, *Visitation of Yorkshire,* ed. Davies, p. 265.

[172] Owing to the generosity of Abbot Caravel of Saint-Vaast the house had been established in 1605.

[173] Weldon, *Chronicle,* Appendix, p. 9.

[174] *Seventeenth Century Studies,* Second Edition, 1885 ; *Sir George Etherege,* p. 237 : " During the first years of the Restoration the principal playwrights were Porter, a sort of third-rate Brome, Killigrew, an imitator of Shirley, Stapylton, an apparently lunatic person, and Sir William Lower, to whom is due the praise of having studied French contemporary literature with great zeal, and of having translated Corneille and Quinault."

[175] Langbaine, *Dramatick Poets,* Oxford, 1691, p. 491.

[176] Metcalfe, *Book of Knights,* p. 199.

[177] Chester, *Registers of Westminster Abbey,* p. 170.

[178] Mr. Dryden in his *Discourse concerning the Original and Progress of Satire,* prefixed—to his *Satires of Decimus Junius Juvenalis,* folio, 1693, has occasion to speak severely—but not too severely—of Stapylton's quality as a translator of Juvenal. See the *Prose Works of John Dryden,* ed. by Edmond Malone, 1800, vol. iii, p. 187.

[179] The war between Philip II and the United Provinces. The first edition is Rome, 2 vols., folio, 1640–7. The work is still much esteemed.

[180] Langbaine, p. 492, also attributes to him translations from De Marmet and Cyrano de Bergerac, but these are from the pen of Thomas St. Serfe.

[181] Langbaine, ibid.

[182] On 29th May, 1663, Pepys saw *The Slighted Maid* " wherein Gosnell acted Pyramena, a great part, and did it very well ". He thought the play " not very excellent " but " well acted ". He also saw Mrs. Gosnell in *The Slighted Maid* on 28th July, 1668, but he does not mention if she acted Pyramena, in which rôle presumably she understudied Mrs. Betterton.

[183] *Dryden The Dramatic Works,* ed. by Montague Summers, vol. v, 1932, p. 15 and p. 409.

[184] *English Stage,* vol. i, p. 46.

[185] See also Pliny Junior, *Epistolae,* III, xvi; and Tacitus *Annales,* xvi.

[186] Edited by Montague Summers, 1914, pp. 66–8, and (notes) 143–8.

[187] The name of this dance, which seems to have been a kind of reel, is said to be derived from the French *haie,* a hedge, the dancers who stood in two rows being compared to hedges. In Playford's *Musick's Handmaid,* 1678, an air is found entitled " The Canaries, or the Hay ". Two partners danced the Canaries, which was a variant of the jig.

[188] Mrs. Pinchwife in *The Country-Wife* during her jaunt to the New Exchange bought *The Slighted Maid* and *Tarugo's Wiles* from a bookseller.

[189] " *Retiarius,* or Net-bearer, so named from a kind of floate Net, which he carryed in his hand ayming to cast it about the head of the *Sequutor,* or pursuer, who played against him, and prest upon him with a Sword and Target." Stapylton, *Juvenalls Satyrs,* London, 1647, The Second Satyr, Annotations, (2) Verse 172, pp. 30-1. For an illustration of Retiarii see the engraving at p. 583, in vol. i of the Suetonius ed. by Samuel Pitiscus, Leovardiae (Leenwarden), 1714-15.

[190] Musaeus the Greek grammarian of the fifth century was thought by scholars of the Renaissance to be the semi-mythical disciple of Orpheus, the morning star of Hellenic song. When Aldus Manutius conceived the noble plan of issuing the entire body of Greek literature from his Venetian press he deemed it fitting that the first book he printed (in 1493) should be Musaeus, " the most ancient poet." There are many English translations of " The Divine Poem of Musaeus, first of all Bookes " as Chapman termed it (1616).

[191] It might almost be thought that here Staplyton is harking back to the old multiple setting, *décor simultané,* but the point has no practical bearing since *The Tragedie of Hero and Leander* was not acted, and in its present form is hardly adapted for production.

[192] Who comes of the old stock, the *nutrix* of Latin comedy, the Nurse of *Dido, Queen of Carthage,* Juliet's Nurse, the Nurse in *The Night-Walker,* Biron's Nurse in *The Fatal Marriage,* and many more.

[193] *English Stage,* vol. i, p. 142.

[194] Thomas Horde, junior, a grammar-school teacher at Stow-on-the-Wold, wrote (and adapted) fifteen bad plays.

[195] *The Complete Works of William Wycherley,* edited by Montague Summers, 1924 ; vol. i, Introduction, pp. 18-24 ; vol. iv, pp. 73-102 and pp. 261-7.

[196] Scarron has a parody *Léandre et Héro, ode burlesque* in the *Ode Burlesque à Fouquet,* Paris, de Sommeville, 1656.

[197] *Heroides,* xviii and xix.

[198] *Ovidius Exulans, or Ovid Travestie.* A Mock Poem on five Epistles of Ovid. Radcliffe subsequently parodied all the Epistles for the enlarged later editions.

[199] For Querno see Gyraldus, *De Poetis suorum temporum* ; although Franciscus Arsillius in his *De Poetis Urbanis* praises Querno as fluent. Pope, *Dunciad,* ii, 13-16, has :—

> Not with more glee, by hands Pontific crown'd,
> With scarlet hats wide-waving circled round,
> Rome in her Capitol saw *Querno* sit,
> Thron'd on sev'n hills, the Antichrist of wit.

It was not Querno, however, but Baraballo of Gaeta, who was led in ridiculous pageantry through Rome, nor did the Pope crown the bard. On 27th September, 1518, Baraballo bedecked with antique gold and purple, mounted an elephant and rode through the thronging streets in solemn state. Paolo Giovio describes the procession in his *Vita Leonis,* X, lib. iv. See also the epigram of Angelo Colocci, *De Abante Baraballo.*

[200] Langbaine, it is true, remarks of Flecknoe, " His Acquaintance with the Nobility, was more than with the Muses," *English Dramatick Poets,* 1691, p. 199.

[201] The suggestion was originally made by Peter Cunningham in an article in *The Gentleman's Magazine,* December, 1850. Flecknoe was certainly very friendly with Edward Howard, to whom he has addressed a copy of complimentary verses.

[202] The " *Civiliz'd Epistle* " is "A Defence of an Essay of Dramatique Poesie ", which was prefixed only to the second quarto, 1668, of *The Indian Emperour.* See Dryden *The Dramatic Works,* edited by Montague Summers, 1931, vol. i, pp. 255-270.

[203] No. 330 in the Second Day's Sale, Tuesday, 12th May, 1931, of the Thorn-Drury Library. Sotheby's Catalogue of the First Portion, p. 39.

[204] In his reprint of *Tomaso the Wanderer,* Prefatory Note, p. iv, Mr. Thorn-Drury says : " It is, of course, impossible now to be sure of the precise nature of the grievances which Flecknoe had, or thought he had, against Killigrew ; there can, however, I think be little doubt but they arose from their relations of theatrical manager and playwright."

[205] The second daughter of Oliver Cromwell. She died in 1658.

[206] The *popa* was the priest's minister, who brought the victim to the altar, and felled it with an axe. Thus Propertius, IV (V), iii, 62 :—

Illa dies hornis caedem denuntiat agnis
Succinctique calent ad nova lucra popae.

See also Ovid, *Fasti*, i, 319–321 ; and Alexander ab Alexandro *Geniales Dies*, iv, 17, " victimarii seu cultrarii, nonnullis popae et agones dicti sunt," with the notes of Tiraquellus on this passage ; ed. Hackiana, 1673, tom. i, p. 1105. See also Turnebus, *Adversaria*, xviii, 5, and xxx, 7 ; Stuck, *Sacrorum sacrificiorumque gentilium . . . descriptio*, p. 109 ; Majorogius, *Quaestiones*, xi, 4 ; Saubert, *De sacrificiis*, vi. Panvinius, *De civitate Romana*, xliv.

[207] In which island Venus was particularly worshipped, whose cult is said to have been introduced there by the Phoenicians. Thus she is named Cypria in the Homeric poems, and by almost all subsequent classical authors. Cf. Horace *diva potens Cypri* ; Odes, I, iii, 1 ; and the epithet of Hesiod Κυπρογενής.

[208] However, Langbaine, *English Dramatick Poets*, Oxford, 1691, p. 201, remarks : " Whether the Play answer the Title-page, or whether *Mr. Flecknoe* have so regularly observ'd the three Unities, I shall leave to the Criticks."

[209] Festa dies Veneri, tota celeberrima Cypro ; Ovid, *Metamorpheon*, x, 270.

[210] *English Stage*, x, p. 249.

[211] *Roscius Anglicanus*, p. 31. Langbaine, p. 202, is blunt in his remark upon *Love's Kingdom* : " the Poet got leave to have it acted ; but it had the misfortune to be damn'd by the Audience."

[212] 12mo, 1664, dedicated to William, Lord Marquess of Newcastle. Flecknoe complains that the people, judges without judgement, " received his play coldly for want of its being rightly represented to them." He owns that it wants much of the Ornament of the Stage ; but *that* (he says) " by a lively Imagination may easily be supply'd ".

[213] Langbaine, p. 201, mistakes when he says of *Erminia*, " This Play . . . was never acted."

[214] Produced at the Palais-Royal, 6th August, 1666.

[215] For Wilbraham see p. 88. Alexander can hardly be identified with the Mr. Alexander (by some once thought to be Verbruggen) who was playing *c.* 1685–1700, and for whom see my edition of *The Works of William Congreve*, 1923, vol. i, pp. 246–8.

[216] It should perhaps be mentioned that Pepys speaks of Flecknoe's play as "a translation out of French by Dryden, called ' The Ladys à la Mode ' ". This mistake of Pepys has in the past given rise to some confusion.

[217] Vol. v, part ii, p. 268.

[218] New Edition by David Patrick, LL.D., 1903, vol. i, pp. 784–6.

[219] Sir Edmund Gosse : *Seventeenth Century Studies*, Second Edition, 1885, p. 224.

[220] Foster, *Gray's Inn Register*, p. 208. Frating is in the north-east of the county, 6 miles east-south-east of Colchester. In the *Complete Baronetage* G. E. C. says that Sir Samuel Tuke was the son of Thomas Tuke of Layer Marney by his second wife Judith *née* North. This seems to lack confirmation, and to be due to some mistake. Layer Marney is about 5 miles south-west of Colchester.

[221] *Diary*, 1st October, 1649. Evelyn refers to Tuke as " my cousin Tuke ". The relationship was through Mary, Evelyn's wife. Sir Samuel Tuke is spoken of several times in the *Diary* particularly 9th May, 1660, 13th February, 1661, 24th February, 1644 ; 9th June, 1664 (Tuke's first marriage) ; 2nd July, 1668 (Tuke's second marriage). Oddly enough, Evelyn, 23rd December, 1662, and 8th January, 1663, speaks of *The Adventures of Five Hours* as written by Sir George Tuke. This must be a slip, although in itself sufficiently curious. Downes (p. 22) says that this comedy was " Wrote by the Earl of *Bristol*, and Sir *Samuel Tuke* ", but there are many inaccuracies in the *Roscius Anglicanus*, and his mention of the Earl of Bristol may be accounted an error, as it does not appear this nobleman had any hand in the play. The confusion arises from the fact that the Earl of Bristol translated '*Tis Better Than It Was* and *Worse and Worse* from Calderón's *Mejor Está que Estaba* and *Peor Está que Estaba*, so that many persons took the three plays from the Spanish to be by the same hand. See Pepys, 20th July, 1664.

[222] Le Neve, *Knights*, p. 180.

[223] There were also two daughters, for whom see *Miscellanea Genealogica et Heraldica*, New Series, i (1874), p. 196. The baronetcy became extinct in Sir Charles, who died of wounds received at the Battle of the Boyne, loyally fighting for King James II.

[224] Wood, *Athenae Oxonienses*, ed. 1721, ii, p. 802. For a fuller account of Sir Samuel Tuke and quotations of tributes paid to him see the Introduction by the present writer to the separate reprint of *The Adventures of Five Hours*, 1927.

[225] Cotalero, *Boletin de la Real Academia Española*, Diciembre de 1918, p. 587.

[226] Pepys *Diary*, 8th January, 1663. There are several other references to this " most excellent play " as also the famous entry, 20th August, 1666 : " Reading ' Othello, Moor of Venice ', which I ever heretofore esteemed a mighty good play, but having so lately read ' The Adventures of Five Houres ', it seems a mean thing."

[227] *Roscius Anglicanus*, pp. 22–3.

[228] See *The Complete Works of William Congreve*, 1923, edited by Montague Summers, vol. i, Introduction, p. 18. Other notable continuous runs recorded by Downes are *The Siege of Rhodes*, 12 Days (p. 21) ; the magnificent revival of *Henry VIII*, 15 Days (p. 24) ; *King Henry V* by Orrery, 10 Days (p. 28) ; *The Woman made a Justice*, Betterton, 14 Days (p. 30) ; *Don Carlos*, 10 Days (p. 36) ; *Oedipus*, 10 Days (p. 37) ; *The Squire of Alsatia*, 13 Days (p. 41) ; *Love for Love*, 13 Days (p. 44) ; and *The Mourning Bride*, 13 Days, (p. 44).

[229] He was baptized at S. Stephen's Walbrook, 27th December, 1626. His father was then rector of this church. *Register of S. Stephen's Walbrook and S. Benet's Sherehog.* (Harley Publications.)

[230] *Black Book of Lincoln's Inn*, vol. ii, p. 396. Wilson dedicates his *Jus Regium Coronae*, 4to, 1688, " To the Honourable Society of Lincoln's Inn," whom he reminds " I served a Double Apprenticeship within your Walls ".

[231] Langbaine, *English Dramatick Poets*, 1691, pp. 512–13, knows practically nothing of Wilson and is even uncertain whether he is still alive. Gildon, how-ever, in the later edition of Langbaine, 8vo, 1699, remarks that Wilson died " near *Leicester* Fields about three years since ". On 3rd February, 1694–5, John Wilson of " Cundit Court, Longaker ", was buried. The entry is in the parish register of S. Martin-in-the-Fields, and almost certainly this John Wilson was the dramatist.

[232] A fraternity of roaring blades dubbed *Tityre tues* (from the Vergilian Tag) engaged the attention of the authorities as early as the reign of James I. The history of these rowdy gangs, who nightly beset London streets and proved a very formid-able danger—Oatmeals, Huffs, Muns, Swashes, Scowrers, Mohocks, and the rest —is old and long. See *The Works of Thomas Shadwell*, 1927, ed. Montague Summers, Introduction, pp. ccxx-ccxxvii.

[233] Loveday, Mrs. Marshall, and Mrs. Margaret are not in the printed quarto, but are supplied by the Worcester College Library MS. For Mrs. Margaret [Hughes], see Chapter II, n. 174.

[234] See *The Restoration Theatre*, by Montague Summers, pp. 287–8, and Plate xxiv.

[235] The first quarto of *The Cheats*, 1664, has " Imprimatur. Nov. 5, 1663. Roger L'Estrange ". It is entered in the *Stationers' Register* under 9th November, 1663.

[236] Probably on Monday, 16th March, or on the following day.

[237] *Familiar Letters*, p. 103. See *Notes and Queries*, 5th Series, vol. iv, 1875, p. 420.

[238] *State Papers*. Domestic, 1663-4, p. 83.

[239] For one instance, and there are many on record, see Pepys, 16th April, 1667.

[240] Oldmixon, *History of England*, folio, 1730, p. 690.

[241] In allusion to the Act of Uniformity which came into force 24th August, 1662.

[242] " *Scribb'd* and *Libb'd*, farmers' terms, or rather they are used as one word—castrated." Robinson, *Whitby Glossary*, 1855.

[243] There is a painting (which has been engraved) by Van Bleeck of Griffin as Tribulation and Ben Johnson as Ananias in *The Alchemist*, III, 1.

[244] John Hippisley (d. 1748), the original Peachum, was a famous droll. " On the death of Pinkethman he succeeded to all his characters, and was received in them by the public with great applause." *Biographica Dramatica*, 1812, vol. i, part i, p. 348.

[245] Since this chapter was written and actually as I am engaged upon the final revision of proofs an edition of *The Cheats* has been published (1935), edited by M. C. Nahm, "From the MS. in the Library of Worcester College, Oxford."

[246] Morglay was the sword belonging to Sir Bevis. Thus Drayton *Poly-olbion*, ii, 1, 332 :—
> "Arundell his steed, And Morglay his good sword."

[247] "Uds Niggers Noggers," swears Simpkin in *The Humours of Simpkin*, ed. 1673. In Dryden's *The Kind Keeper*, iv, 1, when the hypocritical fanatic Mrs. Saintly makes lewd advances to young Woodall she cries : "Delay no longer, or——" "Or ! you will not swear, I hope ?" laughingly answers the gentleman. "*Uds Niggers*, but I will," threatens the anxious dame. "Uds Niggers, I confess, is a very dreadful Oath," banters he. *Dryden The Dramatic Works*, ed. Montague Summers, vol. iv (1932), p. 317, and note, p. 559.

[248] *Shakespeare and the Universities*, 1923, p. 251.

[249] In "The Author, To The Reader", 4to, 1664, Wilson himself says that the humour of Bilboe and Titere Tu "*can be no wise strange, to any man that knew this Town, between the years 46, and 50, ... And further, if there be any thing in their language, that may seem loose, be pleased to consider who they are that speak it*".

[250] *Imprimatur*, 18th January, 1663/4.

[251] In his Dedication, "To My Friend A. B.," Wilson remarks : "To tell you how long since this Tragedy was first written, or why it has not been since acted, were but in effect to suspect your memory. 'Tis enough to me that you know both, and I doubt not will be ready to do me right as you see occasion."

[252] This should be Alice (or Agnes), daughter of Louis VII of France, and relict of the young Emperor Alexius whom Andronicus strangled with the bowstring.

[253] *Stationers' Register*, 15th February, 1664-5.

[254] *Biographica Dramatica*, 1812, vol. iii, p. 182.

[255] Mr. J. R. A. Nicoll, who in his *Restoration Drama*, 1928, p. 200, writes of *The Cheats* as "a would-be imitation of Jonson with little to relieve its incoherent brutality", and who also mentions the "original and boisterous manner" of *The Projectors*, appears to have no acquaintance with Wilson's plays.

[256] Since *L'Avare* was produced 9th September, 1668, Wilson cannot of course have been influenced by Molière.

[257] *The Miser's Daughter* ran through *Ainsworth's Magazine*, commencing with the issue of the first number in February, 1842. It was first published separately, three volumes, 1842 ; second edition, 1843 ; and in one volume, third edition, 1848.

[258] Langbaine, pp. 122-3, says that "The beginning" of Dekker's *If this be not a good Play, the Devil is in it*, 4to, 1612, "seems to be writ in imitation of *Matchiavel's Novel* of Belphegor : where Pluto summons the Devils to Councel." Ward, *English Dramatic Literature*, ed. 1899, vol. ii, p. 465, is mistaken when he writes that Langbaine supposed the source of Dekker's play was Machiavelli's novella. Langbaine does not intend this. Both Dekker's play and Jonson's *The Devil is an Ass* are to some extent suggested by the popular *Pleasant Historie of Friar Rush*. It should perhaps be remarked that Wilson's *Belphegor* has nothing at all in common with *Belphegor the Mountebank* produced at the Adelphi, London, on 13th January, 1851, with Benjamin Webster as the hero. This is an adaptation of *La Paillasse* by MM. Dennery and Marc Fournier, produced at the Gaité, Paris, 9th November, 1850, with Frederic Lemaître as the hero. No less—possibly more —than four versions of *Belphegor the Mountebank* were being played in London contemporaneously, at the Adelphi, the Surrey, the Victoria, and City of London theatres. In 1856 an adaptation was seen at Sadler's Wells. In 1865 in another version Fechter played Belphegor at the Lyceum, and there are yet other versions which achieved great success.

Belphegor ; or, The Wishes, a comic opera in three acts by Miles Peter Andrews, was produced at Drury Lane on 17th March, 1778, with Bannister as Belphegor, a devil. This takes a hint from Wilson. A woodcutter, Booze, shelters Belphegor from his pursuers, and in return the familiar grants him three wishes.

[259] On 17th November, 1672 ; and on 8th January, 1674, there were performances at Court of a play *The Guardian*, which may either have been Cowley's comedy, or (more probably) Massinger's earlier play of the same name.

[260] Thomas Harrison, regicide, 1606-1660. He was executed for High Treason at Charing Cross, on 13th October. The Fifth-monarchy enthusiasts spread a report

that he would rise from the dead, judge his judges, and establish a kingdom of the Saints. To this allusion is made here. See further Pepys, 13th October, 1660 ; and *Cal. State Papers. Domestic*, 1660–1, p. 569.

²⁶¹ *English Dramatick Poets*, p. 81.

²⁶² *Roscius Anglicanus*, p. 25. Cowley's other dramatic pieces, the charming pastoral comedy *Love's Riddle* and the amusing *Naufragium Joculare*, both early works, do not fall within our scope. Charles Johnson's *Fortune in her Wits*, published anonymously, 4to, 1705, is a poor adaptation of the Latin comedy, which was also utilized together with Terence's *Andria* in Daniel Bellamy's *The Perjur'd Devotee ; or, The Force of Love*. This piece which sets out to exhibit " *Terentian* Humour, join'd with *Cowley's* wit " was written according to the *Biographica Dramatica* for presentation to the young ladies of Mrs. Bellamy's boarding-school at Chelsea. It is printed, No. 2, in a collection of *Dramatic Pieces and Miscellanies* by Daniel Bellamy, Senior and Junior, 2 vols., 12mo, 1739–1740.

²⁶³ *Cal. State Papers. Domestic*, 1655, pp. 74 and 577. *Middlesex Quarter Sessions*, 17th July, 1655.

²⁶⁴ *Historical MSS. Comm.*, 9th Rep., II, 123.

²⁶⁵ *Mercurius Politicus*, 22nd–29th March, 1655, p. 5228. *Middlesex Records*, iii, 233.

²⁶⁶ Pepys has very full details of the whole affair, 29th July ; 8th and 12th August, 1667. Langbaine strangely enough knew nothing of Porter's life, for whose plays he expresses great admiration.

²⁶⁷ Fonblanque, *Lives of the Lords Strangford*, pp. 15 and 83. *Memories of Lady Fanshawe*, p. 172.

²⁶⁸ *English Stage*, vol. x, p. 248.

²⁶⁹ Mary Moders continued her fraudulent career after acquittal, and was transported in February, 1671, to Jamaica for theft. She escaped back to England, was taken and found guilty of stealing a piece of plate for which she was hanged at Tyburn, 22nd January, 1673. For the earlier part of her adventures see *The Assignment, Trial and Examination of Mary Moders*, 1663, a pamphlet of 16 pages ; also John Carleton's *Ultimum Vale*, 1663. Her own " Historical Narrative " is, of course, not to be relied upon, and her later " biographies " the most important of which is from the pen of Francis Kirkman are often extravagantly romantic.

²⁷⁰   Damn'd *Holden* with's dull *Garman Princess* appear'd
    Whom if *D'Avenant* he got as some do suppose,
    Apollo said the Pillory should crop of[f] his Ears,
    And make them more sutable unto his Nose.

The Session of the Poets, stanza 40. *Poems on State-Affairs*, 1705, p. 157.

²⁷¹ The mistake probably originated with Genest, *English Stage*, i, pp. 51–2. Most writers have, it is true, been cautious enough to point out that the identity of *A Witty Combat* with The *German Princess* is highly speculative, but Mr. Bernbaum in his eccentric and unreliable monograph *The Mary Carleton Narratives*, 1914, plumps out : " In the spring of 1664, to be sure, 'A Witty Combat,' then called ' The German Princess ', was staged, with Mary herself . . . acting the leading part," p. 26.

²⁷² *Term Catalogues*, Michaelmas (26th November), 1677. The play was licensed for printing 2nd August, 1677. The Epilogue, spoken in the character of a Frenchman, girds at " the *French* troop at toder end o' Town ", by which the Whitehall theatre is intended. On the King's birthday, 29th May, 1677, *Rare en Tout* (printed 4to, 1677) had been given before His Majesty : *Verney Papers, Hist. MSS. Comm.*, 7th Report, Appendix, p. 469. Two French troupes visited London in 1677, the first, at which Porter jeers, in the early part of the year ; the second in November.

²⁷³ *Roscius Anglicanus*, p. 28.

²⁷⁴ The folio *Guzman*, 1693, is an important text as being printed from the prompt-copy and giving a number of prompter's directions and marginalia which were omitted when the piece was included in volume ii of *The Dramatick Works of Roger Boyle, Earl of Orrery*, 1739. See *The Restoration Theatre*, by Montague Summers, 1934, pp. 98, 131, 214, 215. The first edition of *Guzman* was dedicated by Nahum Tate to The Right Honourable Lionel, Earl of Orrery, etc.

²⁷⁵ The permanent Proscenium Doors, see *The Restoration Theatre*, ut cit. sup., pp. 126–144.

²⁷⁶ Downes, *Roscius Anglicanus*, p. 28.

[277] This accident has parallels, not very close perhaps, in Italian comedy ; see Machiavelli's *La Clizia* and other plays. One may also compare the episode of old Gripe and Lucy in Wycherley's *Love in a Wood*, Act III.

[278] Produced at Lincoln's Inn Fields, 28th April, 1703 : 4to, 1703. (The title page has a misprint MDCIII for MDCCIII.)

[279] The Masque should certainly have been mentioned in Alwin Thaler's *Milton in the Theatre, Studies in Philology*, xvii, 3, July, 1920, but Mr. Thaler apparently did not know Cokayne's work.

[280] Licensed by Herbert, 6th June, 1634. Printed 8vo, 1655.

[281] There are other reminiscences of earlier plays. The fantastic travel-talk of Lorece is clearly derived from Freshwater in Shirley's *The Ball*. See the reprint of this comedy in T. M. Parrott's *The Comedies of George Chapman*, 1914.

It may be noted that it is sufficient for Tandorix (Rosinda), iv, 1, to draw off her periwig and her son immediately recognizes her, although till then seeing her daily he had thought her the manservant. For other examples of this convention see my *The Restoration Theatre*, pp. 262–3.

[282] Two vols., Paris, 1644.

[283] In parody of the popular *A King and No King*.

[284] Edward Fitzwilliam, 1788–1852, of Irish parentage was especially famous in Irish characters. He was a great favourite with the town. See Oxberry's *Dramatic Biography*.

[285] For a full and detailed examination of the Don Juan legend and the many dramatic pieces founded upon the story see my edition of Shadwell's *Complete Works*, 1927, vol. i, Introduction, pp. cxxii–cxli.

[286] It may have been that Cokayne was the " worthy gentleman " who told Shadwell of a Play made upon the Story of Don Juan in Italy and acted there " by the name of *Atheisto Fulminato* in Churches, on *Sundays*, as a part of Devotion ". See the Preface to *The Libertine*, Shadwell's *Works*, ut sup., vol. iii, pp. 21 and 379.

[287] *English Dramatick Poets*, 1691, p. 69.

[288] A long and interesting note might be written upon this mechanical chair. Such a device is recorded by Pausanias, and was well known in Italy during the fifteenth and sixteenth centuries. Bandello mentions a chair of this kind, iv, 1, whence it was taken by Barnaby Barnes for *The Divils Charter*, 4to, 1607, i, 5, where Lucretia Borgia catches Gismond di Viselli in her chair and kills him. On 1st November, 1660, Sir William Batten amongst other rarities showed Pepys " a chair, which he calls King Harry's chair, where he that sits down is catched with two irons, that come round about him, which makes good sport ".

[289] It is disputed at which theatre but Lefèvre gives the following cast : Polyeucte, d'Orgemont ; Sévère, Floridor ; Néarque, Desurlis ; and Pauline, Mlle Duclos. This, if correct, implies the Marais. There is, however, reason to suppose that the Hôtel de Bourgogne was the actual house, and that Champmeslé, le Thuillerie, Hauteroche, Beauval, Mlle le Comte, and Mlle Guyot were among the original performers. Polyceute wore a Spanish doublet, buskins, and a hat with large plumes. (See the frontispiece of the first edition.) Voltaire makes himself very merry at the white gloves and large-brimmed hat which formed part of Polyeucte's traditional costume. Pauline has been a favourite rôle with many of the greatest French tragediennes ; Adrienne Lecouvreur, Hippolyte Clairon, Marie-Françoise Dumesnil, and in late days Rachel, the fervour of whose " Je crois " caused an electric effect in the theatre. Donizetti's opera *I Martiri* in which Tamberlik sang Polyeucte, and Madame Jullienne Paulina, is from Corneille's tragedy.

[290] The Greeks keep his festival on 9th January, since he was beheaded 10th January, A.D. 250 (or 257). His Acts were written by his friend Nearchus. For the history see Symeon Metaphrastes and Surius, or perhaps more conveniently Alban Butler under 13th February.

[291] *English Stage*, x.

[292] Add. MSS. 28723.

[293] Curiously enough many of the names in *La Généreuse Ingratitude* occur in Dryden's *The Conquest of Granada*, as I have already noted. *Dryden The Dramatic Works*, edited by Montague Summers, vol. iii (1932), p. 516. The characters, however, are entirely different, and there is no sort of resemblance between the two plays.

[294] In Calderón's original *El Galan Fantasma* we have El Duque de Saxonia.

[295] For example, *The Innocent Lady* from the French of Père de Cerizicis, s. 7 ; *The Triumphant Lady* translated from the same author ; *The Pleasures of the Ladies* (unprinted) from de Grenail. Lower's stateliest production was his *Relation of the Voyage and Residence which . . . Charles the II King of Great Britain &c. Hath made in Holland,* folio, The Hague, 1660, with plates by T. Matham.

[296] *Historiarum Philippicarum,* libri xliv, from the lost work of Trogus Pompeius, which is itself believed to have been a translation of the Greek history of Timagenes. This was based upon Theopompus, Ephorus, Timaeus, Polybius, and other earlier writers.

[297] Liber XXX, xxxii.

[298] *Théâtre François,* tom. ix, pp. 20–2.

[299] Tome i, ed. 1740, p. 236.

[300] See also Livy, i, 3 : " Tiberinus, qui in traiectu Albulae amnis submersus, celebre ad posteros nomen flumini dedit." Cf. Ovid, *Metamorphoseon,* xiv, 614–16. After Ascanius Silvius ruled, then followed Latimus, Epitos, Capetus, Capys, and Tiberinus, whose son was (according to Livy) Agrippa. These legendary lists of kings differ very considerably in various authors.

[301] There is ample material available for a very full account of Sir William Killigrew, whose chequered career I have not been able to do more than touch upon here.

[302] J. A. R. Nicoll, *A History of Restoration Drama,* 1928, p. 129.

[303] This has been quoted above. B.M. Add. MS. 34217, fol. 31b.

[304] *Poems of Edmund Waller,* ed. G. Thorn-Drury, 1901, vol. ii, p. 64.

[305] *Roscius Anglicanus,* p. 15.

[306] Bodleian, Rawl. Poet., 29.

[307] For Ann Marshall, Mrs. Weaver, and Elizabeth Davenport, see my edition of the *Roscius Anglicanus,* pp. 89–91 and pp. 139–140.

[308] Sir William Killigrew did not escape the jeer of Buckingham in *The Rehearsal.* See my edition of that play, Shakespeare Head Press, 1914, p. 102, the note upon p. 26. *Hey day, hey day!* Also p. 93 for *Pandora,* and p. 140 for *The Imperial Tragedy.*

[309] Gibbon, *Decline and Fall of the Roman Empire,* chapter xxxix, ed. 1823, vol. v, pp. 3–5.

[310] John Malas, *Chronicle,* ed. Bekker, 1831, xv, p. 390.

[311] Suidas, s.v.

[312] *English Dramatick Poets,* Oxford, 1691, p. 64 ; and p. 535.

[313] Lope de Vega's *El Galán escarmentado* has been hazarded as a possible source. The difficulty lies in the fact that Lope's play is unprinted and the MS. so far has not been traced. It is mentioned in a list of plays by Lope, 1603. Dryden may, or may not have seen the Spanish comedy in MS. form. See further, *The Dramatic Works of John Dryden,* edited by Montague Summers, vol. i, 1931, pp. 61–3. Unfortunately we only have the altered, not the original version of *The Wild Gallant.*

[314] Cervantes, *Las Dos Doncellas* in the *Novelas Ejemplares* ; Rotrou, *Les Deux Pucelles* ; Quinault, *Les Rivales.* See Dryden, ut cit. sup., vol. i, Introduction, pp. xxxv–xxxvi, and pp. 131–2.

CHAPTER IV

THE TOP-WITS AND THE MEN OF QUALITY

The Duke of *Buckingham's* Name is Panegyrick sufficient . . . and
the *Rehearsal,* the justest and truest Satyr the World ever saw, will
be an everlasting Demonstration of his Wit.—MR. THO. BROWN,
Some Memories On His Grace, George, Late Duke of Buckingham. (Third
Edition, 1715.)

> Wit, sacred Wit, is all the bus'ness here ;
> Great *Fletcher,* and the greater *Rochester.*
> > APHRA BEHN, (*Valentinian,* 4to, 1685.) *Prologue*
> > *spoken* by *Mrs.* Cook the *first Day.*

> She strait pull'd off her Sattin cap, and Band :
> Bade *Wycherly* be bold in her Defence,
> With pointed Wit, and Energy of Sense :
> *Etherege* and *Sidley* join'd him in her Cause,
> And all deserved, and all received Applause.
> > E. FENTON, *Poems on several Occasions,* 8vo, 1717,
> > p. 72 ; " An Epistle to Mr. Southerne."

Although the Court of King Charles returning from France
at the Restoration brought with it the latest Parisian mode in
things theatrical, the very drama reformed by Corneille and
some other Frenchmen—" which before was as much below
ours as it now surpasses it and the rest of *Europe* " [1]— they were
not themselves perhaps conscious how finely the foreign material
must needs be boltered through a native sieve before it was
palatable to English appetites, and, curiously as it may appear,
for a couple of decades after the King's coming-in the hall-mark
of your top-wit, your " high-brow " modern cant would name
him, was not so much a Gallomania, as a particular veneration
for " the greatest man of the last age, *Ben. Johnson* ".[2]

It was not merely that his masterpieces *Epicoene, The Alchemist,
Volpone, Bartholomew Fair,* were the favourite plays of the
Theatre Royal, given to crowded houses, and supported by the
whole strength of Killigrew's company ; that there were impor-
tant revivals of *Every Man in his Humour, Every Man out of his
Humour, The Devil is an Ass, The Magnetick Lady, Catiline* and
Sejanus [3] ; that so great a critic as Dryden could write of Jonson :
" I think him the most learned and judicious Writer which any
Theatre ever had " [4] ; that a dramatist, such as the lively

Aphra Behn, aiming at popularity, had a sharp bob for those of the audience

> *Who swear they'd rather hear a smutty Jest*
> *Spoken by* Nokes *or* Angel, *than a Scene*
> *Of the admir'd and well penn'd* Cataline.[5]

The Jonsonian cult went much further than this. Far beyond any dramatist, ancient or modern, Ben Jonson must be recognized as the supreme master, who gave laws unimpeachable to the stage, who afforded the perfect models of perfect plays, to copy whom was surety of success, to depart from whose canon was damnation, who was the final arbiter in all matters of taste and poetry. The reign of humours in comedy must be upheld to the uttermost; tragedy must not dare to seek further than *Sejanus His Fall* and *Catiline his Conspiracy*. " Our *Ben*," says Langbaine,[6] " lookt upon himself as the only Master of *Poetry*; and thought it the Duty of the Age, rather to submit to, than dispute, much less oppose his judgment." This tyranny the top-wits of the Restoration were vowed to maintain at all costs. Some of their followers, indeed, went so far as scarcely to allow merit to any other save their Father Ben, and in the Epistle prefixed to *The Dutch Lover*,[7] 4to, 1673, Astrea has a sharp tilt at the affectation of the literary Phormios and Curculios of the great. She is replying to the charge that females cannot write plays for they lack " men's great advantage over women, that is Learning; We all well know that the immortal Shakespeare's Plays ... have better pleas'd the World than Johnson's works, though by the way 'tis said Benjamin was no such Rabbi neither, for I am inform'd that his Learning was but Grammar high, ... and it hath been observ'd that they are apt to admire him most confoundedly, who have just such a scantling of it as he had; and I have seen a man the most severe of Johnson's Sect, sit with his Hat remov'd less than a hair's breadth from one sullen posture for almost three hours at *The Alchymist*; who at that excellent Play of *Harry the Fourth* (which yet I hope is far enough from Farce) hath very hardly kept his Doublet whole; but affectation hath always had a greater share both in the action and discourse of men than truth and judgement have ".

" The most severe of Johnson's Sect " was Thomas Shadwell, who by precept and practice never failed to show himself to the town as one who would go through stitch for his Master, one who approved himself again and again foremost among the dogmatic, fanatical, and intemperate worshippers at Jonson's shrine.[8] In the Preface to his first play *The Sullen Lovers; or, The Impertinents*, 4to, 1668, Shadwell explicitly proclaims: " I have endeavour'd to represent variety of Humours ...

which was the practice of *Ben Johnson,* whom I think all Dramatick
Poets ought to imitate, though none are like to come near ;
he being the onely person that appears to me to have made
perfect Representations of Humane Life." He continues that
in comedy he never met with a character to come near those of
" the admirable *Johnson* " who " never wrote Comedy without
seven or eight excellent Humours. I never saw one, except
that of *Falstaffe* that was in my judgment comparable to any
of *Johnson*'s considerable Humours : you will pardon this dispersion when I tell you he is the man, of all the World, I most
passionately admire for his Excellency in Drammatick-*Poetry* ".[9]
The Preface to *The Humorists,* produced at Lincoln's Inn Fields
early in 1671, is wholly in the same strain : " If Mr. *Johnson*
be the most faultless Poet, I am so far from thinking it impudence
to endeavour to imitate him, that it would rather (in my opinion)
seem impudence in me not to do it." [10] The Epilogue to this
comedy is an unbounded panegyric of

> *The Mighty Prince of Poets, learned* BEN,
> *Who alone div'd into the Minds of Men :*

But " *his great Merit is above our Praise* " ; and sighs Shadwell

> *could he imitate that great Author right,*
> *He would with ease all Poets else out-write.*
> *But to out-go all other men, would be*
> *O Noble* BEN ! *less than to follow thee.*

Literary idolatry could hardly reach further, and this adulation
might be paralleled times without number from Shadwell's
writings.

It was this reckless enthusiasm which gained Thomas Shadwell
the entry to the select and high-placed circle of Jonson's professed
admirers, and here he met and was welcomed by some of the
highest names in the land and supremely powerful influences in
literature. No man stood firmer in Royal favour than " the Most
Illustrious Prince George, Duke of Buckingham ", to whom
Shadwell so silkily declared I " can never be prouder of any
thing can arrive to me, than the honour of having been admitted
sometimes into your Graces Conversation, the most charming
in the World ". [11]

Another ardent Jonsonian, whose patronage of Shadwell
proved life-long and truly generous [12] was Charles Sackville,
Lord Buckhurst, afterwards Earl of Dorset and Middlesex,
who years later, when the Revolution came, was as Lord Chamberlain to set on Shadwell's head the laureate's crown of bays, so
nobly discarded by John Dryden for God and honour's sake.

In Dryden's *Of Dramatick Poesie* Buckhurst appears as Eugenius, who upholds the English theatre against the Italian, French, and Spanish plays—" the *Drama* is wholly ours," he asserts—and Crites (Sir Robert Howard) proffers no further argument in converse with him than the example of Ben Jonson, since " you, *Eugenius,* prefer him above all other Poets ". [13] In his epilogue written for the post-Restoration revival of *Every Man in his Humour,* Buckhurst introduced Jonson's ghost, who, waving aside the actor who had commenced to address the audience, delivered some seventeen lines which doubtless voice the writer's own opinions :—

> Hold and give way for I myself will speak ;
> Can you encourage so much insolence,
> And add new faults still to the great offence
> Your ancestors so rashly did commit
> Against the mighty powers of art and wit,
> When they condemn'd those noble works of mine,
> *Sejanus,* and my best love, *Catiline.*
> Repent, or on your guilty heads shall fall
> The curse of many a rhyming pastoral.
> The three bold *Beauchamps* shall revive again,
> And with the *London 'Prentice* conquer *Spain.*[14]
> All the dull follies of the former age
> Shall find applause on this corrupted stage.
> But, if you pay the great arrears of praise,
> So long since due to my much-injur'd plays,
> From all past crimes I first will set you free,
> And then inspire someone to write like me.

The Jonsonians were by their very gospel bitterly opposed to the romantic dramas of such writers as Davenant, Sir William Killigrew, Sir Robert Stapylton, Porter, and the Howards,[15] but above all their especial detestation was the heroic play. In their caustic *Timon,* which is an adaptation of Boileau's third satire *Le Repas Ridicule,* 1665, a fact hitherto I believe not remarked but which I would bring to the notice of the editor, whoever he may be, when Rochester's works receive that much-needed attention, Buckingham and Rochester pour contempt upon Orrery, Elkanah Settle, Crowne, and Dryden's admired *The Indian Emperour.*

The most powerful counterblast to the heroic drama would, of course, be the production of a tragedy by Jonson, and accordingly the Jonsonian enthusiasts arranged a revival of *Catiline his Conspiracy,* the success of which might for ever drive such plays as *The Indian-Queen* from the boards, and restore tragedy upon the true Jonsonian model.   " The Duke of

Buckingham and Lord Dorset were admirers of Jonson to a degree of idolatry; it is very probable that, by liberal promises, they encouraged the actors to bring forward this forgotten tragedy. Certain it is that the play was acted several times during the reign of Charles II. The action of Hart in Catiline was universally applauded." [16] We know from Pepys that *Catiline* was produced at the Theatre Royal on Friday, 18th December, 1668. Hart played the title-rôle, Mohun, Cethegus [17]; Burt, Cicero [18]; Mrs. Katherine Corey, Sempronia [19]; and the whole strength of the company, Kynaston, Beeston, Reeves, Wintershal, Cartwright, Gradwell, and Richard Bell, helped to complete the cast. The King had given the actors five hundred pounds for costumes; the battle was arranged with unusual care, the Senate—in which there were "sixteen scarlett robes",—was mounted with a magnificence that almost foreshadowed Phelps and Charles Kean, Henry Irving and Tree, and no doubt the Jonson enthusiasts spared neither time nor money to make this splendid revival an intellectual and theatrical triumph. [20]

This revival of *Catiline his Conspiracy* was, as it were, a Jonsonian manifesto, but for several years Buckingham had been preparing something more, a dramatic satire, a play, which by the force of sheer ridicule should effectually once and for all banish the romantic and heroic drama from the theatre.

The Rehearsal [21] was produced at the Theatre Royal on 7th December, 1671. As early as 1663 Buckingham had headed the clique resolved by fair means or foul to damn Colonel Henry Howard's *The United Kingdoms,* a play of which we know nothing save that it began with a funeral and had also two kings in it, duly parodied by Buckingham. [22]

The idea of *The Rehearsal,* which was not altogether new to the stage, [23] is simple enough. Johnson meets his friend Smith, who has just come up from the country, and they fall to discussing current events, "all the impertinent, dull, fantastical things, we are tir'd out with here," says the former, and in particular the plays which are so much in vogue, "hideous, monstrous things." As they converse they encounter Mr. Bayes the poet who presently carries them off to see the Rehearsal of his new piece: "This morning is its last Rehearsal, in their habits, and all that, as it is to be acted," explains the author whilst they hie them away to the Theatre Royal. They stand upon the stage, and the play opens with its Prologue spoken by Thunder and Lightning, next to exhibit the two Kings of Brentford and their Gentleman-Usher and Physician who prove traitors, and "the whole State's turn'd topsie-turvy, without any puther or stir in the whole world", with the rare turn of the four soldiers who strike one another dead but who rise to a "note in *Effaut flat*", and dance "worse than the Angels in *Harry* the Eight or the fat Spirits in *The Tempest*". Then we have Amarillis; Prince Pretty-man; Prince Volscius with his wonderful meditation on boots, honour, and love; the fair Parthenope; the funeral of Lardella which at the command of Pallas changes whip-snap to a banquet; a dance; the appearance of the two right Kings of Brentford in the clouds; a wondrous Eclipse, in a new conceit of the Earth, Sun, and Moon, entering upon the stage, all singing "to the Tune of *Tom Tyler*"; a general battle "in *Recitativo*", until the mighty Drawcansir "comes in and kills 'em all on both sides", declaiming

> Others may bost a single man to kill
> But I, the blood of thousands daily spill.

At last Smith and Johnson half-dazed and mused with noise and nonsense take to their heels, and the actors set up bills for another play, whilst Bayes goes off muttering and swearing revenge in lampoon, pasquil, and satire. What his play was all about it passed the wit of man to tell.

> *The Play is at an end, but where's the Plot?*
> *That circumstances our Poet* Bayes *forgot.*

Yet Mr. Bayes can console himself: "What a Devil is the Plot good for, but to bring in fine things?" The burlesque is of the boldest; Buckingham's net is of the widest. We know at least seventy plays of which there is close verbal parody, and we also know that other plays were satirized which have perished and cannot be traced. When Buckingham sketched the first draft of his mordant scenes about 1663-4 he pricked down Sir Robert Howard [24] as the chief butt of his ridicule under the very pertinent name of Bilboa. The Great Plague closed the theatres; the Great Fire ravaged London; the years passed and what time the polishing touches were being given to *The Rehearsal* in 1671, Dryden the poet-laureate [25] was the most eminent dramatist of the day. Bayes is accordingly Dryden,[26] and indeed whilst the burlesque went capering and jiggetting on its merry way additions were continually being made to the script in burlesque of the laureate's new plays as they appeared. Thus there is some bitter ill-natured banter of *Marriage A-la-Mode,* which was produced by Killigrew's company about Easter, 1672, at Lincoln's Inn Fields, their temporary home after the fatal burning of the Theatre Royal in January of that year. Those quips were of course inserted by

Buckingham subsequently to the first production of his farce. *The Assignation; or, Love in a Nunnery,* given by Killigrew's company at Lincoln's Inn Fields in the winter of 1672, also afforded occasion for considerable interpolations towards the end of Act III. New dialogue was written in, and Mr. Bayes was able to boast how once he had " set off a Scene, I gad, beyond expectation, only with a Petticoat, and the Bellyake ".[27]

Dryden himself had a bob at these augmentations, for Mr. Thorn-Drury has remarked upon a couplet in the poet's Epilogue to Etherege's comedy *The Man of Mode* (1676), which although significantly enough not found in the printed texts occurs in a copy included in a large MS. book compiled by Sir William Haward :—

> *True Fops help Natures work, and go to school,*
> *To file and finish god-a'mighty's fool,*
> Labour to put in more, as Master Bayes
> Thrumms in Additions to his ten-yeares plays.

It would, however, be paying Buckingham far too high a compliment to suppose that *The Rehearsal* came from his pen alone. Thomas Sprat, afterwards Dean of Westminster and Bishop of Rochester; Martin Clifford, afterwards Master of the Charterhouse; and, it is said, Butler, Waller, and Cowley, all lent their aid. It skills not to inquire here exactly which points in the parody may be due to Butler; which scene may be traced to Clifford, which to Sprat. Various lampoons, of which several may be found in the collection conveniently called *Poems on Affairs of State,* speak of the heterogeneous authorship of *The Rehearsal* as well known and undisguised; thus one ballad has :—

> With help of Pimps, plays, and table chat,
> And the advice of his own canonical *Sprat,*
> And his family scribe antichristian *Mat,*
>
> With transcribing of these and transversing those,
> With transmitting of Rhyme and transversing Prose,
> He has dressed up his Farce with other mens Cloathes.

Another writer says :—

> I confess the Dances are very well writ,
> And the Time and the Tune by *Haines* are well set.

In *The Duke of Buckingham's Litany* the following petition occurs :—

> From owning twenty other men's Farce,
> *Libera Nos.*

Of the original actors in *The Rehearsal* we only know that Cartwright doubled Thunder (in the mock Prologue) and the Second King of Brentford ; Kynaston played Volscius [28] ; and Mrs. Reeves, Amarillis ; whilst Lacy, specially trained by Buckingham, created Bayes. Not only are Dryden's plays caricatured ; the turn of his speech and his phrases are reproduced, there are frequent references to his own personal tastes, such as his liking for stewed plums, his fondness for snuff, and even his amour with Ann Reeves [29] is alluded to in very unmistakable terms. Theatrical tradition has it that Lacy made up closely to resemble the laureate, whose tones and gait he mimicked, dressing the character in a suit of black velvet, a mode Dryden chiefly affected.

Spence in his *Anecdotes* reports from Lockier, " It is incredible how much pains he (Buckingham) took with one of the actors to teach him to speak some passages in Bayes's part in *The Rehearsal* right. The vulgar notion of that play's being hissed off the first night is a mistake."

" I have heard, indeed," writes Davies, " that the Duke of Buckingham and the Earl of Dorset prevailed on Dryden to accompany them, in the boxes, on the first night of acting the Rehearsal ; and placed the poet between them to enjoy the feelings of his mind during the exhibition of his own picture. The peculiarities of Dryden, when he instructed the players, seem to be strongly marked throughout the piece." [30]

Since an amusing but unauthentic anecdote is still sometimes referred to and quoted in all seriousness as an actual happening it may be worth while yet once again in brief to refute this long-lived canard. There is no foundation for the story which Joseph Spence in his *Anecdotes* (ed. Singer, pp. 61–2) retails from Dean Lockier of Peterborough, that in a certain play of Dryden's an actress, having to speak the following line,

> My wound is great—because it is so small,

accentuated the absurdity by a long pause and a look of intense pathos, when Buckingham, who was seated in one of the side-boxes, rose, and rejoined in a ridiculous mock-heroic voice, which shrilled through the house,

> Then 'twould be greater were it none at all.

The audience promptly burst into fits of laughter, and hooted the piece from the boards. As it was only the second performance Dryden lost his " third night ". No other reference to this incident has been found elsewhere, and had so ludicrous a contretemps occurred it is impossible that Dryden's battalions of enemies, Settle, Shadwell, the Duke himself, Pordage, Clifford,

PLATE XIV

THE REHEARSAL: ACT III: SCENE 5

Collection of the Author

Henry Care, Rochester, and the rest, would have failed to make capital out of such a happy travesty in their ballads and lampoons. The quiz must have been echoed again and again. There is, moreover, absolutely no record of Dryden's ever having lost a benefit night, and had such been the case it is inevitable that some reference to his discomfiture would have somewhere survived.

No such line as the preposterous "My wound is great—" is found in any of Dryden's works, but in *Notes And Observations On The Empress of Morocco*, 4to, 1674 (p. 62), we have : "His argument runs thus : No Traitor can come within the Sphere of *Morena*, but I can come within the Sphere of *Morena*, therefore I am no Traitor : what could his Father reply to this ; but that *his treason greater was for being small ; And had been greater were it none at all.*" If the banter were originally at Dryden's expense he assuredly would not have suffered it to be inserted in a pamphlet in which he joined with Crowne and Shadwell to roast Elkanah Settle, nor on the other hand would Settle have neglected to take so obvious an opening in his riposte *Notes and Observations on the Empress of Morocco Revised,* 4to, 1675. That there was some contemporary joke in reference to an extravagant line "My wound is great—because it is so small " is shown by an allusion in *S' too him Bayes,* 8vo, Oxon, 1673 (p. 7), but the line itself was probably burlesque in the first instance, and at any rate it was not pointed at Dryden, nor is there any reason to suppose it came from Buckingham.

Lacy was succeeded in the rôle of Bayes by Joe Haines, and during the eighteenth century the famous poetaster was played by many of our greatest comic actors, by Estcourt celebrated for his "Wit, and mimic Humour " ; Colley Cibber ; Theophilus Cibber ; Garrick ; King ; Foote, who mutilated the text and gagged unmercifully [31] ; Suett [32] ; Henderson ; and Wilson, who adapted the burlesque, cutting it down to only three acts. Towards the end of the century, indeed, Buckingham's farce was seen less and less frequently with more and more drastic innovations and alteration. To a certain extent, of course, Sheridan's direct copy *The Critic ; or A Tragedy Rehearsed,* produced at Drury Lane on 29th October, 1779, took the place of the earlier play, and it is interesting to find Walpole writing to the Countess of Upper Ossory on 13th January, 1780 : " *The Critic,* I own, was not so new as I expected ; and then my being ill-versed in modern dramas, most of the allusions must have escaped me. Does not half the merit of *The Rehearsal* depend on the notes ? " [33] I once wrote : " The water of *The Critic* is a mean thing to place beside the strong wine of *The Rehearsal.*" Mr. R. Crompton Rhodes has remarked : " *The*

Critic is for all time. Mr. Bayes perished with the plays of his era." [34] Let us rather say that both Bayes and Puff are as immortal as they are different the one from the other, and let us gladly allow that there is ample living room for both.

Garrick appeared as Bayes at the Goodman's Fields Theatre on 3rd February, 1742, and when he first exhibited the part he could not be distinguished from any other gay well-dressed man, which he soon realized was a false conception, for later to suit the conceit and solemnity of the dramatic coxcomb, " He wore a shabby old-fashioned coat, that had formerly been very fine ; a little hat, a large flowing brown wig, high-topt shoes with red heels, a mourning sword, scarlet stockings, and cut-fingered gloves." [35] This rôle was always considered among his greatest impersonations, and to heighten the jest he was wont in voice and gesture to mimic many of the leading actors of the day, Quin, Ryan, Dennis Delane, and other contemporaries, imitations which although they delighted his audiences were judged by not a few to be unfeeling and unjust. In Walpole's opinion Colley Cibber far excelled Garrick in Bayes, since the Bayes of Garrick was " entertaining but it was a Garreteer-bard. Old Cibber preserved the solemn coxcomb ; and was the caricature of a great poet, as the part was designed to be ". " In acting Bayes, Colley Cibber was dressed like a smart coxcomb," and " in the delineation of the character, he made him sufficiently ridiculous ".[36]

As we have seen, towards the end of the eighteenth century *The Rehearsal* was much abbreviated and compressed. At Covent Garden on 22nd June, 1819, cut down to one single act it was given with Farren as Bayes ; Blanchard, Prince Pretty-man ; and Liston, Prince Volscius. On 20th November, 1912, *The Rehearsal* was revived for one performance at Sheffield by the Sheffield Playgoers' Society,[37] and in 1925 it was given for one evening performance and one matinée on the 5th and 6th July at the Regent Theatre, London.

Charles Gildon expresses his surprise that in spite of the fact of the tremendous success of *The Rehearsal* at the Theatre Royal in December, 1671,[38] " those very plays, or others full of all the absurdities exploded in that pleasant criticism, were not less thronged." [39]

It cannot, indeed, be too strongly and persistently emphasized that although London laughed at and applauded *The Rehearsal,* although Buckingham's burlesque held the stage until the beginning of the nineteenth century, and, as we have seen, not a few actors of the first rank—Haines, Estcourt, Colley Cibber, Garrick, Foote, Henderson, King, Farren—strutted and mimicked and gagged as Mr. Robert Bayes, actually this travesty so far from inflicting a death-blow upon the heroic play, as has ineptly been pretended, entirely failed if its object was seriously to damage and to scuttle the heroic drama. Men shook with mirth one night at Drawcansir, the two Kings of Brentford and Lardella's funeral, but the next night they sat in rapt attention to hear Almanzor and Almahide, jealous Boabdelin, Lyndaraxa, and her lovers twain.

The *Indian-Queen* was drawing crowded houses five-and-twenty years after the production of *The Rehearsal,* and was being played at least as late as 1715 ; *The Indian Emperour* kept the stage with unbated popularity, and had a great success at Goodman's Fields in January, 1734 ; *Tyrannick Love* remained in the theatrical repertory for at least thirty years ; *The Conquest of Granada* was frequently acted during the reign of Queen Anne, but it must be remembered that a play in two parts presents especial difficulties, and so elaborate a production entailed great expense ; Wilks and Mrs. Oldfield were sustaining Aureng-Zebe and Indamora at Drury Lane in December, 1721.[40] Crowne's *The Destruction of Jerusalem,* Part II, was revived at Drury Lane by the summer company in July, 1712 ; Lee's *Sophonisba ; or, Hannibal's Overthrow,* which draws its plot from Orrery's *Parthenissa* rather than from history, and enjoyed frequent revivals, was acted at Lincoln's Inn Fields in March, 1735 ; at Drury Lane in July, 1708, Booth (Crimalhaz) and Mrs. Porter (Morena) were appearing in Settle's famous *Empress of Morocco ;* Otway's *Don Carlos,* also given at this House in the same year, drew large audiences to applaud the Carlos of Booth and the Queen of Mrs. Porter.

In no way did *The Rehearsal* [41] undermine the popularity and prestige of the heroic play.

In spite of Buckingham's attack Dryden was generous enough to pay a high compliment to the Duke's alteration of *The Chances,* for in the *Defence of the Epilogue,* that important essay which follows the Second Part of *The Conquest of Granada,* 4to, 1672, he wrote : " *Fletcher's Don John* is our onely Bug-bear : and yet, I may affirm without suspition of flattery, that he now speaks better, and that his Character is maintain'd with much more vigour in the fourth and fifth Acts, than it was by *Fletcher* in the three former."

When Buckingham took *The Chances* in hand he naturally contrived a certain number of modifications [42] throughout to lead up to his new fourth and fifth acts, which, as Genest aptly says, constitute " the happiest material alteration of any old play ever made ".[43] For Swinburne justly spoke of Fletcher's original fifth act as a " hasty and headlong scrawl of a sketch ",[44] and although the old " parcell drunke " Bawd; the Whore " A little guilded o're "; and the " honest Conjurer " Peter Vecchio with his mock apparitions; are not unamusing, Buckingham has introduced us to new and living characters. The Mother to the Second Constantia, " affecting to be politely commode, for her own Daughter," is a real creation of genius ; whilst the short scene between this obliging lady and the Kinswoman to whom she bewails her child's failures in fundamentals—she " calls all the Meniarderies of a *bonne mien* Affectation! "— ; and the first meeting of Don John and the Second Constantia are in the richest vein of comedy.

The date (*circa* 1627 ?) of the original production of Fletcher's *The Chances* is much disputed, and as the play was first printed in the folio of 1647 this must remain a matter of conjecture. During the Great Rebellion a droll *The Landlady,* made up from scenes in Acts I and III, was given here and there as opportunity permitted. Upon the Restoration *The Chances* was revived on Saturday, 24th November, 1660, at Vere Street. Pepys saw the play on Saturday, 27th October, 1661, and again on the following 9th October. The Duke of Buckingham's revision with the new fourth and fifth acts was not printed until 1682, but it had been produced at the Theatre Royal in January, 1667,[45] and it was this alteration Pepys saw on Tuesday, 5th February, 1667, at the King's house, when he observed : "A good play I find it, and the actors most good in it ; and pretty to hear Knipp sing in the play very properly 'All night I weepe ' [46] ; and sung it admirably."

Downes tells us that Don John in *The Chances* was supremely acted by Hart, and the writer of the Preface to the Tonson Beaumont and Fletcher, 1711, vol. i, p. ix, says : " Mr. *Hart* play'd the Part of *Don John* to the highest Satisfaction of the Audience ; the Play had a great run, and ever since has been follow'd as one of the best Entertainments of the Stage." Langgaine under " John Fletcher, *and* Francis Beaumont, *Esq.*", records " *Chances,* a Comedy, reviv'd by the late Duke of *Buckingham,* and very much improv'd ; being acted with extraordinary applause at the Theatre in *Dorset-Garden,* and printed with the Alterations *Lond.* 4° 1682 ".[47] After the Union of the two Companies there was a particular revival of *The Chances* in 1690–1, when Mrs. Leigh played the Mother, and the Second Constantia was acted by Charlotte Butler, who according to Cibber in this rôle far exceeded " Mrs. *Oldfield's* lively Performance of the same Character ".[48] *The Chances* kept the stage throughout the eighteenth century, and during their lifetime

Wilks and Mrs. Oldfield were much admired in Don John and the Second Constantia. It was indeed a recollection by George II of the amusement they had given him which caused Garrick to revive *The Chances* at Drury Lane on 7th November, 1754. He acted Don John with great spirit, but unfortunately he could not refrain from unnecessary and anæmic alterations. Kitty Clive was very great as the Bawd, a rôle which some three and twenty years later was filled by Mrs. Green, the original Mrs. Malaprop. In 1773 at Drury Lane Mrs. Abington played the Second Constantia to Garrick's Don John, whilst at the Haymarket in 1777 Henderson won great applause as Don John to the Second Constantia of Miss Barsanti, the original Lydia Languish. The critics highly praised the Don John of Palmer, of whom there is an admirable portrait in this part. At Drury Lane on 6th February, 1808,[49] Elliston played Don John to the Second Constantia of Mrs. Jordan, but after that season *The Chances* was not given until January, 1922, when it was revived by The Phoenix for two performances at the Shaftesbury Theatre.[50]

Buckingham adapted another play of Fletcher (and Beaumont), *Philaster; or, Love lies a Bleeding*,[51] a romantic tragi-comedy which would have been a yet greater favourite upon the Restoration stage [52] had not the critics protested that this and other pieces of Fletcher outraged " *the Decorum of the Stage* " and were in fine " much below the applause which is now given them " since " he will see *Philaster* wounding his Mistriss, and afterwards his Boy, to save himself", and the Clown " not only has the advantage of the Combat against the Heroe " [53] but is impertinent with his ridiculous and absurd Raillery. It was these strictures of Dryden that Buckingham had in mind when he altered these scenes, for although in *The Restauration : or, Right will take Place* Philander (Philaster) still wounds Araminta (Arethusa) and Endymion (Bellario) he does so from motives of jealousy, and aiming at Endymion unwittingly hurts his mistress. The Clown is worsted by Philander. It remained for Elkanah Settle wholly to vindicate Philaster in his *Philaster : or, Love lies a bleeding*, " Revis'd, and the Two last Acts new Written," produced at Drury Lane late in 1695 ; 4to, 1695.

The writer of the Preface to the Tonson *Beaumont and Fletcher*, 1711, vol. i, p. ix, after mentioning Buckingham's recension of *The Chances* continues : " His Grace, after that, bestow'd some time in altering another Play of our Authors, called *Philaster, or Love lies a Bleeding*; He made very considerable Alterations in it, and took it with him, intending to finish it the last Journey he made to *Yorkshire* in the Year 1686. I cannot learn what is become of the Play with his Grace's Alterations, but am very well inform'd it was since the Revolution in the Hands of Mr. *Nevil Payn,* who was Imprison'd at *Edinburgh* in the Year 1689." *The Restauration,* which never appeared on the stage, was first printed in Buckingham's *Works,* 1714.[54] In the *Miscellaneous Works,* 1705–7, were given *A Prologue to Philaster* and *The Epilogue, to be spoken by the Governour in Philaster,*[55] two clever pieces, of which the latter, which very agreeably satirizes Shaftesbury, was obviously written in 1682–3.

The Battle : or, The Rehearsal At White-Hall, a farce,[56] unacted ; and *The Belgic Heroe Unmasked : or, The Deliverer set forth in his proper Colours,* unacted ; both printed in the *Works,* 1704, are worthless political dialogues whose only merit is their brevity. *The Militant Couple : or, The Husband may thank himself,* Unacted, printed in the *Works,* 1704, " *In a Dialogue between* Freeman *and* Bellair," is a vigorous, amusing, coarse, and brutal piece, not unlike a rough scene from some comedy by Vanbrugh. *A Conference between His Grace, George late Duke of Buckingham and Father Fitzgerald,* " Faithfully Taken by His Secretary " is blasphemous and beastly.

A boon companion of Buckingham, John Wilmot, Earl of Rochester (1647–1680), adapted yet another play of Fletcher's, the tragedy of *Valentinian.*[57] The original date of *Valentinian,* first published in the Beaumont and Fletcher folio 1647, is generally accepted [58] as 1610–1614. This tragedy, which was one of the plays allotted as the particular property of the Theatre Royal, does not appear to have been revived after the Restoration until taken in hand by Rochester, and the reason is not far to seek since the ravishing of Lucina by the Emperor Valentinian III and the episodes of the four cock-bawds and pandresses twain would hardly have been very grateful to the court of Charles II. The play required some adroit refashioning from more points of view than one. Of Rochester's original alteration, *Lucina's Rape, Or, The Tragedy of Vallentinian,* there is a manuscript preserved in the British Museum, Add. MSS. 28692, folios 3a–69a. The handwriting not being that of Rochester this is clearly a copy of the original,[59] and there is evidence from the interpolation of stage directions that we here have a prompter's script. *Lucina's Rape* lists the following cast : Valentinian, Hart ; Aecius, Mohun ; Maximus, Wintershall ; Pontius, Lydal ; Chylax, Cartwright ; Lycias, Clarke ; Lucina, Mrs. Marshall ; Claudia, Mrs. Cox ; Marcellina, Mrs. Boutell ; Ardelia, Mrs. Corey [60] ; Phorba, Mrs. Knepp. Rochester himself died 26th July, 1680 ; William Wintershal died in July, 1679 ; and from these and various other circumstances we may with some precision

PLATE XV

MS. PAGE OF ROCHESTER'S LUCINA'S RAPE

British Museum

narrow down the production of *Lucina's Rape* at the Theatre Royal to 1677-8, probably the former year.[61]

After the Union, at the Theatre Royal, on 20th February, 1684, was produced " the Tragedy of *Valentinian*, wrote by the Lord *Rochester*, from *Beaumont* and *Fletcher*. Mr. *Goodman Acted Valentinian* : Mr. *Betterton, Æcius* : Mr. *Kynaston, Maximus* : Mr. *Griffin, Pontius* : Madam Barry, *Lucina*, &c. The well performance, and the vast Interest the Author made in Town, Crown'd the Play, with great Gain of Reputation ; and Profit to the *Actors* ".[62] From a MS. list we are able to add to this cast. Nokes played Balbus ; Leigh, Chylax ; Alexander, Licinius ; Freeman, Proculus ; Mountford, Lycias ; Mrs. Boutell, Celandia ; and Mrs. Leigh, Marcellina.[63] *Valentinian*, "A Tragedy. As 'tis Alter'd by the late Earl of Rochester, And Acted at the Theatre-Royal," was printed 4to, 1685.[64] A " Preface concerning the Author and his Writings " heavily overloaded with " high-flown surfeiting encomiums " [65] was prefixed by Robert Wolseley. A Prologue, by Aphra Behn,[66] was spoken by Sarah Cook on the first day. The same actress spoke a second Prologue on the second day. There was also printed a Prologue intended for *Valentinian*, to be spoken by Mrs. Barry. The Epilogue " Written by a Person of Quality " was assigned to Lucina.

There are considerable, but in sum not important, differences between *Lucina's Rape* and the *Valentinian* of 1684. We find additions and omissions, as well as a rearrangement and trans-position of certain scenes for the most part made with an adroit effectiveness that seems to speak the practised theatrical hand. Wolseley pleads that indulgence be shown " an unfinish'd Piece ", since " Lord *Rochester* intended to have alter'd and corrected this Play much more than it is, before it had come abroad ". "And yet as Imperfect as *Valentinian* is left . . . my Lord has made it a Play." [67] This is certainly in one respect true. Not only does Lucina's death cut the tragedy in half, but as John Addington Symonds noted : " The second part exhibits Fletcher's weakness as a dramatic poet." [68] He has arrived towards the middle of the third act, and in order to deal out poetical justice to the Emperor he is bound to evolve a number of new incidents, to elaborate fresh characters, and after the death of Valentinian from poison to present a scene, extremely striking in itself, which has the effect of sheer anti-climax.

Rochester made sweeping changes, rewriting whole scenes, compressing others, omitting characters (such as Eudoxia, Afranius, Paulus, Licippus), adding interest and individuality to the figure of Lycias, and wholly altering the catastrophe, for Valentinian at the conclusion is assassinated by Aretus and the soldiery and does not die from poison early in Act V. The action is thus unified and direct, and, whatever criticism may have to urge concerning details of diction and phrase, the play gains immensely by being more closely knit together and determined.

It is plain that the 1685 quarto was set up from a prompt copy for various marginalia are to be found in the printed text,[69] and the question arises does *Valentinian* represent *Lucina's Rape* as overhauled by Rochester alone, or (as I suspect) did another hand assist and complete the final alterations? Wolseley emphasizes that " *Fletcher* might be allowed some Preference in the skill of a Play-Wright (a thing my Lord had not much study'd) ", and I may not perhaps be far out if I suggest that the piece was to some extent shaped for the boards by Betterton, whose knowledge of stagecraft would have helped considerably in more deftly arranging the sequence of the scenes. I do not for a moment wish to imply that Betterton did more than this, and he cannot (of course) in any sense be considered to have adapted or altered Rochester's version. That he carefully superintended the revival of 1684, which had in effect all the force of a *première,* is certain.

The development, or rather the rewriting of the part of Lycias, who in Fletcher's original is quite a sketchy figure—he carries the token of the ring to Lucina in Act II, scene 2, and is present at the Emperor's death, Act V, scene 2—is extremely interesting and significant.[70] In Rochester's *Valentinian* old Chylax comments very plainly upon the homosexuality of this " soft Rogue, this *Lycias* ", who indeed after the death of Lucina is passionately beloved of the Emperor.[71] William Mountford, who at the age of nineteen created Lycias, was certainly himself homosexual, and his uranian amours with persons of the highest quality were notorious, so that when he was so foully murdered in December, 1692, contemporary lampoons declared that the beaux wept even more than the ladies of quality.

Many of the actors were homosexual. This was, of course, quite common in earlier days, and is pretty broadly alluded to in the Epilogue to *The Parsons Wedding*,[72] printed in *Covent Garden Drollery,* 1672, an address commencing :—

> When boys play'd women's parts, you'd think the Stage,
> Was innocent in that untempting Age.
> No : for your amorous Fathers then, like you,
> Amongst those Boys had Play-house Misses too.

It were superfluous to refer to the Sonnets of Shakespeare or the Poems of Barnfield. Homosexuality had its part in the plays as it had in the life of Christopher Marlowe. There are homosexual scenes in such tragedies as John Mason's *The Turke,* 4to, 1610, acted probably in 1608-9, where we have the very outspoken episode in Act I of Bordello, the humorous traveller, with Pantofle his page, a scene reminding one of the Marescalco and Giannicco in Aretino's *Il Marescalco.* Allusion has already been made to Davenant's *Albovine* and *The Cruell Brother.*

In plays written and acted after the Restoration we may note Edward Howard's *The Usurper,* Theatre Royal, January, 1664, Act II, where the comments of Damocles and Hugo de Petra upon the page-boy (who is in reality Calanthe disguised) are frankly uranian. There is a similar scene in Mrs. Behn's *The Amorous Prince,* Lincoln's Inn Fields, 1671, when Lorenzo makes very unequivocal advances to Philibert, a comely country lad, who is actually—though unknown to him—Cloris in male attire. In Dryden's plays there are several markedly homosexual allusions. In Otway's popular *The Souldiers Fortune,* Dorset Garden, spring of 1680, during the tavern-scene in Act IV Sir Davy Dunce very lewdly manifests an inclination to Courtine. There are some curious passages, too, in Lee's *The Princess of Cleve,* produced at Dorset Garden in 1681, but not printed until 1689, as also in Mrs. Behn's novel *The Court of the King of Bantam.*

When Southerne's capital comedy *Sir Anthony Love ; or, The Rambling Lady,* was produced at the Theatre Royal with such triumphant success in November, 1690, the scene in the Fifth Act between the wanton old Abbé and Sir Anthony was omitted in spite of the gap in the Action ; " *not that there is one indecent Expression in it,*" protested the poet, " *but the over-fine Folk might run it into a design I never had in my head : my meaning was to expose the Vice.*" The fact is that it was thought to reflect far too openly upon the homosexuality of William of Orange, whose tastes in that direction [73] were being pretty freely glanced at in contemporary lampoonery and pasquinado. This penchant is very plainly displayed in *The Womens Complaint to Venus,*[74] an unpublished MS. satire of 1698, and there are even more personal attacks which do not spare William Bentinck (1649-1709),[75] first Earl of Portland, and Arnold Joost van Keppel (1669-1718), first Earl of Albermale.

There were in society Wits " uncommon and Facetious ", such as John Hoyle of the Inner Temple, who is said to have helped Mrs. Behn in her comedies, and whose homosexual amours were common town-talk,[76] as also mysterious figures such as Beau Wilson, who was " kept by somebody ", and scandal whispered a very high name. In an unpublished comedy *circa* 1683 I have found some extremely curious details of homosexual practices, a frankness which probably precluded this piece from the public theatre. Homosexuality appears in Dilke's *The Lover's Luck*, Lincoln's Inn Fields, November, 1695, the scene between Goosandelo and his ingle, Jocond, the page; also in Granville's *The She-Gallants*, produced at the same house in the following month; and in the notorious episode between Daddy Coupler and young Tom Fashion in the First Act of Vanbrugh's *The Relapse, or Virtue in Danger*, Drury Lane, November, 1696. In an unpublished poem by Sir Henry Sheeres, *The Strowlers Prologue at Cambridge*, it is very openly said:—

> The Pathic, execrable Gold-finding Rogue
> Wou'd Sin without a Blush, & grow in Vogue—
> Active and passive Villanys wou'd abound
> If honest Satyr did not keep his Ground.

There is a frank enough bob for the audience in Dryden's Epilogue " *Intended to have been Spoken* " to *The Duke of Guise*, before the play " *was forbidden last Summer* ", that is to say in July, 1682. After tilting against the brawls and blackguardism of the pit, as well as lashing the libels and lampoons scribbled by the petty Julians of the hour, the poet gave Sarah Cook, to whom this very candid address was to have been entrusted, the following lines:—

> Nay, and I fear they worse Designs advance,
> There's a damn'd Love trick new brought o'er from *France*.
> We charm in vain, and dress, and keep a Pother,
> While those false Rogues are Ogling one another.
> All Sins besides, admit some expiation;
> But this against our Sex is plain Damnation.

One is reminded of old Mr. Snarl's philippics on the contemporary theatre. It will be remembered how in Shadwell's *The Virtuoso*, half a dozen years before, that indomitable *laudator temporis acti* denounced the young men of the Age with no uncertain voice: " they are vitious, illiterate, foolish Fellows, good for nothing but to roar and make a noise in a Play-house. To be very brisk with pert Whores in Vizards, who, though never so ill-bred, are most commonly too hard for them at their own weapon, *Repartee*— And when Whores are not there, they play Monkey-tricks with one another, while all sober men laugh at them."

It should be remarked that the first edition of *The Duke of Guise*, 4to, 1683, does not reprint the Epilogue, quoted above, which, however, appears with a Prologue, " Written by Mr. *Dryden*: Spoken by Mr. *Smith*," and another Epilogue, " *Written by the*

PLATE XVI

EDWARD KYNASTON
Collection of the Author

[face p. 294

same Authour; Spoken by Mrs. Cooke," in a folio pamphlet without pagination, being a single sheet folded in two, with the signature B, " Printed for Jacob Tonson ", 1683. For a full collation of this rare piece and of the quarto with facsimiles, see T. J. Wise, *A Dryden Library,* 1930, pp. 43–4.

That runagate buffoon, Joe Haines, who during the reign of James II had ostentatiously feigned to be converted, upon his appearance very shortly after the Revolution as Bayes in *The Rehearsal,* spoke a special " recantation " prologue before the play. He had the effrontery to masquerade "*in a White Sheet with a burning Taper in his hand*", and the lines he delivered, which are generally ascribed to Tom Brown, will be found to contain some extremely coarse jests.

Many more allusions, poems, and indeed scenes from plays might be cited but the above catena will sufficiently serve to show the prevalence of uranianism in the theatre. Of the actors that " Compleat Female Stage Beauty " Edward Kynaston— especially during his effeminate youth when he played leading lady, and as Downes [77] says " it has since been Disputable among the Judicious, whether any Woman that succeeded him so Sensibly touch'd the Audience as he "—was notoriously homosexual, and contemporary satires do not spare his intrigues with the debauched Duke of Buckingham. Kynaston indeed became rich from the gifts of his admirers, for to his beauty he added a shrewd business head.[78] Especially famous was he as the Silent Woman, the title-rôle of Jonson's *Epicoene,* in which comedy as Pepys remarks [79] : " Kinaston, the boy, had the good turn to appear in three shapes : first, as a poor woman in ordinary clothes, to please Morose ; then in fine clothes, as a gallant, and in them was clearly the prettiest woman in the whole house, and lastly, as a man ; and then likewise did appear the handsomest man in the house." The great comic actor, James Nokes,[80] who had also played female characters as a youth, and later was much applauded in petticoat parts such as the Nurse in *Caius Marius* (Otway's adaptation of *Romeo and Juliet*) was entirely homosexual. Richard Bell, Tom Clarke, Hildebrand Horden, and many other young actors bore the same reputation. It were easy indeed to prolong the list with anecdote, pasquil, epilogue and satirical song, but it will suffice to mention one actor more, who chronologically lies outside our period, it is true, John Leigh, dubbed " *Handsome Leigh* " who, as Chetwood has it,[81] " might have been in the good Graces of the Fair-Sex, *if his Taste had led him that Way.*" Born in 1689, Leigh died in 1726. He left one comedy, *Kensington-Gardens ; or, The Pretenders* (8vo, 1720, two editions), produced at Lincoln's Inn Fields on 26th November, 1719, as *The Pretenders*. It is a brisk witty piece, and the character of Bardach is very amusing and very significant.

Rochester's obscene farce *Sodom* is a thing of no value [82] with all the filth but lacking the occasional wit of the modern limerick. A slight silly squib in five puny acts, it was printed Antwerp [London], 8vo, 1684. Although the authorship has been disputed [83] there is no doubt that Rochester actually penned the piece.[84] At present it appears that no copy of the octavo, 1684, is known, which is perhaps hardly surprising. The book was, however, in Richard Heber's collection, but was unfortunately destroyed by his executors, and my late friend, Sir Edmund Gosse, had seen an exemplar.

The most interesting lines in *Sodom* are those which parody the heroic play, and once or twice a phrase of Dryden's has been amusingly, if lewdly, caricatured.

The question has been raised whether this piece was ever performed, and some kind of presentation does not seem wholly impossible, especially when one remembers the clandestine performances of libertine little plays so popular in Paris during the eighteenth century,[85] for, as De Villeneuve remarks, these private playhouses were frequented by persons of the highest quality, and " On y jouait sans voiles les priapées de Pétrone et les orgies du Portier des Chartreux ".[86] One writer in describing *Sodom* quite precisely says : " Est Comoedia, quae Londini fuit impressa, ubi tempore Caroli II. spectante Rege aliisque acta est, personis denudatis in scenam prodeuntibus." [87]

There are several extant MSS. of *Sodom*. Of these I have examined three. The best text is that of the Harleian MS. 7312, British Museum,[88] where the piece appears as *Sodom or The Quintessence of Debauchery By E of R*. Written for the Royall Company of Whoremasters. There are two prologues, the first of 72, the second of 29 lines, and two epilogues, followed by ten lines of obscene verse. There is a MS. in the Victoria and Albert Museum, South Kensington ; Dyce MS. 43. There is also a MS. in the Hamburger Staats- und Universitätsbibliothek, *Sodom A Play By The Earl of Rochester,* originally the property of the famous Frankfort bibliographer Zacharias Conrad von Uffenbach (whom Mr. John Davy Hayward, probably thinking of the musician, calls Offenbach). After the death of Uffenbach this MS. came into the possession of Professor Wolff, who was curator of the Hamburg Library, to which he bequeathed it. The Hamburg MS. is so very faulty as to suggest that the copy was made by a German scribe imperfectly acquainted with English.

A fourth MS. with a more correct text but lacking the title-page, prologues, epilogues, dramatis personae, and the whole of Act V is preserved at The Hague. *Sodom* was printed in 1904, 12mo, *Rochester's Sodom Herausgegeben nach dem Hamburger Manuscript mit einer Einleitung von L.S.A.M. v. Römer, med. docts Arzt zu Amsterdam*; Paris, Verlag von H. Welter (xxiv + 60 pp.). The same reprint appeared in vol. ix of Κρυπτάδια Heilbronn et Paris, 1911 : also 8vo, n.d. (1930).[89] Herr Prinz justly says that this text, originally faulty enough, is badly disfigured by numerous inaccuracies, misprints, misreadings, and omissions of whole lines. The introduction seems to a large extent based upon the notice in Pisanus Fraxi's *Centuria Librorum Absconditorum*,[90] which Dr. von Römer [91] has not wholly understood, and therefore has but indifferently reproduced. Mr. Hayward is alone in supposing that the modern reprint has " a painstaking preface wholly in the tradition of German scholarship ".[92]

I fear that the entirely conscientious editor of Rochester's Works—whoever he may chance to be—cannot but include *Sodom* in his text.

Unfortunately we have no edition of Rochester. There is a bad lacuna upon our shelves and the *Collected Works of John Wilmot Earl of Rochester Edited by John Hayward*,[93] The Nonesuch Press, 1926, a most unsatisfactory and infelicitous omnium gatherum, is by no means calculated to fill the place.[94]

Although an ungrateful, it may be a necessary task to vindicate so complete but, I believe, so well-merited a censure, and I will endeavour to do this as briefly as possible. Accordingly I shall not dwell upon the slipshod journalese of the ill-informed and often grossly inaccurate Introduction, although one might mention that Mrs. Barry did not make her début in the King's Company (p. xxxiv) ; that it is misleading to say Pepys found himself in the company of the Ballers (p. xxxviii) ; that there is no such play by Charles Davenant as *Dirce* [95] (p. xli) ; that the account of Rochester's death is offensive and in shocking taste (pp. xliii–xlv). We may also pass over Mr. Hayward's exuberant and stalwart Protestantism, in which he rivals Mr. Kensit himself, as irrelevant. When Mr. Hayward, having occasion to mention (in a very faulty note, p. 394) that Robert Graham took vows under the rule of La Trappe, exclaims : " His death—one may call it suicide—," we smile ; but Mr. Hayward must learn not to speak of the " assumption of the Romanists to afford plenary indulgence and complete absolution of sins in exchange for money ", since this is simply ignorance, and I am very sure that Mr. Hayward has not the foggiest idea what a "plenary indulgence" is. I would also like to inquire what is *incomplete* absolution ? Presumably there is such a thing, as he speaks of "complete absolution".

With reference to the Text, which is vermiculated with misprints and misreadings, and has many serious omissions and gaps, it is quite clear that Mr. Hayward was unaware that there are two issues of the *Poems on Several Occasions* . . . Printed at Antwerpen ; that he has not been at the trouble of carefully collating the earlier editions ; that he too often relies (so far as one is able to judge) upon a worthless reprint of 1731, of which Grässe observes : "Cette édition est nommée l'obscène." Moreover he has swept into his *Collected Works of John Wilmot Earl of Rochester* poems by Randolph (who died more than ten years before Rochester was born), Etherege, Oldham, Aphra Behn—to name no more, for no other reason apparently than, as Mr. Thorn-Drury has observed,[96] that these poems are the sort of thing Rochester conceivably might have written.

It is perhaps in his Explanatory Notes—save the mark !—that Mr. Hayward most fatally exposes himself. He speaks of "a celebrated actor" *Captain* Mohun, which should be Major Mohun ; Shirley's *The Traitor* was revived as early as 6th November, 1660, and thus not for the first time on 20th October, 1674 ; *My Lord, Great Neptune* does not refer to the Davenant-Dryden adaptation of *The Tempest* but to Shadwell's opera. Lady Elizabeth Howard was not Moll Howard, nor is there any relevant note on p. 378 to which we are bidden turn for elucidation. Crowne wrote eighteen (not seventeen) plays in addition to the masque *Calisto*. The term "puzling Otway" does not refer "to Otway's inability to write successful comedies". (These blunders all occur on one page, 358.) A reference (p. 57, l. 31) to John Caryl's tragedy *The English Princess ; or, The Death of Richard the III,* produced at Lincoln's Inn Fields, 3rd March, 1667, is explained (p. 360) as a hit at "'The English Princes', an heroic poem by Edward Howard". There is no poem *The English Princes* by Edward Howard, whose *The Brittish Princes* : "an heroick poem" was published, 8vo, 1669. Joseph Harris (p. 363) was not "a well-known actor and friend of Pepys". Moreover "*fl.* 1661–1681" against his name is absolutely incorrect. The sculptures in *The Empress of Morocco*, 4to, 1673, do not represent "the appearance of the Duke's playhouse in Lincoln's Inn Fields" (p. 363), a bad mistake which is repeated with many additions on p. 396, where we are informed, for illustrations of the Lincoln's Inn Fields Opera "see the engravings to the Empress of Morocco, 1675". The sculptures, of course, represent Dorset Garden. Mr. Hayward tells us that *The*

Empress of Morocco (1673 or 1675 ?) " was priced at 2*s*." *The Term Catalogues,* ed. Arber, vol. i, 1903, p. 152, 24th November, Mich., 1673, have : " The Empress of Morocco . . . In Quarto. Price, sticht, 1*s*." No edition of 1675 is known. On p. 370 we learn that Charles Hart " was a grand-nephew of Shakespeare ", a weary blunder which has been corrected again and again. The Frazier to whom reference is made in *Rochester's Farewell* is not Alexander Fraser as stated on p. 385, but James Frazier of Westminster, a very different person.

On p. 402 we encounter the following : " *Tartar Cox.* Miss Cox was a woman of the Town : little is recorded of her. She may have been the actress who played in Dryden's *Marriage à la Mode.*" On p. 403 we have : " *The Tartar.* i.e. Miss Cox, to whom this epithet was regularly applied." Mr. Hayward knows nothing of Mrs. Cox—he does not even know her Christian name, Elizabeth. Mrs. Cox in *Othello* succeeded Mrs. Hughes as Desdemona. See the note, p. 132, in my edition of Downes' *Roscius Anglicanus.* Sometimes Mr. Hayward is fairly gravelled, and so when he has to annotate *Florid Hunting-don and civil Grey* (p. 382), he leaves a blank, which indeed we prefer to these leaps in the dark.

In the famous *A Session of the Poets,*[97] " Imitation of a Satyr in Boileau "[98] (upon which Mr. Hayward offers no comment, and perhaps discreetly, although a note is most certainly required), allusion is made to Elkanah Settle :—

> Poet S—— his Tryal was the next came about,
> He brought him an *Ibrahim,* with the Preface torn out ; . . .[99]

The important reference has entirely escaped Mr. Hayward, whose note (p. 380) runs : " *Ibrahim the Illustrious Bassa. A Tragedy.* Acted at the Duke's Theatre, 1677." This is not only inadequate but incorrect. Settle's tragedy *Ibrahim The Illustrious Bassa* was produced at Dorset Garden in March, 1676. Mr. Hayward needs to be told that the point of this couplet lies in the fact that Settle prefixed to *Ibrahim,* 4to, 1677, a " Preface to the Reader ", which is nothing other than a violent but not unprovoked attack upon Shadwell. This Preface was almost immediately suppressed by the writer, and copies of the 1677 quarto of *Ibrahim,* which remain intact, are of the utmost rarity.

Three lines later, in *A Session of the Poets,* " cry'd *Newport,*" with an obscene expression, " I hate that dull *Rogue,*" meaning, of course, Elkanah Settle. I do not know what reprint Mr. Hayward used here, but the Antwerpen *Poems* give the passage entire. The later and from a textual point of view, valueless, editions of the eighteenth century for modesty sake corrupt the line to "And *Bank's,* cry'd up *Newport,* I hate that dull Rogue ". Mr. Hayward prints (p. 132, l. 27) " And Bancks, cry'd Newport, I hate that dull rogue ", which has neither sense nor correct metre, but which affords him the opportunity to furnish us with an inaccurate note (p. 381) upon " John Banks, or Bankes, the dramatist ", to whom he obviously supposes allusion is made. Incidentally the date of the quarto of *The Unhappy Favourite* in 1682, Term Catalogues, November, 1681. Mr. Hayward does not know of the first edition, and refers to 4to, 1685, the second edition.

Similar errors and ineptitudes might be cited from almost every page, but I have said enough to show that my stern word of warning was more than justified. Mr. Hayward (p. ix) has made reference to myself as " *a high authority on the literature of the Restoration* ". Be that as it may, in my opinion Mr. Hayward shows himself wholly incompetent to deal with the period in question. As an editor he lacked experience; as a critic his pronouncements are negligible and a bore. I am led to this conclusion not only by this reprint of Rochester, but also by later notices which he has written dealing with Restoration literature, reviews both signed and anonymous.

Owing to his enthusiasm for his subject, a zest (I fear) rather ill-regulated and therefore on occasion more than a trifle over-stressed, Herr Johannes Prinz in his study *John Wilmot, Earl of Rochester,* 1927, has not merely condoned and set out to gloze almost every vice, every fault, but he has further endeavoured to present Rochester in colours so rosy and so fair that many of his pages can from this point of view only be read with astonishment, not to say actual disapprobation and an emphatic dissent. I would not be misunderstood. Rochester has too long been traduced and maligned. He was a very remarkable person ; an acknowledged archwit amongst wits of the first quality ; a true poet of elegance and even beauty ; a keen and biting satirist. Let there be no question here, for example, of the obscenities of his writings, of *the Play call'd Sodom,* foul though it is, of such scandalous bastard pieces as *The Cabinet of Love* so injuriously laid to his door, which have made him for full a century and a half the very Raw-head and Bloody-bones of English Literature. Yet beyond all this there is something which goes deeper still. There are sides of his nature which cannot be overlooked. He was not only profligate and drunken, he was insolent, brutal, false, cowardly, malicious, and vindictive. Even Burnet was bound to confess of Rochester that " none of all our Libertines understood better than he, the secret Mysteries of Sin, had more studied every thing that could support a man in it ". In this connexion it has not, I think, before been remarked that Rochester is drawn in a play by Nathaniel Lee *The Princess of Cleve,* which, although not printed until 1689, had been produced at Dorset Garden several years before, in 1681. The allusion to Rochester as " the Life, the Soul of Pleasure, Count *Rosidore* " has of course long been noted. Thus A. W. Ward who gives but half a dozen lines to Lee's tragedy drew attention to it in his *English Dramatic Literature,* 1875 (and Second Edition, 1899), and indeed the reference cannot but have been a detail of common knowledge since it did not even escape so superficial a writer as Roswell Gray Ham in his trivially journalistic *Otway and Lee,* 1931.

Curiously enough, however, it seems to have eluded observation that Lee with a certain literary duplicity, very Machiavelian but very understandable in the circumstances, having paid his obvious compliment to the late Lord Rochester as Rosidore— of whom nevertheless it is said " I thought his last Debauch wou'd be his Death "—proceeded to draw him full length as Duke Nemours, and when the Town " expected the most polish'd Hero in *Nemours* " the poet " gave 'em a Ruffian reeking from *Whetstone's-Park.* The Fourth and Fifth Acts of the *Chances,* where *Don John* is pulling down; *Marriage Alamode,* where they are bare to the Waste; the *Libertine,* and *Epsom-Wells,* are but Copies of his Villany. He lays about him like the *Gladiator* in the Park ". In Nemours' character, talk, morals and actions Rochester is reflected not once or twice but seen steadily and as a whole. Moreover the tragedy has a scorpion sting in its tail, since the couplet (spoken by Nemours) which concludes the last act runs :—

> He well repents that will not sin, yet can ;
> But Death-bed Sorrows rarely shew the Man.

It is to be hoped that Rochester's repentance was sincere, and whatever our misgivings it is far too solemn a subject upon which to comment now. In the first place I should indeed require some better testimony than that of Dr. Burnet, " a liar and forger " so Hilaire Belloc sums up the man, " whose lies and forgeries can be proved by the clearest of evidence." Burnet's own Christian orthodoxy was something more than suspect. He stands out in fact no better than a plain deist, whilst as an author he was justly condemned by those who knew him as " guilty of shameful omissions and perversions in numerous instances ", as a " false and vain relater ", and one informed by " spite and malice ". With regard to Rochester, even on Burnet's showing the Earl upon his death-bed denied the fundamental beliefs and essential doctrines of Christianity. According to Thomas Hearne, Rochester once told Mr. Giffard, chaplain to the Countess his mother, " I am no Atheist " ; and we must leave it at that, since from his attitude towards religion we can go no further, and indeed it is not altogether easy to go so far.

Herr Prinz laments the " general meagreness " of " the literature of the Restoration period ", and he openly advances that it is on account of this " dryness and sterility " he has set out to vindicate " to the Earl of Rochester in the history of literature the place that is due to his genius ". The pains which Herr Prinz has taken over his study, his thoroughness, his collocation of bibliographical details, are all deserving of very high praise, but unfortunately in his intensive concentration upon Rochester he has neglected all other names in Restoration literature, and he is obviously not equipped to pass any general critical judgement upon this period. It results that his work, valuable as it is, in some sense falls out of proportion.

Yet for all his boundless and indeed exaggerated enthusiasm Herr Prinz has certainly not gone to the lengths of proclaiming that Rochester had a " religious " mind, that he was a man who " pondered long and deeply on the ultimate problems of philosophy and religion ". This absurdity was put forward in all apparent seriousness by a writer in an article " An Unpublished Poem Attributed to Rochester " in *The Times Literary Supplement,* 22nd November, 1934. By the aid of liberal quotations from this Poem, which he transcribed from a MS. copy and " which obviously represents Rochester's own opinions ", a whole structure of theory and argument is elaborated and offered as " a most valuable revelation of the state of Rochester's mind in the years immediately preceding his conversations with Burnet ".

Unfortunately as any student of Restoration literature must at once have recognized the Poem is not by Rochester, and has nothing to do with Rochester at all. It is in fact a continuation of *Gondibert,* written by Sir William Davenant and printed in the posthumous *Works* of that laureate, folio, 1673. It has its place among " Poems on Several Occasions Never before Printed ", and is referred to as " the Death of *Astragon* called, *The Philosopher's Disquisition, directed to the dying Christian* ". Never was so unfortunate and so unpardonable a blunder. Down tumbled the whole house of cards. The thought, ear, style, philosophies of Davenant and Rochester were all as separate and different as any such qualities well can be. To present a poem of Davenant, already in print, as a poem by Rochester now first transcribed from the MS., is an error of so bad a kind as almost to seem impossible. A writer who is guilty of such a fundamental mistake at once puts himself out of court for all time, he has forfeited our confidence, and he can hardly suppose that in future his critical opinions on any literary subject of this kind deserve or should meet with recognition and regard.

We are, of course, none of us infallible. Any student, any authority, however keenly and long he may have studied his period is liable to make mistakes, many mistakes. There are the mistakes which matter; and the mistakes which practically do not count, in that they have no resilience, no reflex, no ultimate bearing. In the face of insufficient data, for example, it is easy enough to hazard the production of a play as in the spring rather than in the winter; and even if details come to light which show that it was given a twelvemonth before, whilst we are of course glad to be accurately informed, the original error of this sort in itself seldom has any essential consequences. It is not a spark which sets a whole train of fallacy ablaze. There exists many a crux concerning which scholars are not decided among themselves. It may be that some day evidence will be found enabling us to pronounce exactly upon one or other of these points. Even so there is no reflection upon the scholars who have from existing data argued on the wrong side. What we do keck at is the eager *réclame* and the tiro's cool pretentious ignorance which is not informed and will not be informed either by study or research. Such circumstances seem exacerbated when after a notorious blunder the writer at fault endeavours to bolster up his false position by futile obstinacy and by what must briefly be termed bounce.

Although a figure of considerable social importance in his day, the boon companion of Buckingham, Rochester, and the rest, Sir Charles Sedley, who " lived mostly in the great city, became a debauchee, set up for a satyrical wit, a comedian, poet, and courtier of ladies, and I know not what ",[100] has now faded away to a thin piping shadow of a writer. The personality of the man must have been everything; for with the exception of a song or two—" Not *Celia,* that I juster am," and " Love still has something of the Sea ", are deservedly remembered—some neat translations from Ovid and Martial, one tolerable comedy (in which Shadwell probably had no small share) the rest of his work is just sifted ashes. Courthope is entirely justified when he says of Sedley : " The brilliance of his conversation carried away men's judgements," and that "nothing that he has left behind him " can account for his contemporary reputation. In his own day he seems to have held his dramatic pieces at a light rate enough, and posterity very fairly has held them at less. As a droll, a wit, a libertine, a dabbler in literature, he is certainly worth attention, and it seems a pity that the only full-length study of Sedley [101] should too often trench upon that imaginative biography, which Mr. Thorn-Drury used to term the "most detestable field for the exercise of human ingenuity ".[102]

Sedley's contribution of an act to *Pompey the Great* " translated out of the French by Certain Persons of Honour ", 4to, 1664, a version of Corneille's *La Mort de Pompée,* which was given at Lincoln's Inn Fields, is negligible. His first play, a comedy, which was originally named *The Wandering Ladys,* was produced as *The Mulberry-Garden* at the Theatre Royal on 18th May, 1668. "The house infinitely full," Pepys tells us. "But the play when it come, though was here and there a pretty saying, and that not very many neither, yet the whole play had nothing extraordinary in it at all, neither of language or design, insomuch that the King I did not see laugh, nor pleased, the whole play from the beginning to the end, nor the company ; insomuch that I have not been less pleased at a new play in my life, I think." There is little to add to this criticism. The opening of the plot is a poor imitation of Molière's *L'École des Maris,* produced at the Palais Royal, 24th June, 1661, for Sir John Everyoung in some sort corresponds to Ariste and Sir Samuel Forecast to Sganarelle, The incidents ramble dully through five acts with obvious borrowing from *The Comical Revenge* and *She wou'd if she cou'd.* Sedley has intermixed in his comedy scenes in rather stocky prose with episodes in truly terrible couplets, and the result cannot be considered happy. *The Mulberry-Garden* was printed 4to, 1668, but no cast is given, although we know from Pepys that Mrs. Knepp played Victoria.[103]

Sedley's next dramatic venture was a rhyming tragedy *Antony and Cleopatra,* produced at Dorset Garden in February, 1677, with Betterton as Antony ; Mrs. Mary Lee, Cleopatra ; Smith, Augustus Caesar ; Sandford, the villain Photinus ; and Harris, Mecaenas, who is in love with Octavia, played by Mrs. Betterton. The action takes place after the battle of Actium, and the historical incidents have been ruthlessly compressed so that the climax of the Fifth Act shows the deaths of Antony and Cleopatra. It is sufficient to say that the verse is execrable and Sedley's *Antony and Cleopatra* cannot but be considered to have plumbed the nadir of all Restoration heroic tragedies.

Many years later Sedley remodelled *Antony and Cleopatra* as *Beauty the Conqueror,* a classical drama with choruses between the acts. It is unfinished, and is if possible even more banal than the original. It was first printed by Captain Ayloffe in the 1702 edition of Sedley's *Miscellaneous Works.*

In May, 1687, was produced at the Theatre Royal *Bellamira, or The Mistress,* a comedy, published, 4to, the same year as "Written by the Honourable Sir *Charles Sedley* Baronet". In the Preface Sedley tells us that whilst one fine morning he was out of "a Curiosity" engaged upon turning Terence's *Eunuchus* into English, a friend came into the room, and so approved the design that Sedley not only finished the piece but presented it to his friend to "get it Acted under his own or anothers Name". The friend in question was Thomas Shadwell,[104] who had given such grave offence by his tearing revolutionary politics, especially as exhibited in *The Lancashire Witches,*[105] a dangerous inflammatory play which was more than once prohibited and drastically excised before it was suffered to appear at Dorset Garden in the autumn of 1681, that the theatre would have no more of his wares and the actors refused to appear in his pieces. "*By G——— my Lord,*" he grumbled to the Earl of Dorset, "*those* Tory-rogues *will act none of my Plays.*"[106] From the autumn of 1681 until May, 1688, no play by Shadwell was given, a circumstance not only entailing considerable pecuniary loss to Master Og, but also pretty severely wounding his literary pride. Sedley, then, presented him with this version of the *Eunuchus* and freely gave him all the profits of the comedy. Yet it could not be produced under Shadwell's name, and Sedley fathered *Bellamira* although there can scarcely be any question that the original script was revised and in some part rewritten by Shadwell himself. This circumstance amply explains why *Bellamira* is incontestably the best of the plays which go under Sedley's authorship.

The *Eunuchus* has been cleverly enough remodelled and fitted to the Restoration world of Spring-Garden, Hyde-Park, St. James's, the Play-house, and the Drawing-Room, where the ladies "Dress, Patch and Curl, and Paint too", the men drink terse and hockamore at the Rose, play at Back-Gammon and Trick-track, and when they have quarrelled with their mistresses make their peace "with a Present of *China* or a *French Petticoat*" or "a dozen pair of *Marshal* Gloves". Even Pisquil, "an Eunuch after the *Turkish* manner," bought for Fifty pound, Terence's Dorus, is wholly in the picture. An essential change in the characterization, affecting the whole play, is that Terence's Thais becomes the wanton Bellamira, whose infidelities are traditionally said to be a satire upon the amours of the Duchess of Cleveland, "the lewdest as well as the fairest of all King Charles's concubines." [107] Characters in comedy of the type of Bellamira are, of course, extremely common in the Restoration dramatists. One may instance D'Urfey's Madam Fickle in the eponymous comedy (Dorset Garden 1676), and Madam Tricklove in *Squire Oldsapp* (Dorset Garden, 1678), from both of which *Bellamira* has borrowed a few hints.

Merryman is a well-drawn character, although sketched in the rough. He has a good deal of Shadwell himself, and certainly derives something from Falstaff. A suggestion for the two rivals, greasy fat Merryman and the scarecrow, the "piece of Shrivil'd Parchment" the "walking Skelleton" Cunningham, both of whom woo Thisbe, was plainly taken from Pinguister and Lean-man in James Howard's popular *All Mistaken,* produced in 1667. Howard himself had drawn upon the fat gentleman and the thin citizen who figure in Shirley's *The Wedding,* 4to, 1629, first produced (according to F. G. Fleay) on 31st May, 1626, at the Phoenix in Drury Lane, and revived after the Restoration on 9th January, 1661, at Vere Street. There is a theatrical tradition [108] that Merryman was created by Anthony Leigh ; Cunningham by Thomas Jevon.

In the theatre *Bellamira,* as so lively a comedy well deserved, proved a great success, although some squeamish folk affected to be a little shocked at the theme, a prudery very agreeably rallied in the Preface. It did not, however, keep the stage.

It is a little doubtful whether *The Grumbler,* an adaptation of *Le Grondeur* [109] by the Abbé de Brueys and Jean de Palaprat, produced at the Théâtre Français, 3rd February, 1691, is actually to be assigned to Sedley. This little play is said to have been first printed with date 1719,[110] and is included in the Second Volume of Sedley's *Works,* 1722. In any case it is a mere trifle, and hardly deserves more than the most cursory notice.[111] Probably nobody save the late Mr. William Archer could seriously consider *The Grumbler* a "gay and sparkling character-farce, crystal-clear and brimful of comic invention", but then Mr. Archer is one of the most extraordinary figures who was ever suffered to assume the rôle of a critic. This gentleman began his career by writing what has justly been termed "a scurrilous libel", *The Fashionable Tragedian,*[112] attacking Henry Irving, who is therein described as "one of the worst actors that ever trod the British Stage". Irving's Hamlet is styled "a weak-minded puppy" ; his Othello an "infuriated Sepoy" ; his Richard "a cheap Mephistopheles". Not only is the thing conceived in incredibly bad taste, but the whole wretched pamphlet gives us the lowest and truest idea of the critical faculty of a writer who could thus assail the supreme genius of one of the greatest names the English stage can boast. Mr. Archer's judgement did not improve with the years, although his command of Billingsgate became even more fluent and flatulent. In 1923 he published *The Old Drama and the New,* originally a series of four lectures delivered at King's College in 1919 and 1920 by the invitation of the Education Authority of the London County Council; and, as was observed at the time, whoever this "Authority" may have been such an invitation was most improper and ill-advised. As criticism the book is beneath contempt. It is ignorant and ill-informed, vulgar, rancorous, and abusive. What are we to think of this crank who sputtering and slobbering praise over *Two Roses* blandly proclaims of James Albery: "I confess I do not see in what way his wit is inferior to Congreve's"! Of these lectures a critic in *The Athenaeum,* 28th November, 1919 (p. 1267), observed: "The first of them (19th November) was enough to show that they can only be attended by susceptible people at imminent risk of an apoplexy."

A friend and boon companion of Buckingham, Rochester, Sedley, and the whole society of wits, "gentle George" Etherege (1634-5—1691), although he gave the world only three comedies, and was chidden for his laziness,[113] is a dramatist of the first importance. His first play, *The Comical Revenge, or, Love in a Tub,* was produced at Lincoln's Inn Fields in March, 1664, with a superlative cast. The serious characters, The Lord Beaufort and Graciana, whom he loves, were sustained by Betterton and his wife; Bruce and Aurelia, by Smith and Mrs. Davies; Lovis, Norris. The strength of the piece, however, lies in the lighter scenes. Harris was Sir Frederick Frollick; Nokes, Sir Nicholas Cully; Price, Dufoy, the French valet who is so ridiculously incarcerated in a tub; Cave Underhill and Sandford, the two sharking gamesters, Palmer and Wheadle.

> *Sir* Nich'las, *Sir* Fred'rick; *Widow and* Dufoy,
> *Were not by any so well done,* Mafoy.

Thus Downes [114] breaks out into rhyme, more enthusiastic than poetic, perhaps, and continues: "The clean and well performance of this Comedy, got the Company more Reputation and profit than any preceding Comedy; the Company taking in a Months time at it 1000*l.*" Nor is the reason far to seek. The very features which may strike us as something incongruous were the highest recommendation to a Restoration audience, since in one play they were given all they relished most. The episodes in themselves partly strike an original note, and partly reflect the dramatists which immediately after the Restoration were the most popular fare of the theatre. Thus we have scenes of a Fletcherian sentimentality conveyed in the ultra-fashionable and most novel of styles, rhyme, alternating with Middleton's realistic pictures of taverns and tipplers, ninnies and rooks and courtezans. Sir Frederick Frollick with his wooing of the Widow Rich, his midnight serenades with a noise of fidlers and link-boys beneath her window in Covent Garden, his rampant bacchanalia and " more qualms than a young woman in breeding " the morning after, might have stepped straight from the pit on to the boards. He is a creation which we recognize in comedy and musical comedy even to-day. It is true that we had rather enjoy Sir Frederick's pranks upon the stage than meet him in real life, where he is apt to prove an intolerable and insolent nuisance. Dufoy taking a " Crown for a Plaister " for his cracked poll, picked up on the " new Bridge in *Parie* " from a mountebank's motion for a Serviteur, drugged and clapped up in a tub with his head through the top so that like a new snail he has to bear his wooden prison about on his shoulders, is broadest farce, crude and were we to take it seriously even a little cruel, but 'tis excellent tomfoolery all the same, and I make no doubt that, as Pepys suggests, funny in the reading, on the stage it was funnier still.[115]

With all its faults and awkwardness—the various parts are somewhat clouterly sewn [116]—*Love in a Tub* is a remarkable play. The latest editor of Etherege,[117] Mr. Brett-Smith, writes : " The Town was waiting for something that should represent its own image ; and neither Cowley's juvenile extravagances [*Cutter of Coleman Street*], nor Sir Samuel Tuke's Spanish intrigues [*The Adventures of Five Hours*], nor Dryden's cumbersome improbabilities [*The Wild Gallant*], had hit that mark. *The Comical Revenge* was the first of the new plays to hold the mirror up to Covent Garden and the Mall." This is more than a trifle ridiculous, but it is quite plain from Mr. Brett-Smith's gritty and jejune Introduction that he should claim little or no knowledge of the Restoration period save what he seems to have imbibed as Mr. Pott's critic obtained his knowledge of Chinese metaphysics—" He *crammed* for it, to use a technical but expressive term."

The Comical Revenge kept the stage with applause until the third decade of the eighteenth century. At the Haymarket on 14th December, 1706, Bowen played Dufoy; Wilks, Sir Frederick; and Mrs. Oldfield, the Widow, in which rôles they were greatly admired. At Drury Lane on 10th January, 1713, Mrs. Knight replaced Mrs. Oldfield as the Widow. At the same house *The Comical Revenge* was played on 29th September, 1720, as "Not acted 4 years". Cibber caused much mirth as the French valet, Wilks was Sir Frederick; and Mrs. Horton, the Widow. Among the latest (if not the last) of the revivals was that given at Drury Lane, on 26th November, 1726, with Wilks, Mrs. Oldfield, and Cibber in their former rôles. It was presented three times that season.

Etherege's second comedy, *She wou'd if she cou'd,* is an immense advance upon *The Comical Revenge* and in every scene shows a firmer and surer touch. In the first place he has learned entirely to discard the pseudo-romantic episodes expressed in rhyme, and therefore he is able to concentrate upon his very delightful and vivacious quartette, Courtall and Freeman, Ariana and Gatty. I hesitate to call them lovers, but certainly they play at being in love amusingly enough, and there is a wholesome hint that the game may prove more dangerous than they know. Lady Cockwood, from whom the play takes its title, is a difficult person, and the rôle might be interpreted in various ways by several actresses. It is possible to conceive her as merely absurd in her erotomania; it is possible to conceive her as extremely unpleasant and bitter when her passion is balked; whilst she might even have that touch of tragedy which is so far more fully developed in Lady Wishfort. Sir Edmund Gosse thought of her as "a female Tartuffe",[118] but to my mind she is only a female Tartuffe in the same sense as my Lady Fidget. Where Lady Cockwood fails is that she hunts her game too openly and too eagerly, thinking more of the assay than the pleasure of the chase, which is unsportsmanlike. Ned Courtall assuredly is not the man to blench from an intrigue with the lady, but he objects to being made the single quarry of this ravenous kite.

The pictures of the Mulberry Garden, the New Exchange, and New Spring Garden are admirably done. Lady Cockwood, confining Sir Oliver at home in his penitential suit, has gone off to the Bear in Drury Lane with the two young ladies, Courtall, and Freeman. Rollicking and rampant Sir Joslin Jolly arrives as the tempter, and has scant difficulty in seducing Sir Oliver abroad to meet little Rake-hell with a bevy of vizard-masks and silk petticoats at the very same rendezvous. No sooner, however, is the knight making merry as he thinks, with rogues and whores than Lady Cockwood counterfeits a fit, the women pull off their masks, and there follows a scene of delicious comedy in which the lady establishes an even more absolute dominion over her spouse. None the less, however she may seek to gratify herself, circumstances prove singularly unpropitious, and as we take leave of her we hear her sigh : " Fortune was never before so unkind to the Ambition of a Lady."

It is very clear upon reading *She wou'd if she cou'd* that it is a comedy which demands a brilliant cast. The original Lady Cockwood was Anne Shadwell, esteemed an excellent actress ; Mrs. Jennings and Mrs. Davies were Ariana and Gatty ; Smith and Young, Courtall and Freeman ; Nokes, Sir Oliver ; and Harris, Sir Joslin Jolly. Yet the first performance at Lincoln's Inn Fields on 6th February, 1668, proved a failure, and the play never perhaps wholly recovered from this initial damp. Pepys has given us a vivid picture of the occasion. A thousand people put back before two-o-clock that could not have room in the house ; himself only able to squeeze into the 18*d*. box at the back where he could see little and hardly hear a word ; the Duke of Buckingham, Lord Buckhurst, Sedley, and the entire galaxy of wits thronging the pit ; the King present ; the whole audience agog with excitement and expectation. And then " how silly the play, there being nothing in the world good in it, and few people pleased in it ". And after the curtain fell that dark wet afternoon, Etherege loitering in the pit curses " the actors, that they were out of humour, and had not their parts perfect " whilst the rest blamed " the play as a silly dull thing ".

With some difficulty the piece gained ground, although in his Preface to *The Humorists,* 4to, 1671, a comedy which was spoiled owing to " imperfect Action ", Shadwell refers to *She wou'd if she cou'd,* and remarks " even that, for the imperfect representation of it at first received such prejudice, that, had it not been for the favour of the *Court,* in all probability it had never got up again, and it suffers for it in a great measure to this very day ". As late as 1702, Dennis in the Epistle Dedicatory to *The Comical Gallant,* that shocking travesty of *The Merry Wives of Windsor,* remarks how barbarously *She wou'd if she cou'd* was treated at the first performance, although since acted with general applause.

Among more notable productions were a revival at the Haymarket on 5th December, 1706, when Underhill played Sir Joslin ; with Wilks as Courtall ; Mrs. Barry, Lady Cockwood ; Mrs. Bracegirdle, Gatty ; and Mrs. Leigh, Mrs. Sentry. At Drury Lane on 5th December, 1716, Wilks was Courtall to the Lady Cockwood of Mrs. Hunt. On 21st March, 1726, at Lincoln's Inn Fields Ryan for his benefit played Courtall, and made this rôle peculiarly his own, only Wilks in his prime excelling the younger actor. The comedy was repeated four times that season. At Drury Lane on 28th April, 1732, Wilks reappeared in his

PLATE XVII

SHE WOU'D IF SHE COU'D: ACT III: SCENE 3

Collection of the Author

favourite old part with great applause. At Covent Garden on 8th December, 1733, about a year after the death of Wilks, Ryan acted Courtall, and the comedy was given six times. At the same house, as " Not acted 10 years ", *She wou'd if she cou'd* was presented on 21st December, 1750, with Macklin as Sir Oliver; Mrs. Macklin, Lady Cockwood; and Ryan, Courtall.

"An instructive rather than an exhilarating evening " was spent at Malvern on Wednesday, 5th August, 1931, when *She wou'd if she cou'd* was revived with Ralph Richardson as Courtall and Margaret Chatwin as Lady Cockwood. The critics certainly, and I fear the producer presumptively, quite plainly did not appreciate the quality of the play. I have also heard it whispered that had Etherege been in the house he would pretty vigorously and with reason have repeated his first night's objurgations.

It may have been owing to a lingering disappointment, it may have been on account of his besetting sin, idleness, that Etherege now kept silence for eight long years. His last play, the very quintessence of his art, *The Man of Mode, or, Sr Fopling Flutter,* was produced at Dorset Garden on 11th March, 1676. Gildon tells us that it " met with Extraordinary Success; all agreeing it to be true Comedy, and the Characters drawn to the Life ".[119] Of plot there is even less than in *She wou'd if she cou'd*; in a series of witty (yet not too witty) scenes we overhear the conversation—so superfine, in one sense so amorously *spirituel* —of a number of elegant but perfectly heartless people. Indeed when some feeling, some sentiment and jealousy break through they go near to wrecking the whole design of the piece, an atmosphere of passionate reality is intruded in which those beaux and belles of society could not have continued to exist. As we listen, we feel that we are walking all the time on the high ropes; the movements so graceful and buoyant leave us full of admiration, but how perilously near it is to a rude tumble and fall!

The comedy opens very agreeably in Dorimant's dressing-room, where his repartee with foggy Nan the orange-woman is refreshing in its vigour and its truth. And so Dorimant, as general an undertaker as Casanova, must pursue Harriet, who is a perfectly callous little baggage with a vile tongue,[120] although exceedingly expert in her pretty cunning simplicity. But Lady Woodvil, Harriet's mother, shudders at Dorimant, who as she truly remarks " delights in nothing but in Rapes and Riots ", wherefore Dorimant must woo his coquette as Mr. Courtage. All this is amusing enough but we are a little disquieted by occasional touches of pregnant realism, and when Mrs. Loveit appears, restless, sick with yellow jealousy and wan hope, crying out that she must love Dorimant be he never so wicked, tragedy, not the tragedy of the green carpet, the dagger and the bowl, but a very bitter tragedy none the less, enters with her upon the scene. She is no doubt intemperate and violent, yet she has cause, for Dorimant entreats her most shamefully. Bellinda, his Juliet of a night, he uses with the utmost brutality, and the result is a little too cruel for comedy.[121]

We can only marvel at the consummate art with which Etherege has glozed over these ruffianisms and degradations, for if one examines the matter quite sincerely I think *The Man of Mode* the most immoral comedy I know.

Sir Fopling Flutter himself is an ornament to but has little to do in the play. He is drawn with the most exquisite strokes and we must approach him very delicately and with care. He is as lovely and as frail as the bloom on a peach. It is, in fine, he who makes the play tolerable, else sure after the first act we could never stomach it.

Downes tells us Betterton created Dorimant ; Harris, Medley ; Smith,[122] Sir Fopling ; Anthony Leigh, Old Bellair ; Jevon, Young Bellair ; Mrs. Barry, Mrs. Loveit ; Mrs. Betterton, Bellinda ; Mrs. Leigh, Lady Woodvil ; and Mrs. Twyford, Emilia. " This Comedy being well Cloath'd and well *Acted,* got a great deal of Money."

At the Haymarket on 9th November, 1706, Colly Cibber played Sir Fopling to the Dorimant of Wilks, the Harriet of Mrs. Bracegirdle, and Mrs. Barry in her original rôle. At Drury Lane, 4th April, 1715, Cibber and Wilks repeated the same parts with Mrs. Oldfield as Mrs. Loveit and Mrs. Porter, Bellinda ; for the benefit of the soubrette actress Mrs. Saunders.

Theophilus Cibber appeared as Sir Fopling at Drury Lane on 21st March, 1738, for his benefit ; Mills was Dorimant ; Mrs. Cibber, Mrs. Loveit ; Kitty Clive, Bellinda ; and Macklin, foggy Nan the Orange Woman. *The Mock Doctor* followed. At Covent Garden on 10th November of the following year young Cibber was again Sir Fopling ; Ryan, Dorimant ; Mrs. Horton, Mrs. Loveit. At the same theatre, 6th February, 1746, Cibber repeated Sir Fopling ; with Ryan, Dorimant ; and Mrs. Pritchard, Mrs. Loveit. On 26th November, 1753, at Drury Lane, the lively and diverting Woodward played Sir Fopling ; with Mrs. Cibber, Mrs. Loveit. At Covent Garden when revived for Woodward's benefit on 15th March, 1766, *The Man of Mode* was a little inaccurately said to have been " Not acted 20 years " at this theatre. Woodward again sustained Sir Fopling to the Dorimant of David Ross, and the Mrs. Loveit of George Anne Bellamy. For one hundred and seventy years, now, *The Man of Mode* has not been seen upon the stage, although in 1926 a London revival was being seriously discussed.[123]

" Satyre, Wit, and Strength " are the three pre-eminent qualities which Dryden assigned to William Wycherley, and indeed save the great laureate himself there is no writer of the Restoration who exhibits to the same degree such irony, such power, and such keen intelligence. Wycherley had the widest knowledge of his own world. He had truly read the hearts of false men, and—what is a more difficult matter—of loose women too. The life, we may candidly say the libertinism of the Restoration, he enjoyed to the full, and yet as he enjoyed, he loathed. His hate—for it was nothing less—found its outlet in his plays, where there are persons and scenes almost savage in their natural brutality, and yet his worst characters are not more callous than the best of Etherege. He is a moral writer, because he sees how vile are his women and his men, his lecherous Olivia, his traitor Vernish. Etherege is immoral since he draws his depraved and cruel Dorimant and his worthless minx Harriet in utter nonchalance without comment or protest, he has no spark of Wycherley's " saeva indignatio ", which alone can excuse the presentation of such deformities. Wycherley is an infinitely greater writer than Etherege. He has not the grace, the airy delicacy of phrase, which please and are forgotten ; but he has force, and an almost fanatical fury, and phrases which bite to the quick. He is Juvenal in a peruke ; Archilochus turned fine gentleman.

Born in 1640,[124] his first play *Love in a Wood ; or, St. James's Park* was produced at the Theatre Royal, Bridges Street, in the spring of 1671.[125] There was an exceptionally brilliant cast. The three young Gentlemen of the Town, Ranger, Vincent, and Valentine, were played by Hart, Bell, and Kynaston. The lecherous old usurer Gripe was Lacy ; Sir Simon, Wintershal ; Dapperwit, Mohun. Mrs. Boutell and Mrs. Betty Cox acted Christina and Lydia, who are respectively loved by Ranger and Valentine. Gripe's sister, My Lady Flippant, fell to Mrs. Knepp ; Mrs. Martha, the daughter, to Mrs. Farlowe ; Mrs. Corey and Mrs. Rutter were the two old trots, Joyner and Crossbite ; and Betty Slade, the hussy Lucy, Crossbite's worthy daughter.

Love in a Wood is an admirable comedy, and for a first play shows a truly astonishing grasp of the technique of the theatre.[126] Wycherley at once saw that his more romantic episodes, the crossgame of Ranger and the jealous Valentine with the tender passion of Christina and the idle escapade of Lydia, would be incongruous in couplets, which, when we consider that the slovenly heroics of Etherege and Sedley were modish to the last degree, was no such careless hit. Moreover the Ranger-Valentine episodes of *Love in a Wood* are far more natural in prose than is the chequering of *The Comical Revenge* and *The Mulberry-Garden* with bad verse. If the over-nice honour of Valentine does not remind us of Shakespeare, it does recall Calderón. I have already suggested elsewhere [127] that the serious intrigue of the play points to a Spanish original, and although I am unable to identify this, I am quite convinced that Wycherley was working upon some piece he had seen at Madrid, or read in one of the huge Spanish collections of *Comedias Nuevas de los meiores Ingenios de España*. The strength of *Love in a Wood* lies, however, in those scenes of amplest comedy which unveil to us the household of Alderman Gripe, and although it may be objected that there is no very close interrelation between the two themes, the love of Valentine for Christina so crossed yet so true, and the rather dirty business of the Gripe *ménage,* yet Lady Flippant, the ubiquitous Ranger, Dapperwit, and Sir Simon in masquerade with their clandestine intrigues and baffled amours, their visits to Pepper Alley and midnight rambles in the park, their mistakes and misadventures afford quite sufficient connexion since the plot is balanced with considerable neatness and acumen. One of the finest scenes in the play is that where the hypocritical old alderman is introduced by Mrs. Joyner to Lucy, and the saucy jade having allowed him to proceed to filthy extremities turns the tables by a rare cross-buttock trick. It is not pleasant ; it is even a little disquieting, with such vigour does Wycherley lay naked the shame of human nature, the horrid lust of an old man who is betrayed by confederates even worse than he. Lady Flippant herself would be enough to lend life and spirits to any play. Her lewd wooing of Sir Simon, the pseudo-Jonas, is in the highest vein of comedy, as also is her ruttish coursing of the Park at night till she is fain cry : " the Rag-Women, and Synder-Women, have better luck then I."

Love in a Wood was not infrequently revived for a period of some forty years. Probably the last production was that during the summer season of 1718 at Drury Lane, where it was given on 15th August.

The Theatre Royal, Bridges Street, having been burned down in January, 1672, and Killigrew's company being hardly housed at Lincoln's Inn Fields, Wycherley was forced to carry his second comedy *The Gentleman Dancing-Master* to Dorset Garden, where it was produced in March, 1672. It was the third new play acted there, yet Downes tells us, " it lasted but 6 days, being liked but indifferently." [128]

The hint of the design—and really very little more—of *The*

Gentleman Dancing-Master is taken from Calderón's *El Maestro de Danzar,* for the treatment of the two comedies differs widely in almost every respect. It has been objected that *The Gentleman Dancing-Master* once or twice trenches too nearly upon farce, but even if such be allowed to be the case the situation is saved by the characters, for these are full of life and drawn by a master-hand. Moreover the technique of the play is admirably knit and contrived. To us Mr James Formal, or Don Diego, the Anglo-Spaniard, and Monsieur De Parris the Gallomaniac, may appear a little exaggerated, but in the London of Charles II they would have been by no means unusual figures. When James Howell dedicated his English and Spanish Grammar (1662) to Queen Catherine of Braganza he signed himself *Don Diego Howel,* and he was indeed well known for his Spanish fopperies. The Hon. James Howard had already drawn full-length Mr. Frenchlove in *The English Mounsieur,* acted in 1663, and very many caricatures of the French in Restoration comedy might be cited.

The tearing cyprians, if not very germane to the plot, are distinctly good, but perhaps the best character in the piece is Mrs. Caution, the ancestress of a long line of jailer-aunts, Argus-eyed duennas, verjuiced and domineering spinsters, and she is an admirable portrait. One may venture to think she was drawn from the home circle at Clive.

It is curious that *The Gentleman Dancing-Master* did not succeed upon the stage, for it is a capital acting play, and although the same situation is repeated or rather prolonged it is so agreeably varied and so neatly handled that far from wearying it seems to gain a fresh interest as the intrigue develops, one should perhaps say as it hastens to its climax for in this piece Wycherley has wisely left us no time for thought, and it must be taken at tip-top speed.

The original cast has not been preserved, but from allusions in the play it is certain that Edward Angel created Don Diego, and Nokes was Monsieur De Parris. There were revivals of *The Gentleman Dancing-Master* at Drury Lane in 1692–3, and again in 1702 ; at the Maddermarket Theatre, Norwich, in the autumn of 1924 ; and at the Regent Theatre, London (one performance) on 20th December, 1925.

The third play by Wycherley to be seen on the stage, *The Country-Wife,* produced at the Theatre Royal in January, 1675, is the very acme of comedy, of its kind unsurpassable, as it is unsurpassed. In no play in the English theatre, or in any other theatre I know, is the wit more sparkling, the humour more cleverly poised, the sequence of events more naturally deployed ; nowhere are the situations more brilliantly sustained, the characters drawn with keener observation and acuter intellectual insight and truth. Wycherley has given us the full-blooded world of his day, the brilliant society in which he moved, their dazzling wit, their finished graces, their lively affectations, their lewd impudence, their multifold intrigues, their eroticism, their vices, all without mitigation, without glozing, without sentiment, without excuse. The province of comedy is not apologetics.

There is the hard selfishness of the gay gallant Horner, whose scheme is planned as much for the sheer intellectual delight in the novelty of the adventure as for the ends to which it serves. Horner's greatest joy is the knowledge of his mental superiority over the silly cuckolds, who for all their busy importance and endless precautions are but puppets dancing to the tune he calls, and he pleases to pipe an amorous lay. But in my Lady Fidget he has met his match, for she is every whit as clever and every whit as selfish as he. With the affectation of an exaggerated care for her dear reputation she combines the morals of Messalina. Utterly egoistical and self-centred, she has no more affection for her lover than for her husband. Yet appearances must be maintained at all costs. And private pleasures must be satisfied —at all costs. A whore, she is a fine lady too, and a *faux pas* will meet with a frown and a rebuff. Even when on the point, one cannot write of yielding, but of giving herself to Horner, she checks a trifling freedom in speech with " Fie, let us not be smutty ". A charming creature, so long as she gets what she wants, and so long as her gallants are careful not to allow sentiment to enter into the case.

Pinchwife is the man who has drunk deep of all the pleasures of town, and in whom satiety has succeeded to enjoyment, and to satiety disgust. His is the crapulence of the morning after the night before. He shuns his former haunts, not out of wisdom learned but out of moroseness, and in some rambling lone house in the country he frets and curries an exacerbated mind with the boorishness and rusticity of companions whom he despises engaged in rustic employments which he detests. He has, as is the quality of most churls, the sordid sense of possession and petty despot power : " So then you only marry'd to keep a Whore to your self " is Horner's biting comment when Pinchwife confesses to matrimony. For his wife he has taken a girl, who is not innocent but merely ignorant, and the opportunities slight though they may be, of acquiring knowledge, social or sexual, she seizes with such eagerness and so obviously desires, that they are to him moments of the most exquisite annoyance and even bitter torment. Mrs. Margery herself is young and beautiful.

But she is a very child both in the simplicity with which—before, an apt scholar, she has learned her lesson—she blabs of her lover to her husband and in the voluble delight with which she welcomes admiration from a man, as also in her bewilderment at her grum spouse's threats and violence and growls and in the school-boy cunning wherewith she circumvents his jailership when the situation gradually dawns upon her. There is a good deal of pathos in her situation ; one feels for her as one feels for a caged bird beating his pretty breast against the bars. Who could better her description of " the *London* Disease, they call Love " ? " I have heard this distemper, call'd a Feaver, but methinks 'tis liker an Ague, for when I think of my Husband, I tremble, and am in a cold sweat, and have inclinations to vomit, but when I think of my Gallant, dear Mr. *Horner,* my hot fit comes, and I am all in a Feaver, indeed, & as in other Feavers, my own Chamber is tedious to me, and I would fain be remov'd to his, and then methinks I shou'd be well." For those who can fully appreciate there are few lines more full of tender beauty than the postscript of the letter wherein she warns her lover against her husband : " let him not see this, lest he should come home, and pinch me, or kill my Squirrel."

Sparkish is a coxcomb who, as the author intended, is somewhat coarsely drawn. He is far, very far removed from Sir Fopling Flutter, and he is not so perfectly genteel as to be of the line of Sir Courtly Nice and Baron Foppington. Tattle—the Tattle of Charles Laughton not the Tattle of Ernest Thesiger—might allow him a cater-cousin ; he is more shrewd than Lord Brainless ; a more elegant and a cleverer lad than Beau Clincher. Yet his father, one imagines, might have been a worthy citizen, and he himself was probably born well within the sound of the bells of Bow. He is a joyous moth, albeit his markings are a trifle garish, and he imitates skilfully enough the imperial butterflies. Alithea is a sensible girl, too good for Sparkish, perhaps too good for Harcourt. But Wycherley with consummate art has left Ned Harcourt a sketch for the actor to fill in, and I have no doubt that Kynaston coloured the outlines with amplest vigour and vitality. It is in one sense the most difficult rôle to cast in the whole play.

It is difficult to conceive a more brilliant troupe than the original actors. Hart was Horner ; Mohun, Pinchwife ; Haines, Sparkish ; Cartwright, Sir Jasper Fidget ; Lydal, Dorilant ; Shatterel, the Quack ; Mrs. Knepp, My Lady Fidget ; Mrs. Corbet, Mrs. Dainty ; Mrs. Wyatt, Mrs. Squeamish ; Mrs. Rutter, Old Lady Squeamish ; Mrs. Boutell, Mrs. Margery ; Mrs. James, Alithea ; and Mrs. Corey, Lucy, the maid.

The Country-Wife was from the first a recognized triumph, and this masterpiece of English comedy at once took its place as a stock play. After the Union of 1682, when most of the members of the original cast had retired, some new allotment of the rôles became necessary, and Cibber tells us in his *Apology* that Mountford excelled in Sparkish.

On 12th April, 1709, *The Country-Wife* was produced at Drury Lane for the benefit of Mrs. Bicknell, who acted Margery Pinchwife to the Horner of Wilks and Sparkish of Colley Cibber. So admirable were these three that the play was frequently given with the loudest applause.

At Lincoln's Inn Fields *The Country-Wife*, " never acted there," was presented on 4th October, 1725, with Ryan as Horner ; Mrs. Younger, Mrs. Pinchwife ; and Quin, Pinchwife, one of the greatest creations of his genius. In 1735 he was playing Pinchwife to the Mrs. Margery of Kitty Clive, whilst Mrs. Pritchard gave a magnificent rendering of Lady Fidget.

The last production of Wycherley's comedy in the eighteenth century was at Drury Lane, 28th November, 1748, with Woodward as Sparkish, and Kitty Clive, Mrs. Pinchwife.

A miserable and muddled version of *The Country-Wife*, with huge omissions, in two sorry acts, was seen at Drury Lane in April, 1765, and the following year at the same theatre on 25th October was presented what is possibly the worst adaptation of any original known, Garrick's eviscerated and offensive caricature of Wycherley as *The Country Girl*. The thing, than which it is impossible to imagine scenes more devastatingly dull, was revived at Drury Lane on 18th October, 1785, with Mrs. Jordan as Peggy (Margery Pinchwife), in which part she won a triumphant success although it is difficult to see how even the greatest actress can have infused life and spirit in such a clot of crystallized boredom. None the less at the Gaiety Theatre, London, in 1881, Miss Litton played Peggy. In 1884 at Daly's Theatre, New York, Ada Rehan appeared as Peggy ; and at Terry's Theatre, London, in June, 1898, *The Country Girl* was revived with Miss Kate Vaughan in the title-rôle.[129]

There yet rings in my ear the howl of horror which greeted the announcement by the Phoenix in their programme of Wycherley's *The Country-Wife*. Mrs. Grundy wailed aloud and wrung her mittened hands ; Comstock blustered and bawled, fearful for his maidenhead. Even after the production a gentleman, rigid with horror, asked in the newspapers : " Did the Phoenix players really give it unbowdlerized ? And did none of the audience suffer from a feeling of sickness retching—

such as I felt when I first read it ? " [130]   The answer is that
the Phoenix certainly gave Wycherley's comedy unbowdlerized,
whilst the raptured audience rocked with laughter.

After a lapse of one hundred and seventy-six years on 17th and
18th February, 1924, *The Country-Wife* was revived by the Phoenix
at the Regent Theatre, London. Baliol Holloway played Horner ;
Howard Rose, Pinchwife ; Ernest Thesiger, Sparkish ; Stanley
Lathbury, Sir Jasper Fidget ; Isabel Jeans, Mrs. Pinchwife ;
Nell Carter, Alithea ; Athene Seyler, Lady Fidget ; and Louise
Holbrooke, Old Lady Squeamish, which small part she made
great. Baliol Holloway and Athene Seyler gave performances
of most exquisitely finished art. As Margery Pinchwife Isabel
Jeans was consummate perfection.

A subsequent presentation of *The Country-Wife* at the Everyman
Theatre, Hampstead, proved far from successful for reasons
only too plain to those who saw this production.

On Friday, 2nd March, 1934, at the Ambassadors Theatre,
London, Mr. Sydney Carroll revived *The Country-Wife* with
Baliol Holloway, who produced the play, as Horner ; Edmund
Willard, Pinchwife ; John Laurie, Sparkish ; Margaretta Scott,
Alithea ; Agnes Lauchlan, Lady Fidget ; and Lesley Wareing,
Margery Pinchwife. Later in the run George Grossmith suc-
ceeded Baliol Holloway as Horner ; and as Lady Fidget Athene
Seyler followed Agnes Lauchlin. This revival proved a sheer
triumph.[131] The critics joined in one unanimous paean of praise.
" The most amusing play in London," plumped *The Evening News*.
" Well performed and well produced," said *The Times* ; " Brilliant
stagecraft and unflagging wit . . . Brilliantly produced," E. A.
Baughan in *The News-Chronicle* ; " Sincere and courageous.
Mr. Carroll has done his task nobly," S. R. Littlewood in *The
Morning Post* ; " One of the most amusing comedies in the
language. A very clever production. A brilliant picture," George
Bishop in *The Daily Telegraph* ; "A very naughty, but very
human Comedy . . . Beautifully produced and dressed," *The
Daily Express* ; " Crescendo sounds of Delight excited by
Wycherley's Comedy, acted with an exquisite sense of wit by
a polished nonchalant cast," M. Willson Disher in *The Daily Mail* ;
" Staged admirably with a fine cast. A vivid sense of a Period
conveyed with all its suggestiveness honestly," P. L. Mannock
in *The Daily Herald*. Such are a few of the tributes paid to
Wycherley and to Mr. Carroll. The play, carrying everything
before it, ran for no less than five months. Where all were
excellent it may seem invidious to single out any one for praise,
but I cannot refrain from paying my tribute of admiration to
Miss Lauchlan's Lady Fidget. " Miss Lauchlan by a brilliant

make-up and by wearing her beautiful costume as if she had been born in the seventeenth century, might be one of Sir Peter Lely's portraits come to life." [132] This lady's acting was superb, exactly right in every intonation, in every look, in every gesture. So must Mrs. Knepp at her most brilliant and best have trod the stage.

The time had now come when, to use Dryden's phrase, " all honest and virtuous Men " were to be obliged, and our stage enriched " by one of the most bold, most general, and most useful Satyrs which has ever been presented on the *English* Theatre ". The fourth and last play of Wycherley was by his contemporaries esteemed as his masterpiece, but great as it is I question whether to-day we can set *The Plain-Dealer* above *The Country-Wife*. This may, of course, depend upon our angle of observation. As an acting play *The Country-Wife* is un-questionably the better of the two. It sparkles with more brilliant wit and the observation is fully as keen, but not so profound, for *The Plain-Dealer* is the more intellectual piece. The theme of *The Country-Wife* is man's appetite, man's jealousy and hot desire, passions which weave close the strands of life, but the remorseless scalpel of *The Plain-Dealer* cuts deeper still into the very agony of the human heart. It is indeed among the most powerful and philosophical plays in our English, or in any other language. The giant strength of the conception and the bold strokes of the painting cannot be denied. The harshness, even the brutality of certain scenes may be disliked but cannot be burked. As Hazlitt says, the play " penetrates to the core ".[133] No doubt many of Wycherley's contemporaries, as many critics since, deemed Manly's pessimistic hatred of the vices and banalities, the shallowness, the petty businesses and fopperies, the hypocrisy and superficiality of the society about him, delivered in too mordant a vein. He strives to stand apart from man, to segregate himself, to be an onlooker, but his strength is not sufficient for that ; with an ill-grace and struggling hard he is drawn into the game, and in his failure to keep aloof lies his tragedy. He is savage, abusing and kicking the sailors who wait on him for their fo'c'sle jests ; and violent, the more violent for his weakness. Yet he is bound to suffer the noise and endless loquacity of a " Litigious She-Petty-fogger ", that fiend the Widow Blackacre, since she may make amends for her visit by discourse of his mistress, her cousin Olivia. There are two, and two only whom he trusts, his mistress and his friend. During his absence his mistress notoriously jilts and cheats him, and upon his return he surprises her in her drawing-room entertaining the idlest coxcombs in Town ; he overhears her insolently discussing

PLATE XVIII

AGNES LAUCHLAN AS MY LADY FIDGET

The Country-Wife, March 1934

[face p. 320

his love with them in terms of the utmost coarseness and callousness ; when he reveals his presence she repels and flouts him with the brazen impudence of a common strumpet ; she is ready " to satisfie Obligations with a quarrel, the kindest Present a Man can make to his Mistress, when he can make no more Presents " ; she listens to his reproaches with a mocking smile and leaves him with a cruel jest upon her lips. She is mercenary, too, and even though his need is pressing, she retains the money and jewels he deposited in her hands, confident he will be too proud to beg 'em again. Vernish, Manly's bosom and only friend, behaves with the foulest treachery, and promptly betrays him in circumstances of ignoblest dishonour and perfidy. He marries Olivia during Manly's absence, but when he discovers Fidelia, whom his wife deeming a young fellow has just invited to her bed, to be a woman disguised in breeches he at once proceeds to rape her, and she hardly enough escapes. This precious couple, man and wife, are at length unmasked, their intrigues and double-dealing all unripped and exposed.

The character of Fidelia Grey is very tenderly and beautifully drawn. Pure and gracious, for love's sake she follows her rough and reckless captain through perils on sea, through perils on shore. At his behest she undertakes with a breaking heart the most difficult and degrading of functions, the rôle of Pandarus. She realizes all the while that his attraction for Olivia is merely physical, that he is fascinated by the wanton's beauty, and she who loves him for his bravery and true courage, for those sterling qualities she has perceived beneath the scurf of anger and bitter mistrust, executes all his commands save one—to leave him. In a situation of peculiar embarrassment she behaves with perfect modesty and propriety. Her loyalty and the pathos of her lot call unashamed tears to our eyes.

Olivia is Vittoria Corombona in private life, a White Devil in domesticity. Portrayed with the most pregnant and biting strokes, she is governed by self-interest and self-interest alone. The stalwart assurance with which, after having confided her guilt to Eliza, she turns round and fortune favouring her denies all she has previously said, even accusing her cousin of maliciously inventing the whole tale, has something almost terrible in its impudence, so base and rotten and lying is she. She has no love, hardly sensuality, but merely animal passion and herd desire. Flamboyantly physical, she immediately captivates men, and is herself as readily attracted by them. There is in particular one acute piece of psychology which should be noted : she does not seem in the least degree attracted by the vigour and strength of Manly, but her lust is at once stirred by the feminine graces and gentle comeliness of the disguised Fidelia. The bold aban-doned woman seeks for the immaturity and softness of a bashful boy, whose embraces she craves with the most unrestrained ardour, whose kisses she snatches in an orgasm of sadistic vampirism. She preys upon the vitals of men, stripping her lovers bare, and casting them aside like empty husks. A true daughter of the horse-leech, crying always, "Give, give," she is as the grave and the barren womb, as the earth that is not filled with water, and the fire that saith not "It is enough". "Elle a été l'Hélène des Troyens . . . Elle a été Dalila, qui coupait les cheveux de Samson. Elle a été cette fille d'Israël qui s'aban-donnait aux boucs. Elle a aimé l'adultère, l'idolâtrie, le mensogne et la sottise. Elle s'est prostituée à tous les peuples. Elle a chanté dans tous les carrefours. Elle a baisé tous les visages . . ."[134]

It is obvious that Olivia has nothing at all in common with Molière's Célimène, and although Wycherley took a suggestion for the character of Manly and the design of certain scenes from *Le Misanthrope,* the material thus borrowed he has so energized and informed with fire of his native genius that *The Plain-Dealer* is an original masterpiece, a new creation. It has been well remarked : "Wycherley has so overlaid his appropriations with the colouring of his own brilliant individuality that his play appears almost equally a masterpiece of originality as of ingenuity. It is scarcely too much to say that in *The Plain-Dealer* we are conscious of a fertility of invention, a richness of wit and satire, which make even *Le Misanthrope* seem tame in comparison." [135]

It says much for Wycherley's genius that the buzzing crowd of impertinents, coxcombs, fops, chatterers, and lawyers, who circle round Manly and incessantly chafe him with their hum and sharp brize-stings, should all be so severally and entirely differentiated, should each one be a real living person, and not mere puppets to vanish away in shadowy fashion before the strong glare of his personality. The Widow Blackacre herself is, of course, supreme. "The Widow Blackacre and her son are like her lawsuit—everlasting. A more lively, palpable, bustling, ridiculous picture cannot be drawn." [136] Litigation rules her life and sways every action. She can only think in legal terms, and can talk of nothing but law, of which she has all the technicalities at her fingers' ends, and to which she can immediately twist any business or any conversation. None so learned in legal invectives, poignant and sour, alias Billingsgate, none so copiously fluent. Vexatious as a dozen attorneys, and as implacable as a parson suing for his tithes, she will listen to a chancery suit as another might listen to a play, she will even purchase the defence of a case from a pure love of friction and quarrel. Her brief bag, her deeds, and her parchments, are never apart from her; she is restless and resistless as the waves of the sea. We know her very looks, her sharp scolding voice, the clothes she wears, her mantle and bedraggled petticoat, the meat she eats, soused venison, and the wine she drinks. She is all bustle and pother, noise and obstruction and hurry. In fine, the Widow Blackacre is, as Voltaire wrote, " la plus plaisante créature et le meilleur caractère qui soit au théâtre." [137]

The Plain-Dealer was produced at the Theatre Royal in December, 1676. The cast entailed the full strength of the house. Hart played Manly, one of the greatest creations of his genius; Kynaston, Freeman; Griffin, Vernish; Clarke, the pert coxcomb, Novel; Cartwright, Major Oldfox; Haines, Lord Plausible; Charleton,[138] Jerry; Mrs. Rebecca Marshall, the leading tragedienne of the day, Olivia; " chestnut-man'd " Mrs. Boutell, Fidelia; Mrs. Knepp, Eliza; and Mrs. Corey, who was (tradition says) supreme in this rôle, the Widow Blackacre. There is an old story that, so biting is the satire, the play did not at first meet with general applause, but that being highly praised by the best judges, and especially by Dryden and the Earl of Dorset, the new comedy began to be appreciated by the Town. This is hardly probable since it is very certain that *The Plain-Dealer* was long the most popular of Wycherley's pieces, that it was continually given in the theatre, and by the end of the century had passed through at least nine editions.

To-day, I acknowledge, there would be few, if any, more difficult revivals to contemplate than *The Plain-Dealer*. In the first place the play demands a method of acting which now may be said no longer to exist, the acting of the school of Macready, Phelps, Kean, and Henry Irving. It is all on the grand scale. Again, not only is the piece very lengthy, but the incidents and episodes are so interlaced that it would prove wellnigh impossible to make any appreciable cuts without loosening and essentially harming the structure and design. The dialogue, replete with force, vigour, and spirit, is none the less far from succinct. It is perhaps this which Dryden was hinting at when in his complimentary poem prefixed to Motteux's tragedy *Beauty in Distress,*[139] 4to, 1698, he says :—

> Thy Incidents, perhaps, too thick are sown ;
> But so much Plenty is thy Fault alone :
> At least but two, can that good Crime commit,
> Thou in Design, and *Wycherley* in Wit.

Downes tells us that after the retirement of Hart the rôle of

Manly was acted by Philip Griffin (the original Vernish), and save his predecessor, who was unapproachable and unapproached, none equalled his admirable performance.

Gildon says that Betterton appeared in *The Plain-Dealer,* and it has been loosely suggested that he sustained Manly, but this is more than doubtful since the part so peculiarly belonged to Griffin.

Wycherley's play was given season after season, but the casts do not (generally speaking) seem to have been recorded, and there is something more than a suspicion that the actors who created the parts were so supreme that other players did not relish the inevitable comparison in the minds of those who remembered the original.

Nearly forty years passed, and at Lincoln's Inn Fields, 29th November, 1715, Theophilus Keen played Manly; with Pack as Jerry; and Letitia Cross, Olivia. At Drury Lane, 15th May, 1723, Barton Booth was Manly; Pinkethman, Jerry; and Colley Cibber, Novel.

Announced as " Not acted 14 years " (at that theatre) *The Plain-Dealer* was revived at Covent Garden on 15th January, 1733, with Quin as Manly, a magnificent creation, which ensured frequent performances season after season until the retirement (1751) of this famous actor. In various years, to his Manly, Jerry Blackacre was played by Macklin, and Olivia by Kitty Clive. In 1743 at Covent Garden Woodward was his Jerry, and the lovely Mrs. Horton, Olivia.

With material alterations by Isaac Bickerstaffe, who should have known better, *The Plain-Dealer* was revived at Drury Lane on 7th December, 1765. Kitty Clive was the Widow Blackacre, and in spite of Bickerstaffe's tinkering at and the stuff he has inserted in the play [140] this version was received with great applause, so much so indeed that it was frequently given during the following thirty years both at Drury Lane and Covent Garden. With yet further alterations by John Kemble, who acted Manly, it was presented [141] at the former house on 27th February, 1796. There was a good cast, with young Bannister as Jerry; Mrs. Goodall, Olivia; Mrs. Hopkins, the Widow; and Mrs. Jordan, Fidelia; but the rifacimento did not please, and was only seen thrice.

Wycherley's *The Plain-Dealer* was revived for one performance at the Scala Theatre, London, on 15th November, 1925.

Not much more than a twelvemonth after the original production of *The Plain-Dealer* in December, 1676, Wycherley fell dangerously ill of a lingering fever, which even when he had at the King's expense spent a winter and spring at Montpellier left him a prematurely aged man hampered and betrayed by a sadly defective memory, a weakness that rapidly increased with the years. Nevertheless he is appointed tutor to a son of Charles II and the Duchess of Portsmouth, the young Duke of Richmond. There followed that ill-starred marriage with Lady Laetitia-Isabella, Countess of Drogheda, whose carking jealousy, passionate ill-temper, and extravagance so embittered their brief wedded life; the instant loss of royal favour; difficulties and litigation; his wife's death; lawsuits concerning the estate; his commitment on 7th July, 1685, to the Fleet, whence he was rescued and pensioned by the bounty of King James II, who deemed it shame that the author of so fine a play as *The Plain-Dealer*, which His Majesty had just applauded and admired, should be thus harassed and distressed. After that, in these later years Wycherley was as often in the country, playing " the humble Hermit at *Clive* ", as in Town. In 1697 Daniel Wycherley dies at the age of eighty-one leaving a new burden of cares to his son. All this while the great Mr. Wycherley is writing miscellany poems; of an evening dipping into his old favourites La Rochefoucauld, Montaigne, Seneca; and the next morning, unconscious of the theft, reproducing their thoughts, their maxims, in halting verses, which he asks young Mr. Pope to correct and review, writhing in agony and dismay at the excisions, the blotting, the alterations and amendments. Sharp words are exchanged, but the quarrel is presently made up with apology and generous excuse. In London when he visits there the new men at Will's hang upon the words of the Plain-Dealer, who has in truth outlived his generation. He marries, by especial licence, at his lodging in Bow Street, Elizabeth Jackson, in order that he may leave her with a jointure and enable her soon to wed Captain Thomas Shrimpton, whom she loves. He signs his will; a Catholic priest administers the last Sacraments, and on 31st December, 1715, the old man passes gently away, almost in his sleep. He is buried in the vaults of S. Paul's, Covent Garden.

" Mr. Wycherley is universally allow'd the first place among the *English* Comick-Poets, who have writ since *Ben. Johnson*. His *Plain-Dealer* (of which he took the first hint from *Moliere's Misanthrope*) is the best Comedy that ever was compos'd in any Language. The only Fault that has been found in it, is its being too full of *Wit*; a Fault which few Authors can be guilty of. He has also writ three other Plays, the best of which is the *Country-Wife*." [142]

There is little to dispute here. Dryden is, of course, an even greater name than Wycherley, but in this we are not considering prose comedy alone. We may prefer *The Country-Wife* to *The Plain-Dealer*. That is a matter of individual taste ; a question for genial discussion, and one which I, at any rate, cannot venture to decide. This I do know, there are not in any language two comedies more supreme in their achievement than *The Country-Wife* and *The Plain-Dealer* by William Wycherley.

NOTES TO CHAPTER IV

[1] Dryden, *Of Dramatick Poesie,* 1668 ; Lysideius (Sir Charles Sedley) speaks *Dryden The Dramatic Works,* edited by Montague Summers, vol. i, 1931, p. 25.

[2] Ibid., Crites (Sir Robert Howard) speaks ; p. 41.

[3] As showing the vitality of genius, the Theatrical Histories of plays, their life upon the stage, which is their appeal through the centuries to contemporary audiences—and plays are written not for the study but for the theatre—are among the most important parts of an editor's work, and essential to the understanding and appreciation of any dramatist. Unfortunately in the latest edition of Ben Jonson, edited by C. H. Herford and Percy Simpson, vols. i and ii, 1925, "The Man and his Work" (vol. iii, 1927 ; vol. iv, 1932), no account of the theatrical histories of Jonson's plays is attempted. In vol. ii, p. 79, there is a cursory reference, quoted from Pepys, to a performance of *The Silent Woman,* and on pp. 131–2 is a similar reference to *Bartholomew Fair.* For the rest, the extremely important revivals of Jonson's plays until the present time are ignored. It cannot but be considered that such omission is a very serious blemish, and materially impairs the value of the edition. The same deficiency mars the latest reprint (1927) of Etherege's three comedies by Mr. Brett-Smith. One is reminded of the very pertinent comment of a great Italian dramatist : " Io mi ridi dei pedanti, i quali si credono che la dottrina consiste nella lingua greca, dando tutta la riputatione allo in *bus* in *bas* della grammatica."

[4] *Dryden The Dramatic Works,* ut sup., Neander (Dryden himself) speaks ; p. 41.

[5] Prologue to *The Amorous Prince ; or, The Curious Husband,* her second play, produced at Lincoln's Inn Fields in the spring of 1671.

[6] *English Dramatick Poets,* 1691, p. 301.

[7] *The Works of Aphra Behn,* edited by Montague Summers, 1915, vol. i, p. 224, and note p. 448.

[8] For a full consideration of the Jonsonian influence see my edition *The Works of Thomas Shadwell,* 1927, vol. i, Introduction, pp. lxxix, and *passim.*

[9] Ibid., pp. 10–11.

[10] Ibid., p. 187 ; Epilogue, p. 254.

[11] Ibid., vol. iii, p. 193. The Dedication to *The History of Timon of Athens,* 4to, 1678.

[12] See the Dedications to Buckhurst of *The Squire of Alsatia,* 4to, 1688 ; and *Bury Fair,* 4to, 1689 ; ibid., vol. iv, pp. 202–3 and 293–4. Also vol. i, Introduction, pp. cxciv–cxcvii, ccv–ccvi, ccviii, ccxxix–ccxxxi, and *passim.*

[13] *Dryden The Dramatic Works* edited by Montague Summers, vol. i, 1931, pp. 11, 16.

[14] *The Bold Beachams,* which is not extant, has been generally attributed to Thomas Heywood, who is the author of *The foure Prentises of London,* to which reference is here also made. *The foure Prentises* is a Red Bull play, acted *c.* 1599–1600 ; 4to, 1615 ; and 4to, 1632. Both these pieces were immensely popular with the groundlings. Cf. the Introduction to *The Knight of the Burning Pestle* when the Citizen's Wife expresses her desire to see *The Bold Beechams.*

[15] Even Edward Howard's professed admiration for Jonson could not save him from the stinging shafts of their satire. Howard recognizes the eminence of

Jonson in more than one of his prefaces, and he did not neglect to pay him the tribute of imitation. He further introduced Jonson's Ghost to speak the second of the leash of prologues before *The Womens Conquest* in November, 1670, at Lincoln's Inn Fields. Edward Howard, however, was a general butt, and is violently attacked by Buckingham, Buckhurst, Rochester, Shadwell, Waller, Sprat, Clifford, and many more of his contemporaries. In most instances his assailants seemed inspired by a purely personal animus. A collection of nine such lampoons will be found in a manuscript volume, Bodleian MS. Eng. Poet., e.4. Buckingham and Shadwell both brought Edward Howard upon the stage in mockery.

[16] *Dramatic Miscellanies*, London, 1783, vol. ii, pp. 88–9.

[17] Rochester in the Epilogue to Sir Francis Fane's *Love in the Dark*, Theatre Royal, 10th May, 1675 ; 4to, 1675 ; in reference to Mohun " the great Wonder of the *English* Stage " asks the young blades who imitate this actor :—

> Could they . . .
> Rage like *Cethegus*, or like *Cassius* die.

[18] " Which they all conclude he will not be able to do well." *Catiline his Conspiracy* upon its original production in 1611 failed mainly owing to the immense oration of Cicero in Act IV, which the audience were unable to endure.

[19] In which rôle on account of her mimicry, at the instance of Lady Castlemaine, of the eccentric Lady Harvey she caused something like a riot in the theatre " and real troubles at Court about it ". Pepys, Friday, 15th January, 1669.

[20] As a *bonne bouche* the Prologue was " merrily spoken " by Mrs. Nell in an Amazonian habit, and an Epilogue by the same. *Catiline his Conspiracy* was reprinted 4to, 1669, to be sold by William Cademan.

[21] See my edition of *The Rehearsal*, The Shakespeare Head Press, 1914, for all references to Buckingham's play.

[22] *The Rehearsal*, pp. vii, 83, 120.

[23] Buckingham may have taken a hint from *The Knight of the Burning Pestle*, and he also doubtless knew Scudéry's *La Comédie des Comédiens*.

[24] As I have remarked, the Christian name " Robert " was even retained for Bayes. Malone in error tried to show that Davenant was the original hero of *The Rehearsal*. As the mistake has been repeated it is worth while to draw attention to and correct it here. Of course Bayes is to a certain extent a composite figure. He has something of Edward Howard whose phraseology is ever in his mouth. The incident at the end of Act II where he injures his nose, to appear " *with a Papyr on his Nose* " is a sharp bob at Davenant's nasal misfortune.

[25] Dryden was created Laureate in April, 1668, immediately after the death of Davenant. See *Dryden The Dramatic Works*, ed. Montague Summers, vol. i, 1931, Introduction, pp. lxvii–lxviii.

[26] In the Introduction, pp. lxxix–lxxx, to my edition of *Dryden*, vol. i, 1931, I have explained : "As to the name Bayes, Dryden did not value the banter a rush ; it stuck to him, and in some sense he even recognized it, writing in the Epilogue to *All for Love ; or, The World Well Lost*, 4to, 1678 :—

> For our poor wretch, he neither rails nor prays, ⎫
> Nor likes your wit just as you like his plays ; ⎬
> He has not yet so much of Mr. Bays. ⎭

In the *Vindication of the Duke of Guise*, 4to, 1683 (p. 22), he says : " Much less am I concerned at the noble name of *Bayes* ; that's a *Brat* so like his own *Father*, that he cannot be mistaken for any other body." In the Dedication to the *Juvenal*, folio, 1693 (p. iv), he further remarks, " I answer'd not the *Rehearsall*, because I knew the Author sate to himself when he drew the Picture, and was the very Bays of his own Farce."

Dean Lockier is the authority for the following, related in Spence's *Anecdotes*, ed. 1820 : Arranged with notes by Malone. Dryden allowed *The Rehearsal* to have a good many strokes in it " though so severe (added he) upon myself ; but I can't help saying that Smith and Johnson are two of the coolest, most insignificant fellows I ever met with on the stage ".

" The greatness of Dryden's reputation," said Dr. Johnson, " is now the only principle of vitality which keeps the Duke of Buckingham's play from putrefaction." *Anecdotes of the late Samuel Johnson, LL.D.*, by Hesther Lynch Piozzi (1786) : ed. Cambridge, 1925 (p. 39).

[27] To jeer *The Assignation*, iv, 1. See my edition of *Dryden*, vol. iii, 1922, pp. 312–314, and notes pp. 557–8. In a revival of *The Knight of the Burning Pestle* at the Theatre Royal, which may be dated about 1669–1670, some burlesque of Dryden's *Secret-Love, Or The Maiden-Queen* was introduced, as can be inferred from a new Epilogue to Beaumont and Fletcher's play, spoken by Nell Gwyn, and printed in *Covent Garden Drollery*, 1672. This address commences :—

> The Prologue durst not tell, before 'twas seen,
> The Plot we had to swinge the *Mayden Queen*, . . .

It should be noted that in his *Beaumont and Fletcher on the Restoration Stage*, 1926 (p. 37), Mr. A. C. Sprague hazards a wrong date for this revival, and he is in error when he supposes that Nell Gwyn " quit the Theatre Royal " permanently in 1667. Her absence was merely temporary, whilst she was for a while under the protection of Lord Buckhurst.

[28] Bodley MS. Eng. Poet., e.4.

[29] Ann Reeves was an actress of the Theatre Royal. She is said to have been extraordinarily beautiful, but apparently of mediocre talent since the rôles she filled were for the most part very small. In the spring of 1675 she disappeared from the theatre to take the veil in a foreign convent. For further details see my *Dryden*, vol. i, Introduction, pp. liv–lv.

[30] Spence, *Anecdotes*, ed. 1820, pp. 102–3. Davies, *Dramatic Miscellanies*, 1783, vol. iii, pp. 289–290.

[31] " The Bayes of Foote was an odd mixture of himself and the Duke of Buckingham." Ibid., vol. iii, p. 304.

[32] Of whom there is a fine portrait in the part by John Graham, in the Victoria and Albert Museum, London.

[33] *The Letters of Horace Walpole*, ed. by Mrs. Paget Toynbee, Oxford, 1904, vol. xi, p. 101.

[34] *Plays and Poems of Sheridan*, edited by R. Crompton Rhodes, 1928, vol. ii, p. 179.

[35] Davies, op. cit., vol. iii, p. 303.

[36] Ibid., p. 302–3.

[37] It proved extremely successful, and save for some minor difficulties of production the burlesque would have taken its place in the Sheffield Repertory Season.

[38] On 14th December, 1671, Evelyn " went to see the Duke of Buckingham's ridiculous farce and rhapsody, called *The Recital,* buffooning all plays yet profane enough ".

[39] *The Complete Art of Poetry*, 12mo, 1718, vol. i, p. 203. Professor Noyes remarks: " Clever as the farce was, it could not and did not overthrow an established reputation. Just as we ourselves can enjoy Calverley's parodies of Browning without one whit abating our admiration of the original, so ' gentlemen of wit and sense ' in the seventeenth century could laugh at Drawcansir and applaud Almanzor."

[40] I would draw attention to the presentation in May, 1934, of *Aureng-Zebe* at the Westminster Theatre. Originally intended to be given for two performances, 13th and 14th May, the revival, owing to its great success, extended to a series of matinées. *The Morning Post*, 14th May, spoke of " this beautiful production of a fascinating play ", and praised the Nourmahal of Sybil Thorndike as " in the truest sense a splendid performance ". On 30th May the same paper recorded the " enthusiastic welcome " of Dryden's tragedy. This admirable revival was due to Mr. Hubert Langley who played Aureng-Zebe.

[41] For the satire on the heroic play in Arrowsmith's *The Reformation*, Dorset Garden, September, 1673 ; D'Urfey's *The Two Queens of Brentford*, 8vo, 1721 ; Gay's *What d'ye Call It ?*, Drury Lane, 23rd February, 1715 ; Fielding's *The Tragedy of Tragedies ; or, The Life and Death of Tom Thumb the Great*, Haymarket, 25th April, 1730 ; of which there is a separate edition by J. T. Hillhouse, 1918 ; *Bombastes Furioso ; A Pantomime Rehearsal ; The Poet and the Puppets* ; and many more, see the Introduction to my edition of *The Rehearsal*, 1914.

[42] Curiously enough in his rearrangement of Act III Buckingham still makes Antonio cry " get me a Conjurer . . . Find me out a Conjurer, I say ", although the Peter Vecchio episodes were expunged. By an oversight the name Peter Vecchio is even retained in the second quarto of Buckingham, 1692.

[43] *History of the English Stage*, vol. i, p. 67.

[44] *Contemporaries of Shakespeare*, 1919, p. 152.

[45] There have been some bad blunders made with regard to the date of the production of Buckingham's alteration. Dyce, who cared nothing for these details, actually wrote : " In 1682 an alteration of this comedy [*The Chances*] by the celebrated Villiers, Duke of Buckingham, was brought out at the theatre in Dorset Garden ! " Sir E. K. Chambers when editing *The Chances, The Works of Francis Beaumont and John Fletcher*, Variorum Edition, 1912, vol. iv, merely reproduced Dyce wholesale, errors and all, a method of recension which does not commend itself to me. To draw attention to no other point, both Dyce and Sir E. K. Chambers ought to have been very well aware that Hart who acted Don John had retired from the stage before 1682. Miss McAfee in her indifferent compilation *Pepys on the Restoration Stage*, 1916, pp. 82–3, n. 1, apparently thinks that Buckingham's alteration was produced early in 1661. All these mistakes are inexcusable. We know from Dryden that Buckingham's *The Chances* had been acted not later than 1671 (*The Conquest of Granada* is in *The Term Catalogues*, Hilary, 7th February, 1672). There is an allusion in the Epilogue to Nell Gwyn's dancing—*When Nell has danc'd her Jigg*—and the first appearance of this actress was in 1665. When Pepys saw *The Chances* (Fletcher) in 1660 and 1661 he makes no comment at all on this comedy, but in 1667 he is expansive in his praises of the piece.

[46] My friend, the late Mr. W. Barclay Squire, in a letter of 30th December, 1921, wrote to me as follows : " I cannot trace 'All night I weep ', but there is a song in *The Chances* ' Washed with sighs ', words by Sir Robert Howard, music by John Eccles, which must date from the end of the 17th century. It is rather elaborate. It was sung ' by Mr. Wiltshire ', whose name is unknown to me." John Wiltshire, when quite young, joined the Theatre Royal in 1676. See my edition of the *Roscius Anglicanus*, pp. 233–4. I will here take leave to correct a mistake I there made. On obtaining a captain's commission Wiltshire left the stage in 1685. I have said : "He was killed during his first engagement in Flanders." Colley Cibber is responsible for my error, since in his *Apology*, at the end of Chapter III he writes : " *Carlile* and *Wiltshire* were both killed Captains ; one, in King *William's* reduction of *Ireland* ; and the Other, in his first War, in *Flanders*." Wiltshire, however, returned home and to the stage. *The Post Boy* 4th–7th December, 1697, tells us that at Lincoln's Inn Fields Mrs. Willis like a Country Girl, and Mr. Wiltshire like a Souldier, sang the Dialogue in the Musical Interlude on the Peace.

[47] *English Dramatick Poets*, Oxford, 1691, p. 207. Langbaine, of course, does not in any case refer to the original production, 1667, but to the revival of the play by the Duke's Company in 1690–1. Both 4tos, 1682 and 1692, have : "As it is Acted at the Theater Royal," so that Langbaine's *Dorset-Garden* is probably a slip, for the united Companies were certainly at the Theatre Royal.

[48] *Apology*, 1740, p. 136.

[49] *The Chances* (Garrick's adaptation from Buckingham) was included in vol. iii of *The British Theatre*, 1811, with a critique by R. Cumberland, who very sapiently assigns Acts I, II, and III to Fletcher, and the prose portion Acts IV and V to Beaumont !

[50] For a detailed Theatrical History see the programme of this performance. At Covent Garden, 20th February, 1821, was produced a foolish operetta *Don John ; or, The Two Violettas* founded on *The Chances*. The thing has been well described as a " literary murder ".

[51] Unfortunately the separate reprint by F. S. Boas of *Philaster* (1898), in the *Temple Dramatists*, contrary to the general rule of this useful series is woefully inadequate and lacking.

[52] *Philaster* was acted at Vere Street, 13th November, 1660, and remained in the repertory of the Theatre Royal. Pepys saw the play on several occasions. " Those darlings of the stage," Hart and Nell Gwyn, in the later 'sixties acted Philaster and Bellario ; Mrs. Marshall, Arethusa. See for further details my edition of the *Roscius Anglicanus*, pp. 118–119.

[53] Dryden's *Defence of the Epilogue*. See my edition of *Dryden The Dramatic Works*, vol. iii, 1932, pp. 167–8, and the corresponding notes.

[54] *The Works of His Grace George Villiers, Late Duke of Buckingham*. In Two Volumes. The Third Edition, 8vo, 1715. *The Restauration* has a separate title-page, 1714.

⁵⁵ *A* Spaniard, *Governour to Prince* Thrasomond (Pharamond), is a new character introduced by Buckingham. He has little to do in the play. The statement by Giles Jacob in *The Poetical Register*, 1719, that *The Restauration* was "Injuriously father'd upon the Duke of *Buckingham*" carries no weight. There is no reason at all to think that this piece is other than the Duke's version of *Philaster*.

⁵⁶ Also termed "The Farce upon *Segmoor* Fight", and in the *Works*, 1715, "The Battle of *Sedgmoor* : Rehears'd At *White-Hall*. A Farce. Never before Printed Entire," with separate title-page, 1714, as "The Battle of *Sedgmoor* ; Betwixt King *James*'s Forces And the Duke of Monmouth, Rehears'd at *White-Hall*, A Farce."

⁵⁷ For an admirable criticism of *Valentinian* see John Addington Symonds *In the Key of Blue*, 1893, "Some Notes on Fletcher's 'Valentinian'," pp. 217–240.

⁵⁸ For a discussion of the Authorship and Date, Sources, and other details see *Valentinian*, edited by R. G. Martin in the Variorum *Beaumont and Fletcher*, vol. iv (1912), pp. 207–321.

⁵⁹ The scrivener could not always read Rochester's writing, and some rather ludicrous blunders have resulted, such as (in the opening scene) "Bower" for "Hour". "Ave" baffled him entirely, and he left a blank—"To give an *Ave Cesar* as he passes." In IV, 2, he wrote "Standard Court" for "Slander'd Court". There are other errors. The passages concerning Lycias (at the end of Act II, and at the commencement of Act V, scene 5) have at some time been scored through by a prudish hand.

⁶⁰ Mr. J. R. A. Nicoll in an article "Dryden, Howard and Rochester", *The Times Literary Supplement*, 13th January, 1921, amongst other "enthralling suppositions", hazarded a wild guess at Mrs. Corbet for the rôle of Ardelia. His knowledge of the actors is so inadequate that he informs us "Neither Cox nor Clark appears in any list of *dramatis personae* subsequent to 1682", which is echoed without acknowledgement by Mr. John Davy Hayward in his *Collected Works of John Wilmot Earl of Rochester*, 1926, "The Text," p. xiv, note. For Ardelia Mr. Hayward prefers "Mrs. Cere". (The MS. spelling of Mrs. Corey is Mrs. Core, which is simple enough.) But any list of Restoration actors seems completely to gravel such an authority on the period as Mr. Hayward.

⁶¹ To *The Times Literary Supplement*, 27th January, 1921, I contributed a letter indicating 1684 as the original production of Rochester's *Valentinian*. This letter was written owing to the strong persuasion and arguments in a private letter to myself (14th January, 1921) of Dr. W. J. Lawrence, in whose authority I then perhaps too implicitly confided, and who urged that "No version of Rochester's *Valentinian* could possibly have been acted before 1684". A maturer and independent consideration leads me to believe that, as I have here stated, *Lucina's Rape* was actually produced, and that the cast given in the MS. is not merely suggested, but a record of the performers who played in Rochester's alteration in 1677–8. For the rest, my correction of Mr. J. R. A. Nicoll in this published letter holds good.

⁶² Downes, *Roscius Anglicanus*, p. 40.

⁶³ After 1692 Bowen succeeded Nokes as Balbus ; whilst Mrs. Mills acted Celandia ; and Mrs. Osborne, Marcellina. When Goodman left the theatre Valentinian was played by young George Powell.

⁶⁴ *Term Catalogues*, Michaelmas (November), 1684.

⁶⁵ The phrase is Anthony à Wood's ; *Athenae Oxonienses*, ed. Bliss, iii, 1231.

⁶⁶ Reprinted in my edition of *The Works of Aphra Behn*, 1915, vol. vi, pp. 401–2. Mrs. Behn also wrote an elegy "*On the Death of the late Earl of* Rochester", ibid., pp. 368–370.

⁶⁷ Compare Shadwell's phrase in his dedication to the Duke of Buckingham of his alteration from Shakespeare, *The History of Timon of Athens*, 4to, 1678, where after praising "the inimitable hand of *Shakespear*", he adds : "Yet I can truly say, I have made it into a Play."

⁶⁸ *In The Key of Blue*, 1893, p. 235.

⁶⁹ In Act III, scene 3, we have at the entrance of Lycias, *A Ring*, a note to remind the prompter that Mountford was to be provided with a property ring, which plays a great part in the scene. In Act IV we have "[*Call Emperor behind*", that is a warning to be given Goodman that he is to enter drawing in Mrs. Barry some thirty lines later. At the commencement of Act V we have : "*Æcius solus.*

A Letter." That is Betterton was to be furnished with the property letter which he hands Proculus to be carried to the Emperor. There are other examples.

In Nahum Tate's *Poems by Several Hands and on Several Occasions*, 1685, p. 17, is included "*A Mask* made at the Request of the late Earl of *Rochester*, for the Tragedy of *Valentinian*". At the conclusion of this masque we have " Enter Satyrs and Dance ". This piece was written by Sir Francis Fane.

[70] Mr. J. R. A. Nicoll, *A History of Restoration Drama*, 1928, p. 166, writes : " Pandarus in Dryden's *Troilus and Cressida*, in a similar way, is made inexpressibly coarse. One might cite in the same connexion the indescribable indecencies introduced by Rochester into his alteration of Fletcher's *Valentinian*." Had Mr. Nicoll read Dryden's *Troilus and Cressida* he must be aware that Dryden considerably softened the character and speech of Pandarus. For an example see my Introduction, vol. i, p. cviii of *Dryden The Dramatic Works*, 1931. It is plain, also, that he has no real acquaintance with Rochester's *Valentinian* or it were hardly possible to chatter of " indescribable indecencies " and similar puerilities.

[71] The final scene should be particularly noted.

[72] The Prologue and Epilogue were written for the revival of Killigrew's comedy in 1672 at Lincoln's Inn Fields, the temporary home of the Theatre Royal company, when the play was presented all by the women players.

[73] For very explicit details see the famous letters of Elisabeth Charlotte, Princess Palatine and Duchess of Orleans. *Briefe der Herzogin Elisabeth Charlotte von Orléans* . . . herausgegeben von Dr. Ludwig Holland. Stuttgart, 1867. (*Bibliothek* von Litterarischen Vereins in Stuttgart.) Vol. 88, pp. 239, 249 ; 257. In a masterly article, " False History Exposed : The Ground Gained," published in *The Universe*, 28th December, 1934, Hilaire Belloc observes that William of Orange cannot be defended. "As for William's personal character, I do not think that in the near future there will be anyone left to defend it. We owe our grateful thanks for this to Macaulay, who by his deliberate advocacy and ' falsehood of the soul ' has helped to produce a reaction . . . he is now found out. It is one of the most satisfactory developments of our time that a man who called the relations between Keppel and William of Orange ' filial ' should be exploded." Either Macaulay (and such is assuredly the case) knew the facts and of intent perverted them, or else he did not recognize the facts and is stamped no historian. A recent writer of authority succinctly summed up Macaulay as " a liar ". There can be little doubt that his misrepresentations have in the past done considerable harm, and it is gratifying to know that he has been stripped and unmasqued, that he is utterly discredited both in his rôle of historian, and in his rôle of literary critic.

[74] Bodley : Rawl. MSS. poet. 159 ; 32, 33.

[75] Groen van Prinsterer says, 1645–1709.

[76] See *The Works of Aphra Behn*, ed. Montague Summers, 1915, vol. i, memoir of Mrs. Behn, pp. xxxiii–xxxvi, and note 1 on last quoted page.

[77] *Roscius Anglicanus*, p. 19.

[78] Kynaston actually was of a bisexual temperament, for on 8th February, 1691, when he was aged nearly fifty, he married Hannah Bunhead at S. Mary le Bone.

[79] Monday, 7th January, 1661. It is incredible that later the rôle of the Silent Woman should have been given to an actress. It was indeed this blunder which caused the play to fall out of the repertory of the theatres. For details see my edition of the *Roscius Anglicanus*, pp. 104–5.

[80] See the *Satyr on the Players* first printed in my edition of the *Roscius Anglicanus*, p. 56. Nokes died 8th September, 1696. He was unmarried, and left his estate to a nephew.

[81] *A General History of the Stage*, 1749, p. 179.

[82] To me *Sodom* appears quite worthless as literature and of no consequence. Yet it has been termed " a document of incontestable value and far-reaching importance " ! I am quite unable to follow this judgement of Herr Prinz, who is manifestly in error, since the versification does not show " incomparable freedom, ease, elegance, and melodious rhythm ". Nor does " the language of the play abound in words and expressions which the poet affected, and which cannot be traced in any contemporary author ". *Sodom* is not well written, and to describe it as " a masterpiece " is sheer nonsense. It is equally absurd to speak of the thing as a " scurrilous attack against Charles II ", whom Dr. von Römer informs us was a homosexual !

[83] Charles Gildon in his *Lives and Characters of the English Dramatick Poets*,

8vo, 1699, p. 56, attributed *Sodom* to John Fishbourne, a young barrister who "belonged to the Inns of Court", a statement which carries no weight at all, but which has been repeated by many books of reference and dramatic catalogues. The extant poems by Fishbourne are of an entirely unexceptional character.

[84] Herr Johannes Prinz in his *John Wilmot Earl of Rochester* (Palaestra 154), Leipzig, 1927, p. 173, says of the authorship of *Sodom*, "There is ample evidence to speak in favour, or rather in discredit of Rochester." Mr. Hayward, *Collected Works of John Wilmot, Earl of Rochester,* 1926, pp. xvii–xviii, argues, or attempts to argue, that Rochester must not be accounted the author of *Sodom.* He mainly bases his contention upon a Poem by Oldham which he incorrectly attributes to Rochester himself; a footnote to the *Poems,* 2 vols., 1731, of the source of which he is ignorant; an allusion in Otway which he misunderstands; and the account in the *Biographia Dramatica,* vol. i, part 1, 1811, p. 243, under Mr. Fishbourne! The authorship of Rochester is accepted by all contemporaries whose opinions carry weight, and some interesting evidence has been brought together by Herr Prinz, op. cit., pp. 172–7.

[85] See the *Théâtre Gaillard,* 2 vols., Glascow [Paris], 1776, which collection contains such plays as Marc-Antoine Legrand's *Le Luxurieux* (1732); Piron's *Vasta, reine de Bordélie; Les Plaisirs du Cloître;* and many more. Also the *Théâtre d'Amour,* four parts, "A Paphos. L'an 4000 . . ." On 1st January, 1741, at a little theatre in the rue de Clichy was given a ballet, *L'art de foutre; ou, Paris foutant.* What Mr. Hayward, op. cit., p. xviii, intends to convey by suggesting "that the Court played *Sodom* at a private performance, in the nature of a charade, in which Rochester may have taken a part", it is impossible to tell. Why a charade?

[86] In reference to the famous pornographic piece, which has been so many times reprinted, *Histoire de Dom B——, portier des Chartreux.* This was written by Gervaise de Latouche, and first appeared in 1745. The work sometimes has the title *Mémoires de Saturnin.*

[87] August Beyer, *Memoriae Hist.—Crit. Librorum Rariorum,* 1734, pp. 150–1. Beyer quotes the bibliophile and scholar Henrich Muhle of Kiel (1666–1733).

[88] Folios, 118–145. This MS. carries no date, no motto (as in the Hamburg MS.), and no indication that the text was ever printed. The third page of the Hamburg MS. has: Antwerp. Printed in the year 1684. Uffenbach made a note upon the first page: Comitis Rochestriae Comoedia versibus Anglicis perobscoenis scripta . . . haec Comoedia in aulâ Regiâ acta perhibetur.

[89] In the Soleinne collection were three MSS. (since destroyed), two of which at any rate seem to have been translations of Rochester's *Sodom. Le Roi de Sodome,* a version said to have been made by Bussy-Rabutin; see Gay, *Bibliographie des Ouvrages relatifs à l'Amour,* etc., 4th ed., Tom. i, c. 501. *Sodome,* comédie en 5 actes et en prose, par le Comte De Rochester, traduite de l'anglais, 1682. *L'Embrasement de Sodome,* comédie, traduite de l'anglais, may be another piece, and to be identified with *L'Embrasement de Sodome* attributed to Voltaire in *La Cauchoise, ou Mémoires d'une courtisane célèbre,* where Rochester's *Sodom* is also mentioned.

There is a German translation by Theophil Marquardt, *Sodom, Ein Spiel,* folio, Leipzig, 1909, illustrated by Julius Klinger. A pirated reprint appeared in the series *Bibliotheca Erotica et Curiosa.*

[90] Privately printed, pp. 330–341. Pisanus Fraxi was the bibliographer Henry Spencer Ashbee, 1834–1900.

[91] Dr. L. S. A. M. von Römer is an eminent psychologist and scientist, and his work *Die Uranische Familie,* which appeared both in Dutch and in German, is of very great importance, hence it is all the more pity that he should have been misled or mistaken in his treatment of Rochester's *Sodom.*

[92] *Collected Works of John Wilmot, Earl of Rochester,* 1926, p. xvii.

[93] Originally (*The Times Literary Supplement,* 5th March, 1925) a Mr. R. Wood was to have collaborated with Mr. Hayward in this edition of Rochester, and presumably to have been principal editor.

[94] When Mr. Graham Greene in *The Spectator,* Friday, 22nd December, 1933, praised Mr. Hayward's *Rochester* as a "noble piece of editorial pioneering" he must have been indulging in banter, and have

Cried "*Superbe !—Magnifique* !"
(With his tongue in his cheek)—

Yet such sarcasm is inadvisable and imprudent, for the quiz might have been taken seriously. Mr. Graham further remarked that Mr. Hayward had done most of the work for future editors ; there remained only to correct a few faults. I have here corrected, not a few, but a very great many blunders, and there remains to correct a very great many more.

⁹⁵ *Dirce*, an opera, music by C. E. Horn, was produced at Drury Lane in 1821.

⁹⁶ *The Poems of Thomas Randolph*, edited by G. Thorn-Drury, 1929. Mr. Thorn-Drury points out (p. 206) that Randolph's famous *A Pastorall Courtship* " has been included among Lord Rochester's works, as being, I suppose, the sort of thing he might have written ". Upon *Love fondly refus'd for Conscience sake* he remarks (p. 208), " This has also received the doubtful distinction of having been included in the last edition of Lord Rochester's works."

⁹⁷ *A Session of the Poets*, p. 111, in the edition " Printed at Antwerpen ", 8vo, 151 pages. In late editions this is termed *A Trial of the Poets for the Bays*, and Mr. Hayward prefers the later title. Herr Prinz, *John Wilmot Earl of Rochester*, 1927, pp. 100-2, is very unconvincing in his argument that *A Session of the Poets* is not even partially to be ascribed to Rochester.

⁹⁸ *A Session of the Poets* looks rather to Suckling than to Boileau, but Mr. Hayward does not even seem to recognize that the *Satyr* commencing " What, Timon, does old age begin t'approach . . ." is a version of Boileau's third satire *Le Repas Ridicule*.

⁹⁹ This is the reading of the Antwerpen edition. I do not know whence Mr. Hayward had his (p. 132) " Poor Settle " for " Poet Settle ". In *Poems on Several Occasions*, 1701, p. 88, the line in question reads : " And Rat him, cry'd Newport, I hate that dull Rogue." *The Works of the Earls of Rochester, Roscommon, Dorset . . .* 2 vols., 1721, vol. i, pp. 134-5 ; and 2 vols., 1731, vol. i, p. 134, both read : " And *Banks*, cry'd up *Newport*, I hate that dull Rogue."

¹⁰⁰ Anthony à Wood, " Life of Sir Charles Sedley," *Athenae Oxonienses*, second edition, London, 1721. This " Life " is not in the first edition of the *Athenae*, Oxford, 1691.

¹⁰¹ *Sir Charles Sedley* by V. de Sola Pinto, 1927. Mr. Pinto's social pictures (pp. 70-6 ; 83-95, *et saepius*) are full of errors. For example, p. 72, Rochester is said to have " looked in at the Play, probably at the King's House at Drury Lane, where Mrs. Gwynne is doubtless acting in a new piece by Mr. Dryden ". This is in 1676, when Nell Gwyn had for some years retired from the stage. No new piece by Dryden was presented in 1676. Again Lord Buckhurst was not in a barge on the Thames on 3rd June, 1665, as Mr. Pinto describes (p. 89), for the very simple reason that he was taking part in the naval engagement between the English and Dutch off the Suffolk coast.

¹⁰² See *The Poems of Thomas Randolph*, edited by G. Thorn-Drury, p. viii.

¹⁰³ Mr. Pinto, to whose inadequate knowledge of Restoration stage-conditions I have already been compelled to draw attention (*The Restoration Theatre*, 1934, pp. xv, 250-1), speaks of Michael Mohun and Charles Hart as " famous veterans " in 1668, and suggests that they " may well have been cast for *Everyoung* and *Forecast* ", the two old men in the play ! In 1668, and for ten years after, Mohun and Hart were playing the heroes, the young leading rôles, e.g. in 1667 Mohun created Philocles and Hart Celadon in *Secret-Love* ; in 1668 they created Bellamy and Wildblood, " Two young English Gentlemen " in *An Evening's Love* ; in 1672 they created the young courtiers Rhodophil and Palamede in *Marriage A-la-Mode*. Mohun was famous as Don Leon in *Rule a Wife and Have a Wife* with Hart as Michael Perez. Mohun was also the recognized Valentine, the young gallant in *Wit without Money* ; and Truewit in *The Silent Woman*. Hart excelled as Amintor in *The Maid's Tragedy*—he is called " young Amintor " and there is an emphatic reference to his " lusty youth "— ; as Don John in *The Chances* ; and Bussy d'Ambois. In November, 1675, he created Aureng-Zebe, the title-rôle in Dryden's tragedy ; in 1677 the fiery young Alexander in *The Rival Queens* ; and in 1678 that gay spark Monsieur Thomas in D'Urfey's adaptation from Fletcher, *Trick for Trick*. A mere haphazard guessing at the casts of plays can have no possible value, and must be accounted altogether unsound.

In his edition of *The Poetical and Dramatic Works of Sir Charles Sedley*, 1928, vol. i, p. 105, Mr. Pinto repeats once again the crusted old error that Nell Gwyn created S. Catherine in Dryden's *Tyrannick Love*. This rôle was originally played by Mrs. Hughes, and afterwards by Mrs. Boutell.

[104] See my edition of Shadwell's *Complete Works*, 1927, vol. i, Introduction, pp. cxciii–cxcvi ; also vol v, pp. 291–2. Shadwell in addressing Sedley mentions : "Your late great obligation in giving me the advantage of your Comedy, call'd *Bellamira, or the Mistress*."

[105] Shadwell's *Complete Works*, ut sup., vol. i, Introduction, pp. clxviii–clxxix ; and vol iv, pp. 87–189.

[106] *The Vindication of the Duke of Guise*, 4to, 1683. See *Dryden The Dramatic Works*, ed. by Montague Summers, vol. v, 1932, p. 326, and notes, pp. 512–13.

[107] Oldmixon, *Critical History of England*, ii, f. 276. Undoubtedly the incident of Cunningham being surprised with Bellamira and escaping out of a lower window by the river reflects upon the young guardsman Churchill being surprised (owing to the malice of the Duke of Buckingham) in bed with the Duchess on the entry of the King. This is alluded to in the satirical novel *Hattegé ; ou, les Amours du Roy de Tamaran*, Cologne, 1676 ; English translation "Amsterdam", 12mo, 1680. *Le Roy de Tamaran* is Charles II ; *Hattegé*, The Duchess ; *Rajep*, Churchill ; and *Osman*, Buckingham. The details differ, but the circumstance is the same.

[108] Entirely unknown, of course, to Mr. Pinto.

[109] 12mo, Paris, 1693. David Augustin de Brueys, 1640–1723. Jean de Palaprat, 1650–1721.

[110] The *Biographia Dramatica*, vol. ii, 1812, p. 274, mentions an octavo edition, 1702, which is probably an error.

[111] *The Grumbler* was adapted as a farce by Garrick in 1754 ; and in 1773 by Goldsmith for the benefit of Quick, when it was given (once only) at Covent Garden on 8th May.

[112] Mr. R. W. Lowe may have been guilty of some share in this disgraceful brochure, but there is reason to believe that Mr. William Archer was mainly responsible. For Archer on Albery see *The Old Drama and the New*, 1923, p. 272. Archer in the same book (p. 270) has the impudence to say that whilst Henry Irving was "establishing his reign at the Lyceum" he was doing practically nothing for the English drama. "He had very little literary or dramaturgic sense." In comment I will merely quote Mr. H. M. Walbrook : "All about Irving's supposed neglect of the modern drama. What more could Irving do for it than he did ? Wasn't Tennyson a modern writer ? Irving produced three of his plays He gave Pinero his first start, also Conan Doyle, also Hichens and H. D. Traill, and simply 'made' W. G. Wills ! This parrot-cry began with Shaw who first said Irving neglected the modern theatre ; in other words Irving neglected G. B. S. ! ! ! And the nonsense goes on being repeated !" To-day Mr. Archer's drugget mantle, "With double portion of his Father's Art," has descended upon or been clutched by Mr. St. John Greer Ervine who never wearies of expressing his dull lack of appreciation of the Restoration drama in general, and of Congreve in particular.

[113] In some well-known lines, *A Session of the Poets*, Rochester's *Poems*, Antwerpen [1680], p. 103, "gentle *George*" is rebuked by Apollo for "th' crying Sin *Idleness*" and his "Seven Years silence" pronounced unpardonable.

[114] *Roscius Anglicanus*, p. 25.

[115] Wednesday, 4th January, 1665. Pepys found *The Comical Revenge* "very merry, but only so by gesture, not wit at all, which methinks is beneath the house".

[116] Thus Sir Frederick is "Cousin to the Lord *Beaufort*" ; Mrs. Rich, "Sister to the Lord *Bevill*," but these relationships are practically unmeaning.

[117] *The Works of Sir George Etherege*, 2 vols., 1927, edited by Mr. H. F. B. Brett-Smith.

[118] *Seventeenth Century Studies*, p. 243. See also J.-E. Gillet, *Molière en Angleterre 1660–1670*, 1913, p. 70.

[119] Dorimant was generally recognized to be Rochester. Sir Fopling represented Sir George Hewett. It is disputed whether Sir Charles Sedley was Medley, and Etherege himself Young Bellair ; or whether Etherege drew himself in Medley. Oldys is the chief authority for these ascriptions.

[120] "Mr. *Dorimant* has been your God Almighty long enough, 'tis time to think of another—" is her last vile and profane sneer at Mrs. Loveit.

[121] Mrs. Behn in the Preface to *The Luckey Chance, or, An Alderman's Bargain*, 4to, 1687, defending her new comedy from the "Indecencys" which had been

charged upon her scenes, takes occasion to draw attention to popular plays which exhibit equal freedoms, among others " the fam'd Sir *Fopling Dorimont* and *Bellinda,* see the very Words ".

[122] This was an exceptional piece of casting. William Smith was notably handsome and athletic. The coxcombs and fops at this date were usually assigned to Nokes ; or (if he happened to be at the Duke's Theatre) to Haines. After the Union, Mountford, and then Bowman, and then Colley Cibber excelled in fop-rôles. Sir Fopling was emphatically an especial creation, demanding a particular actor.

[123] Etherege's three comedies were popular in Dublin. See Chetwood, *A General History of the Stage,* 1749, pp. 53–5, where complete casts are given. In *The Comical Revenge* Wilks played Sir Frederick ; and Mrs. Hook, the Widow ; Bowen, Dufoy. Wilks was Courtall ; and Mrs. Smith, Lady Cockwood in *She wou'd if she cou'd.* In *The Man of Mode,* Wilks was Dorimant ; Sir Fopling, Griffith ; Mrs. Loveit, Mrs. Knight ; Bellinda, Mrs. Schoolding ; and Harriet, Mrs. Ashbury. These casts may be dated about 1695–6.

[124] *The Complete Works of William Wycherley* were for the first time collected and edited by the present writer in four volumes, 1924. This edition is prefaced by a Life and full critical notice of sixty-four pages. In 1921 Mons. Charles Perromat had published a study *William Wycherley, Sa Vie, Son Oeuvre.* Assiduously gleaning from Mons. Perromat and myself, but without acknowledgement of his ample conveyances, a Mr. Willard Connely published in 1930 *Brawny Wycherley,* but this, as *The Times Literary Supplement,* 29th May, 1930, remarked, " is merely what the French call *vulgarisation.* Not only is there no new insight into the man, his work, his time, but the whole of the old material which is used is served up so as to make it repulsive where it does not dull through familiarity."

The exact date of Wycherley's birth is uncertain. Precise details are lacking. I see no reason for assigning it to other than the winter of 1640, but there was some interesting correspondence in *The Times Literary Supplement,* March, 1932, when Mr. H. P. Vincent suggested 28th May, 1641 ; and Mr. H. I. Anderton preferred March, 1641.

[125] The date of production is very doubtful, and I have previously assigned the *première* to October, 1671. I am not at all sure whether autumn rather than spring might not be the nearer time.

[126] Of course, a Restoration theatre. It seems necessary to emphasize this since Mr. H. G. Barker in his *On Dramatic Methods,* " being the Clark lectures for 1930," 1931, chapter iv, has bitterly attacked Wycherley's stagecraft, because it was not *selon le formule de M. Scribe.*

[127] See my edition of Wycherley's *Complete Works,* vol. i, pp. 30–1, where I also draw attention to the fact that Mrs. Centlivre borrowed the central situation of her evergreen comedy *The Wonder : a woman keeps a secret* from *Love in a Wood.* See further p. 67.

[128] *Roscius Anglicanus,* p. 32.

[129] Critics speak of the acting of these three famous ladies as " dazzling " and " unforgettable ". Certainly this may have been the case, but to give life to Garrick's *The Country Girl* would be to raise the dead. At the time of the great vogue of Wycherley in 1924 a small travelling company very ingeniously announced on their bills *The Country-Wife.* When we got to the theatre we were regaled with *The Country Girl.*

[130] Mr. Hubert B. Mathews writing to *The New Statesman,* 8th March, 1924.

[131] " One of the most heartening signs about the theatre is the continued success of ' The Country Wife ' " : *The Observer,* 13th May, 1934. The great success of Mr. Carroll's revival in a modern theatre more than answers the foolish strictures of Mr. H. G. Barker who impugns Wycherley's stagecraft and technique.

[132] *The Referee,* 4th March, 1934.

[133] *The English Comic Writers.* Lecture IV, ed. Bell (Bohn's Libraries), 1906, p. 102.

[134] Flaubert, *La Tentation de Saint Antoine,* IV. Édition Définitive, 1918, pp. 134–5.

[135] W. C. Ward in his reprint of Wycherley in the " Mermaid Series ". For Wycherley's indebtedness to Molière and other writers in *The Country-Wife* and *The Plain-Dealer* see the notes on the Sources of these two plays in my edition,

The Complete Works of William Wycherley, 1924, vol. ii, pp. 3–4 and 91–2. Mr. Hubert B. Mathews seriously urged that *L'École des Femmes* " would require very little bowdlerization to make it actable, either in French or English " !

La Critique de l'École des Femmes has given Wycherley a hint for an excellent lively scene in *The Plain-Dealer*.

It should perhaps be remarked that in the Widow Blackacre we have the dramatist's father, the barratrous Daniel Wycherley, very clearly depicted in petticoats.   It has been absurdly suggested that the Widow Blackacre is from Racine's Comtesse de Pimbesche.   As well say that Dandin is from the old Justice in *The Coxcomb*.

[136] Hazlitt, *English Comic Writers,* Lecture IV, ed. cit. sup., p. 103.   He adds : " Jerry is a hopeful lad, though undutiful, and gets out of bad hands into worse." He also points out that Goldsmith drew Tony Lumpkin and his mother from the Widow and her son.   Certain incidents are the same in both comedies.

[137] *Lettre sur la Comédie Anglaise.*

[138] Curiously enough, little is known of this actor whose name (indifferently spelled, Charleton, Charlton, Carleton) appears rarely and to very minor rôles. I have suggested in Chapter II that he is perhaps to be identified with the pre-Restoration Will Cherrington.

[139] Produced at Lincoln's Inn Fields, April, 1698.   Publication advertised in the *Protestant Mercury,* 24th–29th June, 1698.

[140] Garrick joined Bickerstaffe in his assault on Wycherley.   The thing was printed 8vo, 1776.

[141] 8vo, 1796.

[142] Boyer's *Letters of Wit, Politicks, and Morality,* 1701, Letter III, p. 217.

CHAPTER V

THE MINOR DRAMATISTS : 1660–1682

I cannot chuse but laugh, when I look back and see
The strange Vicissitudes of Poetrie.
Your Aged Fathers came to Plays for Wit,
And sat Knee-deep in Nut-shells in the Pit.
Course Hangings then in stead of Scenes were worn,
And Kidderminster *did the Stage Adorn.*
But you, their wiser Off-spring, do advance
To Plott of Gigg; and to Dramatique Dance :
But when the Reign of Gigg and Dance is past,
Whither the Devil will you go at last,
What yet unheard-of Way can Poets try,
To please the Modern Criticks of the eye.

> Prologue to JOHN CORYE'S *The Generous Enemies ;*
> *or, The Ridiculous Lovers,* 4to, 1672.

It has superficially been supposed, and quite erroneously asserted, that actually there must be very few plays of the Restoration period, the name conveniently given to the forty years from the coming-in of King Charles II to the death of Dryden, of which no record remains, and which indeed were not issued from the press. We know from many sources how great a number of Elizabethan dramas perished, leaving us only their titles to tantalize and torture our imagination. What would we not give for " The History of Cardennio, by Mr Fletcher & Shakespeare " ; " Henry ye first, & Hen: ye 2d. by Shakespeare, & Dauenport " [1] ; " The History of King Stephen," [2] by Will: Shakespeare ; Middleton's *The Puritan Maid, Modest Wife, & Wanton Widow* [3] ; or *A Late Murther of the Sonn upon the Mother* [4] in which the genius of Ford and Webster combined ?

One ill-equipped writer on the Restoration has even gone so far as to say with the regular slap-dash swindge that so often characterizes inefficiency, " It is a fact worthy of notice that very few plays of this time seem to have remained unprinted." Nothing could be further from the truth, and it would not be difficult from the glimpses afforded by Pepys, Downes, and others to draw up a very ample list of dramas whose names alone have thus hardly survived. Even more have entirely vanished ; some after a brief, but not wholly unapplauded, course upon the boards ; some fallen successless, " e scena non modo sibilis sed etiam convicio " explosa, as Cicero has it ; some " perishing unheard " ; all as if they had never been.

Where, for example, are that " play or two " which one Sunday afternoon in November, 1665, John Evelyn read to Pepys, who judged them " very good, but not as he conceits them " ? Where is Ned Howard's *The Change of Crownes,* " a great play and serious ", which " took very much " ; or the same writer's *The London Gentleman* ? Where *The Politician ; or, Sir Popular Wisdom,* a comedy bitterly satirizing " my Lord Shaftesbury and all his gang ", produced on 17th November, 1677, when the King made a particular point of occupying the Royal Box ?

None of the following have come down to us : *The New-Made Nobleman* [5] given at the Red Bull on 22nd January, 1661-2 ; *The Exposure,* which Herbert records as being played at the Theatre Royal, Bridges Street, in November, 1663 ; Henry Howard's *The United Kingdoms,* satirized *in The Rehearsal* ; *'Tis Better than it was* and *Worse and Worse,* two translations from Calderón given at Lincoln's Inn Fields between June, 1661, and June, 1665 [6] ; *Heraclius,* produced at Lincoln's Inn Fields, 8th March, 1664 ; Holden's two plays *The German Princess* and *The Ghosts* ; Stroud's *All Plot, or the Disguises,* a Lincoln's Inn Fields comedy ; Orrery's *The Widow,*[7] a farcical comedy of coprophorian humours, produced in May, 1665 ; the Duke of Newcastle's *The Heiress,* produced at Drury Lane, 29th January, 1668-9 ; Betterton's *The Woman made a Justice,*[8] in which Mrs. Long acted the Justice ; Shadwell's *The Hypocrite,* probably a hurried adaptation of *Tartuffe ; The Armenian Queen* [9] ; *The Romantic Lady ; The Sea-Captains ; No Fool like the Old Fool ; Like Father, Like Son ; or, The Mistaken Brothers,* a rehandling by Mrs. Behn of Randolph's *The Jealous Lovers,* produced at Dorset Garden in March, 1682 ; *Love in, and Love out of Fashion* [10] ; *The Rape Reveng'd, Or, The Spanish Revolution,* a version of Rowley's *Alls Lost By Lust,* which possibly was not brought upon the stage ; *The Gordian Knot Unty'd,* a comedy given at Drury Lane in the winter of 1691 ; *Have at all, or The Midnight Adventures,* produced at the same house in April, 1694 ; *The Strollers* ; Crowne's *Justice Busy, or the Gentleman Quack* ; and very many more of which only the mere titles remain.

A play which has survived in MS. alone [11] and which was acted but never attained the dignity of print is a romantic drama entitled *The Faithfull Virgins,* a script presenting many features of interest. On the first leaf is inscribed : " This Tragedy apoynted to be acted by the dukes Company of Actors only

leauing out what was Cross'd by Henry Herbertt M.R.," and
below, " the Chaster witts, say ; that (luxury) must be pronounc'd
for letchery in the masque throughout acording to the judgement
off Docter, H:C: " The MS., however, gives no cancelled passages
and only four lines are marked (significantly enough) [12] for
omission, whence it seems clear that it is a fair copy, licence
and all, from the original script, which was used as the prompt
copy.   The licence is not exactly reproduced since Sir Henry
Herbert invariably appended the day and month.   There is no
cast, not even a list of characters.   It is possible none the less
to date the piece with some fair attempt at a proximation. About
July, 1663, Herbert appointed Edward Hayward deputy Master
of the Revels, and retired to his country seat at Ribbesford,
Bewdley, comitatu Wigon, where he died some ten years later.
The Faithfull Virgins then was licensed (and acted) between
1661 and June, 1663.

The characters are the Duke of Tuscany ; Cleophon, a prince
of the blood ; Statenor ; Floradine, who is Philammon's sister,
Erasila, disguis'd, in love with Statenor ; Eumenus, Trasilius,
Cleon, Franciscus, lords ; Isabella ; Merantha ; Umira ; 2 witches.
Act I commences with "A Herse discouered with Tapers Burning
Round it at the feet of it Merantha in black weeping ".   She
speaks :—

> What soule's soe weary of her Mansion
> that will at such an hour wander from home
> When much aflicted widowes Cease to weepe
> and ev'n madmen, and sad louers sleepe
> When flowry slumber statesmen does invest
> and jealousie's Charm'd in soft fether'd rest.
> When Natures selfe in sleep's kind Armes does lye
> and nought that Liues does seem to wake but I.

Umira enters, also robed in black, and announces her intention
to watch and weep by the bier :—

> know though philammon did to you prettend
> your loue for him Could not my flame transcend.

The two ladies who (together with Floradine-Erasila) are the
Faithful Virgins, since nothing so commonplace as consummation
with the man they loved had ever entered their heads, resolve
to keep vigil by the hearse together. Cleophon has been betrothed
to Isabella, who rejects him for the Duke. Act I concludes with
"A dumb shew. a temple discouered, the duke with his lords
and attendants on the one side : on the other Isabella and ladies.
Eumenus presents her to the duke a priest seems to joyne them
the duke embraces and leads her oute loud musique and shouts

wthin ". In Act II Cleophon consults a couple of sorceresses. " Enter Cleophon As in a Groue looking aboute on the site of it a Caue discourd." The hags summon two spirits in white like nymphs who give disappointing answers. " witches stampe and Spirits descend ". Other spirits appear from the air, announce that " Cleophon shall be prince of Tuscany ", and " ascend in the scene " (i.e. on the further side of the proscenium arch). Act III is almost entirely taken up with an elaborate Masque of Envy, Detraction, Ambition, Lechery, Chastity, Flattery, Avarice, Virtue, performed before the Duke and Duchess. In Act IV there is a scene between Statenor who is passionately in love with Merantha, and Floradine (Erasila), who in her turn dotes upon him. This is very reminiscent of *Philaster*. Floradine is sent by Statenor to plead his suit with Merantha. The Duke has become enamoured of Umira and neglects the Duchess, who studies revenge. She urges Trasilius who is smitten with her beauty to kill Umira. The last scene is a welter of blood, not unlike a tragedy of Tourneur, but lacking Tourneur's great and sombre power. Merantha and Umira are watching by the bier. Trassilius enters disguised and stabs Umira, only to be cut down by Cleophon. Statenor, who has come to prevent the Duke's designs on Merantha, joins Cleophon, and together they drive off the Duke's attendants. The Duke, who is disguised, is slain, whilst Statenor also falls in the fray. Merantha kills herself, when as Statenor breathes his last, Floradine comes trembling in and seeing her lover pale and dying reveals that she is Erasila, and driving a dagger to her heart expires in his arms. This episode is far the best in the play, and is not without pathos and poetry. " The curtayne is Lett fall, Solemn musique a while as it is drawne up agen, the musique ceases, att one dore Enter Cleophon and the dutches at the other the Lords." Then " The Scean Opens discouering Umira, Merantha ; and Erasila, like a woman in white with sparkeling Wreaths or Coronetts upon their heads dead on a Couch : Statenor's head plac't on Erasila's Lap ; at the other side, the scen Trasilius and the duke are Layde ". (This is borrowed from Davenant's *Albovine, King of the Lombards*.) Explanations follow. Isabella is relegated to a convent ; and Cleophon, uttering a eulogy on the Faithful Virgins, is hailed Duke of Tuscany.

The Faithfull Virgins is on the whole a poor play of the William Killigrew type, and being baldly told in outline it probably may appear weaker than it actually is. The most important point it presents is the use of rhyme. It lacks the grandiose rhetoric and vast canvas of the perfect heroic play, but it has all the flowery sentiment and passionate platonism, as well as in the character of

PLATE XIX

ERNEST THESIGER AS MR. SPARKISH

The Country-Wife, February 1924

[face p. 340

the duke an unbridled red-hot eroticism. This character could hardly have been very agreeable to the court.

The date of *The Lovers Stratagem or Virtue Rewarded,*[13] an unprinted play, is uncertain. The Persons Represented are : Seignior Gilberto a Rich Roman knight husband to Dianora ; Ansaldo Gradenzee, a Noble Baron in love with Dianora ; Abasto his trusty kinsman & Heir in love with Labona ; Roberto, Brother to Dianora, in love with Bellinda ; Rodolpho a Kinsman & Dependant on Gilberto ; A Magitian of Spain ; Rumbulo, his servant ; Merlyns Ghost ; Dianora yᵉ Chast Wife of Seignior Gilberto ; Labona, her Sister (unmarried) ; Bellinda, Sister to Rodolpho (unmarried) ; Macquerella, an old Servant to Gilberto, made in yᵉ Interest of Ansaldo. The Scene is ye City of Udina in ye Country of ffretelium or fforum Julij [Frioli]. The Time is ye first week of January. The Prologue, spoken by Macquerella, commences :—

> Long has ye Husband here been Ridiculd, ⎫
> Long made a Cuckold, and too often foold, ⎬
> and all because that Vice ye Stage has Rul'd. ⎭
> Can you for once forgive a Modest Play,
> Show it by Gracing of us with your Stay.
> But hold whilst I his Modesty Applaud,
> I quite forgot I am to Day a Baud.
> And talk myself so feelingly of Man,
> That sometimes you'l be forc'd to use your Fan. . . .
> He has this Day a loving Couple drawne,
> Such Counterparts they on each other fawne,
> And tho ye ladie's Driven to Distresse
> She comes off Bravely that you must Confesse,
> In such a Manner scarce was known before
> Just when She was design'd to be a Whore.
> A sort of Thing I cou'd not wel passe by,
> And looks as if ye Story was a ly.
> But true or false 'tis such as Boccace Told . . .

The play, which is well written with occasional scenes in rhyme, has as its theme the famous story which Boccaccio first introduced in his *Filocopo,* and afterwards told as novella 5, giornata x, of the *Decameron.* It is the Frankeleyn's Tale of Chaucer, who, however, did not derive the incidents from the Italian, but, as he himself relates, from some old Breton lay.

In *The Lovers Stratagem or Virtue Rewarded* the novella from the *Decameron* is pretty closely followed, whilst the incidents are handled with considerable ability. Dianora lays upon Ansaldo the command she deems impossible : " in this month this nipping January (nay in this week) Raise me a Garden ful of fragrant floures with Beauty Rivaling ye Pride of May . . . with Greenes and Jessamines of every Sorts." Ansaldo bargains with the Magician. With many mystic ceremonies he summons the Ghost of Merlin, who " rises out of ye Stage ". Merlin promises success, and " on this ye Ghost of Merlyn sinks & a Thick Cloud of Smoke arises to warme ye Air . . . Many Spirits hover about ye Sky : some bring Greens, others flowers, & fix them in ye Ground. Then Dæmons rise & dance . . . After this a Song is sung in parts by ye Spirits and Dæmons. Then a Garden suddainly springs up & all variety of Flowers & Greenes are discovered on wch ye Spirits fly away, ye Dæmons sink and ye Scene closes ". The drama concludes as in the novella. Ansaldo moved at length by Gilberto's generosity and Dianora's spotless chastity honourably returns the lady to her husband, craving but the friendship of so noble a knight. The magician with unheard of liberality cancels Ansaldo's bond of 2,000 ducats, a detail which is also directly from the Italian. A witty Epilogue is spoken by Dianora.

It must remain an open question whether *The Lovers Stratagem* was performed or no. There is no record of its production, but this actually goes for little. There is no indication that it was not given upon the stage, although the script is not a prompt-copy.

Other MS. plays that have survived, of which some may have been acted although many certainly were not, are the Earl of Orrery's *The Tragedy of Zoroastres* [14]; James Wright's version of *Le Malade Imaginaire* [15]; Lady Anne Wharton's *Love's Martyr, or Witt above Crowns,*[16] which tells the story of amorous Ovid's love for Julia, a theme also incidentally employed by Lee in his *Gloriana ; Anna Bullen,* whence John Banks perhaps took a hint for his sentimental *Vertue Betray'd ; Tamerlane the Beneficent,*[17] a tragedy, dated 1692.

Jugurtha or The Fait[h]less Cosen german, a poor tragedy, is preserved in Bodley, Rawl. MSS. poet. 195. Octavia, the daughter of Marius, the Roman general, loves and is beloved by Jugurtha, partner in the kingdom of Numidia with the royal brothers Atherball and Hyempsall, who are both enamoured of Seraphina, Jugentha's sister. The drama reads in sentiment like a very indifferent imitation of Lee's weakest scenes ; the verse hobbles and halts in clouterliest fashion.

Try before you Trust,[18] a prose comedy, has the scene laid in Paris. Among the characters are Emillon, a French gentleman of quality ; Emillia, his wife ; his daughters Justiniana and Florida ; Beau Garçon, a courtier ; Chaumont, a rich fool ; Chambrière, the inevitable waiting-maid ; Fripon, Emillia's page. This mediocre piece bears all signs of having been penned *circa* 1695–8.

The Cure of Pride, or, Every one in their Way,[19] an adaptation from Massinger's *The City Madam*, was probably written between 1670 and 1680. *The Faithfull Genius*,[20] an indifferent tragi-comedy, which has many rhyming passages in the style of the heroic drama seemingly belongs to the same decade.

Love's Metamorphosis, or The Disguis'd Lovers [21] is a rococo comedy which may be dated about 1680. The scene is " Sicil ", and the plot turns upon the struggles between the King of Sicil and the King of Thrace. The Duke of Florence also appears. The atmosphere of this brocaded play can be sufficiently gathered from the dramatis personae amongst whom are the two sons of the King of Thrace, Alander and Arnado, who respectively love Amsidea and Juliana, the daughters of the King of Sicil. Phylautus, the son of the King of Sicil, is " knowne by yᵉ name of Lorenzo and sometime Humerozo ". He is enamoured of the daughter to the Duke of Florence, Evadne, who is disguised as a page to Alander. Palerno, a Spanish prince, exhibits himself as " lustfully in love with Juliana ". Cleon and Philon are " two merry gentlemen " ; Zamanthus lends a pastoral touch as a shepherd. Varia, who was originally called Lady Ficklefaire, is Cleon's mistress. There is also a young girl, her sister. Waiting-women ; an Ambassador from Thrace ; Masquers and Attendants ; complete the complement of a pretty motley cast. The intrigue which is complicated enough is further reticulated by the use of disguises, the ultimate discovery of which leads to the felicitous finale :—

> While all hearts sing, Vertue's reward is blisse,
> And joy concludes Love's Metamorphosis.

A few chansons occur : " Now I am free as a bird in the aire " ; " I lately lov'd a lady bright " ; " Within this shady silent grove " ; and a rollicking chorus, "Away with the women and give us some wine." Towards the end of the comedy is introduced a Masque, but a marginal note tells us " if ye play be too long " it may be omitted. The original MS., 91 pages, folio, is inscribed " Nar. Luttrell, his Book, 1682."

Brittannicus or the Man of Honour,[22] " a Comedy. Written in ye year 1695," is a manuscript of nineteen pages. The dedication " To my worthy friend Erasmus Earl of Heydon in ye County of Norff. Esq." is signed E. D'Oyley, who modestly informs his friend : " I need not tell you 'tis ye first Essay I ever made in this nature : that I feare will be too obvious but if it may find you a little diversion in a leisure houre I have all I aime at or covet." Two Songs occur in this play which is duly equipped with a Prologue. Act II, scene 2, presents a room in a Tavern, where Drinkwell and Reveller, two boon companions, are met over a glass of wine.

There is an amusing MS. comedy, which has no name, but which I will call *Mr. Doolittle* from the principal character, and which may be dated 1681-2. The persons are : Old Lovewell, an impotent keeper who has settled part of his estate on his Miss, and seeks to retrieve his fortunes ; Young Lovewell, his nephew, a brisk gentleman in love with Lucia ; Truboy, an ingenious loyall gentleman, amorous of Mrs. Shorter, after in love with Clarinda ; Wildman, a Leud young gentleman of spent fortunes that Lusts after every fine woman he sees ; Doolittle, a presbiterean preacher, stallion to his congregation, a busie seditious fellow, and that writes whiggish pamphlets, proud, leacherous, & revengfull ; Lady Bumbol, one of Doolittle's followers, old & leacherous ; Shorter, her granddaughter, loves Truboy, and drawn in by her grandmother to consent to him, afterward neglected by him ; Rachell Bumbol, an impertinent zealous rich old maid, would fain marry Doolittle, but being slighted by him marries Wildman ; Clarinda, Lucia, two gentle young women in love with Trueboy & Young Lovewell ; Mrs. Trickett, kept by Old Lovewell, proud, leacherous, ungratefull ; Phillis, Lady Bumbol's woman ; Bettie, Clarinda's maid. Scene, London.

If rather coarse, the piece is often very funny, and might indeed have been written by a Tory Shadwell. Act the first commences with " Truboy in his morning gown as just up ", since he only came from the country the day before, and his friends " would have carried me to Mother Creswell's to dispose amongst her damsels—how I loath those creatures ". Young Lovewell is betrothed to Lucia, a fortune of £5,000, left ward to Doolittle, without whose consent she must not marry. Suffice to say that in spite of various crosses, mainly due to the lies and mischief of the jealous Trickett, the two young gallants wed their respective mistresses. Old Lady Bumbol is amusing : "Aloisia comes short of her—she has added 18 of her own invention to make Aretine's 50." Doolittle owes something to Mr. Scruple in *The Cheats,* and is drawn with rougher strokes. When My Lady espies him coming out of no very well reputed house he defends himself : " one may get a great deal of good from a bad place & on the other side one may be in a very good & holy place yett think & doe as ill as if we were in a bawdy House, nay, I know it." In love affairs he betrays *des gouts italiens,* as the modish slang went, a sharp bob at Titus Oates. Young Lovewell is not safe for him. When it is suggested that Wildman shall become an independent preacher under Doolittle, a very lively but not very decent picture is drawn of the duties he will be required to undertake. Doolittle is an author: "I have heard there is a young woman of a very good fortune in love with my brother Baxter. How is my shove to the heavy arst Xtian—that will be ready in a week. Bayl never wrote anything half so well in his life." Stoutly he maintains the primitive evangel: "Do we not call Peter Peter, & Paul Paul without any addition; yes we doe; the Baptists call them St. Peter & St. Paul, we abhor all popish customs, but they who are pure & without generation ought to give them some extraordinary title, but we considering our nearer familiarity with them may call them plain Peter & plain Paul." Even if there is a distinct echo of Scruple, his casuistry on tithes is amusing. "Let me see, tithes, whether or no they are lawfull. No, certainly they are not, to force a man to pay tithes is popish & illegal. Yet this farr they are lawfull, if one of the wicked will of his own free will, give me tithes I may take them: yet not as tithes, but as part of the spoyles of the ungodly." [23]

It may not be improper here to consider a play, which although written many years before, was not printed until after the Restoration, *The Benefice* by Robert Wild, D.D. (1609–1679), a dissenting minister who distinguished himself by bad poetry and effervescent loyalty. Of this comedy there is preserved an imperfect MS. copy[24] comprising eleven quarto leaves of a larger size. This commences with "Act 3. Scen. 4. Enter Sr Homily", and concludes " Ceres after the Epilogue speaks " eight lines. "ffinis actus Q^{ti}/Robert Wild." A few slight alterations seem to have been made in the script by the author, and these corrections are incorporated in the printed text. The play was obviously not intended for production. In 1689 the piece was printed, 4to, and the address to the Reader commences: "'*Tis now several Years, since these Papers, of the most Ingenious Dr*. R. Wild'*s first fell into my Hands*." The title-page has " The Benefice. A Comedy. By *R. W*. D.D. Author of Iter Boreale.[25] Written in his Younger Days; Now made Publick for promoting Innocent Mirth ".

The Dramatic Personae are: Invention; Furor Poeticus, An Humorous Poet; Pedanto A School-Master; Comædia, a Girl; Ceres, The Goddess of Harvest; Marchurch, the Patron of a Living; Ursley, His Kitchin Wench; Mar-Pudding, A Cotquean, newphew to Marchurch; Book-Worm, a young Divine; Sir Homily, an old Curat; Hob-Nail, Marchurch's Hind-Servant; Phantastes, A man Scholar, newly come from the University; Goodman Scuttle, a New-English Basket-Maker; Two Watchmen; A School-Boy; Tinker, and a Gypsie his Wife. *Scena profingentis arbitrio*.

The First Act is merely an Induction. Invention and Furor Poeticus criticize Plautus, Ben Jonson, Shakespeare, Beaumont and Fletcher, and Randolph. Ceres speaks from above, but presently consents to have her temple, a barn, turned into a playhouse, when she even delivers the Prologue. The whole design of the piece is that Marchurch who is Patron of the Benefice will not dispose of it to anyone who does not pay him well. Hob disguises himself as a parson, and Marchurch who has got the kitchen-wench Ursley with child in hopes of marrying his convenient to the new vicar, sells the yokel the living. " Let him be Pulpit-Monger, Desk-Thumper, and Sermon-Braker . . . I care not," he chuckles to himself. In the end Sir Homily secures the presentation by a trick.

Some speeches are amusing enough of themselves, but the intended satire is very feeble. It is, moreover, largely derived from Peter Hausted's *The Rivall Friends,* a comedy printed 4to, 1632, "As it was Acted before the King and Queens Maiesties, when out of their princely favour they were pleased to visite their Universitie of *Cambridge,* upon the 19 day of *March,* 1631." In this play Sacriledge Hooke, a Simonicall Patrone, has a supposed daughter Mistris Ursely, " deformed and foolish." There appear half a dozen " Suiters to Mistris *Ursely* for the Parsonage sake ", a method of procedure which, as Genest notes, is termed smock-simony. Wild has also taken something more than a suggestion from *The Returne from Parnassus ; or, The Scourge of Simony,* a college drama in two parts which were acted at S. John's, Cambridge in 1601–2 and 1602 respectively, and in which Furor Poeticus is a character.

The Poor Scholar, a Comedy, printed 4to, 1662, was probably "Written by *Robert Nevile,* Fellow of Kings Colledge in Cambridge" during the preceding year. Act I, scene 4, Aphobos upon the arrival of Anaiskuntia jeeringly says to the two scholars in tattered gowns :—

> Faith here she comes, now you Rogues quake
> And run like *London* Train-bands when the
> Phanaticks were in armes.

This allusion and a couplet in the Prologue refer to the riots organized by Venner and his Fifth-Monarchy men in London during January, 1661.[26] The Dramatis Personae of *The Poor Scholar* are : Eugenes Senior, Unckle to Eugenes Junior, and President of the Colledge, a very passionate man, although a Clergyman ; Eugenes Junior, the Poor Scholar ; His Father, a Citizen ; Demosthenes, Tutour to Eugenes Junior ; Pege, a young student, Chamber-fellow to Eugenes Junior, a woman-hater ; Philos, a friend of Eugenes Senior, and one that discover'd his nephew's rambles to him, a Fellow of the same Colledge ; Aphobos, a mad Raskel, afterwards married to Anaiskuntia ; Eutrapelus, a quibbling fellow of Eugenes Junior's acquaintance ; Morphe, a beautiful Lady, but of a low fortune, to whom Eugenes Junior was a servant ; Anaiskuntia, her Maid, an impudent scoffing Lass, to whom Aphobos was a servant ; Eugeneia, sister to Eugenes Junior, and courted by Eutrapelus ; Uperephania, her maid, a proud wench, and a great hater of men ; Two Schollars ; Three Fellows of the Colledge.

The chief merits of this comedy and these are not inconsiderable consist in the dialogue, which is often very good, as also in the drawing of the characters who are nicely discriminated and portrayed with apt vigorous strokes. The incidents are few, and the plot actually is rather thin, but the many allusions to Cambridge customs and University life prove extremely interesting,[27] whilst it is certain that Eugenes Senior could be matched twenty times over at Oxford (and I doubt not at Cambridge too) even to-day.

Eugenes Senior, who is President of a College at Cambridge, is very severe upon his nephew, Eugenes Junior, the Poor Scholar. More than once the uncle complains of young Eugenes to his father, when they discuss the lad's immediate expulsion. The President is especially angry upon the discovery that his nephew has " commenc'd an acquaintance with that beggarly gentlewoman call'd *Morphe,* who though she has a little skin deep beauty, yet shee's desperately poor and indigent ". Eugenes Junior even weeps at the jobation he receives, and his tears flow faster when his tutor joins in with " Is this a fit qualification for a student in *Philosophy,* to be a visitant of wenches ? " The President at last locks his nephew up in his chamber to reclaim him from his lewd courses. Nevertheless Eugenes Junior files through a bar and escapes to Morphe. They disguise themselves as country-folk, Philip Lovelass and Mary Allcock, in which rustic rôles they present themselves to Eugenes Senior and request him to exercise his reverend office by uniting them in matrimony. He forthwith performs the ceremony in the College chapel, and when they reveal who they are the father of Eugenes Junior promptly announces "And as for you, *Eugenes,* because you have contriv'd your Plot so well, I declare you my sole Heir : I'le not vex my self in vain."

The Poor Scholar is duly furnished with a Prologue and an Epilogue, but I imagine that it is more than doubtful whether it would have been given to a London audience. The humour is entirely that of the University, and upon the general public this would soon be bound to pall. Nor can I think that scenes so satirical were tolerated in the presentation at Cambridge or Oxford. Langbaine merely remarks of *The Poor Scholar,* " I know not whether ever it was acted."

In some respects not entirely dissimilar is *The Academie; or, The Cambridge Dunns* by Joshua Barnes (1654–1712), a comedy acted by undergraduates at Cambridge in 1675 and 1676. There are preserved in the library of Emmanuel College, Cambridge, two MS. copies of this play, which was not printed. The first copy supplies the names of the undergraduates who played. These do not appear in the second copy which is slightly abbreviated. The same author also wrote *Englebert,* a piece in rhyme, part tragedy, part opera. This was acted at Cambridge. His also is *Landgartha; or, The Amazon Queen of Denmark and Norway,* which he completed on 29th May, 1683, this entertainment being designed for the nuptials of Prince George of Denmark and the Princess Anne. The play has some historical foundation. Neither *Englebert* nor *Landgartha* were printed, the manuscripts being preserved at Emmanuel College.

Of Thomas Forde the author of *Love's Labyrinth* little is known save what may be gathered from his printed works, notably his *Fœnestra in Pectore* (1668), a collection of one hundred and two " familiar letters " addressed to friends. Born in 1613–15, he was in 1647 residing in London, and a MS. note in the British Museum copy of *The Times Anatomized* describes the author as " T. Ford servant to Mr. Sam Man ", the well-known bookseller who had a shop in S. Paul's Church-yard (1616–1674). Although " something related " to John Udall, the notorious Puritan, Forde was himself a staunch Royalist. For a time after the murder of King Charles I he was living " near Maldon " in Essex, and at some date he took Anglican Orders. In addition to his known works, there can be no doubt that he was the author of a good many pamphlets which are unidentified. In 1660 he published *Virtus Rediviva, A Panegyrick on our Late King Charles the I Second Monarch Of Great Britain.* This and other pieces, including " *Love's Labyrinth; Or, The Royal Shepherdess: A Tragi-Comedie:* By Tho. Forde, *Philothal:* ... London, 1660 ", were collected in one volume, 8vo, with a general title-page *A Theatre of Wits,* London, 1661. The year of Forde's death is unknown.

Love's Labyrinth; or, The Royal Shepherdess, is a dramatization of Greene's popular *Menaphon,* 1589, and is certainly intended as a poetical exercise, a closet drama. The scene lies in Arcadia, of which land the King, Damocles, in an access of cruel

" sublimated rage " has set adrift in a small boat sans sail or rudder to perish at sea his daughter, Sephestia ; her husband, Maximus Prince of Cyprus ; and their child.

Maximus is cast upon the Arcadian shore, whilst Sephestia and her babe are reported to have been drowned. Calling himself Melicertus the unhappy prince, " clad in sorrows weeds," resolves to pass his days as a humble shepherd. Sephestia, however, has been saved, and appears as the shepherdess Samela, with whom Melicertus falls in love, deeming her " the living picture of my dear, My dear Sephestia ". There are many accidents and cross accidents which involve King Damocles who, disguised as an Old Shepherd, visits the hamlet where Samela dwells to view the lovely shepherdess. The last scene is the Arcadian court and all difficulties are resolved by a general anagnorisis. It is further discovered that Plusidippas who has been brought up by King Agenor of Thrace and who weds the Princess Euriphyla is none other than the son of Maximus and Sephestia. He was rescued, a mere babe, by pirates and by them presented to the Thracian monarch.

Langbaine remarked of *Love's Labyrinth,* " part of this Play is stollen from *Gomersal's* Tragedy of *Sforza,* Duke of *Millain,*" [28] a somewhat ambiguous charge, which means no more than that Forde has taken twenty odd lines of dialogue from the older drama and with some variation inserted them in his pastoral, Act I, scene 5.

Love's Labyrinth was never acted, but even less fitted for the regular stage is Anthony Sadler's " Divine Masque " *The Subjects Joy For The Kings Restoration,* 4to, 1660, which includes "6 *Shewes.* 10 *Speeches.* 3 *Songs* ". Among the Persons are : Psyche ; King David ; King Abijah ; His Queen-Mother ; Two Dukes, his Brothers ; The High Priest ; The Lord General ; The Prophet Shemaiah. In this " new-mysterious masque " the allegory is very extraordinary, very biblical, and very loyal. In the last Show Oliver Cromwell is presented as " Jereboam, *in a Chair of State : Hell, under him ; the Devil, behind him : and King* Abijah *in a Throne above him* ". The frontispiece is curious, showing Cromwell, over whose head is inscribed *Jereboam,* and a hideous demon, who hold a wheel of fortune, surmounted by a crown, betwixt them.

Anthony Sadler who was born at Chitterne S. Mary, Wilts, in 1610, was according to à Wood " a man of a rambling head and turbulent spirit ", but his eccentricities have probably been much exaggerated. Certain it is he suffered for his loyalty during the Commonwealth. He proceeded B.A. on 22nd March, 1632, from S. Edmund's Hall, Oxford, and was ordained by Dr. Corbet,

Bishop of Oxford.   He was first beneficed at Bishopstoke, Hants. In May, 1654, the triers refused to allow him to occupy when Lettice, Lady Paget, presented him to the rectory of Compton Abbas, Dorset.   At the Restoration he was presented to Mitcham, Surrey, but here and in a subsequent living, Berwick S. James, Wilts, his tenures were brief and unhappy.   He died about 1685.

It may not be out of place here briefly to make mention of two more plays which were never acted, and almost certainly not intended for the English stage.

Following his imprisonment after the battle of Worcester, 3rd September, 1651, Sir Richard Fanshawe (1608–1666), the diplomatist and poet,[29] was afforded an asylum by Lord Strafford at Tankersley Park, Yorkshire, where he resided from March, 1653, to the summer of 1654, being forbidden by the Parliament to go more than 5 miles from the house.   He occupied his time in a translation or rather a paraphrase of Antonio Hurtado de Mendoza's *Querer Por Solo Querer,* which as *To Love only for Love Sake* was published 8vo, 1671.

Mendoza, who was born about 1590 and died in 1644, enjoyed great favour with King Philip IV.   He was a Commander of Calatrava, Secretary of State, and a member of the Tribunal of the Holy Office.[30]   *La fiesta que se hizo en Aranjuez a los anos del Rey nuestro senor D. Felipe IV con la comedia de Querer por solo Querer* was published 4to, Madrid, 1623.

To Love only for Love Sake might be described as an immensely long play, but it is rather a romance of chivalry in dialogue comprising three acts.   The characters are Zelidaura, Queen of Tartaria; Claridiana, Queen of Arabia; Felisbravo, Young King of Persia;   Prince Claridoro;   Prince Florantes;   the Captive Prince; the General; Roselinda, attending Zelidaura; Florinda, attending Claridiana;   Two Gyants;   and Rifaloro, the Droll or gracioso. The play opens with drums and trumpets, and the whole thing is as cumbrous and as stately as the Plumes and fardingales the Queens of Arabia and Tartaria wore upon the stage. An Inchanted Castle, whence " *let there sally out of the mouth of a Serpent a black Gyant armed with a Club, and spitting fire* ", looms largely in Act I. There is glamour galore, and at the end of the first act let " *the whole vanish in a trice* ".   In Act II Cupid, a Gentleman, Claridoro's servant, and a Citizen join the Dramatis Personae who are further augmented in the third act by Mars, Aurelio, a Captain, and others. Felisbravo is torn by conflicting emotions :—

> Love and Honour, pull *two* ways,
>   And I stand doubtful *which* to take :
> To *Arabia, Honour* says,
>   *Love* says, no ; thy stay *here* make.

Eventually Mars appears "*in a Chariot drawn with Lyons*" and when Zelidaura and Claridiana are with rival armies about to contend for Felisbravo, the lord of war cuts the knot by giving the former to Claridoro and the latter to Florantes. Felisbravo loves for love's sake alone, and remains the idealistic platonist complete.

To Love only for Love Sake in spite of its baroque embroideries contains some fine writing, and the sentiment if too exalted cannot but be admired. Dramatic, in the English sense, it is not. By contemporaries it was much esteemed, and not altogether without reason ; for many manuscript copies circulated before it was issued from the press. Thus it was parodied in *The Rehearsal,* ii, 2, where Mr. Bayes says : " now Prince Pretty-man comes in, and falls a sleep, making love to his Mistress, which, you know, was a grand Intrigue in a late Play, written by a very honest Gentleman : a Knight." This burlesques the incident when Felisbravo retiring into a wood to shun the noon-tide heat and taking out the picture of Zelidaura falls asleep under a tree as he is apostrophizing his mistress. Risaloro, his squire, like a trusty henchman does not neglect to follow so good an example. Felisbravo's dilemma between Love and Honour is also jeered in Buckingham's farce, iii, 5.

In the *Oeuvres Meslees* of Saint-Évremond, A Londres, Chez Jacob Tonson, three volumes, 1709, is printed [31] *Sir Politick Would-Be,* " Comedie à la manière des Anglais." The scene is Venice and the principal characters are : Sir Politick Would-Be, Chevalier Anglois, Politique ridicule ; M. de Riche-Source, Homme d'Affaires François, Chimérique en Projets ; La Femme de Sir Politick, grave & sottement capable ; Mde de Riche Source, Coquette & Bourgeoise. Un Voyageur allemand, exact & régulier, qui voit jusqu'aux dernieres Epitaphes des Villes ; Mylord Tancrède, homme d'esprit, qui connoît le ridicule de tous les autres ; Une Entremetteuse faisant la Dogaresse, & ses Demoiselles faisant les Femmes des Senateurs ; Dominico, Venetien Mistérieux, faisant l'Espion ; Le Signor Antonio, Diseur de Concetti, ami de Tancrède ; Agostino, faux Caton & ridiculement grave, Quatre Senateurs ; et Un Huissier. La Scène est à Venise.

The comedy is in the regulation five acts, and as its very name betrays was suggested by the underplot of *Volpone.* It must not, however, be mentioned in the same breath as that immortal masterpiece. The characters are merely a collection of etiolated Jonsonian humours linked together by the thinnest filament. There are perhaps some brisk passages although these are few and brief enough, for the various scenes hang heavy on the meagre skein of plot, if plot it may be called. Sir Politick Would-Be and Mr. de Riche-Source, two noble politicians, are overheard discussing their silly scraps by Dominico, a grison of the State. He catches a phrase here and there of their solemn nonsense—" Secret, République, Doge "—and informs Agostino a silly senator of much self-importance, who scents a black conspiracy. Agostino himself contrives to listen to some of the chatter of these busy twattling fantasts, whence he conceives them to be in the highest degree dangerous to the State. Sir Politick and his Lady give a splendid entertainment to which are invited the Dogaressa and a number of Senators' wives, persons of the first quality. By the contrivance of Tancrède and Antonio a pursy old procuress and her flight of bona-robas appear as the Serene Duchess and the most noble Venetian ladies. During the ball Sir Politick and Mr. de Riche-Source are carried off by the saffi and brought up before a court of senators, in which presence Sir Politick cannot help proudly declaring himself a follower of Nicolas Machiavil and Mons. Jean Bodin. Lord Tancrède privately interviews the Senators and assures them that this precious couple are harmless cranks, a fact already pretty clear to the magistracy, whereupon the gentlemen are dismissed with laughter, although the foolish Agostino still persists that they may be cunning conspirators who ought to be hanged rather than let go scot-free. Thereupon Sir Politick and his lady, M. de Riche-Source and his wife, agree that Venice is not worthy of them; " Venise n'est pas digne de nous posseder," remarks the knight with the utmost self-complacency and off they wag to other scenes of adventure.

Among the earliest original plays produced at the Restoration was *The Life of Mother Shipton*.[32] A New Comedy. Written by T[homas] T[hompson]. It is said to have been "Acted Nineteen dayes together with great Applause ". The question arises, where was it performed? That the actors were George Jolly's troupe is clear, and accordingly the house would be either the Cockpit or Salisbury Court both of which theatres were used by this company.

The Scenes are The City of York and Nazeborough Grove in Yorkshire. The chief characters are : Pluto, King of Hell ; Radamon, a spirit ; The Abbot of Beverley ; Hairbrain, a wild gallant ; his companion, Swagger ; a Captain ; Mr. Shiftwell, a pander ; Mrs. Shiftwell, his wife, and his sister, Maria ; Mr. Moneylack, his companion ; Mr. Scrape, a userer ; Prue, a bawd ; Priscilla, a whore, and two other Whores ; Sir Oliver Whorehound, an old letcher ; his wife, called Mrs. Lovefree ;

Mother Shipton ; and her maid, Abigail. The play opens with young Mother Shipton, who is yet in her 'teens, melancholy, bewailing by the river's side her lot of misery and indigence. As she soliloquizes, Radamon enters as a rich cavalier, and promises her wealth, honour, and power. She consents to wed him, the marriage banquet follows, after which he reveals his secret : " Now I am thy Husband and thou art my Wife, yet know I am no mortal ! I am a Devil ! these my attendants Devils too !" The lady is not unnaturally a little disturbed : " How married to an Immaterial Spirit, this startles me," she exclaims ; yet she resolves to go through stitch with it. The old chap-book episodes of Mother Shipton's career are somewhat crudely shown, and during the progress of the play she becomes aged and deformed as *de rigeur*. Thus the Abbot of Beverley disguised as a layman visits her, and she instantly penetrates his masquerade, prophesying to him the dissolution of the monasteries. He presents her nevertheless with a Holy Relic, which foils the infernal spirits when they come to carry her away. " Pluto with other devils with rakes enters." They are baffled, and Radamon yells : " Too sure she is sheilded [*sic*] by these powers above, to which ours are impotent ! " Nevertheless Radamon bribes Abigail with a heavy purse to steal the jewel from Mother Shipton's neck when she is asleep. Mother Shipton discovers the treachery, and Abigail humbly confesses. The purse is found to contain no coins but " all stones and dirt ". Angels descend and comfort the wise woman,

In thy sorrows be not drown'd
From above thou hast mercy found :
Think not repentance comes too late
If 'tis unfeigned thou art fortunate !
And though the Devil does endeavour
To entrap thy sinful soul, yet never
Yield, but his attempt resist,
And he his suit will soon desist.

Actually Pluto and all the Devils make a final appearance, but only to confess that they have no further hold upon her now. With " horrid musick " they vanish, and Mother Shipton philosophically comments : " So let them roare."

Whilst I do all their Hellish Acts despise
The higher powers make me truly wise.

It is indeed " homely chear ", as the Epilogue avows, very " homely chear ". These scenes of *The Life of Mother Shipton* [33] which do not directly concern the sibyl herself are a curious amalgam of episodes from Middleton's *A Chaste Maid in Cheap-side* and Massinger's *The City Madam* very roughly welded together, and having no connexion with Mother Shipton herself save that in Act IV, scene 3, she is consulted by Hairbrain.

Thomas Thompson's second play to be printed was actually the first written and the first to be performed if we may accept the statements in the Prologue. A new Comedy called *The English Rogue* was issued 4to, 1668, "As it was acted before several Persons of Honour with great Applause." It is dedicated to Mrs. Alice Barret. The scene is laid in Venice. The English Rogue is Plot-thrift, who with Ben Cozen his companion, weaves and successfully carries out a good deal of not very adroit knavery.

There are also some sentimental or serious scenes, written for the greater part in rhyme, which intermingle with the sleights of Plot-thrift and Cozen. Erminia, contracted to Eusames, a young decayed gentleman, is wooed by Gonzetto, a great lord, who involves the faithful pair in various jealousies and mis-fortunes, but the end salves all. The Epilogue, spoken of the English Rogue, is curious. Plot-thrift asks the audience :—

> *Joyn all your forces now and set me free,*
> *One score of Claps and I'm at liberty.* (*Clap.*)

At the conclusion we have " (Clap agen) ". These extraordinary stage-directions for the audience are jeered in *The Rehearsal* when Mr. Bayes contrives his first Prologue, that he shall enter with a great Huge Hang-man behind flourishing a mighty sword, and then he will tell the audience plainly " That if, out of good nature, they will not like my Play, I gad, I'l e'en kneel down, and he shall cut my head off. Whereupon they all clapping—a—" " I, But suppose they don't," queries Smith. Extremely mortified, Bayes can but retort : " Suppose ! Sir, you may suppose what you please, I have nothing to do with your suppose, Sir ; Suppose quotha !—ha, ha, ha."

The English Rogue is at best an awkward piece, and was obviously written for a primitive arras stage. Thus we have " *Exeunt. Enter presently agen in a Tavern with a drawer*", iii, 2. In v, 1, the mock footpads are on the stage ; " *Enter* Plottthrift *with a bag and* Avaritius. They exchange a speech or two, and " *They walk off the Stage and on agen, and they seize on them*". In many respects both Thompson's plays seem more like the scenario of a comedy than the full script, and I conceive that these scenes must have been amply farsed with improvisation and gag.

Rather more skilfully contrived is *The Polititian Cheated*, "A New Comedy," 4to, 1663, by Alexander Greene, of whom nothing is known. This piece was duly equipped with Prologue

and Epilogue, and there seems no adequate reason to suppose
it had not been performed. As Malone remarks in a MS. note
in his copy : " It was, says the author of the *Playhouse Dictionary*,
never acted. Langbaine only says ' *he knows not* whether it ever
appeared on the Stage '." *The Polititian Cheated* is thoroughly
Plautine in design and intrigue *via* Ariosto and the Italian comedy.
Melampus, a Pandar ; Laurinda, his wife, a bawd ; are the
leno and lena of Roman tradition, whence also is derived
their servant Frisco, who reminds one of Boult in *Pericles*.
Signior Gormondino Belbedero, a Captain, though but the
merest *esquisse,* is Il Capitano of the Commedia dell'Arte, Spezza-
ferro, Matamoros, Coccodrillo, Bonbardon—he has a score of
huge bombast names. " I wonder no man dare challenge me,
but who dares lift up a finger against *Signior Gormondino Belbedero ;*
the very names enough to strike them dead," boasts Gormondino;
v, 1. Monsieur Michael, a *French* Merchant, is yet another stock
type. He is Lycus in the *Pœnulus* ; Dordalus in the *Persa* ; Labrax
in the *Rudens* ; Dorio in the *Phormio* ; Lucramo in *La Cassaria ;*
and a score of variants beside.

Beyond those already mentioned other characters in *The
Polititian Cheated* are Hillario, a Merry Old man ; his son
Lysander ; Ananias, a Precisian ; Thersames, his son ; Joculo,
his nephew ; Astutio the Politician ; Jeronimo, his brother ;
Leonora, daughter to Ananias (but unknown), servant to
Laurinda ; Silentio " *aliàs* Eudora *aliàs* Euthusa, Servant to
Thersames and Daughter to Hillario ". It is hardly necessary
to unravel the complicated incidents which are exactly modelled
on stock lines. Old Ananias loves Leonora and wishes to purchase
her of the bawd. Lysander disguises himself as an Ethiop, and
is bought by Laurinda for Hillario. Leonora, however, soots
her face and hands, and escapes in man's attire as the negro.
Monsieur Michael next appears with a real black-a-moor, and
there is a deal of counter and cross-countering. Eventually
Thusames weds Euthusa ; and Lysander, Leonora. Astutio,
for all his wiles and sharp practice is exposed, and after
a broadly farcical scene of a mock-hanging, pardoned.

The chief interest in the play is the conveyance of Commedia
dell'Arte plots and characters, albeit the assimilation as yet is
not very adroitly managed.

Altogether a better and far more important play is *Flora's
Vagaries,* a comedy by Richard Rhodes, which even if not
printed until 1670, must have been acted in London in the
early spring of 1663 since Theophilus Bird, who played Prospero,
was dead by 28th April of that year.

Wood [35] tells us that Rhodes was a gentleman's son of London who was educated at Westminster School. He matriculated at Christ Church, Oxford, 31st July, 1658, and proceeded B.A. 22nd March, 1661–2. In Oxford he enjoyed the reputation of an accomplished musician. He does not seem to have advanced to his M.A., but travelled in France and took a degree in physic at Montpellier. He spent some time also in Spain, where he died and was buried at Madrid in 1668.

Wood further mentions that *Flora's Vagaries* was "publicly acted by the students of Ch. Ch. in their common refectory on the 8th of January, 1663". A few weeks after it was produced in London at the Theatre Royal, Vere Street. The actors' names given in the 4to, 1670, cannot be in every respect the cast as it was then performed, since Nell Gwyn is set down for Flora, and she had not as yet appeared on the stage. It is curious to find "Floras Figarys" recorded by Herbert on 3rd November, 1663,[36] so one can only suppose that the earlier presentations escaped notice.

The 1670 4to of *Flora's Vagaries* has the following cast: Alberto, lover to Flora, Mohun; Lodovico, his friend, Beeston; Prospero, Friend to Alberto and Lodovico, Bird; Grimani, a rich old senator, Father to Otrante and Uncle to Flora, Cartwright; Francisco, Lover of Otrante, Burt; A Fryer, Loveday; Otrante, in love with Lodovico, Mrs. Knepp; Flora, in love with Alberto, Nell Gwyn. The scene lies in Verona. The language is easy and often witty; the intrigue, if intertwined, is interesting and direct. Francisco, who has obtained a false key to Otrante's garden, engages Lodovico to assist in abducting her, a business which he alleges is to be carried out at her own wish. When it proves, however, that the lady loathes Francisco and calls out pretty loudly for help Lodovico rescues her. In revenge Francisco bribes two ruffians, Pietro and Pesauro, to murder him. Otrante, who has fallen in love with Lodovico, adroitly conveys messages to him by Fra Dominico who is quite unconscious of acting as a go-between. In conclusion Alberto and Lodovico run off with Flora and Otrante, and the two couples are married. Francisco, who is severely wounded, confesses his villanies expressing meet repentance. This is an excellent comedy, and particularly good are the scenes where old Grimani is plagued by Otrante and the sprightly Flora. Thus in Act III when he disguises himself as a friar to learn their secrets, they at once smoke the trick and Otrante confides in him how barbarous a domestic tyrant is her father, whom Flora jeers as "old and peevish, covetous and jealous . . . full of filthy humours, he's as nasty too as his own Closet".

Flora's Vagaries long remained a favourite play and there

can be no doubt that the performance of Nell Gwyn as Flora had much to do with its popularity. It was seen on 8th August, 1664, by Pepys, who remarks " by the most ingenuous performance of the young jade Flora, it seemed as pretty a pleasant play as ever I saw in my life ".[37]

On 26th July, 1715, *Flora's Vagaries* was revived at Drury Lane, as " Not acted 6 years ". No cast is recorded.

Otrante's device to let Lodovico know of her affection by means of the unsuspecting Fra Dominico is borrowed from the *Decameron,* giornata iii, novella 3. The rubric runs : " Sotto spezie di confessione e di purissima conscienza una donna innamorata d'un giovane induce un solenne frate, senza avvedersene egli, a dar modo che'l piacer di lei avesse intero effetto." [38] Grimani's attempt to discover the secrets of his daughter and his niece by masquerading in a religious habit seems suggested by the old fabliau " Du chevalier qui fist sa femme confesser ".[39]

It was perhaps this fabliau which suggested an episode (Chapter 46) in G. W. M. Reynolds' powerful romance, *Agnes ; or, Beauty and Pleasure,* when at Naples the Count of Camerino through bitter jealousy and too truly suspecting that his second wife, a lovely girl whom he has but recently married, may have already proved unfaithful, disguises himself as a Dominican friar, Father Falconara, and in the Chapel of the Magdalen sacrilegiously hears her confession only to learn that she has committed incest and adultery with Viscount Silvio Camerino—" the young wife had been guilty with the youthful son of her own husband ! " Such a masquerade was not unknown. In 1796 Joseph Herranz was prosecuted by the Inquisition of Madrid for disguising himself in a religious habit and cowl, and thus hearing the confession of his wife, who (as he believed) had cuckolded him.

In contrast to *Flora's Vagaries* with its quick sure strokes of vigour and good fun *Love a la Mode,* a comedy, printed 4to, 1663, "As it was lately Acted with great Applause at *Middlesex House* " may seem old-fashioned fare, but it is by no means devoid of merit. The title-page announces it to be " Written by a Person of Honour ",[40] i.e. Thomas Southland, the brother-in-law of Sir Richard Colbrand, who has prefixed a most eulogistic copy of verses to the play.[41] On account of the title Southland's comedy had not unnaturally been taken to be an adaptation of Thomas Corneille's extraordinarily successful *L'Amour à la Mode,* acted at the Hôtel de Bourgogne in 1651 with Floridor as Oronte, and Jodelet Cliton ; 12mo, 1653, but which is itself a version of *El Amor al Uso* of Antonio de Solis, who has drawn upon *El Amante al Uso* of Lope de Vega. *Love a la Mode,* however,

has conveyed nothing from Corneille, and Southland commences his address to the Reader by pointing out that his play
gives no "*just cause to any to believe it a Translation: although
(I must confess) there be a* French *Play which bears this Title; and
in Title onely they resemble* ". The chief characters are Gambugium,
a doctor of Physic, whose jealousy of his wife Clittomestra
causes him to pen her and their daughter Acuta as strictly as
Carthusian nuns with his man Glisterpipe to play Argus.
Glisterpipe keeps a diary of their actions to submit to the doctor,
and there is an amusing scene where the ladies infuse an opiate
in a bowl of cream eagerly licked up by the greedy varlet, and
whilst he snores they make such entries as: "*My Mistress and
her Daughter spent their time in Prayer.*" In Act III, scene 1,
Gambugium appears "*shav'd and powdred, in equipage of a young
Gallant*", and, as Mr. Winal, attempts to seduce his wife. The
lady sees through the absurd masquerade, and retaliates by
calling up Glisterpipe and giving him orders to cut and geld
her new admirer, who is delighted with such a reception. Actually
Ticket, a traveller, and Rant his friend, two belswagger "Lovers
A la Mode" [42] pretend to court Clittomestra and Acuta. The
parallel plot is concerned with the wooing of Coelia, Virginio's
daughter, by Philostratus, who assumes various disguises to
obtain access to his mistress. He appears as a Precisian, and
later when Coelia feigns frenzy as a doctor to cure her.[43] There
are some amusing hits at the Puritans, for Coelia who pretends
to have turned conventicler cants at a great rate. Says her old
father :—

> She'll talk you
> Twelve hours of Predestination, Reformation,
> Sanctification, Tribulation, Reprobation,
> Damnation, and such a spawn of Phanatick
> Words, that in plain *English* I think she's mad.

The plays of Lodowick Carliell are of no small interest and
importance, but as actually only one of these is a post-Restoration
work he may be considered somewhat briefly here.[44] Born in
1602 Carliell came of the fine old Border stock of the Carlyles
of Brydekirk, and leaving his native marches at an early age
to seek advancement at Court he proved so successful in his
ambitions as to rise through several lucrative posts to become
one of the two Royal Keepers of the great Forest at Richmond.
In 1626 he married Joan, the daughter of William Palmer of
S. James's Park. He died in 1675, being in his seventy-second
year.

Langbaine [45] speaks of Carliell as "an Ancient Courtier",
and adds that "His Plays (which are Eight in number) were

well esteem'd of", being acted with great applause. Carliell is indeed a typical court dramatist of the days of Charles I. His first play, *The Deserving Favourite,* was acted at Whitehall in 1629, and although "not designed to travel so far as the common stage" was soon after given at Blackfriars. The plot which turns on Lysander's struggles 'twixt love and duty is derived from a famous Spanish novel *La Duquesa di Mantua* (1629) by Don Alonso del Castillo Solorzano. In 1636 Carliell's two-part play *Arviragus and Philicia* [46] was given both at Court and at Blackfriars, being published 12mo in 1639. It is practically one long ten act heroic-romantic drama exhibiting the idealistic friendship and surprising adventures of Arviragus, Prince of Pictland and Guiderius. The incantation scene in Part II is noteworthy.

The Passionate Lovers, also in two parts, turns on the rivalry of Agenor and Clarimont, the two sons of the King of Burgundy, for the hand of their cousin Clarinda. It is all very fashionable Platonism, as Whitehall was then pleased to understand it.

The Fool would be a Fauorit; or, The Discreet Lover is much in the same vein, although we are glad to meet with the simple Bumpkin's son, Young Gudgen, "The Fauorit that would be."

Rather more succinct in its action than these loose-knit and rambling dramas, but by no means so interesting and agreeable, is *The Famous Tragedy of Osmond The great Turk, otherwise called the Noble Servant,* 8vo, 1657, which has some slight basis in history, the famous legend of Mahomet II and the fair Irene being transferred to Tartary.

The Spartan Ladies, which is mentioned in the MS. *Diary* [47] of Sir Henry Mildmay, as also in the advertisements to Middleton's *More Dissemblers besides Women,* 8vo, 1657, and is further listed as one of the plays which were the monopoly of the Theatre Royal (1669), has not survived.

After the Restoration *The Fool would be a Fauorit* [48] was revived at Lincoln's Inn Fields between 1662 and 1665 ; whilst *Arviragus and Philicia* was revived at the same theatre during the tenancy of Killigrew's company, for which production Dryden furnished a new Prologue.[49]

In 1664 was published 4to, " Heraclius, Emperour Of the East. A Tragedy. Written in French by *Monsieur de Corneille.* Englished by *Lodowick Carlell,* Esq " ; and in the Advertisement prefixed to his work Carliell states that "*Another Translation formerly design'd (after this seem'd to be accepted of) was perfected and acted, this, not returned to me until that very day*". Naturally enough the old poet was deeply mortified at such a slight, and it must be allowed that he expresses his very just vexation in the most moderate and decent terms. What exactly happened is all clear enough, but since by some misunderstanding it has been said that " he makes a most confused and confusing statement in regard to the way in which his tragedy was treated ",[50] it may be well to recount that first Carliell submitted his translation of Corneille's *Héraclius* to Lincoln's Inn Fields. The piece was seemingly accepted and (as he understood) put in rehearsal. On Tuesday, 8th March, 1664, the script was returned to him, and that very day to his amaze another version of Corneille's *Héraclius* was produced at the theatre. The actors had not been satisfied with his work, but realizing the excellence of the French play with incredible duplicity they commissioned another adaptation, and this they staged, meanwhile misleading Carliell and keeping him in complete ignorance of their shabby trick by retaining his MS. until the very day of the rival production. *Heraclius,* the second version from Corneille, was not printed and has not come down to us, but we know from Pepys that it attracted much attention and proved a great success. On Tuesday, 8th March, 1663-4, he was present with his wife at the first performance, which they both had " a mighty mind to see ". He was highly pleased with the production. " The garments like Romans very well. The little girle [51] is come to act very prettily, and spoke the prologue most admirably. But at the beginning at the drawing up of the curtaine, there was the finest scene of the Emperor and his people about him, standing in their fixed and different postures in their Roman habitts, above all that ever I yet saw at any of the theatres."

The anonymous *Heraclius* remained in the repertory for a decade or more. When Pepys saw it a second time on Monday, 4th February, 1666-7, he remarks that to his extraordinary content the house was very full, and that the piece was an " excellent play " with which he was " mightily pleased ".

Carliell's *Heraclius, Emperour of the East,* is written in rhyming couplets, and I fear it is true that, as Genest says, this " translation is not a good one ".[52] Corneille's original, *Héraclius Empereur d'Orient* was produced at the Hôtel de Bourgogne in the first week of January, 1647, and proved very successful although the design was generally criticized as being far too intricate and involved. In his *Examen* Corneille himself goes so far as to admit : " Elle n'a pas laissé de plaire ; mais je crois qu'il l'a fallu voir plus d'une fois pour en remporter une entière intelligence." The play was published, 4to, 1647. The plot is taken from the *Annales ecclesiastici* of the Ven. Cesare Baronio, *anno* 602. It has been much discussed whether Corneille derived some important situations from Calderón's *En esta vida todo es verdad y todo mentira,*[53] and it was once maintained, as by M. Viguier,[54] that the French play appeared first. This has now been shown to be an error due to the fact that no earlier edition of *En esta vida* than 1664 had then been traced. Not only could this of itself prove nothing, but actually there has since been found an issue of *En esta vida* anterior to 1637, and furthermore Calderón's play is quoted in a romance issued in 1641. Corneille, for his dénouement, seems to have taken a hint from Lope de Vega's *Fuenza lastimosa*.

A far more indifferent translation from Corneille than Carliell's *Heraclius* was the anonymous version of *Le Menteur,* which as *The Lyar* was given at Vere Street in 1661. To this there is an interesting allusion in Dryden's *Of Dramatick Poesie* (1668) when Neander (Dryden himself) who has been pretty severely criticizing French comedies says : " *Corneille* himself, their Arch-Poet, what has he produc'd except *The Lier,* and you know how it was cry'd up in *France* ; but when it came upon the English Stage, though well translated, and that part of *Dorant* acted to so much advantage by Mr. *Hart,* as I am confident it never receiv'd in its own Country, the most favourable to it would not put it in competition with many of *Fletchers* or *Ben. Johnsons*." This special pleading is ingenuous, for it can but be acknowledged that *The Lyar* is a very poor version, which misses only too much of Corneille. That *Le Menteur* could be used to better purpose on the English Stage is proved by Steele's *The Lying Lover ; or The Ladies Friendship,* produced at Drury Lane on 2nd December, 1703, and since this may not unjustly be voted no particularly good play, a far livelier example is at hand in Foote's *The Lyar,* 8vo, 1764, produced at Covent Garden 12th January, 1762, with the author in the title-rôle, Young Wilding. Although only given four times during its first season, *The Lyar* met with great success when revived that summer at the Haymarket, and remained in the repertory of the theatre. From time to time alterations, slight or more material, were made, but it has always been received with applause, and was acted at the Royalty Theatre, London, as late as 1896.

The Lyar, a comedy in three acts (1763), is described in the *Biographia Dramatica* as " a catch-penny, intended to be imposed on the public for Mr. Foote's play of the same name ".

Goldoni's *Il Bugiardo,* first produced in Mantua, 23rd May, 1750, is from *Le Menteur* and *La Suite du Menteur*. Romagnesi's *La Feinte inutile* was also drawn on for this lively comedy, the first issue of which is 1753, as it appears in vol. iv of the original Venice edition by Bettinelli.

Le Menteur was, as Corneille acknowledges, suggested by

La Verdad Sospechosa of Juan Ruiz de Alarcon y Mendoza, a play which he first took to be by Lope de Vega Carpio. The anonymous *The Lyar* was published 4to, 1661,[55] but the only edition I know is that of 1685, " Printed for *Simon Neale,* at the three *Pigeons* in *Bedford-street* in *Covent-Garden,* over against the New *Exchange,*" as *The Mistaken Beauty, or The Lyar.* The compositor, no doubt, is largely to blame, yet there can be nothing more distracting than the way somewhat indifferent prose suddenly jinkles and giggits into a lamer sluthery versification.

It may be remarked that there is not any attempt to transfer the scene to London. Dorant in his first speech remarks " Now we're in the *Thuilleries* here, the Land o' th better World and Gallantry ", and the allusions of the original to Poitiers, and the German Wars, are retained.

The translator, however, of *The Feign'd Astrologer,* a Comedie, 4to, 1668, a free adaptation of *Le Feint Astrologue* of Thomas Corneille, has shifted the locale to London and opens Act I in Lincolns-Inn-Fields, whilst there is not only some renaming but some shuffling of the characters, who are more numerous in the English than in the French. Thus Don Fernand in *Le Feint Astrologue* opens the play by his conversation with his valet Philipin. The parallel scene in the English provides Endimion (Fernand) with a friend Bernard, as well as Shift (Philipin). Indeed Philipin also gigs another valet, and we have " Shift, Rawman : Two wittie Knaves servants to *Endimion* ". Leonard becomes Sir Christopher Credulous, and Lucrèce, Clarinda. Don Juan is Bellamy ; Leonor, Celia ; Don Lope, Gratian. Beatrix keeps her own name ; Jacinte is Luce ; Mendoce, " *La-gripe,* An old French man, a servant of Sʳ *Christopher's.*" Rudeman, Bellamy's man is a new rôle, as also is Fannie, "A little Cosen of Celia's," " With Song," as the old programmes used to say. This version from Thomas Corneille is far from being altogether a bad one. The dialogue is more than a mere translation, it has acquired a truly native idiom and tang ; it is a little vulgarized, perhaps, but it is none the less spirited and brisk. It is not stated at which theatre *The Feign'd Astrologer* (which has head-titles *The Astrologer*) was given, but one might hazard that this comedy was produced at Lincoln's Inn Fields [56] in 1668 as a rival attraction to Dryden's *An Evening's Love ; or the Mock-Astrologer,* produced at Drury Lane in June of that year, which also has derived some episodes from Corneille.[57] It remained for Dryden, however, to show how foreign material could be utilized, and so supreme a genius does not merely take and convey, he invades and conquers.

L'AMOUR A LA MODE

LE FEINT ASTROLOGUE

[face p. 362

It was probably Southland's title *Love a la Mode* which suggested to John Bulteel the idea of turning into English Thomas Corneille's *L'Amour a la Mode*. This extremely indifferent version, made in rhyming couplets of a kind, was printed 4to, 1665, as *Amorous Orontes : or, The Love in Fashion*; a second edition, 4to, 1675, being issued as *The Amorous Gallant : or, Love in Fashion*. "A Comedie, In Heroick Verse, As it was Acted." It was given at the Theatre Royal in 1664. Perhaps it had been produced earlier at Vere Street, whilst the second edition of 1675 would seem to indicate a revival during the tenancy of Lincoln's Inn Fields by Killigrew's company. As a fair specimen of Bulteel's work one may quote a few lines from the beginning of Act III, scene 6. Erastes has hastily left Dorothea to avoid Orontus who enters with

> What,—is all vanish'd ? this seems strange to me,
> I heard much noise,—yet can no body see !
> To use me thus, is ill, I tell you true,
> I neither came to scare,—nor hinder you.
> *Dorothea.* Surely yo've taken me to task, this day.
> *Orontus.* No,—but free humours hate such boe-peep play
> And 'tis my trouble, that with so much care
> You should disguise your self from what you are.
> What ever Gallant 'tis,—let him come forth :
> My Passion dares all Eyes, to try its worth.

It is hard to see how even the most accomplished actors could have delivered this skimble-skamble stuff with vigour or conviction. The silks and satins of the original have become mere shoddy and scrub.

L'Amour à la Mode is to my mind not altogether a pleasing comedy. Oronte, the philanderer complete, a sort of stingless untragic Don Juan, partly because of his own fickle fancy and partly to be in the swim, lays siege to a leash of women at once ; Dorotée, who is a heartless coquette ; Lucie ; and Lisette, a spruce wench, Dorotée's abigail. To be entirely modish Dorotée sends Eraste a love-letter couched in precisely the same terms as the billet she has just dispatched to Oronte. Eventually the puppy weds the minx, and we are left with rather a bitter taste in our mouths, save that we realize the sentiment of the whole thing is so patently artificial and charlatan. When Argante, the father of Dorotée, roundly informs the pair that after they have so foolishly risked their reputations in this flirtation they must wed, Oronte calmly replies :—

> J'y consens ; il faut bien qu'enfin je me marie.
> Pourrions-nous autrement finir la Comédie ?

It may be remembered that Wycherley has taken a hint from *L'Amour à la Mode* for *The Plain-Dealer,* Act IV, the scene where Olivia sends the same letter, " the names only alter'd," to the brace of coxcombs, Novel and Lord Plausible.

Of John Bulteel little is known. He was of French extraction, and seems to have been born at Dover, where his father Jean Bultel,[58] a Huguenot minister, long resided. He is to be distinguished from the John Bulteel who died (a bachelor) in the parish of S. Martin-in-the-Fields, 1669. Among the works of John Bulteel the dramatist are *London's Triumph,* a piece of tasteless pageantry for the reception " of that honourable gentleman, Robert Tichburn, Lord Major ", on 29th October, 1656 ; *Birinthia, a Romance,*[59] 8vo, 1664, an incredibly pedestrian performance treating of the wars of Cyrus, " a real History " to which the author has " added those Auxiliary Embellishments rather to Illustrate, then Disguize or Corrupt it " ; *Rome exactly described,* 1668, a version of two discourses by the Venetian ambassador to Pope Alexander VII ; a *General Chronological History of France,* 1683 ; *Apophthegmes of the Ancients,* 1683 ; and some other journey-work none of which inclines us in the slightest to regret those works Bulteel informs us he printed without prefixing his name. In 1674 he published "A New Collection of Poems and Songs. Written by several Persons.[60] Never Printed before. Collected by John Bulteel ", which in 1678 was re-issued as *Melpomene, or the Muses Delight.*

In 1663 was printed quarto at Edinburgh *Marciano ; or, The Discovery,* a tragi-comedy, "Acted with great applause, before His *Majesties* high Commissioner, and others of the Nobility, at the Abby of *Holyrud-house,* on St. *Johns* night. By a company of Gentlemen." This is the work of William Clerke (or Clarke), a Scotch advocate, who in his address " To all humours " is at some pains to defend his play which " *appears as a City-swaggarer in a Country-church, where seldom such have been extant* ", and which he prophesies will be pretty rudely assailed by those " *base, greazy, arrogant, illiterate, Pedants*", to whom the drama is anathema. The main intent of *Marciano,* Clerke tells us, was a compliment to John Middleton, First Earl of Middleton (1619–1673), the Lord High Commissioner of Scotland for King Charles II, but lest his play should seem too serious he " *thought fit to interlude it with a comick transaction* ", and in spite of the difficulty, which he emphasizes, of carrying on two different plots in one single Play, he prides himself that he has triumphantly " *arrived at a happy Catastrophe* ". One imagines that the production of *Marciano* in the great hall at Holyrood on Saturday, 27th December, 1662, was somewhat simple in its arrangements.

There is neither Prologue nor Epilogue, and it is clear from the directions in the text that the play was acted upon an arras stage. The characters are Cleon, Duke of Florence ; Marciano, a noble Siennois, his General ; Strenuo, Marciano's friend ; Borasco, Captain of the rebels guard ; Cassio, Leonardo, two gentlemen of quality ; Pantaloni and Becabunga, two rich gulls in favour with the Ladies, who with Manduco, an arrogant pedant, supply the comic relief. The heroine is Arabella, a Siennois Lady, beloved of Marciano ; whilst Chrysolina and Marionetta play a great part in the lighter episodes.

Marciano is not a dull play. The writer has a story to tell, but unfortunately he does not know how to relate it in dramatic form. The piece opens briskly enough on a field of battle : *"A noyse within, Trumpets, Drums, Pistols, Shot, Swords clash, &c. Enter* Marciano, *wounded, chaffing,* &c.

> Lost—By heavens—all lost,
> All our hopes blasted . . .

The vigour of the first moment is not sustained. The scenes are too short, chopped up and disconnected. The comic relief is wedged in most haphazard fashion among the more serious episodes. Clerke's theme is vaguely political. Cleon, Duke of Florence, has withdrawn from his city to Savoy, before the usurpation of Barbaro. Marciano commands the Sienese, who are leagued to restore the Duke, but they are defeated by the rebel Florentines under Borasco. We then have " *Enter* Arabella *sola, as at* Siena, *having got intelligence of the Rebels victory.* Act II commences with " *Enter* Marciano, *a boy with him as in an Inn* ". Borasco and his soldiers capture him here. Arabella is also seized, and there are various meetings between the two lovers. Strenuo is able to make the jailer drunk, so that Marciano escapes. The Florentines had decided to free Arabella, but they alter their decision, and " *Enter* Arabella *sola in Prison, more closely confin'd, then formerly upon the report that she was to be beheaded.* Borasco attempts to seduce her with a promise of life, but is repulsed. At this juncture Barbaro, who does not appear in the play, dies ; all his creatures are driven out, and Florence with great rejoicings " *Trumpets, Kettle-drums, Ho-boyes, with all sort of musick* " welcomes back her lawful Duke, one of whose first acts is to give Arabella to her faithful Marciano.

The Duke obviously stands for Charles II ; Barbaro for Cromwell ; and, as the author tells us, the Earl of Middleton is drawn in the person of the heroic Marciano. A practised hand might have made something of the piece, but essayed by an amateur it falls and fails. In fact so far is this the case that hitherto it has been entirely neglected and may be said to be practically unknown. The only recent reference (I think) is that in Mr. Robb Lawson's *The Story of the Scots Stage*,[61] where *Marciano* is briefly spoken of as " published in Edinburgh, 1668 ",[62] an edition I have not seen, and erroneously attributed to Sir Thomas Sydceff (Thomas St. Serfe, son of the Bishop of Orkney). However, in the *Mercurius Publicus*, No. 2, 15th January, 1662–3, William Clerke is named as the author, and in the *Catalogue of the Printed Books in the Library of the Faculty of Advocates, Marciano* is assigned to William Clark, advocate, who also composed *The grand tryal ; or poetical exercitations upon the Book of Job*, folio, Edinburgh, 1685.

Almost as amateurish in its technique as *Marciano,* and far less dramatic in its movement, is the anonymous *Irena*, 4to, 1664, Licensed (for printing) by Roger L'Estrange, 13th October, 1664. This tragedy apparently was not given on the stage. The theme is the well-known story of the beautiful Irene, a Greek of most exquisite loveliness of form and perfection of mind, who having been made captive at the sack of Constantinople in 1453 was given to the Sultan Mahomet II, whose mistress she shortly became. The Sultan so doted upon her charms, that she swayed the empire, and in his amorous dalliance he neglected all business and affairs of State, until his subjects were discontented and murmured to faction and unrest. Mustapha Bassa, the Sultan's most trusted counsellor, dared to warn his prince of the danger ; whereupon the monarch came to a barbarous and horrid decision. He summoned a meeting of all his nobles, and having previously solaced himself with the fair Irene, he entered the full divan leading by the hand the lady dressed in her richest robes so that she seemed a very goddess for grace rather than of mortal mould. In a brief speech the Sultan made known that he was aware of their malcontentment and vexations, but he added he would let them see that he regarded the honour and conquests of the Ottoman kings before all else in the world. So saying the monster drew his scimitar and twining the tresses of the fair Greek in his hand with one blow he severed her head from her body. " Now by this judge whether your emperour is able to bridle his affections or not," quoth he ; and presently he was preparing for the besieging of Belgrade.

The author of *Irena* draws his characters very differently from this. The Sultan is transformed into a love-sick amoroso of platonic dreams and ideals. If Irena is chaste as unflecked snow, Mahomet is a pattern of heroic honour. When the Turks chafe and rebel, he is saved by Irena's favoured lover, to whom in the true vein of de Scudéry romance he surrenders the lady with the most appropriate and grandiloquent sentiments. In order to secure his dominion over his subjects he has to appear to sacrifice Irena, but actually he kills a slave in her place. Thus all ends happily in that the fair Greek is able to reward her true lover's constancy with her hand. The play is interesting on account of the rhymed couplets, which are so frequently used as to suggest that the author recognized that this was to be held the metre in which tragedies of love and honour must be presented.

The original story was first told by Bandello, who says he learned it from an oral tradition first handed down by contemporaries. It is his tenth novella with rubric: " Maometto imperador de'turchi crudelmente ammazza una sua donna," published in 1554. Thence it passed into Pierre Boaistuau's *Oeuvres Italiennes de Bandel,* 1559 ; and from Boaistuau to Belleforest, 1564. In England it formed the fortieth novel of Painter's *Palace of Pleasure,* 1566. The Latin historians of Turkey, Martinus Crusius and Joachim Camerarius, inserted it in their chronicles, Crusius taking it from the French versions of Bandello, Camerarius more directly deriving it from the Italian. Hence Richard Knolles conveyed it for his *Generall Historie of the Turkes,* but so forcibly did this legend strike his imagination that he turned to the original sources, and told the tale in far greater detail than it appears in either the *Turcograeciae Libri Octo* or the *De Rebus Turcicis.*

Upon the English stage the story was popular. *The Turkish Mahomet, and Hyrin the faire Greeke* [64] was a " famous play " by George Peele, and may tentatively be dated as not later than 1594. This is possibly the same drama as *Mahomet* which the Admiral's men were acting in 1594 and 1895 ; or indeed it may be *The Love of a Grecian Lady* or *The Grecian Comedy* which was being acted by the same company from 5th October, 1594, to 10th October, 1595. It should be noticed that Jacob Ayrer wrote a drama on the siege of Constantinople and the loves of Mahomet and Irene, which probably had some connexion with *The Turkish Mahomet.*

The Marriage Night, a drama by Henry Cary, fourth Viscount Falkland, printed 4to, 1664, and produced at Lincoln's Inn Fields that year, is a mediocre piece. Webster seems to have been Falkland's inspiration, but the noble poet falls immeasurably short of those supreme heights of tragedy. The scene is Castile. The characters are, The King ; his brother, the Duke De Bereo, the villain of the play ; Count De Castro and Count Dessandro, brothers ; De Flame, a count ; Pirez, Sampayo, two courtiers ; De Loome, La Gitterne, attendants on the Duke ; Silliman (who supplies comic relief), Steward to the Duchess; Two Judges; the Duchess Claudilla; Torguina, De Prate, her Ladies; Cleara, sister to De Flame. Claudilla is loved by De Flame and Cleara loves Dessandro. The Duke, who has debauched Claudilla and is a ming at the crown, in policy contrives that his mistress shall be wedded to Dessandro, a marriage which the King honours with his presence. De Flame and Cleara, devoured with jealousy, make their way into the bridal chamber, where Cleara kills Claudilla and stabs Dessandro as he lies in bed by his wife's side. She then destroys herself. News is now brought that the King is dead; and Bereo, who has secretly induced De Castro to poison the late monarch, assumes the crown. At De Flame's trial, however, the King suddenly appears, and it is found that De Castro repented of his murderous design, the more especially as Dessandro's life was saved by a skilful physician. Bereo's villainies are exposed, and he and De Flame, who is stung to madness when he realizes that Claudilla was the Duke's whore, fall by each other's poniards. The conclusion and indeed many of the events of this play are huddled very improperly although one feels that with a little pains the scenes could have been far more effectively contrived. The verdict of Pepys who saw *The Marriage Night* on the 21st March, 1667, is: " some things very good in it, but the whole together, I thought, not so."

" The sillyest thing that ever was writt." Although one must by no means entirely subscribe to this description of *The Spightful Sister* penned by a contemporary hand in Malone's copy of the play,[65] yet it can hardly be disputed that we have here an extremely indifferent piece of work. *The Spightful Sister* was published 4to, 1667,[66] as "A New Comedy. *Written by* Abraham Bailey, *of* Lincolns-Inn, Gent.", concerning whom nothing further appears to be known. The author in his address " To the Reader " apologizes for the following sheets, and informs us : " That as it is a Play, so I made the writing thereof onely my Recreation, not my Study; done in a few hours and youthful years."

Losana is " The Spightful Sister to Berania ", a lady wooed by Litus. In spite of Losana's arguments and admonitions Berania rejects Litus, and loathes his eager suit. Thus baffled he employs " *his Ruffion* ", Harpes, to aid him in abducting the lady, but the scheme is foiled by Petus, " *a young Lord, after-wards* Berania's *Sweet-Heart* ", and his friend, Lidorus. Litus through shame conceals himself, and is given out as dead, whilst Losana who is secretly in communication with him plots mischief. She contrives to embroil Petus and Lidorus in a duel, by persuading the former that Berania is false to him with the latter. She further hires assassinates to dispatch Petus, but in error they kill Litus. Fallen into a distraction she is at last led to confess her evil designs, and as a penitent resolves to immure herself in a cloister, preparatory to which, she prays

> I humbly beg your leave,
> That my devotion may be fitted by
> A pilgrimage to the shrine of *Loretto*;
> By a new favour I may be absolv'd,
> As penitent for all the impious stains
> Of my bad life.

At the end Petus and Berania are joined in matrimony, the celebrations including a kind of Masque of Hymen and other divinities.

Lighter relief is afforded by Beucer, who having got Sarah with child, now courts Thele. However, Winifred, "Sarahs *Humerous Mother*," a fearful harridan, pursues him lustily with her tongue and a stick. Eventually when Beucer thinks he is united to Thele he finds that his bride is Sarah, veiled and in the damsel's gown, whereupon he cheerfully accepts the situation.

Langbaine reviewing *The Spightful Sister* said: "I believe the Author has stollen neither his Characters nor Language from any other," which is true enough, but a very ambiguous criticism at best. Bailey's play was never acted.

It is not to be denied that some of this dramatic undergrowth is jejune and desiccated enough, but at the same time when we consider the immense activity of the forty years from 1660 to 1700 it must be allowed that the quota which sinks to a very low level is remarkably small, and even *The Spightful Sister*, which nearly plumbs the nadir of dramatic accomplishment of this period is not wholly without vigour in the farcical Beucer and Winifred episodes.

The two plays, a tragedy and a comedy, that came from the pen of John Caryl, Baron Caryl of Dunford, are justly esteemed. *Sir Salomon; or The Cautious Coxcomb* in particular is a capital piece of work. John Caryl, who was born in 1625, was of an ancient Catholic family which had been settled from the close of the sixteenth century at West Harting, Sussex. His mother was Catharine, daughter of Lord Petre, and he received at least part of his education at St. Omer's. Succeeding to a fair estate, he was widely known and much esteemed in the Court and literary circles after the Restoration. During the panic of Oates' plot falling under suspicion, he was even committed to the Tower in 1679, but shortly released on bail. Upon the accession of King James II, who had been his constant patron, Caryl was for a while employed as English agent at Rome, whence he returned in 1686 to make room for Lord Castlemaine. He was then appointed Secretary to Queen Mary of Modena, and only death thenceforth severed his intimate connexion with the Royal Family. Thus he retired with the Court to St. Germains, and it is said that, at the especial request of the King, William of Nassau refrained from confiscating the West Harting property. This was little more than a cunning show on the part of the intruder, for Caryl was attainted in 1696, the estate seized and granted to Lord Cutts, from whom however it was redeemed by John Caryl, Lord Caryl's nephew, who was managing the family affairs since his uncle's retirement abroad. In 1695 or 1696 Lord Caryl was appointed Secretary of State to King James II, after whose death in 1701 he was created by King James III Baron Caryl of Dunford. He died on 4th September, 1711, being buried in the Church of the English Dominicans at Paris. His epitaph was written by no less a poet than Pope.[67] Early in life Lord Caryl married the daughter of Sir Maurice Drummond, Margaret, who died childless in 1656.

In addition to his plays Lord Caryl translated the " Epistle of Briseis to Achilles " which appeared in *Ovid's Epistles,* 1680, and also the First Eclogue of Vergil in Dryden's *Miscellany Poems,* 1683. He further wrote a very happily turned copy of verses on the Earl of Shaftesbury, entitled *The Hypocrite.*[68]

The English Princess ; or, The Death of Richard III, Caryl's tragedy, was produced at Lincoln's Inn Fields on 3rd March, 1667, and printed, 4to, 1673. Downes has the following notice : " *Richard* the Third, or the *English* Princess, Wrote by Mr. *Carrol,* was Excellently well Acted in every Part ; chiefly, King *Richard,* by Mr. *Betterton* ; Duke of *Richmond,* by Mr. *Harris* ; Sir *William Stanly,* by Mr. *Smith,* Gain'd them an Additional Estimation, and the Applause fom the Town, as well as profit to the whole Company."

In the Prologue Caryl advises his audience :—

> *You must to day your Appetite prepare*
> *For a plain English Treat of homely Fare :*
> *We neither* Bisque *nor* Ollios *shall advance*
> *From Spanish Novel, or from French Romance ;*
> *Nor shall we charm your Ears or feast your Eyes*
> *With Turkey works, or Indian Rarityes :*
> *But to plain Hollinshead and down right Stow*
> *We the course web of our Contrivance owe.*

The " Turkey works " is an allusion to Orrery's *Mustapha* ; and the " Indian Rarityes " to *The Indian-Queen* and *The Indian Emperour,* the great successes of the rival Theatre Royal.

The characters are Richard III ; the Queen Dowager of

Edward IV ; the Princess Elizabeth, Daughter of Edward IV ; the Earl of Richmond Crown'd Henry the Seventh ; Earl of Oxford ; Lord Stanly ; Lord Strange his Son ; Lord Chandew of Bretany ; Sir William Stanly ; Mrs. Stanly, his sister ; Charlot Page to the Princess ; Lord Lovel ; Sir William Catesby ; Sir Richard Ratcliffe ; Miles Forrest ; and the Prior of Litchfield. The Scenes are laid in the Head Quarters of King Richard and the Earl of Richmond, when they are in sight of one another.

The play is written in heroic verse, the couplets being both vigorous and poetical. Sir William Stanly loves with hopeless passion the Princess Elizabeth, whose heart is Richmond's, whilst Richard III courts her for his policy. Charlot, who is Lord Chandew's daughter disguised as a French page, is enamoured of young Stanly. The Princess doubts Lord Stanly's truth because he seems to be of Richard's party, but a letter conveyed to her by him from Richmond shows that he is a " *conceal'd and faithful Servant* ". In scene 9, the conclusion of Act IV, we have the interior of Richard's tent : " *The Curtain is opened. The King appears in a distracted posture, newly risen from his Bed, walking in his Dream with a dagger in his hand, surrounded by the Ghosts of those whom he had formerly killed.*" This is a powerful episode, but for us somewhat marred by the memory of Shakespeare's great scene. Forrest is suborned to murder the Princess, who, however, escapes in Charlot's attire to a neighbouring convent, and thus Lord Strange, who has undertaken to superintend the murder, actually in order that he may protect Elizabeth, finds Charlot dressed in the royal robes. On Bosworth Field Sir William Stanly dons a suit of armour similar to Richmond's mail and engages Richard, but Richmond himself interposes and slays the King. The last scene is the cloister to which the Princess has retired. Sir William Stanly heroically stifling his love places the crown on Richmond's head amid acclamations and the solemn blessing of the saintly Prior. Charlot, who is recognized, gently rejects Lord Strange's hand and declares that she will rather

> in a Cloister chuse
> The lasting Love of an Immortal Spouse.

There is something extremely beautiful and touching in many passages of this play, and for that reason it is far superior to such dramas as Orrery's *Henry the Fifth* or *The Black Prince* which are merely gorgeously brocaded tapestries of English history. In *The English Princess* the characters are intensely alive ; they scheme, they are torn by emotion and perplexed ; they suffer and love. So admirably acted, as it originally was, it must have proved a very powerful and moving drama.[69]

The characters of *Sir Salomon; or, The Cautious Coxcomb,*
Lord Caryl's second piece, are : Sir Salomon Single ; Mr. Single,
his Son ; Mr. Woodland ; Mr. Peregreen, his Son ; Mr. Wary ;
Mr. Barter, an *Indy*-Merchant ; Sir Arthur Addell ; Mrs. Julia,
Daughter to Wary ; Mrs. Betty, Daughter to Barter ; Timothy,
Sir Salomon's Steward ; Ralph and Alice, Servants of Sir Salomon
and attendants on Mrs. Betty ; Roger, Wary's man ; Harry,
Woodland's man ; A Nurse ; Two Foot-boys ; Constable and
Watch. The scene is London.

This Comedy, which was produced at Lincoln's Inn Fields,
is thus recorded by Downes : " Sir *Soloman Single,* Wrote by
Mr *Carrol,* Sir *Solomon,* Acted by Mr. *Betterton : Peregrine Wood-
land,* by Mr. *Harris : Single,* by Mr. *Smith* : Mr. *Wary,* by
Mr. *Sandford : Timothy,* by Mr. *Underhill : Betty,* by Mrs. *Johnson :
Julia,* Mrs. *Betterton.* The Play being Singularly well *Acted,* it
took 12 Days together." Sir Arthur Addell was created by
Nokes.

The episodes which mainly concern Sir Salomon, Peregreen
Woodland, Timothy, and Mrs. Betty are avowedly taken from
L'École des Femmes by " Molliere *the famous* Shakespear *of this
Age* ", as the Epilogue has it. Sir Salomon settles his estate
upon Mrs. Betty, whose parentage is unknown and whom he has
adopted and disciplines in all simplicity to be his wife. He
discards his son, who is in love with Julia, the daughter of
Justice Wary ; which old gentleman on learning the forfeit
promptly forbids young Single the house. This situation is
further embarrassed by Sir Arthur Addell, " a noisy bawling fop,"
who pretends to Julia, and owing to his affluence secures her
father on his side. Peregreen Woodland confides in Sir Salomon
that he is enamoured of Mrs. Betty who is " lodged in a House
on the back-side of *Holborn,* towards the Fields . . . maintained
and educated in a private cunning way by an old Gentleman
they call Mr. *Evans* ", the name assumed by Sir Salomon in
his rôle of guardian, just as Arnolphe in *L'École des Femmes*
is Monsieur de la Souche. Peregreen continues to open his
heart to Sir Salomon, and presently occasion offers that he
shall entrust Sir Arthur with a note to deliver to Mrs. Betty.
No sooner has the messenger knocked at the door than the
whole garrison of Sir Salomon's spies mistaking him for
Mrs. Betty's lover rush skirling out and beat him so lustily that
by a sleight he tumbles down feigning to be killed. There are
loud cries of murder and all hastily disperse, whilst the dead
man too rubs off only to fall into the hands of the watch who
seize him as the murderer in spite of his protests that he is the
poor victim. Mr. Woodland and Mr. Barter, who have come

to Town, now make their appearance, and the intrigue begins to clear. Betty is recognized as Barter's daughter whom he intends shall wed his old friend Squire Woodland's son. Sir Salomon withdraws—a pathetic figure : " Heart, since thou needs must break, go, break alone, And rob 'em of the pleasure to look on," he groans as he blindly stumbles away. Sir Arthur is haled before Justice Wary, and explains that he was the Man who scoured off at top speed after he was dead, but he is disappointed of his mistress, for Peregreen hands over to young Single the writings of Sir Salomon's estate settled on Mrs. Betty, and Wary piously ejaculates : " I dare not resist the will of Heaven, which shews it self in the wonder full turne of Affairs, which this day has produc'd. Daughter, enjoy your Love ; and my blessing go along with it." Even honest Ralph and Alice are joined in wedlock as the comedy ends, although Ralph naïvely declares whilst he smickers at Mrs. Betty that after looking at so fine and fair a lady " that greasie Wench turnes my Stomack ", and Alice with a sheep's-eye sighs to Peregreen " I shall never love that slobbering Fellow there : An' he were but half so hand- some, as your Worship—"

This is an admirable comedy. If it be objected that too much is conveyed from Molière, a double answer may be given. In the first place *L'École des Femmes* takes from Lope de Vega's *La dama boba,* and also from Scarron's *La Précaution inutile,* which is itself founded upon *El prevenido engañado.*[70] Secondly Caryl has justified his impropriation by the adroitness and skill with which he has refounded his material since in his hands this at once acquires a native air. He has a complete command of technique ; the incidents are varied and natural ; his dialogue characteristic and lively, always animated and often witty.

His persons are drawn with sure and distinctive strokes. They are individuals, not merely the lay figures—the *jeune premier,* the second old man, the soubrette, who appear in so many a comedy which is sustained by the felicitous arrangement and pleasant bustle of its contrivance rather than by any interest in the living characters. Single and Peregreen Woodland are two young men of different temperaments and ideas ; Justice Wary is so real and true that there cannot be many who have not met just such another foxy fellow, a shrewd and rasping old file ; Sir Arthur Addell is no mere buffoon, no mere laughable but ridiculously exaggerated caricature of a coxcomb, for his absurdity and pert fripperies are always well within the bounds of pro- bability. Sir Salomon himself is Caryl's highest achievement. One knows what he would have become under the same con- ditions in a comedy by Ravenscroft, or Otway, or Mrs. Behn—

consummedly unpleasant, highly ludicrous in his green jealousy, always choused, always futile, and yet exquisitely droll withal. Caryl, however, makes us feel the conceit and weakness of Sir Salomon's position ; we realize his heavy and selfish tyranny ; we know him hard and pragmatical, yet he retains our respect, if not indeed in a sense our sympathy throughout. At the last when in agony he quits the scene with an expression of something like despair we are not able to see him go without one short pang, a mere stitch, or just a quick catch in the throat. Yet it could not have happened otherwise.

Genest indeed expresses some surprise that Betterton created Sir Salomon, a rôle which in his opinion " would have suited Dowton or Munden ".[71] Anthony Leigh, as Cibber tells us, was very great as Ralph, the " stupid staring under-servant ".

Sir Salomon ; or, The Cautious Coxcomb remained—as indeed it so amply deserved—in the theatrical repertory for half a century, and Downes tells us that of the four plays [72] " commanded to be *Acted* at Court at St. *Jame's,* by the *Actors* of both Houses " from " *Candlemas* 1704, to the 22d, of *April* 1706 ", " the second was, *Sir* Solomon, *or the Cautious Coxcomb* : Mr. *Betterton, Acting Sir Solomon* ; Mr. *Wilks, Peregrine* ; Mr. *Booth,* Young *Single* ; Mr. *Dogget,* Sir *Arthur Addle* ; Mr. *Johnson,* Justice *Wary* ; Mr. *Pinkethman, Ralph* ; Mr. *Underhill, Timothy* ; Mrs. *Bracegirdle, Julia* ; Mrs. *Mounfort, Betty* : The whole being well perform'd, it gave great Satisfaction."

On 11th March, 1707, at Drury Lane for Mrs. Mountfort's benefit Estcourt appeared as Sir Solomon with Mrs. Mountfort, Mrs. Betty ; Powell, Peregreen ; and Pinkethman, Ralph. At the same house 21st May, 1714, Keen was Sir Solomon ; Norris, Sir Arthur Addell ; Wilks, Peregreen ; Booth, young Single ; Johnson, Justice Wary ; Bullock, Timothy ; Leigh, Ralph ; Mrs. Santlow, Julia ; Miss Younger, Betty ; Mrs. Willis, Alice.

The popularity of Caryl's comedy is shown by the fact that it was one of the two plays Charles II selected to be given during the visit to England of his sister the Duchess of Orleans, who arrived at Dover on Sunday, 15th May, 1670. The Treaty of Dover was signed on the 22nd May, and on the 2nd June she crossed back to France, so short a time was allowed by Monsieur's jealousy.

The next author whose plays it will be convenient to review, John Dover, also left extant a tragedy and a comedy, but unfortunately his work has nothing of the quality which distinguished Lord Caryl's pen.

John Dover, the son of Captain John Dover of Barton-on-the-heath in Warwickshire, was born in 1646. At the age of 15 in 1661 he became a Demy of Magdalen College, Oxford, and matriculated on 12th July of the same year, but he departed from the university without a scholastical degree.[73] Meanwhile he had entered himself as a student at Gray's Inn on 19th May, 1664, and was called to the Bar on 21st June, 1672. According to Wood he " lived at Banbury in Oxfordshire, and practis'd his faculty ", until at the age of eight and thirty in 1684, he took Holy Orders, and four years later " became beneficed at Drayton [74] near the said town, where he is resorted to by fanatical people ". In a MS. description of Drayton, 1688, the following occurs : " It is a Rectory, Incumbent John Dover Rector of Magd. Coll. Oxon. 120£." [75] The Parish Register of Drayton has : " Mr. John Dover, Rector of this parish buried Nov. 6, 1725, aged 81." In the chancel of the Parish Church, S. Peter's, which is of the fourteenth century, remains a stone with the following inscription. *H.S.E. Johannes Dover, qui stipendium peccati hic deposuit cadaver, minimè dubitans, quin Phoenicis instar floriosius e suis resurget cineribus. Vixit, peccavit, pænitiit : obiit tertio die Novembris, A.D.* MDCCXXV.

Dover's first play *The Roman Generalls ; or, The Distressed Ladies* was printed quarto 1667 [76]; it was never acted, and there can be little doubt that the poet was wise when he decided *" to shun A Publick Censure "* (i.e. a verdict, favourable or the reverse) by confining his piece to print alone, for truth to tell it is a most fantastic and incongruous medley. In his Dedication to Lord Brook of Beauchamp Court, Staffs, Dover says : " I have neither altogether followed, nor yet declin'd History, lest by the One, My Play might be took for a Piece translated out of *Livie* or *Lucan,* or by the Other, for an Idle Romance ; but like the Traveller, for Delight, sometimes I follow, and sometimes I quit My Road." He further informs his patron that when weary of poring over Coke and Littleton, to divert himself he " took *Cæsar's* Commentaries, or read the Lives of My *Roman Generalls,* out of *Plutarch* ". The " Roman Generalls " are Caesar and Pompey, and in so far as Dover's scenes have any relation to history he has drawn upon Plutarch's lives of these two heroes. Among the characters in the play are : Julius Caesar ; M. Valerius and Curio, his two Generals ; Pompey ; Crassus *his Ghost ;* Uxama, *"A Spanish Lord, in Love with Selania "* ; Parmeno, *" Servant to* Uxama *taken Prisoner "* and at times going under the extraordinary name of Oránges ; Astragia and her Sister, the two Distressed Ladies ; Selania, a Sardinian Lady. The play is written in rhyming couplets of a sort, and episodes of Caesar in Gaul alternate with Pompey's triumph amid cries of *Io Triumphe ! Subacta Hispania !* until the final struggle between the two great rivals begins. These martial scenes are interlaced with the adventures of two ladies, who make their first appearance in a very striking and novel way. " *The Scene is a Tempetuous Sea. Two Ladies are discover'd as cast on Shoar on a Planck.*" After some elegant and sugary dialogue which would have delighted Cathos and Madelon, they go out " *hand in hand* ". The next scene is an Italian plain, " *Where an Augure is discover'd as amongst Sheep. A Nymph passeth by scornfully. He Sings,*

> *Nymph who so coy? you hope in vain*
> *To cool my Bosom with disdain . . . .*

Presently Fairies appear and pinch him for intruding on their magic ground. He pacifies the good folk by piping whilst they " trip it o're the Plain ", and whilst treading " *an Antick Measure* " they sing

> *We daunce an Antick Round,*
> *Blew Rings on the Ground,*
> *Shall alwayes be found,*
> *Where we keep Rendezvous . . .*

These lyrics are often extremely pleasing and quite the best things in the whole play. Two Ladies, who are not the same as the Ladies recently cast ashore, now appear in a " *Lawrel Grove* ", and become very precious in their talk. The First Lady poetically tells us it is dawn, and the stars " Glow-worms of the Skie " are fading fast :—

> For now the Champion of the day dos rise,
> And routs those Common Link-boyes from the Skies.

" Common Link-boyes " is good. She next proceeds to declare that her real name is not Secreta, but Selania, and that she is following from Spain her lover Uxama, who there called himself Oránges. Uxama appears dressed as a Shepherd, but is un-recognized by Selania. A Shepherdess in man's Apparel enters, and we learn that she is Astragia disguised in order to test the fidelity of her sister's lover, whose loyalty is not to be shaken. Well may Uxama a little later exclaim :—

> What Labyrinth is this ? things seem to me
> Riddles in love, and all a Mysterie.

Selania and " *the associate Lady* " are next habited like Amazons. Parmeno further complicates affairs by his use of this odd name Oránges, which had been employed by Uxama. Eventually owing to Caesar's conquest of Pompey's army, the ladies who have been seized by soldiers flying from the field are released, and Uxama united to Selania. A mediocre confused muss of a play, and poor even for the work of a stripling of twenty. Dover's second extant play *The Mall, or The Modish Lovers,* a comedy, is a far better and brisker piece. It was produced at Lincoln's Inn Fields by Killigrew's company, during their tenancy of that theatre, in January–February, 1674, or possibly in December of the preceding year, and published 4to, 1674. No printed cast is given, but the characters are Mr. Easy, an old husband; Courtwell, his Kinsman, a brisk gallant, newly arriv'd from Spain; Lovechange, privately married to Mrs. Woodbee; Amorous, servant to Grace, and nephew to Mrs. Woodbee; Sir Ralph Spatter, a foolish country knight, rival to Amorous; Jo, Spatter's man; Mrs. Easy, young wife to old Easy; Mrs. Woodbee; Grace, old Easy's niece, in love with Amorous; Perigreen, alias Camilla, a Spanish Lady in disguise; Peg, Mrs. Easy's woman; Clare, Mrs. Woodbee's woman; Betty, Grace's woman. The Scene, S. James' Park and the adjacent places.

Lovechange, who is privately married to " the rich Widdow *Wou'dbee* ", neglects his wife since to use his own phrase " first she's Old, next Jealous, she is, to Damnation, Proud, Expensive, and—very honest, which makes her very insolent ". At the same time he pursues Mrs. Easy, whose husband is of an intolerably jealous humour. Mrs. Easy having no suspicion of the truth shows Mrs. Woodbee a letter from Lovechange making an assignation at night in the Mall, S. James Park. Mrs. Woodbee promptly sends her husband a billet-doux as from Mrs. Easy appointing a rendezvous at the Duckpond. Lovechange discovers from Peg, Mrs. Easy's woman, that the note must be a cheat, and accordingly he meets his mistress in the Mall as originally intended. Mrs. Woodbee goes to the Duck Pond, and here she encounters Courtwell, whom Mrs. Easy has bidden attend there. They retire, and Mrs. Woodbee imagining she is gratifying her spouse grants him the last favours. There is a very amusing scene in which Peg, who is dressed as Mrs. Easy in order to further that lady's intrigue abroad with Lovechange, is taken by Easy for his wife, and conducted to the bedchamber where he tumbles her since she dare not discover the subterfuge. Eventually Lovechange finds out what has happened, and taking every advantage of the situation bestows a pretty severe jobation on his wife. " I will part with you, you know the entertainment which you gave young *Courtwell* on the River-side i' th' Park, I know it too," he cries. They agree to conceal their marriage, and to separate, but he retains half her fortune. " So, I have shook her off, and with very little remorse too . . . I'le to my sweet, pretty, little, dear Mrs. *Easy,* and if she can but contrive to do as much for her Husband, as I've done for my Wife, we'le 'en strike up a match *A-la-mode,*" is the expression of the gentleman's sentiments upon this occasion. Easy who decides that his wife—" my kind, my handsome young Wife "—has grafted him with some fine antlers, makes no bones about handing her over to Lovechange ; " I am a Cuckold that's not my fault, but I will not be a Fool, and so, much good may it do you kindly." There is an underplot of the rivalry of Amorous and Sir Ralph Spatter for the hand of Easy's niece, Grace, who after some crosses and intrigue weds the man she loves, young Amorous, whilst the Knight in high dudgeon consoles himself with Betty. We also have the episodes of Perigreen, a Spanish lady, who disguised as a page follows Courtwell to England, and wins him by her devotion.

Since there has been some extraordinary mystification concerning this play, and blunders are even yet being made, it may be as well here to state the facts of the case quite simply, once for all.

On Tuesday, 15th September, 1668, Pepys went " to the King's playhouse, to see a new play, acted but yesterday, a translation out of French by Dryden, called ' The Ladys à la Mode ' ; so mean a thing as, when they come to say it would be acted again to-morrow, both he that said it, Beeson, and the pit fell a-laughing, there being this day not a quarter of the pit full ". There is, of course, no such piece by Dryden as *The Ladys à la Mode,* and the play in question which Pepys saw was Flecknoe's *Damoiselles à la Mode,* " taken out of several Excellent Pieces of *Molliere,*" 8vo, 1667. The attribution of this very vapid comedy to Dryden by some wicked wit in the theatre was but an intentional jest at the laureate's expense.

Upon the publication of Pepys' *Diary,* however, this mischievous canard was taken as correct, and editors began to inquire concerning *The Ladys à la Mode.* As late as 1891 so careful an investigator as R. W. Lowe in his monograph *Thomas Betterton,* without a word of caution speaks of Pepys' visit on 15th September, 1668, " to the King's Playhouse to see a new play by Dryden, called, *The Ladies à la Mode,* of which, by the way, this is the only record." [77] Again in his study " The Persistence of Elizabethan Conventionalisms ",[78] Dr. W. J. Lawrence blunders most woefully when he writes : " On 15th September, 1668, the diarist [Pepys] paid a visit to the Theatre Royal to see Dryden's indifferent new comedy, *The Ladies à la Mode.*" The error was firmly enough established, and had support.

The next thing was to identify this elusive play. It so happens that Dover signed his Epistle Dedicatory, addressed to William Whitcomb, Junior, Esq., which is prefixed to *The Mall; or The Modish Lovers* with his initials only, J.D., for no doubt the reception of *The Roman Generalls* had made him a little cautionary and diffident. Langbaine in his *English Dramatick Poets*, Oxford, 1691, under the initials J.D. mentions *The Mall; or, The Modish Lovers*, and says : " This Play is ascribed by Dr. *Hyde* (the *Proto-Bibliothecarius* to the University) to Mr. *Dryden*; tho' methinks the Stile of the Epistle Dedicatory, is not like the rest of his Writings.[79] The *Biographia Dramatica* [80] gave a note of warning in its mention of *The Mall* : " This play has been ascribed to Dryden ; but its style and manner bear little resemblance to those of that author ; and therefore it is reasonable to imagine it the work of some more obscure writer." Probably the first person so blunderingly to identify Dover's comedy with the pseudo-Dryden *Ladies à la Mode* was the late Mr. George Saintsbury, who in his extremely inaccurate and uninformed *Dryden*, has a lengthy and confused note in which he suggests that *The Mall; or The Modish Lovers* " may possibly be the very ' mean thing ' of Pepys' scornful mention ". " The difference of title is not fatal," he airily remarks, and he goes on to speak of the quarto of *The Mall*. " The date is 1674, and the printing is execrable." This latter assertion is not correct, for *The Mall* actually is far better printed than many plays of this period, but then Mr. Saintsbury had a very limited experience of such things.[82] Mr. Saintsbury further reprinted (without any attempt at annotation) Dover's comedy in his unfortunate recension of Scott's *Dryden*, vol. viii.

In addition to his extant dramatic work Dover is the author of *The White Rose : or, a Word for the House of York, vindicating the Right of Succession, in a Letter from Scotland,* 9 *Mar.* 1679, folio, 1680. Wood further tells us : " He hath written one or two more plays, which are not yet printed."

As we have noted the influence of the Spanish theatre upon English dramatists was at this time very great, and several Spanish comedies had been translated or adapted for the London stage, especially through the medium of the French. In 1667 Thomas St. Serfe produced under the name *Tarugo's Wiles : Or, The Coffee-House,* a pretty close version of the famous " Gran Comedia di *No Puede Ser* ".[83] This was first given on Saturday, 5th October, 1667, at Lincoln's Inn Fields, when Pepys found the house so full he was unable to secure even standing-room. Downes records that it " Expir'd the third Day " but as I have elsewhere shown he is certainly in error.[84] It was at any rate not acted for three successive days and then withdrawn as on Tuesday, 15th October, Pepys visited the Duke of York's house, " and there saw ' The Coffee-house ' the most ridiculous insipid play that ever I saw in my life, and glad we were that

Betterton had no part in it." The diarist was in an ill-humour, and his sweeping condemnation goes for little or nothing. At the same time the compliments addressed by Lord Buckhurst to St. Serfe upon his printing his play, a copy of verses to be found in the Fifth Volume of Tonson's *Miscellanies*, v, p. 272, as well as the poem, " *To my friend, Master* Tho. St. Serf," in *Covent Garden Drollery*, 1672, must perhaps be judged too partial. They are, however, entirely inconsistent with any such conspicuous failure as Downes suggests and Dennis asserts.[85] Not that *Tarugo's Wiles* remained in the repertory; it was indeed pretty soon forgotten, for less than twenty years after Charles II recommended Crowne to use *No Puede Ser* as the groundwork of a comedy, and it was not until he had written three acts of his new play that the author of *Sir Courtly Nice* discovered how the Spanish piece had been sometime before " translated and act'd and damn'd ".

The cast of *Tarugo's Wiles* is not printed, but the characters are : Don Patricio ; Don Horatio ; Liviana, Sister to Patricio ; Locura, her maid ; Sophronia, in love with and beloved by Patricio ; Stanlia, her maid ; Roderigo, a Knight designed by Patricio to marry Liviana ; Tarugo, a younger Brother, bred in England, and Kinsman to Don Horatio ; Hurtante, a tailor ; Alberto, Patricio's man ; Domingo, Horatio's man. The scene is Madrid, and since the plot is exactly that of *Sir Courtly Nice* it were superfluous to detail the incidents here. It may be remarked that Crowne in his adroit management of the business, his wit and humour, infinitely surpasses St. Serfe, whose Third Act is wholly given to the humours of a coffee-house, and is amusing enough with its " mixture of all kind of people ", but as Genest truly observes, " it would serve for any other play as well as for this."

Thomas St. Serfe, as he signs his name at the end of the dedication of *Tarugo's Wiles*, was one of the four sons of the Bishop of Galloway, the only surviving prelate at the King's coming-in of those removed by the Assembly of 1638. Although a very old man upon the restoration of Episcopacy the Bishop was translated to the richer see of Orkney which he held to his death in 1663. The surname is also spelled Sinserf, Sydserfe, and Sydceff. Thomas St. Serfe, the dramatist, served under Montrose in Scotland, and in the Dedication of *Tarugo's Wiles* to the Marquess of Huntley he has reference to the " *many Reliefs, Shelters and Protections* " he received from that noble family, during the " *late Fanatick Commotions* ". In January, 1661, St. Serfe began a weekly journal *Mercurius Caledonius* but only, nine numbers were issued. In 1669 he occupied a house in the

Canongate, Edinburgh, where " he keeps his theater for acting his plays ". This, the first regularly established theatre in Scotland, was maintained as such until at least 1672, about which year according to Mr. Robb Lawson [86] in his *The Scots Stage,* two brothers Edward Fountain of Lochhill and Captain James Fountain were granted official recognition as " Masters of the Revels " throughout the kingdom.

In Lord Buckhurst's verses Thomas St. Serfe is called " Sir Thomas ", but he does not seem to have received the accolade. St. Serfe translated from De Marmet *The Entertainment of the Cours,* 8vo, 1658 ; and from Cyrano de Bergerac, *The Government of the World in the Moon,* 8vo, 1659. As we have already noted, the attribution of *Marciano,* 4to, 1663, to his pen is an error, since this play is work of William Clerke.

A play which seems almost to have escaped notice is *The Amazon Queen ; Or, The Amours Of Thalestris To Alexander the Great,* a tragi-comedy by John Weston, 4to, 1667.[87] It is briefly mentioned by Langbaine who gives the author's name as John Watson,[88] and hence it is recorded in the *Biographia Dramatica,* but Genest apparently did not know this piece. As Weston informs us in his Preface, it was never acted owing to the fact that he heard of no less than two other dramas intended for the theatre, both of which were written or being written on the same theme, that is to say both of which were to some extent at least founded upon episodes from La Calprenède's *Cassandre.* It is a little difficult to identify these two tragedies, which were then in preparation since it would appear that the immense vogue of Lee's *The Rival Queens* first turned the attention of playwrights to the Alexander romance. Lee's tragedy was not produced until January, 1676–7, that is to say ten years after the publication of *The Amazon Queen,* and it was followed in quick succession by Banks' *The Rival Kings* produced at the Theatre Royal in June, 1677 ; Pordage's *The Siege of Babylon,* Dorset Garden, a few months later in the same year ; and Cooke's *Love's Triumph,* unacted, 4to, 1678. Banks in his Epilogue claims that his play was written a year before Lee's, and it is, of course, possible that Pordage had his *Siege of Babylon* draughted a decade earlier, and that the increased popularity of the subject obtained it a belated hearing on the boards. Weston's language is ambiguous, and his reference to " *a principal Elector, having owned, that he had a child of his own family who pretended to the same Crown* ", implies that some leading dramatist of the day (1666) was engaged upon a drama dealing with Alexander and Thalestris.

Plutarch in his *Alexander,*[89] 46, records how Polycritus, Onesicritus, Antigenes, and many other ancient historians menion that an Amazon queen visited Alexander the Great, and Strabo [90] (505), whose authority is Clitarchus, when he refers to the Amazons tells us : " καθάπερ καὶ περὶ Θαληστρίας, ἥν Ἀλεξάνδρῳ συμμῖξαί φασιν ἐν τῇ Ὑρκρανίᾳ καὶ συγγενέσθαι τεκνοποιίας χάριν, δυναστεύουσαν τῶν Ἀμαζόνων." [91]

La Calprenède in his *Cassandre* substitutes Oronte for Alexander. Talestris, Queen of the Amazons, comes to the banks of the Euphrates in search of Oronte, the brother of Oroondate, who has been tricked into believing her false. She relates her own history in some detail.[92]

The characters of *The Amazon Queen* are Alexander the Great ; Ephestion, his Friend ; Ptolomy, Perdiccas, Leonatus, Eumenes, his Commanders ; Tyreus, the Eunuch ; Statira, Darius his daughter ; Thalestris, Queen of Amazons ; Roxanna, first Wife of Alexander ; Cleona, Statira's woman ; Hesione, Roxanna's woman ; Hippolita and Amalthea, two Amazons.

The Scene is : " The Banks of the River *Thirmodon,* on the Borders of the *Amazons* Country." It is a very rococo piece of work, and I am afraid rather a poor specimen of the heroic play. The sentiment is unreal and often trifling, whilst the couplets without being entirely bad lack enjambment, and result in a kind of lilt which is both monotonous and far from pleasing. There are some terrible dips into bathos. Thus when Alexander and Thalestris meet, the lady begins :—

> You so oblig'd me, Sir, with your kind blanks,
> That for your pass I staid not to give thanks . . .

Alexander replies :—

> He who on earth no equal will endure,
> To keep from you his freedom is not sure.

And later, after she has discoursed, he declares :—

> You fill my soul with wonder and delight,
> Madam, we'l marry if you please this night.
> *Thalestris.* You use me ill to talk of marriage,
> I scorn to be your tame bird in a cage.

Alexander acknowledges " My heart's by fair *Statira* preposses'd ", and the Queen retorts " I scorn to have with half a man to do ". Whereupon the hero philosophically murmurs :—

> There's nothing now that can abate my grief,
> But seeking in *Roxanna's* charms relief.

Statira on learning this resolves : " I'le pine away in *Dian's* Nunnery." Alexander now surprises Roxanna kissing Leonatus, who is forthwith banished :—

Leonatus. If I cann't fight for you, I'l learn to pray.
Roxanna. But I have nothing for my self to say.

Statira next comes in favour again with the philandering Alexander. Ptolomy in a drunken fit attempts to rape Thalestris, but is pretty badly worsted : " *They tug a while, and the Queen o're-throws him.* He has previously remarked :—

> The Queen of *Amazons* now with a frown
> Could not check love, when drink has warm'd my crown ;
> And though, for love, a Queen I would not strike,
> I may for conquest wrestle it is like.

Thalestris again wooes Alexander, who in reply to her jealous disparagement of Statira coldly checks her with

> I should believe this, Madam, were't not known
> She always scorn'd dissimulation.

In Scena Ultima he invites the Amazon Queen to be present at his nuptials with the daughter of Darius. This masculine-minded lady is very cruel in her refusal :—

> Excuse me, Sir, if I resolve to shun
> The witnessing your being both undone.

A dance of Amazons was designed to conclude the play.

William Joyner, the author of *The Roman Empress,* produced at the Theatre Royal, in August, 1670; 4to, 1671, is a noble and indeed a saintly figure. The son of William Joyner (*alias* Lyde) of Horspath [93] and Anne, the daughter of Edward Lupworth, M.D., of Oxford, William Joyner was born in the parish of S. Giles, Oxford, and within a few days baptized at that church, on 24th April, 1622. He received his education at Thame and at Coventry Grammar School, and was elected Demy of Magdalen College, Oxford, 6th May, 1636. He proceeded B.A. 3rd November, 1640 ; and M.A. 7th July, 1643. He was a Probationary Fellow of his College from 1642 to 1645, when he resigned his Fellowship upon his conversion to Catholicism. He then entered the household of Edward, Earl of Glamorgan, eldest son of the Marquess of Worcester, with whom he went to Ireland, afterward accompanying him into France and Germany, " whereby," says Wood, " he improved himself much as to the knowledge of men and various parts of learning." After this he was commended to the service of the Honourable Walter Montagu, Lord Abbot of S. Martin near Pontoise, youngest son of Edward, first Earl of Manchester. Abbot Montagu employed Joyner in a position of trust and confidence, as his domestic steward, in which office he was " much esteemed for his learning, sincere religion, and great fidelity ". The Abbot dying in 1669, Joyner returned to England and " spent several years in London in a most retired and studious condition ". It was then that he wrote his one play *The Roman Empress,* which was produced at the Theatre Royal, as has been noted, in August, 1670. Some seven years later upon the violent commotions and disorders that were fomented by Oates' plot Joyner retired to Horspath, where in 1678 he was seized upon by the fanatical Vice-Chancellor, Dr. John Nicholas, Warden of New, who declared that he was a Jesuit, or at any rate a priest. He was accordingly bound by the Vice-Chancellor to appear at the sessions held at Oxford Guildhall, in January, 1678, but no evidence being forthcoming the matter fell through, and Joyner withdrew to still greater seclusion at Ickford, Bucks, a tiny village on the borders of Oxfordshire and Buckinghamshire, some 4 miles from Thame. In 1686–7 Joyner was restored to his Fellowship by King James II, and thus was to some extent inevitably involved in the troubles when Magdalen College so disloyally and disgracefully resisted the King. On Tuesday, 15th November, 1687 : " The Commissioners came to Oxford. They alighted at Magdalen College, where they were received by the Bishop, the Dean, Obadiah [Walker, Master of University], old Joyner, and others of that gang." On the following day at nine in the morning : " The Lords Commissioners being set, the first thing they did, they sent for the Buttery Book, then called for Mr. Joyner and Mr. Allibone,[94] and entered them actual Fellows." [95] At the Revolution Joyner was deprived of his Fellowship, " and retired to his former recess," living very frugally in a small thatched cottage at Ickford in the greatest obscurity and anchorism. There are several references to Joyner in the Diary of Thomas Hearne, who notes : " On Friday, Sept. 18th [1706] died Mr. William Joyner, who had been Fellow of Magdalen College . . . Upon King James's turning out the Fellows of Magdalen he was restored, but quickly outed again. Afterwards he lived in a retired condition partly near Brill in Oxfordshire, and partly in a house adjoining to the north part of Holywell Church [St. Cross] in Oxford ; in the last of which he died, and was buried in the churchyard of that place. He died pretty wealthy . . . He was a large man, very cheerful and pleasant, and died singing a hymn . . . I was acquainted with Mr. Joyner, and used to visit him at the Manor House at Holywell, where he lodged, after dinner, it being his desire I would come at that time, because of his going to bed always at four in the evening, and rising at four in the morning. . . . He would talk very pleasantly and have a pint of ale by himself, and a very hard crust . . . He was a religious, retired man . . . Mr. Kymber used to tell me that the said Mr. Joyner spent a very great part of his time upon his knees, so that whenever they peeped secretly through the keyhole, where he lodged, they always found him in that posture." A.D. 1712, 21st July, Hearne has: "A white freestone is laid over Mr. William Joyner's grave in Holywell churchyard, with this inscription: *William Joyner, Gentleman, who died Sept.* 14th, 1706, *aged* 84 *years.*"

Wood often used to visit Joyner, who "told him many stories which he, Mr. Wood, penned down in his presence". In addition to *The Roman Empress* Joyner write *Some Observations upon the Life of Reginaldus Polus, Cardinal,* 8vo, 1686 [96]; and he is also the author of lines in *Musarum Oxon-Charisteria,* 1638; and *Carolini Rosa Altera,* 1640.[97]

Joyner in his Dedication of *The Roman Empress* to Sir Charles Sedley tells us that "this Tragedy, in spight of a dead Vacation, and some other impediments, found the applause & approbation of the Theatre is oft as it appear'd". "I am apt to believe," says Langbaine, "that under the Character of *Valentinus,* the Author means *Constantine* the Great; and that *Crispus,* and his Mother-in-law *Faustina,* are shadow'd under the Characters of *Florus* and *Fulvia,*" [98] which much indeed is hinted in the Preface. The cast was as follows: Valentinus, Roman Emperour, Mohun; Florus, whose other name is Vespasius, General of Valentinus, proving at last to be his Son, Kynaston; Honorius, his friend, Epicurean in his opinions, Bell; Statilius, a Military Councellor, Favourite of Valentinus, Lydal; Macrinus, a great Person, vulgarly passing for the Father of Florus, Beeston; Servilius and Carbo, Great Courtiers and Commanders, William Harris and Littlewood; Fulvia, Roman Empress, in love with Florus, the young Mrs. Marshall (Rebecca); Antonia, Lady of Honour to Fulvia, wife to Servilius, Mrs. Mary Knepp; Hostilius, Tyrant of Rome, Watson; Arsenius his General, and thinking himself father of Florus; Aurelia, Daughter of Hostilius, of singular beauty, belov'd of Florus, Mrs. Boutell; Sophonia, her Governess, who proves to be Palladia, first wife of Valentinus, supposed long before dead, Mrs. Corey. "The *Scene* of this Drama or Action is about the Banks of *Tiber*: where *Hostilius* and his Party are suppos'd to be in *Rome,* or on the *Roman* side of the River: And *Valentinus* with his Party encampt on the other side in the nature of Besiegers." The plot to some extent follows the historians. Thus Fulvia, passionately enamoured of Florus, accuses him, when he rejects her love, to Valentinus. In consequence Florus is executed, but Fulvia escapes [99] and Valentinus stabs himself. The Plot is "*variously intricated*" by the love of Aurelia, the daughter of Hostilius (by whom Maxentius would seem to be intended), for Florus. Yet as the author truly points out " *here is nothing Episodical ; which I have not made essential in the construction of the Story* ". Rebecca Marshall was very great as Fulvia, a rôle of which Joyner says : " *if my art fail'd in the writing of it, it was highly recompens'd in the scenical presentation, for it was incomparably acted.*" He further compliments Mrs. Boutell for her "Aurelia, *which, though a great, various, and difficult part, was excellently performed* ". The "*false Pagan Gallantry*" of Honorius is well drawn and distinguished, and it is very certain that no just exceptions can be taken to it.

The diction of *The Roman Empress* is nervous, poetical, and animated. The scenes are always dignified yet natural ; the catastrophe surprising yet consistent ; the situations interesting and pathetic. " Through his Roman tragedy there runs a pensive vein of sadness, as though the poet were thinking less of his Aurelia and his Valentinus than of the lost common-room and the arcades of Magdalen to be no more revisited." This work must in fine be accorded no mean place in the long roll of our dramatic literature.

There is preserved in Worcester College Library, Oxford, a MS. (Plays 9, 20) which was bound as and went under the name *Aurelia* (MS. 120 C.). This I identified as Joyner's *The Roman Empress*. In the Preface to the Quarto Joyner says : " *I wrote the quantity of three or four Playes upon this noble Subject ; of which I conceive this the best extract.*" The Worcester MS. is unfortunately not a prompt copy, but plainly one of these earlier drafts. It consists of forty-four pages of foolscap size very clearly and neatly written on both sides, almost without erasures.

Although no very material alterations occur there are not a few differences between the printed quarto and the MS., which it will be necessary for a future editor of Joyner to collate very scrupulously. Tucca of the MS. is renamed Carbo ; Macrinus " a great Comander " is "A great Person ", Fulvia is described as " Empris, ardently in love with Florus but never practically lascivious "; Aurelia " a Princesse of great beauty whose virtues & vices are almost equal ".

There is no reason to identify Edward Revet, the author of *The Town-Shifts, Or The Suburb-Justice* produced at Lincoln's Inn Fields in March, 1671, with Revet the actor, as Mr. Hotson rather sweepingly asserts in his *Commonwealth and Restoration Stage.*[100] But Mr. Hotson is generally hazardous and never very happy in similar instances of random guess-work ; as when, for example, he imagines that Elizabeth Davenport of the Theatre Royal played Roxalana at Lincoln's Inn Fields,[101] a sorry blunder enough. There was an Eldred Revett, whose *Poems* were published 12mo, 1657. The only copy I have seen of this exceedingly scarce book was that in the library—since dispersed—of my late friend, Mr. G. Thorn-Drury, K.C.[102]

The characters in *The Town-Shifts* are : Ned Lovewell, Cademan ; Frank Friendly, Medbourne ; Tom Faithfull, Westwood ; Leftwell, Edward Angel ; Pett, Norris ; Justice Frump, Sandford ; Stingey, his clerk, Sherwood ; Runwell, Whaley ; Moses, Williams ; Clowt the Constable ; Squeeze the gaoler ; Mold the sexton ; Leticia, Mrs. Mary Lee ; Fickle, Mrs. Long ; Betsy, Mrs. Dixon ; Goody Fells, Mrs. Norris. The plot is simple. Ned Lovewell is in very reduced circumstances, yet he will not give his two comrades Friendly and Faithfull the go-by, as young Leftwell who has just come into an estate and flaunts it, saddled in silk, would have him do. Leticia, the daughter of Pett an East India Merchant dwelling at Hackney, has a great affection for Lovewell, but her father refuses to hear of it, the more so as he designs her for Looby Leftwell. Goody Fells, Friendly and Faithfull's old landlady, is an amusing character, although she applies to Justice Frump, who dispatches Clowt the Constable to deal with her lodgers. Leticia supplies Lovewell with money, and he is thus able to refurnish himself and his two companions with brave new clothes. There is a good scene at Pett's house where all is in a bustle as he directs his cook and Mrs. Snuff the housekeeper to make preparations for his daughter's wedding. Early that very morning while it is still dark Leticia elopes with Lovewell, and Fickle with Frank Friendly. They repair to Mold's dwelling next the church in order that a parson may be procured to tie the matrimonial knot, but unfortunately here they fall in with Clowt and old Goody Fells, who raise a mighty hubbub, and on suspicion the runaways are haled before Justice Frump. So Mr. Pett brings them back home. Leftwell is frightened into believing that Lovewell and Friendly intend to murder him, and allows Betty to conceal him, whilst the two couples are married. Pett declares himself reconciled to the inevitable.

The chief fault of *The Town-Shifts* is that the incidents are a little thin-spun, whilst the humorous scenes, although far from dull, prove not sufficiently droll and ingenious to support so slender a story. This was due to the fact " *that it was thought on, begun, and finished, in a fortnight* ". One point of interest about *The Town-Shifts* is that it may be regarded as in a very real sense a throw-back to the Elizabethan. Goody Fells, Clowt, and Mold smack not merely of Brome, but also of earlier dramatists than Brome. Lovewell with his estimable and almost quixotic ideas of Honour and Honesty as also his healthily sentimental Leticia might have been drawn by Heywood. Another detail worth remark is that here we have realistic scenes of middle-class life and manners. There is not even a knight's title in the play.[103] A brisker if not better piece of work is *The Generous Enemies, Or The Ridiculous Lovers,* the one play by John Corye, of whom nothing is known. This comedy was produced at the Theatre Royal in June–July, 1671, with the following cast : Signior Robatzy, Wintershal ; Signior Cassiodoro, in love with Jaccinta but beloved by Alleria, Lydal ; Don Alvarez, in love with Alleria, Mohun ; Signior Flaminio, in love with Jaccinta, Kynaston ; Don Bertram, An humorous old man, Cartwright ; Sanco, his man, Dick Bell ; Pedro, his groom, Shirley ; Addibar, Flamineo's man, Richard Hart ; Jaccinta, sister to Alvarez, Mrs. Marshall ; Alleria, daughter to Robatzy, Mrs. James ; Lysander, who is Semena, Flamineo's sister in disguise, Mrs. Boutell ; Sophia, Mother to Flamineo and Semena, Mrs. Pratt ; Julia, Alleria's woman, Mrs. Corey ; Livia, Jaccinta's woman, Mrs. Uphill. The Scene is at Seville.

Langbaine who dubs Corye "A Gentleman who is pleas'd to stile himself the Author of a Play call'd *The Generous Enemies or The Ridiculous Lovers* ", is extremely severe in his notice of this comedy and quotes a saying of Apollodorus concerning the works of Chrysippus the Stoic philosopher : " If a Man should extract the things which he hath borrow'd from others, the Paper would be left blank." " Εἰ γάρ τις ἀφέλοι τῶν Χρυσίππου βιβλίων ὅσ' ἀλλότρια παρατέθειται, κενὸς αὐτῷ ὁ χάρτης καταλελείψεταϊ. Καὶ ταῦτα μὲν 'Απολλόδωρος.' (Diogenes Laertius, *De Clarorum Philosophorum Vitis,* VII, vii, 181.) It must be acknowledged that Corye is a great plagiary, and has levied pretty freely both from English and from French authors. Thus the main theme of the play, the " Generous Enemies ", is from Quinault's " Tragi-Comédie-Pastorale " *La Généreuse Ingratitude,* produced in 1654.[104] Semena in the habit of Lysander is very plainly Zélinde disguised as Ormin ; whilst Don Alvarez is Zégri ; Flaminio, Abencerage " sous le nom d'Almansor " ; and Lindarache, Sophia. Alleria has something of Fatime, in her love for Cassidoro, who is in certain respects moulded upon Abidar, amant de Zaide, in the English, Jaccinta. The intrigue is fairly obvious from these premises, and it were superfluous, I apprehend, to follow it in detail. At the conclusion every Jack has his Jill ; Don Alvarez being overcome with love and gratitude weds Semena. In Act I when Lysander-Semena relates her history to Alvarez—" There

PLATE XXI

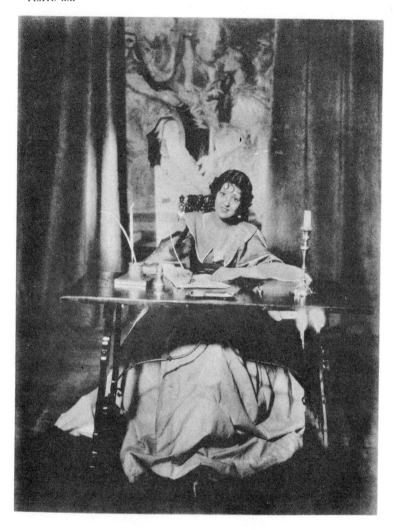

LESLEY WAREING AS MRS. MARGERY PINCHWIFE

The Country-Wife, March 1934

iface p. 388

was a young Lady, Sir, that lov'd me tenderly, who scarce had numbered 15 years," who was betrayed but in a masculine habit pursued and overtook the Insnarer of her faith, there would appear to be some suggestion from *Twelfth Night* were it not that the speech is paraphrased from Quinault, i, 5. But the similarity is striking.

The Ridiculous Lover—for the plural is superfluous and indeed incorrect—Don Bertran of Seggaral is Thomas Corneille's Don Bertran de Cigarral, the principal figure of his homonymous comedy acted in 1650. *Don Bertran de Cigarral* is itself taken from *Entre Bobos anda el juego, ó don Lucas de Cigarral* one of the most fantastic pieces of Franciso de Rojas Zorilla. Don Bertran is thus described by his valet Guzman, i, 2 :—

> Il mouche, il tousse, il crache en poûmon malaisé,
> Pour fluxions sans cesse il est cautérisé ;
> Gouteux ce que doit l'estre un Gouteux d'origine,
> Toujours vers le poignet muny de la plus fine ;
> Joignez à tout cela, vilain, jaloux, quinteux,
> Obstiné plus qu'un Diable, et mutin plus que deux,
> Mal propre autant que douze en mine, en barbe, en linge,
> Rusé comme un renard, et malin comme un singe.

None the less this horrible old apparition enjoys an income of 6,000 ducats, and it is to him that, blinded by the gold, Don Garcie de Contreras Isabelle's father has pledged her hand. The scene is an inn on the road from Madrid to Toledo, and there results an almost infinite complexity of accidents and cross-turns.[105] Eventually Don Bertrand is glad to renounce his pretensions to Isabelle, who weds his kinsman Don Alvar, her admirer but a lover adroit enough to secure from his choused cousin 2,000 ducats as a guerdon for taking the lady. In *The Generous Enemies* Sancho represents Guzman, and the above passage from Corneille appears thus : " Such are the infinite number of diseases that afflict him, he is the Practice of all Physicians ; not only his Garden, but his very Windows are set with Physick-Herbs, he is continually perplexed with Fluxes, and Aches quarter in every bone of him ; then he is as obstinate as a devil, and as Mutinous as Tow ; a most abominable Sloven, yet as crafty as a Fox, and as malicious as a Monkey."

Corye has conveyed a good deal almost verbatim from *Love's Pilgrimage* by Beaumont and Fletcher,[106] much more indeed than was noted by Langbaine, who only draws attention to the quarrels, ii, 1, and iii, 3, between the two choleric old men, Sanchio and Don Alphonso, which Corye conflated for the angry encounter of Don Arnaldo Robatzy and Don Fernando Bertran at the commencement of Act V of his play. The episode of Don Fernando Bertran and his two servants, Sancho and Pedro, Act III, perhaps derives a hint from Colax and Dyscolus in Randolph's *The Muses Looking-glasse,* 1638, ii, 1.

The Generous Enemies or The Ridiculous Lovers proves a mosaic, but it is a cleverly wrought mosaic, and Corye should receive some credit for his adroit workmanship. The first scene of the play, a fire, servants running with buckets, and after the confusion the change to the quiet of the garden where Alvarez enters bearing in his arms the swooning Alleria is a good opening and effective.

A far better writer than Corye, and a dramatist whom even Langbaine dare not tax with plagiarism, was Henry Nevil *alias* Payne. He is further an interesting, and I will add a noble, figure. The date of his birth has not been precisely ascertained, but he was a young man, probably in the early twenties, at the time of the production of his first play in 1672, and we shall not be far out if we hazard 1647–1650. At the time of Oates' plot Payne often stood in considerable danger owing to his staunch loyalty, and he soon attracted the very particular and unfavourable attention of the Whigs by whom since the success of *The Siege of Constantinople* in November, 1674, he had been a marked man. In 1680 Payne assisted Mrs. Cellier in the penning of her *Malice Defeated: Or a Brief Relation of the Accusation and Deliverance of Elizabeth Cellier,* folio [107]; in 1685 he published *The Persecutor Exposed,* a political tract; and two years later issued *An Answer to a scandalous Pamphlet entitled a Letter to a Dissenter concerning his Majestie's late Declaration of Indulgence.* This called forth an abusive and contemptible rejoinder from a scribbler who signed himself T.T. After the Revolution Payne had the distinction of being regarded as " the most active and determined of all King James's agents ", which caused Burnet with his usual indifference to truth, or rather love of a lie, to throw a good deal of mud. Henry Payne indeed is believed to have been the chief contriver of the loyal design to restore King James II to the throne, a project in which Sir James Montgomery, tenth baronet of Skelmorlie took so large a part, but which was unhappily discovered probably owing to the treachery of Robert Ferguson. It is hardly necessary to enter into the long and tangled narrative, the circumstances of which brand William of Orange with eternal infamy. Sufficient to say that it was illegally resolved to put Henry Payne to the question in order that he might reveal the whole business. The Privy Council on 4th August, 1690, sent to Scotland where Payne was confined an order for the infliction of torture, and as this was not immediately acted upon the usurper dispatched a special order on

18th November. So on 10th and 11th December this " dastardly
fellow ", as they mockingly called the King's faithful servant,
suffered the excruciating agony of the thumbscrew and the boot.
However, to their surprise he endured the torments with great
constancy, and they were unable to extract a word. " Torture
had been declared by them against the claim of right of the
people, and illegal and tyrannical, but they inserted a very
necessary clause, and fit for their own occasions, ' except upon
extraordinary occasions,' which made every case extraordinary
and necessary when they found it for their own interest." [108]
Contrary to law, Payne was still kept in prison without being
brought to trial, and this gave Burnet occasion to invent a
specious tale, which will not hold water for a minute, in order
that the worst of the Whiggish blackguardism, too bad to bear
the light of day, might be palliated and excused. On the petition
of his nephew, Francis Payne, for some time after the excessive
torture Henry Payne was allowed open prison and the attendance
of his own physicians and surgeons. This was hurriedly over-
ruled by William of Orange on 23rd December, 1690, and as
late as 1699 Payne was in close confinement in Stirling Castle,
where he was granted for certain hours during each day liberty
over a range of half a mile from the Castle in order to conduct
important experiments in river navigation. On 9th December,
1700, the Duke of Queensberry wrote to Carstares that their
prisoner must be set at liberty as his detention was against
every principle of justice or right. Of Payne's later years nothing
is known, nor (I believe) has the date of his death been traced.

Fortunately our concern is with earlier and happier days.
Downes chronicles :—

" Loves Jealousy, and The Morning Ramble.	Written by Mr. Nevil Pain.

Both were very well Acted, but after their first run, were laid
aside, to make Room for others ; the Company having then
plenty of new Poets."

Loves Jealousy or rather The Fatal Jealousie, a tragedy, was
produced at Dorset Garden on 3rd August, 1672, with the
following cast : Don Antonio, a jealous Lord, Smith ; Don
Gerardo, his friend, Medbourne ; Don Francisco, Young ;
Don Sebastian, his friend, Crosby ; Jasper, a villain, servant to
Antonio, Sandford ; Pedro, another servant, Burford ; Gerardo's
servant, Norris ; Captain of the Watch, Nat Lee (the poet) ;
Caelia, wife to Antonio, Mrs. Shadwell ; Eugenia, her sister,
Mrs. Betterton ; Flora, Caelia's woman, Mrs. Osborn ; Witch,
aunt to Jasper, Mrs. Norris ; Nurse to Caelia, James Nokes.
The Scene is Naples.

Jasper was one of Sandford's most remarkable rôles, and Nokes in petticoats was very great as the Nurse.

The plot of this powerful tragedy concerns the unfounded suspicions of Don Antonio, who is madly jealous of his wife Caelia. These sick and sad self-deceptions are cunningly fomented by the vicious Jasper, a servant, but in reality Jasper de Monsalvo, the son of a traitor, whose forfeited estates had by the King been bestowed upon Antonio, and who thus seeks revenge. In order to further his ends Jasper has to serve as a stallion-drudge to Caelia's lustful old nurse, and from this perfidious trot he learns that Antonio's sister, Eugenia, has allowed Don Francisco to enjoy her, whereupon he also desires a share of her favours. Eugenia's brother is about to bestow her upon Don Gerardo, and when her lover visits her at night it is contrived that she shall wear Caelia's attire, at which Antonio who has been set to watch kills her, deeming it to be his wife who is granting some roving gallant a rendezvous. Gerardo and Francisco duel in the dark with fatal results. When these villainies are discovered Jasper having run his rapier through the Nurse as she is confessing her treacheries, foully stabs Antonio in the back, and at last exultant in his infamy escapes justice by his dagger's point.

The feigned Witch is Jasper's aunt, and to her he applies to aid him in his malignant schemes. At first he believes she is a genuine sorceress, but she disabuses him and frankly acknowledges—

I can raise no Devils,
Yet I Confederate with Rogues and Taylors,
Things that can shape themselves like Elves,
And Goblins—

Her imps, *Ranter* and *Swash, Dive, Fop, Snap, Gilt* and *Picklock,* are slim lads in masquing habits, trained to trickery. None the less at Jasper's bidding they manage an incantation scene further to persuade and convince Antonio that Caelia is untrue. An " Antick Dance of Devils " which follows is interrupted by the forcible entry of the Watch. The Aunt shows Jasper a secret hiding-place, whereupon he murders her and conceals the body in the hole. He pretends that she was in truth a witch and has vanished by art magic. The Captain of the Watch, however, had detected her charlatanry long before, and presently a demon's vizor and a domino are found on the premises. Later a little boy, who is caught in his devil's attire, confesses the impostures, and trembling adds that in one of the secret chambers they have discovered their mistress's corpse poniarded to death.

The Morning Ramble, or, The Town-Humours, produced at Dorset

Garden on 4th November, 1672, was Payne tells us "*nine dayes work*", wherefore "*His Play Pretends neither to Wit nor Plot*", and is merely to be judged as

A thing made up of Fiddle, Song, and Dance.

It is truly a slight enough piece, but the dialogue is extremely vivacious, even if plot be almost wanting. The scene opens at two-o-clock in the morning and fair weather. Will Merry (Harris) has resolved "to make a Night on't", and with Townlove (Betterton) in his company he serenades Honour Muchland (Mrs. Johnson). Rose, her woman (Mrs. Shadwell), endeavours to drive him away, but eventually Muchland (Medbourne), the lady's brother, is persuaded to join in the frolic. Thence they proceed to the house of Ned Rash (Crosby), whom they forthwith gather in their train, also awakening his sister, Betty (Mrs. Long). Meanwhile in order to watch the sport Honour Muchland and Rose venture abroad in men's clothes. There is a very amusing episode when the roistril crew rescue from the round-house four night-wandering whores, who give a very good account of their trade, and of whom one proves to be Mrs. Last, the old constable's wife, in a lewd vizor-mask. There are some gaming-house incidents, Ruffle (Smith) being choused at dice by two confederates, Fullam (Underhill) and Breef (Norris). There is also a duel in Hyde Park at six-o-clock in the morning, for Ruffle has challenged Muchland, and by a trick Rash, Merry, and Townlove find themselves involved. Some very pointed topical satire occurs here, as plainly hinted in the Prologue :

> *you'l see him now*
> *Have a slight pass or two at some of you;*
> *He thinks there's Bullys dare not fight, i' th' Pit*
> *As well as Cricticks, that he's sure want wit.*

Muchland would have Ruffle sign a paper, but this gentleman protests : " Gad, *Mr. Muchland,* the words are too severe, there is no enduring of 'em—let me leave out this sentence : *And like a Cowardly Son of a whore as I am* : Look you, Sir, this is abusing of my Mother, and she had not the least hand in the Quarrel." This is a sharp hit at Otway's challenge to Elkanah Settle, when " Mr. O. a man of the Sword " compelled the author of *The Empress of Morocco* to pen and subscribe the following words : *I confess I Writ the* Sessions of the Poets, *and am very sorry for't, and am the Son of a W——for doing it ; Witness my hand E.S.*"[109]

Lady Turnup is a good character in *The Morning Ramble,* although she only appears in one short episode when she is very familiar with Townlove. The comedy ends agreeably enough in Coleby's,[110] at the Mulberry Garden, about eight-o-clock in the morning.

The Siege of Constantinople, a tragedy, Nevil Payne's third play produced at Dorset Garden in 1674, will be dealt with at length as a political drama in the next volume.

It was during the year 1671, whilst he was living at Broad Chalk, Wiltshire, that John Aubrey bethought himself to compose a realistic comedy of country life as he saw it all around him. The rough draft of this piece is preserved in Bodley, MS. Aubrey 21, and although it was never completed a fair idea of several scenes and of the general conduct of the plot can be formed. Most of the projected play is written in the blank spaces and between the lines of a lengthy legal document. The comedy is entitled *The Countrey Revell, or the Revell of Aldford.* The Scene lies at " Aldford in Cheshire by yᵉ River Dee. Sᵗ Peters day, 1669 ". Act I, scene 1, is " Christian Malford Green ", which shows us that Aubrey had in mind an actual locality, Christian-Malford, a Wiltshire village and parish situate on the Avon, six miles north-east of Chippenham. Among the Dramatis Personae as roughly listed are : Sir Courtoise, Knight of the Bath, a Protector of distressed ladies ; Lady Euphrasia, wife to Sʳ Libidinous (Gregorie) Goatman=cookemayd, and Lady Pamela, wife to Sʳ Surly Chagrin=waiting woman, two Platonics ; Mrs. Salacious ; Ralph yᵉ footman ; Justice Wagstaffe ; Squire Fitz-ale ; Sʳ Fastidious Overween ; Capt. Exceptious Quarrel-some ; Sowgelder ; Sʳ Hugh yᵉ Vicar ; Sir Eubule Nestor, disguised as Sʳ Surly Chagrin ; Sir Eglamour Collin, disguised as Sʳ Gr. Goatman ; Squeaker, a shee-Balladess ; Margery Maquesell, Bawde ; (Peg, her mayd or daughter) ; Lord of May Pole. It must be remembered that these names are very confusedly scrawled with suggested alterations and some erasures. The comedy was to depict the humours of a country wake, when a few gentlemen and ladies of the courtly old school were to be contrasted with the sottish debauchery and general boorishness of contemporary rural life. Sow-gelders, carters, dairy-maids, gypsies, and a motley throng of hinds exhibit the lewd talk and gross loutishness of the villagers. Thus the play opens with the gossip of a number of country wenches. With these, in tavern and in revels on the green, mingles the neighbouring squirearchy. As the plot develops we were to be shown the innocent pastoral loves of a lad and maid of gentle birth, Damon and Phyllis, living in disguise as a shepherd and a dairy-maid, the " Lord and Lady of the Maypole ". Other episodes concern Mrs. Raynes who in page's attire follows her lover Sir Fastidious, and is jealous of his wanton play with other women.

" Raynes comes & invades Sir Fastidious Overween, & is slayne by him; and then Sir Fastidious neglects her; & wooes Pamela, *nulla vis Illata,* &c : she comes & stabbes him, & then herselfe." A character who was to have been considerably elaborated is Mrs. Knolls, " a lady of a good fortune and family : *&* pride : she scornd all govt : Mary Ambree or the pucell d'Orleans had never a higher or more masculine spirit than shee." None the less she runs away with Tom, her father's groom, a native of Aldford. " Let Madam Cockayn come to visit her." Mrs. Knolls very frankly confesses " the great & violent passion that shee had for Tom. Shee fasted & prayed ". There was to be introduced " A ballad on this humour of L. Cockayn ".

Aubrey has jotted down various anecdotes which were to be worked into plot or dialogue, and it is interesting to remark that here and there he has pricked down the initials or name of the person he was drawing under some fanciful title. Thus Sir Eubule Nestor is Thomas Tyndale (1588–1672) " an old gentleman that remembers Queen Elizabeth's raigne and court . . . and with much choler inveighes against things now ", as Aubrey notes in his *Brief Lives.*[111]

It should be mentioned that as Appendix II to his edition of Aubrey's *Brief Lives,*[112] Andrew Clark has given some account of " Aubrey's Comedy of Restoration Manners " and furnished excerpts from two scenes.

It is a little difficult from the rough outline he has left to judge whether *The Countrey Revell* could have been wrought into a good comedy. Much of the theme seems a little unpromising, but by the side of episodes which would appear to be designed as extremely artificial and stilted we have sketches of the rustic ale-house, which are absolutely Hogarthian in their vivid realism of talk and manners. An Elizabethan dramatist, Heywood or Dekker, might have made something too of Mrs. Raynes and Sir Fastidious, but I doubt if we missed much when Aubrey left their tale untold.

Although intended for the stage, and duly equipped with Prologue and Epilogue, *Emilia,* which is described as a Tragedy but more correctly (in the Epilogue) as a Tragi-Comedy, does not appear ever to have been acted. It was " Printed for the Author ", London, 8vo, 1672, and from the prefatory address " *To the Onely Few* " it is plain it was at least offered to the theatre since the writer says : " I Print not this *Play* before it is Acted, to make it more *Publick,* but onely more *Legible* for those who are to judge of it ; who, if they like it in this *Undress,* will much more in its *Theatrical Habit.*"

The play is taken from *La Costanza di Rosmonda* of Aurelio

Aureli, which was performed at the Teatro Grimani di Zanipolo (SS. Giovanni e Paolo), Venice, in 1659; 12mo, 1659. Aureli, a Venetian, was born about 1634 and died in 1711. He was attached to the household of the Duke of Parma, and was much esteemed by his contemporaries for his dramas which were set to music by the eminent composers of the day. Most of these were produced in the Venetian theatres, and received with great applause. His first play was *Eriginda,* 1652, given at the Teatro Grimani. *La Pace fra Cesariani e Pompeiani* was produced in 1709, and in the autumn of 1729 appeared at the Teatro Formagliani, Bologna, a posthumous pastoral *Amore e Gelosia*; 12mo, 1731. A list of his six and thirty pieces is supplied by Giammaria Mazzuchelli in his *Scrittori d'Italia,* Tom. I, parte 2 (1753), pp. 1273–74.

The author of *Emilia* says: "The *Writing* or *Language,* I have accommodated to the Persons; *Verse,* for the most Heroick, and *Prose,* for the rest, with often allay of this with the other, to make it more flexible, which else would be too stiff." Several of his scenes are written in rhyme "which our English Ears by Custom do so expect, as they will scarcely allow *Verses* to be compleat without it", but he scrupulously refrains from commendation "because it has so many Potent Enemies" or condemnation "because it has so many Potent Friends".

The characters of *Emilia* are: The Duke of Micena; the Prince, his son; Calimachus, his General; Palemon, the general's friend; Agenor, a courtier; Cleanthes, a courtier of Argos; Clymias and Cleobulo, Emilia's servants, to supply light relief; the Duchess of Micena; Emilia, the wife of Calimachus; Aurindo Irena Princess of Argos, "*disguised,* En Page"; Cleora, Olinda, women to the Duchess; Althea, Emilia's woman; Masquers. The Scene: Micena. The Unities are strictly observed. The Prince of Micena was intended to marry the Princess of Argos, but being enamoured of Emilia did not seek the lady's hand. Emilia, in the absence of her husband at the war, leads a life of cloistral retirement. The Prince, knowing that Emilia visits the shrine of Mars in her private chapel to pray for her husband, takes the statue's place and leaps from the pedestal, whither he is obliged to return on the arrival of the Duke who begins to court Emilia. Calimachus, who has unexpectedly come home, is seized with jealousy. Meanwhile the Duchess, who is the old Duke's second wife, avows her passion for Aurindo, the Prince's page, who is the Princess of Argos, Irena, following the Prince for love. Calimachus now masquerades as an Ethiop, a dumb slave, supposed to be sent to Emilia by her husband. The Duke attempts to ravish Emilia, but she snatches out his poniard and threatens to stab herself. The Ethiop witnesses this scene, and is filled with joy to find—

> *Emilia* is as pure and chaste,
> As Ice or Chrystal,
> And Ermin on the Snow.

Aurindo visits Emilia to plead the Prince's suit, but she rebukes and reproves the messenger, who thereupon discloses the secret of her sex. They embrace, and are seen by Calimachus, who now suspects the page is the favoured lover, whilst the Duchess who also has caught sight of Emilia and Aurindo vows revenge. Various complications ensue, since both Calimachus and the Duchess seek Aurindo's life. Emilia, however, persuades Aurindo to doff male attire, and news having come that Calimachus is slain, promises to wed the Prince at once and secretly, lest the Duke should prevent the nuptials. Irena (Aurindo) veiled takes Emilia's place, and when Calimachus discovers himself all mistakes are explained. The Duke is careful to ask pardon of Calimachus—

> that I
> So far have tryed *Emilia's* constancy,
> But that you know, with no other intention
> But onely to try her constancy 'twas done.
> *Calimachus.* I know it well, my Lord—or it is best
> To seem to know no otherwise at least.   *Aside.*

Of Thomas Duffett, whose pen was employed by the Theatre Royal to travesty successes at the rival Dorset Garden, actually nothing is known beyond the fact that he was " before he became a Poet, a Milliner in the New Exchange ". He left a volume of Poems, two comedies, a masque, and three burlesques, the merit of which is vastly underrated. In his day he won considerable notoriety, if not fame, by his popular skits on Settle, Dryden and Davenant, and Shadwell. Since his farces, *The Empress of Morocco, The Mock-Tempest,* and *Psyche Debauch'd* will be most fittingly considered in relation to the pieces they parody, there remain only his two more regular plays and the Masque to be reviewed here.

The Spanish Rogue, a comedy written in rhyme, was produced at the Theatre Royal in May, 1673, with the following cast : Don Fenise, William Harris ; Don Alonzo, Lydal ; Don Manuel, Watson ; Larasco, Martin Powell ; Mingo, Coysh ; Sanchez, Griffin ; Alcinda, Mrs. Boutell ; Rosella, Mrs. Uphill ; Teresa, Mrs. Corey ; Leonella, Mrs. Knepp. The plot of *The Spanish Rogue* is extremely complicated. Some nine or ten years before the play commences Don Valasco the father of Don

Fenise died, bequeathing to the guardianship of Don Alonzo's father, Don Pedro de Valiza, his orphan daughter, Calista, to be brought up with Don Pedro's own daughter, Laurina. Don Pedro, having shortly after been appointed to a governorship in Peru, sails for South America, taking the two children with him. Unhappily he fell sick upon the voyage, and in his last moments charged Sanchez, an old faithful servant, and a maid Guttarze who were travelling with him, to conduct Laurina and Calista back to Spain, and there to deliver them into the care of their respective brothers. Sanchez was true to his trust, but as they were nearing Spain they fell in with—

> Gorʒell, a cruel tatter'd Pickaroon ;
> Sancheʒ they murther'd, made the rest their prey.

Guttarze proved a vile traitress and joined with Gorzell, to whom she betrayed her late master's gold which they were carrying on board as well as Calista and Laurina.

Don Valasco and Don Pedro had long ago resolved to cement their friendship by a blood relationship between the families, and in spite of the extreme youth of their children they had contracted Don Alonzo to Calista, whilst Don Fenise in like manner was " oblig'd by vows " to marry Laurina. The years, however, have gone by and inasmuch as no news could be obtained of the vessel in which Don Pedro sailed for Peru it seems pretty certain that all who had embarked upon her must long since have perished. Don Fenise has fallen in love with Alcinda, one of the two daughters of Don Manuel and Donna Teresa, a starch Argus-eyed couple who keep a very strict ward against suitors and gallants.

The play commences at night in Don Manuel's house where Alcinda and her woman, Leonella, are waiting for Don Fenise who is late for his rendezvous. Alcinda retires in some displeasure, but Leonella tarries to inform Don Fenise of her mistress's vexation, whereupon in fury he turns his naked sword on his man, the foolish Larasco, who has delayed him, and whose cries promptly arouse the household so that Don Manuel comes rushing in and bawls " Thieves ! " at the top of his voice. Amid the confusion Fenise who has found his way to Leonella's chamber makes his peace with the lady. After some farcical incidents Larasco also manages to escape. Don Manuel and Teresa debate whether it will not be the better plan to enclose Alcinda and her sister Rosella in a convent. Leonella, who owing to Don Manuel's fears and jealousies cannot receive her lover, Don Alonzo's valet, Mingo (the Spanish Rogue), at the house now suggests he shall counterfeit " An Eunuch handsomely ", as Don Manuel designs to take some such castrato into his service to keep watch over Alcinda and Rosella. Mingo, who for his tricks has been turned off by his master, only too readily falls in with the idea, and is duly engaged by Don Manuel as a cut cock-duenna to play Cerberus over his daughters. It is just about now that Don Alonzo, the bearer of a message for Fenise to Alcinda, meets Rosella, and they instantly fall in love. Hearing that Alonzo requires a valet, one Sanchez, who says he once served Don Pedro de Valiza, applies and is incontinently engaged. Don Manuel informs Alcinda that he is not actually her father, but that he found her,

> Wandring and lost upon some pathless down.
> Forsaken by her Parents, and expos'd
> To fortunes mercy . . .
> Dejected, weary, hopeless, starv'd, and weak
> Where none could see her weep, or hear her speak.

In charity he gave her a home and educated her with his own daughter, Rosella. Her parents are unknown, and when she endeavours to express her gratitude he very frankly replies that this will be best shown by granting him a share of her favours, Upon her refusal he proceeds to force and is only prevented by the entrance of Mingo. It appears that old Teresa dotes upon Mingo, who has confided to her that he is no eunuch, and has made little scruple of telling him all her husband's secrets. There is a good deal of business at cross-purposes, but when Sanchez appears on the scene and strikes terror into Manuel and Teresa, they drop the mask and confess that they are none other than Gorzall and Guttarze, as the woman has already acknowledged to Mingo who very effectually blows the gaff. Alcinda is none other than Laurina, and Rosella, Calista ; so that Fenise and Alonzo by wedding their mistresses actually carry out the contract their parents made long ago, whilst Mingo is rewarded with the hand of Leonella. Manuel and Teresa are with difficulty granted their lives, but bidden leave Spain and warned that should they be discovered within its bound the law will take its course unchecked.

A good Prologue was spoken by Mrs. Boutell, and a racy Epilogue by Mrs. Mary Knepp. When printed, 4to, 1674, *The Spanish Rogue* was dedicated in courtliest compliment to Nell Gwyn.

The device employed by Mingo and his counterfeiting himself to be a eunuch may have been derived by Duffett from Terence's *Eunuchus,* which was so largely utilized by Sir Charles Sedley for *Bellamira, or The Mistress,* if indeed that comedy be wholly his. A more direct adaptation from Terence by L'Estrange and

Echard was performed at Drury Lane in July, 1717, and at the same house twenty years later was produced *The Eunuch; or, The Derby Captain,* a farce from Terence by Thomas Cooke, with Leigh in the title-rôle and Macklin as Captain Brag (Thraso). Almost equally as reticulated as the adventures of *The Spanish Rogue* is the plot of *The Amorous Old-woman; or, 'Tis Well if it Take,* a comedy produced at Drury Lane during March, 1674, and printed quarto the same year. It was reissued a decade later with a new title-page as *The Fond Lady.* The play is vaguely stated to be "Written By a Person of Honour", and Langbaine's ascription to Duffett is certainly correct, for even a cursory reading of these two comedies would unmistakably show that both were from the same author. Michael Mohun spoke the Prologue to *The Amorous Old-woman,* but as was so often the case with a Lenten play the cast is badly balanced, and indeed so far as the men were concerned, seems distinctly second-rate, although curiously enough the female characters were allotted to four actresses of admitted excellence. Lydal played Honorio, in Love with Arabella ; Beeston, Amante, in Love with Clara ; Eastland, Garbato, in Love with Arabella ; Carey Perin, Cicco, a blind Senator that pretends to see ; Coysh, Riccamare, his Brother, in love with Riches ; Chapman, Buggio, a Fellow that delights in Romancing ; Martin Powell, Furfante, servant to Cicco ; and Shirley, Sanco-panco, servant to Strega. Thus it must be acknowledged that these rôles were assigned to very indifferent performers. Incidentally, as no actor of the name Eastland is found elsewhere in any record I have suggested that Garbato was played by Mrs. Eastland, who generally sustained such minor rôles as Cydnon, an attendant in *Tyrannick Love,* June, 1669 ; and Halyma, who speaks two lines in *The Conquest of Granada,* I, December, 1670. For an actress to appear in a male character, we may remind ourselves, would be nothing at all out of the common. Yet the "Women Actors" in *The Amorous Old-woman* included Mrs. Cox as Constantia, sister to Honorio ; Mrs. James, Arabella, daughter to Cicco ; Mrs. Boutell, Clara, in love with Honorio ; and Mrs. Corey, Strega, an old Rich deformed lady. Mrs. Cox, Mrs. Boutell, and Mrs. Corey at least, were performers of the first rank.

The Scene of the play is Pisa. Amante, who had long paid his addresses to Honorio's sister, Constantia, became enamoured of Clara, and accordingly ceased his suit to the lady whom he had formerly admired. Won by Constantia's tears and entreaties, her brother has promised and even bound himself by an oath not to seek satisfaction from the fickle Amante, whom she still tenderly loves. However, he no longer considers himself held by his plighted word when the news reaches him as he roundly tells her erstwhile suitor face to face :

> Y' have given out (thereby
> To justifie your levity) my Sister was unchast,
> And that the reason you forsook her Love ;
> That I (being conscious of my Sisters guilt)
> Durst not confirm't to th' world by my revenge.

The result is a challenge, which Amante accepts. Actually the report that Amante has defamed the lady is false, a malicious invention of one Buggio, a loose gossip than whom none is more eager to disseminate a daily pack of lies and scandal. Honorio himself seeks to wed the fair Arabella, daughter of old Signor Cicco. Her father favours the match and has straitly forbidden her to see Garbato, a young gallant who seeks her hand. Clara dotes upon Honorio, and the further to effect her designs, if haply she may prevent the marriage, disguised as a page, Infortunio, takes service with Arabella. Honorio requests Buggio to be his second in the duel, whereupon the fellow being a poltroon as well as a false witness promptly informs Constantia who contrives to lock her brother fast in the house, and presents herself to Amante at the appointed spot and time, " The Place is *Pantalonies* Grove, the hour Six." She relates what she has done, and Amante promises her not to engage Honorio. As Infortunio, Clara reveals to Honorio the mutual love of Garbato and Arabella, persuading him to cease his claim. She also informs Amante that Clara is dead, and that her last wish was his flame should cease and he should return to his former love. In return for these services the page requests Arabella to be allowed to enter Honorio's household, and is gladly received as an inmate there. Amante and Honorio meet, swords are drawn and both wounded before Constantia and Infortunio can separate them. Owing to the good offices of her Uncle Riccamare, Arabella is wedded to Garbato. Amante now declares he has resigned all pretensions to Clara and is a convert to Constantia's fidelity. Accordingly there is a double wedding, Honorio and Clara ; Amante and Constantia. Upon this glad occasion at the entreaty of Constantia even Buggio is forgiven.

The Amorous Old-woman is Strega, a beldame of great wealth but hideous as a Gorgon. Riccamare, whose Elysium is gold, secures the good offices of Garbato, who is able to introduce him to the hag as a suitor for her hand. The antique Strega fearful lest she should be wooed for her money rather than for her " well-favouredness ", and having already made trial of seven husbands, is resolved that all her sweethearts shall participate the knowledge of her five imperfections ere there is any serious talk of matrimony. Accordingly attended by the venerable Sanco-panco her " Porter, Usher, Steward, Butler, Coach-man, or what You please ", she proceeds to make her toilet whilst Riccamore and Garbato are present. Just as she is about to commence, her parchment hide frame is shaken to pieces by a hacking cough,

> The cold she got in *Nebuchadnezzars* days,
> Doing homage to the Golden Image.

When she is something recovered and set before her dressing-table with its array of phials and caddies and *tazze*, off she sheds her eye-brows, and next out comes an eye to be stored in its proper box. Her teeth vanish and show withered slobbering gums and falling chops ; then a well-fitting wig leaves her pate as bald as a coot.

> She's sufficiently ugly, but still I pray with
> The Man, that was carried away by the
> Devil, God bless us from worse,

mutters Riccamare, whose eyes veritably seem about to pop from his head. When, however, with much creaking and groaning a leg is unscrewed he finally takes to flight fearing what may come next, and the dismembered old scarecrow is left to lament the loss of an eighth husband, croaking hoarsely to her palsied Abigail :

> Come *Sanco,* lead me in, and as we go
> Let's both together sing fortune's my foe.

Howbeit eventually she is not disappointed, for Signor Cicco who is as blind as a buzzard and obstinately persists that he is keener sighted than the hawk, hearing of her fortune and being told by Buggio that Strega is " Fresh as *Aurora,* before the rising Sun ", incontinently sends Furfante as his ambassador of love, and unable to wait follows this up in person, declaring the raddled hag to be a " Miracle of Nature " and besieging her so hotly with " Fair *Strega* " and " *Strega,* do not disdain the humble flame which spouts—blazes, which blazes from a young Lovers heart " that he wins her heart and hand, and the old couple go to church with merry music and dancing at their nuptial feast.

Although the humour is coarse-grained, and even brutal, these scenes are not without a certain hard vigour, and might have been found amusing enough.

Langbaine speaks of Duffett as : " An Author altogether unknown to me, but by his Writings ; and by them I take him to be a Wit of the third Rate : and One whose Fancy leads him

rather to Low Comedy, and Farce, than Heroick Poetry." None
the less that Duffett had a very real vein of poetry is amply proved
by the charming lyrics which are included in his *New Poems,
Songs, Prologues and Epilogues,* 8vo, 1676 (With Permission, 30th
September, 1675). Although the general Dedication (in verse)
is " To Celia ", most of these truly elegant verses are addressed
to Francelia. The Prologues and Epilogues are vivacious
pieces, and certainly not without merit. Indeed this little book
might very advantageously be reprinted, and would be a vastly
agreeable gift not only to scholars but to all lovers of poetry.
The broadside ballad " Amintor's Lamentation for Celia's
Unkindness " could fittingly be added.

Of particular interest is Duffett's *Beauties Triumph,* " A Masque.
Presented by the Scholars of Mr. Jeffery Banister, and Mr.
James Hart, at their New Boarding-School for Young Ladies
and Gentlewomen, kept in that House which was formerly
Sir Arthur Gorges, at Chelsey." Gorges House stood just
behind what is now Lindsey Row, between Beaufort Street and
Milman's Row. It was the property of Richard Morgan of
Marlies, Essex. A Mr. Portman seems to have managed the
School for a few months after Banister and Hart left it, and he
was succeeded by Josias Priest, who removed there from Lincoln's
Inn Fields in November, 1680 : *London Gazette,* 22nd–25th
November, 1680. It was for Priest's School that Purcell composed
Dido and Aeneas, and this was the School where, as it was generally
understood at the time, D'Urfey laid the scene of his *Love for
Money : Or, The Boarding-School.*

One point is worthy of remark. Duffett could not have been
the Bohemian buffoon that has sometimes been supposed if the
two principals of so famous and select a Boarding-School employed him to write them a Masque to be given by their pupils,
who were of the most aristocratic and distinguished families.

Although not comparable to the great Jacobean and courtly
Caroline masques—how different indeed was its scope—*Beauties
Triumph* is none the less a very pleasing piece. The design is
the fable of the Golden Apple of Discord thrown down by Ate
and claimed by the three Goddesses. The scene of the vale of
Ida is " a pleasant Landschape of a flowrie Mountain ", and here
we have a delightful pastoral anti-mask, " an Astrologer with a
Globe in his hand, and a Fortune-telling woman enter, pursu'd
by Shepherds and Shepherdesses ". With Oenone at his side,
Paris bestows the Apple on Venus, the Triumph of Beauty.[115]

The Divine Comedian Or The Right Use Of Plays, " *Improved* in
a sacred Tragy-Comædy " in three Acts by Richard Tuke was
published 4to, 1672, with a Dedication to the Countess of

Warwick. These allegorical scenes, which in their kind are by no means ill contrived, were not intended for the stage. The Dramatis Personae are : Empirea, the Soul; Cosmus, the World, with her two Minions, Profit and Pleasure " *drest like Pages* " ; Satan ; Lust ; Caro, the Flesh ; Reason, Privy Counsellor to Empirea, but disloyal ; Scandal (or Slander), Poverty, Sickness, three Castigators ; Faith, Hope, and Charity, the three Theological Graces attending Queen Empirea ; and the Five Senses, Visus, Auditus, Olfactus, Tactus, and Gustus. The theme of *The Souls Warfare,* an alternate title, is summed up in the Prologue, which commences :—

> *The Life of Man's, a Tragi Comedie,*
> *Varied with Scenes of sorrow and delight,*
> *The World's the Scene and we the Actors be,*
> *Angels spectators, that behold the sight.*

The whole inspiration of the struggle between " Empirea *and her Ghostly Enemies* " is mediaeval. Richard Tuke, of whom nothing is certainly known, stands forth as a poet capable of reaching great height of beauty and sincerity.

"A Comedy call'd *The Reformation,* Written by a Master of Arts in *Cambridge* ; The Reformation in the Play, being the Reverse to the Laws of Morality and Virtue ; it quickly made its Exit, to make way for a Moral one." Thus writes Downes of Joseph Arrowsmith's *The Reformation,* produced at Dorset Garden in September, 1673, and in all seriousness the old prompter's reference is quite inexplicable, since there is nothing at all in the play to which exception can be taken. One can only surmise that his memory after thirty years and more had played him false and he had in mind the vague recollection of some other play.

Joseph Arrowsmith was born about 1647, and having been educated at Manchester Grammar School was admitted a pensioner of Trinity College, Cambridge, 3rd July, 1663. He matriculated the same year, and in 1664 advanced to a Scholar. He proceeded B.A. in 1666-7 ; M.A. in 1670. In 1668 he was elected a Fellow of his College. On 12th April, 1675, he was ordained both deacon and priest by Dr. Edward Reynolds, the aged Bishop of Norwich. For six years Joseph Arrowsmith was Master of S. John's Hospital and Rector of S. John's Church, Bedford, and in 1681 he was instituted Rector of Papworth S. Everard, Cambridgeshire, a parish some 6 miles from Huntingdon, in the patronage of Trinity College. On 5th October in the following year he married at Milbrook, Bedford, Christian Denston, by whom he had one son Joseph, born in

PLATE XXII

THE INDIAN-QUEEN: ACT III

The Incantation in the Opera
Collection of the Author

the spring of 1689. This boy was educated at Westminster and admitted a pensioner of his father's old college, Trinity, Cambridge, on 22nd May, 1706. Joseph Arrowsmith the elder died in 1708–9, or a little later.

The Dramatis Personae of *The Reformation* are : Camillo, an old severe Father, Sandford ; Pacheco, his son, a Reformer, Anthony Leigh ; Tutor to Pacheco, an Englishman, Underhill ; Antonio and Pedro, Reformers, Harris and Cademan ; Leandro, loves Ismena, Crosby ; Lysander, Juliana's husband, Medbourne ; Pisauro, gallant to Juliana, a Reformer, Smith ; Antonio's boy ; Mariana, Mrs. Caff, and Ismena, Mrs. Johnson, Camillo's daughters ; Juliana, Mrs. Betterton ; Lelia, her cousin, Mrs. Osborn ; Æmilia, Lysander's mistress, Mrs. Mary Lee ; Nurse, Mrs. Norris ; and Lucia, Æmilia's woman. Scene, Venice.

Lysander a wealthy merchant is married to Juliana, who feigns to doat upon him and weeps if he must absent for a few days on business. Meanwhile she is only too glad of the opportunity to entertain her lover, Pisauro. Lysander, for his part, often pretends that his affairs call him from home so that he may pass the time with his mistress, Æmilia.

The Reformation, which so scandalized Downes, is nothing more than a society who are eager to afford women a wider freedom and greater privileges than they now enjoy under the jealous watch of fathers or husbands. Camillo keeps his daughters very strictly with an ancient Nurse as their duenna, upon whom they play sad tricks. Pedro marries Ismena, and Antonio, Mariana. Camillo would engage Mariana to wed Leandro, but when Antonio's Boy disguised in petticoats appears and cries " O perjur'd man ! is *Fabia* so soon forgot ? false, false *Leandro* " with a long story of having been betrayed by that gallant the old man is completely gulled.

The intrigue is too slight for a good play, but there are some amusing incidents, and the dialogue is often very happy. Pacheco, Camillo's fopling son, and his Tutor are the two best characters. The Tutor, who is a dramatist, discusses heroic plays at length and lays down the rules for concocting a fine tragedy, something in the style of *The Rehearsal*. His recipes for writing successful plays include for tragedy " a Drum and a Trumpet . . . three or four or half a dozen Kings . . . two Ladies in Love with one man, or two men in love with one woman ; if you make them the Father and the Son, or two Brothers, or two Friends, 'twill do the better. There you know is opportunity for love and Honour and Fighting, and all that . . . you must have a Hero that shall fight with all the world ; yes i' gad, and beat them too, and half the gods into the bargain

... in all you write reflect upon religion and the Clergy, you can't imagine how it tickles ... Last of all be sure to raise a dancing singing ghost or two, court the Players for half a dozen new scenes and fine cloaths ... put your story into rime, and kill enough at the end of the Play, and *Probatum est*". Comedy is perhaps simpler: "Write your Plays with double sence and brisk meaning Songs. Take me, you shall have the Ladies laugh at a little bawdy jest as if they would bepiss themselves, and the young Mounsieurs clap as if they meant to wear their hands out in the service ... No matter what your plot is, your love and honour will do here agen, and 'tis but saving alive and marrying those you would kill in Tragedy, and you have done."

Whether Peter Belon who wrote *The Mock-Duellist, Or, The French Vallet,* produced at the Theatre Royal about Easter, 1675, and printed, 4to, that year as "Written by *P.B.* Gent.", is to be identified with Belon the physician [116] who translated from the French *A new mistery in physick, discovered by curing of fevers and agues by quinquina, or jesuites powder,* cannot definitely be decided, but it seems very likely such is the case. There appears no reason to dissent from Genest's judgement that *The Mock-Duellist* is "an indifferent comedy". The principal characters are: Sir Amorous Frost, an old doating Knight, in love with Kitty Noble; Sir Hope Coggin, suitor to the Lady Lovewealth; Noble, in love with Diana, Sir Hope's sister; Crosby, in love with Phillipa Airy; Peregrine and Dick Airy, brothers; Shift, a cheat; Timothy Clay, a country-bumpkin, a suitor to Lady Lovewealth; Clunch his man and Tray his dog; Slye, Noble's man; Champagne, a French servant to Sir Amorous; The Lady Lovewealth, a covetous old woman; Diana, sister to Sir Hope Coggin; Phillipa Airy, Sister to Peregrine and Dick, in love with Sir Hope; Mrs. Crostitch, mistress of the school; Kitty, Noble's sister; Phanny, betrothed to Crosby; Lysse, Diana's woman; Siss, Phillipa's woman; Prudence, Lady Lovewealth's woman. The scene; Covent-garden. Champagne was probably created by Lacy. "It is one of those parts, which, in the hands of such an actor as Lacy, tell upon the stage, but have little to recommend them in perusal." [117]

Shift has contrived to possess himself of the affections of young Kitty Noble, who by her brother's instructions is straitly mewed up at a boarding-school under the Argus eye of Mrs. Crostitch (a name incidentally adopted by D'Urfey for his Schoolmistress in *Love For Money*). Shift designs to steal away Kitty and hand her over to Sir Amorous, whose head he has filled with fingle-fangles, and who led to believe that the lass dotes upon him, is preparing to marry her and accordingly arranges for a parson to be in readiness. He confides his plans to Champagne and thus they are blurted out to Lysse. Hence Noble learns the design and resolves to catch the eloping parties in the nick. Kitty lets down her rope-ladder, but it is young Dick Airy who climbs up from the street and gets her away, whilst Sir Amorous is groping about only to stumble over Noble, Sir Hope, and Slye. General confusion ensues, but in the end when Dick and Kitty are married there is a reconciliation all round to wind up the comedy. After a good deal of circumstance and intrigue Crosby who plans to marry Phillipa is tied to Phanny, whilst Phillipa secures Sir Hope Coggin. Clay, Clunch, and the dog have some amusing episodes. Clay in his boorish manner wooes Lady Lovewealth who is at last wedded to Peregrine. Champagne affects to be a regular fire-drake, but he is in truth an arrant coward. His soliloquy in Act IV when he appears armed cap-à-pie would be good fun if smartly delivered with the gestures and grimace of a low comedian. Some of the business in this play almost verges upon pantomimic farce. The prose Epilogue is spoken by Champagne.

The one comedy of Sir Francis Fane, *Love In The Dark, Or The Man of Bus'ness,* produced at the Theatre Royal, 10th May, 1675, is a far better and more adroit piece of work. The eldest son of Sir Francis Fane, K.B., F.R.S. (*ob.* 1681) of Fulbeck, Lincolnshire, and Aston, comitatu Ebor, Francis Fane was created a K.B. at the coronation of Charles II. An intimate of Rochester, Sedley, and the wits, Fane was highly esteemed by his contemporaries, although his actual output was small. During the latter part of his life he resided on his estate at Henbury, Gloucestershire, and here he died in the winter of 1689. He married Hannah, daughter of John Rushworth, and in his will, dated 14th November, 1689, and proved 15th September, 1691, he appoints his wife sole executrix. Amongst other legacies he bequeathed forty pounds to the poor of the parish of Olveston.[118]

The locale of *Love In The Dark* is Venice, where appear the following persons : Doge Loredano, Lydal ; Cardinal Colonna, Papal Legate, Burt ; Hircanio and Grimani, Procuratori di San Marco, Cartwright and Griffin ; Cornanti, an old jealous senator, Wintershal ; Intrigo, a curious formal Coxcomb, Lacy ; Count Sforza, Trivultio, and Visconti, three Milanese gentlemen, Kynaston, Mohun, and Joe Haines ; Jacomo, Cornanti's man, Charleton ; Circumstantio, Intrigo's man, Robert Shatterel ; Satana, Advocate-General, William Harris ; Father Scrutinio, the confessor ; Proveditor (" titolo di carica, o dignità nella

Reppublicadi Venezia ", *Manuzzi*), Powell ; Parhelia, the Doge's daughter, Mrs. Susanna Uphill ; Bellinganna, Cornanti's wife, Mrs. Boutell ; Aurana, Hircanio's daughter, Mrs. James ; Melinda, Grimani's daughter, Mrs. Betty Slade ; Vigilia, Bellinganna's duenna ; Hircanio's Wife.

The curtain rises upon the Piazza of San Marco and here the first words of Trivultio who is alone strike the key of this vivacious comedy :—

> The Carnival's begun ; the Feast of free-born Souls,
> Where Nature Reigns, and Custom is depos'd :
> That Magistrate of Fools, Wise men's Usurper, . . .

Intrigo who presently appears is an excellent character. He has "all the mechanick parts of a Statesman ; he's a notable Herauld too, an Antiquary, and Cabalist ; . . . he's as Busy, as if his Head were a Bee-hive ". He frequents the Council of Ten and the Courts of Judicature but "brings away all the Shells of business, and leaves the Kernel behind ". When the stage is presently inundated with masquers and punchinellos he flies in horror, but the bustle of the festa gives Parhelia in her domino occasion to address Count Sforza of whom she is enamoured. Jealous old Cornanti is particularly disturbed during the carnival and closely pens up his young wife Bellinganna, who cleverly sends her lover Trivultio by the medium of the confessor messages seeming to rebuke him for his advances but in reality conveying information how he may obtain access to her. This intrigue is admirably managed, although founded upon a novella of Boccaccio, *Decameron,* iii, 3, which had already been used by Rhodes in *Flora's Vagaries* but which is here agreeably varied in its detail. Trivultio is able to make his way to the lady and gains admittance disguised as her duenna. The plot of Parhelia and Count Sforza is taken from Scarron's *Histoire de l'Amante Invisible,* chapter ix of *Le Roman Comique,* which it follows very closely, and which was afterwards utilized by Otway in *The Atheist,* the story of Beaugard and Porcia.

Bellinganna tells her husband that she is pursued by Trivultio whom she has given a rendezvous in the Moccenigo Gardens, so that he and his men may lie in wait to catch the would-be cuckold-maker. Accordingly they repair thither, but first Hircanio, with whom the lady has made a mock-assignation, arrives and presents her with a fair jewel. In the nick Hircanio's Wife, a very virago, having been privately forewarned by Bellinganna rushes in and loading her husband with abuse conducts him away, scolding at a great rate : "Ah you old Goat you, have I caught you ? Did I ever deny you at home, you false

Man ? " This is from *The Loves of Sundry Philosophers and other Great Men,* Translated out of French, 8vo, 1673, from the original by Marie Catherine Hortense de Desjardins, Madame de Villedieu.[119] The episode will be found in " The Loves of Great Men. Socrates ", pp. 29–62, the story of Socrates, his wife Myrto, and her behaviour on the occasion of her jealousy. It may be remarked that this translation, 8vo, 1673, is of the last rarity. The only copy I myself have ever met is to be found in Bodley.[120]

Trivulto next appears, and after a few soft words, " *she hangs upon him, he shakes her off : she comes and fawns again.*" " Oh you vile Strumpet," he cries, " abuse my noble friend, and an illustrious Senator ! 'Tis private justice, and 'tis publick too, to scourge thy sinful Carcase ! " " *Seems to beat her violently with his Cane.*" Cornanti rushes out squeaking, " O spare my Wife, spare my Wife, she's Honest, she's very honest." The trick has succeeded, and the choused old cuckold exclaims delightedly, " Such a Wife and such a Friend ! " (This sleight was suggested by the *Decameron,* vii, 7 ; although Fane has with some adroitness varied the incidents of the tale whose rubric runs : " Lodovico discopre a madonna Beatrice l'amore il quale egli la porta la qual manda Egáno suo marito in un giardino informa di sè, e con Lodovico si giace ; il quale poi levatosi, va e bastona Egano nel giardino ".[121] Some carnival frolics are taken to be a plot against the State, and a number of masquers including Trivultio are clapped up in prison. He escapes by a trick, and disguised as the Cardinal Legate attends the extraordinary meeting of the Senate, who presided over by the Duke, are met to discuss the crisis. Some declare it to be " nothing but an amorous Gambol ", others fear " Treason in the highest degree ". The learned Satana in a huge pompous speech pronounces it " subversion of the State ", to the great joy of Intrigo, who has obtained admittance in a trunk of records, and busily takes notes of the proceedings. Trivultio, in his cardinal's robes, rises and demands that the prisoners be condemned

To the perpetual Prison of the Nuptial Sheets.

The true Cardinal now enters in state ; there is some confusion, during which Intrigo is discovered, but eventually after the mock-legate has braved it a little, he falls on his knees, and the good Eminence recognizing " the wanton wag Trivultio " pardons the imposture, so all ends happily enough.

Intrigo and Circumstantio are two very droll characters, and their escapadoes do much to enliven this capital comedy. Mrs. Centlivre adapted Intrigo as Marplot in her long-lived *The Busie Body* produced at Drury Lane, 12th May, 1709, with Pack as

Marplot. This favourite piece kept the boards until well within the nineteenth century.

Sir Francis Fane's tragedy *The Sacrifice* was printed quarto, 1686, but not acted. The second edition in the following year has complimentary verses by Tate, John Robins, and Aphra Behn, who do not spare their eulogies. Langbaine is also warm in his praise of this " admirable Tragedy ", but I confess I incline to the opinion of the contemporary reader who noted " ordinary " on the title-page of Malone's copy. The piece was written by Fane in his country retirement at Henbury, and is dedicated to Buckhurst. The characters are Tamerlane ; Bajazet ; Axalla, Tamerlane's general ; Ragalzan, a villain, one of Tamerlane's chief officers ; Zeylan, a Revolted Prince of China ; Irene, Tamerlane's daughter ; Despina, Bajazet's wife ; and Philarmia, Zeylan's mistress. Scene, a Revolted Fort in China. The play treats the story of Tamerlane and Bajazet. The latter indeed is seen in his cage, but Tamerlane is represented as a virtuous heroic figure, who deplores that Bajazet is enraged against him.

> Why will you still afflict me, Sir, to see
> Your malice frustrate all my Clemency ?

he gently queries through the bars to his captive. There is a curious scene in " *an Amphitheatre of Crown'd Mummies* ", deified " *China* Monarchs for ten Thousand years ". Whilst under the conduct of the mummy-priest, who is a sorcerer, Tamerlane is viewing these ghastly relics of mortality, Ragalzan, disguised as the mummy Tzionzon, " *leaps down, Stabs at* Tamerlane : Irene *interposes. He and the Priest leap down the Trap-door,*" and escape through the vaults. Ragalzan, however, is so swathed and disguised that he is not suspected of the attempt. Bajazet, as tradition has it, dashes out his brains against the cage. Tamerlane falls in love with Despina, who learns that it is on this account Bajazet has slain himself. Ragalzan makes no inconsiderable amount of mischief during the course of the play, and some horrid catastrophe is foretold by " *Thunder, Lightning, Rainbows inverted, a bloody Arm, Comet, &c.*" Prince Zeylan is so overcome by Tamerlane's generosity that after various accidents he submits, and is appointed vice-roy of China. Despina, who is working with Ragalzan, has Tamerlane in her toils, and in his dotage of love he has vowed to grant her whatever she will. She demands Irene to be handed to her as a captive to be slain, and Herod-like, bound by his oath, Tamerlane grants this

> Love's Oath, an over-acted Rant,
> A Fugitive Word, that has out-run a Thought
> Forc'd by the violence of self-urging Passion,

Axalla, who is betrothed to Irene, protests against the intended sacrifice, but Despina still urges on her lover, when Axalla swearing he will prevent so black a deed, plunges his dagger to his own heart with " Then thus, Sir, I absolve you ". Irene swoons, and dies poisoned by Ragalzan who feigns to offer her a cordial. He then thrusts his sword into Despina's breast, lest she shall reveal their confederacy. As she falls she confesses she had already administered a noxious drug to the Emperor, but she inculpates Ragalzan, who is led off to tortures and death.

The play is written partly in heroic couplets, and partly in blank verse with one passage in prose, Ragalzan's soliloquy which ends Act II. There can, I apprehend, be little doubt that Rowe had glanced at this piece, for he has utilized some details from it in his ridiculous *Tamerlane*. Thus the name of Axalla is common to both plays ; in both Tamerlane is a heroic figure.

Sir Francis Fane, at the request of the Earl of Rochester, also wrote A Mask which was to be introduced in that nobleman's alteration of *Valentinian*. This represents " a frightfull dreame to Lucina ". There are some pretty conceits, but as a whole this *entretenimiento* is singularly inappropriate. It was not printed with the quarto play, 1685, but is included in Nahum Tate's *Poems by Several Hands,* 8vo, of the same year. In this Miscellany may also be found three copies of verses by Fane, which are elegant and agreeable enough.

The Woman turn'd Bully produced at the Duke's Theatre in 1675, probably about Easter, and in any case not later than the first week of June, is a sprightly agreeable comedy, which Langbaine justly finds " very Diverting ". It has been ascribed without any warrant to Mrs. Behn, but actually it was published anonymously, 1675. The scene lies in London, and the characters are : Jack Truman, a young Templar, possessed of a good estate and lives handsomely ; Ned Goodfeild, a Cantab, his friend, newly come to Town ; Docket, an antient attorney, a very Law-driver ; Dashwel, his clerk, like his master ; Spruce, another clerk to Docket, but a lively fellow ; Trupenny, Madam Goodfeild's Country-Steward, an old formal coxcomb ; Madam Goodfeild, a rich country-widow of Derbyshire, who drinks and takes tobacco,[122] and can't speak a word out of the Country-Element : she hates the Town, but comes up about an immergent Law-affair ; Betty Goodfeild, an aiery young Lady, her Daughter, comes up to London after her Mother, in man's Apparel. She personates a Town-Gallant ; Frank, her maid in the like disguise ; Loveal, the widow's woman, a stale maid who longs for a husband

and is very fond ; Lucia, Docket's niece and ward. Betty Good-feild is an excellent rattle. As Sir Thomas Whimsey, she swaggers in fine style, interlards her repartee with tags from the most toney plays—*Marriage A-la-Mode ; The Assignation ; An Evening's Love ; Love in a Tub ; Love in a Wood*; and half a score beside—sends her brother a challenge, and delivers another cartel to Jack Truman. The plot of the play is slight but there is some first-rate dialogue and clear-cut characterization on which the humour depends. Docket, the sharking lawyer of Clifford's Inn, is employed by Madam Goodfeild to draw up the writings connected with the marriage of Sir Alexander Simple a Derbyshire neighbour, and her daughter Betty, who in fact, unknown of course, to her mother, is ruffling it away as a gallant in Town. The lawyer endeavours to inveigle the old country lady into matrimony with himself, and wellnigh succeeds, but at the last moment, mainly owing to the good offices of Spruce, Docket is united to the man-hunting abigail, Loveal. Lucia, his young niece, whom he keeps secluded and who will forfeit her portion of 6,000 pounds if she marries without his consent is wedded to Ned Goodfeild, whereupon Docket thinking he has fast secured the widow and that the money must remain in the family acknowledges that the clause of forfeiture was a trick which he gave out so that no one would venture on Lucia, and whilst she stayed single he might employ the fortune as his own. Jack Truman wins Betty Goodfeild, although the old lady has a colt's tooth to him herself and designed to take him as her spouse, which in truth induced her to permit Loveal to practice upon Docket. She is metal, however, and if sorely mortified carries it off well, saying 'twas but her design to have sport with him and show that " country dames can have wit upon occasion, as well as your fine flanting Londoners, an' they list ".

There is a good song trolled out right merrily " to the tune of the Sixteenth Psalm, and it will go to *Green sleeves* ", by Stephen Trupenny, who falls into bacchanalian company, and chaunts—" O London, wicked London-Town ! ", a stave *To be sung al' yvrouge, in a drunken humour*.

The three comedies of John Leanerd, a dramatist of whom (I regret once more to have to write the phrase) no particulars are recorded, seem to me far better work than Langbaine will allow. This wrathful critic is frankly contemptuous in his abuse of Leanerd, "A confident Plagiary, whom I disdain to stile an Author [123] ; whilst he would altogether deny him the credit of *The Counterfeits* as " too good to be his Writing ".[124] Leanerd assuredly is not to be absolved from the charges of very ample conveyances from the Elizabethans, but he by no means deserves this wholesale damnation which might suitably have been ladled out by a Muggletonian ranter.

The Country Innocence : Or, The Chamber-Maid Turn'd Quaker, produced at the Theatre Royal in Lent, 1677, Leanerd's first play, is it must be acknowledged for the first three acts little more than a condensed adaptation of Thomas Brewer's [125] *The Countrie Girle,* printed 4to, 1647, "As it hath beene often Acted with much applause." Leanerd has once or twice considerably curtailed and a little refashioned the dialogue ; he introduces in Act I Gillian's song *Shall the Lasses and Lads,* and the song *Charming Beauty, you alone* after the Morris ; as also in Act IV the drinking song *Here is without doubt.* Acts IV and V of the original, however, are materially altered, and Langbaine's sneer that Leanerd has reprinted " another Man's Play, under his own Name " is so entirely misleading, that Genest did not scruple to write of *The Country Innocence* " Leanard calls himself the author of it, but Langbaine says it is only Brewer's Country Girl with a new title ", which is in effect precisely what the older critic intended. The characters are Sir Oliver Bellingham, Lydal ; Sir Robert Malory, Coysh ; Captain Mullineux, Goodman ; Plush, Wiltshire ; Rash, Griffin ; Gregory Dwindle, Haines ; Mr. William, servant to Lady Lovely, Powell ; Old Thrashard, Marmaduke Watson ; Abraham, his son, Styles ; Lady Lovely, a widow, (in Brewer, Lady Mosely), Rebecca Marshall ; Lady Malory, Mrs. Rutter ; Margaret, the Country Girl, and Gillian, her scolding sister, Thrashard's two daughters, Mrs. Baker and Mrs. Sarah Cook ; Barbara, Lady Lovely's maid, Mrs. Mary Knepp ; an Old Gentlewoman, Mr. Carey Perin. The scene, London and Edmonton.

It must, I think, convey a false impression to write as Genest has done that this comedy was acted by the younger part of the Company, since this implies that it was from the outset little esteemed and lightly regarded. The fact is that in 1677 the Theatre Royal was distracted by domestic quarrels and difficulties, and I have no doubt that the cast of *The Country Innocence* was as good a rally as could be contrived. Indeed some excellent actors took part ; Lydal, Goodman, Wiltshire, Griffin, Haynes, Watson, and of the ladies, Mrs. Marshall, Mrs. Rutter, Sarah Cook, Mrs. Knepp, were all well-known names.

In its plot the comedy, as we might expect, presents many Elizabethan characteristics. Sir Oliver Bellingham courts the Lady Lovely, who is retired to solitude and deep set in grief for her first husband, Sir James Lovely, Lady Malory's dead brother. Rash the Mercer, Plush a humorous gallant, and Gregory Dwindle also aspire to her hand. A trick is played upon them as by permission of her mistress Bab entertains them veiled and in weeds. Sir Robert Malory seeks to seduce the fair Margaret, daughter of his tenant, old Thrashard. Lady Malory, learning of this, disguises herself as an old bawd and accosting Margaret pretends to be the bearer of a message and money from Sir Robert. She is received with scorn and indignation, whereupon she delightedly reveals herself. Captain Mullineux, who had once courted Lady Lovely, and Sir Oliver duel, and the former is wounded. It appears that the Captain really loved Margaret, and he contrives that Sir Oliver shall attend him, disguised as a physician. When Lady Lovely visits the sick man she is constrained to reveal her love for Bellingham, who is supposed to have fled, whereupon he discovers himself and claims her hand. The Captain wins Margaret; and by a device of Bab she is wedded to Rash. There is an amusing scene in Act V where the newly married couple assume the dress and manners of puritans, canting at a great rate. The ridiculous suitors are paired, Plush with Gillian, and Gregory with the Old Gentlewoman. Lady Malory reclaims her wanton husband by a design in which the Thrashard family appear dressed in silks and satins, aping gentility and treating the knight with contumely. There is a good song *You that languish'd so long* at the end of Act V. The Epilogue, which is smartly turned, was spoken—and perhaps written—by Haines.

Leanerd tells us that *The Country Innocence* met with considerable success, and was honoured by the presence of the King. Unfortunately one of the actors, who played a leading rôle, fell ill, and the piece was necessarily withdrawn since the " Part was too considerable to be quickly studied ".

The Rambling Justice, Or The Jealous Husbands. With the Humours of Sir John Twiford, was produced at the Theatre Royal, in February, 1678, with the following cast: Sir Arthur Twilight, a lascivious old knight, Powell ; Sir Generall Amorous, Wiltshire ; Contentious Surly, the jealous husband, Disney ; Sir Geoffrey Jolt, the rambling justice, fond of all women, Perin ; John Twiford, a gentleman of no fortune, sometimes lunatic, Power ; Spywell, Sir Generall's man, Nathaniel Cue ; Bramble, Sir Arthur's man, Coysh ; Eudoria, Sir Arthur's wife, Mrs. Farlee ; Petulant Easy, Surly's wife, Mrs. Merchant ; Emelia and Flora, daughters to Sir Arthur by a former wife, Mrs. Bates and Sarah Cook. Scene, London ; time, twenty-four hours. Sir Arthur suspects that his wife is beloved by Sir Generall, and is " as Jealous as he is Old, as Old as he is Crafty, and as Crafty as the Devil ". Surly is also horn-mad, and his wife indulges something more than a liking for Sir Generall who has indeed not been slow to gratify her stomach, but already has begun to find her " a stale, a cast off *Amoret* ". The two ladies, Eudoria and Petulant Easy, for a prank disguise themselves as gipsies, and resort to the romany camp where they meet Bramble, another gentile who is also masquerading as a true zingaro. Sir Generall tricks Sir Arthur into a compromising situation with Petulant Easy, when they are discovered by Surly. Meanwhile Eudoria has given access to her lover, and they entertain each other at a well-known bagnio. A good deal of pantomimic farce follows amid which John Twiford wanders out and about in rather a haphazard inconsequential fashion. In fact he behaves uncommonly like the Clown in an early nineteenth-century harlequinade, and there is an amusing unrelated scene with a trick sedan which might have been exhibited by Grimaldi. Eventually Sir Generall is united to Flora, and Sir Geoffrey who has been befooled not a little to Emelia. There is a laughable episode where the country justice picks up Flora, who is masqued, for a wench, and is led home by her. Whilst he is amorously preparing for the encounter Emelia and Flora enter unvizarded to banter and deride him.

There are many episodes in *The Rambling Justice* which depend entirely upon action of the most farcical kind. It is not a good play to read, and even upon the boards much must have seemed mere burlesque, although it may well have been droll enough when supported by the broadest pantaloon.

The romany episodes (sometimes copied verbatim) are from Middleton's *More Dissemblers besides Women,* which was allowed on 17th October, 1623, by Sir Henry Herbert as an " Old Play ", and which had originally been licensed by Sir George Buc; printed London, 8vo, 1657. *More Dissemblers besides Women* is not among Middleton's best work, and the reason for its revival was the extraordinary success of Jonson's masque *The Gipsies Metamorphosed,* presented to King James by the Duke of Buckingham, which was given on 3rd and 5th August and again in September, 1621. [126]

The Counterfeits which was produced at Dorset Garden in May, 1678, possibly on the first of the month, is altogether a far better play, and can indeed be accounted a capital comedy. There was a strong cast. Anthony Leigh acted Don Gomez de Aranda ; Gillo, Don Luis ; Betterton, Vitelli ; Harris, Antonio ; Medbourne, Carlos ; Smith, Peralta ; Percival, Dormilon, the host ; Underhill, Fabio, Peralta's man ; Williams and Richards, Crispin and Tonto, Vitelli's servants ; Young Will Mountford (he was then fourteen), the Boy ; Mrs. Mary Lee, Elvira, Antonio's sister ; Mrs. Barry, Clara, her woman ;

Mrs. Price, Violante; Mrs. Gibbs, Flora, her woman. Peralta, during his residence at Valentia, had assumed the name of Vitelli. He has whilst sojourning there seduced Elvira, and then deserted her. She informs her brother Antonio of this by a letter: " Vitelli, *a Gentleman of* Cordova, *as he pretended, with promise of Marriage had possession of my Bed; and, as I am inform'd, is fled towards* Castile. *My Retreat is to a Monastery, where, you shall know when my Injuries are reveng'd.*" Don Pedro Vitelli has come from Mexico in order to marry Violante, the daughter of Don Gomez, an alliance long since arranged by Don Gomez and Don Gonzalo Vitelli, the two fathers, who are old friends. Peralta and Vitelli on their way to Madrid slept at the same inn. Here their portmanteaus were exchanged by mistake, and Peralta on opening Vitelli's luggage determines to pass himself off on Don Gomez with the letters and papers as the newly landed suitor for Violante's hand. This he does very successfully, so that when Don Pedro puts in an appearance he is treated as an imposter. Elvira, however, disguised as a Knight of Malta has come to Madrid, attended by Clara in male attire. Don Luis, the uncle of Peralta, does not personally recognize his nephew, whom he has not seen since early boyhood. A good deal of confusion results, but in the end Peralta acknowledges his deceit, begs Elvira's hand, and is forgiven by all concerned, whilst Vitelli is united to Violante.

Of this play Langbaine says: " 'Tis founded on a translated *Spanish* Novel, call'd *The Trapanner trapann'd,* octavo *Lond.* 1655, and I presume the Author may have seen a *French* Comedy, writ by *Tho. Corneille,* on the same Subject, call'd *D. Cæsar D'Avalos.*" The *Trapanner trapann'd* I have not met with, neither in the English translation nor yet in the Spanish original. Corneille's *Dom César d'Avalos* was first given at the Théâtre de Guénégaud on 21st December, 1674, and though not a remarkable success was well received, attaining fifteen performances between the original date of production and 22nd January, 1675. This comedy had been written in great haste at the instance of the actors who stood in urgent need of a new play.

When *The Counterfeits* had fallen out of the repertory the ingenious Colley Cibber availed himself pretty liberally of Leanerd's scenes for his popular comedy *She Wou'd and She Wou'd Not; or, The Kind Impostor,* which was produced at Drury Lane in November, 1702, and which continued season after season to afford unbated pleasure. *She Wou'd and She Wou'd Not* is indeed the plum of Cibber's theatre, and he could handle the best of the material of others with singular dexterity and vigour. He had in truth a flair for telling situations in the older prompt-books, and none

PLATE XXIII

THE MAN OF MODE: ACT I: SCENE 1

Collection of the Author

was more adroit in skimming the cream of half-forgotten comedies. The consequence is that many of his pieces remained stock favourites, when work of far greater merit and importance was either laid on the shelf or but respectfully revived at rarer intervals. When Cibber ventured to be original he generally tumbled pretty badly. Thus the scene, which was once much admired, in *The Careless Husband* where Lady Easy finds Sir Charles and her woman, Edging, in a situation that explains itself only too clearly, is in fact ill-introduced and worse developed.

She Wou'd and She Wou'd Not was played in London as lately as 1884, when it was included in the repertory presented by Augustin Daly at Toole's Theatre for a brief season of six weeks. The company opened on Saturday, 19th July, with *Casting the Boomerang*, an adaptation from the German of Franz von Schonthan. The Hippolyta in Cibber's comedy was Ada Rehan, who was much admired in that vivacious rôle.[127]

In his notice of *Tom Essence : Or, The Modish Wife* Langbaine remarks : " This Play is said to be writ by One Mr. *Rawlins*," [128] who was certainly not Thomas Rawlins the author of *The Rebellion*, acted at Blackfriars in 1639 ; 4to, 1640. This erroneous identification has, however, been accepted, nay, even enlarged upon, so that we have ladled out such nonsense as " Thomas Rawlins, principal engraver at the Mint, published anonymously after the Restoration two such [typical] comedies, *Tom Essence, or The Modish Wife* (D.G. *c.* Sept. 1676), and *Tunbridge Wells, or, A Day's Courtship* (D.G. *c.* March, 1678)." [129] As Thomas Rawlins died in 1670 it is difficult to see how this could be.

With Thomas Rawlins we are hardly concerned. " He was the Cheif [*sic*] Graver of the *Mint* to both King *Charles* the First and Second, and died in that Employment in 1670," [130] says Langbaine. His one play *The Rebellion* lies outside our scope, and it will suffice to say that this is a tragedy of considerable merit.[131] Indeed it is stated originally to have had a quite exceptional run, being " acted Nine days together ", as well as " divers times since with good applause ".

The author of *Tom Essence : or, The Modish Wife,* which was published without the writer's name, may well have been another Rawlins, of whom nothing is known. There were very many men who wrote just their one play, printed it anonymously, and then were content to vanish into obscurity. Hazlitt's guess that this comedy is from the pen of Ravenscroft need not be considered. Indeed a couplet in a lampoon, *A Session of Poets,* 1676,[132] proves that such was not the case :—

> At last Mamamouché put in for a share,
> And little Tom Essence's Author was there.

It will not escape remark that these lines also afford contributory evidence disposing of the attribution to Thomas Rawlins. *Tom Essence* was produced at Dorset Garden in September, 1676, with the following cast : Old Monylove, a credulous old Fool, who has a young Wife, Percival ; Courtly, a sober gentleman, loves Theodocia, Crosby ; Loveall, a wild Debaucht Blade, Norris ; Stanly, gallant to the Old Man's wife, Gillow ; Tom Essence, a vendor of gloves, ribbons, essences and the like, a jealous coxcomb of his wife, Anthony Leigh ; Laurence, Loveall's man, Richards ; Mrs. Monylove, the Old Man's wife, and mother-in-law to Theodocia, Mrs. Hughes ; Theodocia, Monylove's daughter, Mrs. Barry ; Luce, a widow disguis'd and passes for Theodocia's maid, Mrs. Osborn ; Mrs. Essence, very Impertinent and Jealous of her husband, Mrs. Gibbs ; Betty, Mrs. Monylove's maid, Mrs. Napper. The Scene, London. That part of the plot which concerns Loveall and Luce is from Thomas Corneille's *Dom César d'Avalos,* a comedy already mentioned as the source of *The Counterfeits.* Luce is a rich widow who has been kind to Loveall. To keep in with his uncle he forsakes her for Theodocia, with whom Luce contrives to place herself as a maid. Theodocia loves and eventually marries Courtly, whereupon Loveall craves Luce's forgiveness and being taken into favour is united to her. Mrs. Monylove, who has been dispatched to Tunbridge Wells by her husband, dresses as a young gallant, pretending to be her own brother, and returns to visit Old Monylove at whose house Stanly is sleeping. Monylove offers her a night's lodging, and puts her in the same bed as Stanly. Accordingly we have, Act IV, " *Malfey's* Chamber. Scene the Second : Scene a Chamber in Old *M.* House. Stanly *dressing himself. Mrs.* Mon. *dressing her self at a Table, have Night-cloaths on her head, in her half Shirt, and her Breeches on. A Letter for Mrs.* Monylove. Mrs. *M.* Your Raptures are too violent to last—and know Sir, I had not yielded now, had not my Old Man warranted, or rather justified my proceedure ; for his Penuriousness I cou'd no other way requite, and he was instrumental to his being a Cuckold, for laying two so full of Love together."

The intrigues of Tom Essence and Mrs. Essence are Molière's *Sganarelle, ou le Cocu Imaginaire,*[133] which is rather neatly chequered with the other episodes. *Tom Essence* is a brisk amusing comedy, and must have played admirably in the theatre. Act IV, scene 3, where Tom Essence is serving his customers is particularly good. This has no counterpart in the French. As the above quotation shows it was printed from the prompt-copy. " *A Letter for Mrs.* Monylove," is a warning to the prompter to provide a letter which is needed a little later for the business of the scene. "*Malfey's* Chamber" refers to a recent revival of *The Dutchesse of Malfy,* with new costumes and scenes, of which this Chamber was utilized in *Tom Essence.*

There was printed 4to, 1678,[134] *Tunbridge-Wells : Or A Days Courtship,* "Written by a Person of Quality." Langbaine notes : " This is said (in the Title-page) to be writ by a Person of Quality : tho' I have been told it was writ by Mr. *Rawlins.*" [135] This Rawlins, I take it, is the same dramatist as the author of *Tom Essence.*

Tunbridge-Wells was produced at Dorset Garden in the spring of the year, possibly February–March, and the piece was printed without actors' names. The characters are Tom Fairlove, a gentleman of the Town ; Jack Owmuch, a gamester ; Mr. Wilding, a modish husband ; Sir Lofty Vainman, a baronet of great means and little sense ; Squire Fop ; Alderman Paywel, an indulgent City Husband ; Dr. Outside, a man made up of Physical terms and little Art ; Parson Quibble, a Welsh Vicar in love with the Widow, and strangely addicted to puns ; Poet Witless, a conceited Rhimer ; Farendine, a quondam mercer, from a sedentary Fool being turned a Riotous Coxcomb ; Alinda, beloved by Fairlove ; Courtwit, a great Pretender to Wit, Fairlove's sister ; Paywel, a pampered Aldermans Wife, that imployes more of her Husbands Estate in Lewdness than Charity ; Parret, Parcel Midwife, parcel Bawd, the Confident of Mrs. Paywel ; Brag and Crack, two whores.

The intrigues of Tunbridge with its London visitors are exhibited in this comedy which has some easy felicitous dialogue, but rather lacks incident. Mrs. Paywel very fashionably keeps Jack Owmuch as a *beau garçon* to supply her pressing needs, but just as he is about to give her a cast of his office they are interrupted by the Alderman. The gallant is hurried into a closet, whilst Mrs. Paywel and Parret pretending the old gentleman's eyes are sorely inflamed, lay him in a chair, and gently drop a lotion into them. Meantime Owmuch slips away unperceived, but his would-be mistress conveys a jewel into his hand as an earnest of future service. Brag passes herself off as a rich London widow, upon which report she and Crack are besieged by suitors. Thus Sir Lofty is entrapped into matrimony by Brag, but when she is recognized as a Whetstone whore it is found that on this occasion the parson has been none other than Courtwit muffled up in Quibble's canonicals and a peruke. It is this female parson also who has performed a like service for Farendine and Crack, whom he married in a vizor, thinking her to be the rich widow. So the two trulls boomerang back to London Town. Fairlove having rescued Sir Lofty from the strumpet, secures as his reward the baronet's sister, Alinda, a witty discreet lady.

On account of the similarity of the title, *Tunbridge-Wells* has been compared with *Epsom-Wells,* but actually save in so far as both comedies portray the humours of an inland spa there is little in common between the anonymous piece we have been considering and Shadwell's vivacious scenes.

An unacted play, *Cytherea Or The Enamouring Girdle,* " Written by *John Smith* of Snenton[136] in York-shire, Gent.," was printed quarto, 1677. John Smith, who dedicates his play " To the Northern Gentry " speaks of it as " *a Comick Poem made and fashioned in your own Country* " which lacks " *the seal of applause obtained from a smiling* Theater, *for as yet it hath not been presented publickly upon the stage* ". He continues : " *further (as I am informed) one of the best Comical Poets in* London (*whose judgment is without exception*) *did approve of it,*" and recommended it to the players, who proved unwilling since " *it was not writ in so plain familiar words as the taking Comedies of the Time* ", and " *they could not act it to the life without much expence in contriving* Scenes *and* Machins *to their great loss* " if the play did not take. It was also urged that the " *Scene being laid at the City of* York " the characters were too elegant in their diction for plain lads and lasses who dwell 'twixt Humber and Tyne.

Cytherea is a most amazing production, and we are not surprised that the actors flinched before it. The characters are : Sir Adrian Somerfield, Cytherea's father, disguised as Oblivio ; Sir Eucosmus, a Noble Burgess and Justice of Peace in York ; Tibullus, a well-bred Gentleman ; Warran, the Justice's Clerk, found to be Adrastus ; Master Seeker, a Phanatich Minister at last turn'd Conformist ; John Clay, a half-bred Gentleman ; Fidelio, a faithful Trustee ; Julian, a treacherous friend ; Tax and Simia, his followers ; Andrew Grant, a pedlar ; Grex, Chapmen to the pedlar ; Cytherea, Lady to Sir Eucosmus ; Delia, Sister to Sir Eucosmus ; Mariana, the Lady's woman, found to be Placilla. Scene, City of York.

The Prologue, which is spoken by Venus, " *having on a rich flaming girdle,*" commences :—

> Dramatique *Poems famous in this age,*
> *As they are acted on your* English *stage,*
> *Invite a Goddess from above to day*
> *At the Dukes* Theater *to see a Play* . . .

But I am afraid Mr. Smith was altogether too optimistic, for as we have noted, the management of Dorset Garden declined to produce *Cytherea*. The dialogue, indeed, is difficult, and stuffed with classical allusions—Paphos, Erycina's needle, Phaeton, Tethys lap, Orpheus, Favonius, Arabia Fælix, Ormus, the Fortunate Isles, Sabæan Odours, Ganymede, Hebe, Endymion, Pygmalion's Statue—all of which are rather inconsequential and impertinent. Sir Adrian, who calls himself Oblivio, pretends to have lost his memory, and appears in various masquerades, in one of which " Like *Trincalo* transform'd ", as Andrew Grant, the pedlar, he sings a rollicking Pedlar's Ballad which is the best thing in the piece. A marginal note tells us : " *This part of Oblivio was intended for Mr.* Underhill." The villain is Julian, but eventually Adrastus (found to be Sir Adrian's son) weds Delia ; and Tibullus is united to Placilla (found to be Sir Adrian's daughter). An Epilogue is spoken by Venus who casts her girdle into the pit, whereupon some lady takes it up and strikes with it a gallant who is incontinently enamoured of her.

Cytherea, altogether too fantastic and loose-knit, seems like the first effort of a rather precocious school-boy, who having just read *Cynthia's Revels* and *The Muses Looking-Glass* sets out to rival Jonson and Randolph.

The author of *The Constant Nymph : Or, The Rambling Shepheard* produced at Dorset Garden in July, 1677, and printed anonymously with date 1678, in his Dedication makes the same complaint of the actors as had been voiced by Smith. He deplores the economies of the theatre in these words : "As for Adornments in Habit, Musick, and Scene-Work, it was Vacation-time, and the Company would not venture the Charge." Perhaps he is to some extent justified, for, as he points out, a Pastoral largely depends upon the elegance and beauty of the *décor*. This, however, was not his only grievance. The script had suffered pretty badly : " The chief Parts Acted by Women ; and, for their Ease, and somewhat of decorum, as was pretended, whole scenes left out, and scarcely any one Speech unmangled and entire." It is not very difficult to gather that *The Constant Nymph* proved anything but a success.

Yet on the fact of it the cast was strong enough, and the racy Prologue delivered by Mrs. Mary Lee should have put the house in a right good humour. The characters are : Sylvanus, chief Shepherd of Lycea, father of Traumatius and Astrea ; Astatius, the rambling Shepherd, Mrs. Mary Lee ; Philisides, a young Shepherd of Dipea, in love with Astrea, and disguised as a Shepherdess by name Euplaste, Mrs. Barry ; Traumatius, supposed dead, but disguised in the Habit of a Priest, by name Evander, Medbourne ; Ismenius, a priest, Gillow ; Melibeus, a Shepherd, Jevon ; Clinias, a merry Shepherd, Servant to Astatius,

Richards; Darmetas, servant to Sylvanus, Percival; Lilla, mother to Alveria, and aunt to Philisides, Mrs. Norris; Alveria, her daughter, in love with Traumatius, Mrs. Betterton; Astrea, daughter to Sylvanus, Mrs. Anne Quin; Lipomene, Cloris, Sylvia, three Shepherdesses. The Scene, Lycea in Arcadia. Traumatius is believed to have been killed in a fray by Philisides, whereas disguised as a priest he serves the temple of Esculapius under the name of Evander. The pastoral commences on the nuptial morn of Astatius, who is to be married to Astrea, when his vagrant fancy is caught by Euplaste (who actually is Philisides concealed as a girl), and he promptly makes love to his new flame only a little after to transfer his wayward affections to Alveria. Act III opens with Astatius and Euplaste, Courting :—

> *Euplaste.* 'Twould be indecent ; urge it not, I pray :
> Make the first Day we meet, our Wedding-Day !
> *Astatius.* Why not ? Deserves it Blame, or rather Praise,
> To take our Happiness the nearest wayes ?

In Act IV Astatius is pursuing " th' incomparable Alveria ", the " Constant Nymph ". He even flaunts his fickle humour, and speaks scornfully of Astrea to Euplaste. Presently Euplaste doffs the female gear, and enters as Philisides, who bitterly resents the affront put on the fair Astrea, his mistress. Astrea had only consented to wed Astatius, since it was supposed Philisides had killed her brother. Philisides forces the rambling Shepherd to a duel. Astatius falls, but is conveyed to the Temple of Esculapius, and here he is healed of his hurt. Philisides in his flight seeks refuge in the vault tenanted by the lorn Alveria keeping her vigil o'er the coffin of Traumatius, whereupon he is seized as a murderer to be sacrificed to the shade of his supposed victim. However, what time the temple is thronged for this event, the altars are blazing and the keen knife about to cut the youth's throat, Traumatius discovers himself so that all ends happily. Alveria is united to Traumatius, and Astrea to Philisides. Astatius, his sensuality purged by his recent part, renounces the world declaring

> My Heart ingulphs all Love in the Divine

and is at his prayer appointed a priest in the sanctuary of the god.

It was beyond question a mistake to assign male rôles, Astatius and Philisides, to a couple of actresses, and the author had very just cause to protest. It is difficult to see what curtailments were demanded by modesty and good manners. Indeed this pretext was obviously mere fudge. One cannot be surprised that so seriously hampered by these disadvantages *The Constant Nymph* enjoyed no great favour, and our sympathies are with the poet whose charming pastoral was so hardly used by the actors.

The dialogue in in heroic couplets. Some hints have been taken from Fletcher's *Faithfull Shepheardesse,* in particular the devotion of Alveria to Traumatius, suppos'd dead, which resembles the meditations of Clorin by her lover's grave where she sojourns forgetful of all joys. In Fletcher also Alexis, the wanton Shepherd, is cured of "looser thoughts, ill-tempered fires" after he has been wounded by the spear of the Sullen Shepherd. So Astatius is reclaimed in this play. His pristine loose caprices are a copy of the humour of Hylas in D'Urfé's *Astrée,* whence also is derived the episode of Astatius falling in love with Philisides disguised as Euplaste. So Hylas is enamoured of Céladon disguised as Alexis, the daughter of Adamas. Pausanias has no mention of Lycea. It is indeed the Lignon which waters this Arcady.

In September, 1677, was given at Drury Lane *Wits Led by the Nose; Or A Poet's Revenge* with the following cast : Antellus, King of Sicilia, Goodman ; Oreandes, his General, Lydal ; Zannazarro, a young Lord in Rebellion, Carey Perin ; Arratus, an old Courtier, Watson ; Vanlore,[137] a decayed gentleman, Power ; Sir Symon Credulous, Joe Haines ; Sir Jasper Sympleton, Styles ; Jack Drayner, Servant to Credulous, Nathaniel Cue ; Dick Slywit, servant to Sympleton, Coysh ; Heroina, Princess of Regium, Mrs. Frances Baker ; Glorianda, Princess of Cyprus, sister to Antellus, Mrs. Boutell ; Amasia, Zannazarro's sister, Mrs. Katherine Baker ; Theocrine, daughter to Arratus, Mrs. Farlee ; Julia, Theocrine's Maid.

Langbaine leaves an incorrect impression when he says : " The greatest part of this Play (except a Scene or two) is stollen from *Chamberlain's Love's Victory.*" *Wits Led by the Nose* is actually an alteration of *Loves Victory,* but with very considerable omissions and some additions. The lighter episodes in the two plays differ very considerably. In *Loves Victory* we have Cosmo Buffonie, a simple clown, nephew to Arratus ; Buffonie's Father and Mother, and Gudgeon, his man. Creon and Lewcippus, two knaves, practise upon young Cosmo, cheat and chouse him, involving him with a bawd and whores, and other accidents. In *Wits Led by the Nose* we meet Sir Symon Credulous and Sir Jasper Sympleton, a couple of Englishmen who are travelling in Sicily. Credulous is favoured by Arratus as a suitor to Theocrine, who loves and eventually is united to Vanlore. Sympleton also pretends to the lady's hand. They serenade their mistress, declare themselves rivals, meet in a wood to fight ridiculously, and call son of a whore ; equip themselves in full armour for their duel; drink and pretend to poetry; there is some satire on Settle here, for Slywit who is disguised compels each to subscribe " I am an Arrand stinking Coward, a Poetical Thief, and a damn'd Son of a Whore if ever I writ these Verses ". The play derives its name from the Tavern Scene in Act V, where " *Enter Led by the Nose, Sir* Jasper Sympleton *by* Drayner, *and Sir* Symon Credulous *by* Slywit, *disguis'd* ".[138] Sir Jasper is married to Julia disguised whom he takes to be Theocrine. It must be allowed that all this underplot is very farcical, and very indifferent fooling. The trick episode in Act III where Sir Jasper and Sir Symon, both armed cap-à-pie have rubbed off from the field deeming they are pursued, and to avoid detection both stand upon pedestals imitating statues, after which they descend and dance in antic postures round about the officers, is just madcap pantomime.

Loves Victory, a play of considerable merit, is in blank verse with some prose for Buffonie and his fellows. There are not a few striking passages which may be read with pleasure, but in *Wits Led by the Nose* the serious scenes are almost uniformly reduced to prose with a small admixture of heroic verse, and sadly spoiled in the process. The rococo figures of the Sicilian monarch, of Oroandes, Zannazarro, and the rest fit in very awkwardly as criss-crossed by the cruder episodes of Credulous and Sympleton.

Their story, romantic and rather artificial, has moreover been roughly mishandled by the adaptor, whoever he may have been, and episodes which in *Loves Victory* were presented in an interesting and agreeable manner, so that the poetry salved the incongruities, are in *Wits Led by the Nose* unfortunately denuded of their embellishments, and so drabbed and dulled that there is little to commend in a performance which must reluctantly be pronounced far from pleasing or meritorious.

This is very unfair, for William Chamberlayne was no mean poet, and it may be remarked that a new edition of his works would be exceedingly acceptable. Southey speaks of him as " a poet to whom I am indebted for many hours of delight ".

Chamberlayne,[139] who during the Great Rebellion was distinguished for his loyalty to the King, practised as a physician at Shaftesbury in Dorsetshire, and here he died on 11th January, 1679, being buried in the churchyard of Holy Trinity, where his son Valentine erected a monument to his memory. *Loves Victory* was published 4to, 1658, with a dedication to Sir William Portman (*ob.* 1690), to whom also is addressed *Pharonnida : A Heroick Poem,* 8vo, 1659, a piece of great beauty, " remarkable for happy imagery and rich expression," which the late Mr. Bullen was wont to compare to *Endymion*.

Of Edward Cooke, who in the spring of 1678 published *Loves Triumph; or, The Royal Union*,[140] practically nothing is known. It has with some probability been suggested that the dramatist was the translator from Le Grand of the *Divine Epicurus or the Empire of Pleasure over the Virtues* (1676), but this indeed may be from the pen of another Edward Cooke of the Middle Temple. *Loves Triumph* " *an absolute stranger to the World, being never yet seen upon the publick Theatre* "—no matter for surprise —was dedicated to " Her Highness The Most Illustrious Mary, Princess of Orange ", and concerns the oft-told amours of Oroondates *and* Statira, who, says the author, " *now being forc'd again from the peaceful Shades of their happy Retirement, do throw themselves at Your Princely Feet with the Reverence and Humility of Idolaters, devoutly begging their Protection might be in Your* High-ness's *Umbrage*." There are, I apprehend, few readers who will not wish that Oroondate and Cassandre (Statira) had not been left by Cooke unmolested in their heroic Elysium. The Dedication proceeds to celebrate the Princess Mary with a fulsomeness that is both nauseating and grotesque, but what one particularly kecks at is the praise of William of Nassau, when adulation swells to a strain of braggart blasphemy which is more intolerably offensive and repellent than anything of the sort I have met with in any such address whatsoever.

Of *Loves Triumph* Langbaine writes : " This Play is founded on *Cassandra,* a fam'd Romance, as you will find by reading Part 5th, Book 4th, to the End [141]; " *Cassandra : The Fam'd Romance. The Whole Work* : translated by Sir Charles Cotterell, folio, 1661 ; " The Continuation of the Fifth and Last Part of Cassandra," The Fourth Book and The Fifth Book, pp. 1–80. For once Langbaine has very considerably understated the matter. *Loves Triumph* is not merely founded upon, but it is for the most part a paraphrase from Cotterell's translation of La Calprenède's *Cassandre.* The play is written in heroic couplets, and it is hardly an exaggeration to say that Cooke only varies the diction when he is in labour for a rhyme, whilst all too frequently his pains end in abortion. Some short connecting scenes are, it is true, not so palpably taken from the English version. It may be remarked that Pordage in his *The Siege of Babylon,* acted at Dorset Garden in the autumn of 1677, has dramatized the same incidents as Cooke.

Loves Triumph abruptly commences with the discovery by Roxana that Statira (Cassandre), whom she has seen put to death, still lives. False Perdiccas, one of the Four Successors of Alexander the Great, to whom the task of beheading Statira and her sister Parisatis was assigned, being enamoured of the former concealed them both in the house of Polemon, on the banks of the Euphrates, not far from the walls of Babylon. To deceive Roxana he caused two condemned slaves to be killed and the bodies being thrown into a well are covered with stones. Statira and Parisatis live in close retirement under the names of Cassandre and Euridice. Later the two ladies are brought back into Babylon when Perdiccas and his brother Alcetas endeavour to force them into marriage. Briefly we may remind ourselves that Oroondate, Prince of Scythia, besieges Babylon to rescue Statira and her sister. He is taken prisoner, but is courted by Roxana, who is madly in love with him. Various adventures succeed, and finally the fall of the city delivers Oroondate and Statira, who are then united. Roxana stabs herself.

To judge candidly in *Loves Triumph* we have the very lees and lurt of the heroic school.

An infinitely better, and indeed an extremely interesting rhyming tragedy is Thomas Shipman's *Henry the Third of France, Stabb'd By A Fryer, With The Fall Of The Guises,* 4to, 1678.

Thomas Shipman, eldest son of William Shipman (1632–1680), an ardent royalist, and his second wife, Sara, daughter of Alderman Parker, of Nottingham, was born at the little village of Scarrington, 2 miles from Bingham, Notts, and was baptized there in November, 1632. Dr. Thoroton alludes to him as "a good Poet, and one of the Captains of the Train Bands of this County", whilst Flatman esteemed him as "a Man every way accomplish'd". He was educated at Sleaford School, and on 1st May, 1651, was admitted a member of S. John's College, Cambridge. In addition to one tragedy *Henry The Third Of France* he is the author of a number of poems, which were collected and published posthumously as *Carolina ; or, Loyal Poems,* 8vo, 1683. The verses comprised in this collection were for the most part written in his "quiet recess" during "the Calamities of the last rebellion". Although whilst in London Shipman frequented the society of the wits and was esteemed by literary men of the day, he none the less proved a careful economist and nursed his Nottinghamshire property to some effect. He married a daughter of John Trafford, Esquire, Margaret, by whom he had twelve, if not thirteen, children. He died at Scarrington, and was buried there 15th October, 1680. His wife who had brought him an estate at Bulcote survived until about 1696. Their third son William settled at Mansfield, and in 1730 was high sheriff of Nottinghamshire.

Henry The Third Of France Stabb'd by a Fryer, With The Fall of the Guise was produced by Killigrew's company during the early months of their tenancy of Lincoln's Inn Fields, very shortly after the fatal fire of Thursday, 25th January, 1672. This address which is printed in *Carolina* (pp. 208-9) as spoken by a Woman, "*soon after the Royal Theatre was fir'd,*" commences :—

> *'Tis very hard, whilst* Fortune *was our Foe,*
> *You should dissert us for her being so.*
> *We were your* Fav'rites ; *and none before*
> *Lost that preferment, by their own being* poor.
> *Small cause, that you should with that* Whore *conspire,*
> *To send us* Famine, *'cause she sent us* Fire.
> *The* Scenes, *compos'd of* Oyl *and porous Firr,*
> *Added to th' ruine of the* Theater.
> *And 'twas a judgement in the Poets Phrase,* ⎫
> *That* Plays *and* Play-house *perisht by a blaze* ⎬
> *Caus'd by those* gaudy Scenes, *that spoil* good Plays. ⎭
> *But why for this should we forsaken be ?*
> *It was our House, alas, was* burnt ; *not we.*
> *And yet from hence might some suspition come,*
> *Since it first kindled in our* lowest Room ;
> *The* Fire *did seize on all both* Brick *and* Wood ;
> *But we more lucky were in* Flesh *and* Blood.

The Prologue was " Intended, and Part Spoken by Mr. *Hart* ".

There was an important revival of *Henry The Third Of France* in June, 1678, and the play was then given to the press. No less than three Epistles are prefixed. The first, a Poem addressed to the Duke of Monmouth, is dated *Novemb.* 1678 ; the second, a prose dedication to the Marquess of Dorchester, is dated 30 *August,* 1678 ; the third is a letter to Roger L'Estrange. This last is the most interesting of the leash, as discussing the use of rhyme upon the stage, and defending the heroic couplets of the author's own tragedy. He tells us that it was endeavour to keep to history. " I alter'd not the *Story,* nor made the *Guises* speak, or not worse than really they did. I branded not that *damn'd League* with such characters, as I might have done, and they deserv'd. . . . I made both the *Kings Amorous, Generous and Valiant,* and so indeed they were. . . . If *Grillon* [142] seem'd overbold and rough sometimes in some places, I do but keep my self to that character which Monsieur Girard and D'Avila (with others) have bestow'd upon him." A vigorous defence of the use of rhyme follows. Shipman is sad when he hears " some are *Fugitives* to their own *perswasions* ", a bob for Dryden. " *Miltons Paradice* is a work noble, strong, and fanciful, but had his humour of contradiction soften'd it into his own sweet *Rhime,* what a *Poem* had it been!"

The cast of *Henry The Third Of France* is not printed, but the characters are: Henry the Third, Loves Chateauneuf and Gabriel; Henry King of Navar, Loves Gabriel; Henry, Duke of Guise, Loves Gabriel; Francis, Cardinal of Guise; Grillon, Collonel of the Guards, Loves Gabriel; Guessle, Proctor General; Revol, Secretary of State; Plessis, Secretary to Navar; Pericart, Secretary to Guise; Larchant, Captain of the Guards; Commolet, a Jesuit; Burgoin, Prior of the Jacobines; James Clement, a Jacobine Novice; Gabriel de Estree, Mistress to Henry the fourth; Chateauneuf, Mistress to Henry the Third; Armida, friend to Gabriel; Bonneval, friend to Chateaunef. The Scene, "*Blois,* remov'd at th' Fourth Act to the Camp at St. *Clou,* before *Paris.*"

The play does not materially deviate from history in its main episodes. The ambition of the Guise is developed, and there is an undercurrent of much contention between the various lovers of Gabriel, who when about to be ravished by soldiers in a wood near Blois is rescued by Henry of Navarre. An elaborate Incantation Scene concludes Act II. The locale is the Cave in the Wood, and hither Guise and the Cardinal resort to consult the Fryer, a Conjurer. This worthy evokes various astral spirits of Endor. Incidentally the magi comes of staunch old warlock lineage, for he tells us:—

> Thrice fifty years ago, one *Gyles-de-Raiz*
> (*Marshal of France*) my great Grand-father was,
> 'Twas he who first with Necromantick art,
> Taught *Joan of Orleans* to act her Part.
> Whose pow'rful charms made th' *English* quit the Field;
> No mortal force else could have made 'em yield.
> 'Twas he (as by my bloody Roll appears)
> Who hir'd two Spirits for two Hundred Years.

It is curious here to meet with this foul and dark tradition concerning S. Joan, which had already been so abominably exploited on the English stage in *Henry VI, Part I.* The Fryer withdraws to the inner recesses of the cave. "*A Table brought, A Censer of burning Coals, a Cabinet, &c. He returns, a Cap on, a Wand, and book in 's hands; taking out of the Cabinet a piece of Chalk,*" he draws mystic circles, burns and strews perfumes, whereupon are seen apparitions of Henry the Third crown'd, holding a cypress branch; Navarre, crowned, holding a laurel; the Guise, wearing a ducal crown with a drawn sword. The Planets descend with music. An Earthy Spirit ascends accompanied by Rebellion and Murder. As they are about to descend the Friar stays them, but they return an ambiguous answer and vanish. Act III concludes with the killing of the Duke of Guise. He goes out to the King's audience, then re-enters fighting with six armed guards. There is a *mêlée* and he has a dying speech of twenty lines. Next the Cardinal is brought in by two soldiers. "*He Eyes 'em seriously*," but is dispatched, for although the first soldier refuses to kill a churchman and hastens away, the second has no such scruples and soon does the business.

Act IV is largely occupied with Gabriel and her lovers. The King in his bedchamber, whilst asleep, is visited by Murder and attendant fiends, whom his Guardian-Angel drives away, but "*Vengeance (personated) descends in a bright Cloud*" and in spite of angelic intervention declares he has been sent by Heaven to strike the monarch. "*The Angel first flies up, then Vengeance ascends in the Chariot, and the Scene closes.*"

In a Dominican convent the Prior and Father Commolet, S.J., have arrayed "two *grand Scenes* of horrour and of blisse" to help "mould the soul of Novices". Accordingly "a Scene of Paradice" and a "Scene of Hell" (both painted new) are exhibited to Jacob Clement, who goes forth to kill the King, convinced he will merit Heaven by his Act. (It was long actually believed by the vulgar that such devices and trickery were employed on like occasions.) [143] Clement presses into the presence of Henry the Third whom he stabs. The wounded monarch snatching the knife from the gash pierces the friar, who falls as Grillon runs him through with his sword. The last scene is the royal bedchamber. Gabriel and Chateauneuf kneel at the death-bed, and curiously enough two of their speeches are in quatrains, breaking off from the heroic couplets. When Henry the Third expires, Navarre is recognized as King, whereupon he declares he will present Gabriel "with a double Crown" and "*The Curtain falls*". (This direction is exceedingly unusual at the conclusion of a Restoration play, since normally the curtain did not fall until after the Epilogue had been spoken. Perhaps the reason for this exception here is that the body of the King, who has died in his bed, could not well be disposed of by being carried off the stage.) [144]

There are some sorry lapses in Shipman's verse and he does not seem able to manage the turns of dialogue in rhyme with sufficient facility. His scenes are often frankly melodramatic, but in the theatre may have proved effective enough. Yet it remained for Dryden to show what genius could do with the history of the Duke of Guise.

Carolina: Or, Loyal Poems was published 8vo, 1683, a posthumous collection ushered in by Thomas Flatman who signs his address " To the Reader ", 7th February, 1682–3. The earliest poems in this miscellany, which contains many complimentary verses to friends were composed in 1652, and the latest in 1679. One of the most interesting pieces is entitled " The Representation. 1677. *Upon the Honourable Mrs.* Bridget Noel, *acting the Part of* Almahide, *in* Dryden's Granada, *at* Belvoir ". There is also a Prologue, " *The Huffer,* 1677 : *Spoken by* Ant. Eyre Esquire, . . . *when he acted* Almanzor *in the* Granada, *at* Belvoir." Shipman's verses are always fluent and facile, and not unseldom felicitous. That he should often echo Waller seems inevitable, but his conceits are never other than graceful and well turned with something new and much prettily said.

Although never performed on the regular stage, and indeed composed for particular pleas and special occasions, two pieces printed in 1678 may be considered here.

The Traitor To Him-Self, Or Mans Heart his greatest Enemy, by William Johns, is described as "A Moral Interlude In Heroic Verse. Representing

$$\text{The } \begin{cases} \text{Careless} \\ \text{Hardned} \\ \text{Returning} \\ \text{Despairing} \\ \text{Renewed} \end{cases} \text{Heart.}$$

With Intermasks of Interpretation at the close of each several Act ". It was "Acted by the Boys of a Publick School at a Breaking up, And Published as it may be useful on like occasions ", Oxford, 4to, 1678. In his address " To the Reader " Johns explains why he preferred for this Entertainment native English to the more formal Latin, and how carefully he refrained from introducing "Womens Parts, which I never thought fit to put on Boys ". When it is noted that among the chief characters are Cardian (the Heart of Man), Governor of the City ; Idos and Sunidos (Knowledge and Conscience), Two Faithful Councellors but Slighted ; Pathus and Anoetus (Passion and Folly), Two mean Servants who by flattering grow great Favorites but prove Traitors ; Kerux (the Word of God), A Leiger Embassador ; Lupa (Affliction) ; Interpres, Interpreter of the meaning of the several passages ; the allegory will be quite plain. It is indeed by no means badly worked out and managed. Johns has even contrived to catch something of the old morality plays ; he has a vein of real poetry, and his sincerity adds a certain human interest to this Interlude, which otherwise might have become a very dull and wholly artificial piece.

Johns, who was born in 1644, was the son of William Johns, of Matherne, Monmouthshire. In Michaelmas Term, 1663, he became a chorister of All Souls, Oxford, but never proceeded to a degree. He conducted for several years a very successful school at Evesham, finally taking Orders. In 1691 he was the minister of a church near Evesham, and although the precise record of his death has not been traced, this seems to have taken place early in the eighteenth century.

W.M. who signs the Dedication of *The Huntington Divertisement,* 4to, 1678, is not easily to be identified. This " small Fascicle of Rustick-Drollery ", as the author terms it, is but an Interlude presented at the County Feast held at Merchant Taylors Hall, which is situate on the south side of Threadneedle Street, on 20th June, 1678. Only a part of it could be given, and indeed although not divided into Acts and Scenes it is of some length. The place is " Hinching-Brook, Grove Fields and Meadows ". Hinchingbrooke House stands in the parishes of SS. Mary and John, Huntingdon. A small Benedictine nunnery founded here by William the Conqueror was given by Henry VIII to the Cromwells. It now belongs to the Earl of Sandwich, and carries with it the title of Viscount.

There are more than three and forty actors in *The Huntington Divertisement,* which comprises a number of dialogues of topical and purely local import, the interlocutors being such figures as Sir Jeofry Doe-Right, a Justice of Peace ; Generous Goodman ; Sedulous Prudent, an Alderman of Huntington ; Tom Clodbrain, the farmer, with Dorothy, his wife ; Will Catlin ; milkmaids, women hay-makers, and a rout of rustic clowns. Much is said and sung in praise of a country life, and many of the allusions are of considerable interest. The whole ends with an elaborate masque of huntsmen, presided over by Huntingtonia, " attir'd like *Diana,*" and surrounded by damsels representing a wool-carder, a spinner, a knitter, a lace-maker, with other folk to exhibit the staple industries of the county.

Charles Lamb in his *Specimens of English Dramatic Poets* printed the dialogue between Sir Jeofry and Goodman, the " *Humour of a retired Knight* ", where the former so eloquently praises the practice of rising at cock-crow and " the pleasures of an early contemplation ".

In 1680 was published, quarto, " The Muse of New-Market : Or Mirth and Drollery Being Three Farces. Acted Before the King and Court At New-Market ; Viz., [1] The *Merry Milkmaids* of *Islington,* or the *Rambling Gallants* defeated. [2] *Love Lost* in the *Dark,* or the *Drunken* Couple. [3] The *Politick Whore* or the *Conceited Cuckold.*" Each one of this leash is duly equipped with its own Prologue and Epilogue, and very smartly turned these addresses are.

The three farces are by no means original, but merely consist of excerpts from older plays, scenes jointed together with no little skill by a practised hand, and so arranged as to supply a quintessence of merriment and broad fun. Thus *The Merry Milkmaids of Islington* in three short acts is from Thomas Nabbes' *Tottenham Court*,[145] produced at Salisbury Court in 1633; 4to, 1638. *Love Lost in the Dark* is from Massinger; *The Guardian* (acted in 1633) being pieced out by *A Very Woman* (licensed 1634) and *The Bashful Lover* (licensed 1636). *The Politick Whore* consists of excerpts from Robert Davenport's *The City Night-Cap*,[146] licensed by Herbert on 14th October, 1624, but not printed until 1661.

These farces seem to have been from time to time acted upon the regular stage as afterpieces, and proved very acceptable to the Town. Thus at Covent Garden on 2nd May, 1746, *The Merry Milkmaids of Islington* under the title *May Day* followed Howard's *The Committee*. A letter in the *General Advertiser* says : " May Day or the Merry Milkmaid of Islington, was written by the particular desire of Charles the 2d, and first performed at New-market." It was announced as " not acted 20 years ".

In January or February, 1679, was produced at the Theatre Royal a fine rhetorical tragedy *Sertorius* by John Bancroft, a figure of some note in the world of letters. Giles Jacob in the *Poetical Register*,[147] tells us : " This Author was by Profession a Chirurgeon, and by a frequent Conversation with a Set of Witty young Gentle-men (to whom his Business led him after their Sportings with the Substitutes of *Venus*) he was very much inclin'd to Poetry." " I suspect," wrote Sir Edmund Gosse, " that John Bancroft was a very interesting man. . . . One fancies the discreet and fervent poet-surgeon, laden with his secrets and his confidences. Why did he not write memoirs, and tell us what it was that drove Nat Lee mad, and how Otway really died, and what Dryden's habits were ? Why did he not purvey magnificent indiscretions whispered under the great periwig of Wycherley, or repeat that splendid story about Etherege and my Lord Mulgrave ? " [148]

Bancroft was a particular friend of William Mountford, and when the young actor was so foully assassinated by that fine couple of blackguards Charles, Lord Mohun, and Captain Richard Hill in Howard Street, Strand, on the night of 9th December, 1692, it was he who was called in to attend the dying man. He also gave evidence at the trial of Lord Mohun, and repeated several of Mountford's ante-mortem statements. (It is not convenient here to correct even the more glaring errors made by Mr. R. S. Forsythe in his *A Noble Rake,* 1928, but it must suffice to say that the account of Mountford's murder there given is extremely unreliable and inexact.) [149] The question of the two historical plays *King Edward the Third* and *Henry the Second,* in which Bancroft certainly had a considerable share, but the Dedications of which, when they were issued from the press, appeared under Mountford's signature, will be discussed in dealing with the dramatic work of the actor-author. Bancroft died towards the end of August, 1696, and was buried in S. Paul's, Covent Garden, on 1st September of that year.

The cast of *Sertorius* is unfortunately not given but the characters are : Sertorius, exil'd from Rome, chose head of the Lusitanians in opposition to Sylla ; Bebricius, A Lusitanian, true Friend to Sertorius ; Tribunius, Captain of Sertorius's Guards ; Cassius, a Roman Tribune ; Norbanus, Ligurius, Crassus, Decius, Exil'd Roman Senators ; Perpenna, General of the Italian Bands, a Villain ; Manlius, Aufidius, Grecinus, his Officers ; Pompey, a Roman General, of Sylla's faction ; Aquinias, his Lieutenant ; Two Pontic Ambassadors ; Terentia, wife to Sertorius ; Fulvia, wife to Perpenna. Scene, Lusitania.

As Genest observes, Bancroft does not depart very materially from history, except as to the death of M. Perpenna Vento. Plutarch, upon whose Life this drama is founded, relates that Perpenna having been defeated in the first battle he fought against Pompey after the death of Sertorius, whom he and other conspirators treacherously slew at a banquet in 72 B.C., was captured and in order to save his life he showed Pompey the letters of certain noble Romans, who had invited Sertorius to come to Italy and effect a political revolution. Pompey not only burned the letters unread, but incontinently put Perpenna to death lest he should divulge the names of those who had thus corresponded with Sertorius. In the play, as Perpenna is insulting Tribunius whom he has betrayed and who is in chains, the prisoner snatches a sword and wounds him mortally. Terentia and Fulvia are fictitious characters, and Bancroft has done well to introduce this interest.

The story of the fawn of Sertorius is extremely pleasing, and there is a romance which should not have been so entirely forgotten entitled *The Fawn of Sertorius,* 2 vols., Longmans, 1846.

Bancroft has borrowed nothing from Pierre Corneille whose *Sertorius* [150] was produced at the Hôtel de Bourgogne (not as is sometimes supposed the Théâtre du Marais) on 25th February, 1662, and achieved so extraordinary a success that in the *Muse historique,* 4th March, 1662, Loret speaks of " le grand Sertorius " of Corneille—

> Qui selon le commun créit,
> A plus de beautés que son *Cid,*
> A plus de forces et de grâces
> Que Pompée et que les *Horaces,*
> A plus de charmes que n'en a
> Son inimitable *Cinna,* . . .

The rôle of Viriate, Queen of Lusitania, was created by Mlle des Œillets, and Pompée by Hauteroche. Baron was a famous Pompée in later years. Perhaps the most celebrated Viriate was Mlle Clairon. At a revival in 1758 Madame Vestris was much applauded in this part, when Grandval sustained Sertorius.

Lewis Maidwell, the author of *The Loving Enemies,* produced at Dorset Garden in the early spring of 1680, was a figure of some importance in his day, but Giles Jacob only briefly mentions him as one who " had the Care of Educating some young Gentlemen privately in the City of *London* ",[151] whilst Langbaine terms him "An Ingenious Person, still living (as I suppose) in *London*; where some time ago he undertook the Care and Tuition of young Gentlemen, and kept a Private School; during which Employment, besides some other Performances, (with which he has obliged the World) he has borrow'd so much time as to write a Play ".

From Westminster School, where he had been a pupil of Busby, Lewis Maidwell went up to Cambridge to S. John's, and proceeded B.A. in 1671. He acted as amanuensis to the Master of the College, Dr. Peter Gunning (Bishop of Chichester, 1669; of Ely, 1675). Next he was for five years tutor to the sons of Sir Stephen Fox, the " favourite with twelve successive parliaments, and with four monarchs ", and by him was recommended for employment (the original letter is in Bodley, MS. Tanner, 40, 149) to Sancroft on his election to Canterbury in December, 1679, upon which occasion Maidwell published a florid Latin Poem in the true Palladian style. Maidwell, under the patronage of the Archbishop, now opened a school in London and proved extremely successful, although Aubrey has nothing to say of him save that his fees were exorbitant. A new Ode by Purcell, *A Welcome Song at the Prince of Denmark's Coming Home,* was performed at the house of Mr. Maidwell, the eminent schoolmaster, on 5th August, 1689. A considerable number of educational treatises and charts flowed from his prolific pen and Nahum Tate who in *Majestas Imperii Britannici,* 4to, 1706, englished three of Maidwell's Odes, in his Dedication to Charles, Earl of Carlisle, speaks of " the Signal Services Mr. *Maidwell* has done his Country in the Happy Education of many Persons of Quality, very Eminent in both Houses of Parliament. But He has Reason to Glory in Nothing more than in the Honor He had, of being Serviceable to your Lordship in that capacity ".

Latterly Maidwell came very prominently before the world in connexion with his scheme for establishing and supporting a Public School, designed amongst other things for the sea service of the nation. His first petition was considered by the House of Commons on 3rd February, 1699–1700, and referred to a Committee.

His proposals, however, for converting a great house of his, near Westminster, " into a publike *Academy* . . . of which he might be Master " caused a vast fluttering in the academical dovecotes of Oxford and Cambridge, and amongst others Dr. Hough, Dutch William's President of Magdalen, Oxford, opposed the projects tooth and nail. Hearne in his diary, 27th September, 1732, speaks of this business as once " much talked of in the University ",[152] and adds " I think it was wisely stopped ". In 1705 in his *Essay on Education* Maidwell was still urging a Scheme for a School of Languages and Navigation.

It is, however, Maidwell's dramatic work alone with which we are here concerned. *The Loving Enemies* was given with an excellent—one might say an all-star—cast. Betterton and Smith played Lorenzo and Marcello, " Two Noblemen Enemies to one another from a long fewd in their families "; Joseph Williams, Antonio " In love with *Lucinda,* but pretends it to the Widow "; Anthony Leigh, Paulo del Campo, " a brisk old Gentleman in love with the Widow "; Underhill, Circumstantio, " a formal *Valet de Chambre* very troublesome with impertinent Rhetorick "; Richards, Albricio, Lorenzo's servant; Mrs. Mary Lee, Julia, " Sister to *Lorenzo,* in love with *Marcello,* yet never seen by him "; Mrs. Barry, Camilla, " Sister to *Marcello,* in love with *Lorenzo,* yet never seen by him "; Mrs. Shadwell, Lucinda, " Old *Paulo's* daughter, in love with *Antonio*"; Mrs. Leigh, Paulina, " a rich Widow "; and Mrs. Norris, Nuarcha, "An old Maid almost undone for want of an Husband." The scene lies in Florence. Circumstantio, who vows he would " not for the Universe be without those tropes, and flowers that my discourse adorn ", is a good character and must have proved extremely diverting upon the stage. Paulo who has a mind to make his daughter Lucinda a nun has placed to lodge with the relict of his friend Ferdinand, Paulina, to whom therefore Antonio is forced to pay court to obtain access to his real mistress. The widow's lascivious old abigail, Nuarcha, is forward in managing this intrigue, and is better bribed by kisses than by gold. The wooing of Nuarcha by Circumstantio is very happy, although it must be allowed that the valet with " a certain immoderate Guilt he has of impertinent *Eloquence* " is very closely modelled upon Shadwell's Sir Formal Trifle, often to verbal echoes, especially the Description of " a *Magpy* sucking of an *Hen's Egg*" (iv, 1), which is obviously inspired by Sir Formal's famous oration upon the Mouse taken in a Trap. There is an amusing scene when Antonio conceals himself within the hollow wooden effigy of Paulina's late husband and speaking in oracular tones feigns to be the spirit of the deceased forbidding any new bans. Antonio and his mistress are in the act of eloping at midnight when an accident raises the house, and Lucinda is only able to effect her lover's escape by feigning that Ferdinand's ghost has again appeared. Nevertheless eventually Antonio and Lucinda are united, whilst Paulo and Paulina both resolve not to change their state, so the match is happily blessed and approved.

The more serious episodes show two young men of quality, Lorenzo and Marcello, at variance. Now Julia, Lorenzo's sister, loves Marcello ; whilst Camilla, Marcello's sister, loves Lorenzo. The accidents and complications which develop from this situation may be easily surmised. There is a duello on a moonlit night in a wood, where presently appear the two heroines, each masquerading in a boy's habit. Love effects in the end a general reconciliation.

The Loving Enemies is an exceedingly well-written and interesting play, both as regards the romantic incidents and the lighter scenes. One can only be surprised that it did not keep the stage, more particularly as many a worse comedy long maintained a place in the theatre. It is not improbable that this disregard was the reason why Maidwell did not make another essay in the drama.

The Epilogue to *The Loving Enemies* was written by Shadwell, and spoken by Mrs. Barry. When printed, 4to, 1680, the play was dedicated to Charles Fox, a son of Sir Stephen Fox, and a former pupil of the author.

From the Prologue, written by Ravenscroft, it would appear that William Whitaker's tragedy *The Conspiracy ; Or, The Change of Government* was produced at Dorset Garden in March, 1680. This address commences :—

> *Gallants, in this good Godly time of Lent*
> *I am come forth to bid you all repent.*[153]

No cast is given with *The Conspiracy,* which presents the following characters : Ibrahim, the Sultan ; Mahomet, his son, a youth ; the Mufti, or Chief Priest ; Solyman Aga, chief Eunuch ;

PLATE XXIV

GARRICK AS DON JOHN IN THE CHANCES

Collection of the Author

Kuperli ; Ipsir ; Oglar, enamour'd with the Queen Formiana ;
Meleck Hamet, the grand Vizier, a Traitor ; Bectas, a Rebel ;
Kara and Kulcaiha, two of his adherents ; Kiosem, the Queen-
Mother ; Formiana, the Sultaness ; Flatra, the Sultan's sister ;
Lentesia, a lady of the court.

The Sultan Ibrahim is enmeshed amongst plotters. The old
Queen, Kiosem, who is in league with Bectas, has already killed
three sons, Ahmet, Osman, Morat, and is now planning the
destruction of the fourth. The ambitious Flatra urges her husband
Meleck Hamet to dispatch her brother and enjoy his throne.
We move in an atmosphere of suspicion, blood, and guilt, and
the young Queen Formiana falls senseless at the vision of a
carious skeleton that seems to beckon her Lord to a Tomb.
Ibrahim exclaims :—

> I nothing saw, and yet me thinks the mirth
> Of my calme soul is damp't with smells of earth :
> Moist vapours rise as from some Vault or Cave ;
> Sure—I am in a Charnel house or Grave.

When the Sultan and Sultana are together in the Seraglio Oglar
intrudes to announce

The City Rages in Rebellious Flame :

Oglar puts on the Sultan's state robes to turn the fury of the
assailants on himself, but takes advantage of his disguise to
attempt Formiana's virtue. She feigns and hesitates in order
to make time, and before retiring to her bedchamber conceals
him for a few moments in a closet as the rebels are on the point
of entering. Suspecting a ruse Oglar steals out of his hiding
and persuades the Sultan to take his place in order to escape the
soldiers. The Sultaness directs the Vizier and Bectas to the
closet supposing they will discover Oglar and slay him in her
husband's stead. However, owing the treacherous exchange,
they drag out the real Sultan who is thus led to believe the
Queen has betrayed him and is about to stab her when Oglar
interposing receives the blow, and has but time to confess to
the Mufti and other loyal nobles his crimes ere he expires.
Sultan Ibrahim is cut down by Meleck Hamet, whilst the Queen
as she weeps over his body is comforted by a vision : " There
Descends an Heavenly Shape, in the Clouds, and Sings :—

> *He's dead, he's dead ; seek not in vain*
> *To weep the dead to life again :*
> *Spare, O spare those Orient show'rs,*
> *They fall too late on wither'd Flow'rs . . ."*

The proud Flatra is now " *discover'd, habited in the Robes of a*

Sultaness, sitting in a Chair of State ", around her slaves make obeisance and worship. She does not, however, long enjoy her sovranty as her husband driven mad by the haunting spectre of the murdered Sultan, suddenly exclaims :—

> 'Cause you love Honor and a Crown so well,
> I do intend you shall go Reign in Hell,

and drives a dagger to her heart, afterwards accomplishing the same office for himself, whereupon the " Queen-Mother *and* Lentesia *squeak* ".

Kiosem, planning to dispose of her daughter-in-law and grandson, invokes Heaven's blessings on them to be repulsed by Formiana with

> The Witch prays backward, if she prays at all ;
> Her tears, like Mildew, blast where e're they fall.

Events hasten to a conclusion : " the Scene being drawn ; young Mahomet is discover'd on a Throne, in Imperial Robes, attended by Mufti, Solyman, Aga, Ipsir, Kuperli, Bectas, Kara, Kulcaiha, and several others : who upon the opening of the Scene, make their obeisance, and cry, Long live Sultan Mahomet Han the fourth : Then they all enter " ; that is to say they advance well down front on to the apron. The new Sultan appoints his counsellors, and Bectas with his friends are chagrined not to be of the divan. They resolve to depose Mahomet Han and set on the throne his younger brother, Solyman, who will be a puppet in their hands. An extraordinary episode, worthy of Beddoes, is next exhibited : " *Scene draws, discover a Room hung all with black ; the Old Queen, Lentesia, Bectas, Kara and Kalcaiha seated, while several of the Royal Party are plac'd in Order, with Coffins before them, on which stand a dim Taper, and Mutes standing ready as to strangle them : then Enter eight or ten Blackmoors, drest like Fiends, and dance an Antic ; having done, they go out, and after fearful groans and horrid Shriekings ; some of them return with burnt Wine, which they fill out in Sculls to the King's Friends, who, as fast as they drink, dy : at which the Queen and all the rest seem pleas'd.*" Retribution is swift, for as the conspirators are congratulating themselves " *The* Sultan's *Ghost appears, leading Death by the hand : He passes the stage beck'ning to them severally* ". There is now a sudden and alarming descent to absolute bathos, for Bectas remarks :—

> I never knew till now what 'twas to fear,
> S'death, who are you ? or, what's your business here ?

The royal troops surprise the plotters, whereupon Lentesia " *snatches up a Pistol, and kills one of them* " with the very salutary reprimand :—

Dy, Rascals, some of you, for being so rude
In to the Queen's retirements to intrude.

It only remains for Sultan Mahomet to condemn the traitors to
their fate,whilst Kiosem is to be immured in a shadowed dungeon
with the prospect of impending doom. There is a good Epilogue
by Ravenscroft.

The Conspiracy is the work of a very young man. The fable
is well designed, but the execution is not equal to the planning.
Dryden would, and Lee might have given us a crowded but
splendid picture of Turkish intrigue and have thrilled us with
the horrors and villainies of Bectas and Kiosem. Whitaker
almost uniformly fails and falls flat, for, worst of all, where he
strives to be most impressive and macabre he is merely ridiculous.
Flatra, his best character, is clearly modelled on Lyndaraxa in
The Conquest of Granada. Thus the magnificent dying speech
of the Moorish princess is copied, closely enough but how weakly !
Flatra's last words are :—

O, I am dead ; and by a subject slain !
But shall I not have Time one hour to reign ?
Yet make him Emperor before I go :
Or if you cannot make him, call him so.
But fancy must your unkind sloth supply ;
For, in conceit, I will an Empress dy.

A far better tragedy, and one of the last original plays to be
given at the Theatre Royal before it temporarily closed prior
to the Union of the Two Companies was *Tamerlane The Great*
by Charles Saunders "A Young Gentleman, whose wit began
to bud as early, as that of the Incomparable *Cowley* ; and was
like him a King's Scholar, when he writ" this piece. *Tamerlane
The Great* was produced in February, 1681, and was received
with great favour, although a faction sharply attacked the new
poet, for "*no sooner can a young Writer appear in the World, but he
is look'd upon by those squint-ey'd pretenders, to wit, no less than some
Notorious Malefactor, or Branded Outlaw, whom all may Prosecute,
Attaint, Judge, Condemn, or what they please, cum Privilegio*". This
tragedy, Saunders says in his Preface, "*as it was Writ only for
my divertisement at Vacant Hours or Recreation after severer Studies,
was never design'd to see the light,*" but certain friends of the young
author were so pleased with his talent that they praised it highly
"*about the Town and University*", raising so great an expectation
that the author was perforce obliged to let his work appear.
Even then he insisted on submitting his scenes to the judgement
of "*the greatest part of the Witty and Judicious Men of the Town*",
nay, more he would not sanction its production "*untill it had*

receiv'd some Rules for Correction from Mr. Dryden *himself, who also was pleas'd to Grace it with an Epilogue, to which it ows no small part of its success* ".

Even if they were baffled in one point the critics were nevertheless resolved to damn the piece, " *and the means they took, was to give out, that this was only an Old Play Transcrib'd,*" Marlowe's *Tanburlaine the Great* refurbished, and that not by the young poet's pen alone. Saunders very convincingly asserts " *I never heard of any Play on the same Subject, untill my own was Acted, neither have I since seen it, though it hath been told me, there is a Cock-Pit Play, going under the name of the* Scythian Shepherd, *or* Tamberlain the Great, *which how good it is, any one may Judge by its obscurity, being a thing, not a Bookseller in* London, *or scarce the Players themselves, who Acted it formerly, cou'd call to Remembrance, so far, that I believe whoever was the Author, he might e'en keep it to himself secure from invasion, or Plagiary; But let these who have Read it Convince themselves of their Errors, that this is no second Edition, but an entirely new Play* ". It is indeed plain at a first glance that Saunders has taken nothing from Marlowe, but a phrase of great interest in the above passage plainly alludes to some post-Restoration revival of *Tamburlaine the Great.*[154] This may be dated very early in 1660–2, when many of the older plays were, as it would seem, somewhat roughly and perfunctorily presented.

Saunders, moreover, continues : " *I must acquaint you that I drew the design of this Play, from a late* Novell, *call'd* Tamerlane *and* Asteria, *which I'm sure bears not half the Age of the Tragedy before mention'd, and I am confident the Characters are quite different,*" which is most certainly the case.

Asterie, ou Tamerlan was first published at Paris, 2 vols., 12mo, 1675. It is the work of the daughter of Charles de Guilhen, sieur de La Roche,[155] although it has sometimes in error been ascribed to Madame de Villedieu.

Asteria And Tamberlain ; Or, The Distressed Lovers : "A Novel. Written in *French* by a Person of Quality. And rendred into *English,* by E. C. Esq " ; London, 12mo, 1677, is an uncommonly scarce book.[156] Charles Saunders in his tragedy has followed and selected the incidents in the story with great judgement, and he has certainly done well in altering some of the harsher names in his original for more euphonious appellations. The Dramatis Personae are : Tamerlane, Emperor of the Tartars ; Bajaset, Emperor of the Turks ; Arsanes, Mandricard, Sons to Tamerlane ; Odmar, Abdalla, Counsellors ; Axalla, Zanches, friends to Arsanes ; Asteria, Bajaset's daughter ; Ispatia, wife to Mandricard ; Zayda, confidante to Asteria. Scene, Samarcanda. The cast is not printed.

The tragedy opens with the Temple of Mahomet. Priests are hymning Tamerlane's victories, and presently Bajaset and Asteria are brought forth in chains. When, however, Mandricard declares his love for the captive princess the fury of Tamerlane blazes out, and he condemns Bajaset to instant execution. The next scene is a wood. To his friend Axalla Arsanes laments his father's injustice to himself and declares his love for the fair Nerina, who proves to be none other than Asteria. Bajaset has mounted the scaffold, about to lay his head on the block when Arsanes interrupts, and falling at his father's feet declares his exile and his wrongs. Tamerlane receives him with joy, confessing that he has lent too ready a ear to the slanderers of his son. Mandricard, who has contrived the disgrace of Arsanes and who has discovered his love for Asteria, now lays deep and bloody plots. Meanwhile by his coldness he has aroused the jealous anger of his wife Ispatia. The news is brought that Bajaset has been locked in an iron cage by his conqueror and led about in mockery, and Zayda tells Asteria that as the Royal Captive was conveyed thus through crowded Sarmarcand

> Against the massy Bars with rage he dash'd
> His Royal Head, while from the fatal Wound
> Gush'd out that Blood, which long the greatest Life
> The World cou'd ever proudly boast preserv'd . . .

The villain Odmar bribes slaves who swear on the Koran to Tamerlane that Arsanes is conspiring to slay Mandricard,

> To poison *Tamerlane* our Royal Master
> And with *Asteria* to usurp his Throne.

Mandricard forces his way into Asteria's apartments upon receiving a missive from her, and here is surprised by Ispatia. He feigns to be reconciled to his wife, and bids

> one Kiss upon
> The Sacred Alcoran, and our Love is Seal'd.

No sooner has she pressed her lips to the volume than he cries as she falls swooning :—

> The Book was poison'd, and thou hast drunk the Venom.

Saunders here probably had in mind the scene in Webster's *The Dutchesse of Malfy,* Act V, where the Cardinal poisons his mistress Julia by a precisely similar device.

Ispatia expires acknowledging she wrote the letter in Asteria's name which drew him to the spot. The soldiers rise in favour of Arsanes, whom Tamerlane dare not dispatch, as he would. Odmar, who is lurking near Asteria's lodging, sees Arsanes at her door, and in the dark drives his dagger to the Prince's heart, only to discover he has slain Mandricard. Tamerlane enters with his retinue, and Odmar who is wailing over the corpse, acknowledges that twenty years before he substituted his own son Themyre for the royal Mandricard who " a tender Infant dy'd ", and it is for Themyre he has woven his plots and schemed. To prevent a traitor's doom he slays himself as the guards are seizing him. Arsanes enters leading Asteria, and Tamerlane joins the hands " of the blest Loyal Pair ".

Saunders died young, and one cannot help feeling that we lost an excellent dramatist, since *Tamerlane the Great* is a good stirring tragedy with some vigorous writing, and the technique in particular is extraordinarily well wrought for the earliest attempt of " *the first Boy-Poet of our Age* " as Dryden termed him. It proved a lucky handsel, for older pens and more practised have written far worse tragedies and not wanted applause.

Banks highly commends this tragedy in a copy of verses prefixed to the quarto, and it was sufficiently esteemed, so Langbaine [157] tells us, to have been given " at *Oxford,* before his late Majesty King *Charles* the Second, at his meeting the Parliament there ". The King entered Oxford on Monday, 14th March, 1681, and having dissolved Parliament about half-past ten on Monday morning, 28th March, His Majesty left the town at one-o-clock the same afternoon, and so came to Windsor in the evening.

It is hardly necessary to do more than record the names of the three translations from Seneca by Sir Edward Sherburne (1618–1702), Clerk of the Ordnance, who published the *Medea,* 8vo, 1648 ; *Troades,* 8vo, 1679 ; and *Phaedra and Hippolitus,* 8vo, 1701. Langbaine considered that these versions showed " the Translator a Gentleman of Learning and Judgment ", but they were not, of course, intended for the stage.

The *Troades* was also translated " Into our Vernacular Tongue " by " lame *Mephiboseth* the Wisard's Son ",[158] Samuel Pordage (1633–1692),[159] and printed in his *Poems Upon Several Occasions, By S. P. Gent.,* 12mo, 1660.

We may now review a play written by no less a critic than Thomas Rymer, 1641–1713, for whilst he was engaged upon *The Tragedies of the Last Age Consider'd and Examin'd,* 1678, licensed 17th July, 1677, a treatise in which he devotes him to a hypercritically unjust review of *Rollo, A King and no King,* and *The Maid's Tragedy,* Rymer was composing a Tragedy which might put precept into practice and demonstrate how the thing ought to be done. Accordingly with date 1678,[160] Rymer published quarto *Edgar Or The English Monarch* ; An Heroick

Tragedy, in the Advertisement to which he announces : " This I call an *Heroick Tragedy,* having in it chiefly sought occasions to extoll the *English* Monarchy . . . The Tragedy ends Prosperously ; a sort of Tragedy that rarely succeeds . . . Yet this sort seems principally to have pleased *Euripides.*"

The Persons Represented are : Edgar, King of England ; Lewis the IV, King of France, *incognito* ; Kenneth, King of Scotland ; Ethelwold, Edgar's Favourite ; Editha, Sister to Edgar ; Gunilda, Sister to the King of Denmark ; Alfrid, the Duke of Cornwall's Daughter; Ethelgede, Ethelwold's daughter; and Dunstan, Arch-bishop of Canterbury. The Time of the Representation, from Twelve at Noon to Ten at Night."

The outlines of the familiar story as told by William of Malmesbury are that King Eadgar (944–975) hearing of the beauty of Ælfthryth, daughter of Ordgar, Ealdorman of the western shires, thinks of taking her as his consort, but first sends his favourite Æthelwald to see if report has spoken truly. Æthelwald visits her father's house, falls in love with and himself marries her, reporting to the king that she is wholly unworthy of a royal alliance. After a time Eadgar learning of the deception proposes a visit to Æthelwald, who in much alarm tells his wife how he obtained her, and begs her to masque her beauty from the king. The lady instead of obeying her husband so adorns herself so that her charms irresistibly enslave the amorous monarch, who slays Æthelwald at a hunting-party. Eadgar then marries the widow Ælfthryth. The Brompton Chronicles and other sources give varying stories, but Freeman in *The Fortnightly Review,* May, 1866, was of opinion that these are almost wholly legendary, although William of Malmesbury's account may contain some germ of truth.

Rymer mainly based his tragedy on the Geoffrey Gaimar version of the tale, but even so he departs very widely from tradition. " I question," wrote Rymer in his *Tragedies of the Last Age Consider'd,* " whether in Poetry a King can be an accessary to a crime " ; and thus in accordance with his own canons he refuses to " make *Edgar* point-blank guilty of *Ethelwold's* Death " ; the more especially, perhaps, because in his rhymed dedication " To The King " he protests that

You alone, great Edgar's *Person bear.*

The first scene is a " *Landschap of a River, Trees, Palace,* &c.". The River is apparently the Dee, since presently " *The King in a Triumphant Barge appears within the Scenes, rowed by eight Kings towards the Stage,* &c. *The Kings enter in procession with their gilded Oars ; after them* Edgar, *with* Alfrid *in his hand, his eyes fixt on her,*

Ethelwold *behind*. *The Kings successively salute* Edgar " in terms of adulation which scarcely Domitian would have tolerated. Their praises are in some sense prophetic of Britain's naval power, for Rymer is nothing if not jingoistic to absurdity.[161] Ethelwold has previously disclosed to Alfrid the ruse by which he gained her hand and begged her to shroud her beauty.

> Cover those Beams, and let that natural Light,
> Obscur'd by Art, less fiercely strike the Light.

The lady objects, and he storms, whereupon she replies :—

> To calm your mind, my utmost power I'll try.
> If I receive advantage from my Dress,
> 'Tis that I you might with advantage please.
> If, wanting this, your Love be not impair'd,
> These Ornaments I readily discard.   [*Pulls off her Patches.*

Ethelwold. Those Trifles did your Beauty but rebate.
> If this be all you'll doe, how desperate is my state !
> Pull out those Eyes—and then my work is done.
> To what extremes will my resentment run !

> [*Pulls her away. Exeunt.*

Queen Ethelgede, who is Ethelwold's daughter, acclaims her husband's majesty as he is rowed on the river in lines which bid defiance to burlesque :—

> He sits on high, illustrious and large :
> They blow, and tugg and launch along his Barge.

We understand that it is only three days since Ethelwold and Alfrid were married, and as she has denied him her person for three nights she rests a virgin-bride. Learning that Alfrid is to meet the King, Queen Ethelgede resolves to take her place at the bower, a stratagem Alfrid suggests may bind them always in love. Ethelwold having discovered the secret appointment lurks in the dark to kill his wife whom he deems false. He drives his dagger to the Queen's heart and then stabs himself, leaving Edgar to marry Alfrid. Suddenly S. Dunstan enters and forbids the union, only to be dismissed very summarily and rudely by the amorous monarch. This is a gross indecorum which we might well have been spared, especially in the writings of one who so piqued himself upon the civilities and courtesies of poetry.

In fact *Edgar, Or The English Monarch* is not merely a bad play, but a ridiculously bad play, and something very ironical appears when we consider that it was printed as a sort of companion and complement to the author's dissolving criticism of three masterpieces of drama. It may seem strange that *Edgar* did not become the veriest butt and white for the shafts of pasquil and lampoons, but inasmuch as it made no appearance in the theatre it was simply ignored. It was printed, and it was left unread by contemporaries, a reasonable neglect which has persisted for two centuries and a half and which there are no grounds to suppose will not steadfastly endure. Thus Rymer, and—as Butler has it—

> all the Lewd Impeachers
> Of witty Beumonts Poetry, & Fletchers,

reap their own reward of completest oblivion.

With some sense of relief we turn to the one and only Opera of the son of Sir William, Charles Davenant (1656–1714), whose *Circe* described on the title-page of the first (1677) edition and subsequent editions (1685, 1703) as a Tragedy, was produced at Dorset Garden during the first week of May, 1677, and is thus noticed by Downes : " *Circe,* an Opera Wrote by Dr. *Davenant; Orestes,* was *Acted* by Mr. *Betterton; Pylades,* Mr. *Williams: Ithacus,* Mr. *Smith; Thoas,* Mr. *Harris: Circe,* Lady *Slingsby: Iphigenia,* Mrs. *Betterton: Osmida,* Mrs. *Twiford.* All the Musick was set by Mr. *Banister,* and being well Perform'd, it answer'd the Expectation of the Company."

The play is written in heroic verse, nobly equipped with a Prologue by Dryden and an Epilogue by Rochester. We must at once dismiss any idea of Greek drama, and incontinently enter the rococo realm of Italian opera, which is not without its own fragrant fascination, smelling of neroli and frangipan. The Scene is Taurica Chersonesus. Act I opens with Circe's cave, shadowed and terrible. Here are seen Iphigenia, the priestess —albeit all unwilling—of Diana Taurica, "A Goddess, who in humane blood delights." She is pursued with guilty passion by King Thoas of Scythia, and is also wooed by Prince Ithacus, Circe's son by Ulysses, both of whom she imperiously rejects. Ithacus is beloved by the daughter to Thoas, the fair Osmida, who sighs in vain. Circe, Queen of Scythia, by her magic arts is aware of the infatuation of Thoas, and also of the love of her son Ithacus. In a fine incantation scene she summons Pluto, " th' Infernal King," and bids him

> Vouchsafe in Fates mysterious Books to read,
> What for my Son and Husband is decreed.

The deity of Tartarus, called from Eternal night, replies that both must " meet a cruel fate this day " unless Iphigenia shall sacrifice "A bloody Victim to attone for all ", whichever one she may choose of the " two Noble Youths from *Argos* come ", who are newly landed, driven " hither by *Apollo*'s doom ".

These are none other than Orestes and Pylades, whom Circe, warning her husband of the dusky rede, by her arts compels to fall into an enchanted slumber so that they are easily captured. Iphigenia is now obliged to select the victim. She hesitates and falters, for she has fallen in love with Pylades, when Orestes claims that grown weary of the world he alone has the right to seek " Death's quiet Cell ". Circe, however, has begun to dote upon Orestes, and she determines that Pylades must bleed on Diana's horrid altar. Thoas suspecting her design at once commands Iphigenia to immolate Orestes, whereupon Circe reveals that the Priestess is about to offer her own brother, Agamemnon's son. None the less the weeping Iphigenia is forced thence, whilst the grim priests proceed to the murderous rites. Suddenly *"As they go to kill* Orestes, *two Dragons rise out of the Earth, and bear him away* ; Circe *appears in a Chariot drawn by Dragons* ". The weird woman conveys Orestes to her " Inchanted Palace, with a beautiful Garden " on Mount Parnassus, and here the hero is lulled to sleep on a bed of flowers whilst Orpheus plays on his lute and Circe's maidens sing. Circe wraps Orestes in amorous dalliance, which is interrupted by King Thoas, who, aided by Vesta, half-dissolves the charms. " Fiercer than Thunder is his jealous Rage," and he is about to slay Orestes when Ithacus rushes in crying that the Greek warriors have not only seized Osmida but threaten his life and throne, whilst his own people hating the tyrant's yoke are revolting to the foe. After a tender parting from Circe, Orestes goes to head his soldiers. Ithacus is mortally wounded in the fray, and Osmida expires broken-hearted over his body. Circe, realizing that Orestes having escaped her spell does not intend to return, by the force of necromantic runes and baleful evocations wrecks the Greek fleet driven back on the Scythian shores and sends him mad. The shade of Clytemnestra, pale and bloody, arises to goad her son to raving frenzy. In his paroxysms Orestes kills Thoas who has attempted to cut him down, whilst Circe overwhelms sky and earth in a fearful storm with hurricanes of wind, blazing levin, and crashing thunder. Orestes in his delirious calenture imagining Circe to be his mother's ghost stabs her to the heart, then buries the steel into his own breast. Pylades and Iphigenia are struck with horror amid the whirl of elements as the whole " *City of a sudden is a Fire* ", and Circe is lost in death's dark mist.

Circe is an excellent tragedy, and although Charles Davenant has given the incidents a turn neither Aeschylus nor Euripides ever knew, he has skilfully managed his new-minted story, and sustained the interest to the end. The verse may be operatic, but it is not without merits in its kind. Circe's Inchanted Palace in Act IV and her wantonness with Orestes, who there despises glory for love, are clearly suggested by Tasso's description of Armida's palace, and the amorous ease of Rinaldo in her circling arms.

A piece, not intended to be acted, *Youth's Comedy; Or, The Souls Tryals and Triumph*, described as a "Dramatick Poem", and published 8vo, 1680, may be dismissed in a few words. The address "To The Reader, Especially The Younger Sort" is subscribed T.S., who would seem to have been a minister of Calvinistic views. Calderón has shown us with what wealth of poetry such an allegory may be vested. *Youth's Comedy,* written in halting rhymes that recall the metrical effects of Sternhold and Hopkins, is a production of the utmost tedium. It largely consists of duologues between the Soul and the Body. A Nuncius declaims between whiles, and the Soul is tempted of Pleasure, Honour, Riches, and the like. We are right glad when the thing concludes with "*The Soul and Bodies mutual Valediction to each other*".

The compass of this chapter which covers some very miscellaneous work renders a summary more than ordinarily difficult; and, perhaps, at best a matter of supererogation. "It is odd, however," once wrote Sir Edmund Gosse in his charming essay "A Volume of Old Plays", "that the very worst production, if it be more than two hundred years old, is sure to contain some little thing interesting to a modern student." [162] There have been passed in review plays, both tragedies and comedies, which rank only just below the first place; there has been— as I hope—sufficiently described one piece which is among the meanest and weakest of the Restoration theatre. In the former category are to be placed Payne's *The Fatal Jealousie* and Lord Caryl's *Sir Salomon,* nor are these solitary examples. To the neap must be assigned Edward Cooke's feebly amateurish and chlorotic *Love's Triumph* with its splayed couplets and ormolu nobilesse.

Even so fantastical and unrelated an extravaganza as is honest John Smith's *Cytherea* presents certain points of attraction, and is by no means wholly without flashes of wit and censure. In Dover's *The Mall,* Payne's *Morning Ramble,* Rawlins's *Tom Essence* and *Tunbridge Wells,* Fane's *Love In The Dark,* Rhodes's *Flora's Vagaries,* the anonymous *Woman Turn'd Bully,* Leanerd's *Counterfeits,* and others we have comedies of great merit. Written in more serious vein, Joyner's *Roman Empress* and Bancroft's *Sertorius,* are truly poetical and worthy of regard.

It was inevitable that when the theatres once again reopened their doors busy poetasters and bantling wits should break silence by urging their own performances upon the stage, and that when these were refused by the actors, some one or two at least should slink and slither into print amid the well-fed applause of puffers and parasites. What was not inevitable is that during the twenty years from 1660 to 1680 the general standard of writing among the lesser men should have maintained so high a level, whence comes it that both tears and jest keep something of their original appeal, their sadness and their joy, even after the long intervention of two and a half centuries of time.

NOTES TO CHAPTER V

[1] *Stationers' Register,* 9th September, 1653.

[2] Ibid., 29th June, 1660. Chambers, *William Shakespeare,* 1930, vol. i, p. 538, has : " 29th June, 1600."

[3] Ibid., 9th September, 1653.

[4] Licensed by Herbert, September, 1624. *Dramatic Records of Sir Henry Herbert,* ed. J. Q. Adams, 1917, p. 29.

[5] See a letter by Miss Ethel Seaton, *The Times Literary Supplement,* 18th October, 1934. There must be, of course, a good deal of uncertainty as to this play, since it might prove the revival of an older piece, and I am unaware that any serious attempt has been made to identify it. Incidentally it may be remarked how inconsequent are Mr. J. R. A. Nicoll's conjectures and guesses, which Miss Seaton quotes. It is not " fairly likely " but most highly improbable that the piece was a mere droll.

[6] Downes, *Roscius Anglicanus,* p. 26.

[7] Henry Savile to Sir George Savile. *Savile Correspondence,* Camden Society, 1858, p. 4.

[8] *Roscius Anglicanus,* p. 30.

[9] Duffett wrote the Prologue and Epilogue. See his *New Poems,* 8vo, 1676, pp. 84–7.

[10] *Roscius Anglicanus,* p. 41. For *Justice Busy,* p. 45, and my note pp. 257–8.

[11] Bodley, Rawl. MSS. Poet. 195.

[12] In Act I Cleophon to Isabella :—

go shackle with the duke and be Admir'd ;

and, spoken of the Duke :—

he must haue mistreses and often change.

Act V, with reference to the Duke, who is killed :—

for it is fitt
all that so sinn, should punisht be for itt.

[13] Bodley Rawl. MSS. Poet. 18. The old story is world wide. It is incorporated (from the Vetála Panchavinsati) in the great Sanskrit collection *Kathá Sarit Ságara,* " Ocean of the Rivers of Story," and is found in numberless tongues. Boiardo has it in the *Orlando Innamorato,* canto xii. Beaumont and Fletcher employ it in their *Foure Playes in One* as *The Triumph of Honour.* It also forms part of the plot of John Cumber's *The Two Merry Milkmaids, or the best Words wear the Garland,* 4to, 1620.

[14] This drama was first examined and described by myself in an article, *Modern Language Review,* January, 1917, vol. xii, pp. 24 sqq., reprinted in *Essays in Petto.*

[15] Forty-two pages. See Colbeck, Radford & Co., *Catalogue of Autograph Letters and MSS.*; No. 105 (3).

[16] B.M., Add. MS. 28693.

[17] B.M., Add. MS. 8888, f. 2.

[18] B.M., Add. MS. 37158, f. 17.

[19] Dobell, *Catalogue*, 1918, " The Literature of the Restoration," p. 98 ; 1262.

[20] Ibid., p. 98 ; 1263.

[21] Colbeck Radford & Co., *Catalogue*, pp. 12–13 ; No. 105 (1).

[22] Ibid., No. 105 (2).

[23] There are in addition to the plays I have mentioned a number of MS. separate and incomplete scenes to be found in various libraries as also in private collections.

[24] B.M., MS. Lansd. 807⁴.

[25] 4to, 1660. This poem " upon the Successful and Matchless March of the Lord General George Monck from Scotland to London, The Last Winter, &c.", proved so popular as to run into several editions. In his *Of Dramatick Poesie,* Dryden dubs Wild " the very *Withers* of the City ".

[26] See Pepys, 10th January, 1661.

[27] There are several references to the whipping of undergraduates by their tutors. For the use of the rod at both Universities see T. Warton's *Milton's Poems*, p. 421, and for a threatened castigation upon the posterior at Queen's College, Oxford, in 1680, see *Hist. MSS. Comm.*, Report XII, App. 7, pp. 166 and 168. Dr. Johnson in his *Life of Milton* declares that he is ashamed to relate how the poet as a sizar of Christ's College, Cambridge, " suffered the publick indignity of corporal correction."

[28] 8vo, 1632.

[29] There is an ample account of Fanshawe in the *Dictionary of National Biography.*

[30] Nicolas Antonio in his *Bibliotheca Hispana nova* gives Mendoza seven or eight *comedias*, all of which were highly esteemed.

[31] Vol. i, pp. 251–348.

[32] An anonymous tract *The Prophecies of Mother Shipton in the Raigne of King Henry 8th*, . . . London, 4to, 1641, seems to be the earliest published account of this famous figure. Ursula Shipton is believed to have been born near Knaresborough in 1488, and to have died at Clifton, Yorks, in 1561. Although many and the wildest legends are attached to her name she is by no means to be regarded as a mythical personage. Richard Head's *Life and Death of Mother Shipton*, 1667, proved extremely popular and was more than once reprinted with variants.

[33] Mother Shipton has been the subject of many pantomimes, of which the earliest was probably that produced at Covent Garden, 26th December, 1770. At the same house on 16th April, 1787, there was a trifling entertainment *Mother Shipton's Review of the Audience.*

[34] Licensed for the press by Roger L'Estrange, 28th July, 1669.

[35] *Athenae Oxonienses*, ed. Bliss, vol. iii, 1817, p. 819.

[36] *Dramatic Records,* ed. Adams, p. 138.

[37] See also the *Diary* under 5th October, 1667, and 18th February, 1667–8.

[38] The story is also told by Massuccio, *Il Novellino*, 30 ; by Henri Estienne in his *Apologie pour Hérodote*, xv, 30 ; by Bonaventure Des Périers, Nouvelle 114. A similar device is employed by Marston , in *Parasitaster* ; by Otway in *The Souldiers Fortune* ; and by Molière in *L'Ecole des Maris*. Cf. the old German story in V. d. Hagen's *Gesammtabenteuer*, I, xiv.

[39] This is *Le Mari Confesseur* of the *Cent Nouvelles Nouvelles*, 78, imitated by La Fontaine as *Le Mari Confesseur*. It is No. 92 of Celio Malespini's *Ducento Novelle*. Cf. Boccaccio, *Decameron*, vii, 5 ; and Bandello i, 9, who, however, gives the tale a tragic turn.

[40] On Sunday, 19th July, 1663, Pepys " fell to read over a silly play writ by a person of honour (which is, I find, as much as to say a coxcomb), called ' Love à la Mode ' ".

[41] The eulogy by J. Kelynge is absurdly extravagant, and concludes :—

> Were *Shakespeare, Fletcher,* or renowned *Ben*
> Alive, they'd yield to this more happie pen
> Those lawrells that bedeckt their brows ; and say
> *Love a la mode's* the best-accomplish'd Play.

[42] There is a good description of the type of lover who
> when he cannot
> Lie with your person, he'll be sure to do it
> With your reputation.

[43] Compare Molière's *L'Amour Médecin,* produced at Versailles on 15th September, 1665 ; and on the 22nd of the same month at the Palais-Royal, Paris.

[44] The more so since ample analyses and criticisms will be found in Genest, vol. x, pp. 24–30 ; Ward, *History of English Dramatic Literature,* ed. 1899, vol. iii, pp. 160–1 ; and Schelling, *Elizabethan Drama,* 1908, vol. ii, pp. 352–6. C. H. Gray's monograph *Lodowick Carliell,* Chicago, 1905, furnishes a text of *The Deserving Favourite.* In 1926 were issued reprints of *The Fool would be a Fauorit* and *Osmond, the Great Turk.* Although the editor—whose vast labours in one case consist of a brief four-page Introduction, and in the second actually run to a couple of pages— called in the help of an auxiliary, the thing has been feebly enough done.

[45] *English Dramatick Poets,* Oxford, 1691, p. 45.

[46] There are two MSS. extant : Bodleian, MS. Eng. misc. d. 11 ; and a copy with Carliell's signature in the possession of Lord Leconfield, Petworth House, *Hist. MSS. Comm.,* 6th Rep., 1877, p. 312.

[47] B.M., Harleian MSS., 454.

[48] *Roscius Anglicanus,* p. 31. " *Two Fools well met,* by Mr. *Lodowick Carlile.*" This is taken to be *The Fool would be a Fauorit,* and not James Carlisle's *The Fortune-Hunters ; or, Two Fools Well Met.* See my note on the *Roscius,* p. 202.

[49] Printed in *Miscellany Poems,* 8vo, 1684.

[50] D. F. Canfield, *Corneille and Racine in England,* pp. 64–9.

[51] This " little girl " was one of the great attractions of Lincoln's Inn Fields in the early days of that theatre. Thus Davenant in his sorry amalgam *The Law against Lovers,* February, 1661–2, wrote in a new rôle for this juvenile favourite.

[52] *Some Account of the English Stage,* vol. x, pp. 138–9. Miss Canfield in her monograph, to which reference has just been made, speaks of the " incoherence . . . involving one at once in obscurity " which she finds in Carliell's version, but this is an exaggeration, no doubt due to her confessedly " hasty perusal " of the play (pp. 64–9).

[53] For a detailed account of this piece see my *Shakespeare Adaptations,* 1922 ; Introduction, pp. l–liii.

[54] *Oeuvres de P. Corneille,* éd. Regnier : " Les Grands Ecrivains de la France," tom. v, pp. 134–140.

[55] *Biographia Dramatica,* 1812, vol. ii, p. 401 ; vol. iii, p. 48. Sir Edmund Gosse had seen and examined a copy of the rare 1661 quarto of *The Lyar.*

[56] Fannie was doubtless played by the " little girl ".

[57] Thomas Corneille has taken much of *Le Feint Astrologue,* produced in 1648, from Calderón's *El Astrologo Fingido,* published on 7th March, 1632.

[58] At least one of his discourses was printed : " Un sermon sur 1 Cor., ix, 16, avant l'imposition des mains de Mons. Stouppe," 8vo, 1653.

[59] Imprimatur *Octob.* 16, 1663. Roger L'Estrange.

[60] The Collection includes Dryden's address to the Duchess of Cleveland, "As Sea-men shipwrackt . . .," and *The Imperfect Enjoyment,* attributed to Rochester.

[61] Paisley, 1917, pp. 95–6.

[62] Mr. Lawson is sometimes a little inaccurate, and this may be an error. There was a reprint of *Marciano,* Edinburgh, 4to, 1871, ed. by G. Logan.

[63] Vol. ii, p. 247.

[64] Pistol's " Have we not Hiren here ? ", 2 *Henry IV,* ii, 4, is a tag from Peele's play. See also *Merrie Conceited Iests of George Peele,* black letter, p. 14 : " How George read a Play-booke to a Gentleman."

[65] Bodley : Malone 65 (4).

[66] Licensed *April* 10, 1667. *Roger L'Estrange.*

[67] Since the mistake has been made (e.g. by Macaulay) it should be remarked that John Caryl to whom *The Rape of the Lock* is addressed was the nephew of Baron Caryl, and not the dramatist himself.

[68] Nichols, *Select Collection of Poems,* 1780, ii, 1; and iii, 205.

[69] Pepys, 7th March, 1667, considered *The English Princess* " a most sad, melancholy play ", but was delighted when " little Mis. Davis did dance a jig after the end ".

[70] It is very unlikely that Molière was acquainted with Scarron's Spanish source.

[71] *Some Account of the English Stage,* vol. i, p. 90. " Dowton's passionate old men are pronounced faultless." In acting, says Boaden, he was of " the chastest, and therefore the best " school. It must be remembered that Munden created Old

Dornton in *The Road to Ruin,* and in spite of his genius for grimace Talfourd remarked that in him (so fine was his art) it was " natural that a strong relish for the ludicrous should be accompanied by a genuine pathos ".

[72] The three other plays were *All for Love ; The Merry Wives of Windsor ;* and Ravenscroft's *The Anatomist.*

[73] Wood, *Athenae Oxoniensis,* 3rd ed., 1820 ; vol. iv, 597. See also J. R. Bloxam, *Magdalen College Register,* vol. v (1876), pp. 239–240.

[74] Drayton lies about 2½ miles north-west from Banbury. In 1911 the population was 164.

[75] Bodley ; Rawl. MSS., B. 400, F. f. 62.

[76] Licensed 7 *Novemb.* 1667, by Roger L'Estrange.

[77] *Thomas Betterton,* 1891, p. 13.

[78] *The Elizabethan Playhouse,* second series, 1913, pp. 187–8.

[79] *English Dramatick Poets,* 1691, p. 518. Thomas Hyde, D.D. (1636–1703), was elected Bodley's Librarian on 2nd December, 1665. A distinguished Orientalist, he was hardly in touch with the contemporary theatre.

[80] 1812, vol. iii, p. 12.

[81] " English Men of Letters," 1881, p. 58.

[82] Sir Edmund Gosse, from whose Library Mr. Saintsbury derived his knowledge of *The Mall,* may once have thrown out some casual suggestion with reference to this play, but my old friend certainly did not hold this view for long, nor yet did he seriously press it.

[83] A convenient edition is in Tomo xiv of *Pensil de Apolo en Doze Comedias Nuevas de los meiores Ingenios de España,* Madrid, 1661. *No puede ser guarda una mujer,* one of the best comedies of Agustin Moreto y Cabaña (*c.* 1600–1669), is something indebted to Lope de Vega's *El Mayor impossibile.* In the Third Volume of *Le Théâtre Espagnol,* Paris, 12mo, 1770, *No puede ser* is translated as *La Chose Impossible.* On 4th October, 1786, was produced at the Palais Royal *Guerre Ouverte, ou Ruse contre Ruse,* a version of Moreto by Dumaniant (Antoine-Jean Bourlin, 1752–1828). Frontin, the scheming valet (Tarugo ; Crowne's Crack) was created by Michet. *Guerre Ouverte* was published in 1787, and adapted for the English stage by Mrs. Inchbald as *The Midnight Hour,* Covent Garden, 22nd May, 1787, a comedietta which long remained popular.

[84] *Restoration Comedies,* 1921 ; Introduction, pp. xlii–xliii.

[85] *Letters Familiar, Moral and Critical,* 2 vols., 1721. Vol. i, p. 48. Dennis's letter is dated, 23rd June, 1719.

[86] 1917 ; p. 96. Curiously Mr. Lawson does not mention St. Serfe, except to ascribe to him *Marciano,* which is an error.

[87] Licensed, *Febr.* 11, 1666/7, by Roger L'Estrange.

[88] *English Dramatick Poets,* 1691, pp. 510–11.

[89] Teubner ed., 1881 ; vol. iii, p. 331.

[90] *Geographica,* ed. Meineke. Teubner, 1895 ; vol. i, p. 709.

[91] See also *Scriptores Rerum Alexandri Magni,* Didot, Paris, 1846. These fragments are printed as an appendix to *Arrian,* ed. Müller ; Clitarchus, *Fragmentum* 9 (p. 78) ; and Onesicritus, *Fragmentum* 5 (p. 49).

[92] *Cassandre,* Paris, 10 vols., 1642–1650 ; vol. iii, pp. 383–472, continued in vol. iv, pp. 467–654. This lengthy episode was suggested to La Calprenède by the story of Theocrine in Barclay's Latin romance, *Argenis,* Liber iii, c. viii, etc. The *Argenis* was published in 1621, the year of Barclay's death. An English translation appeared in 1636.

[93] About 4 miles from Oxford. In 1911 the population was 382.

[94] Job Allibond, or Allibone, Dean of Arts.

[95] Cobbett's *State Trials.* " Proceedings against S. M. Magdalen College in 1687–1688."

[96] Printed as by G. L., i.e. Guilielmus Lyde, the Ancient name of his Family. Dr. Bloxam also attributes to Joyner *Vita Reginaldi Poli,* 8vo, 1690, but this would seem to be an error.

[97] Wood, *Athenae Oxonienses,* ed. Bliss, vol. iv, 1820, pp. 587–590. See also *A Register of Saint Mary Magdalen College, Oxford,* ed. J. R. Bloxam, vol. ii, 1876, pp. 144–8.

[98] *English Dramatick Poets,* 1691, p. 309.

[99] " *In the escape of* Fulvia *I have follow'd the example of* Medea, *which by the subtile*

and judicious Castelvetro *is only censur'd for want of preparatives : the foregoing parts having nothing contributed to this strange action, which is here contrary ; and the conveyance more rational.* Joyner ; Preface.

[100] *The Commonwealth and Restoration Stage,* 1928, p. 215. See also Chapter II, n. 171.

[101] Ibid., p. 248.

[102] The only other exemplar known seems to have been the Britwell copy, which wanted a leaf (F 12), and had the first seven leaves defective.

[103] The article dealing with *The Town-Shifts* in *Anglia,* 1913, vol. xxxvii, pp. 125 sqq., *An Early Sentimental Comedy,* by C. M. Scheurer, is pretentious and superficial.

[104] Parfaict, *Histoire du Théâtre François,* t. viii, 1746 ; pp. 27–39.

[105] Colley Cibber's evergreen comedy *She Wou'd and She Wou'd Not,* Drury Lane, November, 1702, also opens in an inn at Madrid. There are other resemblances, but Cibber was drawing from Leanerd's *The Counterfeits,* as noted later in this chapter.

[106] Oliphant, *Beaumont and Fletcher,* 1927, p. 433, adds " altered by Massinger and Jonson ".

[107] See a pretended answer to Mrs. Cellier : *Modesty Triumphing over Impudence : Or, Some Notes upon a Late Romance . . .,* folio, 1680.

[108] Colin [Lindsay], Earl of Balcarres, *Memoirs Touching the Revolution in Scotland,* 1688–1690 ; Edinburgh, Bannatyne Club, 1841, p. 67.

[109] For a full account of this see *The Works of Thomas Otway,* edited by Montague Summers, 1926, vol. i, Introduction, pp. lxxi–lxxii.

[110] The landlord of the tavern in the Mulberry Garden. There are references to him in many plays, e.g. Sedley's *The Mulberry-Garden ;* Wycherley's *Love in a Wood, or, St. James' Park.*

[111] Ed. Clark, 1898, vol. ii, pp. 266–8.

[112] Vol. ii, pp. 333–9.

[113] Vol. i, parte 2, 1753 : pp. 1273–4.

[114] Op. cit., p. 177.

[115] A word of warning should be added against the meagre and inexact account of Duffett in *The Dictionary of National Biography.* The contributor was manifestly unacquainted with Duffett's work.

[116] He was certainly not M. Ballon, a celebrated French dancing-master, whose arrival in England is noted by Luttrell on 8th April, 1699, and who had been engaged to dance for five weeks at the Theatre in Lincoln's Inn Fields at a salary of 400 guineas. Yet one of our more recent authorities is so completely at sea as airily to assume that M. Ballon was the author of *The Mock-Duellist.* For this sapient suggestion see J. A. R. Nicoll, *A History of Restoration Drama,* 1928, p. 65, n. 2 ; and pp. 353, 391.

[117] *History of the English Stage,* vol. i, p. 173.

[118] Olveston is near Thornbury, and 10 miles north of Bristol.

[119] For a study of Madame de Villedieu, 1631–1683, see Arno Kretschman's *Madame de Villedieu ; Leben, Romane und Erzählungen,* 1907. Bibliographies, on the authority of Deschamps and Brunet, date the first edition of *Les Amours des Grands Hommes,* Cologne, 1676. No exemplar is forthcoming, and hence many prefer Paris, 1679. However, the English translation is 1673, which points to an *editio princeps* of 1671–2, this being confirmed by Fane's use of the work in his play.

[120] Shelfmark : 8°, 62/1, E. Art.

[121] The same device is utilized by Ravenscroft in *The London Cuckolds.* See my *Restoration Comedies,* 1921 ; Introduction, pp. xxxvii–xxxviii.

[122] Cf. the Widdow Ranter, played by Mrs. Currer, in Mrs. Behn's posthumous play of that name, Drury Lane, November, 1689.

[123] *English Dramatick Poets,* 1691, p. 319.

[124] Ibid., p. 528.

[125] Kirkman's play-lists, 1661 and 1671, ascribe *The Countrie Girle,* printed as by T. B., to Anthony Brewer, author of *The Love-sick King* (*c.* 1607), 4to, 1655, and *The Perjured Nun,* 4to, 1680. Malone conjectured that T. B. might be Tony Brewer (MS. note in his copy of *The Countrie Girle*). Archer in 1656 names Thomas Brewer as the author of *The Countrie Girle,* which Oliphant (*Modern Philology,* viii, p. 422) on no grounds at all supposed might be a revision by Massinger (!) of

an early work by Thomas Brewer, who is then to be identified with the writer of a pamphlet, *The Life and Death of the Merry Devil of Edmonton*, 1608.

[126] This also suggested to Middleton and Rowley *The Spanish Gipsie* (1623), derived from two tales by Cervantes, *La Fuerza di Sangue* and *La Gitanella*.

[127] *The Theatre*, a monthly review, edited by Clement Scott, New Series, August, 1884.

[128] *English Dramatick Poets*, 1691, p. 552.

[129] J. A. R. Nicoll, *A History of Restoration Drama*, 1928, pp. 203–4. This writer ingenuously tries to save the situation by a footnote : " It is possible that neither of these were by him."

[130] Langbaine, op. cit., p. 424. The notice of Rawlins in the *D.N.B.* is very untrustworthy.

[131] Genest, vol. x, 113–15, gives an adequate outline.

[132] Bodley, Rawl. MSS. Poet. 159. " Mamamouchi " is Ravenscroft in allusion to his first play, *The Citizen Turn'd Gentleman*, 4to, 1672, re-issued 4to, 1675, as *Mamamouchi ; or, The Citizen Turn'd Gentleman*.

[133] First played at Paris on 28th May, 1660. *Sganarelle* is from an Italian farce, *Il Ritratto, ove Arlecchino cornuto per opinione*.

[134] *Term Catalogues*, Easter (14th May), 1678.

[135] Op. cit., p. 554.

[136] Sneaton is a village in the North Riding of Yorkshire. It stands high, overlooking Whitby and the sea.

[137] This name also occurs in *Pharonnida*, IV, canto iii.

[138] Saintsbury, who clearly had not read the play, speaks of *Wits Led by the Nose* as " a title not obviously applicable " ; *Minor Poets of the Caroline Period*, vol. i, 1905, p. (3) ; sig. B. 2, n. 1.

[139] Of William Chamberlayne there is an excellent account in *The Retrospective Review*, i, pp. 21–48 ; and 258–271. See also Sir Edmund Gosse's pages in *From Shakespeare to Pope*. Julius Gottlieb Ernst Kilian's dissertation, 1913, on *Pharonnida* is negligible. Singer's reprint of Chamberlayne's poems, 3 vols., 1820, is admittedly out of date, but Saintsbury's *Minor Poets of the Caroline Period* will not be used if any other edition is available. Chamberlayne wrote *England's Jubile*, 1660, to celebrate the Restoration, and paraphrased part of *Pharonnida* as *Eromena, or The Noble Stranger, A Novel*, 8vo, 1683.

[140] *Term Catalogues*, Easter (14th May), 1678.

[141] Op. cit., p. 72.

[142] Grillon is the famous Louis Des Balbes, or Balbis De Berton De Crillon, 1541–1615. The form Grillon is from Davila's Italian *Griglione*.

[143] See Heckethorn's *The Secret Societies of All Ages and Countries*, new ed. 1897, vol. i, pp. 288–9 ; pars. 336–7.

[144] See *The Restoration Theatre*, 1934, by Montague Summers, pp. 153–165.

[145] *Old English Plays*. New Series. Ed. by A. H. Bullen. *The Works of Thomas Nabbes*, vol. i, 1887. It should perhaps be remarked that *The Dramatic Works of Thomas Nabbes*, a thesis by Charlotte Moore (University of Pennsylvania), 1918 (Preface signed 21st May, 1915), is entirely valueless. We meet with such errors as the date 1703 (p. 52) given for the year of production of Lee's *Sophonisba*, 1675. Similar blunders are only too much in evidence.

[146] *Old English Plays*. New Series. Ed. by A. H. Bullen. *The Works of Robert Davenport*, vol. iii, 1890. The plot of *The City Night-Cap* is from Cervantes' novella *The Curious Impertinent*, and from the *Decameron*, giornata vii, novella 7.

[147] *Poetical Register*, 1719, p. 8.

[148] *Gossip in a Library*, ed. 1891, pp. 103–4.

[149] Chapter ii, pp. 22–47.

[150] The first edition is 12mo, 1662. A Monsieur Tronchin included *Sertorius* with some alterations (tom. iv) with other of Corneille's tragedies " revues pour être remises au théâtre " in *Mes récréations dramatiques*, 5 tomes, 8vo, Geneva, 1779–1784.

[151] *Poetical Register*, 1719, p. 166.

[152] For a detailed account of the controversy and a reprint of the letter by the Savilian Professor, Dr. Wallis, directed against Mr. Maidwell, see *Collectanea*, First Series, ed. by C. R. L. Fletcher, 1885, pp. 269–337.

[153] The same prologue as a *bonne bouche* is printed with Ravenscroft's *Titus*

Andronicus ; or, The Rape of Lavinia, 4to, 1687, but acted at the Theatre Royal nearly a decade before.

[154] Miss U. M. Ellis-Fermor in her edition of Marlowe's *Tamburlaine the Great,* 1930, pp. 61-2, has missed this revival. I have earlier in this chapter called attention to the MS. *Tamerlane the Beneficent,* a tragedy, 1692.

[155] Mlle de la Roche-Guilhen was born about 1640 of a wealthy Huguenot family. Upon the Revocaton of the Edict of Nantes she retired from Paris to Holland, and in 1697 she came to England. She is a very prolific writer of novels, which, however, evince but a mediocre talent. She died in 1710.

[156] The only copy I know is that contained in the Bodleian ; shelfmark, Art. 8°, V. 82. This small 12mo, runs to 190 pages.

[157] Op. cit., p. 439.

[158] The " wisard " is John Pordage (1607-1681), rector of Bradfield, Berks, who published astrological and devotional works. Baxter described him as chief of the Behmenists.

[159] It should be remarked that in spite of the ascription by Narcissus Luttrell to Samuel Pordage, the authorship of *Azaria and Hushai* remains doubtful. Wood gives Settle as the author, and there is reason to think that at any rate the piece was not from Pordage's pen.

[160] Licensed for printing, 13th September, 1677.

[161] Thus in Act IV we have a feeble masque of Neptune, Proteus, Nereus, Tritons, and Sirens, who laud England's navy in jolting doggerel.

[162] *Gossip in a Library,* ed. 1891, p. 100.

GENERAL INDEX

INDEX OF PLAYS